The Law & Society Reader

THE LAW & SOCIETY READER

Edited by
Richard L. Abel

NEW YORK UNIVERSITY PRESS
New York and London

NEW YORK UNIVERSITY PRESS
New York and London

Library of Congress Cataloging-in-Publication Data
The law & society reader / edited by Richard L. Abel.
    p. cm.
   Includes bibliographical references.
   ISBN 0-8147-0617-7.—ISBN 0-8147-0618-5 (pbk)
   1. Sociological jurisprudence. I. Abel, Richard L. II. Title:
The law and society.
K376.L3695 1995
340'.115—dc20   95-6532
                CIP

New York University Press books are printed on acid-free paper, and
their binding materials are chosen for strength and durability.

10   9   8   7   6   5   4   3   2   1

Contents

Preface

The chapters in this book all appeared in the *Law & Society Review*. In order to maximize the number and range of articles I have edited them extensively, eliminating or drastically reducing graphs, tables, figures, footnotes, methodological discussions, and references. I am grateful to the authors for their assistance and for foregoing royalties, all of which will benefit the Law and Society Association. I also am grateful to its Executive Officer, Professor Ronald M. Pipkin, for preparing camera-ready copy from an often jumbled disk. The authors wish to thank their funding sources, which include: National Science Foundation, National Institute of Mental Health, National Institute of Justice, National Institute of Law Enforcement and Criminal Justice, Council for International Interchange of Scholars, University of Texas, American Bar Foundation, NAACP Legal Defense and Education Fund Inc., Chicago Resource Center, Amherst College Fund, and British Economic and Social Research Council.

About the Authors

Richard L. Abel is Professor of Law at UCLA and a former editor of the *Law & Society Review* and president of the Law and Society Association. He has written or edited *The Politics of Informal Justice* (2 vols. 1982), *Lawyers in Society* (with Philip Lewis) (3 vols. 1988–89), *The Legal Profession in England and Wales* (1988), *American Lawyers* (1989), *Speech and Respect* (1994), and *Politics by Other Means: Law in the Struggle Against Apartheid, 1980–1994* (1995).

Albert W. Alschuler is Wilson-Dickinson Professor of Law at the University of Chicago. A fomrer federal prosecutor, he has written on sentencing guidelines, plea bargaining, jury selection, search and seizure, civil procedure, and American legal theory. One of his most recent articles continues his history of plea bargaining (*University of Chicago Law Review*, Summer 1994).

Erhard Blankenburg has been Professor of the Sociology of Law and Criminology at the Free University of Amsterdam since 1980, having taught sociology and sociology of law at Freiburg University (1965–70) and having served as consultant with the Quickborn Team Hamburg (1970–72) and senior research fellow at Prognos AG Basel (1972–74), the Max Planck-Institut Freiburg (1974–75), and the Science Center Berlin (1975–80). His books concern police, public prosecutors, civil courts, labor courts, legal aid, and sociology of law generally.

Kitty Calavita is Associate Professor in the Department of Criminology, Law and Society in the School of Social Ecology, University of California, Irvine. She has written extensively on administrative lawmaking, immigration policy, theories of the state, and white-collar crime. Her most recent book is *Inside the State: The Bracero Program, Immigration and the INS* (1992).

John M. Conley is Professor of Law at the University of North Carolina at Chapel Hill and Adjunct Professor of Anthropology at Duke University. He is co-author of *Rules Versus Relationships* and *Fortune and Folly: The Wealth and Power of Institutional Investing*. He also has written a treatise on statistical evidence for lawyers and numerous articles on the law of intellectual property.

Kathleen Daly is a Visiting Associate Professor of Sociology at the University of Michigan. She has written on gender- and race-based disparities in sentencing, gender and white-collar crime, the control of prostitution in the Progressive Era, civil remedies for battered women, and the relationship of feminist theory to crime, law, and justice. Her recent book, *Gender, Crime and Punishment* (1994), examines problems of equality and justice in criminal courts.

Sheldon Ekland-Olson is Professor of Sociology and Dean of the College of Liberal Arts at the University of Texas at Austin. He is co-author of *Justice under Pressure* (1993) and *The Rope, the Chair and the Needle: Capital Punishment in Texas, 1923–90* (1994).

Robert M. Emerson is Professor of Sociology at the University of California, Los Angeles. He has written extensively on ethnographic and field research methods, including *Contemporary Field Research: A Collection of Readings* (1988) and *Writing Ethnographic Fieldnotes* (with Rachel Fretz and Linda Shaw, forthcoming). Using qualitative methods, he has analyzed social control decision-making by a variety of different institutional agents, including juvenile court personnel, psychiatric emergency teams, school disciplinarians, probation officers and district attorneys.

David M. Engel is Professor of Law and Director of the Baldy Center for Law and Social Policy at the State University of New York at Buffalo. His research explores law, culture, and change in Southeast Asia (particularly Thailand), in a midwestern American community, and among persons with disabilities and their families.

William L. F. Felstiner is Visiting Professor of Sociology at the University of California, Santa Barbara, and Distinguished Research Fellow at the American Bar Foundation. His book with Austin Sarat on divorce lawyers and their clients is forthcoming from Oxford University Press. He is currently studying the nature, origins and consequences of lawyer "inattention."

Marc Galanter is Evjue-Bascom Professor of Law and South Asian Studies and Director of the Institute for Legal Studies at the University of Wisconsin-Madison. A past editor of the *Law & Society Review* and past president of the Law and Society Association, he is the author of *Competing Equalities, Law and Society in Modern India,* and *Tournament of Lawyers* (with Thomas Palay) and numerous articles on lawyers, litigation, and dispute processing.

Janet A. Gilboy is a Research Fellow at the American Bar Foundation. She has written several articles on immigration administration and regulation and is currently exploring the legal, organizational, and political factors shaping the exercise of discretion in agency contexts.

Stuart Henry is Professor of Sociology at Eastern Michigan University. He has written or edited *Self-help and Health* (1977), *The Hidden Economy* (1978), *Informal Institutions* (1981), *Private Justice* (1983), *The Informal Economy* (1987), *Degrees of Deviance* (1990), *Making Markets* (1992), *Classical and Contemporary Perspectives on the Informal Economy* (1993), *The Deviance Process* (1993), *Inside Jobs: A Realistic Guide to Criminal Justice Careers for College Graduates* (1994), and *Criminological Theory* (1994), as well as numerous articles. His current research on the relationship between state law and private justice focuses on the drafting of the Uniform Law Commissioners' Model Employment Termination Act.

Milton Heumann is Professor of Political Science at Rutgers University in New Brunswick, New Jersey. He is the author of *Plea Bargaining: The Experiences of Prosecutors, Judges and Defense Attorneys* (1978) and *Speedy Disposition: Monetary Incentives and Policy Reform in the Criminal Courts* (with Thomas Church) (1992). He has also written on mandatory sentencing, the Federal Sentencing Guidelines, and the civil settlement process. His current projects include an examination of college speech codes, as well as the design of a new course on the proposed federal funding for a police corps.

John Lieb is a lawyer in private practice in Atlanta, Georgia.

Steve J. Martin is co-author of *Texas Prisons* (1987). He has been legal counsel to the Texas Department of Corrections and is now in private practice in Austin, specializing in litigation and legislation on prison reform.

Sally Engle Merry is Professor of Anthropology at Wellesley College, author of *Urban Danger: Life in a Neighborhood of Strangers* (1981) and *Getting Even: Legal Consciousness among Working-Class Americans* (1990), and co-editor with Neal Milner of *The Possibility of Popular Justice: A Case Study in American Community Mediation* (1993). She has been president of the Law and Society Association and a member of the editorial boards of the *Law & Society Review, Journal of Legal Pluralism, Negotiation Journal,* and *The Mediation Quarterly.*

Elizabeth Mertz is Assistant Professor of Law at Northwestern University and a Research Fellow at the American Bar Foundation. Her research focuses on the role of language in legal settings; at present, she is studying law school classroom language.

William M. O'Barr is Professor of Anthropology and Sociology at Duke University. His books include *Language and Politics* (1976), *Linguistic Evidence: Language, Power and Strategy in the Courtroom* (1982), *Language and Power* (1984), and *Culture and the Ad: Exploring Otherness in the World of Advertising*

(1994). He has also conducted ethnographic research among the Pare people of Tanzania and studied bilingual courts in Canada. He is the editor of volumes 29–31 of the *Law & Society Review*.

Glenn L. Pierce is Director of the Center for Applied Social Research and Director of the Center for Academic Computing at Northeastern University in Boston. His current research interests include youth and violence, disinvestment in children and youth, and the role of information technology in organizational re-engineering.

Michael L. Radelet is Professor of Sociology at the University of Florida. His last two books both concern the death penalty: *In Spite of Innocence: Erroneous Convictions in Capital Cases* (1992) and *Executing the Mentally Ill* (1993).

Austin Sarat is William Nelson Cromwell Professor of Jurisprudence and Political Science and chair of the Department of Law, Jurisprudence, and Social Thought at Amherst College. He is co-editor of *Studies in Law, Politics and Society* and the University of Michigan Press Series on Law, Meaning and Violence. He is co-author (with William L. F. Felstiner) of *Fragile Power, Elusive Meaning: Lawyers and Clients in Divorce* (1995) and co-editor (with Thomas R. Kearns) of *The Rhetoric of Law* and *Law in Everyday Life* (1993).

Sebastian Scheerer is Professor of Criminology at Hamburg University. He writes about drug policy, political violence, and the general theory of crime.

Takao Tanase is Professor of Law at Kyoto University and the author of numerous books and articles on the judicial process, legal professions, and dispute settlement.

Louis Zurcher was Ashbel Smith Professor of Social Work and Sociology at the University of Texas at Austin until his recent death. Among his numerous books on poverty, natural disaster, the parole system, pornography, bureaucracy, divorce, and the family, his last included *Social Roles: Conformity, Conflict, and Creativity* and (with Ruth G. McRoy) *Transracial and Inracial Adoptees: The Adolescent*.

What We Talk About When We Talk About Law

Richard L. Abel

When asked what I study, I usually respond gnomically: everything about law except the rules. This may be oxymoronic, but it is also accurate. Lawyers seek to understand rules—ascertain, criticize, change, organize, apply, and manipulate them. Social scientists examine everything else: institutional structures, processes, behavior, personnel, and culture (Abel, 1973). Disciplines usually resist colonization: religion is suspicious of philosophy, medicine of sociology, science of feminist epistemology. Law has not always been hospitable to external scrutiny. Some lawyers feared that efforts by political scientists to explain decisions in terms of judges' backgrounds or ideology would undermine judicial authority. Efforts by psychologists to understand jury dynamics were stymied by rules against recording their deliberations. Many legal scholars still resent the imperialistic ambitions of economists.

Nevertheless, there is a long tradition of interdisciplinary approaches to law. For several millennia philosophers have pondered the basis of legal obligation and the nature of legal reasoning. Historians have charted and interpreted changes in legal rules and institutions at least since Jean Bodin in the sixteenth century (Franklin, 1963) and Montesquieu in the eighteenth (Montesquieu, 1756; Ehrlich, 1916). Historical jurisprudence revived strongly in Germany in the nineteenth century (Savigny, 1831; Kantorowicz, 1937) and Russia in the early twentieth (Vinogradoff, 1920; see generally Pound, 1923). Evolutionists sought to extrapolate Darwinian theories of living organisms to social organization generally and legal institutions in particular (Maine, 1861; Bachofen, 1861; Briffault, 1927; Morgan, 1877; Rivers, 1968; Sumner, 1907; Tönnies, 1963; Tylor, 1865; Westermarck, 1906; Hobhouse, 1915; Lowie, 1927; Robson, 1935; Sorokin, 1937; Ginsberg, 1953; Nagel, 1962; Schwartz & Miller, 1964; Redfield, 1964; Parsons, 1966; Kluckhohn, 1960; Rheinstein, 1960).

Two of the three founders of classical social theory were trained in law. Although Marx said little on the subject (Hirst, 1972; Cain & Hunt, 1979; Phillips, 1980; Collins, 1982), Engels wrote an influential book (if misguided by speculative ethnography) (Engels, 1902). Weber emphasized the nature of authority and its relation to varieties of legal reasoning (Weber, 1978; Rheinstein, 1954; Trubek, 1972; Hunt, 1978: chap. 5; Kronman, 1983). And Durkheim, though not a lawyer, chose law as a fundamental index of social morphology (Durkheim, 1964; 1973;

Hunt, 1978: chap. 4; Lukes & Scull, 1983).

Empirical studies of law began in earnest with the emergence of legal realism in the early twentieth century in both the United States (Hunt, 1978: chap. 3; Twining, 1985; Kalman, 1986; Fisher et al., 1993) and Europe (Ehrlich, 1922; 1936; Eckhoff, 1960). Malinowski (1926a; 1926b; 1942) and Radcliffe-Brown (1933; 1934; 1952) inspired other anthropologists to study and analyze legal phenomena (for overviews of this extensive literature, see Cairns, 1931; Bohannan, 1967; Moore, 1969; Hoebel, 1954; Collier, 1975; Roberts, 1979). After World War II political scientists became interested in legal decision-making (e.g., Schubert, 1960; 1963; 1964; 1965). Psychologists began studying such issues as legal compliance, law and public opinion, and jury decisions (e.g., Moore & Callahan, 1944; Cohen et al., 1958; Rose & Press, 1955; Kalven & Zeisel, 1966; see generally Górecki, 1975; Tapp & Levine, 1977). And sociologists and psychologists investigated deviance and social control.

Interdisciplinary studies of law have developed rapidly in the last 30 years for several reasons. First, societies have placed greater demands on law to regulate social, economic, political, and even cultural life. Second, universities have enlarged and transformed both law schools and social science departments. Lawyers qualified by apprenticeship until the early twentieth century in the United States and the early postwar period in Canada, the UK, and Australia. The creation and expansion of university law schools stimulated innovation in legal scholarship. Similarly, the social sciences have matured greatly in recent decades. This introduction surveys what social scientists talk about when they talk about law.

The Origins of Rules

Lawyers and legal theorists tend to take legislation as a given, an exogenous and arbitrary datum, which courts must then process. (By contrast, legal theorists are deeply concerned with how courts make and apply rules.) Social scientists seek to understand the forces that create rules, perpetuate them, and foster change. They are interested in all rule-making institutions: legislative, administrative, and judicial. Three bodies of theory have emerged from this effort.

The first, and most commonly deployed, is liberal pluralism or interest group politics. Rules are one of the prizes in the political arena; interested parties organize and enter temporary alliances to secure them. Among the innumerable examples of such competition we might include contemporary discussions about a national health care program (among providers, insurers, consumers, employers, and unions), environmental controversies, international trade policy, and debates over how to raise taxes (progressivity, capital gains, corporate, estate and property) and spend them (benefits, farm price supports, military bases, government contracts).

Sociologists have adapted this approach to advance a second theory: the object of competition is not only material gain but also respect and social status; the medium is symbols, values, and ethical positions. Again it is easy to cite instances:

pornography and media violence, birth control and abortion, welfare and immigration policy, church–state relations (especially in the schools, e.g., sex education, creationism), animal rights, sexual harassment, alcohol and drug policy, gun control, commemorations (monuments, parades), apology and restitution for past offenses (slavery, the extermination and removal of Indians, Japanese internment).

The third approach differs not about the content or medium of controversies but their structure. Instead of shifting alliances between individuals and groups, with no consistent outcome, these theorists see a systematic pattern of domination and subordination. For Marxists, the central actors are classes, defined by their relations to the means of production. For conflict theorists the categories are more complex and amorphous, but there are clear and persistent winners and losers. Such theories might be applied to disputes over union recognition, wages, workplace health and safety, workers' compensation, capital flight, strikes and boycotts, and international trade.

These approaches are not mutually exclusive. Affirmative action, for instance, can be seen as an interest group struggle over scarce resources (access to education and jobs), symbolic politics about social status, and a challenge to the reproduction of racial domination. Debates about comparable worth could be construed similarly. The regulation of smoking can be interpreted as a conflict between tobacco companies and health promoters, or between smokers and anti-smoking lobbies (categories that overlap class and race).

In the past, the locus of rule-making was clear: the state (usually unitary, although Americans take their federalism for granted). Social scientists emphasize the legal pluralism produced by the wide range of non-state collectivities that promulgate rules. Today, the nation-state is being challenged from both above and below. Supranational economic and political groupings are gaining power: the European Union, NAFTA, the UN; multinational corporations and financial institutions (World Bank, IMF). At the same time, localism, ethnicity, and religion are demanding decentralization and even fission: the breakup of the Soviet Union, Czechoslovakia, and Yugoslavia; separatism in Spain, France, Italy, Canada, and the UK; ethnic conflict in Africa and Asia.

Rules and Norms

Because rules are not self-enforcing, social scientists look at sanctioning mechanisms (discussed below) and the relationship between formal rules and internalized norms. They investigate the similarities and differences between rules and norms, as well as the knowledge (and misinformation) that laypeople (and lawyers) possess about legal rules. They examine how knowledge is disseminated and thus how it is distributed: are there systematic disparities between landlords and tenants, for instance, or manufacturers and consumers, employers and employees? Even if laypeople correctly understand their legal rights, lawyers may discourage claims because of ignorance or antipathy—of the warranties manufacturers must make to consumers, for example (Macaulay, 1979).

Social scientists ask whether embodying a norm in a formal rule strengthens or diminishes the disposition to comply. What explains variations in the obligatoriness of different rules: speed limits, income tax, various kinds of debt, liability to those you injure? Conversely, what are the consequences of enacting rules that violate fundamental beliefs? One response is civil disobedience: the underground railroad to evade fugitive slave laws, suffragists, labor organizers, civil rights sit-ins, anti-war protesters. This, in turn, can lead to jury nullification: the refusal to convict draft resisters during the Vietnam War, or soft drug users, or Dr. Jack Kevorkian for euthanasia. Social scientists also ask whether enacting distasteful rules impairs the legitimacy of the legal system as a whole—did the pervasive criminality of Prohibition erode respect for law generally? does the contemporary failure of the War on Drugs? Does respect for law vary over time? across nations or subgroups within them?

Cultural attitudes toward legal phenomena are complex and contradictory; they both reinforce and are reinforced by the phenomena themselves. Americans believe that courts coddle criminals, although we have the highest rate of imprisonment among advanced capitalist nations, impose the longest sentences, rely most heavily on the death penalty. Americans believe that crime is our greatest national problem, although the middle class and wealthy are unlikely to suffer violence. Americans believe in the slot-machine theory of justice—law as the mechanical application of unambiguous rules to uncontested facts. At the same time that they feel passionately about judicial appointments, as shown by the debates over the Supreme Court nominations of Robert Bork and Clarence Thomas. Belief in the basic fairness of the legal system survives repeated disappointments in actual experience. Americans demand civil rights and liberties for themselves—equality with superiors, free speech for those with whom they agree—while opposing them for inferiors or those whose views they abhor (Sarat, 1977). American stereotypes of welfare recipients and immigrants resist repeated empirical falsification. Americans condemn "big government" for bureaucratic inertia, waste and inefficiency but demand increased protection from environmental degradation and health hazards.

Mobilizing Rules

Social scientists distinguish two kinds of regulation: reactive regimes depend on the initiative of a complainant; in proactive processes an official takes responsibility for investigating, prosecuting, and punishing an offender. Yet even the archetypical proactive enforcement mechanism, the police, relies heavily on citizen complaints; and many other regulatory mechanisms are entirely reactive (e.g., the maintenance of ethical standards by the legal profession). The centrality of private actors to any regulatory regime introduces important forms of variation. The victim must perceive an injury, connect it with a normative violation, and blame a violator (Felstiner et al., 1980–81; Mather & Yngvesson, 1980–81).

In recent years, an aggressive propaganda campaign seems to have convinced Americans that we have become a nation of whiners, that everyone is claiming to be a victim, that litigiousness is out of control. The creation of this moral panic is an appropriate subject for social scientific investigation (British colonial authorities in Africa and India also complained about excessive litigation by their subjects). One ingredient is media dissemination of atrocity stories like the following. Ronald T. Williams claimed that his Dannon yogurt had glass, which cut his mouth, paralyzing his lip; his Revlon Flex protein conditioner burned his head; his Rise shaving cream exploded in his face; his Magnavox television caught fire and burned his clothes; and his Nuprin tablets caused severe kidney damage, putting him in a coma. He filed five lawsuits within five months, three on the same day! It turned out, however, that Mr. Williams had unusually low opportunity costs: he was serving two life terms for murders. The court in which the lawsuits were filed ordered forfeiture of his computer, typewriter, and printer, barred him from filing new actions without its consent, and ordered him to pay $5000 to the clerk of the court *(The New York Times*, A16, March 29, 1994).

Social scientific study of litigation rates requires the very difficult task of calculating the population of events that could warrant lawsuits—the number of Rise shaving cream containers that explode, for instance. If litigation rates are normalized in the crudest way—the ratio to population—they appear to have declined dramatically since the nineteenth century. Furthermore, the categories of lawsuit that have been rising most rapidly are those filed by business, not consumers. Social scientists study the variables that explain readiness to complain: relations between victim and offender (social distance, intimacy or ignorance, permanence or transience, equality or domination), national cultures (Western versus Eastern, degree of normative consensus), transaction costs (expense, delay, emotional trauma). They also consider who is the stakeholder, who must mobilize the process in order to get redress (landlords holding security deposits, tenants occupying premises without paying rent). Finally, litigation can be used as a weapon of terror even when there is little or no chance of success: Robert Maxwell filed libel actions against anyone who dared to criticize him; landlords claim back rent even when the premises were uninhabitable, threatening their former tenants' credit ratings.

Forum Shopping

Those who decide to mobilize norms must choose where and how to do so. Most negotiate directly with their adversaries; some simply take revenge, often anonymously. If they resort to third parties, there is a wide range of potential forums: public and private, courts and administrative agencies, civil and criminal. Each social environment may have its own dispute process: residential communities (small claims courts, neighborhood justice centers); the media (ombudsmen); schools and universities; manufacturers, retailers, and consumers (trade associations of dry cleaners or moving companies, professional organizations of lawyers or doctors, Better Business Bureaus); settlement procedures for mass torts (Agent Orange, asbestos, the Dalkon Shield, silicone gel breast implants, heart valves); labor-management disputes (often specialized by industry); commercial arbitration (both domestic and international).

These institutions differ along a number of variables. Personnel may be lay or professional, full-time or part-time. They may enjoy decisional authority (adjudication, binding arbitration) or rely on persuasion (mediation, conciliation). The institution may be highly visible or private, expensive or free. The complainant may exercise control (civil actions) or relinquish it to the state (criminal prosecutions). The process may be formal or informal, fast or slow. Each forum may have different substantive rules. The outcome may favor one party (zero-sum) or compromise between them; it may consist of money damages, criminal punishment, an order to act or refrain from action, a declaration, an apology. Such legal pluralism requires rules governing which forum has jurisdiction, which must respect the decisions of others, and which can review and change those decisions.

The Mediation of Lawyers

For millennia citizens mobilized the law without any professional assistance; they still do most of the time. In recent decades, however, the number of lawyers has grown rapidly in almost every country. How has this shaped the experience of law? How does access to lawyers vary by class, race, gender, and geography? What legal matters do lawyers seek, and what do they reject? How do clients find lawyers and lawyers seek business? What has the state done to redistribute legal services? Who uses lawyers, for which purposes, and how often? How does the quality of lawyers vary? All of these matters are influenced by the structure of the legal profession: entry barriers (difficulty and kind—education, apprenticeship, examination), numbers, composition (class background, race, gender), distribution among practice settings (independent/employed, partner/associate, public/private, firm size, multidisciplinary and multinational partnerships), self-governance and self-regulation.

The goals of lawyers and clients inevitably diverge. These may be shaped by how the lawyer is paid: hourly fee, contingent fee, percent of the transaction, fixed fee. The accommodation that each makes to the other may be influenced by the importance of the matter and past or expected interaction. A critical question is whether lawyers intensify or moderate legal conflict, encouraging clients to make excessive demands or using their knowledge of likely outcomes and connections with opposing counsel to facilitate settlement.

Deviance and Social Control

Although citizens can mobilize law for their own ends, the state also deploys law through the criminal justice system and regulatory agencies. We are accustomed to think of the state as responding to crime; but social scientists emphasize the ways in which deviance is constructed as behavior is labelled criminal. We can see this most clearly in the aftermath of decriminalization: the repeal of Prohibition, state lotteries and legalized gambling, homosexuality, pornography, contraception and abortion. But even behaviors that remain criminal fluctuate between center-stage during moral panics and public amnesia: drug epidemics (marijuana, heroin, cocaine, and now crack), muggings, gang violence, car-jacking. Crime, as Durkheim observed, is the raw material of modern morality plays. It suffuses both news and entertainment (newspapers, television, movies, fiction, and comic books). It also can be a form of political theater. Repressive regimes stage show trials of traitors to justify their authoritarianism. State crimes are exposed after such regimes are overthrown—the Nuremburg and Tokyo war crimes trials, the trials of Nazis and collaborators in France and Israel; disclosure of the "dirty war" in Argentina; the present effort by former communist nations to come to terms with their past through the "lustration" of apparatchiki and nomenklatura.

Even the most aggressive forms of policing and inspection rely heavily on citizens' complaints. What proportion of deviant acts are observed and recognized as criminal, and by whom? Which of those are reported? How do police and regulators deploy their limited resources to investigate and prosecute? What biases does this introduce? It is equally important to inquire how potential deviants perceive the sanctioning mechanism: do they under- or over-estimate the likelihood of detection, apprehension, and punishment and the severity of sanctions? Do they respond by reducing deviance or insulating it from scrutiny and correction? How do their social and cultural environments encourage or discourage criminal behavior?

The state can intensify social control by increasing either the likelihood or the severity of punishment. Because the former has high costs (hiring more police, curtailing individual liberty), governments—particularly our own—prefer the latter, endlessly lengthening prison sentences and expanding prison populations. Almost as soon as most politicians jumped on the bandwagon of "three strikes and you're out," the slogan was trumped with a "one strike" bill for sex crimes. Senator Marian Bergeson, the sponsor, deplored that "we release 250 convicted sex offenders from prison in California each month. ... I don't want to give them a chance at that second victim" (*The Los Angeles Times*, A3, April 12, 1994). In the aftermath of the caning of an American youth in Singapore there have been calls to use the cane against grafitti artists in the United States and restore the paddle to schools (*The New York Times,* May 21, 1994). Communities erect physical barriers to insulate themselves from crime: fencing homes and residential enclaves, closing streets, barring gangs from parks, imposing curfews on youths, expelling the homeless.

If excessive stringency creates its own problems (overcrowded prisons, the erosion of civil liberties, class and race polarization), so does excessive leniency. For more than half a century criminologists have documented the dramatically different response to street crime and white-collar crime. Partly because of overload, partly out of deference, the state devolves a great deal of regulatory responsibility to professions, industries, management, private police, schools, families. Some of the greatest injuries can be traced to lax enforcement: the underpolicing of poor neighborhoods, the poverty of women and children from nonpayment of support by absent fathers; the Exxon Valdez and other environmental disasters; the hundreds of billions of dollars lost in the savings and loan debacle; underpayment of taxes; the failure to regulate DES or the Dalkon Shield.

The Perversity of Institutions

The decisions by citizens or officials to mobilize the law introduce a great deal of variation. Legal institutions further compound this. They are not ciphers, mechanically delivering a predetermined solution. Social scientists recently have emphasized the relative autonomy of state institutions, their "autopoietic" character. From a more critical perspective, they can be seen as self-interested, bureaucratically obstructionist, staffed by a "new class" pursuing their own ends. Legislators seek to amass campaign funds and maximize their chances of re-election; police need to "clear" complaints, and some are corrupt; prosecutors want to move their dockets and advance their careers by securing convictions in highly publicized cases; judges have to get through their calendars; lawyers maximize fees and sometimes fame; bureaucrats stick to the rules and may also cultivate those they regulate as potential employers when the bureaucrat passes through the revolving door into the private sector.

Plea bargaining is the most notorious distortion of the legal process: only a tiny fraction of criminal cases go to trial. Social scientists have long debated whether this is a function of case overload or laziness or simply an efficient method to dispose of cases where guilt is not in doubt. Lawyers also settle most civil cases, partly to maximize their earnings (if paid a contingent fee), partly because they are insecure about trying cases. Efforts to eliminate or reduce discretion at one point (bans on plea bargaining, sentencing guidelines) inevitably increase it elsewhere (arrest or charge), suggesting to many the metaphor of a water bed.

Equality

We judge the legal system not only by its adherence to official norms, effectiveness in implementing them, and efficiency but also by criteria of equality. Violations of equal justice provoke outrage and even violence: the beating of Rodney King by the Los Angeles Police Department, lenient sentences for shopkeepers who shoot

African Americans accused of shoplifting, early release of high-profile criminals like Michael Milken. More subtle forms of bias are revealed in the disparate treatment of victim-offender pairs (e.g., whites accused of crimes against blacks compared to blacks accused of crimes against whites). The extraordinary overrepresentation of men of color in American prisons and on death row is a source of deep shame. We are properly concerned that the racial and gender composition of our population is reflected in all legal institutions: legislature, executive, bench, jury, legal profession, and police force. Yet efforts to correct the effect of historical discrimination through affirmative action are hotly contested.

Bias can enter the system at each decision-point: arrest, charge, bail, legal representation, prosecution, plea bargain, conviction, sentence, and parole. Perhaps the most pernicious form is the application of equal justice to unequal experience, best captured in Anatole France's famous epigram: the law in its majesty equally forbids the rich and poor to sleep under the bridges of Paris. Bias is likely to be greatest at the early stages of this process, when discretion is broadest and visibility lowest, although we often lose sight of this during show trials, like the second prosecution of Los Angeles police officers for violating Rodney King's civil rights. Bias accumulates and amplifies as the effects of earlier decisions create a criminal record, which then influences subsequent decisions.

Resources for Studying Law in Society

The essays that follow offer an overview of the questions social scientists ask about law and the methods they use to answer them. Students who wish to pursue these subjects further can draw on a wealth of resources.

There are a number of American readers (e.g., Friedman & Macaulay, 1977; Evan, 1980), collections of essays (e.g., Lipson & Wheeler, 1986), and texts (e.g., Friedman, 1977; Chambliss & Seidman, 1982; Kidder, 1983; Lempert & Sanders, 1986; Black, 1989; Evan, 1990; McIntyre, 1994), as well as texts by authors from Norway (Aubert, 1983), Australia (O'Malley, 1983), and Britain (Roshier & Teff, 1980; Cotterrell, 1984), and international overviews (Arnaud, 1988; Ferrari, 1990).

The *Law & Society Review*, from which these essays are taken, is nearly 30 years old and contains a wide variety of empirical and theoretical articles as well as special thematic issues. Other leading journals include the *Journal of Law and Society* (formerly the *British Journal of Law and Society)*, *Law & Social Inquiry* (formerly the *American Bar Foundation Research Journal*), *Studies in Law, Politics and Society* (formerly *Research in Law, Deviance and Social Control*), the *International Journal of the Sociology of Law* (Britain), *Social and Legal Studies* (Britain), *Law in Context* (Australia), the *Australian Journal of Law and Society*, the *Journal of Legal Pluralism* (formerly *African Law Studies*), the *Legal Studies Forum*, *Law & Policy* (formerly the *Law & Policy Quarterly*), *Canadian Journal of Law and Society*, *Droit et Société* (France), *Sociologia del diritto* (Italy), *Jahrbuch für*

Rechtssoziologie und Rechtstheorie (Germany), *Kritische Justiz* (Germany), *Recht en Kritiek* (Netherlands), *Nieuwsbrief voor nederlandstalige rechtssociologen, rechtsantropologen en rechtspsychologen* (Netherlands), *Windsor Yearbook of Access to Justice* (Canada), and *Law and Human Behavior.*

A number of American universities offer undergraduate and joint-degree or graduate programs in law and society, including Jurisprudence and Social Policy at University of California-Berkeley, the School of Justice Studies at Arizona State University, Department of Law, Jurisprudence and Social Thought at Amherst College, New York University, University of Massachusetts-Amherst, University of Wisconsin, and Northwestern University. Major research institutes are found in the United States (e.g., the American Bar Foundation, the Institute of Legal Studies at the University of Wisconsin, Center for Law and Society at Berkeley, the Institute for Law and Society at New York University), France (Centre de Recherche Inter-disciplinaire de Vaucresson), Britain (Centre for Socio-Legal Studies at Oxford, Institute for Socio-Legal Studies at Nottingham), Italy (Centro Nazionale di Prevenzione e Difesa Sociale), Spain (Oñati International Institute for the Sociology of Law), Portugal (Centro de Estudos Sociais), Australia (Center for Socio-Legal Studies, La Trobe University), Colombia (Istituto Latinamericano de Servicios Legales Alternativos), and the Netherlands (Hugo Sinzheimer Institute at Amsterdam, Willem Pompe Instituut voor Strafrechtswetenschapen at Utrecht). There are national associations for law and society in the United States, Canada, Britain, Germany, Japan, Argentina, the Netherlands, Portugal, and Finland, as well as associations concerned with legal pluralism, law and political science, law and economics, law and psychology, third-world legal studies, legal history, and criminology. The (primarily American) Law and Society Association and the (primarily European) Research Committee on Sociology of Law of the International Sociological Association held the first international meeting in Amsterdam in 1991 and will hold another in Glasgow in 1996.

Disputing

1

The Oven Bird's Song: Insiders, Outsiders, and Personal Injuries in an American Community[1]

David M. Engel

Introduction

Although it is generally acknowledged that law is a vital part of culture and of the social order, there are times when the invocation of formal law is viewed as an *anti*-social act and as a contravention of established cultural norms. Criticism of what is seen as an overuse of law and legal institutions often reveals less about the quantity of litigation at any given time than about the interests being asserted or protected through litigation and the kinds of individuals or groups involved in cases that the courts are asked to resolve. Periodic concerns over litigation as a "problem" in particular societies or historical eras can thus draw our attention to important underlying conflicts in cultural values and changes or tensions in the structure of social relationships.

In our own society at present, perhaps no category of litigation has produced greater public criticism than personal injuries. The popular culture is full of tales of feigned or exaggerated physical harms, of spurious whiplash suits, ambulance-chasing lawyers, and exorbitant claims for compensation. Scholars, journalists, and legal professionals, voicing concern with crowded dockets and rising insurance costs, have often shared the perception that personal injury litigation is a field dominated by overly litigious plaintiffs and by trigger-happy attorneys interested only in their fees.

To the mind agitated by such concerns, Sander County (a pseudonym) appears to offer a quiet refuge. In this small, predominantly rural county in Illinois, personal injury litigation rates were low in comparison to other major categories of litigation and were apparently somewhat lower than the personal injury rates in other locations as well.[2] Yet Sander County residents displayed a deep concern with and an aversion toward this particular form of "litigious behavior" despite its rarity in their community.

Those who sought to enforce personal injury claims in Sander County were char-

Abridged from *Law & Society Review*, Volume 18: 551 (1987).

acterized by their fellow residents as "very greedy," as "quick to sue," as "people looking for the easy buck," and as those who just "naturally sue and try to get something [for] . . . life's little accidents." One minister describing the local scene told me, "Everybody's going to court. That's the thing to do, because a lot of people see a chance to make money." A social worker, speaking of local perceptions of personal injury litigation, particularly among the older residents of Sander County, observed: "Someone sues every time you turn around. Sue happy, you hear them say. Sue happy." Personal injury plaintiffs were viewed in Sander County as people who made waves and as troublemakers. Even members of the community who occupied positions of prestige or respect could not escape criticism if they brought personal injury cases to court. When a minister filed a personal injury suit in Sander County after having slipped and fallen at a school, there were, in the words of one local observer a "lot of people who are resentful for it, because ... he chose to sue. There's been, you know, not hard feelings, just some strange intangible things...."

How can one explain these troubled perceptions of personal injury litigation in a community where personal injury actions were in fact so seldom brought? The answer lies partly in culturally conditioned ideas of what constitutes an injury and how conflicts over injuries should be handled. The answer is also found in changes that were occurring in the social structure of Sander County at the time of this study and in challenges to the traditional order that were being raised by newly arrived "outsiders." The local trial court was potentially an important battleground in the clash of cultures, for it could be called on to recognize claims that traditional norms stigmatized in the strongest possible terms.

Social Changes and the Sense of Community

Sander County in the late 1970s was a society that was strongly rooted in its rural past yet undergoing economic and social changes of major proportions. It was a small county (between 20,000 and 30,000 population in the 1970s), with more than half its population concentrated in its county seat and the rest in several much smaller towns and rural areas. Agriculture was still central to county life. Sander County had 10 percent more of its land in farms in the mid-1970s than did the state of Illinois as a whole, but the number of farms in Sander County had decreased by more than one-third over the preceding twenty years while their average size had grown by almost half. Rising costs, land values, and taxes had been accompanied by an increase in the mechanization of agriculture in Sander County, and the older, smaller farming operations were being rapidly transformed. At the same time, a few large manufacturing plants had brought blue-collar employees from other areas to work (but not always to live) in Sander County. Also, a local canning plant had for many years employed seasonal migrant workers, many of whom were Latinos. In recent years, however, a variety of "outsiders" had come to stay permanently in Sander County, and the face of the local society was gradually changing.

To some extent these changes had been deliberately planned by local leaders, for it was thought that the large manufacturing plants would revitalize the local economy. Yet from the beginning there had also been a sense of foreboding. In the words of one older farmer:

A guy that I used to do business with told me when he saw this plant coming in down here that he felt real bad for the community. He said, that's gonna be the end of your community, he said, because you get too many people in that don't have roots in anything. And I didn't think too much about it at the time, but I can understand what he was talking about now. I know that to some extent, at least, this is true. Not that there haven't been some real good people come in, I don't mean that. But I think you get quite a number of a certain element that you've never had before.

Others were more blunt about the "certain element" that had entered Sander County: union members, southerners and southwesterners, blacks, and Latinos. One long-time rural resident told us, "I think there's too many Commies around. I think this country takes too many people in, don't you? ... That's why this country's going to the dogs." Many Sander County residents referred nostalgically to the days when they could walk down Main Street and see none but familiar faces. Now there were many strangers. An elderly woman from a farming family, who was struggling to preserve her farm in the face of rising taxes and operating costs, spoke in troubled tones of going into the post office and seeing Spanish-speaking workers mailing locally earned money to families outside the country. "This," she said, "I don't like." Another woman, also a longtime resident, spoke of the changing appearance of the town:

[It was] lots different than it is right now. For one thing, I think we knew everybody in town. If you walked uptown you could speak to every single person on the street. It just wasn't at all like it is today. Another thing, the stores were different. We have so many places now that are foreign, Mexican, and health spas, which we're not very happy about, most of us. My mother was going uptown here a year ago and didn't feel very well when she got up to State Street. But she just kept going, and I thought it was terrible because the whole north side of town was the kind of place that you wouldn't want to go into for information or for help. Mostly because we've not grown up with an area where there were any foreign people at all.

There was also in the late 1970s a pervasive sense of a breakdown in the traditional relationships and reciprocities that had characterized life in Sander County. As one elderly farmer told me:

It used to be I could tell you any place in Sander County where it was, but I can't now because I don't know who lives on them.... And as I say in the last 20 years people don't change work like they used to—or in the last 30 years. Everybody's got big equipment, they do all their own work so they don't have to change labor. Like years ago ... why you had about 15 or 20 farmers together doing the exchange and all.

Many Sander County residents with farming backgrounds had warm memories of the harvest season, when groups of neighbors got together to share work and food:

When we had the threshing run, the dining room table it stretched a full 17 feet of the dining room, and guys would come in like hungry wolves, you know, at dinner time and supper again the same thing.... And they'd fire the engine up and have it ready to start running by 7:00.... You know, it was quite a sight to see that old steam engine coming down the road. I don't know, while I never want to be doing it again, I still gotta get kind of a kick out of watching a steam engine operate.

And all could remember socializing with other farming families on Saturday evenings during the summertime. In the words of two longtime farmers:

A: Well, on Saturday night they used to come into town, and the farmers would be lined up along the sidewalk with an ice cream cone or maybe a glass of beer or something....

B: If you met one to three people, you'd get all the news in the neighbor hood....

A: If you go downtown now, anytime, I doubt if you'll see half a dozen people that you know. I mean to what you say sit down and really, really know them.

B: You practically knew everybody.

A: That's right, but you don't now.

B: No, no, no. If you go down Saturday night ...

A: Everything is dead.

Injuries and Individualism

For many of the residents of Sander County, exposure to the risk of physical injury was simply an accepted part of life. In a primarily agricultural community, which depended on hard physical work and the use of dangerous implements and machinery, such risks were unavoidable. Farmers in Sander County told many stories of terrible injuries caused by hazardous farming equipment, vehicles of different kinds, and other dangers that were associated with their means of obtaining a livelihood.

There was a feeling among many in Sander County—particularly among those from a farming background—that injuries were an ever-present possibility, although prudent persons could protect themselves much of the time by taking proper precautions.

It would be accurate to characterize the traditional values associated with personal injuries in Sander County as individualistic, but individualism may be of at least two types. A rights-oriented individualism is consistent with an aggressive demand for compensation (or other remedies) when important interests are perceived to have been violated. By contrast, an individualism emphasizing self-sufficiency and personal responsibility rather than rights is consistent with the expectation that people should ordinarily provide their own protection against injuries and should personally absorb the consequences of harms they fail to ward off.

It is not clear why the brand of individualism that developed over the years in Sander County emphasized self-sufficiency rather than rights and remedies, but with respect to personal injuries at least, there can be no doubt that this had occurred. If the values associated with this form of individualism originated in an earlier face-to-face community dominated by economically self-sufficient farmers and merchants, they remained vitally important to many of the longtime Sander County residents even at the time of this study. For them, injuries were viewed in relation to the victims, their fate, and their ability to protect themselves. Injuries were not viewed in terms of conflict or potential conflict between victims and other persons, nor was there much sympathy for those who sought to characterize the situation in such terms. To the traditional individualists of Sander County, transforming a personal injury into a claim against someone else was an attempt to escape responsibility for one's own actions. The psychology of contributory negligence and assumption of risk had deep roots in the local culture. The critical fact of personal injuries in most cases was that the victims probably could have prevented them if they had been more careful, even if others were to some degree at fault. This fact alone is an important reason why it was considered inappropriate for injured persons to attempt to transform their misfortune into a demand for compensation or to view it as an occasion for interpersonal conflict.

Attitudes toward money also help explain the feelings of longtime residents of Sander County toward personal injury claimants. While there might be sympathy for those who suffered such injuries, it was considered highly improper to try to "cash in" on them through claims for damages. Money was viewed as something one acquired through long hours of hard work, not by exhibiting one's misfortunes to a judge or jury or other third party, even when the injuries were clearly caused by the wrongful behavior of another. Such attitudes were reinforced by the pervasive sense of living in what had long been a small and close-knit community. In such a community, potential plaintiffs and defendants are likely to know each other, at least by reputation, or to have acquaintances in common. It is probable that they will interact in the future, if not directly then through friends and relatives. In these circumstances it is, at best, awkward to sue or otherwise assert a claim. In addition, in a small community one cannot hide the fact of a suit for damages, and the disapproving attitudes of others are likely to be keenly felt. Thus, I was frequently assured that local residents who were mindful of community pressures generally reacted to cases of personal injury, even those that might give rise to liability in tort, in a "level-headed" and "realistic" way. By this it was meant that they would not sue or even, in most cases, demand compensation extrajudicially from anyone except, perhaps, their own insurance companies.[3]

Given the negative views that local juries adopted toward personal injury cases, terms such as "realistic" for those who avoided litigation were indeed well chosen. Judges, lawyers, and laypersons all told me that civil trial juries in the county reflected—and thus reinforced—the most conservative values and attitudes toward personal injury litigation. Awards were very low, and suspicion of personal injury plaintiffs was very high. A local insurance adjuster told me:

> [T]he jury will be people from right around here that are, a good share of them will be farmers, and they've been out there slaving away for every penny they've got and they aren't about to just give it away to make that free gift to anybody.

And one of the leading local trial lawyers observed:

> [T]here's a natural feeling, what's this son of a bitch doing here? Why is he taking our time? Why is he trying to look for something for nothing? ... So I've got to overcome that. That's a natural prejudice in a small [community], they don't have that natural prejudice in Cook County. But you do have it out here. So first I've got to sell the jury on the fact that this man's tried every way or this woman's tried every way to get justice and she couldn't. And they now come to you for their big day.... And then you try like hell to show that they're one of you, they've lived here and this and that.

The prospects for trying a personal injury case before a local jury, he concluded, were so discouraging that, "If I can figure out a way not to try a case in [this] county for injury, I try to."

Where there was no alternative as to venue, potential plaintiffs typically resigned themselves to nonjudicial settlements without any thought of litigation. And, as I have already suggested, for many in the community the possibility of litigation was not considered in any case. One woman I spoke with had lost her child in an automobile accident. She settled the case for $12,000 without filing a claim, yet she was sure that this amount was much less than she could have obtained through a lawsuit. She told me that since she and her family knew they were going to stay permanently in the community, the pressure of the local value system foreclosed the possibility of taking the matter to court:

> One of the reasons that I was extremely hesitant to sue was because of the community pressure.... Local people in this community are not impressed when you tell them that you're involved in a lawsuit.... That really turns them off.... They're not impressed with people who don't earn their own way. And that's taking money that they're not sure that you deserve.

Others had so internalized this value system that they followed its dictates even when community pressures did not exist. A doctor told me that one of his patients was seriously burned during a trip out of state when an airline stewardess spilled hot coffee on her legs, causing permanent discoloration of her skin. This woman refused to contact a lawyer and instead settled directly with the airline for medical expenses and the cost of the one-week vacation she had missed. Regarding the possibility of taking formal legal action to seek a more substantial award, she said simply, "We don't do that." This same attitude may help to explain the apparent reluctance of local residents to assert claims against other potential defendants from outside Sander County, such as negligent drivers or businesses or manufacturers.

Thus, if we consider the range of traditional responses to personal injuries in Sander County, we find, first of all, a great deal of self-reliant behavior. Injured persons typically responded to injuries without taking any overt action, either because they did not view the problem in terms of a claim against or conflict with another person or because membership in a small, close-knit community inhibited them from asserting a claim that would be socially disapproved. Some sought compensation through direct discussions with the other party, but such behavior was considered atypical. When sympathy or advice was sought, many turned to friends, neighbors, relatives, and physicians. The County Health Department, the mayor, and city council representatives also reported that injured persons occasionally sought them out, particularly when the injuries were caused by hazards that might endanger others. In such cases, the goal was generally to see the hazard removed for the benefit of the public rather than to seek compensation or otherwise advance personal interests.

Insuring Against Injuries

Persons who had been injured often sought compensation from their own health and accident insurance without even considering the possibility of a claim against another party or another insurance company. As a local insurance adjuster told me:

> We have some people that have had their kid injured on our insured's property, and they were not our insured. And we call up and offer to pay their

bills, because our insured has called and said my kid Tommy cracked that kid over the head with a shovel and they hauled him off to the hospital. And I called the people and say we have medical coverage and they are absolutely floored, some of them, that it never even crossed their minds. They were just going to turn it in to their own little insurance, their health insurance, and not do anything about it whatsoever, especially if [Tommy's parents] are close friends....

By moving quickly to pay compensation in such cases before claims could arise, this adjuster believed that she prevented disputes and litigation. It helped, too, that the adjuster and the parties to an accident, even an automobile accident, usually knew each other:

In Chicago, all those people don't know the guy next door to them, much less the guy they had the wreck with. And right here in town, if you don't know the people, you probably know their neighbor or some of their family or you can find out real quick who they are or where they are.

The contrast between injuries in a face-to-face community and in a metropolis like Chicago was drawn in explicit terms:

I think things are pretty calm and peaceful as, say, compared to Chicago. Now I have talked to some of the adjusters in that area from time to time and I know, well, and we have our own insureds that go in there and get in an accident in Chicago, and we'll have a lawsuit or at least have an attorney ... on the claim within a day or maybe two days of the accident even happening. Sometimes our insured has not any more than called back and said I've had a wreck but I don't even know who it was with. And before you can do anything, even get a police report or anything, why you'll get a letter from the attorney. And that would never, that rarely ever happens around here.

This adjuster estimated that over the past 15 years, her office had been involved in no more than 10 automobile-related lawsuits, an extraordinarily low number compared to the frequency of such cases in other jurisdictions. Of course, once an insurance company has paid compensation to its insured, it may exercise its right of subrogation against the party that caused the accident, and one might expect insurance companies to be unaffected by local values opposing the assertion or litigation of injury claims. It is not entirely clear why insurance companies, like individuals, seldom brought personal injury actions in Sander County, but there are some clues. This particular adjuster, who had grown up in Sander County, shared the local value system. Although she did not decide whether to bring suit as a subrogee, she may well have affected the decisions of her central office by her own perceptions and by her handling of the people and documents in particular cases. Furthermore, her insurance company was connected to the Farm Bureau, a membership organization to which most local farmers belonged. The evident popularity of this insurance carrier in Sander County (over 75 percent of the eligible farm families were estimated to be members of the Farm Bureau; it is not known how many members carried the insurance, but the percentage was apparently high) meant that injuries in many cases may have involved two parties covered by the same insurance company.

Occasionally, an insurance company did bring suit in the name of its insured, but given the unsympathetic attitudes of local juries, such lawsuits seldom met with success in Sander County. The adjuster mentioned above told me of a farm worker from Oklahoma who was harvesting peas for a local cannery. He stopped to lie down and rest in the high grass near the road and was run over by her insured, who was driving a pickup truck and had swerved slightly off the road to avoid a large combine. When the fieldworker's insurance carrier sought compensation, the local adjuster refused, claiming that the injured man should not have been lying in the grass near the road and could not have been seen by her insured, who, she insisted, was driving carefully. The case went to trial and a jury composed largely of local farmers was drawn:

> I was not even in there because our lawyers that represent us said, how many of those people do you know out there? And I said, I can give you the first name of everybody on the jury. He said, you stay over there in the library ... don't let them see you.... So I stayed out in my little corner and listened to what went on and we won, we didn't pay 5 cents on it.

Thus, even a lawsuit involving insurance companies on both sides was ultimately resolved in a manner that accorded with traditional values. The insurance companies' knowledge of jury attitudes in Sander County undoubtedly affected their handling of most injury cases.

Lawyers and Local Values

Sander County attorneys reported that personal injury cases came to them with some regularity, although they also felt that many injury victims never consulted an attorney but settled directly with insurance companies for less than they should have received. When these attorneys were consulted, it was by people who, in the opinion of the attorneys, had real, nonfrivolous grievances, but the result was seldom formal legal action. Most personal injury cases were resolved, as they are elsewhere (Ross, 1970), through informal negotiation. Formal judicial procedures were initiated primarily to prod the other side to negotiate seriously or when it became necessary to preserve a claim before it would be barred by the statute of limitations. The negotiating process was, of course, strongly influenced by the parties' shared knowledge of likely juror reaction if the case actually went to trial. Thus, plaintiffs found nego- tiated settlements relatively attractive even when the terms were not particularly favorable.

But expectations regarding the outcome of litigation were probably not the only reason that members of the local bar so seldom filed personal injury cases. To some extent Sander County lawyers, many of whom were born and raised in the area, shared the local tendency to censure those who aggressively asserted personal injury claims. One attorney, for example, described client attitudes toward injury claims in the following terms: "A lot of people are more conducive to settlement here just because they're attempting to be fair as opposed to making a fast buck." Yet this same attorney admitted that informal settlements were often for small amounts of money and were usually limited to medical expenses, without any "general" dam- ages whatever. His characterization of such outcomes as "fair" suggests an internal- ization of local values even on the part of those whose professional role it was to assert claims on behalf of tort plaintiffs. (This contrasts strongly with Ross's finding [1970: 239] that general damages were a substantial part of most insurance settle- ments.)

The local bar was widely perceived as inhospitable to personal injury claimants, not only because there were few tort specialists but because Sander County lawyers were seen as closely linked to the kinds of individuals and businesses against whom tort actions were typically brought. Although plaintiffs hired Sander County attor- neys in 72.5 percent of all non-tort actions filed locally in which plaintiffs were represented by counsel, they did so in only 12.5 percent of the tort cases. One law- yer, who was frequently consulted by potential tort plaintiffs, lived across the county line in a small town outside of Sander County. He told me, "I get a lot of cases where people just don't want to be involved ... they perceive it to be the hierarchy of Sander County.... I'm not part of the establishment."

Thus, even from the perspective of insurance company personnel and attorneys, who were most likely to witness the entry of personal injury cases into the formal legal system in Sander County, it is clear that the local culture tended in many ways to deter litigation. And when personal injury cases were formally filed, it usually was no more than another step in an ongoing negotiation process.

Why was the litigation of personal injury cases in Sander County subjected to disapproval so pervasive that it inhibited the assertion of claims at all stages, from the moment injuries occurred and were perceived to the time parties stood at the very threshold of the formal legal system? The answer, I shall argue, lies partly in the role of the Sander County Court in a changing social system and partly in the nature of the personal injury claim itself.

The Use of the Court

In the recent literature on dispute processing and conflict resolution, various typologies of conflict-handling forums and procedures have been proposed. Such typologies usually include courts, arbitrators, mediators, and ombudsmen, as well as two-party and one-party procedures such as negotiation, self-help, avoidance, and "lumping it." Analyses of these alternative approaches incorporate a number of variables that critically affect the ways in which conflict is handled and transformed. Such variables include, among others, procedural formality, the power and authority of the intervenor, the coerciveness of the proceedings, the range and severity of outcomes, role differentiation and specialization of third parties and advocates, cost factors, time required, the scope of the inquiry, language specialization, and the quality of the evidence that will be heard. When variables such as these are used to analyze various approaches to conflict resolution, the result is typically a continuum ranging from the most formal, specialized, functionally differentiated, and costly approaches to the most informal, accessible, undifferentiated, and inexpensive. The court as a forum for dispute processing and conflict resolution is typically placed at the costly, formalistic end of such continua.

Yet common sense and empirical investigations consistently remind us that trial courts rarely employ the adjudicative procedures that make them a symbol of extreme formalism. Very few of the complaints filed in courts are tried and adjudicated. Most are settled through bilateral negotiations of the parties or, occasionally, through the efforts of a judge who encourages the parties to reach an agreement without going to trial. This was true of the Sander County Court, as it is of courts elsewhere, and it applied with particular force to the relatively infrequent personal injury complaints that were filed in Sander County. Adjudication on the merits was extremely rare. In my sample only one of fifteen personal injury cases went to trial, and the judges and lawyers to whom I talked confirmed the generality of this pattern. Yet the court did play a crucial role in the handling of personal injury conflicts. It did so by providing what was perhaps the only setting in which meaningful and effective procedures of any kind could be applied. To understand why this was so, we must examine some distinctive characteristics of the relationships between the parties in the personal injury cases that were litigated in Sander County.

Among the relative handful of personal injury cases filed in the Sander County Court, almost all shared a common feature: the parties were separated by either geographic or social "distance" that could not be bridged by any conflict resolution process short of litigation. In at least half of the fifteen personal injury cases in the sample, the plaintiff and the defendant resided in different counties or states. These cases were evenly split between instances in which the plaintiff, on the one hand, and the defendant, on the other hand, was a local resident. In either situation, geographic distance meant that the parties almost certainly belonged to different communities and different social networks. Informal responses by the injured party, whether they involved attempts to negotiate, to mediate, or even to retaliate by gossip, were likely to be frustrated since channels for communication and shared value systems and acquaintance networks were unlikely to exist. This is reflected in the disproportionate presence of parties from outside the county on the personal injury docket.

A more elusive but no less significant form of distance was suggested by interviews with the parties as well as by the court documents in several personal injury cases. In these cases, it became apparent that "social distance," which was less tangible but just as hard to bridge as geographic distance, separated the parties even when they were neighbors.

Social distance could take many forms in Sander County. In one personal injury case, the plaintiff, who lived in one of the outlying towns in Sander County, described himself as an outsider to the community although he had lived there almost all his life. He was a Democrat in a conservative Republican town; he was of German extraction in a community where persons of Norwegian descent were extremely clannish and exclusive; he was a part-time tavern keeper in a locality where taverns were popular but their owners were not socially esteemed; the opposing party was a "higher up" in the organization for which they both worked, and there was a long history of "bad blood" between them.

In a second personal injury case, a Mexican immigrant and his family sued a tavern keeper under the Illinois Dram Shop Act for injuries he had suffered as a bystander in a barroom scuffle. Latino immigration into the community had, as we have seen, increased greatly in recent years to the displeasure of many local residents. Cultural misunderstandings and prejudice ran high, and little sympathy could be expected for a Latino who was injured in the course of a barroom fight. Thus, the plaintiff's wife was quite worried about bringing the lawsuit. She feared that they would create more trouble for themselves and told me, "I was afraid that maybe they'd say our kind of people are just trying to get their hands on money any way we could...." The decision to sue was made because they believed that people behind the bar had contributed to the injury by passing a weapon to the man who had struck the plaintiff (although, under the Dram Shop Act, the tavern could have been found liable without fault), and because they saw no other way to recover the income they had lost when the plaintiff's injury had kept him from working.

The tavern keeper, who considered herself a member of the social underclass (although in a different sense from the Mexican immigrants), was bitter about the case and about the Dram Shop Act. When I asked her how the plaintiffs had known that she was liable under the act, she answered, "I haven't any idea. How do they know about a lot of things is beyond me. They know how to come here without papers and get a job or go on welfare. They are not too dumb, I guess."

In this case, then, the two parties were separated from each other and from the community by a great chasm of social distance. One person was set apart from the general community by ethnicity and was well aware that his injuries were unlikely to be regarded with sympathy. The other party was also, by self-description, a "second class citizen." As a tavern keeper, she told me, "you come up against many obstacles, prejudices, and hard times, you wouldn't believe." Both descriptions of social alienation were accurate. Yet the defendant had an established place in the traditional social order. She owned a small business in a town dominated by the ethos of individual enterprise. Her line of work was widely recognized and accepted, although not accorded great prestige, in a community where taverns were among the most important social centers. Her acquisition of Dram Shop insurance made her a "deep pocket" comparable to other local business enterprises that might provide substantial compensation in appropriate cases to injured persons. The plaintiffs in this case, far more than the defendant, were truly social "outsiders" in Sander County. For them, nonjudicial approaches appeared hopeless, and passively absorbing the injury was too costly. Only formal legal action provided a channel for communication between the two parties, and this ultimately led, despite the defendant's reluctance, to settlement.

Social distance also played a part in an action brought by a woman on behalf of her five-year-old daughter, who had suffered internal injuries when a large trash container fell on her. The little girl had been climbing on the trash container, which was located in back of an automobile showroom. The plaintiff and her husband were described by their adversaries as the kind of people who were constantly in financial trouble and always trying to live off somebody else's money. The plaintiff herself stated frankly that they were outsiders in the community, ignored or avoided even by their next-door neighbors. As she put it, "Everybody in this town seems to know everybody else's business ... but they don't know you."

Her socially marginal status in the community precluded any significant form of nonjudicial conflict resolution with the auto dealer or the disposal company, and the matter went to the Sander County Court, where the $150,000 lawsuit was eventually settled for $3,000. Since initiating the lawsuit, the plaintiff had become a born-again Christian and, from her new perspective on life, came to regret her decision to litigate. The little money they had obtained simply caused her to fight with her husband, who sometimes beat her. She came to believe that she should not have sued, although she did feel that her lawsuit had done some good. After it was concluded, she observed, signs were posted near all such trash containers warning that children should not play on them.

In my interviews with local residents, officials, community leaders, and legal professionals, I presented the fact situation from this last case (in a slightly different form, to protect the privacy and identity of the original participants) and asked them how similar cases were handled in the segments of the community with which they were familiar. From our discussion of this matter there emerged two distinct patterns of behavior which, the interviewees suggested, turned on the extent to which the aggrieved party was integrated into the community. If the parents of the injured child were longtime residents who were a part of the local society and shared its prevailing value system, the consensus was that they would typically take little or no action of any sort. Injuries, as we have seen, were common in a rural community, and the parents would tend to blame themselves for not watching the child more carefully or, as one interviewee put it, would "figure that the kid ought to be sharp enough to stay away" from the hazard. On the other hand, if the parents of the injured child were newcomers to the community, and especially if they were factory workers employed in the area's newly established industrial plants, it was suggested that their behavior would be quite different. One union steward assured me that the workers he knew typically viewed such situations in terms of a potential lawsuit and, at the least, would aggressively seek to have the auto dealer and the disposal company assume responsibility for the damages. Others described a kind of "fight-flight" reaction on the part of newcomers and industrial blue-collar workers. One particularly perceptive minister said, "Those ... that feel put down perceive everything in the light of another putdown and I think they would perceive this as a putdown. See, nobody really cares about us, they're just pushing us around again. And so we'll push back." He also noted, however, that it was equally likely that aggrieved individuals in this situation would simply move out of the community—the "flight" response.

There was, then, some agreement that responses involving the aggressive assertion of rights, if they occurred at all, would typically be initiated by newcomers to the community or by people who otherwise lacked a recognized place in the status hierarchy of Sander County. Such persons, in the words of a local schoolteacher, would regard the use of the court as a "leveler" that could mitigate the effects of social distance between themselves and the other side. Persons who were better integrated into the community, on the other hand, could rely on their established place in the social order to communicate grievances, stigmatize what they viewed as deviant behavior, press claims informally, or, because they felt comfortable enough psychologically and financially, to simply absorb the injury without any overt response whatever.

Interestingly, this was precisely the picture drawn for me by the evangelical minister who had converted the mother of the five-year-old girl to born-again Christianity. Lifelong residents of the community, he told me, reacted to stressful situations with more stability and less emotion than newcomers to the community, who were less rooted and whose lives were filled with pressures and problems and what he called, "groping, searching, grasping." For this minister, born-again Christianity offered socially marginal people a form of contentment and stability that was denied them by their lack of a recognized position in the local society. He argued that external problems such as personal injuries were secondary to primary questions of religious faith. He told me, "[I]f we first of all get first things straightened out and that is our relationship with God and is our help from God, all of these other things will fall into order." This was precisely the message that the plaintiff in this case—and many other socially marginal people in the community like him—had come to accept. On this basis, many social outsiders in Sander County could rationalize passivity in the face of personal injuries, passivity that was at least outwardly similar to the typical responses of Sander County's longtime residents.

The picture of the Sander County Court that emerges from this brief overview of personal injury cases differs substantially from that which might be suggested by conventional typologies of conflict resolution alternatives. In processual terms litigation, although rare, was not strikingly different from its nonjudicial alternatives. It was characterized by informal negotiation, bargaining, and settlement in all but the extremely infrequent cases that actually went to trial. Yet these processes occurred only as a result of the filing of a formal legal action. Because of the distance separating the parties, nonjudicial approaches, even with the participation of lawyers, sometimes failed to resolve the conflict. Resorting to the Sander County Court could vest socially marginal persons with additional weight and stature because it offered them access to the levers of judicial compulsion. The very act of filing a civil complaint, without much more, made them persons whom the other side must recognize, whose words the other side must hear, and whose claims the other side must consider. The civil trial court, by virtue of its legal authority over all persons within its jurisdiction, was able to bridge procedurally the gaps that separated people and social groups. In a pluralistic social setting, the court could provide, in the cases that reached it, a forum where communication between disparate people and groups could take place. In so doing, it substituted for conflict-handling mechanisms which served the well-integrated dominant group but which became ineffective for persons who were beyond the boundaries of the traditional community.

The communication that the court facilitated could, however, give rise to anger and frustration. Plaintiffs often viewed the process negatively, because even when they went to court they could not escape the rigid constraints imposed by a community unsympathetic to claims for damages in personal injury cases. Thus, the plaintiff whom I have described as a Democrat in a Republican town told me that the experience of filing and settling a personal injury claim was "disgusting ... a lot of wasted time." Low pretrial settlements were, not surprisingly, the rule.

Defendants viewed the process negatively because they were accustomed to a system of conflict resolution that screened out personal injury cases long before they reached the courthouse. Even though settlements might turn out to be low, defendants resented the fact that personal injuries had in the first place been viewed as an occasion to assert a claim against them, much less a formal lawsuit. Being forced to respond in court was particularly galling when the claimant turned out to be a person whom the core members of the community viewed with dislike or disdain.

In short, the Sander County Court was able to bridge gaps between parties to personal injury cases and to promote communication between those separated by social or geographic distance. It did so, however, by coercion, and its outcomes (particularly when both parties resided in the community) tended to exacerbate rather than ameliorate social conflict. In the court's very success as a mechanism for

conflict resolution we may, therefore, find a partial explanation for the stigmatization of personal injury litigation in Sander County.

The Preservation and Destruction of a Community

> In rural and archaic Japan ... people used to believe that calamity that at-
> tacked the community had its origin in an alien factor inside the community
> as well as outside it. The malevolent factor accumulated in the community.
> It was related also to the sins committed wittingly or unwittingly by members
> of the community. In order to avoid the disastrous influence of the polluted
> element, it was necessary for the community to give the element form and
> to send it away beyond the limits of the village. However, the introduction
> of the alien element, which could turn into calamity at any time, was abso-
> lutely necessary for the growth of the crops. Thus the need for the alien
> factor had two facets which appear contradictory to each other on the sur-
> face: that is, the introduction of the negative element of expiation as well as
> the positive element of crop fertility. (Yamaguchi, 1977: 154)

The social and economic life of Sander County had undergone major changes
in the years preceding this study, and the impact of those changes on the world-view
of local residents and on the normative structure of the community as a whole was
profound. Small single family farms were gradually giving way to larger consolidated agricultural operations owned by distant and anonymous persons or corporations. The new and sizeable manufacturing plants, together with some of the older
local industries, now figured importantly in the economic life of Sander County and
were the primary reasons why the population had become more heterogeneous and
mobile.

These changes had important implications for traditional concepts of individualism and for the traditional relationships and reciprocities that had characterized the
rural community. Self-sufficiency was less possible than before. Control over local
lives was increasingly exercised by organizations based in other cities or states (there
were even rumors that local farmlands were being purchased by unnamed foreign
interests). Images of individual autonomy and community solidarity were challenged
by the realities of externally based economic and political power. Traditional forms
of exchange could not be preserved where individuals no longer knew their neighbors' names, much less their backgrounds and their values. Local people tended to
resent and perhaps to fear these changes in the local economic structure, but for the
most part they believed that they were essential for the survival of the community.
Some of the most critical changes had been the product of decisions made only after
extensive deliberations by Sander County's elite. The infusion of new blood into the
community—persons of diverse racial, ethnic, and cultural backgrounds—was a
direct result of these decisions. The new residents were, in the eyes of many

old-timers, an "alien element" whose introduction was, as in rural Japan, grudgingly recognized as "absolutely necessary" to preserve the well-being of the community.

The gradual decay of the old social order and the emergence of a plurality of cultures and races in Sander County produced a confusion of norms and of mechanisms for resolving conflict. New churches were established with congregations made up primarily of newcomers. Labor unions appeared on the scene, to the dismay and disgust of many of the old-timers. New taverns and other social centers catered to the newer arrivals. Governmental welfare and job training programs focused heavily (but not exclusively) on the newcomers. Newcomers frequently found themselves grouped in separate neighborhoods or apartment complexes and, in the case of blacks, there were reported attempts to exclude them from the community altogether. The newcomers brought to Sander County a social and cultural heterogeneity that it had not known before. Equally important, their very presence constituted a challenge to the older structure of norms and values generated by face-to-face relationships within the community.

Perceptions of Contract and Personal Injury Claims

The reaction of the local community to the assertion of different types of legal claims was profoundly affected by this proliferation of social, cultural, and normative systems. The contrast between reactions to claims based on breaches of contract and those based on personal injuries is especially striking. Contract actions in the Sander County Court were nearly ten times as numerous as personal injury actions. They involved, for the most part, efforts to collect payment for sales, services, and loans. One might expect that concerns about litigiousness in the community would focus upon this category of cases, which was known to be a frequent source of court filings. Yet I heard no complaints about contract plaintiffs being "greedy" or "sue happy" or "looking for the easy buck." Such criticisms were reserved exclusively for injured persons who made the relatively rare decision to press their claims in court.

In both tort and contract actions, claimants assert that a loss has been caused by the conduct of another. In contractual breaches, the defendant's alleged fault is usually a failure to conform to a standard agreed upon by the parties. In personal injury suits, the alleged fault is behavior that falls below a general societal standard applicable even in the absence of any prior agreement. Both are, of course, long-recognized types of actions. Both are "legitimate" in any formal sense of the word. Why is it, then, that actions to recover one type of loss were viewed with approval in Sander County, while far less frequent actions to recover the other type of loss were seen as symptomatic of a socially destructive trend toward the overuse of courts by greedy individuals and troublemakers? The answer appears to lie in the nature of the parties, in the social meanings of the underlying transactions, and in the symbolism of individuals and injuries in the changing social order.

Most of the contract litigation in Sander County involved debts to businesses for goods and services. Typically, the contracts that underlie such debts are quite different from the classic model of carefully considered offers and acceptances and freely negotiated exchanges. Yet many townspeople and farmers in the community saw such obligations as extremely important. They were associated in the popular mind with binding but informal kinds of indebtedness and with the sanctity of the promise. Longtime Sander County residents viewed their society as one that had traditionally been based on interdependencies and reciprocal exchanges among fellow residents. Reliance upon promises, including promises to pay for goods and services, was essential to the maintenance of this kind of social system. One farmer expressed this core value succinctly: "Generally speaking, a farmer's word is good between farmers." Another farmer, who occasionally sold meat to neighbors and friends in his small town, told me:

> We've done this for 20 years, and I have never lost one dime. I have never had one person not pay me, and I've had several of them went bankrupt, and so on and so forth. I really don't pay any attention to bookkeeping or what. I mean, if someone owes me, they owe me. And you know, I've never sent anybody a bill or anything. I mean, sooner or later they all pay.

In these interpersonal exchanges involving people well known to one another there was, it appears, some flexibility and allowance for hard times and other contingencies. On the other hand, there was a mutual recognition that debts must ultimately be paid. When I asked a number of people in the community about a case in which an individual failed to pay in full for construction of a fence, the typical reaction among longtime residents was that such a breach would simply not occur. Of course, breaches or perceptions of breaches did occur in Sander County, and the result could be, in the words of one farmer, "fireworks." I was told stories of violent efforts at self-help by some aggrieved creditors, and it was clear that such efforts were not necessarily condemned in the community. A member of the county sheriff's department observed that small unpaid debts of this kind were often viewed as matters for the police:

> We see that quite a bit. They want us to go out and get the money. He owes it, there's an agreement, he violated the law.... You see, they feel that they shouldn't have to hire an attorney for something that's an agreement. It's a law, it should be acted upon. Therefore, we should go out and arrest the man and either have him arrested or by our mere presence, by the sheriff's department, a uniformed police officer, somebody with authority going out there and say, hey, you know, you should know that automatically these people give the money and that would be it. So therefore they wouldn't have to go to an attorney. Boy, a lot of people feel that.

Other creditors, particularly local merchants, doctors, and the telephone company, brought their claims not to the police but to the Sander County Court. In some cases, contract plaintiffs (many of whom were longtime residents) appeared to litigate specifically to enforce deeply felt values concerning debt and obligation. As one small businessman explained:

> I'm the type of a person that can get personally involved and a little hostile if somebody tries to put the screws to me.... I had it happen once for $5 and I had it happen once for $12.... I explained to them carefully to please believe me that it wasn't the money, because it would cost me more to collect it than it'd be worth, but because of the principle of it that I would definitely go to whatever means necessary, moneywise or whatever, to get it collected. And which I did.

Even those creditors for whom litigation was commonplace, such as the head of the local collection agency and an official of the telephone company, shared the perception that contract breaches were morally offensive. This view appeared to apply to transactions that were routinized and impersonal as well as to the more traditional exchanges between individuals who knew each other well. As the head of the collection agency said, "When you get to sitting here and you look at the thousands of dollars that you're trying to effect collection on and you know that there's a great percentage of them you'll never get and no one will get, it's gotta bother you. It's gotta bother you." Certainly, business creditors felt none of the hesitancy of potential tort plaintiffs about asserting claims and resorting to litigation if necessary. Equally important, the community approved the enforcement of such obligations as strongly as it condemned efforts to enforce tort claims. Contract litigation, even when it involved "routine" debt collection, differed from tort litigation in that it was seen as enforcing a core value of the traditional culture of Sander County: that promises should be kept and people should be held responsible when they broke their word.

Conclusion

In Sander County, the philosophy of individualism worked itself out quite differently in the areas of tort and contract. If personal injuries evoked values emphasizing self-sufficiency, contractual breaches evoked values emphasizing rights and remedies. Duties generated by contractual agreement were seen as sacrosanct and vital to the maintenance of the social order. Duties generated by socially imposed obligations to guard against injuring other people were seen as intrusions upon existing relationships, as pretexts for forced exchanges, as inappropriate attempts to redistribute wealth, and as limitations upon individual freedom.

These contrasting views of contract and tort-based claims took on special significance as a result of the fundamental social changes that Sander County had experienced. The newcomers brought with them conceptions of injuries, rights, and obligations that were quite different from those that had long prevailed. The traditional norms had no doubt played an important role in maintaining the customary social order by reinforcing long-standing patterns of behavior consistent with a parochial worldview dominated by devotion to agriculture and small business. But the newcomers had no reason to share this worldview or the normative structure associated with it. Indeed, as we shall see, they had good reason to reject it. Although they arrived on the scene, in a sense, to preserve the community and to save it from economic misfortune, the terms on which they were brought into Sander County—as migrant or industrial workers—had little to do with the customary forms of interaction and reciprocation that had given rise to the traditional normative order. The older norms concerning such matters as individual self-sufficiency, personal injuries, and contractual breaches had no special relevance or meaning, given the interests of the newcomers. Although these norms impinged on the consciousness and behavior of the newcomers, they did so through the coercive forces and social sanctions that backed them up and not because the newcomers had accepted and internalized local values and attitudes.

Indeed, it was clear that in the changing society of Sander County, the older norms tended to operate to the distinct disadvantage of social outsiders and for the benefit of the insiders. Contract actions, premised on the traditional value that a person's word should be kept, tended to involve collection efforts by established persons or institutions against newcomers and socially marginal individuals. Such actions, as we have seen, were generally approved by the majority of Sander County residents and occurred with great frequency. Personal injury actions, on the other hand, were rooted in no such traditional value and, although such claims were infrequent, they were usually instituted by plaintiffs who were outsiders to the community against defendants who occupied symbolically important positions in Sander County society. Thus, a typical contract action involved a member of "the establishment" collecting a debt, while the typical personal injury action was an assault by an outsider upon the establishment at a point where a sufficient aggregation of capital existed to pay for an injury. This distinction helps to explain the stigmatization of personal injury litigation in Sander County as well as its infrequency and its ineffectiveness.

Yet personal injury litigation in Sander County was not entirely dysfunctional for the traditional social order. The intrusion of "the stranger" into an enclosed system of customary law can serve to crystallize the awareness of norms that formerly existed in a preconscious or inarticulate state (see Fuller, 1969: 9–10; Simmel, 1971). Norms and values that once patterned behavior unthinkingly or intuitively must now be articulated, explained, and defended against the contrary values and expectations of the stranger to the community.

In Sander County, the entry of the stranger produced a new awareness (or perhaps a reconstruction) of the traditional normative order at the very moment when that order was subjected to its strongest and most devastating challenges. This process triggered a complex response by the community—a nostalgic yearning for the older worldview now shattered beyond repair, a rearguard attempt to shore up the boundaries of the community against alien persons and ideas, and a bitter acceptance of the fact that the "stranger" was in reality no longer outside the community but a necessary element brought in to preserve the community and therefore a part of it.

Local responses to personal injury claims reflected these complexities. In part, local residents, by stigmatizing such claims, were merely defending the establishment from a relatively rare form of economic attack by social outsiders. In part, stigmatization branded the claimants as deviants from the community norms and therefore helped mark the social boundaries between old-timers and newcomers. Because the maintenance of such boundaries was increasingly difficult, however, and because the "alien element" had been deliberately imported into the community as a societal act of self-preservation, the stigmatization of such claims was also part of a broader and more subtle process of expiation, a process reminiscent of rituals and other procedures used in many societies to deal with problems of pollution associated with socially marginal persons in the community.

Local residents who denounced the assertion of personal injury claims and somewhat irrationally lamented the rise in "litigiousness" of personal injury plaintiffs were, in this sense, participating in a more broadly based ceremony of regret that the realities of contemporary American society could no longer be averted from their community if it were to survive. Their denunciations bore little relationship to the frequency with which personal injury lawsuits were actually filed, for the local ecology of conflict resolution still suppressed most such cases long before they got to court, and personal injury litigation remained rare and aberrational Rather, the denunciation of personal injury litigation in Sander County was significant mainly as one aspect of a symbolic effort by members of the community to preserve a sense of meaning and coherence in the face of social changes that they found threatening and confusing. It was in this sense a solution—albeit a partial and unsatisfying one—to a problem basic to the human condition, the problem of living in a world that has lost the simplicity and innocence it is thought once to have had. The outcry against personal injury litigation was part of a broader effort by some residents of Sander County to exclude from their moral universe what they could not exclude from the physical boundaries of their community and to recall and reaffirm an untainted world that existed nowhere but in their imaginations.

Notes

1. The title refers to Robert Frost's poem "The Oven Bird," which describes a response to the perception of disintegration and decay not unlike that described here. The poem portrays a woodland scene in midsummer, long after the bright blossoms and early leaves of spring have given way to less attractive vistas and to age, fallen leaves, and "highway dust." With the approach of fall (in both of its senses), the "loud song" of the oven bird echoes through the woods. "The question that he frames in all but words/Is what to make of a diminished thing."

2. The average annual litigation rate for torts in Sander County Court in 1975 and 1976 was 1.45 cases filed per 1,000 population, compared to 13.7 contract cases (mostly collection matters), 3.62 property-related cases (mostly landlord-tenant matters), and 11.74 family-related cases (mostly divorces). McIntosh (1980–81: 832) reports approximately 6 tort actions per 1,000 population in the St. Louis Circuit Court in 1970. The National Center for State Courts (1982: 51) reported 4.47 tort cases per 1,000 in New York State in 1977. None of these figures distinguishes personal injury from other tort actions.

3. I heard of only a few cases where injured persons negotiated compensatory payments from the liability insurance of the party responsible for their harm. In these cases expectations (or demands) appeared to be modest. One involved a woman who lived on a farm. When visiting a neighbor's house, she fell down the basement stairs because of a negligently installed door, fractured her skull, was unconscious for three days, and was in intensive care for five days. As a result of the accident she suffered a permanent loss of her sense of smell and a substantial (almost total) impairment of her sense of taste. Her husband, a successful young farmer, told me that their own insurance did not cover the injury. Their neighbor had liability insurance, which paid only $1,000 (the hospital bills alone were approximately $2,500). Nevertheless, they never considered seeking greater compensation from their neighbor or the neighbor's insurance company:

> We were thankful that she recovered as well as she did.... We never considered a lawsuit there at all. I don't know what other people would have done in the case. Possibly that insurance company would have paid the total medical if we would have just, well, I have a brother who is an attorney, could have just wrote them a letter maybe. But, I don't know, we just didn't do it, that's all.

DISCUSSION QUESTIONS

1.   In thinking about American attitudes toward litigation, consider it as a social service, which government subsidizes by creating, staffing, and paying for courts. Sometimes we encourage or even compel consumption of government services: schooling, innoculations, libraries. We are much more ambivalent about the consumption of other services: welfare, unem-

ployment compensation, prisons. Where does litigation fit in this spectrum and why?

2. Is there a tort litigation crisis? What makes you think so? What evidence would prove or disprove its existence? Which residents made use of tort litigation? Have you ever suffered a tort? Did you sue? Have you ever committed a tort? Were you sued? If you were not involved in litigation in either of these settings, why not?

3. If hostility to litigation partly reflected fear of outsiders and of change, how else do those sentiments manifest themselves in contemporary America? What are other instances of romantic nostalgia?

4. If the residents of Sander County are correct in thinking that rates of personal injury litigation vary widely between their community and large American cities, what are some possible explanations?

5. Why did residents exhibit such different attitudes toward tort and contract litigation?

6. Did the article change your attitude toward the "tort litigation crisis"?

2

Going to Court: Strategies of Dispute Management in an American Urban Neighborhood

Sally Engle Merry

Introduction

In recent years, legal anthropologists have increasingly focused on the process by which disputes are settled, rather than on the substance of the law which emerges from legal decisions. These studies adopt a transactional perspective, investigating the strategies actors use to manage disputes and the choices they make between alternative modes of dispute settlement. Of recurring interest are the conditions under which disputants resort to courts rather than more informal modes of dispute settlement such as gossip and scandal. Although we know something about the role of courts in dispute settlement strategies in relatively stable, homogeneous, and close-knit communities such as Mexican, Lebanese, and Turkish peasant villages, small Ghanaian towns, and Atlantic fishing villages, we know relatively little about the situation in complex, heterogeneous urban neighborhoods. This paper investigates the role of criminal courts in dispute management strategies in a polyethnic American urban neighborhood. Many of the poor, relatively uneducated residents of this neighborhood use criminal courts extensively as part of their arsenal for managing disputes and have become quite sophisticated in manipulating the courts for their own ends.

A detailed analysis of disputing in this heterogeneous urban housing project supports Schwartz's (1954) hypothesis that disputants turn to formal mechanisms of social control in social settings where informal social controls are ineffective. However, despite frequent appeals to the criminal courts in disputes within ongoing relationships, the formal legal system fails to resolve most disputes in the sense of providing a mutually acceptable settlement that terminates the dispute. Consequently, courts come to serve simply as a sanction—a way of harassing an enemy—and an alternative to violence for those unable or unwilling to fight. Ultimately, the only resolution of disputes occurs through avoidance, the "exit" of one or both disputants from the neighborhood.

Abridged from *Law & Society Review*, Volume 13: 891 (1979).

⤚ This analysis of urban disputing addresses four general questions: 1) To what extent do the residents of this neighborhood, including minorities and the poor, have access to courts and to precourt hearings? 2) Under what conditions do they appeal disputes to court? 3) How are these disputes handled by the court? 4) How are disputes terminated, and what role does the court play in ending disputes? My findings suggest that the nature of the social structure surrounding disputants significantly affects their strategies of dispute management.

The appeal to courts to settle disputes in a heterogeneous urban neighborhood conforms with the general hypothesis that formal mechanisms of social control assume greater importance when informal controls are not effective. Black suggests this relationship as a general theoretical proposition: "Law tends to become implicated in social life to the degree that other forms of social control are weak or unavailable" (1973: 53). However, Felstiner argues that in technologically complex, rich societies, such as the United States, disputants do not turn to courts to settle interpersonal disputes when economic stakes are low (1974; 1975). The courts' specialized and alien rules demand hiring an expensive lawyer, and the backlog of cases slows down adjudication. Instead, they use avoidance, a strategy of "limiting the relationship with the other disputant sufficiently so that the dispute no longer remains salient" (1974: 70). He argues that avoidance is a common and relatively inexpensive way of settling disputes in complex societies (1974: 76–77) and criticizes Black's hypothesis, arguing that "he does not consider the possibility that as 'communities' and their informal controls disappear, the need for any external civil dispute processing between individuals may also substantially fade" (1974: 83). He points out, however, that we have very little data on patterns of self-help, negotiation, and avoidance and do not know if avoidance is an empirical reality or simply a sociological possibility (1974: 86). My study suggests that law intrudes into urban social life where informal controls are absent, as Black hypothesizes, but that because courts fail to settle cases, avoidance is ultimately the only successful mode of terminating disputes, as Felstiner argues.

The decision to appeal to court in this neighborhood depends to a great extent on the nature of the relationship linking the disputants and the wider network of social ties enveloping them. Unlike patterns of disputing described in small, close-knit, and isolated communities, residents use courts as a resource against insiders as well as outsiders. In small, bounded societies, disputants often fear that court action will disrupt important social ties and that the gains of an uncertain victory are not worth the cost of social opprobrium. Recourse to court also appears to be disruptive to social relationships within this urban setting, but the implications of such disruption are quite different in the urban context. If the hostility of neighbors is too intense, urbanites have the option of withdrawing from the social system, though usually at some cost, and initiating new social relationships elsewhere. Such a shift is far more difficult in an isolated, rural society. In the complex urban environment, disputants have greater freedom to terminate ongoing relationships, to offend their neighbors and escape social pressure, and to move away from stressful situations. Many social relationships between neighbors in this neighborhood are fragile, and residents are relatively indifferent to their perpetuation in the future. Consequently, they are far less constrained from seeking redress in court than are members of bounded, closed societies. Although studies have frequently discussed the significance of ongoing social relationships to modes of dispute processing, the crucial variable here is not the duration of a relationship in the past, but its future.

The Social Organization of Heterogeneity

Dover Square is a pseudonym for a ten-year-old housing project of 1,150 inhabitants in a polyethnic East Coast port city. Located in the inner city, Dover Square is surrounded by ethnic neighborhoods and the city's skid row. Chinatown abuts the project on one side; and James Hill, a mixed neighborhood of Syrian-Lebanese, Greek, Irish, Chinese, black, Hispanic, and white professional residents borders it on the other. The area has almost the highest crime rate in the city: in the summer of 1976, according to police statistics, it had the highest per capita rate of robberies and assaults in the city; and in 1969 it ranked third in rate of robberies, fourth in assaults, and eighth in residential burglaries among 81 neighborhoods in the city. The project was constructed on the rubble of a white ethnic neighborhood destroyed in conjunction with a major urban renewal project. It contains 300 low-rise garden apartments for families (two-, three- and four-bedroom units). Dover Square houses a very heterogeneous population: 55 percent Chinese, 26 percent black, 9 percent white, and 9 percent Hispanic, living primarily in nuclear families. Although income ceilings restrict tenancy to families with low or moderate incomes, the occupations of the tenant families are highly diverse, ranging from a few teachers and social workers to welfare families. This is not conventional public housing but mixed housing for moderate-income families, with 20 percent leased for poorer, public-housing tenants. Much of the population holds steady, semi-skilled jobs; 14 percent are on welfare. Sixty percent of the families have lived in the project since it opened. The rate of turnover is only 5 percent a year; yet this is not an urban ethnic village with deep roots in the past. The heterogeneity of the population and its limited history maintain anonymity between ethnic groups and consequently undermine informal social control in the project as a whole.

The four ethnic groups in the project are culturally and economically very different. In the Chinese population of 650 individuals, most of the adults were born in mainland China and speak little or no English, while their children are American-born and speak little Chinese. Economically, the Chinese families are tied to the Chinatown commercial establishment. Eighty-six percent of the heads of house work as chefs or waiters in Chinese restaurants or clerks in Chinatown shops. Sixty-five percent of the women work, 89 percent of them in garment factories in Chinatown or nearby downtown areas. Ninety-nine percent of the families have two parents living in the household.

The black population of 300 individuals displays a wider range of occupations. One-fourth of the families are on welfare, while another quarter do skilled manual and technical work; 12 percent have white-collar, professional, or managerial occupations. About half the families are female-headed, at least 10 percent of which are headed by widows. Some black residents are recent immigrants from the South, but most have lived in the North for 15 to 20 years or longer. About 25 black youths, the children of 20 project families (about 7 percent of all project families), form a stable group which has grown up in the project together and whose members are one another's best friends, lovers, and bitter enemies. Four children have been born to unions between group members. Several of the leaders of this group are active in crime and have spent one or more terms in prison. These youths form a local social group, which lounges regularly in the playground in the center of the project, where they are joined by a few white and Hispanic youths.

The 100 white residents are the remnant of a larger white population which moved in when the project opened. Most are older couples whose children have grown and left; only about four white families with young children still live in the project. One-third of the white families form a cohesive Syrian-Lebanese community, while the other families are a potpourri of white ethnics including Irish, Italian, Greek, and Jewish families. The white families are largely working class, with two-thirds engaged in skilled or unskilled manual work. Forty-two percent of the households are female-headed. The 100 Hispanic residents are a small minority, marginal to the social life of the project. About half are on welfare, and one-tenth are young couples with white-collar jobs.

No ethnic group occupies a distinct territory within the project. The policy of the project management is to integrate the neighborhood, and as a result, members of each ethnic group are scattered evenly throughout the project. Residents find that their neighbors are often members of different ethnic groups. Since friendships and kin ties are generally restricted to members of the same ethnic group, neighbors of different ethnicity are usually strangers. The social organization of the project consists of nonlocalized social networks linking members of the same ethnic group in different parts of the project.

This situation persists because members of each ethnic group maintain close social and work relationships with their own ethnic neighborhood. The nearby ethnic neighborhoods provide friends, social services, recreational opportunities, and jobs. These ties serve to bind members of a single ethnic group both to the ethnic neighborhood and to their co-ethnics living in the project. In contrast, ties with neighbors of different ethnicity are fleeting. They are strangers, in Simmel's classic formulation: people who come today and stay tomorrow, but never give up the potential of leaving; people who are in a social system but not of it (1950: 402). Further, substantial cultural differences between neighbors of different ethnic groups foster misunderstanding and suspicion and serve to maintain social distance. No leaders in the project are able to draw together residents of different ethnic groups. The project lacks even local shopowners or business people who could serve as a social center for the whole project.

Strategies of Dispute Management

A dispute is a disagreement which stems from the perception by an individual or group that rights have been infringed and is then raised into the public arena. Nader and Todd's (1978: 14–15) division of disputes into three stages is useful in this context. The first stage is *grievance*, a situation which one person or group perceives to be unjust and grounds for a complaint. The second phase is *conflict*, when the aggrieved party opts for a dyadic confrontation with the offending party. The third stage is the *dispute* itself, when a conflict escalates to the public arena and a third party becomes involved.

Disputes in Dover Square are rarely settled by an agreement that satisfies both parties and terminates the conflict. Most disputes persist for years, with varying levels of salience and intensity, ending only when one of the disputants moves out of the project. Thus, it is more appropriate to discuss dispute management than dispute settlement.

Gossip is the most common dispute management strategy employed by Dover Square residents. While gossip accompanies all kinds of disputes, it appears to have little impact within ethnic groups and virtually none across ethnic boundaries. It is most influential within the Chinese community, where some disputants manage their cases using gossip as their sole strategy, but even here it does not stop the errant husband from sleeping with white women or the stingy woman from failing to reciprocate enough tea cakes. One Chinese woman, for example, lived with both her handicapped husband and a lover, despite considerable gossip about this very irregular union. Gossip within the black community appears to have even less impact. A black woman, for example, discovered that the new redwood gate on her back fence had vanished and reappeared gracing the back fence of a black neighbor whose son had a reputation for stealing. She discussed the incident freely, and it became widely known throughout the black community. When the victim confronted the possessor of the gate, however, the latter claimed that her son had found it. Despite the widespread gossip and consensus that the boy had stolen the gate, it was not returned.

Not unexpectedly, gossip by members of one ethnic group about the misdeeds of individuals in another has no impact at all. Some of the black youths who are leaders of the youth group and active in crime have a project-wide reputation as "bad characters," but they are quite indifferent to their notoriety among Chinese, white, and Hispanic residents. To be effective in managing disputes, gossip must rely on implicit threats to reputation. Whatever potential exists for using gossip this way within an ethnic group, little or no impact is likely across ethnic boundaries.

A second common mode of managing disputes is actual or threatened violence. The injured party gathers friends and attacks the offender. This option demands skill in street fighting and/or a pool of readily mobilizable allies who can fight. It can only be used in disputes when the aggressor can be identified and located again if retaliation is not immediate.

Disputants also appeal to third parties outside their social system. Grievances about dogs, noise, and trash are regularly taken to the office of the project manager with requests for restraining or evicting the offender. The project managers perceive their role as purely custodial, however, and make no effort to mediate such disputes or to evict families on the basis of disputes with neighbors. Managers in the project have always been white and middle class; none has spoken either Chinese or Spanish. They listen sympathetically but do not intervene.

The police are a frequent resource for stopping events perceived as crimes and for halting some kinds of offensive behavior by neighbors. If they arrive in time, they will stop the offending behavior, but their intervention rarely leads to significant mediation or arbitration of the underlying conflict. One woman, for example, summoned the police to stop her Chinese neighbors from exploding firecrackers on their shared porch during Chinese New Year, unaware of how that holiday was traditionally celebrated. The police did stop the firecrackers but did not formulate a compromise which would avoid such conflicts in the future. Nor did they address the wider range of other issues which had persistently led to conflict between these two families.

A third outside party to which disputants appeal is the court. Courts are also instruments of the state, but the mode of access to them and implications of turning to them differ significantly from calling the police. Once the police have stopped an altercation, their role, for the most part, is completed. But the consequences of filing criminal charges are more enduring. In this jurisdiction, any person can file an application for a complaint in the clerk's office of the local district court alleging some form of criminal behavior on the part of the defendant, usually assault, kidnapping, attempted murder, or occasionally rape. Incidents must be serious crimes; this strategy is not used in disputes over noise, trash, or slovenly neighbors. The process of filing an application is easy and cost free: the courthouse is a five-minute subway ride away, and a police officer or clerk of court is always available during working hours to write out the application. The application must specify both the charge and the name and address of the accused. This information is essential, since the accused then receives a summons to appear for a hearing in the court to determine if a complaint should be issued. Without this identifying information, such a strategy is impossible. Therefore it is never used against a stranger.

In this state, district courts have jurisdiction over misdemeanors and minor felonies. They also conduct probable cause hearings in more serious cases, which are then heard in the superior court, the higher criminal court. Before the district court will issue a complaint (a criminal charge), it conducts a "show-cause" hearing to determine whether the evidence is sufficient. In many district courts these hearings are conducted by clerks, but in the court that serves Dover Square it is held by a judge. Almost all who apply for such a "civilian complaint" are granted this preliminary hearing, but the judge often does not issue a complaint. He may feel that the case is too weak or that another mode of handling the conflict would be superior. No records are kept of these hearings, and judges have considerable discretion. In some "show-cause" hearings, the representative of the court, either judge or clerk, makes some effort to mediate the dispute. Often, based on the defendant's promise to correct the offending behavior, the case is continued for a period of time.

Thus, a civilian complainant is assured a preliminary hearing before a judge in a courtroom, although it is likely that the judge will not actually issue a criminal complaint. Nevertheless, this precourt arraignment procedure has several benefits for the complainant. The complainants I talked to believed that defendants were forced to appear for the hearing; and in all the cases I recorded, the defendants did appear. This procedure also carries the possibility that a criminal charge will be issued, with the attendant inconvenience of a trial and risk of a permanent criminal record and incarceration. In a few cases, defendants were convicted. Recourse to the courts suggests to the offender that the complainant has access to a powerful set of sanctions which, even if they are not imposed in the present, might be in the future if further offensive behavior occurs. And finally, it is free for the complainant, requiring neither a court fee nor payment for a lawyer, since the state conducts the hearing and prosecutes the case if a complaint is issued.

Avoidance is a very common response to conflict. One party may move out of the project, or both may strive to avoid one another within the project. Moving out is not an easy or inexpensive solution, however, despite the fact that this is a tenant population not rooted by home ownership. The project offers good housing at low rents, particularly for racial minorities, and the waiting list is long. Rates of turnover are under 5 percent a year. Avoiding a neighbor in such a dense settlement is also difficult, so that unresolved conflicts are frequently exacerbated by periodic encounters. But even successfully avoiding one's adversary does not necessarily terminate the dispute. Thus, it is useful to distinguish between avoidance and "endurance," the latter a situation in which a disputant simply endures an ongoing state of conflict because the costs of real avoidance—i.e., moving out—are too high. This may seem identical to the phenomenon Felstiner describes as "lumping it" (1974: 81). However, the term "lumping it" simply refers to the end point in a dispute in which the offended party gives up and declines to assert his rights. It does not describe situations in which a dispute persists for long periods, broken by periodic eruptions of conflict, before it is finally terminated either by a settlement, real avoidance, or "lumping it" in the sense of giving up. In other words, "lumping it" is a mode of terminating disputes, while endurance is a phase in the disputing process. Avoidance can be a strategy for either managing disputes or ending them. Endurance persists as long as the disputants find the costs of avoidance or resolution higher than the costs of putting up with a conflict situation. Endurance is a frequent pattern in Dover Square, where disputants have relatively few alternatives for settling disputes and are financially constrained from moving out.

Categories of Disputes

Disputes in Dover Square typically fall into three categories, differing according to the substance of the dispute, the time depth, the nature of the relationship between the disputants, and the characteristic modes of managing and settling the disputes.

Property Crimes (Pre-Dispute)

Crimes initiated by an impersonal desire for gain are very common in the project but do not themselves constitute disputes. Robbery, burglary, larceny, and some cases of assault typically occur between strangers and across ethnic lines. Crimes are intended to enrich the thief, not to express personal animosity toward the victim. Victims are selected according to apparent wealth and vulnerability. The victim rarely learns the culprit's identity. According to my victimization survey of 200 households, these families suffered 89 burglaries; 50 robberies, attempted robberies, and purse snatches; 19 larcenies; and 42 auto thefts during their residence in the project. These property crimes are frequent but rarely lead to a dispute, in the sense of a confrontation moving into the public arena. They can more appropriately be described as grievances. Time depth is very short, usually not extending beyond the incident itself, and the only mode of managing such events is to call the police. Settlement, in the sense of the termination of the conflict, rarely occurs, and the prevailing mode of dealing with such grievances is "lumping it."

Crime-Initiated Disputes

In a few cases the victims knew or discovered the identities of the culprits and initiated one or more responses. In about half of these incidents the aggrieved party simply confronted the offender with an expression of injustice; thus it only reached the level of conflict. But half moved into the phase of dispute itself by drawing in an outside third party. I recorded ten cases of this latter type, all but one occurring between individuals acquainted with one another and members of the same social network but not close friends or kin. In one case, the robber assumed a false identity but inadvertently selected one the victim knew; she was able to detect the deception and trace the real culprit.

Only four out of ten occurred across ethnic boundaries. In most of the cases time depth was short, involving a grievance (the crime) and only one or two "moves" in response. A "move" is any act designed to prosecute the dispute and can itself constitute a grievance, which initiates a new move. The most frequent moves are calling the police or coercive self-help, primarily violent attacks or threats against the person who commits a crime or retaliation against those who call the police. In half of the ten cases observed, the infringed party gave in and "lumped it." Two were settled by the court and two by violence. One case was still in court and not yet resolved at the end of my research.

Neighborhood Social Order Disputes

A second kind of dispute erupts between neighbors over physical and social order: over the disposal of trash, barking and biting dogs, noise late at night or through the walls, and standards of cleanliness for shared porches, stairwells, and back yards. The inevitable frictions of dense living are exacerbated by differences in life style and culture. One Chinese family, for example, found its white neighbor's dog noisy, dirty, and frightening, since they came from a world in which dogs are not common. I heard of nine neighborhood order disputes, and I suspect there were many more.

These disputes occur between people who are acquainted with one another but are not friends and do not share a similar culture or life style. Five crystallized between neighbors of different ethnic groups, and the other four erupted between individuals who belonged to the same ethnic group but were divided in other ways. One older couple, for example, had emigrated from a peasant village in rural China, where they had lived much of their lives. They fought bitterly with their American-ized Chinese neighbors, whose teenage children spoke no Chinese and lived a very American way of life. The older couple accused them of making too much noise and throwing beer cans into their back yard.

The time depth in such disputes is typically long, perhaps as long as ten years. In that time the feuding neighbors may execute many moves against each other. The most common, utilized in about half the cases, is to appeal to the management office to curtail the offensive behavior and/or evict the offender. The management is loath to get involved, however; so disputants adopt a number of other strategies–principally calling the police, threatening court action, violence, or avoidance. Settlements, in the sense of a termination of the conflict, occur only when one of the disputing parties moves away. By the end of the research period, two families had moved out; but in six cases, the neighboring disputants simply endured an ongoing state of enmity and conflict over dirty stairs, loud noises, and offensive dogs. In the last case, neighboring families constructed a fence between their shared back yards, an example of more or less successful avoidance rather than simply endurance.

Interpersonal Conflicts

The third kind of dispute concerns breaches in ongoing social relationships stemming from personal rivalry, sexual jealousy, public insult, or physical injury. Most are sparked by some act of violence between friends, lovers, and neighbors of long standing. I recorded 14 cases of this kind of dispute, 9 within the same ethnic group and the other 5 between close friends or the allies of close friends in different ethnic groups. Eight took place between blacks and one between Chinese residents, although the latter, involving a man who had affairs with white women and neglected his wife, as already noted, never moved beyond the stage of gossip.

These are usually complex disputes in which the parties engage in numerous moves and countermoves over the years. Emotional involvement with the other party and with the conflict is high. Such disputes are rarely "settled" except by avoidance. Eleven ended when one of the parties left the project. The other three were not settled; at the end of my research period the disputants continued to endure a situation of unresolved conflict. Even in those disputes ended by avoidance, this termination was preceded by a long and stressful period of conflict. Avoidance appears to be a very prevalent mode of terminating interpersonal disputes, but only after a phase of endurance.

In sum, all of these disputes concern conflicts between individuals involved in ongoing relationships, yet each category is quite different in substance and process. They contrast markedly with most crimes—incidents between strangers that do not evolve into disputes. Disputes in all categories are appealed to third parties, but none of these third parties is very effective in providing satisfactory resolution. Violence seems to be effective and is thus frequently employed. The most frequent mode of "settlement" is avoidance. Of the cases I observed, 44 percent were settled in this manner. Six percent were settled by court action and 6 percent by violence. Some form of nonsettlement, and an enduring state of conflict in which one party temporarily or permanently refrained from pressing its legitimate claims, occured in 44 percent of the cases.

Since the crime-initiated and neighborhood disputes occur between people who are distantly acquainted but not intimate and between people different in ethnic and cultural traits, this use of outside third parties conforms to Black's hypothesis about the role of formal social controls where informal ones are absent. However, disputes between intimates are also commonly appealed to an outside third party, the court, although in these relationships one would expect informal social controls to be more effective. As a detailed analysis of patterns of court use reveals, this anomaly occurs because the heterogeneity and complexity of the city undermine informal social sanctions and allow disputants to jettison hostile or disapproving relationships if necessary. Thus, the costs of using formal mechanisms for resolving disputes are less than in isolated, small-scale societies where one must continue to confront the consequences of disruptive actions long into the future. Breaking off an ongoing relationship or moving away, although often undesirable, is at least possible in this urban setting.

Recourse to Court

Analysis of when and why disputants in Dover Square seek court intervention
uncovers a complex pattern of moves and counter-moves aimed at dispute
resolution. Indeed, disputants often lose track of who is ahead and which moves may
exacerbate the conflict or restore an uneasy truce. As disputants become more
emotionally committed to the dispute, their moves and reactions to counter-moves
of their opponents intensify and often escalate in frequency and level of violence.
Recourse to the courts and resort to violence are most frequent. The following cases
illustrate the complexity of these patterns of interaction.

The Case of the Jilted Lover's Slap

The case of the jilted lover's slap erupted between a young black man and his
ex-lover, a young black woman, both about 20 years old. They had lived together
for three years and had a baby, but two weeks before the incident, the young woman,
Renee, packed up her belongings and the baby and moved back to her mother's
apartment in another part of the project, where she had lived the previous eight
years. George, her boyfriend, was lounging in the project one morning after her
departure when she walked by. Surrounded by a group of their mutual friends, he
complained that she had taken their daughter for a ride in the car of his bitter enemy
and rival, and she responded that she was free to do as she pleased and didn't like
him "jumping up in her face." He was angered and slapped her. Infuriated, she raced
home to her mother.

A few minutes later, Renee's older brother Bill, aged 21, and a close friend of
his, Fred, who lived in the project and had a reputation as a tough person, appeared
in the local hangout in the project looking for George. Bill had a pipe thinly concealed in his pants pocket. Renee's mother appeared brandishing a bent aluminum
lawn chair leg, not an effective weapon but a symbolic one, followed by her
boyfriend feebly waving a wooden chair leg. Bill told his mother to go home, that
he would take care of George. George was nowhere to be seen, but no one made any
effort to look for him, remaining in the same hangout for two hours waiting for him
to return. When I asked why no one even went to George's apartment, about 100
yards away, to look for him, Bill explained to me that it would be risky as well as
inappropriate, since according to "people's law," if you break into someone's house,
they have the right to do whatever they want to you since you have no right to be
there.

An audience of other project residents, mostly black, quickly gathered to join the
vigil waiting for George's return and his punishment. Renee's mother announced that
George was a homosexual, that "he does it with little boys, right here in the
playground." Several said that George had no right to slap Renee. Yet no one
mentioned that while George and Renee were together, he had hit her frequently. I
suspect that the slap generated this response because once the relationship was

terminated, he no longer had the same rights to hit her. Further, as one of his friends observed, his real offense was not simply that he hit her but that he hit her in public.

Later that afternoon, Renee's mother, whose brother was a policeman, went to the courthouse and took out an application for a complaint against George. When the news traveled through Dover Square, listeners were impressed with the severity of her action. She charged George with assault against her daughter. I have only reports of what happened in court, since I did not attend. The first day the case was heard, both Bill and George were in the courtroom. Bill threatened to beat up George, so George filed an application for a complaint against Bill, charging him with assault. At the next hearing, both cases came up before the judge at the same time, and he dismissed them both.

Two weeks after this incident, George spotted his bitter enemy and rival for Renee's affection a few blocks away and attacked and injured him. He also gossiped that Renee was robbing him by clearing out the apartment that he had deserted and that her daughter was actually not his but belonged to his rival.

The incident of the slap and the surrounding events did drive George from the project. He did not return to his apartment but left all his clothes and belongings there and moved in with a friend a few blocks away. Five months after the incident, when I last observed the state of the conflict, he had still made only fleeting visits back to Dover Square and regularly "hung" in another park.

Thus, the festering dyadic conflict between George and Renee expanded to a dispute when a public breach occurred, drawing in other members of the community who had their own long-standing grudges. Renee's family used several strategies simultaneously, and George reciprocated. Renee's family threatened violence, slurred George's reputation, and took him to court. George employed similar strategies. The court did not adjudicate the case, however, and termination of the conflict occurred only when George moved out (unwillingly).

The Case of the Neighbor Rapist

Two black families, the Smiths and the Jacksons, lived next door to one another for ten years and, during this time, alternately fought with and socialized with one another. On at least three previous occasions one family had filed a complaint against the other. One of the women, Mrs. Jackson, was about 40 and lived alone with her six children. One of her children had been arrested several times, was friendly with the local teenage gang, and invited them to her parties. A leader of this group, James Smith, lived next door with his three sisters, a brother, grandmother, and his girlfriend and baby. James had been arrested several times and served at least one prison sentence. In the past, Mrs. Jackson had taken two neighbors to court over disputes arising from fights between her children and others in the neighborhood.

Following a minor quarrel Mrs. Jackson accused James Smith and his brother of breaking into her apartment and attempting to rape her and took out a complaint to this effect. James was angry and confronted her on the stairs between their apartments wielding a gun. Mrs. Jackson then charged him with intimidating a witness. The two brothers were arrested and sent to jail for two weeks pending the hearing on this charge. Mrs. Jackson was working as a traffic supervisor for the police department at this time and was encouraged to take this action by the policeman she worked with, who was anxious to develop a case against James Smith because the police considered him a "troublemaker."

While the two brothers were in jail pending trial, a robber broke into the Smith house with a shotgun and ransacked the house, holding the family up. The Smiths could not identify the culprit since he had a stocking over his face, but called the police afterwards to report the incident. Through the gossip network they heard that the robber was a long-standing enemy of James and blamed the incident on Mrs. Jackson, whom they suspected of inciting the robber in order to get revenge.

When the case came to court, James was convicted on charges stemming from a previous arrest for a burglary, while his brother was acquitted. The day the brother returned home, Mrs. Jackson moved out of her apartment to another part of the city. She did not want to leave her apartment but moved because she feared retaliation by James and his brother. (James was released periodically during his sentence on a prison furlough program.) He and his family blame Mrs. Jackson for his conviction.

The Case of the Averted Robbery

An older white man averted a robbery by warning an elderly Chinese man that he suspected a group of youths was plotting to rob him on his way home from the laundromat. One of the youths, a white boy, was furious at the old man and verbally threatened and abused him. The older man then went to the courthouse and filed an application for a complaint against the youth. When the clerk of the court told him he could not make a strong case on the basis of a verbal assault, he changed the charge to physical assault, explaining to me that the judge would believe him, an older respectable citizen, not the youth who had a record. The case did not come to court, however, since the boy was on probation and his probation officer warned the boy not to give the older man any trouble or he would be in jail. The boy did not harass the older man any further, and was actually quite polite to him. The older man moved out of the project three months later and had been planning his departure at the time of the incident. He told me that his plans to move had given him courage to confront the local gang of criminals.

The Case of the Revengeful Brothers

This final case suggests the conditions under which disputants resort only to violence and do not appeal to an outside third party. In this case the plaintiffs, young Chinese males, were able to fight and were wary of the court. A teenage white boy who lived in the project began to date a teenage Chinese girl, also a project resident. The boy tried to persuade this girl to work for him as a prostitute and introduced her to drugs such as Valium. The Chinese girl did spend at least one night out with a customer, to my knowledge. Late that night when she did not return home, her brothers came to look for her boyfriend, angry that he had turned their sister to drugs and prostitution. The boy was nowhere to be found. The next day the brothers did find him and beat him up. The white boy and Chinese girl were not seen together again.

These four cases reveal a complex process of unfolding moves and counter-moves in which some parties used violence and others resorted to the police and the courts. The threat of court did serve as a deterrent, since court action did occasionally lead to the imposition of sanctions. However, it was most effective when the accused already had a reputation for crime with the police. These cases also suggest that gossip has little impact in deterring misbehavior, although it did play an important role in providing information. In contrast, violence appears to be a very effective mode of dealing with disputes.

When all the cases in which violence or the courts were used as disputing strategies are broken down into their component moves, it is possible to analyze the characteristics of individuals who resorted to each. Of 32 such moves, 15 were appeals to the court through the civilian complaint procedure and 17 violence or threats of violence. In only one case did the same individual use both strategies. Overall, those who considered or actually did resort to the court reflected the economic and educational diversity of the population. Of the 15 court moves, 12 were by individuals with temporary, unskilled jobs or those on welfare and three by persons with steady, skilled jobs. Nine of the 15 were by individuals who had less than a high school education, and of the six with high school or further education, only two had any college training.

Striking differences existed between those who used the court and those who turned to violence. Courts were used by physically weaker individuals less capable of defending their interests by fighting. It was primarily women who went to court and men who resorted to violence. Of the four men who used the court, one was elderly and another a juvenile transvestite unskilled in fighting. Those who used violence were almost entirely young males experienced in street fighting.

Second, court use was disproportionately high among whites and low among Chinese. About half the blacks turned to court and half to violence, but three quarters of the whites used courts, and no Chinese did. This difference probably reflects each group's familiarity and past experience with American courts. Third, those with a criminal record or a history of arrests did not turn to the court but used violence instead. As one older white man said, he expected that the judge would believe him rather than his protagonist, a youthful offender with a long record. Insofar as the judge, lacking clear evidence and being a stranger to both parties, must rely on his own assessment of the credibility of the parties in making a decision, the party without a record is clearly at an advantage. Fourth, those who turned to court generally had some special, inside knowledge of court operations, either through a close friend or relative on the police force or the past encounters of kin with arrests and court appearances. One exception was a nun who was persuaded to press charges against an armed robber. However, an equal number with inside knowledge of the court chose violence instead, some because they had a record and did not expect to be treated favorably.

Special knowledge seems to be a precondition for using the court but does not guarantee it. Here, in an interesting twist on Galanter's (1974) argument, the "repeat players" who were knowledgeable about the courts were the "have-nots" rather than "haves." The youths involved in crime were often quite sophisticated about criminal courts. One youth, for example, said that he avoided kicking or knocking down old women when he robbed them since he believed that would change the charge from a minor one, larceny, to a more serious one, assault. Another youth pointed out that he sometimes committed crimes which a judge would find so improbable that he would be acquitted. For example, he once robbed a clerk who knew perfectly well who he was, in the laundromat in broad daylight. In fact, the victim did not prosecute, justifying his inaction on the basis that the offender already had so many other charges against him. These youths knew several detectives and even a few judges by name, and discussed their propensities and foibles. This knowledge of court operation extended to their families as well. When one youth's sister was, in her opinion, unjustifiably beaten by a police detective, she lodged a complaint with the city's police commissioner.

Chinese residents, on the other hand, had no experience in court and shied away from any involvement in American legal institutions. Because of immigration laws in effect from 1882 to 1965, excluding most categories of Chinese immigrants, a large proportion of Chinese entered the country illegally and have studiously avoided American police and courts. Many spoke little or no English. Only in the last two years has this Chinatown had a Chinese-speaking lawyer.

The nature of the relationship between the disputants also influenced the decision to appeal to court. It was neither the "relational distance" nor the ongoing quality of the relationship but rather its future that was most significant. Residents filed charges against opponents who were known personally but with whom their relationships were terminating or could easily be terminated. In each case in which a Dover Square resident took another to court, the relationship, despite its long duration, had a limited future. In the conflict between George and Renee, for example, their relationship had ended. One boy took his friend to court over a bike after he had eased out of his friendships in the project. Both Mrs. Jackson and the older white man moved out of the project soon after taking their protagonists to court. In ten of the 15 moves using the court, one of the disputants subsequently moved out of the project or broke off his social relationships with its residents. In a neighborhood with such separate, disjunctive social worlds and so few institutions to tie neighbors together, it was sometimes possible to avoid an enemy without moving away. However, for neighbors or individuals involved in the same social networks, avoidance without departure from the project was difficult. Moving out of the project was usually an expensive and undesirable solution to conflicts, but it is generally easier to move away and construct a new set of relationships elsewhere in an urban setting than in isolated rural villages.

Residents' choice of the court was also influenced by the extent to which they were encapsulated in a cohesive community. Disputants who were not linked into a tightly knit ethnic community were more likely to appeal to court for settlement than those who were. This partially explains the substantial differences between ethnic groups in patterns of dispute management. The Chinese residents of Dover Square, who were closely tied to the cohesive Chinatown community, did not go to court to settle disputes within the group, while the black and white groups, neither of whom was involved in a close-knit social network and community, used courts to settle disputes between intimates as well as strangers.

Chinese residents of Dover Square were dependent on connections to Chinatown for jobs in Chinese restaurants and shops, where most of them worked, and for partners and capital if they chose to establish their own restaurant. This represented the only chance for economic mobility for Chinese who spoke no English. Chinese residents were socially tied to Chinatown as members of family associations, churches, political parties, martial arts clubs, and circles of friends and relatives. Most of their social and recreational life took place in Chinatown, whether shopping in Chinatown shops or attending large wedding banquets, family association outings, traditional holiday celebrations, or social gatherings of kin from the same village in China. Those who spoke no English were dependent on Chinatown for Chinese-speaking bankers, doctors, social workers, and lawyers. Community opinion was a powerful form of informal social control in Chinatown, and Dover Square residents took this into account when contemplating a deviant act such as dating a white person. Chinese residents could not easily escape the social consequences of their misdeeds against other Chinese without severing their ties to Chinatown altogether, a difficult and costly experience.

Moreover, heads of family associations and leaders of the Chinatown Benevolent Association served as mediators for internal disputes. Every individual belonged to a clan or family association, which traditionally handled disputes between clan members. Cases between members of different clans and appeals from family associations were mediated by the Chinese Consolidated Benevolent Association, an umbrella organization that included all Chinatown associations but was controlled by the wealthy owners of Chinese restaurants and businesses. Decisions by these associations were not legally binding but were enforced by social pressure and the considerable economic power of the merchants. The Benevolent Association even punished Chinese criminals for incidents in Chinatown. According to a Dover Square resident, for example, a Chinese youth who robbed a Chinese man on the main street of Chinatown was tracked down through the girl he was visiting and punished by receiving a beating from representatives of the Benevolent Association.

Neither blacks nor whites were implicated in this kind of cohesive, organized community with its own community mediators. Their jobs, friends, churches, and voluntary associations were scattered throughout the black and white neighborhoods of the city, and no more than three or four residents participated in the same organization. Similarly, their networks of friends and kin extended to diverse neighborhoods. Only the Syrian-Lebanese residents shared ties to a small ethnic community, as the Chinese did. Relations between black or white neighbors were fleeting: they expected that sooner or later they would move out of the project and never see one another again. In contrast, even if Chinese residents moved out, they were still implicated in ongoing relationships with their neighbors through ties to Chinatown organizations and social networks. Blacks and whites recognized no leaders with the ability to mediate disputes either within or between their groups and did not even agree who the overall leaders of the project were. Consequently, blacks and whites turned to the courts to manage disputes within the group, but Chinese did not.

These ethnic differences in use of the court also reflect different values about disputing. Most of those who appealed to the court, both black and white, belonged to cultures that value open confrontation in dealing with disputes, protecting one's rights, and avoiding exploitation by others. Chinese residents, in contrast, stressed the importance of pressing claims indirectly while preserving the pretense of amity and gossiping about one another's misdeeds.

The Role of the Court

When Dover Square residents take their cases to court, however, they do not always obtain a negotiated settlement. American criminal courts are not designed to settle interpersonal disputes, in the sense that anthropologists conceive of settlement, but rather to determine if a law has been violated and, if so, to punish the offender. Anthropologists view dispute settlement as a restoration of harmony in social relationships, something that "makes the balance" (cf. Nader, 1969). In an American court, however, facts that are relevant to restoring a balance, such as the past history of the dispute and the community reputation of the disputants, may be excluded as irrelevant to the particular case. This style of court procedure contrasts markedly with the Zapotec court style described by Nader, in which the goal of the court proceeding is to arrive at a mutually acceptable compromise that restores equilibrium in social relationships rather than a verdict specifying a winner and a loser (1969: 87–88). American courts are—at least conceptually—formal, public, narrow in their conception of relevance, and "all-or-nothing" in their style of decision making, in contrast to other modes of settlement, such as a Zapotec court or Kpelle moot, which are informal, define much more of the context and history of the dispute as relevant, seek a compromise decision and restitution, and operate with reference to community norms—not specialized, alien rules. This latter form of court can also exist in a complex urban setting such as a squatter settlement in Chile (Spence, 1978).

Because of the number of cases American courts must handle, they are unable to take the time for a full airing of the dispute. Judges often decide not to hear a case at all if the evidence seems inadequate. Since I did not observe what happened when Dover Square cases arrived in court, I am relying on the perceptions of the participants. They frequently mentioned that the judge "threw the case out" and never said that a judge "settled" a case. Furthermore, since the judge is a stranger to the disputants, he cannot rely on his personal knowledge of the situation or on the opinions of their neighbors. When George and Renee's brother accused one another of assault, for example, the judge threw the case out. In an earlier incident between the Jacksons and the Smiths, the judge noted the long history of charges and countercharges between the two families and refused to hear the case. Of the ten cases actually taken to court whose outcome I discovered, six ended before adjudication, and one was handled by a probation officer. In only three did the judge make a decision.

Even the decisions the judges did make did not always address the fundamental conflict between the disputants and succeed in restoring harmony. In one case, for example, although the court's decision appears to be reasonable and conciliatory, it failed to deal with the underlying issues of the conflict and was not carried out.

Bill, a 15-year-old, appeared one day in the project with a new ten-speed bike. His friend, Vernon, aged 20, asked if he could ride it, and Bill refused. Vernon then grew abusive, pushed Bill around, insulted him, took the bike, and rode off on it. Bill never saw the bike again. A policeman standing across the street watching the incident approached Bill and urged him to file a complaint against Vernon for stealing his bike. Vernon was suspected by the police of being responsible for many crimes in the project. Bill agreed, although he was somewhat afraid of Vernon, who was a leader of the youth group and had a reputation as a tough person. Both Bill and Vernon lived in Dover Square and had been friends for years, but in the last few months preceding this incident Bill had been gradually withdrawing from the local youth group and had formed his own group of gay male friends. Consequently, although his relationship with Vernon was of long duration it had a limited future.

The judge required Vernon to repay Bill for the bike within a certain time period and continued the case until then. However, one day before that deadline Vernon had paid Bill none of the money and did not have it. As a clerk explained the system to me, unless Bill reappeared in court on the day of the deadline and reported that he had not received his money, the case would be automatically dismissed. Bill was too frightened of Vernon and his threats of violence to do that. Furthermore, he was angry less about the bike than about Vernon's abusive treatment of him, and since the bike had been stolen in the first place, Bill was more interested in revenge for the insult than in restitution of the bike.

Cases taken to court in Dover Square rarely produce an outcome that settles the dispute and restores good relations. At least for this low-income population, the court serves as a sanction, a way of harassing an enemy, rather than as a mode of airing and resolving disputes. It serves as an alternative to violence for those unable or unwilling to fight.

Conclusion

Disputants in Dover Square thus use courts frequently, but rarely successfully, as a mode of settling disputes. Although courts are used where informal sanctions are absent, they cannot fill this vacuum effectively. Rather, courts function as a potential sanction by intimidating opponents, and as an alternative to street violence. Courts are used extralegally, not as a forum for adjudicating disputes according to shared legal principles but as a weapon marshalled by disputants to enhance their power and influence. Disputes taken to court are not adjudicated but in Gulliver's terms, "negotiated." Negotiation, as used in this sense, is simply a discussion between the parties in which they must come to a mutually satisfactory agreement based on their relative strength (1969: 17–19). The disputant's ability to appeal to court and probability of success in that arena influences his or her relative power to "negotiate" a settlement. The victor is the contender with the greater power, not the party with superior rights.

Although the court is employed in disputes within ongoing social relationships, it is primarily used in those with a limited future. An ongoing relationship has both duration in the past and potential for the future. A relationship with a long past has little binding power if the participants expect that they will never see one another again. Conversely, even a relationship of relatively short duration may have considerable force if the participants realize they will have to deal with one another for a long period of time in the future. A limited future changes the calculations of costs and gains, making confrontation cheaper. It is the expectation of the future of the relationship, rather than its simple duration, which constrains residents of Yngvesson's fishing village (1976) from taking one another to court over their conflicts.

The extent to which individuals must take account of one another in the future depends, in turn, on the degree to which they are implicated in durable social networks with one another and whether or not they are free to escape these networks. This is a question of the social structure of the community and its articulation with the larger society. The Chinese residents' reluctance to use the court resembles the behavior of disputants in bounded, small-scale societies, suggesting that a cohesive and closed social structure may discourage the use of zero-sum courts to settle disputes.

Felstiner's hypothesis that avoidance is a common strategy for dealing with conflicts in American society is well supported in this neighborhood, but, as Danzig and Lowy argue, it is both more costly and less satisfactory than he implies (1975). Moving away may cost too much, and withdrawal from a social relationship with someone who shares one's stairwell, porch, balcony, and trash area is difficult. Residents resort to court and self-help strategies first, and avoidance only when other approaches fail. It is the inability of the courts to settle disputes effectively that compels residents to rely on avoidance to deal with their disputes. Further, they are often forced to tolerate situations of enduring conflict and hostility. Although it has frequently been noted that courts rarely resolve disputes, few have pointed to the costs of enduring relationships of conflict.

This study suggests that in some settings legal machinery is accessible to the poor, minorities, and women. American courts are often described as costly, slow, and alienating, yet members of this community use criminal courts and the threat of criminal courts skillfully to further their own interests. Many may be more familiar with the functioning of the courts than are middle-class people to whom courts are thought to be much more accessible. It may be primarily the civil courts which are more available to the more educated parts of the population, while criminal courts are open to all segments of society. However, it is also true that although legal machinery is available, it often does not lead to adjudication and it does not necessarily serve this population well.

Even when disputants do not actually go to court, the option of court action may still influence their behavior. Even if a judge does not adjudicate a case, the accused is still pressured to appear in court, and there is always the chance that he will be arraigned, convicted, and sentenced. Since disputes are managed according to the relative power of the disputants rather than by a third party, the threat of court action increases the power and bargaining position of people such as women and elderly men, who can neither resort to violence nor mobilize others who can. The process of dispute management at the local level is influenced by the possibility of recourse to the police and court.

The availability of the judicial sanction has empowered about ten black women and one white woman in Dover Square to take an active role in maintaining order and restraining crime in the project. These women call the police when they observe crimes and are not afraid to identify local criminals in court or to testify against them. The criminals see these women as dangerous and pointedly avoid committing crimes in their vicinity. During the 18 months of my research, all of the local youths who were convicted of crimes were caught as a result of the action of someone who knew them personally, despite the fact that the vast majority of their crimes were committed against strangers. The courts provide these women with a weapon that enables them to play a role in controlling crime in the neighborhood. Although the courts do not see their role as settling local disputes, they will take advantage of local disputes to convict individuals whom the police have labeled as criminals.

Intriguingly, other studies of relatively egalitarian societies in which a court is one possible mode of settling disputes similarly find that the weaker parties, either social marginals (Todd, 1978) or lower-caste groups (Jones, 1974), appeal to the courts for redress against the stronger parties, while the latter rely on informal modes of settlement within the community.

The fact that these urbanites are resorting to courts to deal with conflicts when informal sanctions are inadequate may have implications for the American court system. As society becomes increasingly urban and mobile, and more and more Americans find themselves living in communities where informal sanctions are ineffective for managing disputes with neighbors, growing numbers may turn to courts. Meanwhile, the fleeting quality of most social relationships in a mobile society could lessen the traditional reluctance to resort to courts even in interpersonal disputes. If courts are used more often by Americans at all levels of society, the burden on them could increase. Some form of neighborhood mediation has been suggested as one solution to this problem.

Finally, the apparent inability of the courts to adjudicate disputes effectively in this heterogeneous urban community may actually increase the use of violence for managing disputes. When there is no third party able to mediate or arbitrate a dispute, the disputant with the greatest power triumphs. Colson notes that the Bushmen seek out Tswana courts to settle their disputes; this frees them from the burden of using violence to negotiate disputes (1974). Where a third party listens to the entire course of a dispute and arrives at a mutually acceptable compromise, as apparently occurs among the Kpelle and the Zapotec, violence is less necessary. In the Hobbesian world of the inner city, however, where neither courts nor informal sanctions function to settle disputes, the use of force may be an essential strategy for protecting one's personal as well as property rights.

DISCUSSION QUESTIONS

1. Is your own experience consistent with the proposition that resort to formal legal mechanisms varies directly with the social distance between the disputants? Hirshmann categorizes the responses to conflict as: exit, voice, and loyalty. These might be paraphrased as: lumping it, disputing, and negotiation. What circumstances influence parties in choosing among them?

2. In what ways are the patterns of disputing in Dover Square and Sander County similar, and in what ways are they different?

3. Merry focused on the neighborhood. What significant disputes involving its members are missing from her account?

4.   Under what circumstances is gossip an effective mechanism of social control? Where has it been influential in your experience?

5.   Self-help is often seen as an extralegal or even illegal response to conflict; yet, it is widely employed and often very successful. Where have you encountered it?

6.   Appeal to a third party is the model of a legal system. When have you made such an appeal or been involved in a dispute where a third party was invoked? How was the third party chosen? How effective was the appeal? What is the influence of what Mnookin and Kornhauser call the "shadow of the law"—the threat of a formal legal proceeding—on bargaining or strategizing outside formal legal institutions?

7.   Avoidance or endurance may be the most common responses in urban America. Can you think of examples from your own experience? Under what circumstances are they chosen? Merry suggests that this is the response to stranger crime; is that consistent with your experience?

8.   Consider the cases Merry describes:

a. Jilted ex-lover's slap. What was the real content of this case? Why did the parties choose these remedies? What was the "outcome"?

b. Neighborhood rapist. We tend to think of the criminal justice system as a mechanical application of penalties to transgressions. In what ways did this case deviate from that model?

c. Averted robbery. Are you surprised by the actions of the protagonist? Would you take such actions?

d. Revengeful brothers. What are the conditions of self-help?

9.   Merry explains party choice of response in terms of several variables. What others can you suggest?

10.   What differences among the various ethnic communities influenced their responses to conflict?

11.   Are you surprised that courts rarely adjudicate these kinds of disputes? What is the relationship between the courts and the 11 women who seek to reduce crime? Is this likely to be an effective mechanism of crime control?

3

The Management of Disputes: Automobile Accident Compensation in Japan

Takao Tanase

Introduction

The Japanese are nonlitigious compared to the people in other industrialized countries. For example, by any measure, courts are used less often in Japan than in the United States. If we look at ordinary litigation in courts of general jurisdiction, in which the mobilization of legal resources is the most intense, the per capita litigation rate in Japan was 9.8 per 10,000 population in 1986, while in California it was about 10 times higher, reaching 95.4. The difference is all the more striking if we look at the litigation rates broken down by types of cases. For example, fewer than 1 out of 100 automobile accidents (0.9) involving a death or an injury in Japan produces a litigated case; in the United States, the comparable figure is 21.5. A similar disparity arises for cases in which the legality of an administrative action is contested: in Japan, only 1,003 new cases were filed in 1986, while in the United States in federal courts alone the government was named as a defendant in 31,051 cases. The data are clear, but why do the Japanese resort to courts so infrequently?

Models of Nonlitigiousness

Attitude Model

The most popular explanation attributes nonlitigious behavior to a nonlitigious attitude in the mind of the Japanese people. While the explanation has many variations, Kawashima (1963) has thus far given the most explicit formula. He notes, "for Japanese, the right is indeterminate, conceived as something situationally contingent. Consequently, the people are repelled by the judiciary, which takes rights as being fixed." In other words, under the conventional social order of Japan, acknowledgment of a claim depends so much on the particular relation of one party to the other that the only appropriate way to handle the claim is through negotia-

Abridged from *Law & Society Review*, Volume 24: 651 (1990).

tions, during which the complicated web of interconnecting relationships is brought out and given due consideration.

Functionally, this contingent character helps embed the ideas of "equity and solidarity" into the social relationship, whereas the concept of justice, which is blind to the very person who asserts the right, is considered a menace to the integrity of the community. Therefore, the Japanese, who live in a closely knit community, naturally developed the concept of contingent rights, and concurrently abhorred the idea of legalistic justice. That the Japanese often refer to such legalistic justice as "inflexible" and its claimant as "egotistic" attests to this attitude.

Although this conventional social order is no longer found in its pure form in contemporary Japan, it still lives in the minds of the people, more as an aesthetic sense than as a straightforward ideology. Therefore, according to Kawashima, attitudinal nonlitigiousness represents an element of traditional culture carried over into modern society long after the underlying structure has changed. Popular acceptance of this cultural-lag model was aided by its appearance just at the time when the vestiges of a premodern "feudalistic" order were clearly visible in all aspects of social life and "modernization" was a national goal.

As Japan developed, however, the portrayal of Japan as clinging to her premodern order was more and more at odds both with the reality of an economically prosperous society and an emerging self-consciousness of the people. If the behavior pattern of the Japanese is different from that of Westerners, it cannot be so much a manifestation of the remaining feudalistic elements as a reflection of the deep-rooted sociopolitical, as well as cultural, structures unique to Japan, which have proved stable enough to survive the impact of modernization or, more positively, have enabled Japan to industrialize, if not to modernize, herself. Therefore, within the same attitude model, this shift of general perspective precipitated a search for unique properties of Japanese society that are conducive to the observed nonlitigiousness.

The search for unique-culture explanations proves elusive. Not only does the analysis of the cultural element supposedly underlying nonlitigiousness fail any rigorous scientific test, but because no macro-theory, like Kawashima's modernization/time-lag theory, places the chosen cultural element into a wider theoretical framework, the whole effort is something of an ad hoc process whereby concepts are created to suit the explanation at hand. Moreover, the concept of litigiousness itself confuses the analysis, for it refers both to the innate propensity and to the observed behavior of the people. Thus, nonlitigiousness as observed behavior is easily "explained" by positing nonlitigiousness as an attitude of the people. The unique-culture type of explanation is always in danger of degenerating into, and in fact often does fall into, the circular "the Japanese do not litigate because they are not litigious in nature" type of explanation.

Institution Model

The institution model rejects attitudinal explanations for low rates of litigation in Japan. According to this perspective, the Japanese are not nonlitigious at all, at least in the sense of loving peace and harmony and of readily sacrificing their own interests for the sake of others' well-being. In a radical departure from Kawashima, a leading proponent of the institution model, Haley (1978: 359), notes that the Japanese regularly engage in a great deal of fierce, cutthroat competition as well as many rancorous disputes not amenable to easy solutions. If the Japanese are in nature not different from other human beings, an explanation of the observed nonlitigiousness must be sought elsewhere. Citing the fact that there was more litigation in the prewar period than in the postwar period as evidence that directly contradicts the attitude model (especially its cultural-lag version), Haley offers an alternative explanation for the paucity of litigation in postwar Japan. According to his institution model, the Japanese refrain from litigation because the institutions are structured to discourage it. For example, the Japanese judiciary is clearly under-staffed; the number of judges per capita population has remained low or even decreased in the postwar period. Moreover, the Japanese judiciary is ineffective in enforcing the law and its decisions (Haley, 1982a: 265). Therefore, the people who would be interested in pursuing their rights in court are discouraged from doing so.

While Haley's observations about the availability and efficacy of the courts are correct and potential disputants no doubt take a utilitarian view of courts when deciding whether to litigate, we must still ask why the judiciary remains understaffed and ineffective. If judicial services do not meet the needs of the Japanese public, why has the defect not been cured? Haley answers that it is a deliberate policy of the government elite. The Japanese government intends to keep court utilization low. The court-annexed mediation, established in the 1920s and 1930s, reflects this policy. As is well documented by the remarks of government officials at the time, the government established mediation to curb the increasing assertiveness of the people and to deflect disputes away from the courts (Haley, 1982b: 125–47). But why has the Japanese elite wished to establish and carry out such a policy? And why has the elite been so successful in implementing its policy? Is the elite so all-powerful as to be able to force on the public what it wants? On these questions, Haley remains silent. Moreover, he seems to be too hasty in denying entirely the role that culture plays in bringing about the observed nonlitigiousness. The Japanese may not be so different in their egotistic motives, but certainly they have their own image of the good social order, which in some significant way affects the shape of institutions that channel individual behavior.

In this regard, Ramseyer (1985: 604) has offered an interesting hypothesis that while the low utilization of courts is in fact created by the ineffectiveness of the Japanese judiciary, the people attribute it erroneously to their own cultural preferences, thus perpetuating the myth of nonlitigiousness. Here, the power elite not only reaps the benefits of low court utilization—of reducing both the cost of dispute management and the risk of governmental policies challenged in court—but also gains from the very myth of nonlitigiousness. The image of a harmonious, dispute-free society, which this myth embodies, gives government bureaucrats the appearance of being technocratic rulers, above political strife, and hence free from active, participatory democratic controls. It is this elite's concern for legitimacy that is the key to understanding why contemporary Japanese collectively entertain the myth of nonlitigiousness despite the contradictory manifestations of their underlying individual claims-consciousness. Presumably the government elite is implicated in fostering this myth.

Management Model

Although Ramseyer's model has a unique strength in acknowledging the persistence of a nonlitigious culture, while positing the institutional defect as a major determinant of low court utilization, it is still limited in that the elite seems to wield a free-handed control over the people. Clearly, the elite is not omnipotent. If an elite is to be effective in leading a society, it cannot depart too radically from the aspirations of the people. Especially in a highly developed society like Japan's, where the people enjoy the protection accorded by the legal order and where they freely express their policy preferences through various political channels, the elite's manipulation of the people's propensity to sue must be a subtle one, subtle in the sense that people must be led to feel that they themselves wish for the level of opportunity the elite has provided. In fact, to limit the supply of judicial services when an unmet demand does exist would strain the very notion of a harmonious, dispute-free society. Thus, in order to hold down court utilization while avoiding any discontent by disputants who are denied effective access to the courts, a restricted supply must be accompanied by a limited demand. The notion that the demand must be controlled leads to the management model, which I propose in this article as an alternative explanation for Japanese nonlitigiousness.

The control of demand should not be equated with its suppression or substitution. The disputants must be provided with real alternatives to fulfill their needs and secure full satisfaction. From the very definition of what should be disputed to the provision of accessible forums for dispute resolution, the disputants must be guided toward alterative means of satisfaction.

However, as the word "alternative" implies, this involves an evaluative aspect—reckoning different things as being of equal value. Therefore, for management, the value premises of the people also must be controlled. But in contemporary Japan, compromising claims for the sake of peace and harmony does not appeal to the people, who are no longer so ready to relinquish their entitlements. To curb the demand for court utilization, a more subtle technique must be employed; that is, a differential weight must be given to the costs and benefits of utilizing judicial as opposed to alternative services. If the differential weighting is so arranged as to make the disputants "find" judicial services less efficient and alternative services more satisfactory, then the state, without any coercion, can effectively induce the people voluntarily to use fewer judicial services. In the end, when the demand is diverted to alternative services, the elite also vanishes from the fore. The people now believe that the system is created only to benefit them, not contrived by an ill-willed agent with a hidden agenda. Control is maximized when the people are unaware that they are controlled. When the choice becomes so natural that the disputants innocently start saying, "I will not use the court, for I do not need it," management has succeeded in controlling demand. It is the creation of this "myth of functionalism" that is the ultimate goal of dispute management.

This article demonstrates through a detailed case study of dispute settlement in Japan that management, rather than litigants' attitudes or institutional barriers, provides the best explanation for why the Japanese rarely litigate. By sublimating demand and eliminating apparent agency, management recreates the nonlitigious society in a contemporary setting. Before beginning this analysis, however, two explanations are necessary, one on the operational measure of litigiousness and the other on the choice of a particular dispute for illustration.

Measure of Litigiousness

The most obvious measures of litigiousness are counts of the number of litigated cases per capita, or per total number of disputes. Although these measures give us a first approximation of the propensity of the people to use the courts, on a closer look, they have some inherent weaknesses. First, a large portion of the lawsuits filed are resolved before ever reaching the trial stage. Further, the extent to which judicial services are used in such pretrial stages differs significantly according to the type of civil proceedings adopted by a particular nation's judicial system. In Japan, for example, when a suit is filed, court proceedings begin immediately, and intermittent hearings ensue, usually at the rate of one hearing per month or two, with about 30 percent of the cases going the entire way to a final decision. In the United States, on the other hand, the number of cases that go on trial is much more limited, and there is a long interval between the filing of a complaint and the trial, during which the involvement of the judiciary is minimal. Thus, comparisons depend heavily on whether one measures the number of lawsuits initiated or the number of cases that reach the hearing stage.

An even more serious problem is how to treat cases when disputants mobilize the law but not the courts. We can avoid the problem by simply defining litigiousness to exclude out-of-court settlements and by looking only at actual cases of court utilization. However, such a definition would blind us to subtle differences in the readiness of the people to assert their legal rights in extrajudicial settlements. Disputants in some settings consciously refer to the law in reaching settlements, while disputants in other settings rarely do so. Some negotiations, especially those assisted by lawyers, are so finely attuned to what the court would have done that court utilization is said to have been preempted by such an alternative law mobilization.

Even if it is not possible to measure directly the extent to which legalistic justice is invoked in each type of dispute resolution, it is still possible to approximate a society's use of legalistic justice by measuring the resources invested in the legalistic resolutions of disputes. One indicator is the use of lawyers' services. Since a disputant must engage the services of a lawyer not only to win a court battle but also to mobilize those legal arguments that will attain the most favorable resolution legally possible in an out-of-court negotiation, the use of legal services fairly sensitively reflects the disputant's determination to use the law. To ordinary people, the critical decision is not whether to file a suit but whether to retain a lawyer; the decision to file is often a matter of strategic choice counseled by the lawyer. In this sense, dispute management that controls litigiousness in a given society should, above all, hold down the total consumption of legal services. In this article, I consider mainly the level of lawyer involvement in dispute resolution to see how the demand for such services abates in the process of dispute management.

Focus on Automobile Accidents

I focus here on automobile accident compensation for two reasons. First, it is one of the most common disputes in which the public uses lawyers' services. Every year in Japan as many as 12,000 persons are killed and more than 600,000 persons are injured in automobile accidents. The majority of these accidents hold the potential for disputes between two parties regarding compensation. In addition, such disputes are mostly between strangers and often involve sizable damages. Therefore, people are likely to be less restrained in seeking redress and in getting needed legal services. Furthermore, personal injury cases are often handled on a contingency basis, thus reducing the costs to a potential plaintiff. The sheer weight of legal services in automobile accident compensation should naturally precipitate the elite's intervention for the efficient management of the system. Note, however, that lawyers are sensitive to any system change that may affect adversely their continued involvement, and thus management efforts must involve political conflict.

A second reason to focus on automobile accidents is that management to scale down the use of legal services has been most successful in this area. As Japan plunged into motorization in the 1960s, personal injury cases rose sharply to reach the postwar peak of 12,624 in 1971. But various measures in the late 1960s began to undercut this upward trend and reduced litigation by two-thirds in just a decade (3,626 cases in 1981). Now, less than 1 percent of total accidents end up in court, and the rest are resolved in out-of-court negotiations, where lawyer involvement is minimal (estimated to be less than 2 percent). By comparison, in the United States, 21 percent of all claims were litigated, and another 29 percent were represented by lawyers in out-of-court settlements. Thus, while in the United States, except in minor injuries, people routinely bring their claims to lawyers, in Japan nearly all the injured parties handle compensation disputes themselves without the aid of lawyers. Only when they encounter extraordinary difficulty and feel that, as a very last resort, they will have to use the court, do the Japanese ask the help of lawyers. Hence, auto accident cases provide an ideal ground to test whether prudent management can explain the current state of low consumption of legal resources.

The Nonconfrontational Compensation System

To manage the disputes so that legal services are not used, or to stimulate people to say, "I will not use a lawyer (or court) for I do not need it," three interrelated measures are necessary: (1) the system must enhance the capability of the victims to prosecute the claims on their own; (2) it must simplify the law so that professional services are not needed; and (3) it must provide alternative forums in which the unresolved disputes can be settled short of full legal war. Concretely, the first measure is taken in Japan by providing extensive free legal consultation, the second by standardizing the compensation scheme, and the third by establishing court-annexed mediation and a special forum.

These measures are bolstered by the norm in Japanese society, which demands that the injurer take a personal responsibility for the accident. When attention is diverted from strictly legal arguments to moral concerns, the lawyer offers less specialized authority in obtaining restitution. In the following section, I look in detail at how these techniques are used to manage the compensation disputes in Japan.

Legal Consultation

When legal knowledge exists as a system of abstract rules, persons extracting relevant rules from such a system and applying them to specific situations provide an indispensable service. While these services are supplied almost exclusively by private practitioners in the United States, in Japan they are provided extensively by free legal consultations. Consequently, the disputants need not retain lawyers in Japan to obtain legal information.

Although in sheer numbers the insurance companies and the police are the most conspicuous providers, in terms of the quality of the information provided the two most important consultation centers are the local government centers and the bar association centers. The government consultation centers provide free consultation by special traffic accident counselors (there are 361 such counselors in Japan; they are nonlawyers, and most are retired government officials). These centers are usually located at government office buildings and, in large cities, are open daily. The consultation, lasting typically 40 minutes to an hour, covers all aspects of compensation. When a complex legal issue arises, clients are referred to a lawyer of the general legal consultation center, usually located in the same building. The local bar association's consultation center provides consultations exclusively with lawyers, and in addition it offers mediation services in which the consulting lawyer contacts the other party on behalf of the client and tries to resolve the dispute. (In 1986, 723 cases, or 4 percent of all consultation sessions, led to mediation services, and two-thirds of these were resolved by the mediation.) In addition, the Legal Aid Society and the Traffic Accident Dispute Resolution Center together provided 3,000 consultations by lawyers. In all, these four organizations offered close to 180,000 consultations, 13 percent of which were provided by lawyers. Since lawyers are retained privately by the injured in approximately 3 percent (about 18,000 cases) of the accidents involving death or injury, these specialized organizations provided ten times as many consultations as did private practitioners. Lawyers working in these consultation centers provided 30 percent more consultations than did those in private legal services.

Some government bodies also give free consultations regarding automobile accidents in connection with services they regularly provide. The police also give extensive consultations. As many as 230,000 drivers or victims sought such services. Moreover, insurance companies offer free consultation as a consumer service. Two quasi-public organizations in the insurance business provided 95,000 consultations, while insurance companies provided 450,000 such consultations. In total, these services offer an enormous amount of information, almost two consultations per accident, free of charge so as to meet the disputant's need for individually tailored information.

1. *Function of legal consultations.* Each center assumes a partly overlapping but slightly different role. Typically a police officer is the first person the victim is likely to contact concerning an accident and thus is the person who gives overall guidance as to how to proceed in handling the accident. But the police do not usually provide specific legal information. Such information is provided by both local government and bar association centers. Here, we should note that lay consultants are viewed as sufficiently competent to give an independent opinion concerning such legal issues as the liability of the parties and the proper amount of damages. Although this trust is related to the fact that the Japanese in general have great confidence in government and its officials, the standardization of compensation payments (discussed in the next section) plays an important part. Timing is also important: 45 percent of all visits to these centers take place within a month of an accident and 65 percent within three months. So, as the authority first contacted for specific legal advice, these centers have a great deal of influence on the course the dispute will take.

There are no readily available data on the total cost of these consultation services. However, if we tentatively assume that one consultation session with a lawyer costs 5,000 yen, and with a nonlawyer 2,000 yen, the expenses borne by public organizations and insurance companies add up to 2 billion yen, which is 0.2 percent of the total amount paid to the injured. Although we do not know exactly how much these free consultations cut the demand for private legal services, certainly they account at least partly for the relatively insignificant earnings of

Japanese lawyers in representing the disputants in automobile accident cases; legal fees comprised only 2 percent of the total compensation paid to the injured. If we compare this with the U.S. figure (legal fees amounting to 47 percent of the net compensation received by the injured), the savings of potential costs are enormous. Even if all the consultations are with lawyers, still their involvement is limited and their expertise is offered at a discounted price within the consultation system; thus their active participation in the system hardly contributes to an overall increase in the demand for legal services.

Conceivably, however, the consultation system could act as a springboard to more intense involvement of lawyers at a later stage. An injured party informed of his legal rights at a consultation center could as a result define the dispute essentially as a legal matter and begin seeking full legal recourse by retaining counsel. In fact, to encourage this development, some local bar associations have lifted the traditional ban on taking a private case directly from a public consultation session. However, this channeling function of consultation has not yet materialized. In fact, the norm is to divert disputes away from the legal system. For example, in Osaka, where the bar association is most aggressive in promoting the program, in only 2 percent of the free legal consultations was the consulting lawyer later retained privately. In a society in which lawyers do not yet handle a significant portion of such traffic accident disputes, the extensive legal consultation system fills the information gap and thus reinforces the tendency of people to do without lawyers. As a survey on pre- and post-consultation behavior reveals, one-third of disputants who visited one of the bar association's fee-charging, general legal consultations had already received free legal consultations (on average 1.5 sessions per person). After the consultation, 30 percent planned to or did attend yet another consultation session. Apparently disputants were not inclined to seek full legal recourse merely on receiving advice about their legal rights. Rather, disputants returned to consultation at successive stages of their negotiations, or visited several institutions to shop around for information to enhance their bargaining positions or, more modestly, to guard against losing entitlements at the hands of a shrewd opponent. Many of these disputants themselves read law books. They seemed to view legal consultations essentially as a means of enabling them to resolve the dispute by themselves.

2. *Consensual nature of legal consultations.* Because consultations provide information that is consensual in nature, they contribute to the diverting function of the system. Generally speaking, two types of legal information for the pursuit of rights can be provided: partisan and consensual. The former attempts to provide a person with legal weapons to further his interests, while the latter attempts to promote agreement between the parties by providing both with the same legal information. When the information assumes a strong partisan character, the assertions of one party are more likely to conflict with those of the other and an intervening third party may be requested to adjudicate the conflicting claims. On the

other hand, when the information is less partisan and more consensual, it moves the parties toward a middle ground and thus facilitates autonomous agreement.

The consultation in automobile accident compensation has a consensual character in a double sense. First, since most consultations are provided by the government or insurance companies, they inevitably reflect the bias of their providers against legal action. As nonlawyers committed to the efficient handling of claims, government officials and insurance agents often express the view that lawyers unnecessarily complicate the case and, for the victim's sake, are to be dispensed with. But more important, the very nature of free consultations predisposes them to assume the consensual character. Since the consultant cannot do an independent investigation and relies entirely on information provided by a party, he naturally becomes cautious in giving legal advice too aggressively. Even if the consultant is a lawyer and does recommend aggressive legal action, he cannot provide close follow-up. The burden to put the legal strategy into effect falls on the lay party, and thus the consultation counselor is discouraged from becoming a true partisan advocate. As a result, the consultation center, whether government or bar association, tends to provide consensual information to all parties, the injured and the injuring alike, and thus promotes consensual solutions among the parties.

Yet consensual consultation cannot work effectively unless the whole compensation system is constructed to keep partisan conflicts to a minimum. Otherwise, the information meant to provide a common legal framework would simply be discarded by disputants as being ineffective for their legal fights or would encourage them to pick only opportunistically favorable bits of information, lessening the integrity of negotiations. Therefore, we should expect the proliferation of consultation services in Japan as a way of managing disputes to be complemented by an effort to create a nonconfrontational compensation system.

Standardization

At the heart of the nonconfrontational system is standardized compensation, which, because of its simplicity and accessibility to the wider public, reduces the legal knowledge required to resolve compensation disputes. Thus, it neatly fits with the consultation system, avoiding the need to educate the people in the technicalities of the law.

1. *Compulsory insurance*. Standardized compensation has come to Japan with nationwide compulsory insurance, which pays an overwhelmingly large percentage of overall compensation. This insurance, which every automobile owner must carry, covers up to 25 million yen ($180,000) for death or injury resulting in serious disability and up to 1.2 million yen ($8,600) for less serious injuries. Amounting to 748 billion yen ($5.3 billion) a year in all, compulsory insurance accounts for 69 percent of the total compensation paid to automobile accident victims (1.1 trillion yen). Although this insurance is liability insurance, in practice it closely resembles

no-fault insurance in that the confrontation between the injured and the insurance company that inheres in ordinary liability insurance is conspicuously absent here.

The standards set for the assessment of damages by insurance companies are clearly defined and uniformly applied nationwide. When fundamental data such as detailed accounts of medical expenses and the age and annual income of the injured party have been collected, the amount of compensation, including damages for pain and suffering, is automatically calculated.

Furthermore, some precautionary measures are taken to handle any remaining controversial points. For instance, as to the liability of a driver, a very strict policy is taken. To absolve himself of liability, a driver must prove not only that he was paying due care to avoid an accident but also that he was strictly conforming to all traffic rules. Furthermore, while under Japanese tort law the degree of a victim's own negligence is calculated to offset the compensation he will receive, this comparative negligence rule is applied only sparingly. Under current practices, only if the victim's own fault is more than 70 percent is his fault considered an offsetting factor at all, and if it is, he receives only a 20 percent reduction. Altogether, less than 1 percent of the cases fall within this category. Thus, by tipping the liability scale in favor of the injured party, the compulsory insurance in Japan comes close to no-fault insurance (for example, in 1986, compensation was paid for as many as 80 percent of all persons who died in traffic accidents). From the management perspective, potential disputes are avoided by providing generous compensation to injured parties.

At the same time, documentation used to substantiate a claim must meet strict criteria. For example, only income authenticated by a copy of the person's tax returns or expenses clearly accounted for by medical receipts is taken into account. Although this places a strict burden of proof on the injured party and may create hardships in some cases, disputes are certainly minimized.

The elimination of disputes in insurance payments is also manifested in the peculiar place insurance companies occupy within the overall compensation system. An insurance company is, in the eyes of the injured party, not so much an adversary as an agent. The insurance business has lost much of its private, profit-seeking nature and has been transformed into a quasi-official administrative organ. While insurance is sold through private companies, which are then individually responsible for payment, an independent organization assesses damages, and losses and profits are spread evenly among the insurance companies. In the case of compulsory insurance, all claims against individual companies must be processed first by the investigation office, which then recommends to the companies the amount to be paid. Thus, individual companies lack discretion to negotiate compulsory compensation awards. In addition, the government holds 60 percent of all policy coverage through reinsurance, which further diminishes the private nature of the insurance. Although the purpose of reinsurance is presumably to even out losses among insurance companies in exchange for the compulsory underwriting of even high risk drivers under the same policy and premium, it also diffuses compensation disputes between claimants and individual insurance companies into the overall compensation system. If an injured party wishes to fight individually for higher compensation, he must be prepared to challenge the system itself.

2. *Optional insurance.* In Japan, through the standardized, quasi-administrative system, nearly three-quarters of all compensation is paid routinely without any serious disputes. This alone limits lawyers' involvement in automobile accident cases. In addition, the basic standardization techniques are also applied when optional insurance is involved, which further reduces the need for legal services. For example, while a death in a fatal accident is expected to be compensated, on the average, 27 million yen ($194,000), 70 percent of this amount is paid under compulsory insurance through its strictly standardized system, and thus any potential dispute with the insurance company is limited to the excess portion of 8 million yen. Note, further, that only 36 percent of the beneficiaries of compulsory insurance ever recover under optional insurance. The effect of this containment of potential disputes is more strongly felt in the case of minor injuries. In contrast to the 908,000 claims paid under compulsory insurance, only 313,000 of the injured in automobile accidents received any compensation from optional insurance, and over 70 percent of them got less than 500,000 yen ($3,600), an amount that would not encourage any lawyer to take the case. Furthermore, an insurance company that pays for the excess portion through optional insurance must avoid an assessment that is out of line with the compulsory insurance assessment. Otherwise, a dispute may arise with the company handling the compulsory insurance over the assumption of losses. Therefore, the insurance company generally has a strong incentive to apply the standardization scheme utilized in compulsory insurance to the optional insurance also. In practice, if a driver has an optional insurance policy (about 60 percent of all drivers), the insurance company, on behalf of the driver, directly negotiates with the injured party and later reclaims internally from the overall compulsory insurance system the amount to be borne by compulsory insurance. So, naturally, the insurance company tries to keep in line with the assessment made under the compulsory insurance system so that this internal reclaiming process will go smoothly.

The fact that compulsory insurance is sold as private insurance by the same companies that sell optional insurance makes this transfer all the easier. With this identical representation in mind, the claimant generally regards the insurance company not so much as an opponent with its own interest in keeping the assessment as low as possible but rather as a third party that dispenses justice while maintaining a neutral stance toward the injured and the injuring parties alike. In other words, the private, interested-party character of insurance companies is effectively checked by their transformation under this quasi-public system. This transformation is precipitated by close governmental supervision over the entire insurance industry which, on the one hand, restrains companies from taking unfair advantage of weak claimants and, on the other, enables the company to diffuse potential disputes into the system as a whole. This quasi-public nature can be no more clearly revealed than by the common expression that an injured person gets compensation by "following the instructions" of the insurance company. It is no wonder people feel this way if the information obtained independently from legal consultation is identical to that given by insurance companies.

3. *Discretion and containment of contentiousness.* Optional insurance, however, does not always produce the idyllic rapport described above. Unlike compulsory insurance, which is meant, as a matter of government policy, to provide only basic protection to injured parties, optional insurance must cover the remaining compensation for the injured party and thus must take into consideration potentially conflicting issues.

As a result of this expanded scope of concern, the standards used to set the amount of compensation are relaxed. Although, as in the case of compulsory insurance, the nationwide uniform guideline approved by the Ministry of Finance is used as the payment policy for companies regarding voluntary insurance, it is not legally binding on the parties, and leaves room for further adjustment. Phrases like "to pay the amount that is socially acceptable" or "to take into consideration the trend of judicial decisions" are often added in the payment standards here. Take, for example, a person who has suffered a permanent injury and has thus lost some ability to work. Under compulsory insurance, a set percentage of work-ability loss, which is set forth in a table (classifying first the type of injury into twelve categories and then giving each type a definite figure for work-ability loss) is uniformly applied. Under optional insurance, using the same table, the determination of lost ability is made by taking into consideration not only the type of injury but also such factors as the seriousness of a particular injury, the age, sex, and occupation of the injured, and the actual decrease in income.

Such discretion is not only inevitable in the case of optional insurance, which covers total liabilities mandated by tort law, but also indispensable as a safety valve for the rigidity of the standardized scheme itself. For example, it may be argued that if two persons each have lost an arm, justice requires paying them the same amount of consolation money for their losses. Alternatively, it may be argued that if two persons differ in the extent of the particular worth of the arm, justice requires that this difference be reflected in the amounts paid to them. Standardized compensation in Japan assumes that the first version of justice, namely, that two similarly injured persons should receive the same amount of compensation, resonates more with the equitable sense of the Japanese than the alternative version. Moreover, to the Japanese, whose idea of fairness means above all "fair share" rather than "fair play," individualized treatment smacks of arbitrariness, for the resulting award rests with the disputant's ability to assert and prove the merits of his case as well as with the intuitive determination of the judge (or jurors) concerning the monetary value of the individual's sufferings. The Japanese would view the resulting irregularity of compensation as a sign of the inherent weakness of the system rather than the inevitable price of dispensing justice properly.

It is undeniable, however, that pain and suffering do vary according to the individual involved and the particular circumstances of the accident. Thus, if standardized compensation is followed too closely, it may on occasion conflict with the public's sense of justice. Furthermore, strains on the system may arise if obstinate claimants try to obtain excess payments alleging special circumstances. A certain leeway to pay the so-called nuisance value forestalls unnecessary contention, thus lowering transactions costs.

On the other hand, if the public perceives that discretion is widely exercised, injured parties will be stimulated to seek higher settlement awards, and the very effort to standardize compensation awards in order to contain potential contentiousness will come to naught. To avoid this, two related measures are required. First, the court itself must endorse standardized compensation; otherwise, court decisions will constantly disturb standardization efforts carried out by the government and insurance companies. Second, the injured must be discouraged from attempting to profit from possible discretion, for contentiousness depends in large part on the perception that aggressiveness will produce a sufficient payoff.

In Japan, the standardization of court awards has been pushed to the limit. In fact, the courts took the initiative in standardizing traffic accident compensation awards. In 1962, in response to a drastic increase in traffic accidents, a Traffic Section was set up within the Tokyo District Court. The section developed a unified policy for handling traffic accident cases, standardizing the amounts awarded by that court. Further, judges in the section communicated the standards to other courts by writing articles as well as through the usual channel of case reporting. As a result, judicial handling of traffic accident cases was swiftly standardized throughout the country. The Traffic Section, consisting of one presiding judge and several associate judges, acts as a unit with one unified, guiding policy. In the background, the central judicial administration (the Supreme Court Secretariat and the Directorate of Tokyo District Court) acted as the stage manager of this standardization, by establishing the Traffic Section and by sending to it for disposition all traffic accident cases and also by subtly approving the court's policy. Moreover, career judges themselves, who are bureaucratically organized, tend to value uniform treatment more than individualized treatment. The pursuit of individualized justice would, of necessity, encourage attention to the individual character of the presiding judge, an outcome these judges would not be prepared to accept. Thus, the judiciary and the government form a natural pair in bringing about standardization, which illustrates the maxim that dispute management requires a unified, concerted effort by societal elites.

This subtle coordination is further manifested in the effort to make the inevitable discretion in payment as invisible as possible. Here such a crude measure as withholding information from potential litigants does not suffice. It would be far more effective to design a compensation system in which it is difficult to take advantage of existing discretion and induce the people to believe in the uniformity of standard payments. That is, even if an injured party learns of such discretion and decides to exploit it, the system is so organized as to make very burdensome the party's opportunistic determination to litigate. At the same time the system enables such a party, without a lawyer, to recover through out-of-court negotiation a rough approximation of what he would have obtained in court. As individual parties are thus discouraged from exhausting the possibilities of discretionary benefits, the system as a whole eliminates discretion.

4. *Disposition of factual disputes.* Along with the relaxation of standards, the indeterminacy of the facts is another explosive factor in optional insurance, which may lead to an increase in contentiousness. Three schemes are used to minimize the potential factual disputes.

The first effort is to give special weight to the police report of the accident. Under the Road Traffic Act the parties to an accident, even a minor one involving only property damage, are under a duty to report the accident to the police. If the accident is not reported to the police, the insurance company may refuse to pay compensation. This reporting obligation is well known to Japanese drivers and is widely obeyed. Ordinarily, when such a report is made, several policemen specializing in traffic accidents immediately come to the scene of the accident, conduct a detailed investigation, record the testimony of the parties involved, and report on their findings. This reporting system greatly reduces contention concerning the facts of a case, for the police report is accorded such weight that the facts as recorded are hardly ever challenged later in court. Indeed, because the parties, the police, and often the witnesses, consult at the scene of the accident as soon as possible, and the police adjust differences in factual assertions of the parties and hammer out a consensual story, which the parties accept and formally endorse by signing, it is very difficult for the parties later to refute the facts recorded in the police report.

Factual disputes are also avoided by standardizing the offset ratio used to allocate comparative negligence. Since there is no objective way to assess exactly the level of negligence of each party, in practice the determination of the comparative negligence is simply entrusted to the arbiter, a procedure not conducive to the containment of contentiousness. To handle the problem, the Tokyo District Court's Traffic Section adopted a standardized system in which accidents are classified into a manageable number of patterns using only the facts apparent in the police accident report; each pattern is assigned, somewhat arbitrarily, a set percentage for the negligence of each party. This classification scheme has been modified somewhat since first introduced and is now used in all courts in Japan.

The third scheme set up to contain contentiousness deals with the practice of bill padding employed by some injured parties. The continuation of unnecessary medical treatment not only inflates medical bills but also results in excessive payments for matters like work missed and consolation money, since under standardized compensation the calculation of such awards is mechanically linked to the period over which medical treatment is received. Therefore, insurance companies are interested in contesting such claims. But to contest an injured party's claim endorsed by a physician, however dubious the medical judgment in a particular case, is at odds with the whole effort of objectifying the dispute, for under the system whereby documentation is to be given great weight for efficiency, the opinions of the police and physicians must play a central role in fact finding. Thus, rather than contest the claim on an individual basis, a systemic approach to forestall possible abuses is adopted. Insurance companies, keeping in close contact with the central office for compulsory insurance, regularly refer suspicious cases to a nationwide investigating network. The Compulsory Insurance Investigative Bureau engages physicians from among the larger national hospitals as consultants (47 physicians) and designates authorized hospitals to carry out reexaminations (211 hospitals nationwide). On request of an insurance company, these physicians and hospitals are commissioned in dubious cases to give an expert opinion on the physical condition of an injured party. Moreover, because it processes practically all personal injury cases occurring in Japan, the bureau also investigates on its own and gives informal guidance to hospitals that are suspected, based on statistics, of providing excessive medical treatment ("excessive" in the sense of charging statistically significantly larger fees for a given type of accident than the average hospital does). Further, the bureau regularly consults with medical associations to request that internal controls be applied to such hospitals. Currently the bureau is working out a plan with the Japan Medical Association to standardize the medical fees charged to the injured in traffic accidents.

Nonjudicial Forum

In spite of these efforts, some claims do erupt into full-fledged disputes. But even in these cases, a lawsuit is rarely instituted or a lawyer involved, for there is another buffer. Extrajudicial machinery often settles the dispute before it escalates into a full-scale legal war.

1. *Court-annexed mediation.* The most important extrajudicial machinery is the court-annexed mediation (*chotei*). At its peak in 1971, 16,396 disputes were submitted to it; and in 1986, 5,374 were submitted, accounting for 0.9 percent of the total number of automobile accident cases. Lawyer participation in mediation has increased in recent years to about 46 percent for plaintiffs and 23 percent for defendants. Still, in most cases, the parties are not represented and mediation is used by parties who have attempted in vain to settle the matter of compensation by themselves and continue trying to resolve it without resorting to litigation or lawyers.

The advantages for claimants of resorting to mediation rather than litigation are clear. On the average, it takes 6 months to conclude a case by mediation, in contrast to 14 months for litigation. Furthermore, since a lawyer's average fee is less in a mediation case, more than half of the mediation claimants are not represented by a lawyer, and the amount claimed as compensation is also smaller in mediation, the total costs borne by a disputant in mediation are one-seventh those of litigation. But mediation carries its own costs—the risk of not being able to reach a settlement and the likelihood of compromising a legitimate claim for the sake of settlement. These risks are reflected in two measures: the settlement/win ratio (the percentage of cases settled or found for plaintiff), and the recovery ratio (the amount awarded divided by the amount claimed). Here mediation naturally trails behind litigation. Moreover, in every type of injury the amount awarded in litigation is higher than that awarded in mediation. It is difficult, however, to determine whether these costs are balanced by the greater efficiency of mediation. If we consider the interest that would accrue on a mediation award (between the time of filing and that of settlement in litigation) as well as the difference in costs (court costs plus lawyers' fees), the difference in awards between litigation and mediation decreases. If mediation is pursued without the help of lawyers, the financial advantage of litigation, except in serious injury cases, almost disappears. In such cases when an injury involves permanent disability, aggressive use of the law produces a higher settlement because of the uncertainty involved, while in the rest of the cases, mediation pursued by the claimant himself produces as satisfactory a result as litigation.

2. *Traffic Accident Dispute Resolution Center.* An additional institution, the Traffic Accident Dispute Resolution Center, deals exclusively with automobile accident disputes in Japan and offers mediation outside the official court setting. It was first established in 1974 as a nonprofit corporation, financed by investment profits from compulsory insurance. It now has eight branch offices in major cities. As it is a new, private institution, it lacks to some degree the authority and acceptance by the public that court-annexed mediation enjoys. However, by tactful management, and by assuming a quasi-public character, it has gained a strong foothold within the automobile accident compensation system. Annually more than 4,000 disputes are brought before the center (4,166 cases in 1986), and approximately 40 percent of them are settled there. Although it focuses on mediation, the center is unique in that it incorporates elements of legal consultation and adjudication in order to cater to individual needs as well as facilitate a settlement.

In about two-thirds of the cases, serious efforts are not made by center consultation lawyers to settle disputes, because the time is not ripe for conciliation (e.g., the injured party is still in the hospital, or substantial negotiation has not yet taken place with the other party) or because the center was visited only to obtain advice on how to proceed with a claim or to get an objective, third-party estimate of damages. The center's ability to offer such consultation services nonetheless contributes to its overall effectiveness by enabling it to become involved in diverse cases at early stages. In that way the still relatively weak center can carefully cultivate a clientele among the general public, as well as acquire cases for its mediation services.

The center is unique in furnishing adjudicatory services. In difficult cases in which the parties cannot reach agreement even with the help of a lawyer-mediator, the center refers the case to adjudication by its own panel of legal experts. For example, in 1981, mediation was attempted in 1,181 cases (37 percent of the new cases), out of which 751 cases (64 percent) reached agreement (typically involving multiple sessions, an average of 4.9 sessions per settled case, before an agreement was reached). In addition, 91 cases (8 percent) were referred to adjudication. Although the judgment rendered by the center's panel is not legally binding, it is regularly honored by insurance companies as a matter of courtesy. Furthermore, claimants very seldom challenge decisions, for the decision rendered by the tripartite panel of a retired judge, a lawyer, and a legal scholar seems to have, at least in the eyes of the lay disputants, the authenticity of a "correct" legal decision and hence to be impervious to lay challenge. In fact, this aura of authenticity is the very policy of the center. In order to reproduce a judicial decision as accurately as possible, the center tries not only to apply legal standards meticulously but also to update its judgment standard by systematically collecting judicial decisions and holding periodic conferences with judges working in the traffic section of the courts. As this effort to simulate a judicial decision is completed, any net gain to be derived from full-scale litigation diminishes rapidly so that an incentive for pursuing formal litigation is lost. Through this center injured parties can obtain at low cost (i.e., without a lawyer) the benefits the judiciary would otherwise be called on to provide at a higher cost.

Thus, in Japan, not only is confrontation between injured parties and insurance companies kept to a minimum, but the occasional confrontation that arises between the parties themselves is mostly absorbed by these extrajudicial institutions, leaving only a few cases to be resolved by full legal measures.

Moral Confrontation

Paradoxically, however, there remains a deep-rooted confrontation between the injured party and the injurer over the moral responsibility for the accident (i.e., the injured trying to hold the injurer morally accountable for the accident), which further biases the parties against bringing lawyers into the dispute.

This unique type of confrontation comes from the sense of justice or moral reasoning prevalent in Japan. Because the maintenance of good social relationships is accorded the highest consideration, "giving trouble to others" is itself considered a serious offense. Therefore, a person who has inconvenienced another, for whatever reason, by his own fault or not, is obliged to fulfill his moral duty to make up for the inconvenience independent of his legal obligation to do so. This duty, above all, requires the inconveniencing party repeatedly to express his sincere apologies for the inconvenience. In automobile accidents, this necessity to apologize is best represented by the frequent use of the word "sincerity." For example, if an injurer takes an "insincere" attitude by failing to inquire after the injured party at the hospital or fails to offer condolences to the deceased's relatives, the injured party or his relatives will harden their attitude, and negotiations will become very difficult or may even deadlock.

In this respect, Japan contrasts sharply with the United States, where the insurance company literally acts as a proxy for the injurer in attempting to reach a settlement. Since insurance companies in the United States take charge of handling all the injurer's responsibility, including not only liability for compensation but also conducting negotiations, the injurer usually remains completely uninvolved in the dispute over compensation. It is not at all unusual for the injurer to be unaware of the final outcome of his own dispute. The injured party himself regards the dispute purely as a matter of monetary compensation, and while allowing the injurer to remain completely uninvolved in the negotiations, he entrusts his own part of the negotiation to an attorney, who has no emotional involvement in the accident.

On the other hand, in Japan, strong resentment toward the injurer on the part of the injured party, which is refueled by a moralistic interpretation of responsibility for the accident, makes it difficult for the injurer to remove himself from personal involvement in the negotiations. The injured party himself is anxious to take part in negotiations and keeps demanding that the injurer express his "sincere" apologies for the accident. Of course, in compensation disputes where a large monetary stake is involved, the demand for sincerity does not simply mean a verbal apology. In practice, it also means "show your sincerity through generous compensation," requiring that the insurance company, sharing the moral burden of the original injurer, add a little to the standard payment, or as is quite often the case, requiring the injurer himself to pay some consolation money out of his own pocket. But no matter how calculating a motive may underlie the demand for sincerity, as long as the process of negotiations is couched in terms of moral responsibility, lawyers cannot satisfactorily take over the role of the disputants. Or to put it differently, lawyers' special expertise can have little relevance in these highly moralistic negotiations.

A Paradox of Management

The Successes and Failures

The nonlitigious society of Japan has not developed spontaneously. Instead, it has been cultivated by well-planned management. Under the ostensibly efficient Japanese compensation system, the people seem content with what they get and do not resort to law to recover damages. Moreover, the myth of functionalism prevails; people apparently believe in the benevolence of the system and have not seriously challenged it in the courts or legislature. They have even looked down on the occasional campaign against the system waged by Japanese lawyers, suspecting it to be motivated by their parochial interests. In view of the apparently satisfied public, the system is not likely to change its basic structure in the near future.

In fact, the automobile accident compensation system has been applied to other disputes as well. For example, in medical malpractice, where the number of disputes has sharply increased, a third-party reviewing panel was recently established. A doctor against whom a complaint is lodged must report the complaint to the local medical association, which reviews the complaint and recommends whether the insurance should be paid. If either party or the insurance company is not satisfied with the local association's finding, the case is referred to a central reviewing panel, the Medical Dispute Investigation Council, which consists of representative members of the Japan Medical Association and the insurance companies along with members of the bar. Although the findings of this panel are not legally binding, insurance companies regularly honor them. Interestingly the panels, both in local associations and in the central body, review the case in closed sessions, based not on the adversary arguments of both parties but only on a report compiled by the special staff of the medical association. Furthermore, in view of the strong supervisory power of the Ministry of Finance over insurance companies and that of the Ministry of Public Welfare over the medical associations, this seemingly private panel in reality assumes a semiofficial character. In other areas as well, such as product liability, construction disputes, environmental pollution, real estate transactions, and unpaid wages, similar dispute management has been designed and sanctioned by the government, although implementation has not been uniformly successful.

Note that these nonconfrontational systems are also consonant with the cultural heritage of Japan. Two cultural themes recur throughout dispute management: authority and morality. Although in the United States authority often carries a negative connotation, in Japan it has an intrinsic value; it breeds a sense of orderliness in an otherwise chaotic social world. While an authoritarian person is disliked in Japan, just as in any other society, the authority figure can expect respect so long as he cares for and guides subordinates properly. The resulting hierarchical order makes the nonconfrontational system work. The government, through administrative guidance, directs insurance companies; the judiciary, which is itself hierarchically organized, unifies the interpretation of the law; and the police authoritatively determine the facts on the spot. The third-party neutrals also rely implicitly on this hierarchical control when they set forth the just resolution to the parties.

Morality is also important. In the United States, because morality is left entirely to individuals and cut off from meaningful community sanctions, it has lost much of its binding force. Moreover, as people are overwhelmed by the legal consequences, they are discouraged from showing such fundamental human concern for the victims by, for example, expressing sincere apologies for their fault. By contrast, in Japan, not only is the moral dimension of the accident clearly retained, but also all actors in the system are mutually bound by moral obligations. If the insurance companies did not genuinely honor, or at least, appear to value, morality above legality, and hence live up to the people's expectations, liability insurance could not have been transformed into the quasi-public system. Judges also activate moral concerns. Although committed to maintaining the standardized compensation system, judges nevertheless step beyond the neutral umpire role and urge insurance companies to settle at higher levels when the standardized compensation would work a hardship in a particular case. Otherwise, the rigidity and unconcern for individual plight often associated with bureaucratic justice would strain the system too much. Morality, then, adds a touch of "social justice," if not individual justice, to an otherwise efficient but rigid bureaucratic justice, encouraging support for the system from the people of Japan.

Behind the appearance of consensus and stability, however, one can detect some inherent structural weaknesses in the compensation system. The very effort to create a nonconfrontational system produces problems, for a system that does not employ legal resources is defenseless against overly aggressive parties. The result is a series of irregular payments when persistent claimants wield undue influence or, more troubling, when innocent claimants are subtly induced to accept lower than standard payments. Moreover, the very paucity of litigation weakens the legal system. Only daily experience with law, testing its premises under different circumstances through vigorous, partisan advocacy, can invigorate the law, adapting it to an ever changing society. As the standardized compensation system itself stands on the principle of tort law, this stagnation of the law may in the long run diminish public support for the system.

Although at the moment only a few critics have noted these systemic defects, if the nonconfrontational system harbors the seeds of its decay, it is possible that in the future, when the underpinnings of cultural consensus further erode, and when people with an emerging law consciousness deem the system less satisfactory, it may collapse or evolve into another form. It is too early to predict any major change, but the recent upward turn of litigiousness may reflect the growth of this divergent consciousness. Since 1983, the litigation rate has continued to climb, and mediation is increasingly legalized; the claimants are represented more often, and their cases are less likely to result in settlement. If the problems of unjust compensation and the weakening of the law, which inhere in the system of management, do in fact explain these developments, dispute management has an insoluble contradiction in it; as management is perfected, it creates the problems that undermine its very foundation.

Unjust Compensation

The first problem, unjust compensation, comes about when parties, unaware of any possible leeway in compensation, fail to mobilize available advocacy resources. For example, in a fatal auto accident case, the insurance company first offered 25,000,000 yen, which, on subsequent negotiations, was raised to 35,000,000 yen. However, the plaintiff (the widow who undertook the negotiation) considered this inadequate and consulted a lawyer, who took the case to the Traffic Accident Dispute Resolution Center and settled for 50,400,000 yen. The issue in dispute was whether the economic loss of the deceased (a 38-year-old truck driver temporarily employed) should have been calculated on the basis of his actual income or the average income for all workers of the same age, which was substantially higher. The insurance company relied on the payment standard in the official guideline for optional insurance, which specified that compensation should be made on the basis of actual income. However, the lawyer argued for a higher compensation (68,000,000 yen), relying on the Japan Federation of Bar Associations' handbook, which elucidated the alternative principle that "as a general rule, lost income should be calculated on the injured party's actual income. But if it is probable that such party would, in future, receive the average income for all workers in the same year bracket, the compensation may be calculated on such an average income."

We are struck by the enormous difference in the two figures, both of which are derived from authoritative standards. Without the help of the lawyer, the plaintiff could not have learned of the proviso spelled out in the bar's handbook and would have been forced, albeit reluctantly, to accept the standard shown by the insurance company as "the law." At most, she would have asked the company as a favor to go a little above the "standard" compensation.

Herein lies a major paradox. Since ordinary people lack the resources to utilize the system by themselves, they must engage a lawyer if they wish to obtain the most advantageous settlement. However, to be interested in obtaining legal services they must at first know the possible leeway in compensation that could yield a net increment of compensation. It is a chicken-and-egg problem. How could an injured person know, before engaging a lawyer, that it would pay to engage a lawyer?

The situation could be rectified by a policy that would make this leeway more widely known. It is doubtful, however, that a government with a vested interest in dispute management will voluntarily adopt a policy of informing the public of leeway even in a limited way. Instead, the policy in Japan is to limit individualized adjustments and foster a kind of false consciousness among the public that the leeway in compensation is more limited than is actually the case. Thus, in a recent case study of seven fatal accidents in a local city, a lawyer was retained in only one case. Although several parties in these cases remarked angrily that "the insurance company negotiated high-handedly by alleging the fault of the deceased," or that "the economic loss was calculated by the low wage scale in Akita Prefecture," nonetheless they accepted less compensation by saying that "that's the way it is. It can't be helped."

While an image of standardization with little leeway discourages some valid claims from being pressed, the structure of the management system tolerates some overgenerous awards. When a claimant is overly assertive, the relative non-assertiveness of the insurance company may produce an overgenerous payment. This passivity by the insurance company comes directly from the system of compulsory insurance. Since insurance companies must provide the compulsory policy to every person at a uniform rate regardless of the insured's particular risk, the national government reinsures 60 percent of all such policies and the remaining 40 percent is shared among all insurance companies. As any individual loss is thus spread out among all automobile insurance companies, an insurance company has little motivation to fight overzealous claimants. Moreover, as a repeat player with a good corporate reputation to maintain, an insurance company will be more motivated than an individual one-time claimant to behave like a "good Japanese" by refraining from aggressiveness.

This negation of private interests necessarily weakens defenses against fraudulent claims For those who are not well integrated in the community and influenced by its norms, the insurance companies' self-restraint offers ample opportunity for exploitation. The persistence of unsavory settlement brokers (*jidanya*) in Japan behind the elaborate, well-managed compensation system best attests to this weakness. Some disputants, who are themselves motivated to take unfair advantage of the companies' nonassertiveness, voluntarily refer their cases to such a broker, anticipating that he will fix a settlement larger than that due to them. Thus, the system produces an anomalous situation in which one claimant achieves less than full realization of his entitlement due to his ignorance of the possible leeway in compensation, while another extorts a larger settlement by taking advantage of the excessive restraint of the insurance company. The compensation system, which is predicated upon noncontentiousness, rests on a fragile balance of the negotiating powers of the parties and is maintained not so much by the parties' strength as by their restraint. If one party acts unreasonably, the system easily dissolves, making the less insistent the prey of the more aggressive. Although third-party machinery such as legal consultations and the Traffic Dispute Resolution Center, which occupy an integral part in Japan's compensation system, work to ward off such a disjuncture of negotiating powers, their success is limited. As neutral agents working generally to hold down contentiousness, they are not well equipped to assist the weak party to regain control of negotiations and fight against the predatory party.

Weakening of the Law

Inadequate investment of legal resources, however, does not merely affect the appropriateness of compensation. It may also affect the very maintenance of the whole compensation system by weakening the evolution of law. Without sufficient input from party initiatives, the law stops growing and soon loses its vitality. No law ever achieves perfection, and the standardization scheme in Japan is no exception. By making litigation superfluous, it forfeits the opportunity to adapt itself to the ever changing society. This hindrance of doctrinal development is best illustrated by the ironic admonition of a former judge of the Traffic Section at Tokyo District Court: "Lawyers should litigate more and argue more aggressively before the court than they do now to get the award that best suits for the individual case at hand. The standard should not be applied mechanically." But people do not advocate purely for abstract rules. Private parties sue for private gains, and lawyers litigate if it is worth doing. By litigating out of self-interest, they nonetheless contribute to the growth of law by constantly putting the law in a new light. The arguments made with great partisan zeal imbue the law with new life experiences. In fact, the precedent is only a tip of the iceberg. Without the infinite number of arguments, most of which are never recorded formally, the law would never evolve. And if the vigor of the law is lost, the whole compensation system that derives ultimate legitimacy from it must collapse from public disfavor. After all, the viability of the standardization scheme rests on the recognition, not only by the public but also by the legal profession, that it is the correct representation of true tort principles. Once the faith is shattered, the standardization scheme is nothing but an elite ploy to suppress demand for efficiency's sake.

Again, within the system, there is no cure for this problem. The Japanese judiciary, deeply committed to standardization, is unlikely to encourage party initiative. In fact, unlike the situation in the United States, where people talk about too much law and the overlegalization of the government, in Japan, at least to some critics, bureaucratization of the judiciary is considered a problem. Critics contend not only that the government is insufficiently subjected to judicial control but also that the judiciary itself assumes an administrative outlook toward disputes. That is, the judiciary is accused of actively directing its efforts toward the noncontentious resolution of disputes, implicitly rejecting the aggressive assertion of legal rights. If the law thus becomes stagnant, it does more than just weaken the compensation system. It weakens the entire legal system. As the people become less vigilant in defending their rights, the legal order slackens, and an abuse of power may ensue. Although this weakening of the legal system may be precisely what the government elite wishes to have, still the price is high; it impairs the very power to govern the society. The people accept enforcement of the government policy only when they at the same time are given the protection accorded by the law. In that sense, the current mixture in Japan of strong administrative guidance (*gyosei-shido*) on one hand, and weak regulative power on the other, as rampant tax evasion and widespread insider trading in Japan attest, may be simply a choice by default, which satisfies neither the government nor the people.

If the people in Japan, increasingly sophisticated about law, someday find informal guidance more obtrusive than useful, it will be all the more difficult for the government to regulate the society without law. Thus, if the government assumes an even more aggressive role in regulating the society today, the checks-and-balances function required of the courts must be an equally aggressive one. This much, of course, is known to the elite in Japan, and at least to the degree that the people would not be offended, it avoids the appearance of naked power in exercising its governmental authority. More important, just as insurance companies refrain from exploiting the unwary disputants, the government is trying hard not to abuse the power, which after all is in its self-interest. But to strike the right balance is not an easy task. The bureaucratic management used to create the nonlitigious society tends to go to extremes. Paradoxically, then, the very success of the Japanese elite in disarming the legal weaponry of the people inadvertently sows the seeds of its failure—the loss of legitimacy.

DISCUSSION QUESTIONS

1. What can we learn from comparing litigation rates cross-culturally? What are the methodological problems of doing so?

2. Why do attitudes toward litigation vary across societies? What explains those attitudes? Are there settings in America where "Japanese" attitudes toward litigation prevail? Does "modernization" in Japan inevitably imply an increase in rights-consciousness? Would this be good or bad?

3. What institutions encourage or discourage litigation? How do such factors operate in the United States? What explains these institutional characteristics? Are there situations in which our government discourages litigation? Should it do so?

4. What alternatives to litigation exist in the United States? Have you experienced any of them? Should government create more?

5. How should we measure litigation rates: cases filed? trials conducted? lawyers consulted? What are the reasons for and consequences of each choice?

6. Can Americans obtain legal advice and counselling other than by retaining a private lawyer? How do people learn about their legal rights and obligations? How would you expect American bar associations to react to proposals to introduce lay legal advisers in the United States? Consider the parallels between this debate about the delivery of legal services and contemporary debates about the delivery of medical care. What is gained and what is lost by moving from an adversary model of automobile accident litigation to a more consensual model?

7. Could the American law of automobile accidents be simplified to facilitate consensual resolution of disputes? What would have to be changed? What would be lost or gained by such changes? Would you prefer a no-fault compensation scheme? What are the relative advantages of rules and discretion, routine and custom-made decisions? What criteria of justice and fairness do people use in Japan and the United States in assessing outcomes? Would Americans accept the degree of state intervention, surveillance and control necessary for the Japanese scheme of accident compensation to operate? Would they trust the state to rectify fraud and error?

8. If Japanese litigants seem more able than American to resolve the economic consequences of automobile accidents without litigation, they also seem more preoccupied with the moral consequences. Is this true—do Americans treat accidents as morally indifferent? If so, why? Should we reinvest accidental injury with moral significance? Should those who cause accidents apologize to their victims? Why does this not happen today?

9. Would you rather be a tort victim in Japan or the United States? a tort defendant? Is the emergence of *jidanya* (settlement brokers) analogous to ambulance-chasing personal injury lawyers in the United States?

4

Community Justice, Capitalist Society, and Human Agency: The Dialectics of Collective Law in the Cooperative

Stuart Henry

This article is about the relationship between the structure of whole societies and the rules and sanctions of collective social forms existing within them. Taking the recent debate over the role of informal community justice as a starting point, the article moves through a series of critical arguments to develop a new theoretical perspective for the analysis of the relations between social structure and collective normative orders. It concedes that advocates of community justice have been justly criticized for ignoring the influences of a society's wider political and social structure. But it also argues that the critics are wrong when they claim that the power and influence of the wider society are so pervasive that they necessarily shape and constrain all but the most radical normative orders, using institutions of community justice to sap the strength of any serious challenge to the overall system.

My view is that the independence of community justice institutions is not an either/or phenomenon. The positions of both the advocates and critics of community justice are partial perspectives rather than fundamentally conflicting ones. Recognizing this, I attempt to resolve the debate over the role of community justice institutions by formulating a theory that acknowledges the integrity of both social structures and local normative orders and recognizes that relations at each level are affected by those at the other, in a dialectical fashion.

The article begins with a discussion of the theoretical limitations of current thinking about community justice. Then I build on a series of stimulating articles by Peter Fitzpatrick (1983a; 1983b; 1984) to develop an integrated theoretical perspective that posits a dialectical relationship between social elements and more encompassing forms. Finally, I speculate on the implications of the theory I have developed for the attainment of socialist legality. Throughout, the argument is illustrated with data on the collective justice systems of a group of British cooperatives that I studied (Henry, 1983).

Abridged from *Law & Society Review*, Volume 19: 651 (1985).

Theoretical Limitations in Thinking about Community Justice

The sense that the system of law in capitalist societies has become increasingly formalized, bureaucratic, and routine (Danzig, 1973) has led a number of writers to propose various forms of decentralized informal justice. Two not completely separable goals are sought. The first is to increase most people's contact with and access to legal functionaries. Here the call is for "access to justice" and "justice with a human face" (Capelletti & Garth, 1978), through the introduction of informal dispute processing institutions such as arbitration, conciliation, and mediation (Eckhoff, 1966). Cynically summarized, this goal requires no more than that judges and lawyers discard their wigs and robes. It has been described by Whelan (1981) as "informalizing law."

The second goal is to achieve greater popular involvement in the justice system through increasing participation in the actual administration of law (Versele, 1969). Some who advocate this goal also call for the increased use of arbitration or mediation, but the favored institutional forms are community-based, democratically structured popular courts or tribunals (Christie, 1977). Although some say these should form "a complementary decentralized system of criminal justice" that only handles certain matters (Statsky, 1974), others favor "independent alternatives." Thus, Fisher (1975: 1278) takes the view that "A true community court...should be an alternative to the formal system" and "remain independent of any political organization and influence if it is to operate effectively as an instrument of justice." Likewise, Longmire (1981: 22) argues for "popular" radical alternatives that are "a complete replacement for, rather than complement to, the existing law enforcement system."

There have been a number of criticisms of proposals for increasing democratic participation in the administration of justice through local popular courts that dispense collective justice. The most virulent attack has come from those who analyze the proposed changes from a societal or "macro" perspective. This group includes both supporters of the existing system of law in capitalist society and, perhaps surprisingly, those who are radically opposed to existing arrangements and would prefer a socialist society.

Kamenka and Tay (1975; 1978) are the leading defenders of the status quo. They dismiss the yearning for community and its concomitant personification of law, with its preference for "people's courts" and "people's judges," as a sentimental, romantic, utopian quest to return to the dark ages, and as no more than a "humanizing cosmetic" for the growing bureaucratic practices in law—one that contains "great dangers to liberty and human dignity." Indeed, they ridicule the growing disenchantment with objectivity and with those rational legal methods that hold that people must be judged by universal principles grounded in long pondered and carefully recorded experience. Kamenka and Tay believe the move to community justice reflects an excessive growth of bureaucratic regulation, and they argue that the resultant "crisis in legal ideology" can be resolved by fighting the drift to bureau-cracy and returning to an earlier equilibrium in which capitalist legality, embodying due process principles, was the core integrative mechanism of society.

Those critics who are opposed to the existing organization of society and its system of law acknowledge that community justice institutions may well increase popular participation in the administration of law. They believe, however, that in doing so these institutions help maintain the overall system of societal organization because they are concerned only with relations between individuals and small groups and not with relations between larger powerful collectivities like multina-tional corporations or those between social classes. Community justice institutions, these critics tell us, do not confront fundamental social problems; they serve to reinforce existing social arrangements and to preserve the stability of the state rather than to reallocate power between groups. For example, Brady (1981) believes that popular justice, community participation, and neighborhood justice are being actively promoted and funded by the very government agencies their supporters criticize, precisely because these forms of citizen participation actually serve the dominant legal order, handling low priority cases that would otherwise lay claim to professional and judicial resources. Moreover, according to Abel (1981; 1982a), the restriction of alternative dispute settlement mechanisms to trivial and systemically inconsequential matters—such as neighborhood disputes over noise, pets, and fences—coupled with a mandate for intervention that treats disputants as atomized individuals, has the effect of dispersing conflict. Any discontent is channeled away from societal-level class and structural issues toward personal and individual conflicts. Abel argues that under the guise of providing more humane, more accessible justice, informalism in law shapes conflict so that what are essentially political struggles about the ownership and distribution of property are translated into interpersonal disputes that draw attention away from the capitalist structure of domination and exploitation. Echoing this view, Brady (1981: 31) says that the true nature of popular justice is revealed by the fact that whenever experiments in popular justice begin to challenge powerful interests, they are abandoned by government. They serve merely to "extend the legitimacy and power of the state in a time of fiscal and political crisis."

The positions of both the radical and conservative critics of community justice are themselves open to criticism. As Nelken (1982) points out, Kamenka and Tay's position, that the eclipse of due process law by both bureaucratic and informal community-based developments has led to a crisis in legal ideology, is neither clear nor well founded. Indeed, Kamenka and Tay (1975: 141) note an inevitable tendency toward coexistence among community, due process, and bureaucratic kinds of law "in all, or at least most societies." This seemingly calls into question their assertion that "in the western world there is no doubt that the immediate trend is toward the immeasurable strengthening and extension of the bureaucratic administrative strain" (1975: 142). In short, Kamenka and Tay recognize the integral nature of community and bureaucratic forms to law in a capitalist society, but they apparently do not recognize that, by their own analysis, changes in one element might be expected to give rise to changes in another, as the system returns to equilibrium.

The critics from the left, on the other hand, are guilty of both one-sidedness and inconsistency. In suggesting that capitalist society inevitably shapes systems of community justice to serve its ends and maintain the existing social order, these critics (Abel, 1981; Brady, 1981) overemphasize social structural influences and underplay the degree of autonomy that community justice institutions can have. Santos (1980) recognizes this when he points out that informal institutions of community justice do not merely reflect the ideology of capitalism but instead symbolize ideals of participation, self-government, and real community, which express popular aspirations. Whether such sentiments can be coopted into the wider social control system of a society without meaningfully affecting that overall system is what is at issue in this paper. As I shall demonstrate in the next section, I believe that cooptation cuts both ways.

The inconsistency of the argument becomes clear when we contrast the radical critics' analysis of community justice with their proposals for a structural transformation from capitalism toward socialism and a concomitant transformation from capitalist to decentralized socialist legality. Here the independence that was denied to institutions of community justice is granted to conflicting normative orders. Thus, Brady envisions social movements for equality that seek to bring about social change through raising consciousness, challenging social and economic inequalities, and criticizing the state and its justice system. Similarly, Abel (1981) sees the possibility of radical conflict in capitalist society only in those non-legal institutions that "transform parties, disaggregating those that were corporate and organizing previously atomistic individuals" (Abel, 1981: 255). In neither vision does the pervasive power of capitalism coopt the movement and lead it to serve systemic needs. In neither case do the authors explain why the cooptation they see as inevitable in the case of institutions of community justice does not endanger other movements whose premises differ from those of the dominant capitalist order. Abel (1982b), in particular, recognizes that the transformation to a socialist order may be gradual and that partial advances are meaningful accomplishments, but he, like others writing from the radical perspective, fails to recognize the possibility that community justice institutions themselves may represent a gradual and partial transformation of the capitalist system of dispute processing.

Toward an Integrated Theoretical Perspective

The structural analyses of radical theorists such as Abel, Santos, and Brady reflect an overly mechanistic and deterministic theory of change that focuses on only one aspect of the link between social structure and dispute resolution processes. To develop a more convincing perspective without discarding the insights of the structural theorists requires us, first, to allow for the possibility of mutually interconnecting relationships between parts and wholes, in this case between local normative orders and capitalist legality, and second, to consider the relationship between human agency and legal and normative orders.

A useful starting point for addressing the first issue is Moore's concept of the "semi-autonomous field," a social unit that can "generate rules and customs and symbols internally" and "has the means to induce or coerce compliance," but that is also "vulnerable to rules and decisions and other forces emanating from the larger world by which it is surrounded" since "it is set in a larger matrix which can and does invade it" (Moore, 1978: 55). Fitzpatrick (1983a: 159) draws on Moore's concept and argues that semi-autonomous fields have their own discrete normative orders which, as in the case of the family, both shape and are shaped by state legal order:

> the state legal order itself is profoundly affected by the family and its legal order. There is a constituent interaction of legal orders and of their framing social fields. One side of the interaction cannot be reduced to the other. Nor can both sides be reduced to some third element such as the capitalist mode of production.

As Fitzpatrick (1983b: 8) argues elsewhere,

> It is not ... so much that family relations function in support of relations of reproduction within the totality; family relations are some of those relations of reproduction ... the family cannot be reduced to this totality or seen as only subordinate to it.

In his later statement, Fitzpatrick (1984: 115) offers a sophisticated elaboration of this approach as he introduces the dialectical concept of "integral plurality." Here, "state law is integrally constituted in relation to a plurality of social forms." Drawing on an interpretation of Hegel's concept of dialectic, Fitzpatrick argues that state legal orders tend both to converge with and maintain a distance from other social forms. Relations with state law tend to converge because, "elements of law are elements of the other social form and vice versa" (1984: 122). For example, custom and law can have the same imperatives for behavior because law has incorporated custom into its codes and derives support from such incorporation. During incorporation, Fitzpatrick argues, "law transforms the elements of custom that it appropriates into its own image and likeness" (1984: 122). This process of appropriation and transformation involves mutual influences, such that "Law in turn supports other social forms but becomes in the process part of the other forms" (1984: 122). These mutual relations can have both supportive and opposing aspects, as illustrated by my study of the normative orders of cooperatives in capitalist society.

Cooperatives develop their own normative orders, which are partially rooted in their own social forms and, to this extent, tend to be organized along different lines from state law. The coops surveyed in my study generally developed normative orders similar to those that Abel (1982b) describes as consistent with the needs of decentralized socialism, and to that which Schwartz (1954; 1957) found in his study of the Israeli kibbutz. For example, in most of the coops studied, a decision about someone who had broken the coop rules was made by a general meeting of the cooperative. It was felt that coop members should take personal responsibility on an equal basis within the collective structure and, through their shared individual contributions, reach a collective decision.

Efforts at social control in the coops I examined (Henry, 1983), like those in the kibbutz Schwartz (1954: 476) studied, "must be considered informal rather than legal." Written rules were thought to be incompatible with the kinds of spontaneous, collective decision making that provide the only context in which individuals can be fully and personally responsible, so rules were generally not fixed in advance or written down. As a member of a housing cooperative said to me, "the cooperative spirit is actually doing the right thing without the formality." This, as a member of an electronics commune explained, took the form of a continual openness to correction, which by its nature forestalls disciplinary problems: "All the time I'm asking them what they think about the standard of what I'm doing." Thus, as in the kibbutz (Schwartz, 1954: 477), social control was a consequence of "continuous face-to-face interaction." This is not, however, necessarily effective. For example, three members of the electronics commune left,

> because they had trouble fitting in with the way the rest of us worked....
> They were told in the way the rest of us are always criticizing each other.
> This hurt their pride too much and they left.

Similarly, a member of a housing coop described how "people had just had just enough" of two

> obnoxious sort of dominant figures ... and people decided to give them the boot by no other way than making them feel unwelcome at committee meetings.

Nor are social control efforts in coops limited to purely informal, interpersonal messages. For example, in dealing with those who failed to pay their rent, a housing cooperative in my study found that the relatively more formalized collective meeting was useful because, "If friends are there, they find out you're not paying rent; then there's much more pressure to pay ... group pressure." Here, consistent with the findings of Schwartz (1957) and Rosner (1973), an organized forum focuses the control effort, but the sanction remains one of collective opinion.

Schwartz (1954: 473) also argued that when disturbing behavior is not adequately controlled through the informal process, law develops, in the sense of control by "specialized functionaries who are socially delegated the task of intragroup control." Schwartz thought that this development came at the expense of collective justice, but my evidence, consistent with that of Shapiro (1976), suggests that this tendency toward "legalistic" control coexists with informal controls. Thus, when a member accused of breaking a cardinal coop rule by "not participating" fails to attend the collective meeting, discipline is conducted in a communal way, via a "visit" from a delegation of the collective. A number of housing cooperatives used this system, with varying success, to encourage their members to pay their rent arrears. While such systems have legalistic elements (Shapiro, 1976), they may be institutionalized in a spirit of collective justice that is alien to the spirit of capitalist legality. For example, at one of the regular housing coop meetings that I attended, volunteers were invited to go on a "visit." There was much humor and joking, showing self-consciousness about how the visit might be viewed. One member asked, "What is it going to be then? A knee job?" Another replied, "They're not going to break his legs, just bruise him a little—where it can't be seen!"

Social forms like the cooperative and associated institutions of collective communal justice have complex relations with state law and the wider capitalist society in which they are embedded. Relations of support and opposition may simultaneously exist. For example, in spite of its proclaimed opposition to the existing structure of capitalist society, a housing cooperative is likely to benefit from laws that provide its members with certain rights, such as privacy and freedom from harassment. Similarly, even though its method of production and system of income distribution are diametrically opposed to the predominant forms of capitalist society, a workers' cooperative may depend on contract and corporate law for rights that are essential in dealings with its customers and suppliers as well as with its own members (Weisbrod, 1980). As Shapiro (1976: 429) observes of the kibbutz:

> The possibility that the kibbutz will not prevent the initiation of police action
> ... has a subtle influence in strengthening internal controls in the kibbutz.
> This parallels the way in which tribal societies use the colonial power to
> strengthen traditional leaders.

Insofar as the rules and sanctions that constitute the conflicting normative order of a cooperative are concerned with fundamentally different issues from those of state law, such as rules enforcing participation in coop activities and rules against individual domination of the collective, enforcement of the cooperative's rules will only occasionally lend support to the larger normative order (as when a member is socially sanctioned for stealing by shaming and ostracism). However, a conflicting normative order can support state law by its very separation from it. As Fitzpatrick points out, law "assumes some separate, some autonomous identity in positive constitutive relations with other social forms.... Law would not be what it is if related social forms were not what they are (and vice versa)" (1984: 123). This should be understood in the same sense as Durkheim's famous dictum that "crime brings together upright consciences and concentrates them" (1893: 102). By this Durkheim meant that crime provides an occasion for the celebration and mainte- nance of law by evoking collective shock and generating a cohesive response against activities defined as unacceptable. We might say, to paraphrase Durkheim, that conflicting normative orders bring together capitalist legality and concentrate it. A good illustration of this can be found in one housing cooperative's use of the "visits" system for controlling its rent arrears. When a group of coop members were sent to another's house, without prior warning, to discuss why that member has not paid rent, the visit was intimidating and provoked hostility on both sides. As one member explained:

> It freaked me out. We went as a group of six and stood around shuffling our feet feeling very uncomfortable.... One girl in particular ... was taken aback and abusive.... If there isn't hostility, then the person who is being visited is bound to get overwhelmed. It is rather intimidating when six people suddenly descend on you with no prior notice at all. It's not a good forum to discuss personal things like, "Are you going to pay your rent?" and "Why are you not paying it?"

Not only does such an experience reinforce for both the visitors and the visited the capitalist view of credit and debt, but it also demonstrates the value of capitalist legality's impersonal, rational, and predictable procedures. As a result it may infuse aspects of capitalist legality into the collective system. Weisbrod, for example, shows how nineteenth-century American utopian communistic religious societies used an orthodox legal framework to "create and defend their quite unorthodox institutions" and asserts that "they tended to use that device with considerable sensitivity" (1980: 11, xv). Similarly, the visits system of communal control was sufficiently stressful and insufficiently rewarding that the housing cooperative discussed above switched to a rationally organized model in which the ultimate sanction was the use of state law. The following extract from an interview with one of the members shows how state law can support the cooperative even though the cooperative's normative order conflicts in many ways with the ideology that underlies the state's legal norms.

> We reached a stage then when we sent out eviction notices and nobody believed we'd carry them out. People just saw it as an empty threat ... and meetings just delayed things further. We invited them to come along and

explain. But I mean you can talk till you're blue in the arse and still nothing gets done about it....Then the visits were a bloody disaster. There was a rumpus which was over totally personal things. It had nothing to do with rent.... The reason for people getting at each other's throats about those visiting and calling them the "heavy mob" was because of their own personal feelings towards those people that came.... You see, the problem when you're trying to use discipline or just logic is that people get in the way....To run an efficient rent system you've got to get the human element out as much as possible because that's what messes the whole thing up—people's emotions.... A system where you don't have to go and explain why you haven't paid and involve yourself in totally irrelevant personal problems has to be preferable.... So that's why we introduced the new system. Now, if they are four weeks behind with their rent, they get a warning letter; if they're eight weeks behind, they get a notice to quit, and when that expires, we take court proceedings. Of course the main objection...is "Oh that's a bit heavy, isn't it?" or, if it's a possession order, "getting the law involved." But if the law wasn't involved, people wouldn't be secure in their short-life housing.... So the law is already involved.... I'd much rather not get the law involved.... I think it's a drag giving credibility to the law in this sense because the law doesn't particularly like coops or the people who are in them.... We are allowing the police to harass our members, more or less, which is very heavy, but there's no option.... If there isn't another way, then you've got to do it.

Note the dialectical aspect. By resorting to ordinary landlord-tenant law, the cooperative helps validate for both society and its members a body of law to which it is, in principle, fundamentally opposed. At the same time, it is supported by that law; thus, an institution providing an alternative to capitalist forms of landlord-tenant organizations becomes more viable and more likely to be heard.

Finally, conflicting normative orders like that of the cooperative and the capitalist state may challenge and oppose each other. Fitzpatrick identifies two ways in which this may occur. The first and more obvious way is by "outright rejection," as when state law restricts the activities of conflicting normative orders. For example, the law may demand that worker cooperatives shape their disciplinary actions to the practices of capitalist industry, or the judgmental and compensation standards of capitalist legality may apply when individuals sue their former cooperatives for unfair dismissals (Weisbrod, 1980).

Law may, on the other hand, accept the validity of other norms within their own spheres.

[L]aw sets and maintains an autonomy for opposing social forms keeping them apart from itself and purporting to exercise an overall control, but this control is merely occasional and marginal.... In this limited nature of its involvement with other social forms, law accepts the integrity of that which it "controls." Its penetration is bounded by the integrity of the opposing social form. (Fitzpatrick, 1984: 126)

Thus, cooperatives may have the right to police their own members even to the point of harassing or otherwise victimizing them because the law refuses to intervene in matters that are seen as the "private" concern of the coop and its members. In these circumstances cooperatives can reject and to some extent undercut capitalist legality. For example, by invading members' privacy and subjecting them to intimidation, as in the case of "visits," the collective justice of the coop rejects, sometimes contemptuously, state laws that elevate individual protections over group aims.

Thus, Fitzpatrick concludes that, "law is the unsettled resultant of relations with a plurality of social forms and in this, law's identity is constantly and inherently subject to challenge and change" (1984: 138). The same is true of alternative normative orders in their relations with state law.

Fitzpatrick's contribution to dialectical or integrated theorizing in his series of well-crafted expositions increases our understanding of law by enabling us to grasp the complexity of the relations between the law of society and the normative orders of the social forms that make up a society. Before examining the implications of this analysis for socio-legal change, I should like to point to a number of areas where Fitzpatrick's theory of integral plurality might be developed and to illustrate, with the aid of examples from my research on collective justice within cooperatives, how these developments might be used to examine the relations between law and normative orders.

Incorporating the Action-Structure Dialectic

Fitzpatrick does not tell us what counts as a social form or what counts as a normative order. It is possible to abstract parts from a whole, such that what is originally seen as a part becomes the whole. A cooperative, for example, is both a part of the capitalist society and a whole made up of its own constituent parts, such as factions and subgroups. These parts may be similarly broken down until only individuals remain. At all levels, however, each element is a part of something larger that exists in relation to both the larger whole from which it is extracted and to the other parts that make up the original whole.

The possibility of this dual perspective raises two crucial issues. First, how far should one abstract parts from wholes or, to put the question another way, how many stages of abstraction should there be? Second, how does one meaningfully and intelligibly cope with the myriad of mutually supportive and opposing relations between parts and wholes that may exist at different levels of abstraction? Fitzpatrick's analysis does not go beyond the first stage to consider the constituents of the parts he examines. In particular, his analysis never penetrates to the level of the individual and so ignores all relations of human agency. Thus, in discussing the dialectical relations between law and social forms, Fitzpatrick talks of law maintaining an identity, having an autonomy, etc., but he ignores the fact that it is through human interaction that law relates to other normative orders. Social action and the social structure, social action and the law, and social action and particular normative orders all exist in mutually constitutive relations. Ignoring the action-structure dialectic can lead one to take for granted the forms institutions take and to overlook the implications of the fact that institutions are social constructions.

Theorists have addressed these issues in different ways. Giddens (1979; 1982; 1984), for example, argues that any examination of structure without reference to human agency or to agency without reference to structure is essentially misleading because action and structure presuppose one another in a mutually dependent relationship. He argues that the structural properties of societies are both the medium and the outcome of the practices that constitute these societies and that structure both enables and constrains actions that can change it. Each action is at once new and performed in an historical context that, without either barring or mandating the action, shapes it by setting constraints and providing the medium through which the meanings of action are expressed. Thus, Giddens maintains, "institutions do not just work behind the backs of the social actors who produce and reproduce them"; rather, "all social actors, no matter how lowly have some degree of penetration of the social forms which oppress them" (1979:72).

Incorporating this insight into Fitzpatrick's theory provides a more coherent perspective that not only recognizes the dialectical relationship between state law and other normative orders but also considers the relationship between these orders and the structures in which they are embedded, on the one hand, and social action as human agency, on the other. Humans, in other words, are shaped by and shape the groups in which they are involved just as these groups are shaped by and shape the larger social structure. A theory that seeks to explain institutions of communal justice and their place in capitalist society must recognize this.

Just as the social institution is an abstraction from social structure, so it is possible to identify a second level of abstraction, which I shall refer to as "factions," and a third level, which, following Giddens (1979; 1982), I shall describe as "human agency." The structural correlates of these abstractions are the subgroups that exist within institutions and the individuals who are members of subgroups.

Factions

Take the case of a workers' cooperative as an illustration. Factions are formed by all subgroups within a cooperative, whatever their basis. Thus, within a cooperative of foreign language teachers one faction was "a little clique who did not attempt to consult other members of the cooperative." Factions can include as few as two members who have common interests they seek to promote. The coalition strategies that such interest groups generate may be accommodated, or they can split a group. A member of a collective designing software for computers spoke of the inevitability of factions: "Find some equilibrium size, which might be 7, 10, 15.... Anything bigger than that and problems start to arise, so the best thing is to split."

Factions, like the social institutions of which they are a part, may generate their own rules and sanctions that specify acceptable ways of proceeding. These ways of proceeding may apply only to faction members, or the faction may seek to impose the behavior it legitimates on the larger institution. What is legitimated at the factional level may, but need not, reflect the core norms of the embedding institution. A cooperative that expressly adopts informal reintegrative disciplinary procedures may or may not generate factional forms that espouse similar norms. Thus, a clique within a cooperative that is committed to reintegrative collective justice may legitimate for its members formalized, elitist, and hierarchical methods of social control. This may create tensions that transform both the clique and the cooperative. As a member of a cooperative arts group said:

> We are actually struggling with two systems, and the fact that we have two systems means we never fully commit ourselves to either. There are the two different wheels. They [elite clique] will always step in if you want them to. They will always say, "I'll wield the big stick." It's there in the background.... To that extent we are not using one or the other.

Here, the elite clique's willingness to eject those who fail to abide by the cooperative's rules at one level serves the interests of the cooperative but at another contradicts the cooperative's core ethic and basic organizing principles. Harsh discipline by the elite faction may induce particular individuals to conform to particular rules but in the process may reduce the overall level of compliance with cooperative norms. For example, an elite clique's effort to enforce participation may diminish the average member's involvement both by making the cooperative less attractive and by reducing the average member's responsibility for social control. The result is likely to be a reduced willingness to participate and even greater need to resort to the use of discipline. The cooperative may hang together because of attractions extraneous to the cooperative ideal, such as access to markets, or such factionally legitimated activity may cause the coop to collapse.

> We put together this motion: "Every member of the coop shall assign themselves to one predetermined area of work in List A within which their skills may lay, and can be called upon to utilize their skills and assist in the running of the coop. Anyone who persistently fails to help when asked will have their membership questioned by the participation subcommittee.... In

addition no member shall be exempt from assisting in any one of the activities in List B."

On precisely this motion people just happened to be wandering out. They were going home to tea or something and the finger was pointed: "These people are leaving the meeting. Isn't it a disgrace?" Well there was no evidence to suggest that they were acting in the wrong way so they took offense. They said, "Fuck you!"

Human Agency

Factions are, of course, composed of individuals whose action, following Giddens, I shall refer to as "human agency."

> To be a human agent is to have power to be able to "make a difference" in the world.... In any relationship which may be involved in a social system, the most seemingly "powerless" individuals are able to mobilize resources whereby they carve out "spaces of control" in respect of their day-to-day lives and in respect of the activities of the more powerful.... There are many ways in which the seemingly powerless, in particular contexts, may be able to influence the activities of those who appear to hold complete power over them; or in which the weak are able to mobilize resources against the strong.... Anyone who participates in a social relationship ... necessarily sustains some control over the character of that relationship or system ... actors in subordinate positions are never wholly dependent, and are often very adept in converting whatever resources they possess into some degree of control over the conditions of reproduction of the system. In all social systems there is a dialectic of control, such that there are normally continually shifting balances of resources altering the overall distribution of power...an agent who does not participate in the dialectic of control *ipso facto* ceases to *be* an agent. (1982: 197–99)

The social action of individuals, like social action at each level we have examined, may conform to special sets of rules. The normative order rooted in human agency is that which is referred to as "personal self-control," "self-discipline," or "conscience." It is not, of course, independent either of the person in whom it is rooted or of other social forms with which it exists in a dialectical relationship.

The personal rules that human agents adopt are like the rules of the various subgroups we have discussed in that they both shape and are shaped by the groups of which they are a part. When association with a group is voluntary, as it is with a cooperative or a faction, one would expect personal norms and values to be largely congruent with those of the group to which the person belongs. However, groups have multifaceted attractions, and individuals are complex characters. Thus, human action may both support and challenge the core norms of membership groups, sometimes at the same time. For example, one member of a housing cooperative that I studied was renowned for excusing his rent arrears by blaming his uncooperative behavior on the wider structure of capitalism. In doing so, he confirmed the cooperative ideology while threatening its financial stability. The material advantages of this dual posture led inevitably to resentment, concern, and suspicion:

> People think "Oh he's got a lot of problems!" But it's only because we know about his problems, because he's made damn sure everybody knows about them, whereas other people in the coop ... who've got really serious problems ... haven't made it their business to say so.

A member of the same cooperative explained that they were particularly vulnerable to this kind of individualistic exploitation because

> none of us wants to get our fingers burned or to be seen to be heavy so what happens? ... We'd be nice to them and make an arrangement for them to pay.... We start feeling sorry for them. "Ah poor dears. They've got all these problems. Let's make it easier for them.... Perhaps we ought to restructure the coop to make it more accessible!"

A member of a whole-food coop explained how this kind of toleration could eventually be disastrous.

> Because everybody believes in being nice to everyone, one person could put a complete spanner in the works.... Apart from being bad from the financial side ... it can have a very negative effect on all the other people.

Moreover, individuals subject to the collective discipline of the normative order can challenge it by arguing that individual vindictiveness rather than collective concerns is the motivating force. Cooperatives are especially vulnerable to such defenses because the members all know one another intimately. As a member of another housing cooperative said of those with rent arrears:

> the individuals concerned almost expect to be taken to task but they are surprised and resentful when they see ... a comrade knocking on the door. Quite a lot react aggressively ... feel that they have to hit back. People think they are victimized.

This can be seen in the account of a member of an arts collective who blamed her expulsion on a feud she was having with the wife of a member of the disciplinary committee:

> It seemed to me that it was rigged all the way through by these people this particular woman who wanted me out. She'd got a lever through her husband to every committee.

Another member of the same collective pointed out that the size and close-knit nature of coop relations meant that "it's more likely than you might imagine...[that] the committee you get is possibly going to be influenced in that kind of way."

One may ask why organizations like cooperatives contain members and factions whose rules of proceeding contradict core cooperative norms and threaten to destroy it. The reasons are too numerous and complex to explicate here, but one aspect must be mentioned. The wider capitalist order both stimulates and supports the oppositional actions of both the human agents and factions that are found in cooperatives. Thus, the social structure threatens oppositional institutions from below. These institutions are not foredoomed to failure, but even when they are not overtly challenged by capitalist society, they have a constant struggle to maintain themselves. As a member of a theater cooperative expressed it:

> Specialization is exactly the sort of contradiction that happens when you try and behave in a way that is contradicted by life ... by the particular form of our society.... You can't avoid it.

A member of a housing coop pointed out that it is difficult for people used to a hierarchical system to suddenly change their whole approach and assumptions. They expect a landlord and tenant relationship and cannot imagine how Joe and Mabel from up the road can actually evict them, nor can Joe and Mabel easily contemplate this!

> It's a question of people having been traditionally in a very weak position, and suddenly they are in a position of power but are not aware of it ... cannot comprehend it.

Others point to contamination by the sexist divisions in the wider capitalist society. A member of the electronics commune made the point this way:

> Meetings themselves are sexist.... The men seem to enjoy meetings as a sort of social interaction, a bit like being down the pub together or boys in the back room, and ... it's quite a strong interaction for them.... The women are stronger in terms of one-to-one interaction during the course of the ordinary

productive process, of talking, just sort of chatting over the shoulder.... Both are methods for achieving the same thing, which is to find opinions, interact, and through that you could make decisions. But if you're then going to say meetings are how this coop makes its decisions, it may be that there is a slight sexual bias to it.

Undoubtedly, one of the most important ways in which the wider capitalist society can be seen as shaping the collective is through the necessary interaction of its members with other capitalist organizations. A member of a whole-food coop, for example, noted that the wider capitalist structure means that cooperatives have to compete with capitalist companies on their terms.

Profit means ... having a surplus at the end of the year rather than a deficit. And if you keep having a deficit, you go bankrupt.... I see a lot of coopera-tives very concerned with the superficial image of whether or not they are a kind of far out place ... no authority structure, everybody just does their own thing. They're not actually concerned with building something up that is strong, that is actually going to generate some money and take the capitalists on at their own game.

A member of the theatre collective also accepted the inevitability of some capitalist contamination.

No more do I believe we operate perfectly as a collective could operate. Obviously it's contradicted by lots of things in the outside world. We are on one level a cooperative experimenting with new ways of doing things and on another we are a small company ... concerned with developing plays.... One thing beyond anything else that makes that possible is economic survival. If you want to eat and do community theatre, it's necessary to earn money, and that means endless concessions.... In order to exist legally there are certain accounting skills which you must have.... For Greg, who's learning about performing, to interest himself in the details of administration would destroy his ability to perform. Everything would numb out into a vague blandness.... It's clearly a division of labor, but I don't think a division of labor necessarily means a division of experience, nor does it imply hierarchy.

It is, however, as I have already suggested, a mistake to explain entirely in structural terms the tendencies toward individualism, factionalism, specialization, and sexist role allocation that existed in the cooperatives I studied and were reflected in their normative orders. Human agency was also important. People are different in their abilities, motives, and values, and these differences, both as an inescapable fact and as particular constellations of personalities, necessarily affect the organizations that people create. As a member of an electronics commune put it:

> Although we are very much a coop of equals, I do think we inevitably move away from this ideal ... because we are all different people with different levels of confidence to work.

Another member of the electronics commune observed:

> Even if you think you've got a consensus system, it is possible to find that people with the strongest personalities so often carry everyone else with them that it's almost as if they control the direction in which we go.

And a member of the computer collective said:

> I think a division of labor has to be inevitable in some fields....There's going to be some things that I might find interesting that ... somebody else doesn't.

The wider system of capitalism, with its individualist rewards and competitive ethic, may strengthen and lend support to these kinds of differentiation, but this does not mean that capitalism determines how or the extent to which differentiation proceeds within collectives nor that collectives or other efforts at communal government are doomed to fail or inevitably to support the capitalist enterprise. The tendency toward differentiation that is associated with human agency is, no doubt, reinforced by the encompassing capitalist system, but it exists under socialism as well. And from this human agency arise the values associated with communalism and the commitment to work toward collective ends.

Conclusion

In conclusion, let me sketch the most important implications of this paper for those who espouse socialism and who, like Abel (1982b), believe that the creation of small-scale collectives is fundamental to achieving it. First, my study of cooperatives suggests that in a capitalist society even radically independent collective structures are permeated by influences of the larger system. Second, we have seen that such collective institutions are especially vulnerable to crisis and collapse. This is not due just to the mutually opposing relations that the collective and its normative order have with the capitalist society and its law. It stems also from the sometimes anti-communitarian tendencies of factions and individuals within these institutions, which may be fostered by the wider society and its law. Third, the number of institutions, such as cooperatives and collectives, that are organized around principles inconsistent with capitalism is small in relation to the number of institutions permeated by the capitalist ethic. Even if it were possible for communally oriented institutions to remain free of capitalist influences, we could not expect these forms to be a vanguard for total social change unless we had some reason to believe that the example or efforts of such institutions would transform capitalist institutional structures. Abel offers neither theoretical support for this expectation nor evidence that communal institutions have such effects.

This study provides both, but not in the direct way that this expectation suggests. Alternative institutions and their associated normative orders do not work transformations on capitalist structures and rule systems but instead interact with them in a dialectical way such that both the alternative system and the capitalist order are vulnerable to incremental reformulations. Since capitalist rules and institutions predominate among the norms and organizations of capitalist society, the greatest potential for a social transformation lies in these dialectical processes. At one level the communitarian concerns of human agents are likely to interject more communal elements into capitalist society by penetrating and modifying capitalist institutions than are injected through the creation of alternative collective structures. At another level institutions of communal justice within employee work groups, neighborhood residence groups, mutual support, and self-help groups, none of which challenge the core organizing principles of capitalist society, are likely to do more to modify the shape of capitalist legality than the collective justice of cooperatives, communes, and other more socialistically oriented orders that are rarely encountered within capitalism and are generally marginal in the larger society. Indeed, capitalism may, as we have seen, successfully undercut opposing orders, but it cannot destroy its own institutions and therefore must continually contend with opposing internal tendencies. Thus, it is likely that the collective justice of factions that form within capitalism has a degree of persistence that is not found in conflicting orders. An implication of these observations is that, short of revolution, change towards socialist legality is more likely to be fostered by mechanisms of communal justice within institutions that do not challenge the basic premises of capitalism than through the development of more radical conflicting institutions.

Those who value socialist forms of interpersonal government should recognize that the desired communal collective form is already an existing, if unacknowledged, underemphasized, and undervalued, component of the capitalist legal order. Failing to see this, those who espouse socialism will miss the most promising ways of institutionalizing schemes of socialist legality. Moreover, in evaluating attempts to institutionalize socialist legality, those who are blind to the integrative perspective are likely to be continually frustrated by what are in fact inevitable imperfections in the socialist ideal and will not recognize what they have achieved.

The spirit with which the movement toward socialist legality in capitalist society must proceed, if it is to proceed at all, is nicely captured in the remarks of a member of a theater collective whom I interviewed.

We are trying to glimpse possible relationships in the present world. Unless you know what it would be like to have a society where people cooperate, unless you've got some glimpse of it, I really don't see what you're doing trying to get it. Or even if you manage to get it, what on earth are you going to do with it? ... The only way things change, in my experience—all the things I'm referring to are a very intricate set of relationships ranging from personal ones to huge ones involving organizations—is in an imaginative, cooperative, creative way, where someone offers a possibility with a degree of conviction, energy, and forethought about how that possibility will be organized, so that it becomes evident to the other people that that's what happens. I really want to make it mundane, because I think it's very important to make it mundane. I don't want to end up talking about mass party organization. I'm not convinced that someone running a socialist center, however *au fait* he is with contemporary political ideas, is going to be able to handle society better than Sue Smith, who's 19, because she's doing it now. You know, she's actually trying to work out what happens when she's got a better idea than someone who is older than her, or apparently usually knows better, and how to explain to them without causing an argument and wasted time.

In conclusion, then, I would invert Abel's (1982b) observation that "partial advances need not await a total victory." Total victory is contingent upon partial advances, but such advances will be inconsequential in bringing about the desired end if they are restricted to peripheral institutions that reject capitalism at their core. While such advances are a form of progress, broad-based change requires transformations within mainstream institutions that do not begin by challenging the premises of capitalism and the capitalist legal order. As I have tried to show in this paper, there exists the potential for such broad-based change. It is rooted in the ability of human agents to "make a difference," and in the dialectical interplay of factions and the groups that contain them. Ironically, forces that often undercut bold attempts to achieve socialist legality, like those in the collective systems I studied, provide the greatest hope of ultimately achieving it.

DISCUSSION QUESTIONS

1. How do we explain the interest in community justice, informalism, people's courts, etc., which emerged in the 1970s? Who were the advocates? the critics? Are you surprised by the political alignments?

2.   What are the primary structural conflicts within contemporary American society? Which institutions handle them? What are semi-autonomous social fields? Can you give some examples? How autonomous are they?

3.   What are the conditions for effective informal social control? Where do these exist in contemporary America? When do such settings resort to formal law? What is the effect on informal social control of resort to formal law? Could housing coops remain entirely outside the formal legal system? Under what circumstances does state law recognize "private" ordering and decline to interfere? Must coops retain the ultimate power to expel? Can they exercise this without reliance on the state? If so, how might it be enforced?

4.   How do cooperatives influence the larger society, and how are they shaped by it? How are dispute processes in one affected by processes in the other? Is informalism fated to be marginalized, coopted, or formalized? Under what conditions might cooperatives and collectives be prefigurative or transformative?

5.   Is there an optimum size for cooperatives? If so, how can they coordinate their activities? Is state law necessary for such coordination?

6.   How do individuals resist or evade informal social control? How does this differ from deviance from state law?

7.   What are the elements of socialist legality within capitalist institutions, and what is their transformative potential? Why do some theorists argue that these contradictions are inevitable?

8.   Are tendencies toward specialization, hierarchy, and sexism present in humans regardless of the social structure in which they are imbedded? or are they generated by those structures? How does our knowledge of cooperative organizations help us examine the question? Are some social structures more facilitative of those differences than others? How far can we rely on structural changes to bring about changes in social interaction and social forms?

Social Control

5

The Selectivity of Legal Sanctions: An Empirical Investigation of Shoplifting

Erhard Blankenburg

Scope of the Study

If "deviance" were to be defined statistically as behavior engaged in by only a minority of people, shoplifting might have to be considered as "normal." Stealing in certain situations is apparently such "normal behavior" that attempting to detect and prosecute all shoplifters would immediately clog the criminal justice agencies with masses of files and cases.

Obviously, there are two ways to deal with such a mass phenomenon. The first would be to handle all cases of recorded shoplifting bureaucratically, as is done with many classic offenses. Legal authority could be given to the person who observes the shoplifting to issue some sort of "ticket," requiring payment of a fine, and developing a record of those who are habitual offenders. Although there have been attempts to devise such a bureaucratic procedure in Germany (as in many other countries), these have never been widely used. Instead, department stores, police and courts employ a second strategy to deal with the mass phenomenon of shoplifting: they look the other way in most cases, and they initiate formal prosecution very selectively. Deliberate inaction and selective prosecution occur at various stages and involve a number of choices.

The first is the means used to detect shoplifters. Department stores and smaller shops have an inherent interest in displaying their goods so that customers are stimulated to buy. Most measures of surveillance and protection from theft would interfere with this suggestive display. Thus, most small shops and some department stores in Germany are very reluctantly introducing special methods or personnel for protection from shoplifters, and do so as unobtrusively as possible. In any case, whether detecting devices are absent or whether they are very elaborate, all estimates agree that the number of undetected shoplifters far exceeds the number of those detected.

Abridged from *Law & Society Review*, Volume 11:109 (1976).

Detection itself is selective, because detectives follow a "strategy of suc-cess-oriented suspicion" (Feest & Blankenburg, 1972; Cameron, 1964: 26–32). For example, Cameron reports that store detectives single out persons with big bags or wide coats, or blacks. Whether such strategies are derived from prejudice or represent an instrumental identification of characteristics proven by previous experience to be associated with offenders is not the issue. For our purposes it is essential only that all strategies of suspicion exhibit some kind of selectivity.

After detection, selective practice continues (Cameron, 1964: 20–24). Fear is not the only reason that creates hesitance in reporting detected shoplifters to the police. There are a number of other reasons, including the social consequences of penal prosecution for the offender, a desire to avoid exposure of conflict in front of other customers, or even a wish to retain the patronage of the offender. But even if shops declare vehemently that all apprehended shoplifters will be prosecuted (e.g., because inventory shrinkage is particularly high), there are still economic reasons not to invoke court procedures. Since each case will take several hours of the time of detectives or sales personnel, frequent prosecution will lead to a substantial increase in personnel costs (Cameron, 1964: 32–38).

Thus, there are very good reasons for the victims of shoplifting not to invoke the criminal process. On the other hand, shopowners seem to believe in the symbolic value of criminal sanctions and in their general preventive effects. Therefore, they frequently publish rising crime rates together with estimates of total losses, often leading to arguments for more severe punishment of this type of mass criminality. The effect of these contradictory motivations is selectivity: among all detected shoplifters some are reported to the police (perhaps to satisfy the symbolic function of the criminal law), and others are not. Though there have been speculations on the likelihood of systematic class or racial discrimination, research on the patterns of selectivity has been difficult because statistics at the different stages of criminal process are often not comparable.

This essay makes an attempt to bring together empirical studies at each stage of the factors influencing the sanctioning process. It examines data on self-reporting, the files of each shoplifter reported to the police by the biggest department store and the biggest chain of supermarkets in Freiburg (a university town in southwest Germany with a population of 140,000 at the time of this study), the files of the police, the state prosecutor's office and the courts, and finally experiments on the conditions of being detected and reported for shoplifting. The focus of the study is not the conditions or motivations of shoplifters but rather the factors that determine the chances of being detected, reported, and penalized.

Terminology and Methodological Considerations

If we reflect on our everyday behavior, we realize that we commonly act on the assumption that norms are effective; we underestimate how often there are deviations that will not be sanctioned. The trust in normative efficiency seems to be particularly high if the norm is legal, i.e., supported by an agency responsible for the sanctioning of deviations. We shall define an "agency" as one or more persons who have been designated and equipped with the power to execute sanctions within the confines of certain rules. Sanctioning is a duty as well as a privilege: if there is information about deviance, there "ought" to be a sanction. In actuality, this "ought" knows many exceptions, for which the reasons may frequently be obvious, but so far our need to make legal rules look legitimate has hindered us from seeing this fact clearly.

In studying the application of sanctions we should, for practical purposes, pick a kind of behavior that can readily be observed and that furnishes us with enough instances to generate a statistically significant population at the different stages of the sanctioning process. As our theoretical interest is in the relation of legal and moral norms, the observed behavior should be salient to both. Shoplifting fits all of these conditions: here we have a delinquent action which is quite frequent and which can be observed with some confidence that the enumeration of instances is reasonably comprehensive; there is an active interest on the part of the owners of department stores and shops in preventing the crime; there is some moral indignation in the population; and it is a norm which—according to the law—should only be sanctioned by judicial agencies. However, shoplifting is also peculiar in that detection and sanctioning are institutionally separated. The agency for detecting shoplifters is the department store itself; however, it is the privilege of judicial agencies to decide upon the sanction. This institutional separation makes it possible to separate the conditions of detection from those of sanctioning.

We have developed a taxonomy which should help clarify the analysis. In any normative phenomenon there are two types of compliance to be discussed:

(1)   compliance with the "primary norm": behavior x should be observed;

(2)   compliance with the "secondary norm": deviance from the primary norm should be sanctioned.

In our analysis we focus mainly on the conditions of compliance with the secondary norm. Here the normative claim is directed toward a number of agencies, as well as toward accidental bystanders observing deviance. If we want information about compliance with primary and secondary norms, we should know the quantitative distribution of norm-relevant behavior in these categories. In how many cases will a norm be followed, in how many cases will it be broken? Has the deviant act been detected at all? Does the sanctioning agency know who the actor is? In how many cases will a sanction follow, in how many cases will it not? Which conditions lead to a decision not to sanction? Has the deviant actor been caught?

In answering these questions, we make use of the following categories:

a. Behavioral compliance: norm-conforming behavior
b. Sanctioning compliance: deviant behavior, actor known, sanction implemented
c. Decision not to sanction: deviant actor known, not sanctioned
d. Deviance not cleared: deviant actor unknown, deviance known
e. Deviance not discovered (dark field): deviant actor unknown, deviance unknown

First we ascertain the frequency of deviant events by interviewing a group of students (a/a+b+c+d+e). Then we analyze the conditions under which a deviant act can be detected by using both observational and experimental data (b+c+d/b-+c+d+e). Finally, we examine the sanctioning process in those cases where the deviant act has been detected by using another experimental design and by analyzing the files of department stores, police, and courts (b/c).

The Effectiveness of the Behavioral Norm (a/a+b+c+d+e)

The most common method of sociological research, the interview, usually misses the goal of getting valid data on norm-relevant behavior: the interviewees either do not admit how often they break a norm or they brag about actions they would never dare to perform. They try to evade an answer by giving an opinion: they tell the interviewer what should be done, not what they do in fact. Interviews are very good if we want to know something about attitudes or opinions, but it is always dangerous to make inferences about actual behavior from such data.

In spite of all these difficulties a methodology has been developed to study undetected crime. "Self-reported crime interviews" start with instances of deviance that almost everybody has committed (staying away from school, passing a stop sign) and then slowly progress to more serious crimes such as theft, robbery, or embezzlement. If the interview situation is well designed and the interviewees trust that their responses will be kept truly anonymous, this method may lead to valid data. The first study of this sort in Germany was carried out in Giessen in 1967 and involved 220 vocational school students, 15–18 years old, who belong to the lower social strata. The subjects were asked: "How often have you taken something in a department store or in a self-service store?" Thirty-nine percent admitted that they had shoplifted before, 12 percent three or more times. Of the 89 who admitted shoplifting, only 4 had been known to the police.

Conditions for Detecting Shoplifters (b+c+d/b+c+d+e)

Self-reporting studies give us data on the "dark figure" of shoplifting behavior as far as it relates to unknown *actors*. They show what percentage of the population has committed a certain delinquent act and how many of them have been detected. In examining the effectiveness of norms, however, we are more interested in the dark figure relating to delinquent *acts committed*. What is the likelihood that a shoplifter will be detected? And what conditions influence this probability?

In order to be quite sure that we knew the total population of deviant acts to be detected, we used an experimental design in which we performed the shoplifting ourselves. As we wanted to know something about the sanctioning process, not about the motivation of shoplifters, we could rely on data pertaining to cases where we had controlled all the circumstances of the shoplifting. The management of the firm was informed and consented. Sales personnel were not informed of the experiment, either by us or by the management. This way we made certain that our experiment was truly unobtrusive. On the other hand, we ensured that no information about the reactions of individual employees was reported back to the management, because we wanted to avoid giving rise to any personnel decisions.

We went into each of the branches of the largest supermarket chain in Freiburg between 3 and 6 p.m. and committed, in all, 40 acts of shoplifting while one of our observers took notes on the "thief's" behavior and that of customers and personnel. As we wanted to know the risk run by a shoplifter acting with "normal" skill, we had to simulate the behavior of a shoplifter without any training. Since our "thieves" would gain training during the experiments, we standardized their strategy well below the level of their skills. The behavior of the observer was standardized, too, in order not to attract attention.

The observer entered the supermarket first. He selected his goods in the prescribed manner, using the basket furnished by the store. He unobtrusively noted the size of the store, the number of customers and personnel, and how these were occupied. After a while the thief entered. He also took a basket, put one sizable item into it, and then a second which he could pack into his private bag at the most suitable opportunity. Then he took a third item, went to the cashier, paid for the two items in his basket, and left the store. The observer took notes on the behavior of the other customers, taking care not to draw attention to the thief, whom he had to treat with complete neutrality. When the thief had paid and left the store, the observer also went to the cashier. The goods bought or "stolen" were standardized: the "thieves" had to "steal" a pound of coffee or a can of meat or vegetables, any of which is too big to disappear in a sleeve, and cost DM3–8 ($1–2). They carried a bag of the sort commonly used by young people and they looked "orderly" but not elegant. Immediately after the action, thief and observer independently filled out a standardized "protocol."

The strategic reflections of our "thief" may give us insights into those of real shoplifters.

As there is more danger of being detected by the personnel than by the customers, I was always sticking to the customers and avoiding the sales personnel. Furthermore, I looked around when entering to see whether there were any mirrors, etc. I was trying to find a place in a dead corner, which the sales personnel could not look into. At the same time I tried to act as a "normal customer." In cases when I felt insecure, i.e., I was afraid that I was being observed, I asked for some information. This made my role more believable, and also had a quieting effect on myself. Furthermore, I tried to impress more positively than negatively: I acted as a polite and helpful young man, thinking that if the theft were detected, the people around me would have to admit that they wouldn't have expected a person like me to do that. This way I hoped to have a good bargaining position with the sales manager.

In each store I tried to follow these rules: move around like a real customer, look for a dead corner to transfer the goods into your bag, keep near other customers, try to use favorable situations which might arise suddenly (e.g., if a sales girl is occupied by some other customer). As to the latter tactic, it seems to me important to note that there was a learning process: by and by I learned to use such situations without hesitating.

The learning process was also described by an observer.

During the first days the theft was observably a test situation ("thief" got a red face when packing, he was tired after three tries, he was very hectic in his movements). These symptoms disappeared afterwards, though not entirely. Besides remaining more cold-blooded, there was an improvement in his technique. The first day he withdrew into some dark corner, in order to avoid being near any other person—a technique which could have signaled an intention to steal. Afterwards he used other customers as a protection-shield against potential disturbance by the personnel in cases where there was no other possibility of hiding. As a rule, he used to keep near the customers who were busy choosing goods, and tried to give the impression that he was busy doing the same. To size up the situation in a quick, cognitive way was a learning process which could hardly be excluded (orientation in the shop, taking in the possibilities). Added to this, there was the usual effect that the quota of successes renders a person self-assured.

Managers of department stores estimate that about 10 percent of all shoplifters are detected. However, these are mere guesses. In our experiments we expected to have a "dark figure" of about 90 percent, i.e., about 10 percent of our thieves would be apprehended, and there would be a chance of studying the sanctioning process. However, as a matter of fact, not one of our "thieves" was detected. Thirty-nine "thefts" were carried out successfully, and only in one case did our "thief" give up stealing because he felt he was being observed too closely. Thus, our prognosis was far too high. Although our thieves were not unusually sophisticated, the rate of detection was even lower than we had expected.

The observers' "protocols" give us some clues to why the shoplifters had no trouble in remaining undetected. The difficulties of shoplifters vary with three factors: the construction of the store and arrangement of goods, the behavior of sales personnel, and the behavior of other customers. With respect to the first, it seems quite plausible that a department store which is easy to survey will facilitate detection and will keep potential thieves from stealing. For example, one of our thieves did not carry out his theft because there was no point at which he was sure he could not be observed. Some of our conclusions are less obvious. Our "thieves" reported that they felt much safer in small stores because there were fewer persons whose view they had to avoid. This is not because small shops are arranged for greater visibility; the observers' protocols show that the arrangement of goods varies independently of the size of the shop. But in a small shop that allows high visibility it is still much simpler to steal because there are fewer persons who participate in the situation—the "thief" can judge more easily whether they are observing him or whether they are otherwise occupied. In a big store he cannot keep an eye on the whole place and hence must look for a dead corner in order to recreate the situation characteristic of smaller stores. If criminal statistics show that shoplifting occurs in big department and other self-service stores, this could indicate the increased likelihood of detection and prosecution rather than a higher rate of theft.

The second factor, the behavior of the sales personnel, plays a decisive role in preventing and detecting shoplifters. Our "thieves" stole successfully even in shops affording high visibility supplemented by mirrors. The observers' protocols show why: a nearby saleswoman was busy talking to another client; the cashier was fully occupied in looking for change; a young man had just knocked over a load of cans and was busy putting them back. The more the sales personnel are busy with their regular duties, the less they look for shoplifters. Preoccupation can also be a by-product of polite behavior. On one occasion our "thief" had paid for goods he carried in his basket and had put them into his bag next to the package of coffee he had "stolen." Then he remarked that he had not gotten a receipt. When he asked the cashier she unexpectedly looked into his bag, rearranging the goods he had bought, as well as the "stolen" coffee, in order to look for the receipt. Had she been even slightly distrustful, she might have noticed that there were three packages in the bag, but that only two had been paid for. Her behavior, however, was so completely oriented to politeness and helpfulness that there was no room for developing distrust. From this we draw the conclusion that the definition of the role of a salesperson does not include behavior necessary to detect shoplifters. A good salesperson is characterized by polite and helpful behavior; a true detective, however, has to be suspicious and not preoccupied with helping. The behavior of salesperson and detective are inconsistent.

We tested these conclusions by interviewing twenty-one saleswomen from the department store chain. Eighteen, all of whom had held the job for at least two years, had observed shoppers putting away some goods without paying. They knew that this occurred quite frequently: "several times in a week," "almost every day." They know, too that the "dark figure" is very high. Of the thirty-two stores in which we conducted our experiments, eleven had not reported any shoplifters within the preceding fifteen months; among the other twenty-one stores, a shoplifter was reported on the average of once every seven weeks. Often salespeople would observe something that aroused suspicion but were not sure whether the shopper had put the goods under his coat or into his bag. Asked what they would do in such situations they responded without exception, "nothing." "There you cannot do anything: you have to wait until the person comes another time. Then I am more suspicious and can observe more closely."

Our hypothesis that sales personnel do not regard it as part of their role to be distrustful of customers was confirmed by our respondents. We asked suggestively: "As a sales person you have to look after many different things—do you have enough time to look for shoplifters?" Fifteen replied that they were not able to do so. "Detection is purely accidental. That is not my business. I cannot bother about that." Some declared quite explicitly: "There should be a special person to be a detective," or "Service to our clients is more important to me." When saleswomen were asked what they would do if they actually saw a shoplifter, they typically responded that they would tell the cashier so that he could make sure that the goods were carried out without being paid for. The cashier, however, passed the buck to the manager, and it was up to him to accost the shopper. This avoidance of responsibility shows that nobody likes to sanction a shoplifter; consequently, his chances of escaping apprehension are quite high.

If the sales personnel do not like to accost the thief and accuse him, customers are even more reluctant to do so. In two of our experiments the observer was quite sure that other customers had observed the "theft." One stared at our "thief" for a long time, trying to punish him with her eyes; another young man observed one of our "thieves" when he was packing his bag. Yet neither of them reported the "thief." In order to test this observation, we designed another standardized series of thefts. Our "thief" concealed some article inside his coat while standing next to a woman customer who seemed to be more than thirty years old. It was not easy for our experimental "thieves" to act so that the customers actually observed the "theft"; they had to repeat their attempts quite often because the clients were too busy looking after their own goods. If the "thief" was sure that the customer had observed his theft, he slowly went to the cashier and paid for the goods in his basket. Then he left the store without paying for the "stolen" item. An observer confirmed that the other customer showed signs of noticing the shoplifting. When the other customer had passed the cashier the observer asked her for an interview; eight of the twenty-five refused, and we excluded three more because our observer could not be sure that the customer had noticed the "theft." The interview began with some neutral questions: whether the client had used this shop for a long time, how she found the service. Then there were general questions about shoplifting. Finally she was asked whether she had seen a theft herself and what she would do in such a case. Eleven of the fourteen interviewees responded that they would report any thief to the cashier or at the manager's office. Two were uncertain what they would do. Only one said: "I wouldn't say anything to anybody, I wouldn't run around—that is the risk of the store." But despite this verbalized readiness to report, only two customers reported our "thieves." And none of our customers thought of accosting the "thief" herself or of imposing a sanction on her own.

Our question, therefore, confronted the customer with what we knew about her actual behavior. First we described the "thief" and asked the customer if she had seen him. Then we informed her that we were engaged in an experiment and asked whether she had seen the young man putting something into his bag. Of the twelve interviewees who had reported the theft, nine admitted that they had seen something "suspicious" about our "thief." The other three pretended that they had not seen anything, although our "thief" and the observer were quite sure that they had seen the actual stealing. There is often a gap between verbal expressions of a readiness to report and actual reporting. But this is not because of ambiguities in the norm against stealing. Few of the women interviewed offered any excuse for the shoplifter. When the interviewer elicited reactions to the statement: "If somebody steals in a big warehouse it doesn't matter as much as it would in a small store," only two of the fourteen women agreed. Half of our interviewees accepted the view: "Even if it is only a petty theft, punishment should be severe in order to deter others from stealing." It was only when the interviewees were asked whether the thief should be reported to the police that nine of them stated a preference that the store-manager settle the matter with the shoplifter privately. Customers, like sales personnel, apparently take refuge in the fact that there are others responsible for sanctioning the thief; this, of course, results in their not doing anything.

The client who observes a theft experiences a conflict between following or violating the norm of sanctioning. Lewin's analysis of the psychology of punishment is equally applicable to the person who is punished as it is to those who are punishing. The task of punishing is attended by many disagreeable circumstances. To accost a young man and tell him bluntly that he is a thief demands considerable courage. Even reporting to the manager of the store might be unpleasant enough. The client has to testify and possibly even show where the thief has concealed the stolen goods. There may be arguments and the thief may become aggressive or try to get away. It is much simpler not to follow the sanctioning norm. The customer only has to feign ignorance; there will be no sanction for not sanctioning. Though our interviewees accept the norm of sanctioning, they do not have to follow it in practice because there is no sanction for noncompliance.

But despite this absence of external sanctions, violation of the norm appears to generate pangs of conscience. Of the eight customers who refused to be interviewed, half were so upset by what they had observed that they interrupted their buying in order to hurry out of the store. In our first experiment there was an equally clear case: a young man observed our "thief" queueing for the cashier. He immediately turned, rushed to the cashier, paid, and left the store in a panic. This helped him to solve the uncomfortable conflict between the normative expectation that he invoke a sanction and the unpleasant consequences this might have entailed.

Thus two conditions are lacking for compliance with the norm that third persons report thieves. There is no risk in violating it and there is nothing to prevent the third person from fleeing the conflict-ridden situation.

Selective Enforcement of Sanctions (b/c)

Since shoplifting is a crime with a victim, it would seem to be in the victim's interest to detect the offense and apprehend the offenders. Department stores and their managers have developed many different methods. Because shoplifting occurs frequently, they sometimes keep a record of all detected shoplifters. However, they are not entitled to administer their own sanctions (even if they sometimes try to do so) but are supposed to report the case to the public penal agencies. They usually report to the police rather than the public prosecutor because then evidence is established immediately. If they do so, the police investigate, taking the stolen goods into their custody. At the time of our study German law allowed the police two choices: if the shoplifting concerned food, which could be consumed immediately, the accused could be charged with illegal consumption, a minor offense that could be reported by the police directly to the courts with a suggested penalty. The police could also drop the charge. In none of our cases did they do this, but in a few they asked the courts to drop the charge "because there is no public interest." If the accused were not charged with illegal consumption, the theft was a major offense and had to be reported to the state prosecutor, who advised the court whether the charge should be dropped or which penal measure was appropriate.

At each step there is a possibility of terminating the formal procedure. The department store may not summon the police; the police may charge the accused too late to initiate a formal prosecution; the policeman may suggest to the store owner that it is not worth filing a charge because the act has not adequately been proven; the department store may withdraw the charge. Legally the police have little discretion; they have to report even trivial cases to the court and at best may make suggestions. The state prosecutor, on the other hand, can drop the charge; and though, at the time of our study, this decision had to be countersigned by a judge, in practice it was rarely questioned. The prosecutor must also decide whether the theft should be punished by fine (*Strafbefehl*), or whether it should be taken to a court session. Only when there actually are court proceedings are decisions made by a judge.

In order to analyze the process of sanctioning shoplifters we sought data on the proportion of known offenders who are punished, the number of cases in which the prosecution is dropped, the agency which decides this, and the variables governing this decision. We began by investigating all known shoplifting in the biggest department store in Freiburg and in thirty-two branches of the largest chainstore in town. Both firms had a list of all known shoplifters. Looking through these we identified four hundred shoplifters who had been caught and learned whether or not they had been reported to the police. We looked up these cases in the police books for the day on which they had been reported and then followed their progress in the administration files of the "Bureau of Order" of the City of Freiburg, the state prosecutor's office, and the courts.

We discovered that 50 percent of all known shoplifting had been reported to the police or prosecutor; in 10 percent of all known cases the agencies had dropped the charges; of the remaining 38 percent, slightly over half (20 percent of known cases) were sanctioned by the courts at the instance of the state prosecutor, and slightly under half (18 percent of known cases) were sanctioned through a simplified court procedure. However, these figures cannot be generalized. The propensity to report and the decision to sanction depend on policies that vary from town to town, especially between rural and urban areas. Some department stores report the greater part of all shoplifters, others only major cases. Some department stores make categorical exceptions for children or regular clients. Smaller department stores and small shops are more reluctant to report and often decide on a case-by-case basis. Furthermore, the penal agencies of smaller towns, which tend to be less well organized, prosecute a smaller proportion of reported cases; the high rate of prosecution for Freiburg, where 80 percent of known cases are reported to the police, may be typical only of the larger cities.

The effectiveness of the sanctioning process is thus dependent on the policy followed by the agencies involved. Our research shows this in a dramatic way. Our overall statistics turned out to be an average of figures from two years, which show quite different characteristics. We compared the first three months of 1966 with those of 1967, because late in 1966 the companies we investigated had changed their policy. They formally resolved to sanction shoplifters more severely and, at the urging of the police, to report all cases, "without exception."

The statistical result was striking: The number of cases of shoplifting known to the two companies hardly changed at all; indeed, there was a decrease of approximately 5 percent (perhaps employees grew more reluctant to report shoplifters, knowing that they would be punished more severely). But the police statistics tell another story, an increase in reported cases from twenty-nine to fiftyseven. The newspapers interpreted this as "an alarming rise of shoplifting—from 1966 to 1967 the figures rose about 100 percent!" What had actually happened? The number of known shoplifters had fallen slightly, but the proportion of cases reported had risen dramatically, from 31 percent to 68 percent. The resolution by department stores and police to report "without any exception" had been followed in two-thirds of all the cases, which meant an increase in actual sanctions from 25 percent to 55 percent of all known cases. At the same time we observe some interesting changes in the judicial response: while in 1966 no cases of insufficient evidence were found, in 1967, 8 percent of all cases reported were dropped because "evidence was not sufficiently established." Apparently shop managers had previously omitted all cases in which the evidence was doubtful, while in 1967 the screening had to be done by the state prosecutors.

Criteria for Terminating Formal Proceedings

Shoplifting may be an extreme example of the discretion whether to treat observed deviance as "criminal." But our suspicions about the ambiguity of criminal and court statistics can be generalized. We cannot draw conclusions about actual criminality from trends in crime rates if we do not know how far the behavior patterns of the sanctioning agencies have changed (Black, 1970; Seidman & Couzens, 1974). Even with more serious offenses, rising crime rates may be explained by a strategic decision to devote police resources to certain crimes, or by improved means of detection. The more variable the rate of detection and the more discretionary the decision to prosecute, the more will crime statistics reflect administrative rather than criminal behavior. This is true not only of aggregate statistics but even more of statistics purporting to describe specific crimes or criminals: the social characteristics of the offender, the time and place of the typical crime, etc. The propensity to report and the persistence in prosecuting often correlate poorly with the actual frequency of crimes. Of the 398 instances of shoplifting on which we have data, a high proportion occurred at times when many people were present—between 10 a.m. and noon, after 4 p.m., and on Saturday mornings—but the propensity to report at these times is very low. And many shoplifters are caught between 6 p.m. and closing time, but the rate of reporting is lowest at this time because the sales personnel want to go home.

The social characteristics of the accused can also influence whether he is reported to the police. Of the 398 shoplifters who were apprehended by the stores, 8 percent were foreigners; but of the 156 who received a sanction, 15 percent were foreign. This greater tendency to report foreigners is independent of the value of the object stolen and persists if we compare only thefts of objects worth less than five Deutschmarks (then little more than a dollar). This same bias is found in the discretion exercised by public officials in dropping charges.

Age also has an influence on the exercise of official discretion. Both the young and the old have a better chance of being excused without a sanction. Children under fourteen cannot be legally punished, but those between fourteen and eighteen and people older than sixty-five are more likely to have the charges dropped than any other age group. The result is that, once again, statistics on crimes reported and punished do not give an accurate picture of criminal activity.

Unfortunately, the files contain only fragmentary data on other characteristics, such as occupation and income, so that we can make only a rough estimate of the influence of class on the exercise of official discretion. Occupational bias does seem to be present: blue-collar workers are punished more often than white-collar. But income has the opposite effect—likelihood of prosecution diminishes as income falls. Some differences may be an artifact of age differentials: housewives are more often punished than pensioners or students, especially if evidence has been established. Both social status and age may explain the willingness of officials to drop more than a third of the charges against poorly paid actors, on grounds that the case lacked public importance or the statute of limitations had run.

From detection to punishment, the cumulative effect of the numerous choices made by stores and officials is to overrepresent certain social groups: foreigners, adults, and blue-collar workers. Yet the crime statistics that result from this selectivity do not represent actual behavior, for these categories are only apprehended by stores in proportion to their share of the population. Inversely, the statistics under-represent the predisposition of youths under eighteen to shoplift, because of the greater leniency of the sanctioning agencies toward this category.

Selective Sanctioning and the Definition of "Norms"

Shoplifting as an everyday infraction of a norm is subject to changing judgments depending upon the normative levels by which it is measured: as a normative rule it is found in custom, it is asserted in a private claim, and it is stated in a formal law.

Though the shopowner's property right is protected by law against shoplifting and though he is clearly interested in conformity with this norm, he is not necessarily anxious to sanction the shoplifter. Punishment is of no immediate use to the owner, and in small shops there could be serious disadvantages: regular customers could be lost and goodwill in the neighborhood dissipated. Maintaining friendly social relations may be more important than sanctioning a deviant. The strength of this motivation to mitigate punishment is shown by the behavior of the shopowners in Freiburg after their formal decision to report "every shoplifter without an exception." Thirty percent of those apprehended were still not reported; "every" shoplifter apparently could not mean more than 70 percent. Police and prosecutors do not initiate action to detect shoplifting; unlike certain other crimes—e.g., drug use, murder, or traffic violations—where the police have their own "strategies of suspicion," in shoplifting cases they do not engage in surveillance but react only to other people's complaints (cf. Black, 1973). Prevention and detection are private matters; there are not even any norms against displaying goods in a manner that facilitates, even invites, the crime. At the same time, legal agencies have a monopoly of authority to sanction.

This division of labor increases the chance that sanctioning will be aborted. The effectiveness of a social norm is dependent on the ability of private individuals to impose a sanction when they see it violated by another; but this process is frustrated when a special agency has a monopoly over sanctions. The effectiveness of a legal norm, on the other hand, lies in the existence of an agency endowed with a specialized staff devoted to the maintenance of conformity. But in shoplifting, the agency is in turn dependent upon the shopowner, who often prefers not to sanction. If a norm is maintained by legal sanctions, this inhibits spontaneous sanctioning by victims or third persons. But legal agencies, by themselves, must always be highly selective in imposing sanctions.

In addition to these theoretical conclusions, our study produced confirmation of some doubts about the use of crime statistics. Comparison of store and police files for two successive years showed that the doubling of instances of shoplifting in official crime statistics could be explained entirely by a change in the store policy of reporting offenses to the police. The number of undetected and unreported instances of shoplifting is so high, and practices of detection and reporting depend so heavily on organizational conditions, that any trend in official statistics is just as likely to indicate an administrative change as it is to describe a change in actual patterns of criminal behavior.

DISCUSSION QUESTIONS

1. Why is it impossible for the criminal justice system to punish all deviance? For which crimes are apprehension and punishment highly likely? For which are they very unlikely? What explains the differences? What are the alternatives to the formal criminal justice system?

2. If selectivity is inevitable, what influences the choices made? What should influence those choices? Who makes them? Who should be making them? For what other crimes are detection and prosecution functionally separate?

3. How reliable are self-reported data on deviance?

4. Does the design of this study raise any questions about the ethics of social research? Could the design be used with other crimes?

5. Are you surprised that so few thefts were observed? What explains this? Is there a presumption of legality among observers? Would you expect to find a higher rate of detection in the United States? a higher rate for other crimes? Why are salespeople indifferent to shoplifting? Why are customers? Why do customers claim that they would report crime but actually fail to do so?

6. Under what conditions do those whose primary role is not detection report or discourage crime? Why do they choose "voice" rather than "exit"?

7.   Victims, police, and prosecutors have considerable discretion whether to proceed and how. Should they? Could we reduce or eliminate this discretion? How do these decisions vary by crime? criminal? victim? locality? What prompts change over time? If discretion and flexibility are removed from one part of the system, do they reappear elsewhere?

8.   Has this article made you more skeptical about the meaning of crime rates?

6

The Paradoxical Impact of Criminal Sanctions: Some Microstructural Findings

Sheldon Ekland-Olson, John Lieb, and Louis Zurcher

Commentators on deterrence research have long noted both the gap between objective sanction properties and perceptions of those properties and the importance of studying mechanisms that connect the two (e.g., Geerken & Gove, 1975; Erickson & Gibbs, 1979). For example, Tittle (1980: 240) suggests:

> it seems unlikely that objective sanction characteristics have a direct and specific relationship to individual perceptions.... Hence an important challenge for future research is to identify the processes involved in the formation of individual perceptions of sanctions and to specify the role of objective sanction characteristics in those processes.

In this paper we report data gathered from extended interviews and field observations as they relate to interpersonal mechanisms that link objective sanction properties and perceived sanction severity and certainty. The basic argument can be briefly stated. Sanctions are perceived as more severe the more they threaten to disrupt the subject's life. Furthermore, actions that disturb interpersonal relationships are particularly disruptive (Ekland-Olson, 1984). These propositions together imply that perceived sanction severity depends to some extent on the relationships in which a person is embedded and on the perceived resilience of those relationships. Put another way, persons rich in associations will fear sanctions more than loners, and those who expect that after a sanction their friends and associates will treat them as before will fear that sanction less than those who expect to be shunned. Also, given the mediating influence of interpersonal relationships, we would expect that, for those involved in illegal activity, the organization of interpersonal relationships is closely connected to perceptions of sanction certainty.

Our research suggests that for many offenses this microstructural perspective better explains the deterrent impact of criminal sanctions than does a more strictly psychological approach to fear. Moreover, attention to the organizing influence of fear facilitates discussion of what might be called the anti-deterrence doctrine: the

Abridged from *Law & Society Review*, Volume 18:159 (1984).

idea that criminal sanctions do not deter subsequent criminal activity but rather facilitate engulfment in a criminal way of life. Our research suggests that fear of criminal sanctions may paradoxically encourage encapsulation in a deviant life style at the same time it restricts the frequency of illegal behavior.

Study Design

Six years of qualitative data collection included extensive contact with nineteen dealers of illicit drugs as well as a series of taped and transcribed structured conversations. Each of the nineteen respondents was involved in at least the middleman (one dealer was a woman) level of dealing. Middlemen bought goods directly from a producer or broker and then sold to other dealers. All the respondents sold marijuana. Several also sold cocaine, amphetamines, LSD, mescaline, and other hallucinogens. The observations and interviews with these nineteen respondents were supplemented with field notes from prolonged contact with fifteen additional middlemen dealers who would not agree to taped interviews.

There are obvious limitations in a study based on an availability sample of thirty-four respondents. However, these limitations are of a different sort from those of official record studies (e.g., Gibbs, 1968; Bean & Cushing, 1971; Logan, 1975; Ehrlich, 1975; Bowers & Pierce, 1975; Greenberg & Kessler, 1982) or self-report surveys (e.g., Waldo & Chiricos, 1972; Meier & Johnson, 1977; Erickson et al., 1977; Tittle, 1980; Akers et al., 1979; Grasmick & Green, 1981). Thus, data such as ours can be used to supplement deterrence research based on official records or self-report surveys (Anderson et al., 1977: 113; Tittle, 1977: 586). For example, Meier and Johnson (1977) and Akers et al. (1979), using self-report surveys, found that the best predictor of marijuana use was the presence of similarly oriented friends. Neither study was able to explore in any detail how interpersonal influence was related to perceptions of legal standards and sanctions. Our detailed information gathered over several years allows us to describe this connection.

Since our data are from individuals actively involved in the drug trade, we have no examples of absolute deterrence (Gibbs, 1975: 32–33). Indeed, most of the respondents in the study were engulfed in their deviant role (Schur, 1971: 69–81). They defined themselves as dealers. They organized their daily routines as well as their yearly plans around the rhythm and seasons of the illicit drug business. They developed linguistic conventions and codes of behavior that shaped their relations with others.

Our findings are relevant, however, to what Gibbs (1975: 33) has defined as restrictive deterrence:

> a reduction in the frequency of offenses, including any strategies or tactics employed by individuals to evade detection, identification, or apprehension that have the effect of reducing the frequency of offenses.

The dealers used various tactics to avoid detection, identification, and apprehension. This article focuses on the dealers' interpersonal networks and asks three related questions: (1) How are perceptions of sanction severity and certainty and consequent levels of fear rooted in interpersonal relationships? (2) Is the fear of sanctions an important organizing focus (Feld, 1981) for interpersonal relations among dealers? (3) Does the resulting organization of interpersonal ties restrict, encourage, or have no effect on dealing activities?

Fear and Conventional Others

The dealers we interviewed and observed are obviously fearful of criminal sanctions. Their level of fear is clearly tied to interpersonal relationships and the ways these relationships are likely to respond should the dealers be sanctioned. This is true at all levels of involvement in dealing.

During the early stages of dealer involvement, the intensity of fear depends in large measure on the implications sanctions have for relationships with conventional others. For some, such as the former football player in the following interview, the early stages of dealing are accompanied by a gradual shift in interpersonal relations. This dealer had grown up in a rural Texas atmosphere. He attended his first year of college in a town of 4,500 people, 1,000 of whom were students. When he moved to a larger Texas city to attend college on a football scholarship, he made friends with some drug-using students, used drugs himself, and then eventually began to sell them. Sanction-induced fear during this early stage of loose, friendly dealing was not centered on the severity of punishment per se (i.e., the possibility of jail or the number of years on probation) but simply on the possibility of being caught and what that would mean for his relationships with those who were "straight."

> My paranoia resulted from my being straight. It was a straight kind of paranoia. It was also like I had a lot to lose if I got busted. Going to jail was never really a consideration. The problem wasn't the thought of going to prison or jail, you always assumed probation, just a hassle, but you certainly didn't want to get caught doing anything like I was.

For other dealers we observed and interviewed, the possibility of disturbing ties to conventional others was less important. Their interpersonal relationships were already so weak that an arrest would make little difference. The level of sanction-induced fear was correspondingly lower. This comparison across dealers suggests the tentative generalization that among initial deviants, the higher the perceived risk that interpersonal ties with conventional others will be disrupted by sanctions, the higher the level of perceived sanction severity.

Given the limitations of our data set, it is instructive to compare this conclusion with other findings. It is consistent with the suggestion of Geis (1972) that white collar criminals may be more responsive to the risk of arrest and incarceration than persons connected to less conventional circles of friends and activities. It is also consistent with Tittle's (1977; 1980) findings, using self-report survey data, that the perceived risk of relational disruption was a better predictor for a wide range of deviant behavior than the risk of community exposure, arrest, and incarceration.

As those we studied became increasingly involved in drug dealing, two major changes took place in the strength and structure of their interpersonal ties. First, there was a weakening of ties to conventional others (i.e., those not involved in dealing). The weakening was measurable by both objective (e.g., number of contacts, amount of information flow, opportunities for interaction) and subjective (e.g., the degree of mutual affect, interdependence, and moral consensus) phenomena. Second, there was a strengthening of ties among a small group of fellow dealers. Again, this had both subjective and objective dimensions. Shifts in the objectively defined pattern of interpersonal attachments had a dramatic impact on available opportunities for dealing drugs.

As one dealer noted, after recalling how a deal fell through and another developed:

> You jump into it and it's like you're in a different stream of consciousness when you're doing it—totally. At least it is with me as a middleman because my time table is so weird. I never know when I'm going to have to be where, because people are making appointments, and there are samples to be picked up, people to meet.... You're in it twenty-four hours a day. As it turns out, by being in contact suddenly I got this other thing just in being in touch with the peers that I have now, some suppliers and some buyers who don't know one another.

This same theme of how dealing activities tended to build their own momentum was noted by several dealers.

> You know, it just started out with taking a couple of lids here and selling maybe three lids and getting one free, selling four lids and getting one free.... It just came up from there. As long as I was involved in it and knew this thing that was going on, the more I kept getting pulled toward the middle of it.
>
> It seems to me that the events of my life over the past six or seven years have just carried me along, sometimes with a little bit of effort on my behalf and sometimes with no effort at all, just through circumstances that created themselves, that I had nothing to do with. Just an awareness of it [dealing marijuana] is what brought me into it or made me participate in it.

This pattern of shifting levels of involvement and commitments, as well as the accompanying relational changes, appears to parallel the spiral of involvement and options noted among compulsive gamblers (Lesieur, 1976). It also more generally parallels the process of role engulfment and conversion (Ekland-Olson, 1982). The intensity with which our respondents interacted with other deviants appeared to be a prime determinant of the degree to which they took on the life style, language, and general perspective of drug dealing (cf. Snow & Phillips, 1980: 442). This conversion to a drug dealing life style was accompanied by a marked weakening of relationships with more conventional others (cf. Lofland & Stark, 1965). The question we now address is: "What role, if any, did the fear of sanctions play in this process?"

Fear, Constraint, Network Density, and Closure

It is conventional wisdom that environmental factors influence the organization of social life. Feld has linked this basic idea to recent studies of interpersonal networks. He first defines a focus as a social, psychological, legal, or physical entity around which joint activities are organized (1981: 1016). Aspects of the environment that help determine the strength and structure of interpersonal ties are conceived of as organizing foci. These differ in a number of ways. Of particular importance is the idea of constraint, which, by definition, increases with an increase in demands on the participant's time, effort, and emotion (1981: 1025). Among the dealers we observed and interviewed, the drug market was one important organizing focus. The organizing influence of criminal sanctions was superimposed upon market-determined interaction.

The possibility of apprehension, prosecution, and punishment affected our dealers' drug market activities because of the demands these placed on their emotional energy and time:

> Each time somebody got busted that you knew, it affected you. You'd think about it for sure, and you'd realize it's becoming a simple law of averages and chance. That's when I began to be aware of preparing for a fluke, a freak thing to happen.
>
> I was becoming aware of the fact that there was a possibility of getting busted and I needed to have thousands of dollars around for the defense or to leave the country.

The certainty of punishment was perceived in part in terms of the law of averages. Dealers knew from the experiences of acquaintances that being caught was often a matter of luck, a matter of being in the wrong place at the wrong time. The element of chance meant that success was not totally under their control. This put an increased emotional edge on dealing, as well as what many referred to as "paranoid behavior," such as compulsive planning or a tendency not to trust anyone. Thus, by increasing the amount of effort and emotion put into dealing, fear of apprehension and punishment maximized the degree of constraint dealing imposed.

As Feld (1981) has argued, constraint tends to increase both network density and network closure. Put less abstractly, where constraint is high, one's associates tend to be well acquainted with one another and tend to be only weakly tied to persons not generally known within the close circle of friends. This tendency toward what approximates a secret society (Simmel, 1950; Hazelrigg, 1969) is not lost on those who come in contact with drug dealers. Recalling clients he had represented, a prominent drug lawyer suggested in an interview:

> People that are involved in large-scale dealing for the most part are going to deal with people they know—that they have done business with in the past, and that they are not very suspicious of.

Thus, one manifestation of dealers' fear of sanctions is that their interpersonal ties become increasingly circumscribed. The goal is to reduce the likelihood that bad luck will lead to apprehension. Certainty of punishment is not assessed globally (as it is in both official record and self-report survey deterrence research) but is evaluated with respect to particular dealing situations. Thus, dealers do not think in terms of the general likelihood that they will be caught. Rather, they attempt to assess and minimize the chance that they will be caught while striking a particular deal. Codes of interaction are developed to structure behavior in ways that are thought to minimize the risk of apprehension. Where codes are violated, dealers tend to withdraw from interaction because the association is likely to prove dangerous.

One of our respondents described how he was put off by excessively nervous buyers:

> It's a communication between people that enables the business to be transacted with the least waves. Say you've got a person that's real excited. Like the guy is jerky with his money, quick to find out how much it would cost and always looking out, always worried about when it [the dope] is going to come in. You know, you just quit dealing with these kinds of people eventually, you keep all this [nervousness] within you if you've got it. You certainly don't show it. It's always laid back, cool....

Another respondent described a dealer who was simply too flashy for anybody's good.

> Well, I met a guy who tipped himself immediately by exposing his entire operation. Just because he thought we knew the right people. We knew

everything he was doing for a while and we had no reason to, you know, LOOSE.

Interviewer: How come?

Big time, big fancy car, lots of dope, dealing lots of dope but he definitely didn't have the cool about him as far as being careful.

Another important cue to the risk of apprehension inherent in an encounter is the amount one knows about a potential contact. Strangers as a general rule are to be avoided, but the importance of this cue and its effects on dealer behavior depend on police practices. During the six years covered by our study, police efforts to control illicit drugs increased dramatically. At the state level, money spent on drug-related evidence and surveillance (primarily "buy busts") rose from just under $50,000 to just under $300,000, and the number of narcotics agents rose from roughly 25 full-time officers to 112. The state strategy was to establish a system of undercover buys and informants. We collected information on all drug cases processed by the district courts during the six years: 3067 contained information on how the arrest was initiated. Of these cases 60 percent (1,870) were initiated by informants, and 20 percent (601) were the result of undercover buys.

As these "insider" control strategies evolved, both the control agents and the dealers adjusted their activities. Initially, when informants and buy busts were relatively rare, drug dealing among the predominantly university-related dealers was unguarded. As a result, undercover buys were comparatively easy. In an interview, one former narcotics officer recalled:

> We would go to places that were frequented by people that we knew dealt with drugs. We would go to their residences. At that time it was not unusual to have ten, fifteen, twenty people living in a three or four room house. Nobody knew anybody else. You had a sleeping bag, you were welcome to sleep, eat, or do anything.

Police sought to build up trust through a series of small purchases with the aim of securing an introduction to and arresting someone more deeply involved in the drug traffic. As dealers became aware of this strategy, dealing became a more closely guarded operation. One tactic for reducing the probability of arrest was a cautious approach to strangers. If the potential customer was not well known, suspicion and fear were easily aroused. Often the result was a breakdown in the transaction.

> If someone brought over a stranger, I'd probably take it real friendly, "Come in..." then take them to another room and tell them, "Get your ass out of my house. I told you never to bring anybody over to the fucking house. I don't know these people, I don't know where they are coming from. You do that

kind of crap again and I will not deal with you again. Now get out and get away." You had to do things like that.

Not surprisingly, we found that our dealers perceived a greater risk of apprehension and were more likely to pull out of deals the less they knew about their customers and associates and the more unplanned or reckless the latter's behavior. The deterrent influence of sanction certainty was thus filtered through the properties of relationships among dealers. Interactions like this between the organization of sanctions and relational properties are an important frontier for deterrence research (cf. Lempert, 1982).

Among the dealers in our study, adaptation to the organization of buy-bust/informer strategies resulted in network closure. For those who survived, the circle of contacts became quite tight.

By the third season [in dealing] I was one of the few dealers I knew that had survived that long. It was the law of the jungle. Twenty, thirty, maybe forty people that I had contact with, worked with in the community, had been busted, were awaiting pretrial hearings, or had gone to prison.... Those who survived were coming closer together. It got to a point where I knew what they had, when they would get it, and how much they had. A nucleus was developing.

Sanctions and Relational Tolerance

The level of concern when dealing with relative strangers was not totally a function of the increased possibility of legal sanctions. Dealers were often suspicious of one another, especially when contact was sporadic and reputations not well known. Such was the case with the following dealer when he was trying to establish a source of marijuana in Mexico.

It was a paranoid scene because the Mexicans looked at us as a profitable connection and nothing else. Particularly the oldest sons who had the closest ties with the Mexican end of it. They just really hated gringos and you could tell that they just as soon shoot you, if anything went wrong, as look at you.

Mutual racial biases, sporadic contact, and language difficulties (dealers spoke "Tex-Mex," a hybrid of English and Spanish) meant that our dealers' relations with Mexican connections were largely restricted to the exchange of money for a product. Without much friendship, trust, or social credit they had little to fall back on if things went badly, except, as one dealer put it, "fast talking."

Dealers in such situations were often more concerned with the actions of their connections than with official sanctions. In describing such contacts, it is difficult to untangle the paranoia due to the possibility of getting caught from that attributable to the strains inherent in the dealing relationship. The perception of sanctions was mediated by the quality of the dealing relationship. If dealing partners were thought to be tolerant, which generally meant willing to absorb losses and forgive mistakes if things went wrong, the fear of legal sanctions was reduced.

> I was down one time real bad, _____ got busted and I got busted and lost about fifteen thousand dollars in short order. I stayed with _____. He fronted me a gram [of LSD—four thousand hits]. That brought me up and the next thing you know I was comfortable and I went on to start getting acid in the mail from San Francisco and it worked out real well. I bought the connection from my contact and then I started going out there myself.... I had like four or five steady dealers that I just fronted it all to anywhere from one thousand hits to a gram and then I'd come around a week later and hand out more and pick up my bucks.

With the help of an acquaintance, then, this dealer was able to recover from an arrest and legal fees, make new contacts, and increase his market. In return, the individual who staked him could call in a favor if needed. "Professional" exchanges often led to more personal friendships. For example, after a period of association in business, two dealers eventually became roommates.

> That mescaline turned out to be a good deal because that guy that we got it from in San Antonio was getting it from a guy in Houston, who was like a central distributor type guy. I got to meet him because he'd moved to Austin also at the same time that I did. He lived only a few blocks away, and he didn't know anybody here in town, and I knew only a few people. His roommate got drafted and he needed a place to live, so this guy moved in. So like in the period of a couple of months, we started out doing hits and ended up being roommates with this guy.

People involved in relationships based on extended contact, friendship, and trust, as well as the exchange involved in dealing, tended to be more tolerant of one another's mistakes than less personal connections. Those who were personally close to other dealers expected any penalty they faced to be partially absorbed by supportive relationships, and thus the perceived severity of such sanctions was diminished.

Although the reservoir of relational tolerance served as a buffer against the perceived certainty and severity of sanctions, the sanctioning process was capable of draining that reservoir by disrupting relationships. For this reason an arrest and the accompanying investigation were often perceived to be just as threatening as a prison sentence. Not only was the person arrested affected, but a network of relations built over a period of years could instantly collapse. In one case we learned of, such a collapse resulted from the chance discovery of a load of marijuana.

> As fast as I could I would come down here, get five hundred [pounds of marijuana], drive it back to Chicago, sell it. As soon as I had sold it and had the money, I would come right back down here and get another five hundred and take it back. I did this as long as it lasted—meaning that the source here in Austin dried up. My connection was receiving a load of grass, several tons, and the truck tipped over and the police found the marijuana.... His whole source system dried up because of the police investigation. So he was out of business, and that not only put me out of business but it put the guy in Kansas City out of business.

The concern for relational damage may explain why in deterrence research the certainty of a sanction is almost always a better predictor of law-abiding behavior than its severity. The relational threshold for sanction impact is easily reached since any official reaction to deviance—including arrest, a conventional measure of certainty (but see Lempert, 1982)—is likely to disrupt a deviant's network.

The link between sanction fear and the threatened disruption of ties to deviant others nicely parallels the link between sanction fear and the threatened disruption of ties to conventional others that is found in the literature. Focusing on these links calls into question the assumption common to both self-report and official record studies that the severity of a given sanction is constant across situations (see also Erickson & Gibbs, 1979; Cook, 1980: 216–18). Likewise, the neglect of arrest in most specific deterrence studies is probably a mistake. Research that considers the disruptive potential of all stages in the criminal justice system (e.g., Feeley, 1979) holds more promise. The perceived severity of any sanction, from arrest to incarceration and the conditions attached to eventual return to the community, is determined in large measure by its impact on interpersonal networks and the way in which those networks will adjust.

The Paradoxical Impact of Fear

Deterrence researchers have repeatedly noted that deterrence theory is, at base, a theory about the behavioral implications of subjective beliefs (e.g., Erickson et al., 1977; Cook, 1980). Lempert (1982) emphasized the importance of the subjective dimension but also argued that the research agenda should be broadened to include organizational differences in the ways sanctions are imposed.

Although our experience is within one jurisdiction, there were changes in enforcement policy that clearly made a difference over and above the perceptions of sanction certainty and severity. Thus, we underscore Lempert's suggestion. In addition we believe that greater attention should be paid to "strategies or tactics employed by individuals to evade detection, identification, or apprehension" (Gibbs, 1975: 33). Such practices, while not "deviant" in themselves, can affect rates of illegal behavior in ways that extend far beyond their implications for the subjective fear of punishment.

In our research, tactics of avoidance and the organization of control strategies came together in the related tendencies of dealers to avoid strangers and to form close relationships with a rather restricted number of fellow dealers. The result in terms of deterrence was paradoxical. By increasing network density and closure, fear of sanctions enhanced the probability that dealers would be closely tied to one another and emotionally committed to dealing as a way of life. At the same time, by discouraging the formation and maintenance of "weak ties," the perceived possibility of sanctions reduced the scope of the opportunities available to individual dealers and thereby acted as a restrictive deterrent. Because weak ties are structurally so significant, to restrict them was, in our study, to substantially reduce the sale of illicit drugs. The possibilities of making a profit by dealing drugs within any given friendship circle are limited. It is persons able to bridge otherwise separated groups who are in a particularly profitable position. Thus, in our study, these were the individuals most likely to progress from low-level dealing to middleman brokerage. A dealer who had risen to middleman noted:

> Probably one of my strongest points was I knew everybody on campus....
> They're isolated from the outside dealers and the outside dealers are totally
> isolated from the people on campus and so I had a locked-in market and had
> a big spread of people.

To establish and maintain bridging ties was, however, no easy matter. The bridging ties we observed tended by their very nature to be characterized by less frequent contact, less familiarity, and lower levels of affect than the more intimate ties among dealers. Suspicion and fear were easily aroused. As noted, the result was often a breakdown of the transaction.

Granovetter (1973: 1366) has noted the importance that bridging ties have for the diffusion of information and other commodities.

> The contention here is that removal of the average weak tie would do more
> "damage" to transmission probabilities than would that of the average strong
> one.... Intuitively speaking, this means that whatever is to be diffused can
> reach a larger number of people, and traverse greater social distance.... when
> passed through weak ties rather than strong.

Thus, the deterrent influence of the informer/buy-bust strategies utilized by various police agencies was ultimately more structural than psychological. To be sure, these control strategies depended on their ability to engender a certain amount of fear, but fear did not lead to "going straight." Instead, it led dealers to take on attitudes and to adopt tactics that made it difficult for them to expand their markets. The mistrust of strangers is not conducive to the development of bridging ties.

What expansion did occur was generally facilitated by a set of references. Dealers were concerned about the same kinds of things that concern prospective employers and employees in more conventional businesses. How long had the contacts been dealing? What was the scope of their operations? What drugs had they been dealing? How knowledgeable were they about the product? What kind of people were they? Or, in other words, could they be trusted in tight spots? When answers to these questions were unknown or did not suggest a safe relationship, persons would generally not deal. The only exception we observed was when economic pressures from deals gone bad or pressures inherent in trying to build capital for a bigger deal were present. In these situations normal caution might be relaxed. At the same time, paranoia about the deal increased.

Dealers knew from their own experiences, as well as from those of others, that the risks of failure were greatest when one was trying to recover losses too quickly or when greed suppressed more conservative, long-range planning. The parallels between this and conventional investment strategies were too obvious to miss. Many dealers felt that their experiences, in what was humorously referred to as "grassroots capitalism," were the ideal preparation for entry into the mainstream economy. Two dealers went together and eventually set up a computer business. Stories abounded of restaurants and other thriving legitimate businesses started with "drug money."

We cannot say whether fear of sanctions increased or restricted involvement in dealing illicit drugs without specifying the meaning of involvement. If involvement means commitment and emotional attachment to dealing activities, as well as to others similarly engaged, the constraining influence of fear apparently increased involvement. If involvement refers to the amount of drugs sold, sanction-induced fear apparently decreased involvement. This decrease was largely the result of structural limitations imposed by the perceived danger of dealing with strangers.

It is instructive to note the way these findings relate to the labeling-deterrence debate concerning the impact of sanctions. Articles and books from the labeling school have emphasized how sanctions increase involvement in criminal activities (e.g., Schur, 1971), involvement being defined in terms of self-concept and emotional commitment. Deterrence research has emphasized the behavior-reducing potential of sanction-induced fear, the criterion being reduced probabilities of behavior (e.g., Gibbs, 1975). What our findings suggest is that both may occur at the same time.

With respect to the level of behavioral and emotional involvement in dealing drugs, drug market activities and criminal sanctions acted together. As persons became more heavily involved in drug dealing, the demands of the activities became greater. The monetary stakes were higher, the possibilities of violence increased, and ripoffs from other dealers were increasingly frequent. It is difficult to separate the influence of these marketplace "restraints" from the influence of the perceived certainty and severity of criminal sanctions.

Toward a Microstructural Approach to Deterrence

The mechanisms that link objective sanction properties and perceptions of those properties are not well understood. The same sanction, say a year in jail, may be perceived in quite different ways by individuals in different life circumstances. Different sanctions, e.g., a fine as opposed to thirty days in jail, may be ranked similarly by persons of different economic means. It is difficult even to conceptualize the severity of some sanctions. How severe is an arrest? Which is more severe, a flogging or five years in prison?

The mechanisms that link the objective and subjective sides of punishments to produce general, specific, or restrictive deterrence need not be the same. We have limited our attention to restrictive deterrence and have found that the quality of interpersonal relationships is an important determinant of how sanction threats are perceived. For example, we found in our interviews that if a set of relationships was unlikely to be affected by an arrest, the perceived severity of the arrest was low—just a hassle. If, however, it was believed that an arrest would threaten a friendship circle or operating network, the threat of arrest was taken quite seriously and arrests were to be avoided at all costs. It is in this sense that sanction severity is situationally determined. This situational nature of sanction properties has escaped the scales and indicators employed in official record and self-report survey research. In this body of research an arrest and a year in prison are generally assumed to have the same meaning for all persons and across all situations.

The situational grounding of sanction properties suggests that we look beyond official definitions of sanctions and the attitudinal structure of individuals to the properties of situations. Lempert's (1982: 565) suggestion that deterrence research "attend more closely to group processes and organizational variables" is a step in the right direction. Feeley's (1979) analysis of the process as the punishment also recognizes the structural, interpersonal nature of sanctions. Feeley's ideas were developed in the context of lower criminal courts, where the eventual punishment, in terms of time in jail or prison, is low. But a similar case can be made where charges are difficult to prove and the sanction strategy is as concerned with disrupting the activity as it is with punishing the offender.

Interpersonal relationships also mediated the perceived certainty of punishment. When dealers talked about how a particular deal "felt," they generally referred to what they perceived to be the likelihood of arrest. If the deal was "unusual," if the other dealer's style was too flamboyant, if the connection was not well known, the perceived certainty of arrest and its attendant consequences increased. Like perceptions of sanction severity, the perceived certainty of punishment had important situational components. If asked to talk about the probability of sanctions in the abstract, dealers gave no definite assessments but talked instead of "bad luck" or the possibility of their "number coming up." However, this fatalistic attitude was belied by the dealers' behavior. They were careful in choosing customers and associates and in structuring transactions. These precautions made the dealers feel more secure since they believed, no doubt correctly, that their care influenced the actual certainty of punishment. Thus, the threat of sanctions restricted drug sales primarily by inducing cautions that increased the difficulties of dealing. The structural restrictions that the reluctance to form "weak ties" placed on dealing tell us more about how the threat of sanctions deterred the dealers we interviewed than we would have learned had we concentrated on the psychological processes of fear and avoidance.

A structural approach to deterrence goes beyond the concern with psychological fear. Consequently, it is not a strict reflection of classical deterrence arguments (Gibbs, 1975). However, it is consistent with Tittle's suggestion (1980: 5):

> The deterrence problem really consists of three parts: identifying sanctions or sanction threats in a meaningful way, determining how much and what kind of effect they have on deviance, and specifying the mechanisms by which the effects occur.

Focusing on the structural implications of sanctions and on the interpersonal dynamics of adjustment promises to identify many of the important dimensions and effects of sanctions, as well as the mechanisms through which these effects take place.

In summary, we offer the following as tentative, yet promising, generalizations:

1. The perceived severity of sanctions is in large measure tied to the degree of interpersonal disruption caused by the sanctioning process.
2. Criminal sanctions are socially complex. The degree of interpersonal disruption is determined in large measure by the organization of the sanctioning process and the tolerance or resilience of the affected network.
3. Network tolerance, the ability and willingness of a network of actors to withstand the impact of the sanction process, is in large measure a function of the strength of relationships among actors.
4. Sanctions become more disruptive as they reduce the degree of trust, affect, and normative agreement within the deviant target population and as they inhibit or throw out of balance exchange relationships among deviants. Thus, relational tolerance and the sanctioning process are often highly interdependent.
5. The sanctioning process has an important organizing influence on relationships among those engaged in criminal activities. This is revealed in many ways. For example:

    a.   By increasing the constraining nature of activities, the fear of sanctions tends to increase network density and closure.

    b.   Network closure and density reduce the chances that bridging ties to alternative networks will form. The structural influence of the hesitancy to form "weak ties" accounts for a substantial reduction in criminal activity not explained directly by the psychological processes of fear and avoidance.

6.   The perceived certainty of punishment depends in large measure on what persons know about particular situations, as well as on the degree to which they trust their co-actors.

7.   Persons engaged in criminal activities manipulate the perceived and actual certainty of punishment through choices of associates and the structuring of interaction.

What all these generalizations taken together imply is that perceptions of sanction severity and certainty are situational. Deterrence research, especially when restrictive deterrence is at issue, must move beyond official indicators of certainty and severity and beyond scaling procedures that assume stable attitudinal structures. Further understanding requires data that are sensitive to the dynamic relationship between the organization of the sanctioning process and the adaptive strategies of those who are the target of sanctions.

DISCUSSION QUESTIONS

1.   What psychological processes mediate between the formal legal sanction (arrest, prosecution, fine, jail, probation) and deterrence? What shapes potential offenders' perceptions of sanction severity? What are the relative advantages of qualitative and quantitative methods for studying deterrence?

2.   What is the strongest initial deterrent against beginning to deal drugs? What causes it to fail? How are people recruited to deviant subcultures? What explains their behavior within such subcultures? What social structural characteristics differentiate deviant subcultures? How different is drug dealing from legal business activity?

3.   How do police respond to the closure of deviant subcultures? How do they destroy the trust necessary for deviant activity? How did the drug networks mitigate the severity of sanctions? In what ways does the criminal justice system suppress deviance, other than by imprisonment?

How could we study those other effects? What is the importance of weak ties?

4.   Are you persuaded that the certainty of sanctions is more important than severity, in their capacity to deter? If so, why do we devote so much more effort to increasing severity rather than certainty?

5.   How does this article reconcile the approaches of deterrence and labeling theory?

6.   Test the authors' concluding hypotheses against your own experience of deviance.

7

Plea Bargaining and Its History

Albert W. Alschuler

The Early History of the Guilty Plea

The Judicial Discouragement of Confessions

From the earliest days of the common law, it has been possible for an accused criminal to convict himself by acknowledging his crime [*The Constitutions of Clarendon*, chap. 3 (1164); *The Assize of Clarendon*, chap. 13 (1166)]. "Confession" was in fact a possible means of conviction even prior to the Norman conquest. Nevertheless, confessions of guilt apparently were extremely uncommon during the medieval period. In hundreds of reported cases, medieval defendants denied "word for word, the felony, the king's peace, and all of it," but historians have found only a handful of recorded instances of confession.

When common law treatises first adverted to the guilty plea, they indicated that the courts were extremely hesitant to receive it. By 1680, Sir Matthew Hale had written: "[W]here the defendant upon hearing of his indictment ... confesses it, this is a conviction; but it is usual for the court ... to advise the party to plead and put himself upon his trial, and not presently to record his confession, but to admit him to plead" (1736: 225). In 1609 Ferdinando Pulton wrote that the plea of not guilty was "the most common and usual plea" and that "it receiveth great favour in the law."

Statements like Hale's persisted in criminal law treatises until the end of the nineteenth century. For example, Blackstone's *Commentaries on the Laws of England* (1765–69, vol. 4: 329) observed that the courts were "very backward in receiving and recording [a guilty plea] ... and generally advise the prisoner to retract it." Most of the English and American writers who noted this judicial phenomenon did so approvingly, but the established procedure in guilty plea cases did have a notable critic. In his *Rationale of Judicial Evidence*, Jeremy Bentham declared:

> In practice, it is grown into a sort of fashion, when a prisoner has [entered a plea of guilty], for the judge to endeavour to persuade him to withdraw it,

Abridged from *Law & Society Review*, Volume 13:211 (1979).

and substitute the opposite plea, the plea of not guilty, in its place. The wicked man, repenting of his wickedness, offers what atonement is in his power: the judge, the chosen minister of righteousness, bids him repent of his repentance, and in place of the truth substitute a barefaced lie. (1827, vol. 2: 3161)

Bentham, however, did not propose a more liberal acceptance of guilty pleas. Instead, he urged abolition of the guilty plea and the substitution of a more careful and rigorous examination of the defendant, an examination designed "to guard him against undue conviction, brought on upon him by his own imbecility and imprudence" (1827, vol. 3: 127).

Official reports of guilty plea cases remained infrequent until the last quarter of the nineteenth century, but John H. Langbein's study of the Old Bailey during the late seventeenth and early eighteenth centuries (1978a) offers a glimpse of the English criminal justice system in operation. Working from journalistic accounts designed for a popular rather than a professional audience, Langbein discovered that jury trials were extremely rapid in an era when neither party was represented by counsel, when an informally selected jury might hear several cases before retiring, and when the law of evidence was almost entirely undeveloped. Trials were in fact so swift that between twelve and twenty cases could be heard in a single day. The administrative pressure for plea bargaining was accordingly small, and Langbein found no indication of this practice. He did find a number of cases in which the court urged defendants to stand trial after they had attempted initially to plead guilty.

The case of Stephen Wright in 1743 seems especially revealing. Wright announced that he would plead guilty to robbery in order to spare the court trouble, and he expressed hope that the court and jury would recommend executive commutation of the death sentence mandated for this crime. The court responded, in effect, that the defendant had it backwards, for the court could not take notice of any favorable circumstances in his case unless he agreed to stand trial. Wright then yielded to the court's advice (Langbein, 1978a: 278).

The earliest reported American decision on the guilty plea [*Commonwealth v. Battis*, 1 Mass. 95 (1804)] reveals that the practice in America was no different. A 20-year-old black man was accused of "raping a 13-year-old white girl, breaking her head with a stone, and throwing her body into the water, thereby causing her death." When the defendant pleaded guilty to indictments for rape and murder,

the court informed him of the consequences of his plea, and that he was under no legal or moral obligation to plead guilty but that he had a right to deny the several charges and put the government to the proof of them. He would not retract his pleas—whereupon the court told him that they would allow him a reasonable time to consider of what had been said to him—and remanded him to prison. They directed the clerk not to record his pleas, at present. When the defendant was returned to the courtroom, he again pleaded guilty.

   Upon which the court examined, under oath, the sheriff, the gaoler, and the justice [who had conducted the preliminary examination of the defendant] as to the *sanity* of the prisoner; and whether there had not been tampering with him, either by promises, persuasions, or hopes of pardon, if he would plead guilty. On a very full enquiry, nothing of that kind appearing, the prisoner was again remanded, and the clerk directed to record the plea on both indictments.

The report concluded that the defendant "has since been executed."

Even at the end of the nineteenth century, courts sometimes followed a procedure reminiscent of the one that Hale had described more than two hundred years earlier. In the first United States Supreme Court opinion to uphold a guilty-plea conviction [*Hallinger v. Davis*, 146 U.S. 314, 324 (1892)], the Court observed: "The [trial] court refrained from at once accepting [the defendant's] plea of guilty, assigned him counsel, and twice adjourned, for a period of several days, in order that he might be fully advised of the truth, force and effect of his plea of guilty."

A few compilations of early nineteenth-century judicial records confirm the apparent absence of a regular practice of encouraging guilty pleas. Theodore N. Ferdinand (1973: Tables 1 and 2) examined the work of the Boston Police Court in 1824 and reported that only 11 percent of the 2,208 defendants who came before the court entered pleas of guilty. Raymond Moley (1928: 108) computed the percentage of felony convictions "by jury" and "by confession" in New York State for 88 years beginning in 1839. At the outset of this period, only 25 percent of all felony convictions throughout the state were by guilty plea, and in the urban counties of New York and Kings the figure was even smaller, 15 percent.

There were several reasons for the reluctance of the courts to receive pleas of guilty during the formative period of the common law and for centuries thereafter. First, these pleas were apparently distrusted. William Auckland observed:

   [W]e have known instances of murder avowed, which never were committed; of things confessed to have been stolen, which never had quitted the possession of the owner.... It is both ungenerous therefore, and unjust, to suffer the distractions of fear, or the misdirected hopes of mercy to preclude that negative evidence of disproof, which may possibly, on recollection, be in the power of the party; we should never admit, when it may be avoided, even the possibility of driving the innocent to destruction. (1771: 167)

Probably more important than the judicial distrust of guilty pleas was the fact that English felony defendants were not represented by counsel. It was a basic duty of trial judges to see that these defendants "should suffer nothing for [their] want of knowledge in the matter of law" [*Rex v. Twyn*, 6 How. St. Tr. 513, 516 (1663)]. The common advice to stand trial may have been presented, not in what we would regard today as a judicial capacity, but in the judge's role as counselor.

Still another reason for the courts' discouragement of guilty pleas was that death was the prescribed penalty for every felony. When a guilty plea is an act of suicide, it is understandable that it should evoke squeamish feelings. One should not suppose, however, that the English penalty structure was simply too rigid to permit any development of plea negotiation. When capital punishment reached its high-water mark in England in 1819, death was the authorized punishment for 220 offenses (Michael & Wechsler, 1940: 236). Of the 1254 defendants convicted of capital crimes during the preceding year, however, only 97 were executed (Cottu, 1822: 69n.). An extensive system of executive reprieves had developed alongside England's system of capital punishment (Bressler, 1965). A recommendation by the trial judge ensured a royal pardon, and other techniques were also available for nullifying the death penalty. In practice, therefore, judges did exercise substantial sentencing discretion through their recommendations of executive clemency, but this exercise of discretion apparently did not lead to the exchange of leniency for pleas of guilty.

The Requirement of Voluntariness

Common law courts apparently took a negative view of guilty pleas of any description, not of plea bargaining specifically. They therefore discouraged even guilty pleas that would plainly qualify as voluntary. Nevertheless, the formal requirement that a guilty plea be voluntary is at least as old as the first English treatise devoted exclusively to criminal law, Staundforde's Pleas of the Crown (1560), which declared that a guilty plea arising from "fear, menace, or duress" should not be recorded. A half century later, Ferdinando Pulton wrote that the plea must "proceed freely, and of [the defendant's] own goodwill."

Perhaps because guilty pleas were infrequent and even voluntary guilty pleas were discouraged, the courts articulated the meaning of the voluntariness requirement exclusively in cases involving out-of-court confessions. The principles developed in these cases, however, suggest a basic incompatibility between plea bargaining and traditional common-law assumptions. The most famous of the confession cases was probably *Rex v. Warickshall* [1 Leach 298 (1783)], which held inadmissible any confession obtained "by promise of favor." The court declared: "[A] confession forced from the mind by the flattery of hope, or by the torture of fear, comes in so questionable a shape ... that no credit ought to be given to it."

The basic rule was, and still is, that a promise of leniency by a person in authority invalidates an out-of-court confession (McCormick, 1954: §111). Were this rule applied to pleas of guilty, every bargained plea would be invalid. Although some modern courts and scholars have attempted to escape this conclusion by suggesting distinctions between guilty pleas and out-of-court confessions, such a distinction probably would not have occurred to courts or legal scholars of the past. Indeed, although the legal phenomenon that we call a guilty plea has existed for more than eight centuries, the term "guilty plea" came into common use only about a century ago. During the previous 700 years, what we call a guilty plea was simply called a "confession."

Common law treatises revealed that a "judicial confession" was not a pleading at all. Hale, for example, declared (1736: 225): "When the prisoner is arraigned, and demanded what he saith to the indictment, either he confesses the indictment; or pleads to it." Early treatises contained elaborate catalogues of the pleas that a defendant might offer in a criminal case, but these catalogues did not mention confessions or pleas of guilty. The sections of the treatises on evidence, however, set forth the law of the guilty plea. The work of John Frederick Archbold (1824: 73) is typical. Confessions, he said, are of four kinds: extrajudicial confessions, confessions during preliminary interrogations by magistrates, confessions that we would now call pleas of *nolo contendere,* and confessions that we would now call pleas of guilty. "All of these several species of confessions, to be of effect, must be voluntary," he concluded. The early decisions on the voluntariness of confessions, coupled with the fact that pleas of guilty were not regarded as different from other confessions, strongly suggest that the courts would have condemned the practice of plea bargaining had they had occasion to do so.

Approvement and Other Oddities

Even a sketchy history of the guilty plea requires mention of some early practices that resembled plea bargaining but that did not involve the exchange of leniency for self-conviction. In an early form of diversion from the criminal process, a felon who fled to a church without being captured was entitled to sanctuary there. If he then confessed his crime, he was permitted to "abjure the realm"—that is, suffer exile and a forfeiture of goods rather than conviction and judicially imposed punishment (Hunnisett, 1961: 37–54). In addition, criminal cases were commonly compromised through the payment of money for the victim's refusal to prosecute. "Compounding," as this practice was called, was a criminal offense from the earliest days of the common law but remained a problem for centuries (Radzinowicz, 1956: 313–18).

Particularly instructive in an assessment of attitudes toward plea bargaining was the common law's earliest form of bargaining for information, the practice of approvement. An accused felon might confess his guilt and offer to "appeal"—or bring a private prosecution—against other participants in the crime with which he was charged (Hale, 1736: 226–35). A judge would then balance the benefits of the proposed prosecution against the danger of pardoning the accused, for if the defendant were successful in his appeal, he would be entitled automatically to a pardon. Whether to accept the defendant's offer to become an approver was "a matter of grace and discretion."

Even this limited and regularized form of bargaining was sometimes criticized. Sir Matthew Hale argued that "more mischief hath come to good men by these ... approvements ... than benefit to the public by the discovery and convicting of real offenders" (ibid.). By at least the mid-seventeenth century, approvement had fallen into disuse. Nevertheless, judges regarded this practice as "very material" [*Rex v. Rudd*, 1 Cowper 331, 335 (1775)] in shaping a closely related form of bargaining for information that persisted into the late nineteenth century. Informants were no longer required to bring private prosecutions or to secure the judicial condemnation of their confederates, but whenever a felon was permitted to testify against his accomplices, he gained "an equitable title" to a pardon. The courts therefore refused to allow an offender to testify against less culpable accomplices, and until the mid-nineteenth century they also forbade bargaining for testimony by the prosecutor. They said that the power to grant leniency in exchange for information was "by its nature a judicial power" [*People v. Whipple*, 9 Cow. 707, 711 (1827)].

In 1878, however, the United States Supreme Court noted that a number of American jurisdictions had permitted the public prosecutor to displace the trial judge in deciding whether to allow an accomplice to testify and thereby gain a pardon. The Court apparently favored this development, for it noted that, unlike a trial judge, a prosecutor could assess the need for an accomplice's testimony in light of the other evidence available to the state [*Whiskey Cases*, 99 U.S. 549, 603 (1878)].

In endorsing prosecutorial bargaining for testimony, the Court plainly did not endorse plea bargaining. The case in which the Supreme Court considered the issue was, in fact, a case of plea negotiation—the first such case to come before the Court. A federal prosecutor had struck a complex bargain in a number of internal revenue cases. The defendants had agreed to plead guilty to one count of a criminal indictment, to testify fully concerning a corrupt agreement involving internal revenue officials, and to withdraw their defensive pleas in a civil condemnation case. In exchange, the prosecutor had agreed to forego prosecution of the other counts of the indictment and to forego action on some other civil claims as well. The defendants alleged that they had fully performed their part of the bargain and that the prosecutor, in violation of the agreement, had pressed the civil claims that he had agreed to abandon. The Supreme Court held that the prosecutor had exceeded his authority in entering the agreement and that the bargain was therefore unenforceable. Because the defendants had been permitted to testify, they had an equitable claim to a pardon—a claim which the Supreme Court expressed confidence that the Chief Executive would honor. Nevertheless, the prosecutor's agreement had purported to guarantee nonprosecution of the government's civil claims, and it was therefore improper.

As this Supreme Court decision reveals, the common law did permit a sacrifice of the public interest in punishing a single offender in order to gain his assistance in convicting other criminals. It devised an open and regularized form of bargaining to accomplish this result. Nevertheless, the courts apparently did not countenance bargaining for pleas of guilty.

The Emergence of Plea Bargaining

Plea Bargaining Before the Civil War

During most of the history of our legal system, guilty pleas were more discouraged than welcomed, but four specific indications of plea bargaining prior to the American Civil War have come to my attention. First, John H. Langbein's study of the preliminary examination in renaissance England (1974: 70) noted a statute enacted in 1485 that authorized the commencement of prosecutions for unlawful hunting before Justices of the Peace. As Langbein interpreted this statute, it authorized a Justice to convict the defendant of a summary offense when he confessed his crime and to hold him for prosecution as a felon if he denied his guilt. The statute thus rewarded defendants who brought about their own convictions, but Langbein's study of the early preliminary examination did not reveal any other evidence of this practice.

A second indication of plea bargaining prior to the Civil War emerges from J.S. Cockburn's examination of approximately 5,000 indictments at the Home Circuit assizes between 1558 and 1625 (1978: 73). For the first thirty years of this period, confessions of guilt were virtually unknown. Then, quite suddenly, for a two- or three-year period, "five or six prisoners [at every assize]—sometimes as many as half the calendar—confessed to their indictments and were sentenced without further process." In some cases, the indictments to which the defendants confessed had been altered: burglary charges had been reduced to larceny charges, thus entitling the accused to claim benefit of clergy, and larceny charges had been reduced from felonies to misdemeanors by substituting lesser values for the stolen property. These charge reductions seemed plainly to bespeak plea bargaining, and they occurred at a time when judges traveling the counties of the Home Circuit faced "a rising crime rate, a ludicrously inadequate local law enforcement system, negligent and absentee justices of the peace, ignorant and absentee jurors, and [a] high acquittal rate" (Cockburn, 1975: 230). Cockburn noted that plea negotiation was part of a much broader pattern of lawlessness that came to characterize the administration of justice outside of London at this time. Nevertheless, during the final thirty-five years of the period that Cockburn studied, the altered indictments disappeared, and defendants entered confessions in only 15 to 20 percent of the cases heard at the assizes (1978:73–74).

In a study of criminal justice in colonial Massachusetts, David H. Flaherty noted a third instance of plea bargaining, a case in 1749 in which three defendants pleaded guilty to theft from a brigantine after the Attorney General announced that he would not prosecute them for the burglary charged in the indictment. Flaherty's examination of the records of the Court of Assize and General Jail Delivery prior to this time had uncovered no evidence of plea bargaining, and he reported: "Guilty pleas were uncommon for the crimes tried at the Assizes; even if a defendant had signed a confession upon a preliminary examination, he normally rescinded it and sought trial by jury."

A French jurist, Charles Cottu, observed the English courts during the early nineteenth century, and his report for the French government (1822: 95) provides the fourth indication of plea bargaining. Cottu reported that when a defendant was charged with forging bank notes, two indictments were prepared, one for forgery and the other for possessing forged notes with the intention of uttering them. The punishment for the first offense was death; for the second, it was transportation to the colonies for a term of years. When a defendant charged with forgery was brought into the courtroom, an attorney representing the defrauded bank would approach the defendant's attorney and ask whether the defendant would be willing to plead guilty to the second indictment. If the answer were affirmative, the defendant would be convicted of the lesser offense "upon his own confession," and because the bank's solicitor would then fail to offer any proof of the forgery, the jury would find the defendant not guilty of the capital offense. Cottu commented: "Let it not be thought that such an incredible transaction takes place in darkness and secrecy: no, the whole is done in open court, in the presence of the public, of the judge, and the jury." In other cases, however, Cottu noted that a defendant who sought to plead guilty was strongly discouraged: "[T]he judge ... the clerk, the gaoler, almost all counsel, even prosecutors, persuade [the defendant] to take the chance of an acquittal" (ibid.: 73).

These instances of pre-Civil War plea bargaining seem to stand alone, but Raymond Moley's compilation of guilty plea rates in New York State (1928: 108) suggests that attitudes toward the guilty plea were changing throughout the final two-thirds of the nineteenth century. Although only 15 percent of all felony convictions in Manhattan and Brooklyn were by guilty plea in 1839, the figure increased steadily at decade intervals to 45, 70, 75, and 80 percent. This last figure remained steady until 1919, when it grew to more than 85 percent. By 1926, 90 percent of all felony convictions in Manhattan and Brooklyn were by plea of guilty, and the figures for New York State as a whole revealed a comparable increase. Today approximately 97 percent of all felony convictions in New York City are by plea of guilty (Vera Institute, 1977: Fig. 3).

The Early Judicial Response to Plea Bargaining

It was only after the Civil War that cases of plea bargaining began to appear in American appellate court reports. In the first such case [*Swang v. State*, 42 Tenn. (2 Caldwell) 212 (1865)], the defendant pleaded guilty to two counts of gambling. In accordance with an agreement that he had entered with the prosecutor, eight other charges of gambling were dismissed. The defendant was fined twenty-five dollars on one count and ten dollars on the other. The Tennessee Supreme Court said that this:

statement of fact [was] unprecedented in the judicial history of the state.... [The defendant was,] among other things highly improper, told by the Attorney General, that if he did not submit, he would have to go to jail, and that he could certainly prove his guilt. The plea of guilty was entered ... while the prisoner was protesting against his guilt, but as the best, under the circumstances, he could do.

The court ordered a new trial on a plea of not guilty and said: "By the Constitution of the State, the accused, in all cases, has a right to a 'speedy public trial...' and this right cannot be defeated by any deceit or device whatever."

As guilty plea cases came before the courts with increasing frequency in the late nineteenth and early twentieth centuries, the usual judicial response was expressed in statements like these:

The least surprise or influence causing [the defendant] to plead guilty when he had any defense at all should be sufficient cause to permit a change of the plea from guilty to not guilty. [*State v. Williams*, 45 La. Ann. 1356, 1357, 14 So. 244, 245 (1893)]

The law favors a trial on the merits. [*Griffin v. State*, 12 Ga. App. 615, 622, 77 S.E. 1132, 1136 (1913)]

No sort of pressure can be permitted to bring the party to forego any right or advantage however slight. The law will not suffer the least weight to be put in the scale against him. [*O'Hara v. People*, 41 Mich. 623, 624, 3 N.W. 161, 162 (1879)]

[W]hen there is reason to believe that the plea has been entered through inadvertence ... and mainly from the hope that the punishment to which the accused would otherwise be exposed may thereby be mitigated, the Court should be indulgent in permitting the plea to be withdrawn. [*People v. McCrory*, 41 Cal. 458, 463 (1871)]

As the plea of guilty is often made because the defendant supposes that he will thereby receive some favor of the court in the sentence, it is the English practice not to receive such plea unless it is persisted in by the defendant after being informed that such plea will make no alteration in the punishment.... [J]udicial discretion ... should always be exercised in favor of innocence and liberty. All courts should so administer the law ... as to secure a hearing upon the merits if possible. [*Deloach v. State*, 77 Miss. 691, 692, 27 So. 618, 619 (1900)]

The plea should be entirely voluntary by one competent to know the consequences and should not be induced by fear, misapprehension, persuasion, promises, inadvertence, or ignorance. [*Pope v. State*, 56 Fla. 81, 84, 47 So. 487, 489 (1908)]

In more detailed statements, the courts offered a catalogue of theoretical and practical objections to plea bargaining. In 1877, the Wisconsin Supreme Court considered an agreement in which a defendant had secured a lenient sentence by pleading guilty and offering his testimony against other offenders. It called this agreement "hardly, if at all, distinguishable in principle from a direct sale of justice," and it also noted that "such a bargain ... could not be kept ... in any court not willing largely to abdicate its proper functions in favor of its officers" [*Wight v. Rindskopf*, 43 Wis. 344, 354-55 (1877)]. Perhaps the most serious problem that the Wisconsin court saw in plea bargaining, however, was its secrecy:

The profession of law is not one of indirection, circumvention, or intrigue.... Professional function is exercised in the sight of the world.... Private preparation goes to this, only as sharpening the sword goes to battle. Professional weapons are wielded only in open contest. No weapon is professional which strikes in the dark.... Justice will always bear litigation; litigation is ... the safest test of justice.

The following year, the Michigan Supreme Court expressed concern about the motives of prosecutors in bargaining, and it plainly did not view the conservation of public resources through plea bargaining as a virtue. "[T]here was danger," the court said, "that prosecuting attorneys, either to save themselves trouble, to save money to the county, or to serve some other improper purpose, would procure prisoners to plead guilty by assurances they have no power to make of influence in lowering the sentence" [*Edwards v. People*, 39 Mich. 760, 762 (1878)].

The Louisiana Supreme Court was troubled by what plea bargaining might mean to innocent defendants:

In the instant case the accused accepted the certainty of conviction of what he took to be a minor offense not importing infamy. Not only was there room for error, but the thing was what an innocent man might do who found that appearances were against him, and that he might be convicted notwithstanding his innocence. [*State v. Coston*, 113 La. 718, 720, 37 So. 619, 620 (1904)]

The Georgia Court of Appeals invoked the analogy to out-of-court confessions:

A plea of guilty is but a confession of guilt in open court, and a waiver of trial. Like a confession out of court, it ought to be scanned with care and received with caution.... The law ... does not encourage confessions of guilt, either in or out of court. Affirmative action on the part of the prisoner is required before he will be held to have waived the right of trial, created for his benefit.... The affirmative plea of guilty is received because the prisoner is willing, voluntarily, without inducement of any sort, to confess his guilt and expiate his offense.... It has been said that withdrawal of the plea should be allowed whenever interposed on account of "the flattery of hope or the torture of fear." [*Griffin v. State*, 12 Ga. App. 615, 622–23 (1913)]

The judicial decisions that did uphold guilty pleas during this period included an 1883 federal case in which the defendants' pleas had been induced by prosecutorial bargaining [*United States v. Bayaud*, 23 Fed. 721 (1883)]. In the main, however, the courts affirmed guilty plea convictions only in cases in which there had been no bargains (or at least no explicit bargains) and in which the defendants' alleged expectations of leniency seemed to lack a plausible basis.

The United States Supreme Court did not directly address the propriety of plea bargaining during this era, but there are indications of the position that the Court probably would have taken. For example, this paper has noted the *Whiskey Cases* [99 U.S. 594 (1878)], in which the Court insisted that defendants who had been permitted to testify against their accomplices were entitled to pardons, and that a plea agreement that had led instead to a reduction in punishment and an abandonment of the government's civil claims was invalid.

The Court's reluctance to permit bargained waivers of procedural rights was more strikingly illustrated by *Insurance Co. v. Morse* [87 U.S. (20 Wall.) 445 (1874)]. In this case, the Court invalidated a Wisconsin statute, which required insurance companies, as a condition of doing business in the state, to waive their right to remove civil lawsuits from state to federal court. The Court thus manifested its hostility to a less sweeping procedural waiver than a waiver of the right to trial through plea bargaining. It said:

Every citizen is entitled to resort to all the courts of the country, and to invoke the protection which all the laws or all those courts may afford him. A man may not barter away his life or his freedom, or his substantial rights.

In 1892 in *Hallinger v. Davis* [146 U.S. 314 (1892)], the Supreme Court upheld a guilty plea conviction in a case in which there had been no bargain and in which the trial court had been extraordinarily solicitous in affording the defendant an opportunity to reconsider his plea. A New Jersey statute provided that, following a guilty plea to murder, the trial court should conduct a hearing to determine whether the murder was of the first or second degree. The defendant contended that any waiver of the right to jury trial on this issue, even through a knowing and voluntary guilty plea, violated the due process clause of the Fourteenth Amendment. Although the defendant's argument was rejected, the fact that it was seriously made and considered may indicate how far the Supreme Court was from countenancing any form of plea bargaining.

The Growth of Plea Bargaining

The gap between judicial denunciations of plea bargaining and the behavior of many urban courts at the turn of the century and thereafter was apparently large. In these courts, notorious political corruption apparently contributed to a growing practice of plea bargaining. Richard Canfield, later an operator of elegant gambling casinos in several cities, testified that as early as 1885 his friend, the Mayor of Providence, Rhode Island, had acted as an intermediary in arranging a plea agreement with the State Attorney General (Gardner, 1930: 77). By 1914, there were accounts of a New York defense attorney whose financial arrangements with a magistrate enabled him to "stand out on the street in front of the Night Court and dicker away sentences in this form: $300 for ten days, $200 for twenty days, $150 for thirty days." The Dean of the University of Illinois Law School, Albert J. Harno, later noted:

> When the plea of guilty is found in records it is almost certain to have in the background, particularly in Cook County, a session of bargaining with the State's Attorney.... These approaches, particularly in Cook County, are frequently made through another person called a "fixer." This sort of person is an abomination and it is a serious indictment against our system of criminal administration that such a leech not only can exist but thrive. The "fixer" is just what the word indicates. (1928:103)

Although most of the reported decisions on plea bargaining involved bargains struck by prosecutors, police officers may also have played a significant role in the development of this practice. Arthur Train, an assistant district attorney in Manhattan, wrote:

> Court officers often win fame in accordance with their ability as "plea getters." They are anxious that the particular Part [courtroom] to which they are assigned shall make as good a showing as possible in the number of cases disposed of. Accordingly each morning some of them visit the pens on the floor below the courtroom and negotiate with the prisoners for pleas.... The writer has known of the entire population of a prison pen pleading guilty one after another under the persuasion of an eloquent bluecoat. (1924: 223–24)

An early twentieth-century edition of Wharton's *Criminal Evidence* (1912: 1326 n.22) ascribed a corrupt motive to bargaining police officers and asserted that they commonly made false promises to jailed defendants in order "to earn the transportation and mileage incident to conveying [them] to prison." The work concluded: "[I]t has become a `business' to misuse the power given [to policemen who have charge of detention], and this, too, when both court and prosecution are entirely innocent of the wrong so shamelessly inflicted."

In the late 1960s, when I interviewed participants in the criminal justice system about the plea bargaining process, a number of older attorneys reported that corruption had been the norm at the outset of their legal careers. One recalled a former prizefighter who became an attorney and worked out of a bondsman's office. This attorney commonly offered half his fee to a police inspector to arrange a plea agreement, and if the inspector turned him down, the attorney returned the money to his client. "In that respect, this attorney was more honest than most of the guys in the criminal courts 35 years ago," my source commented (Alschuler, 1975: 1185).

In its infancy the practice of plea negotiation undoubtedly produced many satisfied customers just as it does today, and serious judicial review of the process was rare. This fact, coupled with the corrupt atmosphere of urban criminal justice in the late nineteenth and early twentieth centuries, may help to explain the growth of plea negotiation despite its condemnation by appellate courts.

The Discovery of Plea Bargaining by the Crime Commissions of the 1920s

During the 1920s a number of states and cities conducted surveys of criminal justice. These surveys, which offered a far more complete picture of the workings of American criminal courts than has generally been available in later years, revealed a lopsided dependency on the plea of guilty. In Chicago, 85 percent of all felony convictions were by guilty plea; in Detroit, 78; in Denver, 76; in Minneapolis, 90; in Los Angeles, 81; in Pittsburgh, 74; and in St. Louis, 84 (Moley, 1928: 105).

The dominance of the guilty plea apparently came as a surprise. The first of the criminal justice surveys, the Cleveland survey, noted that 77 percent of all convictions in that jurisdiction were by guilty plea, but its discussion of prosecution focused only briefly on this phenomenon and concentrated primarily on abuses in the granting of dismissals (Fosdick, 1922). Until the Missouri survey in 1926, investigators largely ignored plea negotiation, apparently because its importance was unsuspected (Moley, 1928: 110). Nevertheless, the Missouri, Illinois, and New York surveys soon brought the practice into focus and, in the words of Raymond Moley, "the public learned how much the spirit of an auction had come to dominate the process of justice" (1928: 114).

The surveys commonly revealed a substantial increase in the percentage of guilty pleas in the period just prior to their publication, and they also indicated that plea bargaining became routine in different jurisdictions at different times. In urban jurisdictions in Virginia, half of all convictions were by guilty plea in 1917, but three-quarters were by plea in 1927 (Fuller, 1931: 81). Between 1916 and 1921 the number of guilty pleas in urban misdemeanor courts in Georgia increased approximately three times as rapidly as the total number of cases (Georgia, 1924: 190). In New Haven in 1888, fully 75 percent of all felony convictions were by plea of guilty. A steady increase brought the figure to over 90 percent by 1921 (Moley, 1928: 107).

In the federal courts, the statistics date from 1908, when only about 50 percent of all convictions were by plea of guilty (American Law Institute, 1934: 56, 58). This percentage remained fairly constant until 1916, when it increased to 72 percent. Because the number of cases in the federal courts actually declined during 1916, the increase cannot be attributed to caseload pressures. The American Law Institute commented: "It would appear that the habits of the prosecution suddenly changed in that year.... A method of handling cases which may be referred to as the guilty plea technique came into extensive use" (ibid.: 12). Soon, a flood of cases under the federal prohibition laws seemed to preclude any retreat. By 1925, the percentage of convictions by guilty plea had reached almost 90 (ibid.: 56), approximately the same level as that of recent years.

The surveys of the 1920s indicated that increased plea bargaining might have led some defendants to plead guilty although they could not have been convicted at trial. As the percentage of convictions by guilty plea grew in the period just preceding the 1920s, both the percentage of convictions at trial and the percentage of acquittals showed a sharp decline. If one assumes that the character of the cases coming before the courts did not change significantly during this period and that prosecutors did not significantly alter their screening practices, it seems probable that, although most of the increased numbers of guilty-plea defendants would have been convicted had they stood trial, a substantial minority would have been acquitted.

A reward to defendants who waive their rights to trial lies at the heart of any system of plea negotiation, and many of the surveys focused specifically on the nature of this reward. In Chicago in 1926, 78 percent of all guilty pleas in felony cases were to offenses less serious than those originally charged. Indeed, most of the guilty pleas in cases in which felonies had been charged were not to felonies at all but to misdemeanors (Illinois, 1929: 47). In New York City in 1926, 85 percent of all guilty pleas were to offenses less serious than those initially charged (Moley, 1928: 111).

The rewards associated with pleas of guilty were manifested not only in the lesser offenses of which defendants were convicted but also in the lighter sentences they received. The *Missouri Crime Survey* declared: "[A] plea of guilty upon arraignment reduces the chances of a penitentiary sentence in the cities by about one half" (Missouri, 1926: 149). The *Illinois Crime Survey* reported: "[T]he chances of getting probation are roughly two and one-half times as great if one pleads guilty to begin with as they are if one pleads not guilty and sticks to it" (Illinois, 1929: 84). The New York survey found that suspended sentences were more than twice as frequent when guilty pleas had been entered than when defendants had been convicted at trial (New York, 1927: 135).

A few of the surveys noted that the increased volume of guilty pleas in the early 1920s had been accompanied by an enhancement of the concessions offered to defendants for pleading guilty. Even in 1917, a defendant in Virginia who pleaded guilty was 2.3 times more likely to receive a suspended sentence than a defendant convicted at trial. In 1927, however, this ratio increased to 6.3 (Fuller, 1931: 17). In Georgia, 38 percent of all defendants convicted at trial were sentenced to prison. During a five-year period from 1916 to 1921, while this figure remained unchanged the proportion of defendants receiving a prison sentence following a plea of guilty declined from 24 percent to 13.5 percent (Georgia, 1924: 191).

Although plea bargaining had become a central feature of the administration of justice by the 1920s, it had few apologists and many critics. Most of the criticism came from the hawks of the criminal process rather than the doves. The president of the Chicago Crime Commission condemned plea negotiation as "paltering with crime" and demanded the immediate removal from office of three Criminal Court judges, solely on the ground that they had permitted the reduction of felony charges to misdemeanors in exchange for pleas of guilty. The judges ultimately kept their jobs, but only after an inquiry by a committee of Circuit and Superior Court judges had cast primary responsibility for the reduction of felony charges upon the State's Attorney (Haller, 1970: 633–34).

The *Illinois Crime Survey* argued that plea negotiation "gives notice to the criminal population of Chicago that the criminal law and the instrumentalities for its enforcement do not really mean business. This, it would seem, is a pretty direct encouragement to crime" (Illinois, 1929: 318). The Virginia survey added: "[Persons who boast of their real or fancied bargains] are the best and most persistent advertisers in the world for the bargain counter. Surely this does not make for deterrence" (Fuller, 1931: 154). Dean Roscoe Pound (1930: 184) observed: "[P]rosecutors publish statements showing 'convictions' running to thousands each year. But more than ninety percent of these 'convictions' are upon pleas of guilty, made on 'bargain days,' in the assured expectation of nominal punishment, as the cheapest way out, and amounting in effect to license to violate the law."

Observers who saw plea bargaining as a threat to the rights of criminal defendants occasionally added their voices. Dean Justin Miller wrote in the first issue of the *Southern California Law Review* (1927: 22–23):

> There can be no doubt that [our undercover system of criminal law administration] is dangerous, both to the rights of individuals and to orderly, stable government.... [T]he poor, friendless, helpless man is most apt to become the one who helps swell the record of convictions. The necessity for

making a good record...may well result in prosecutors overlooking the rights, privileges and immunities of the poor, ignorant fellow who ... is induced to confess crime and plead guilty through hope of reward or fear of extreme punishment.

In its *Report on Crime and the Foreign Born*, the Wickersham Commission found that a frequent complaint of foreign-born prisoners was that their appointed attorneys had urged them to plead guilty after discovering that they lacked money to pay legal fees (National Commission, 1931a: 180).

Some observers denounced the irrationality of the guilty-plea system without characterizing it as either too lenient or too harsh. The *Wickersham Commission's Report on Prosecution* labeled plea bargaining an "abuse" without further analysis (National Commission, 1931b: 95–97). *The Chicago Tribune* (April 27, 1928: 1) called it an "incompetent, inefficient, and lazy method of administering justice." The Virginia survey noted that the practice of bargaining had enhanced the power of prosecutors. It said: "[T]he usual case is now decided, not by the court, but by the commonwealth's attorney, [who is] often young, often rather inexperienced" (Fuller, 1931: 155–56).

Other critics looked to the motives of prosecutors in bargaining, and they did not accept the view that a prosecutor's acquiescence in a bargain ordinarily ensures that it serves public interests. "Many prosecutors," the Missouri survey observed, "have an inordinate fear of trying a weak case. As a matter of fact, the case may be weak because the prosecutor himself is weak" (Missouri, 1926:150). Raymond Moley (1929: 157, 187, 190) suggested other reasons why prosecutors entered plea agreements—reasons irrelevant to penology but highly relevant to local politics:

[When the prosecuting attorney accepts a guilty plea to a lesser offense, he] is not compelled to carry through an onerous and protracted trial. He does not run the risk of losing the case in court. He runs no risk of having to oppose an appeal to a higher court in case he wins in the trial.... Most important of all to the prosecutor is the fact that in such record as most prosecutors make of their work, a plea of guilty of any sort is counted as a conviction. When he goes before the voters for reelection he can talk in big figures about the number of convictions secured. In reality these "convictions" include all sorts of compromises.... [I]t is easy for a prosecutor to avoid labor in this way merely for the purpose of expending his best energies upon sensational and politically advantageous exploits in court.... It is not surprising, then, that prosecutors have indulged in the politically profitable enterprise of making friends among the friends of accused persons while atthe same time and by the same acts they were building a record of vigorous and successful prosecutions.

Prosecutors answered that they bargained for guilty pleas only in cases that would be difficult to try (Miller, 1927: 6 n.24, 7 n.25; Baker, 1933). They insisted that "half a loaf is better than none." The *Illinois Crime Survey* responded: "[T]he interpretation of `the best he can get' is left to [the prosecutor]. Such a course ... may ... be used to excuse weak and careless prosecution" (Illinois, 1929: 262).

Just as critics in the 1920s took a different view of why prosecutors engaged in plea bargaining from that of some contemporary observers, they also differed about the motivation of defendants. Modern courts and scholars sometimes argue that an acknowledgment of guilt provides a sign of repentance and that defendants who plead guilty should therefore receive lighter sentences than those who stand trial. The *Missouri Crime Survey* commented: "The popular impression is that when an offender enters a plea of guilty he throws himself upon 'the mercy of the court.' As a practical proposition he does nothing of the kind" (Missouri, 1926: 149). The Illinois survey added: "This tendency to plead guilty is no abject gesture of confession and renunciation; it is a type of defense strategy" (Illinois, 1929: 310). The New York survey, after noting the increase in the number of guilty pleas, observed: "This is not because those accused of crime are becoming to a greater degree repentant of their misdeeds.... It is a development of the tactics of the defense combined with the rise of certain conditions in the machinery of justice" (New York, 1927: 129).

The conditions to which the New York survey referred included growing caseloads caused in part by an expansion of the substantive criminal law. Dean Roscoe Pound (1930: 23) observed that "of one hundred thousand persons arrested in Chicago in 1912, more than one half were held for violation of legal precepts which did not exist twenty-five years before." In 1931, the Wickersham Commission noted the effect on the administration of justice of federal prohibition, the most important victimless crime in American history:

> [F]ederal prosecutions under the Prohibition Act terminated in 1930 had become nearly eight times as many as the total number of all pending federal prosecutions in 1914. In a number of urban districts the enforcement agencies maintain that the only practicable way of meeting this situation with the existing machinery of the federal courts...is for the United States Attorneys to make bargains with defendants or their counsel whereby defendants plead guilty to minor offenses and escape with light penalties.
>
> Lawyers everywhere deplore, as one of the most serious effects of prohibition, the change in the general attitude toward the federal courts.... [T]he huge volume of liquor prosecutions ... has injured their dignity, impaired their efficiency, and endangered the wholesome respect for them which once obtained. (National Commission, 1931c: 561)

The Recent History of the Guilty Plea

The high rates of guilty pleas in the 1920s left little room for dramatic increases. In recent years, however, prosecutors may have found it necessary to offer greater concessions simply to keep those rates constant. This hypothesis is supported by the statements of participants in the criminal justice system whom I have interviewed in various jurisdictions and also by a study of the United States District Court for the District of Columbia between 1950 and 1965 conducted by the President's Commission on Crime in the District of Columbia (1966). During the period of this study, guilty pleas accounted for approximately 74 percent of all felony convictions; there was little fluctuation in this figure. In 1950, however, 58 percent of the District of Columbia's guilty pleas were to the charges originally filed, with no reduction in the number or seriousness of offenses. By 1965, only 27 percent of all guilty pleas were to the indictments originally drawn (ibid.: Table 5 and p.243). In view of the greater frequency with which charges were reduced, it is not surprising that sentences became lighter during this period (ibid.: 245). At the same time, the crimes charged in the District Court became more serious (ibid.: 248–49).

Although the length of the average criminal trial in the District of Columbia increased notably during the period of the Crime Commission's study (ibid.: 263), the growth of plea negotiation probably cannot be explained by caseload pressures. Indeed, as greater concessions were offered to persuade defendants to plead guilty, the number of felony cases reaching the District Court declined (ibid.: 248–55), and the staff of the United States Attorney increased substantially (ibid.: 236). One possible explanation for the enhanced concessions to defendants who pleaded guilty is simply that the attitudes of bureaucracy, emphasizing the maximization of production and the minimization of work, became more pronounced as the prosecutor's staff grew. As Judge Arthur L. Alarcon noted in discussing what he regarded as a growing reliance on plea bargaining in Los Angeles: "The increase in the number of deputy district attorneys has fully kept pace with the increase in cases. Prosecutors say that bargaining is a way to reduce the backlog, but in reality it is simply a way to reduce the work."

In other jurisdictions, growing caseloads probably did contribute substantially to judicial dependence on the guilty plea. The "crime wave" of the 1960s, produced in part by the post-World War II baby boom and the increased proportion of young people in American society, was no figment of Richard Nixon's imagination (Wilson, 1975: 3–20). As the volume of traditional crime increased, the courts also confronted marijuana cases and other cases of victimless crime in greatly increased numbers. These developments led to an administrative crisis in the courts. Criminal caseloads commonly doubled from one decade to the next, while judicial resources increased only slightly.

In 1967, both the American Bar Association Project on Minimum Standards for Criminal Justice (1967) and the President's Commission on Law Enforcement and

Administration of Justice (1967: 134–37) proclaimed that, properly administered, plea bargaining was a practice of considerable value. Nevertheless, a case that reached the United States Supreme Court in 1958 suggests that only a few years before the beginning of today's reign of "realism," the legality of plea bargaining had been very much in doubt [*Shelton v. United States*, 356 U.S. 26 (1958)]. In *Shelton*, a three-judge panel of the Court of Appeals had held plea bargaining unlawful, and when this ruling was later set aside by the full court, the defendant sought Supreme Court review. Officials of the Justice Department may have assessed the probable votes of individual Supreme Court Justices and feared that the Court would condemn all bargained guilty pleas as involuntary. Whatever the reason, the government proceeded to confess error on a narrow, highly questionable ground that prevented the Court from deciding the substantive issue. It seems possible that, even at this late date, the history of plea bargaining might have taken a dramatically different turn.

In the decade following this inconclusive episode, the Supreme Court had other opportunities to consider the legality of plea negotiation but did not use them. Instead, during the period of its "due process revolution," the Court seemed to treat the police as the principal villains of the criminal process. In a regime in which the pressures for self-incrimination ordinarily were far greater at the courthouse than at the stationhouse, the Court repeatedly ignored the leverage that prosecutors exerted upon criminal defendants at the courthouse.

A major effect of the "due process revolution" was to augment the pressures for plea negotiation. For one thing, the Supreme Court's decisions contributed to the growing backlog of criminal cases. Prosecutors' offices were required to devote a larger share of their resources to appellate litigation, and both prosecutors and trial judges spent a greater portion of their time on pretrial motions and post-conviction proceedings. In addition, the Court's decisions probably contributed to the increased length of the criminal trial. In the District of Columbia, the length of the average felony trial grew from 1.9 days in 1950 to 2.8 days in 1965 (President's Commission on Crime in the District of Columbia, 1966: 263), and in Los Angeles the length of the average felony jury trial increased from 3.5 days in 1964 to 7.2 days in 1968 (San Francisco, 1970: 1).

The "due process revolution" also led directly to more intense plea negotiation. In the words of Oakland Public Defender John D. Nunes, "rights are tools to work with," and rather than insist on a hearing on a motion to suppress illegally obtained evidence, a defense attorney was likely to use a claim of illegality to exact prosecutorial concessions in plea bargaining. New York defense attorney Stanley Arkin explained: "As the defendant gains more rights, his bargaining position grows stronger. That is a simple matter of economics." Donald Conn, an Assistant Attorney General in Massachusetts, observed: "If guilty pleas are cheaper today, it is simply because Supreme Court decisions have given defense attorneys an excellent shot at beating us."

As American criminal courts became more dependent on plea bargaining, a return to the historic principle that a guilty plea should be entered "freely and of the defendant's own good will" and without "inducement of any kind," began to seem unrealistic; and the legal profession apparently decided that this principle was sour anyway. By 1970, the due process revolution had run its course, and the Supreme Court, which bore a share of responsibility for the dominance of the guilty plea, was ready at last to confront this central feature of American criminal justice. In a series of decisions that seemed to imply that any other course would be unthinkable, the Court upheld the propriety of plea bargaining. It insisted that plea bargaining was "inherent in criminal law and its administration" [*Brady v. United States*, 397 U.S. 742, 751 (1970)] and that "disposition of charges after plea discussions is not only an essential part of the [criminal] process but a highly desirable part for many reasons" [*Santobello v. United States*, 404 U.S. 257, 261 (1971)]. Indeed, even those Justices who criticized the Court's approach took pains to distinguish the practices then before them from what they called "the venerable institution of plea bargaining."

Some Concluding Observations

Americans tend to view history as progress and often assume that throughout history the law has afforded increasing dignity to persons accused of crime. The lash, the rack, and the thumbscrew have given way to *Miranda* warnings, and lynchings and blood feuds have become rare. The history of plea negotiations, however, is a history of mounting pressure for self-incrimination, and in explaining this phenomenon, the growing complexity of the trial process over the past two-and-one-half centuries seems relevant. Lawrence M. Friedman (1979: 257 n.16) discovered that one American felony court could conduct a half-dozen jury trials in a single day in the 1890s. This was only half the number of cases that an Old Bailey jury had been able to resolve in a day in the early eighteenth century (Langbein, 1978a: 277), but it contrasts dramatically with the 7.2 days that an average felony jury trial required in Los Angeles in 1968 (San Francisco, 1970: 1). One may fairly conclude that if there was a golden age of trials, it was not one in which trials were golden. The rapid trials of the past plainly lacked safeguards that we consider essential today. It may be equally true, however, that our system of resolving criminal cases has now become absurd both in the complexity of its trial processes and in the summary manner in which it avoids trial in the great majority of cases. For all the praise lavished upon the American jury trial, this fact-finding mechanism has become so cumbersome and expensive that our society refuses to provide it. Rather than reconsider our overly elaborate trial procedures, we press most criminal defendants to forego even the more expeditious form of trial that defendants once were freely granted as a matter of right.

The paradox of our current criminal justice system has a notable parallel in history (Langbein, 1978b). During the late Middle Ages and Renaissance, as English courts were discouraging guilty pleas, confession assumed an overwhelming importance on the European continent. Both torture and false promises of pardon were commonly used to induce defendants to confess (Currie, 1968; see Langbein, 1977a). Indeed, what is probably history's most famous case of plea bargaining arose in 1431 in an ecclesiastical court in France. When Joan of Arc yielded to the promise of leniency that this court made, she demonstrated that even saints are sometimes unable to resist the pressures of plea negotiation. Joan, however, was able to withdraw her confession and go to her martyrdom (see Sackville-West, 1936).

Part of the explanation for the greater importance of confession on the Continent lay in the fact that standards of proof were much higher there than in England. Neither the testimony of a single witness nor any amount of circumstantial evidence could warrant conviction of a serious crime. Confession was, therefore, essential to conviction in a great many cases, and this fact led to the exertion of extraordinary pressures to secure it. Formal courtroom requirements apparently designed to protect defendants were transmuted into something like their antitheses through the adoption of expedient shortcuts.

Today, in a sense, the situation is reversed. Methods of proof are far more formal, expensive, and time-consuming in Anglo-American justice than on the Continent, and the elaboration of safeguards surrounding the trial process has provided one source of pressure for plea bargaining. Our supposedly accusatory system has in fact become more dependent on proving guilt from the defendant's own mouth than any European "inquisitorial" system (see Langbein, 1977b). The lessons of both comparative and historical study are therefore essentially the same: the more formal and elaborate the trial process, the more likely it is that this process will be subverted through pressures for self-incrimination. The simpler and more straightforward the trial process, the more likely it is that the process will be used.

The growing complexity of the criminal trial was not the only factor that contributed to the development of contemporary plea bargaining. Urbanization, increased crime rates, expansion of the substantive criminal law, and the professionalization and increasing bureaucratization of the police, prosecution, and defense functions may also have played their parts. For a variety of reasons, we have come a long way from the time when guilty pleas were discouraged and litigation was thought "the safest test of justice." We have also come a long way from the first appellate decision on plea bargaining, in which the court refused to permit the right to trial to be defeated "by any deceit or device whatever." Indeed, the view advanced by the Supreme Court one hundred years ago that "a man may not barter away his life or his freedom, or his substantial rights" is disparaged by the Supreme Court today, and judges no longer proclaim, "No sort of pressure can be permitted to bring the party to forego any right or advantage however slight. The law will not suffer the least weight to be put in the scale against him."

How very far we have traveled is illustrated by the Supreme Court's decision in *Bordenkircher v. Hayes* [434 U.S. 357 (1978)]. The prosecutor in this case offered to permit the defendant, a prior offender charged with uttering a forged check, to plead guilty in exchange for the recommendation of a five-year sentence. When the defendant rejected this offer, the prosecutor carried out a threat that he had made during the negotiations to return to the grand jury and obtain an indictment under the Kentucky Habitual Criminal Act. The defendant was then convicted at trial, and the court imposed the life sentence that the Habitual Criminal Act required. The Supreme Court upheld the constitutionality of the penalty that the defendant had incurred by exercising his right to trial. Indeed, even the four Justices who dissented indicated that they would have upheld this penalty if only the prosecutor had observed some additional niceties in the timing of his threat and offer. The Supreme Court thus gave its imprimatur to a bizarre system of justice in which the crime of uttering a forged $88 check is "worth" five years, while the crime of standing trial is "worth" imprisonment for life. The road from common law principles to the Supreme Court's decision in *Bordenkircher v. Hayes* has been long, and although Sir Winston Churchill once observed that "the treatment of crime and criminals is one of the most unfailing tests of the civilization of any country," Americans can hope there are other yardsticks.

DISCUSSION QUESTIONS

1. Did you assume, before reading this article, that plea bargaining was an ancient practice? Or that it was the contemporary product of overcrowded dockets? What was the source of your belief?

2. Why were pre-modern courts hostile to or suspicious of guilty pleas? What is the difference between extrajudicial confessions and guilty pleas? Should courts treat them differently? Are you surprised that even in the sixteenth century accused were offered leniency in return for testifying against co-accused? Is there anything wrong with that? Is it different from plea bargaining?

3. Are you convinced by Alschuler that nineteenth-century American appellate courts almost uniformly condemned plea bargaining?

4. How should we understand the co-existence of appellate court denunciations of plea bargaining with widespread and increasing use of plea bargaining by trial courts? Are you surprised to find calls for "law and

order" a hundred years ago? Are you surprised that the crime surveys of the 1920s sound so contemporary?

5. Why did the proportion of cases resolved by plea bargaining increase during the early twentieth century? Why have prosecutors found it necessary to offer steeper discounts to induce guilty pleas? Do convicts serve less time as a result? Or is this like businesses that raise prices to appear to offer deeper discounts? Perhaps causation goes in the other direction: the "due process revolution" allowed defendants to compel deeper discounts by invoking procedural protection, forcing prosecutors to raise the original charges?

6. Are you persuaded that plea bargaining is not caused by caseloads?

7. Most civil cases are settled before trial. Is this objectionable for the same reasons as plea bargaining? If not, what is the difference? List the objections to plea bargaining; the justifications. Where do you come out?

8. If Prohibition explains part of the rise of plea bargaining in the 1920s, what is the effect of the "war on drugs" on the criminal justice system today?

9. Do you agree that the most serious threat to the privilege against self-incrimination has moved from the police station to the courtroom? If procedural complexity explains increased reliance on guilty pleas, what explains procedural complexity?

10. Could we operate our criminal justice system without plea bargaining? Should we?

8

Holistic Effects in Social Control Decision-Making

Robert M. Emerson

Sociologists analyzing the decision-making aspects of social control have become increasingly sensitive to the effects of organizational factors on decision outcomes. Yet despite the strong theoretical interest in and recent flurry of research on this topic, one critical organizational dimension—the way in which social control agents process and respond to cases in relation to, or as part of, some larger, organizationally determined *whole*—is seldom explicitly treated. Most studies of social control decision making treat the individual case as the central if not the exclusive unit of analysis.

The individual case provides an adequate unit of analysis only if social control agents themselves examine and dispose of cases as discrete units, treating each on its own merits independently of the properties and organizational implications of other cases. A central point of this article is that under a variety of circumstances, the individual case is not the sole or even the most important unit for categorizing and disposing of cases. Particular cases are in fact processed not independently of others but in ways that take into account the implications of other cases for the present one and vice versa. These wider, *holistic* concerns and influences are an important organizationally based factor that shapes decision outcomes. The following analysis explores a variety of such dimensions.

By way of introduction, consider the following examples of how holistic influences constrain the ways in which individual cases are assessed and decided:

(1) A number of accounts note a recurrent conflict between the client perceptions of the seriousness, priority, and depth of problems and the perceptions of those same problems by agents processing those clients. Bloor (1976), for example, notes that while a number of medical doctors specializing in tonsillectomies accept parental accounts of their child's symptoms at face value, "where specialists do form their own independent assessments of troublesomeness these are likely to be more conservative than parental assessments" (1976: 59).

This "conservatism" reflects several factors, including "specialists' familiarity with the symptomatology—a familiarity which if it doesn't breed contempt may

Abridged from *Law & Society Review*, Volume 17:425 (1983).

breed a dispassionate relativism" (1976: 60). Yet more is involved here than simply familiarity. What the parents see as exceptional and unique the specialist sees as but another instance of a routine case regularly encountered in the course of work. The more general lesson is that the makeup of the overall "stream of cases" that an agent handles provides a background against which the classification of particular cases in organizationally relevant ways will be made.

(2) Many control agents, notably many social workers and probation and parole officers, organize their work around *caseloads*. In this respect, the focus of much of their routine decision-making is not so much the individual case as it is this larger set of cases for which they are organizationally and administratively responsible. One commonly observed consequence is that such agents must allocate time, energy, and other organizational resources on the basis of how they assess the demands and "needs" of any given case relative to the competing demands of other cases within the caseload. Lipsky (1980: 36) has recently emphasized the prevalence of such caseload concerns in the organization of work in a variety of "street level bureaucracies":

> Case loads are often informally divided into active and inactive categories. The inactive cases are often not truly inactive but represent cases to which the street-level bureaucrat is unable to attend in the ordinary course of the day. They are regarded as low priority for reasons having little to do with the client but a lot to do with the pressures on the workers.

To the extent that allocative and other decisions about particular cases are oriented toward the worker's overall caseload, those decisions reflect and must be analyzed in relation to the larger caseload as a whole.

(3) In a variety of social control circumstances, the fact that a particular case is the *first* of a known or anticipated *sequence of cases* can have major implications for how it is handled. Classroom discipline provides a revealing example. School folklore often emphasizes the importance of "the first day" and first impressions for subsequent control in the classroom. Levy (1970: 50) provides an extreme example:

> When children challenge the teacher's power, it is crucial that they be defeated. So, on the first day of school a teacher picks out the potential rebel leader, and, at the first sign of disobedience, makes an example of him. He grabs the disobedient child and threatens to beat him up if he doesn't stop what he is doing. In many instances he smacks the child in front of the class. If the leader is decisively defeated, other children are less likely to rebel.

For teachers concerned with "establishing 'Who's boss' on the first day" (Levy, 1970: 51), the "first offense" may be treated more severely than later offenses because it is seen as the likely precursor of subsequent offenses unless strict action is taken.

Response to the "first offense" reflects its perceived relation to a sequential whole of expected, subsequent offenses. The same behavior occurring at other points in this sequence will be understood and responded to in very different ways.

In the pages that follow I analyze the conditions under which the responses of social control agents to individual cases are fundamentally shaped by reference to larger, organizationally relevant wholes. Three such wholes, paralleling the three illustrations previously presented, will be considered: first, the relativity of judgment in social control decision-making, a relativity reflecting the composite character of the "kinds of cases" processed by a particular agent; second, the ways in which the handling of some current case becomes competitive with the handling of other, "like" cases, a situation epitomized by working within a "caseload"; and finally, the situation in which a current case is treated as part of an organizationally relevant sequence, a situation that is most striking where initial cases are regarded as precedent for the treatment of subsequent cases.

Relativity in Judgment in Social Control Work

In a variety of social control settings, assessments of the "seriousness" of particular cases (on whatever organizationally relevant dimensions) tend to be made in relation to the kinds of cases regularly encountered in that particular setting. Thus, the decision to treat a case as an instance of something serious depends in part on the overall range and character of the case set processed by the agent or agency.

Consider, for example, Freidson's (1970: 257) summary of a 1934 study (reported in Bakwin, 1945) examining doctors' judgments on the advisability of tonsillectomy operations for 1,000 school children. Of these 1,000 children, 611 had already had their tonsils removed. The remaining 389 were then examined by other physicians; 174 were selected for tonsillectomy and 215 adjudged not to need the operation. Then: "Another group of doctors was put to work examining these 215 children, and 99 of them were adjudged in need of tonsillectomy. Still another group of doctors was then employed to examine the remaining children, and nearly one-half were recommended for operation." Freidson concludes: "Since it is very unlikely that each group of physicians would overlook the severity of signs in fully one-fourth of the cases it saw, it seems more plausible to conclude that each used a sliding scale of severity rather than an absolute criterion" (1970: 257).

Freidson's suggestion of a "sliding scale of severity" implies that diagnostic assessment of any particular case is made relative to other cases actually under examination—in this instance, relative to the specific set of cases presented to particular doctors for tonsillectomy diagnosis. Additional evidence of such a "sliding scale of severity" is provided by experimental research on the "relativity of judgment." Parducci (1968: 84), for example, reports the following experiment conducted in a large undergraduate class:

Each student was asked to rate the moral value of different acts of behavior in terms of his "own personal set of values." His task was to assign each act to one of five categories: "1— not particularly bad or wrong," "2 — undesirable, a good person would not do this," "3 — wrong, highly questionable," "4 — seriously wrong," and "5 — extremely evil." Half of the students were given a list made up mainly of relatively mild acts of wrongdoing; the other half got a nastier list, consisting principally of acts that could be counted on to evoke strong disapproval. The crucial feature of the experiment was that, embedded among the other items, each list contained six items that were common to both.

Despite instructions to "judge each act just as though it were the only one you were judging," students' evaluations were made relative to the context created by the different lists: "The six acts appearing in both lists were rated more leniently by students who judged them in the context of the nasty list than they were by those who encountered them in the context of relatively mild wrongdoing" (1968: 87).

Such findings suggest that the makeup or shape of the total collection of cases processed by an agency provides a contextual gestalt relative to which particular diagnostic assessments will be made. This gestalt can assume different qualities under different organizational circumstances. At one extreme, a discrete and bounded *set* or *panel* of cases might provide the larger whole relative to which particular judgments are made. At the other extreme, discriminations between cases may be made relative to the gestalt created by a continuing flow of cases through a particular agency. Here one might speak not of a panel of cases but of a *case stream*, a stream whose characteristics (kinds of cases, relative frequency of each kind) provide a background against which assessments of a particular case are made. Cases on hand at any one time are assessed by reference to what is "normal" and expected in that stream. Such streams tend to be more open and less bounded than relatively fixed case sets. Workers in criminal courts, for example, usually deal with a continuing flow of cases rather than with fixed sets of cases (except in the immediate short term) and come to hold a variety of locally specific expectations about the "normal" character and overall distribution of particular kinds of cases within this stream (Sudnow, 1965). Again, the character or makeup of this stream provides a gestalt against which determinations of seriousness are made.

Where there are significant differences in the case sets of two agencies, we can expect the agencies to define seriousness differently. Hence, the same kind of case may be evaluated differently in the different settings. Sanders (1977: 95), for example, observed the following variation between two organizational units within an urban police department.

[I]n the context of the cases a detective or detail typically received...what was considered a "big case" for one detective was a "little case" for another.

For instance, the Major Crimes Detail received all reports of battery. As compared with the other crimes the detail investigated, batteries were "little" and therefore were rarely investigated. On the other hand, if the Juvenile Detail received a battery case, it was treated as fairly important in the context of the usual crimes they received, such as petty theft or malicious mischief.

Foote (1972: 29) points to a similar phenomenon in comparing the concerns of the criminal courts in sentencing defendants to prison with those of the Adult Authority in fixing actual time served under then prevalent indeterminant sentencing policies:

Courts...are dealing with the felon whom they are about to send to prison in the context of a population most of which is not going to prison at all, thus a population in which the less serious offenders predominate. The administrative sentencing board operating within a prison, however, draws its cases from a population in which it is the most serious offenders who predominate. As sentence-fixings are comparative ratings— e.g.,"this guy's not as bad as the others we've seen this morning"—the company a man is keeping when he comes up for disposition may be just as important a determinant of his fate as his own individual characteristics.

If different agencies classify similar cases in different ways because of their case sets, the transfer of cases from one agency to another can become highly problematic. The juvenile court, for example, often identifies as essentially "good kids" youths who seem to be serious delinquents to agencies with different and less troubled case sets (see Emerson, 1969: 71–72, 84). Similar differences may be at work in the referral of parolees to various sorts of special programs. McCleary found, for example, that social welfare agencies registered formal complaints about parole officers "who send 'bad risks' or 'inappropriate profiles' to the program" (1975: 233). Parole officers termed such agency selectivity "cherry picking," assuming that the goal was to obtain "better" cases and hence to inflate agency "success rates." But this sort of interorganizational conflict might also result from the way that perceptions of the likelihood of successful outcomes with parole cases are rooted in the distinctive case sets of parole workers and welfare agencies.

The internal deliberations of even a single agency may reflect and try to anticipate these sorts of interorganizational variations in case evaluation. Consider, for example, a judge's reflections on how to treat a delinquent who had committed what was thought to be a very serious offense.

During a staff conference on a 16-year-old youth charged with a shooting and armed robbery, the judge discussed several sentencing alternatives, including trial as an adult (with sentencing to State Prison a likely outcome), commitment to the Youth Correction Authority, and commitment to Stillbrook, a special maximum security institution for juveniles. Stillbrook, he noted, had a policy of discharging inmates at the age of 17 and getting them off parole quickly so that if caught again they would not be sent back to them. So if the youth were sent there he would probably be discharged after one year and discharged from parole two weeks later. In fact, juvenile murderers averaged only two years there. And, if the boy were sent to the Youth Authority, he would soon be "back on us." Armed robbery, though a serious offense, is not something the YCA is not used to. Once in an institution the fact that the armed robbery involved guns and masks would be lost sight of, and become simple armed robbery, which was routinely discharged after a brief stay. Similarly at Stillbrook: "If he's not a murderer or acting out, he can get out of Stillbrook." I could send him there, but if I did, "it's 10 to 1 if he doesn't commit mayhem he will be back on the street in 11 months" (when he turns 17). "If he were a murderer we'd get a lot more attention."[1]

Here the judge's deliberations over the most appropriate disposition explicitly take into account "known" differences in assessments of seriousness, differences stemming in part from the fact that these correctional institutions deal with case sets containing high concentrations of serious offenders.

Even greater complexities can arise in the movement of cases between agencies. For just as different case sets can produce varying assessments of case seriousness, so too can the distinctive sets of sanctions or "normal remedies" (Emerson, 1981) employed in two settings produce perceived differences in the seriousness of similar sanctions. A strict punishment in one agency may be regarded as a slap on the wrist in another, depending upon how the particular sanction compares to the range of remedies routinely employed at each agency. This relativity of sanction severity to organizational context has an interesting implication. Both the "advantage" which accrues to those whose cases appear minor in the context of a setting dominated by more serious cases and the "disadvantage" visited on those whose cases appear serious against a backdrop of trivial offenses may be reversed at the sanctioning stage. For what appears to be a minor sanction to an agency used to meting out harsh sanctions to relatively serious offenses may, in fact, be more stringent than the most serious sentences that an agency used to dealing with trivial cases would consider.

Consider what Foote (1972) tells us about those few marijuana offenders who were sent to prison in California and so fell under the jurisdiction of the Adult Authority. The judges who sent them to prison believed that in giving prison time for marijuana offenses they had sentenced severely, and they often recommended release after the minimum time served. "The perspective of the Adult Authority, however, is one of dealing with a population in which most prisoners serve at least thirty months...a parole after eighteen months, for example, is giving the inmate a break even though the minimum may be six or twelve months" (1972: 29). Foote concludes that such an offender "is prejudiced by being thrown into the Adult Authority's pot, for they rate his penalty not against those imposed on his peers in crime but against their own average dispositions" (1972: 29–30). Thus, a case which one decision-maker believes to be serious may, for that reason, be channeled to another decision-maker, who, because of a very different case set, regards the matter as minor. The second decision-maker, applying what for him is a minor sanction, may in fact select a more severe penalty than the first would have considered appropriate.

The contour of the case set against which judgments of seriousness are made is largely a product of the frequency with which different kinds of cases within it are encountered and handled. The greater the absolute frequency with which a particular kind of case is encountered, the more familiar, typified, and routinized it becomes for those processing such cases. Thus, the frequency with which specific kinds of cases and events are encountered lies at the heart of the socialization experience in a variety of settings (Hughes, 1971).

In medical hospitals, for example, death is a frequent event, and medical novices can provide specific counts of the number of deaths they have witnessed (Sudnow, 1967: 36–42). Yet such "frequently occurring events are counted only for a short time, among newcomers," and as the worker comes to witness a growing number (no specific counts were provided higher than eight), the question "How many have you seen?" will be answered by something on the order of "[S]o many I've lost count" (1967: 35–36). As Sudnow emphasizes, how the number of deaths witnessed is reported both reflects and expresses the worker's experience. Such changes involve evaluative components as well. What is countable is also remarkable and memorable and hence consequential to the person providing the count in ways that do not hold for the worker who has seen "a thousand cases like that."

In general, then, the frequently encountered case or event, even if acknowledged to be inherently serious, loses some of its aura of seriousness as "other cases like it" are encountered over time. Workers tend to accumulate knowledge and expectations of the typical attributes of such cases, classifying them into known categories of "normal cases" (Sudnow, 1965). As a class of case becomes typified, it is treated in more routine ways. "Seriousness" becomes routinized, institutionalized, built into the typification, as it were, rather than standing as an experiential feature of the case for the worker.

Heumann's (1978) research on the socialization of criminal court personnel provides several excellent examples of these processes. Heumann notes a "propensity for the new prosecutor or state's attorney to be 'outraged' by the facts of a case" that the experienced attorney would appraise as routine (and not particularly serious) and hence as appropriately plea bargained to some standard reduction (1978: 98). Not surprisingly, new prosecutors noted that they had frequently felt "way out of step" with the standard recommendations of their more experienced co-workers (1978: 99).

> I evaluated a case by what I felt a proper recommendation should be, and my recommendations were almost always in terms of a longer time. I found that the other guys in the office were breaking things down more than I expected. As a citizen, I couldn't be too complacent about an old lady getting knocked down, stuff like that. I thought more time should be recommended. I might think five to ten, six to twelve, while the other guys felt that three to seven was enough.

As the prosecutors became integrated into local office culture, familiar with its procedures, and accustomed to the shape of their caseloads, they came to see and treat offenses that had earlier struck them as "outrageous" in more neutral, routine, and "lenient" ways.

The tendency to routinize cases is to some extent offset by another factor that differentiates the cognitive sets of the novice and the experienced worker. As experience with a given kind of case accumulates, the worker increasingly notes and emphasizes specific subcategories of cases within the general category. Thus, an agency dealing regularly with homicides not only becomes "familiar" with, hardened to, and less affected by such cases but also makes finer, more varied distinctions between types of homicides. This distinction, between a small number of serious "murders" and more numerous and routine "killings," is evident among urban police detectives regularly encountering homicides (Waegel, 1981: 270).

> [A barroom homicide] was termed a "killing" and viewed as a routine case because the victim and the perpetrator were previously acquainted and information linking the perpetrator to the crime could be easily obtained. The term "murder" is reserved for those homicides which do not correspond to a typical pattern.

In these circumstances, where killings make up the routine and regular work of detectives, not just any killing, but only some killings, are seen as serious.

This analysis suggests that changes in the makeup of a case set will produce changes in the processing of specific categories of cases relative to that case set. In general, we may expect that if an institution no longer encounters its previously most serious cases, it will "upgrade" those cases that had been regarded as only somewhat serious. And if it no longer receives what were once its most trivial cases, cases previously seen as somewhat serious will come to be regarded as less consequential. To suggest a specific application: If a juvenile court loses jurisdiction over its previously most serious offenses through more automatic transfer to the adult system what were previously regarded as only marginally serious cases will be regarded with more concern.

To this point the analysis has focused on contextual factors that affect judgments of "seriousness." But the categorization of cases as serious or not is only one aspect of the broader process of decision-making; it is but a step toward implementing a particular decision outcome and as such is part of, but analytically distinct from, the wider process of actually treating or disposing of cases. Categorizations must be implemented under conditions that lead to less than perfect correlations between how cases are seen and the treatment they ultimately receive.

Thus, we must expand our analysis from the more limited cognitive assessments of seriousness to the broader processes of actually responding to cases that have been assessed in such ways; that is, from the question of how a case is classified to that of what is done about it. In doing so, we are led to appreciate the pervasive relevance of *resource availability* for such decision outcomes. For the constraints created by limited resources, notably the need to allocate what is available among cases, can fundamentally affect how particular cases are treated. For example, suppose that serious felonies were withdrawn from the jurisdiction of a juvenile court. The court staff might well come to perceive more severe responses to some previously less serious cases as appropriate, but the change in jurisdiction may have brought with it the withdrawal of organizational resources (e.g., probation staff needed to carry out more intensive supervision, access to special treatment programs) needed to implement more stringent dispositions. Similarly, if reformatory bed space declined while certain kinds of cases were being upgraded in perceived seriousness, the resources needed to treat such cases in the desired, more severe way, would not exist.

Resource Allocation Problems

Issues of resource allocation, although seldom explicit, are critical in the categorization processes discussed in the prior section. For categorizing cases as serious or not so serious is fundamentally *practical* in character and impetus. It is done not for its own sake but *in order to act*; hence, recognized categories both reflect the options available in a particular setting and facilitate choice among options. In this respect, categorization decisions are inherently tied to decisions allocating resources among cases. For example, in street-level bureaucracies, a whole variety of resources, including time and energy, "are chronically inadequate relative to tasks workers are asked to perform" (Lipsky, 1980: 27). As a result, workers unofficially divide their caseloads into active and inactive categories, allocating more resources to the former and as few as possible to the latter. There is, then, an implicit allocation of scarce resources built into any such system of classification. Case types both determine the amount and kind of resources received and are products of the organization's sense that it should provide different kinds of treatment to different kinds of cases.

McCleary's (1978) analysis of parole work in Chicago provides a concrete illustration. He found that while parole agents had large caseloads, most cases received little attention.

> Well, that's how many men I've got on paper. Actually I've only got a dozen men that I worry about. I spend a lot of time with my men the first week they're out of the joint. If they look like they're doing okay, I don't bother them any more. I only see most of my men two or three times a year. But they're still on paper. (1978: 127)

In contrast to such "paper men," the parole agent devotes a great deal of time and energy to two types of cases. First, there are "the few dangerous men [who] are watched closely and returned to prison at the first opportunity" (1978: 126). Second, there are those parolees, termed "sincere" by parole agents, who are willing to be counseled and thus assume the role of "client." The parole officer's relationship with this latter group typically includes frequent, informal, and often "supportive" interaction.

Resource problems are implicated in this set of parole categories in several ways. These types provide workers with preexisting formulas for allocating time and other resources among cases. Paper men require minimal time, while dangerous men and sincere clients merit closer attention. At the same time, the categorization of cases reflects the established pattern of resource distribution within the agency. The category "sincere client," for example, reflects standing organizational practices on just how much time and effort can be devoted to apparently deserving cases. Thus, parole officers come to identify "sincere clients" within the first week or two of contact through the investment of a realistically limited amount of time and effort. Were more resources available for initial contacts, parole officers might classify more parolees as sincere. With more time, for example, the parole officer might work actively to break through to initially resistant and hostile parolees and so "convert" into sincere clients those who would otherwise have become paper men.

To generalize, changes in the resources available to process and treat cases, as well as changes in the number of cases to be handled, will transform the categorization and handling of cases. This can happen in several ways. First, where cases may be roughly ordered on a scale that runs from the more to the less attention worthy, if resources increase, the cutoff point between those cases that are attention worthy and those that are not will tend to move down, and so the ratio of active to inactive cases will increase. Second, the substantive treatment of cases, however categorized, will be transformed. Consider cases that are attention worthy. Such cases will attract attention by definition, but the amount and quality of the attention they draw will vary with the resources that the agency has available. For example, a sincere client in a parole office where workers handle 300 cases each might be seen twice a month in office interviews, while a similar client whose officer in charge has only 30 cases might be seen for weekly counseling sessions as well as in the course of home and job visits. "Inactive" cases might not be seen at all where caseloads are high, but they might be seen at least once a month where caseloads are low. Again context is important. When some cases are the subject of weekly attention, those that are seen only monthly might be considered inactive. Thus, the substantive meaning and implications of similarly perceived categories will vary across settings so as to reflect the availability and distribution of resources.

From the worker's perspective the availability of resources is often a "given." The agency, more than the individual, determines the kind and quantity of resources that will be available. The worker, however, may play a critical role in determining how available resources are actually deployed among particular cases. The scope for worker influence is greatest where workers have responsibility for a *caseload*.

Caseloads involve a relatively fixed collection of cases for which a particular worker is organizationally responsible. They are key units in the routine organization of social control work. In working with a caseload, the worker knows at any point in time not only the number of cases s/he is responsible for but also (at least in principle) the specific cases that are involved. Cases can be added (usually on the basis of some established principle, such as geographical assignment or type of case, or with the aim of equalizing caseload size among workers; see Zimmerman, 1970) and lost, but workers can nonetheless organize their work routines around some collection of cases of relatively known parameters. Furthermore, cases in a caseload tend to be dealt with on a long-term, continuing basis rather than in one relatively brief encounter. As a result, the worker will have cases at different stages in the decision-making process, and the workday will be organized around the need to perform various organizational tasks on a succession of cases that have been seen before and will be seen again. Social workers (sometimes called "caseworkers") and probation and parole officers are prime examples of those whose work is often organized around caseloads.

A critical process in social control decision-making is how to allocate resources among the particular cases that make up a larger whole. While different resources may be at issue in different settings, allocation of the following are especially important in handling caseloads: the amount of *time* that a worker can make available; the amount of energy and *commitment* to be invested in particular cases; and the variety *of special options* that might be employed. Caseloads, in general, accentuate problems of allocation since what is done in one case has implications for what can be done in others. In distributing time, commitment, special options, and other organizational resources, a worker has to decide any instant case with an eye toward what that decision implies for other cases.

These sorts of allocative decisions are analytically distinct from those involved in categorizing cases. The problem is not to decide whether this is a serious case (and implicitly, whether this case needs active handling) but is the more pragmatic one of whether active treatment in this case is desirable given the demands of other cases within the caseload. The distinction between the abstract problem of categorization and the more immediate problem of what to do with a case given competing demands results in *caseload-specific effects*. One such effect is the decision to treat inactively cases that the worker recognizes "should be" treated actively. To reiterate Lipsky's argument (1980: 36):

> Inactive cases are often not truly inactive but represent cases to which the street-level bureaucrat is unable to attend in the ordinary course of the day. They are regarded as low priority for reasons having little to do with the client but a lot to do with the pressures on the workers.

Under these circumstances, the worker comes to treat the instant case with less attention than s/he recognizes it "really" deserves because other cases are seen as even more pressing or deserving. In this respect, caseload-specific effects are not indicated simply by the fact that some cases are treated inactively, or even by high ratios of inactive to active cases. What is critical is not the distinction between active and inactive cases but the fact that such distinctions are made "by necessity" (Lipsky, 1980: 36) rather than on the basis of what in general is considered appropriate for cases of that particular type. When a worker allocates little or no time to a case that in the worker's opinion "needs," "deserves," or "should receive" active treatment, and this is because the case appears less pressing, serious, or otherwise demanding of attention than others in that caseload, caseload-specific effects are evident.

Several implications flow from this analysis. To begin with, the identification of distinctive caseload effects presupposes a prior determination that some cases within the caseload need or deserve attention and others do not. Caseload effects arise in parole work, for example, only when resource pressures prevent a parole officer from giving sufficient time to parolees seen as "sincere" or "dangerous." Thus, the identification of caseload effects in parole work requires both the typification of cases as "sincere" or "dangerous" and the recognition that such cases are not getting the active treatment they need or demand.

Furthermore, the number of cases in a caseload (caseload size) is not the sole and need not be the major factor producing caseload-specific effects. If no case is thought to require more than minimal handling, for example, caseload-specific effects would not arise. Of course, the relationship between caseload size and available resources may, as I have already noted, play a critical role in shaping largely taken-for-granted understandings about the appropriate treatment for cases of given types.

Such an argument underlies several recent analyses, which hold that large caseloads are not the fundamental factor behind high rates of plea bargaining in the criminal justice system (Feeley, 1979; Heumann, 1978). It is not the number of cases but the substantive character of those cases (as understood by attorneys and judges in typified, organizationally relevant terms) that generates and sustains proclivities to plea bargain. For plea bargaining is a mechanism for obtaining "mutually satisfactory outcomes" or "fair dispositions" (Heumann, 1978: 116). What is seen as "satisfactory" or "fair" depends upon attorney assessments of the "worth of the case" (Feeley, 1979: 158–77), which in turn involves consideration of the seriousness of the offense, the nature of the offender, the strength of evidence, and a variety of other factors. Thus, plea discussions often focus on such factors as attorneys try to reach an agreement on what constitutes a fair bargain (Maynard, 1982). Caseload effects arise only when the actual disposition of a case does not accord with this constructed sense of its "worth," an outcome that might result, for example, from the need to process a large number of cases through the system quickly. Seen in this light, plea bargaining is not directly dependent upon the size of caseload, a fact often emphasized by court personnel. Heumann (1978: 116) quotes one prosecutor as saying, "If there were only ten cases down for one day, it still would be something that would be done."

Finally, caseload effects of this sort are member *accounts* (Garfinkel, 1967), in that decision-makers themselves often identify how the overall demands of managing a caseload lead to the "inappropriate" treatment of specific cases. As an example, consider what one parole officer told McCleary about parole revocation decisions.

> In the long run, you can't have too many or too few returns. You usually don't have to worry about having too few because there's a natural recidivism built into your caseload. Usually you have to worry about too many returns. Sometimes you have to take it easy. You have to ignore things you don't really want to ignore.

In noting that he has "to ignore things you don't really want to ignore," the parole officer tells us specifically how his prior decisions to revoke parolees now affect his decisions in current cases. Through such statements, agents formulate the conditions relevant to making some current decision—in this case, the organizational injunction not to revoke "too many" cases — conditions thereby signaled as "necessitating" a disposition at odds with the "most appropriate" or "ideal" disposition.

When an agent talks of caseload effects, his/her account may serve several important purposes. First, it tells others that the agent recognizes the discrepancy between what "ought to be done" in a case like this and what s/he is actually doing, or what has been done. The agent thereby acknowledges the overriding legitimacy of the organizational goals, at the very moment of seeming to violate their specific terms (Zimmerman, 1970; Emerson & Pollner, 1976). Second, by showing how "caseload pressures" have necessitated the "inappropriate" disposition of a particular case, the agent provides a "good reason" for the action that has been taken and hence establishes its rational character. Finally, such accounts may serve more conventional political purposes. Rosett and Cressey (1976: 111), for example, argue that while courthouse personnel frequently tie plea bargaining in general to high caseloads, in fact "attributing negotiated pleas to overwork is a political explanation of court practice." It obscures these workers' assessments of substantive justice which underlie plea bargaining processes, highlighting instead politically more expedient "causes" of the problem (see also Feeley, 1979: 269–70).

Partial Caseload Effects

It is easy to depict working with a caseload as a highly ordered and systematic process in which workers orient their total caseloads in some sustained, rational way. Yet as Studt (1972:50–51) emphasizes:

> the [parole] agents in our samples gave minimal attention to the systematic analysis of and planning for individual cases, and almost none to the examination of their total caseloads in terms of types of needs represented. Instead, most agents' work revealed an ad hoc, reactive approach to problem solving....

In general, it appears that workers rarely attend to their total caseloads in their decision-making activities. Typically, they orient themselves to segments of their total caseloads, as these segments become relevant to some immediate organizational task.

Thus, in weighing how the decision in a given case will affect other decisions, agents typically consider not all other decisions (i.e., their total caseload) but only those that are more directly implicated in the immediate situation at hand. Consider, for example, the process of parole revocation and return to prison. Prus and Stratton (1976: 51, 53) found that parole agents felt constrained by a loose, informal quota system.

> These agents are not concerned with the difficulty of revoking someone at this point [e.g., the uncertainty of success, the "costs" in terms of time, energy, paperwork, conflict, etc.], but they are concerned over what another revocation will do to their image within the organization.... Agents felt that those who counted in the organization, lacking other criteria, tended to evaluate on the basis of their revocation rates. There was the feeling among the agents that those agents who revoked over 10 per cent of their cases were suspected of not performing their jobs adequately.

Thus, for parole agents, particular decisions are conditioned by the emerging overall pattern of decision-making within their caseload as a whole (see also McCleary, 1977: 579). Yet the whole caseload is not rationally and systematically reviewed with an eye toward identifying the most problematic 10 percent for revocation. Rather, decisions are made one at a time, but with a sense of the implications that past decisions have for current ones and current ones for the future. Here a holistic effect derives from the anticipated effects of some next revocation decision given a series of prior decisions. This means that holistic concerns arise only episodically, on occasions when "sufficient" revocations have already been made or are seen as likely in the near future.

The point at which such concerns arise is significantly shaped by agency policies. If the agency evaluates its workers periodically and then wipes the slate clean, as may occur when statistics are reported on an annual basis, workers may be relatively unconstrained by past performances at the start of a "statistical" year but may grow more so as the year progresses. This is most obvious when an agency has an annual budget, which does not allow for any carryover to the subsequent fiscal year. Decision-making late in the fiscal year may lead to what, by the agents' own accounts, is inappropriate underspending or overspending, depending on the pattern of spending to that point.

Caseload effects are based on partial rather than total caseloads where impending decisions are conditioned by only a subset of cases. Hence, at different times within the same organization, different decisions will make relevant or "occasion" (Zimmerman & Pollner, 1970) partial caseloads composed of very different collections of cases. For example, a decision regarding possible revocation of parole will be made with a very different set of cases in mind than a decision about which of several parolees should receive an opening in a drug treatment program. Furthermore, partial caseload effects can influence those whose work is not organized within fixed, bounded caseloads. For partial caseload effects can arise in any situation in which a particular collection of cases competes for the same local, limited resources. A patrolman on skid row, for example, confronting half a dozen inebriated men on the street but having room for only a few in the patrol car, will have to decide whom to arrest and whom to let go or handle in some other way (Bittner, 1967). The group of six becomes a partial caseload for purposes of this immediate decision. More generally, partial caseload effects occur whenever a decision in one case is tied to or has implications for the treatment of a set of other cases, which are conceived of as a set precisely because of the way they relate to the first decision.

The highly situational or occasioned character of partial caseload effects is dramatically illustrated by processes of plea bargaining in which ongoing exchanges between attorneys generate groups of cases whose dispositions become mutually dependent. The so-called "package deal" between defense and prosecution attorneys provides a flagrant instance. As Cole (1970: 340) reports:

> In this situation, an attorney's clients are treated as a group; the outcome of the bargaining is often an agreement whereby reduced charges will be

achieved for some, in exchange for the unspoken assent by the lawyer that the prosecutor may proceed as he desires with the other cases.

Feeley (1979: 192–95) suggests that such blatant package deals are relatively rare but that standard plea bargaining procedures involve a subtle "process of exchange which weights actions in one case against actions in others" (1979: 192). In general, Feeley emphasizes that courtroom negotiations involve a "subtle equilibrium ... maintained by a give-and-take not only within but between cases" (1979: 193). References to how what has been done in some cases is relevant to what is to be done in a current one, for example, permeate attorney interchange (1979: 192–93).

> This process becomes most apparent when a prosecutor and defense attorney sit down to negotiate several cases at one time. After they have discussed a few, the prosecutor might say rhetorically, "Jesus, I've already given you three nolles today, do you want me to go out of business?" Or, he might urge, "That judge is tough; I can't give you anv more nolles today." Conversely, the prosecutor might hear a defense attorney plead, "You've put me through the wringer this morning; give me a break on this one!"

Note that in such instances attorneys explicitly invoke the treatment accorded prior cases as a lever for negotiating the outcome of the current one. Indeed, the standard overture, "do me a favor," may well be "punctuated with a reminder of a particularly favorable or unfavorable treatment in an earlier case" (1979: 193). The issue of who owes whom, therefore, may turn on just which cases are to be counted as relevant to the current decision, and this in turn can be a matter of explicit negotiation. To the request to "do me a favor," for example,

> a prosecutor might retort, "Christ, I gave you the moon on the _____ case; I can't do it here too. The guy has got to do some time in jail." Or a defense attorney might press, "You've been screwing me all week. Give me a break for the weekend." (1979: 193)

Not only are striking partial caseload effects produced in these instances, but these effects are the product of situationally specific negotiations over just which prior cases should be taken into account in achieving some momentary equilibrium or balance.

As in the case of total caseload effects, partial caseload effects can arise when workers confront problems of allocating resources differentially among a group of competing cases. The allocation problem may appear to a decision-maker in several different forms, each giving the process a somewhat different shape and character.

One characteristic situation approximates the economic model of marginal decision-making in which problems of allocation become acute only after the point at which resources become scarce and competitive. Thus, cases arising early in a case stream may be given or denied resources solely on the basis of assessed "need." But as the resource is used up, each next (marginal) decision becomes increasingly competitive with other actual or anticipated cases. The process of managing rates of parole revocation, discussed earlier, provides a substantive illustration. A parole agent may seek revocation rather freely, that is, without explicit reference to other cases or to total caseload, until the 10 percent quota is approached. At that point, each next possible revocation must compete with other possible or anticipated revocations. Mental hospital admissions and bed space may be similarly related. When the hospital census is much below 100 percent, there is little need to compare patients who seek admission. The need arises and caseload effects become apparent when virtually all beds are filled (see Mendel & Rapport, 1973: 202–3).

Under other circumstances allocation problems may be constant and acute. Here the worker from the very start confronts a situation of scarcity, and resource competition influences every decision. The allocation of desired placements for delinquent youths often has this quality. Juvenile courts typically have access to only a few "beds" or openings in desirable treatment programs, yet they have a large number of strong, needy candidates for such positions (Bortner, 1982: 82ff.). Under these conditions, candidate cases are not evaluated individually on the basis of need. Instead, cases are extremely competitive with one another, and actual placements involve the conscious choice of one case over others. These caseload effects are only partial, however, since only some delinquents are candidates for placement, and only some of these are candidates for placement in the same type of facility.

Such allocation problems, whether they assume a more marginal or a more constant form, become particularly pressing in the distribution of what can be termed "special commitments" among some subset of exceptional or deserving cases. A special commitment entails doing more than is usually and routinely done in a particular case. This extra effort often involves support for a more favorable (especially, more "lenient") outcome than the actual circumstances appear to warrant. Exceptional commitments of this sort are a limited resource that must be selectively employed. Workers must orient their decisions to the way that others, particularly their organizational superiors, assess their recommended departures from the normal handling of such cases. Under these circumstances, decisions as to how to allocate special commitments inevitably affect and implicate the workers' reputations as competent organizational members.

For example, psychiatrists in juvenile court clinics feel they cannot recommend probation for every delinquent on the verge of incarceration since, when some of these youths again get in trouble (a statistical inevitability), the psychiatrist who, by organizational standards, has been overly lenient is to some extent discredited in the eyes of the judge and other court staff (Emerson, 1969: chap. 9). S/he not only loses standing on that particular case but can also anticipate that future recommendations will receive greater scrutiny from the court (ibid.: 265). This does not mean that recommending a disposition that is more lenient than normal is not an available option. It is, but it must be done sparingly, because to generate a pattern of cases that disproportionately involve lenient decisions leads others to question one's judgment. So, cases compete. If there are two or three in which leniency seems a viable option, the psychiatrist cannot go to bat for all of them without considerable risk. The inevitable failure rate means that credibility may be irretrievably lost (see also Daniels, 1970). In court psychiatry, as in parole work, we see the tendency noted by McCleary (1978: 94): The agent "routinely underrepresents some clients and overrepresents others."

Cases may also be underrepresented or overrepresented where processes of exchange and equilibrium are involved because of the strategic demands of the exchange. For example, consider the following comments by a parole officer on his good working relations with the prosecutor (McCleary, 1978: 92–93).

> You know why Auslander likes me? Because every so often I help him burn one of my men. It's usually a case where I can't help the man anyway but Auslander doesn't know that. Then the next time I ask him to give one of my men a break, he thinks he owes me a favor.

Presumably in this case, the parole officer "gives away" a case that is hopeless anyway, thereby creating a situation where he has a debt to collect when he wants to give someone a "break."

Since strategic caseload effects are the products of negotiated exchanges, they vary with the resources available to the parties to the negotiation. Where parole agents control resources of interest to prosecutors—for example, information obtained from "tips" by "snitches" (McCleary, 1975: 219)—they can obligate prosecutors without making case concessions. Hence, caseload effects are stronger when exchange resources are limited to the relative treatment of cases held in common. Package deals epitomize this tendency, as here the treatment of other cases is for each attorney the only available concession.

Sequence and Precedent

I would now like to consider one final sort of holistic effect. Under a variety of organizational circumstances, the place in which a particular case occurs in a known sequence of cases has critical implications for the treatment and handling of that case apart from the issues of resource allocation that I discuss above. Control agents orient to some organizationally derived order that renders the sequence of cases a highly salient feature of the disposition of particular cases.

There are a wide variety of organizationally relevant orders that render the sequential placement of any particular case consequential. In this section I want to analyze two circumstances in which sequential order affects how workers treat cases. The first involves constraints posed by quotas, and the second arises from concern with precedent.

The prior discussion has suggested that decisions subject to quotas are likely to produce distinctive caseload effects. But such decisions also exhibit the sequence-oriented concerns currently at issue. Explicit (if unofficial) ticket quotas are familiar to the traffic cop (e.g., Skolnick, 1966; Rubinstein, 1973). Peterson (1971) describes a jurisdiction where officers felt they had to issue between 40 and 50 citations a month in order to satisfy superiors. In practice this rate was so low that officers routinely had "to find ways to limit their rate" (1971: 358). Most officers tried to pace their citations "to be sure that their performance shows a uniformity throughout the reporting period," hence operationalizing the monthly quota as a daily one (1971: 358–59).

> To meet what they regard as a duty shift quota some officers may patrol for six or seven hours of an eight hour tour without stopping any cars or issuing any citations, and then proceed to locations where they know violations occur regularly. Then they will write two or three quick tickets and call it a day. In the same way, other officers will write several tickets soon after they come on duty, then coast for the remainder of the tour.

Depending upon an officer's preferences, then, cases encountered at the beginning or at the end of a shift may receive dispositions reflecting the relationship between their position and the demands of the quota.

Acute problems can arise, however, as the end of the longer quota period nears. On the one hand, the officer may be short and so try to meet the quota with a rush of citations. On the other hand, the officer may find he has accumulated citations too quickly and so change his orientation to potential offenses. Peterson quotes one officer. "I've written a lot of citations this month, so now a guy would have to run over me to get a ticket" (1971: 358).

In this quota system, the officers' orientation to particular decisions as they fit into the unfolding quota order is not visible to motorists affected by their decisions. In other organizational circumstances (often not involving quotas), the sequential order may be visible and relevant to both the decision-maker and those affected by decisions. This occurs, for example, when the precedential value of cases handled as part of a sequential order is important. It appears in its most striking form in lower level criminal and traffic courts.

The handling and outcome of the "first case" heard during a session can be very influential for subsequent cases. As a number of studies have shown, defendants whose cases are heard later in the sequence learn from observing earlier cases.

Brickey and Milier (1975: 692), noting that the physical setting of the court they studied "allowed everyone in the situation to hear and see the interaction between the judge and the defendants," found that the incidence of guilty and not guilty pleas within any particular session correlated strongly with the plea resulting from the interaction with the judge in the first case heard in that session. Where the first defendant offered a guilty plea, most of those pleading subsequently in the same session did likewise; and when the first defendant pleaded not guilty, a disproportionate number of the later cases followed suit. The influence of the initial plea is nicely revealed in the following comments (1975: 693).

> Mr. L: I was thinking about pleading guilty but I figured if they [the defendants who pleaded not guilty prior to his case] could get off, I might as well try it.

> Mr. T: Well, the woman pleaded not guilty to speeding and her excuse isn't any better than mine. Maybe there's a chance I can save some money.

Pollner's analysis of the "self-explicating features" of traffic courts extends and deepens these observations. For Pollner notes not only that "defendants monitor and analyze preceding transactions and use them as grounds and guides for further action and inference" (1979: 239) but also that judges are very much aware that defendants are doing so and through "case management work" seek to control the sorts of inferences and actions defendants might come to. Judges were especially concerned with the ways in which their treatment of early cases could provide later defendants with precedents to use in their own cases. Pollner quotes a handbook for traffic court judges, which suggests that the first case be handled with special care "in order that it may serve as an example for all subsequent cases" (ibid.: 240). Some judges do just this.

> One judge took some pain to review pending cases prior to the beginning of a session, selecting certain serious violations such as speeding in excess of 85 or 90 miles an hour. He would then begin the session with one or two cases, which seemed likely candidates for a jail sentence or a substantial fine, and intersperse other serious offenses over the course of the session. In this manner, the judge felt that it was possible to display the fact that highly discriminative activity was taking place, or, in the words of the judge, that "the good men were being separated from the bad." (ibid.)

In this instance the judge deliberately structures the sequence of cases to achieve desired consequences within the session. Where such advance ordering is not carried out, the judge must deal with the precedential implications of first decisions in other ways. Here he may come to dispose of first cases more strictly than later cases with an eye toward session precedent, giving rise to what can be termed "sequential effects." As Pollner reports (1979: 240–41):

> The judge also noted the dysfunctional effects of giving reduced fines and dismissals at the outset of a session. In sessions where time or circumstances did not permit the a priori ordering of cases (or simply as a supplement to that procedure), the judge imposed standard bail schedule fines (at least) to most cases at the beginning of a session. The disposition of early cases, the judge felt, furnished yet-to-be-arraigned defendants with a baseline with which to gauge the extent to which he had discriminated among explanations. Insofar as defendants were led to believe that everyone received, say, a five dollar reduction, the judge felt that he was denied a valuable resource for revealing to defendants that their case had received special and individual treatment.

Sequential effects also appear when subsequent cases are decided so as to preserve precedents established by earlier cases. For example:

> In Small City I, a young man was the defendant in the first traffic arraignment of the morning. His case was dismissed because of "lack of evidence." The judge felt compelled to dismiss several subsequent cases which he implied would not have been dismissed had the first defendant not been so young. Subsequent defendants were considerably older and by appearance more substantial members of the community. (Pollner, 1979: 243)

Here later cases receive the response that they do because of the judge's commitment to preserving an appearance of consistency.

It should be apparent that the strength of such sequential effects will vary depending upon a variety of structural and situational factors. Such effects presuppose, for example, that decisions are rendered before an attentive audience and, where proceedings are intended to instruct future litigants, before an audience composed specifically of those whose cases will be heard subsequently in that session. Where those subject to such decisions are segregated from one another, as in juvenile court proceedings, establishing precedent is of little concern because future litigants cannot be instructed by what occurs in earlier cases, and they are unlikely to know enough to hold the decision-maker to what was done on earlier occasions. Moreover, to the extent that an audience can be prevented from effectively monitoring the processing of ongoing cases, sequential effects will be weakened. This frequently occurs in felony and misdemeanor courts, where a variety of factors (e.g., the codified and technical nature of much of the talk, whispered conferences between judge and attorneys at the bench, etc.) inhibit full, effective monitoring. In addition, concern with sequence and precedent requires that the same kind of cases be processed. To the extent that cases differ substantially (or can effectively be made to so appear), sequential effects will be diminished. Finally, the constraints resulting from managing precedent decline as cases are completed and the audience witnessing the session dwindles. This fact provides traffic court judges with a way of reducing or eliminating entirely the precedential import of first decisions for subsequent ones:

> In Small City II, a defendant asked the judge for additional time to pay the fine which had just been imposed. The judge, who was sensitized to court costs incurred by the paperwork of a great number of similar requests, was generally reluctant to give any extensions, particularly in public. Though the judge felt that this woman's request had some merit, a concession in public would have meant that he might be besieged by similar requests in the future. After stating that he did not give time, he had the woman sit until the end of the session, at which time she was granted an extension.
>
> In Small City II, a judge, rather than dismiss a case in public, would request that a defendant whose case the judge felt warranted a dismissal be seated so that he—the judge—could "think about it." Near the end of the session, he recalled the defendant and dismissed the case. (Pollner, 1979: 243)

When a decision-maker is unable to make use of this natural mechanism for segregating decisions, or conversely, is unable to arrange that appropriate cases are heard as "first cases," sequential effects will be more evident.

Sequential effects are also maximized in situations where creating the appearance of consistency has special benefits for the organization. Pollner emphasizes, for example, that traffic court judges had very compelling "practical interests" for appearing to follow precedent strictly. For judges sought to maximize the speed of hearings and minimize court costs—goals directly furthered by sustaining the appearance of strict consistency. Such goals were also indirectly supported by such procedures. To the extent that defendants felt that the dispositions of their cases were like those given others, and hence consistent and perhaps even just, they would spend less time raising objections, presenting excuses, and the like. In sum, judges sought to avoid furnishing "a precedent which if invoked by subsequent defendants would greatly increase the length of a session or commit the judge to a course of action which would increase court costs and paper work" (ibid.: 25). Under other circumstances practical interests in cost containment and efficient case processing might not lead to pressures for consistent decision-making. Where the power to impose ad hoc decisions is clear, efforts to shape one decision in the light of past decisions or future cases may not be necessary to the organization's smooth functioning.

Conclusion

The analysis of social control decision-making has in recent years been moving away from the highly atomistic imagery that underlies much research in the area. Waegel (1981: 264), for example, has recently criticized the "individualistic conception" of discretionary decision-making that assumes "one person legal units making decisions." Rather, Waegel argues, such decisions are deeply collective products, reflecting and constrained by the local work culture, notably by "the shared categorization schemes used by members in organizing their day-to-day activities" (1981: 264). In this paper I sought to identify the limitations of a different sort of individualizing assumption common to social control research, the assumption that the individual case invariably provides the sole or the most salient unit for organizing decision-making work and hence for studying that work. Pursuing a phenomenologically oriented understanding of social control work, I have explored a variety of ways in which decisions regarding particular cases reflect, or are embedded in, wider organizational projects and orderings that derive from a variety of highly local, very practical work concerns.

Notes

1. These materials are taken from unpublished field notes compiled as part of the juvenile court research reported in Emerson (1969; 1974).

DISCUSSION QUESTIONS

1. Can you think of other examples of situations where particular decisions are shaped by associated decisions? Is this like "grading on a curve"? Rate-busting by fellow workers? Do you have a "caseload"? Does it influence the way you treat individual "cases"? Can you give other instances where the first of a series of events is treated differently?

2. In what situations does the reference frame for decision-making change? To what extent is routinization of processing related to "professionalization" of officials?

3. How is the scarcity of resources discussed here related to that which contributed to plea bargaining, as described by Alschuler? How do you deal with scarcities of time and energy? What qualitative factors influence the "weight" of a caseload (beyond absolute numbers)? Under what

circumstances are caseloads used as methods for evaluating productivity? Can you give instances of variation in decision-making from the beginning to the end of a statistical accounting period? When is it inappropriate to aggregate individual cases?

4. When do decision-makers offer exceptional treatment? What are the consequences for future decisions? Can you give other examples of the negotiation between decision-makers, in which favors are given and debts created? Have you encountered decision-makers who operate according to a quota? Do you ever do so? Have you observed instances in which the first in a sequence of decisions acts as a precedent for those that follow? Are the pressures for uniformity peculiar to legal decision-making? How do decision-makers under such pressure reconcile exceptions with uniformity?

9

Mandatory Sentencing and the Abolition of Plea Bargaining: The Michigan Felony Firearm Statute

Milton Heumann and Colin Loftin

Introduction

Two features of the American criminal justice system most often criticized are unbridled prosecutorial and judicial discretion. Prosecutors engage in a wide variety of plea bargaining practices unencumbered by appellate court constraints, or any other formal control for that matter. Judges similarly have a wide range of sentencing options for any particular defendant or charge. Frequently, sentencing possibilities range from a suspended sentence or probation to a lengthy prison term or even life imprisonment.

Critics of plea bargaining and indeterminate sentencing are quick to point out the shortcomings of the present system. On the one hand it is argued that undue leniency results from prosecutorial and judicial eagerness to grant concessions to the defendant who pleads; on the other hand, defendants who do not plead or who are "singled out" by the prosecutor or judge are subject, almost whimsically, to harsh treatment. What emerges, in the critic's eyes, is a system of wide disparities in charging and sentencing similarly situated individuals, a system that has lost sight of its goals in its eagerness to dispose of cases.

In this context, two reform proposals are currently fashionable. One calls for the abolition of plea bargaining for all crimes (National Advisory Commission, 1973: 41–49; *Iowa Law Review,* 1975) or for some subset of particularly violent or serious offenses (see Church, 1976). The second urges the introduction of mandatory minimum sentences, again either generally or for certain crimes. Though these proposals, and variants on them, are justified in ways that differ depending on the advocate's ideology, the common theme is that discretion in the criminal justice system must and can be reduced.

The literature is not barren of admonitions, often supported by research, about the consequences of attempting these innovations. Several scholars have predicted

---

Abridged from *Law & Society Review*, Volume 13:393 (1979).

that mandatory sentences would simply enhance the prosecutor's plea bargaining powers.

> While the judge can no longer select from a wide variety of sanctions after conviction, the prosecutor's powers to select charges and to plea-bargain remain. (Zimring, 1977: 111)

> In the future, mandatory sentences or sentencing guidelines for judges probably won't decrease the overall discretion of judges and disparities of treatment that is [sic] experienced in trial courts. Instead, prosecutorial discretion will probably increase to provide the kind of substantive justice more difficult for the trial judge to give. (Sarat, 1978: 326)

> The parts of the criminal justice system are so interdependent that benefits gained by altering one aspect of the system can quickly produce costs in another. If, for example, sentencing discretion is limited, prosecuting discretion will probably be enhanced. It is by no means clear that the latter is preferable to the former. Efforts to effect planned change in the criminal justice system often flounder on such displacement effects. (Horowitz, 1977: 232; see also Levin, 1977: 187; Wilson, 1975: 179)

Similarly, studies suggest that when an attempt is made to proscribe prosecutorial plea bargaining, judges take up the slack and either implicitly or explicitly become involved in sentence negotiations. For example, Thomas Church (1976: 399) examined one such attempt and concluded:

> When the prosecutor stopped making the most prevalent form of concession to drug sale defendants—a reduced charge—the pressures to grant considerations in exchange for pleas moved to the judge. Those judges prepared to make sentence concessions to defendants had little trouble securing pleas.

In short, mandatory sentences reduce judicial discretion but are handled by an increase in prosecutorial discretion; plea bargaining proscriptions reduce prosecutorial discretion but are handled by an increase in judicial discretion. Plug up the system at one point and analogous processes seem to emerge at another.

The question that concerns us in this paper is what happens if both reforms are introduced simultaneously, if mandatory sentences are coupled with a policy that forbids plea bargaining? Are the defendants left no option but to go to trial in every case? Does the system collapse under the sheer weight of these restrictions? Or, does the system adapt, does it somehow work things out so that the status quo is not dramatically altered, in spite of the seemingly major innovations? A new statute in

Michigan and a Prosecutor's decision relating to its implementation in Detroit afforded us the opportunity to explore these questions.

The Michigan Felony Firearm Statute

The Michigan Felony Firearm Statute (hereinafter referred to as the Gun Law) went into effect on January 1, 1977. It mandates a two-year prison sentence in addition to the sentence for the primary felony for any defendant who possesses a firearm while engaging in a felony. This consecutive sentence cannot be suspended nor can an individual be paroled while serving it.

Most state action designed to reduce the illegal use of firearms also restricts legitimate use and thus tends to polarize the public and provoke conflict between organized political interests. Because the Gun Law is intended to reduce the illegal use of firearms without imposing additional costs on those who use them legally, it elicited less political opposition. Though questions can be raised about the assumptions concerning deterrence on which the law is based, there is little question about its political popularity. Prior to its passage and since implementation a wide variety of political interests have supported it, including groups such as the National Rifle Association and the United Auto Workers/Community Action Program, which, in the past, have disagreed with each other over the appropriate policies for reducing firearm violence.

The Michigan law differs from the widely publicized Bartley-Fox Law in Massachusetts, which imposes a one-year mandatory sentence upon anyone convicted of carrying a firearm in violation of the state's firearm laws. In Michigan, the Gun Law does not apply to offenses such as carrying a concealed weapon or illegal possession of a firearm since these are considered to be included in the offense of "carrying or possessing a firearm at the time of committing or attempting to commit a felony." Thus the conduct to which the law applies is more serious but also more diverse: any felony in which the defendant used or possessed a firearm.

The law itself does not impose any restrictions on prosecutorial plea bargaining. A prosecutor is free to decide whether to charge the Gun Law and, if he does, to drop it subsequently in the interests of justice. Nothing in the law precludes the shifting of discretion from the judge to the prosecutor and, as we have seen, this is a common prediction of precisely what will happen when mandatory sentencing is imposed.

However, in Wayne County (Detroit and its environs), the Prosecutor publicly announced that his office would not engage in any plea bargaining in cases in which the Gun Law applied.

Leave the gun at home if you set out to commit a felony after December 31, or count on at least two years in prison if you're caught and convicted. There

> will be no plea bargaining under a new law, no probation, and
> no parole. *(Detroit News,* December 1, 1976: 3A)

In addition to these media proclamations a widespread publicity campaign about the new law was mounted, replete with billboards and bumper stickers proclaiming: "One with Gun Will Get You Two."

The Prosecutor's intraoffice behavior was quite consistent with his public posture. Shortly before the law went into effect, the following memo outlining the procedures to be followed in gun cases was sent to all assistant prosecutors working in the Wayne County Prosecutor's Office.

> 1. At the warrant stage, the Prosecutor will recommend warrants under the statute if the elements of said statute are present. This will be a second count in the charging documents, inasmuch as the underlying felony or attempt to commit a felony will also be charged. Said count will be charged even in those cases wherein a man is charged with possession of heroin and is found to possess a firearm at the same time.
>
> In those cases wherein more than one defendant is arrested on the underlying felony, if there is any evidence that the co-defendants in said felony had knowledge that the possessor of the firearm had same, they will also be charged in the second count of possession of firearms in the course of a felony on the aider and abettor theory.
>
> If there is no evidence that the other co-defendant knew of the gun; i.e., the gun was in the pocket of one defendant at all times, was never displayed nor were there conversations concerning same, the other defendants will not be charged with the second count of possession of a firearm.
>
> 2. At the pretrial, no reduced plea will be accepted on the count of possession of a firearm during the commission or attempt to commit a felony. Pretrial prosecutors should exercise care, however, so that the underlying felony or attempt to commit a felony is not reduced to a crime which would not support the second count. (Intraoffice Memorandum, Dec. 20,1976)

The Prosecutor appeared determined to cast the net of the Gun Law as widely as possible at the warranting stage and to stand firm on the charge once warranted. No room for exceptions was left in the memo or in public pronouncements. An unwavering proscription against plea bargaining was to be followed with the expectation that "every one who commits one with a gun" now would "do two."

The Prosecutor's Policy: Rhetoric or Reality?

We have seen that the Wayne County Prosecutor adopted a firm public and intraoffice policy with regard to the Gun Law. In some jurisdictions, this sort of prosecutorial policy would be greeted with great skepticism by those familiar with the criminal justice system. Typically, assistant prosecutors have wide latitude: as professionals, they are free to make judgments about the strength of the case and the reasonableness of a negotiated disposition (see Heumann, 1978: 99–114). One would expect them to resist constraints on their discretion, and perhaps even suspect that the Prosecutor's posture was more a rhetorical display than an attempt to secure compliance.

However, long before passage of the Gun Law, the Wayne County Prosecutor had taken steps to bureaucratize the disposition process and had instituted policies for certain cases (see Eisenstein & Jacob, 1977: 151–54; Nimmer & Krauthaus, 1977: 10–11). The office was divided into warranting, pretrial, trial, and appellate divisions, and specific guidelines also structured their operation. In short, the probability of compliance with the ban on plea bargaining in Gun Law offenses was higher in Detroit than it would be in other large jurisdictions that are frequently unaccustomed to stringent organizational constraints.

Nonetheless, we cannot assume automatic compliance with the directive. Given the size of the Prosecutor's staff (approximately 110 assistant prosecutors), the volume of business handled annually (approximately 13,000 felony warrants), and the impossibility of constant supervision, it is still possible that the policy was circumvented in practice. There are several points at which assistant prosecutors could undercut the Prosecutor's policy. They could refuse to authorize a warrant if they felt the equities did not justify a two-year penalty or could authorize only a misdemeanor, not a felony, warrant. Similarly, they could ignore the firearm and simply warrant on the primary felony. During the preliminary examination and at subsequent hearings prosecutors could silently acquiesce in a judge's dismissal of the charge. Finally, during the pretrial conference, the assistant prosecutors have the same options as the warranting prosecutors: to drop the gun count, reduce the felony to a misdemeanor, or drop the whole case.

The interview and quantitative data lend qualified support to a conclusion that in fact the Prosecutor was successful in obtaining the compliance of his subordinates. Consider, for example, the comments of a defense attorney who initially feared that the prosecutors would use the Gun Law as a plea bargaining tool only to learn that it was being used in what he viewed as an even more dangerous way—not as a plea bargaining tool.

> Well, I was involved in ... an attempt to stop the law from being passed in the sense of any law that has mandatory minimums.... There wasn't too much of a lobby to stop the law, but our main concern working in Recorder's Court was that it was simply gonna be used as a plea bargaining tool. And that simply they would add that count and when it came time to plea bargain, they would knock that count out.

Q. That comports exactly with my expectations.

That was my understanding of what happened in Florida, and, it hasn't happened in Wayne County. My understanding is that just about in every case, if there's a gun, they're charging it ... even some ridiculous circumstances. We had a case ... where the person was robbed. Thought it was a gun. They caught the people around there, a few blocks away, I don't know, it was a half an hour later or something, and found a toy gun on them. The prosecutor still brought the charge because the prosecutor claimed: "Well, they could have used a real gun which they got rid of."

Other defense attorneys echoed these views, frequently pointing to extreme situations in which the law was charged and subsequent prosecutorial unwillingness to reduce the felony or trade off the Gun Law charge.

[B]asically what they've done over there in Recorder's Court is the Prosecutor's office has adopted a very rigid policy. They charge people with the Gun Law, it seems like they charge it every time they possibly could, whenever there's a gun, they charge felony firearm. And they never drop it as part of pleading, no matter what the circumstances are, who the client is and what kind of equities there are ... so [they are charging it] for first offenders who ordinarily would be absolutely a candidate for probation, and somebody like that comes with a felony firearm and they've got nowhere to move, and it doesn't make sense to send someone like that to jail for two years.... Or a F.A. [felonious assault] when it's not necessarily a serious crime involved, but if there's a gun used, then that's it. And that person's options are gone ... I mean, sometimes, you'll have an individual prosecutor in the courtroom, the courtroom prosecutor who doesn't want to try the case. They may not want to try the case at all. But the policy comes from upstairs and they're helpless to do anything about it.

I have a motion in now on a case where the prosecutor would have recommended a high misdemeanor, but he can't recommend it, since they're applying the felony firearm all over the place.... It's ludicrous.

Most of the assistant prosecutors we interviewed agreed with the general goals of the Gun Law and the Prosecutor's support of it but objected to his rigid policy. Their comments and sense of frustration about their inability to make exceptions in particular cases provide further evidence of the "successful" implementation of the policy.

For a long time I absolutely wanted them [mandatory minimum sentences] on every single offense. I now have some reservations about that. I'll tell you what's happened, the experience with the Gun Law. I mean if this were a wise office, if every prosecutor's office were a wise office, I would absolutely believe in mandatory minimums for everybody and I would allow discretion to be in the prosecutor to take out those 5% of the cases where it shouldn't be charged, and it wouldn't be charged. But [this office] has drawn lines, and we rigidly impose them. As a result I see judges put in incredible pressure situations.

I personally disagree with the office policy of across-the-board recommending felony firearm where warranted by the investigation of the police. There are many cases of equity, certainly, where we should be permitted to exercise our discretion whether or not we recommend it. Because I think you could easily imagine all sorts of domestic and neighborhood squabbles, we have people with otherwise perfect criminal records, who might technically commit a felony while he possessed or used a firearm. Certainly equity indicates that the felony and felony firearm should not be taken in. I don't like to be boxed in to that type of across-the-board policy. But I don't make the policy.... See, my feeling is I'm a prosecutor and if I'm allowed to exercise my discretion then we have a perfect system. Now I'm confident that I can properly exercise my discretion. I'm confident and I know, generally speaking, that the office is confident that the greater majority of these people could exercise their discretion. I think I should be permitted to. But, I can't in the face of office policies. I'm boxed in. What many of us would want is to be able to do so and so, and be held accountable for it. Certainly I'm not going to give the store away.

This grudging willingness to abide by the Prosecutor's policy was not simply a result of institutional loyalty. The Prosecutor ordered his administrative staff to keep close tabs on all cases in which the felony firearm charge was dropped and to monitor carefully all plea bargaining by assistant prosecutors of such charges. When deviations from the policy were uncovered, they were quickly called to the attention of supervisory personnel.

In fact I think we had two or three blow-up type cases that came to our attention very shortly after the statute was enacted, where judges on their own motions did it [dismissed felony firearm], and we ordered transcripts of those cases, just to find out how the prosecutor responded. And in one of those cases a very experienced trial attorney, who was scheduled for a much more responsible job in this office, did not object. We have reason to believe after looking at the transcript, that in fact, he and the judge had worked it out

192 Heumann and Loftin

sort of in chambers, and then the judge had gone out and reduced an assault with intent to do great bodily harm to an aggravated assault [a high misdemeanor] and as a result let the felony firearm go. And, I mean, what happened is the influence, or shall we say the stock of that trial assistant went measurably down, and I think people generally on the staff knew about it. It was not publicized as such, but there was grousing.

I have discretion on most cases but not on the ones with felony firearm. Take the _____ case, a FA [felonious assault] and a gun charge. I reduced it to simple assault after speaking to the cop, and he said "O.K." The defendant had just raised a gun at the cops. Well, higher up in the office the case blew up and....

Assistant prosecutors might be more immune from administrative monitoring at the warranting stage. Though the office policy calls for warranting the gun charge whenever dictated by the facts, a warrant prosecutor's decision not to authorize the charge or to authorize only a misdemeanor would never get into the system and thus would be less likely to blow up at a later stage. Our quantitative data do not allow us to measure decisions not to warrant because our case sampling, using the PROMIS system, assumed warranting and began tracing cases at that point. Interviews, however, suggested some slippage at this stage, though the consensus seemed to be that exceptions were relatively infrequent and made only in borderline cases.

As far as I can determine they've been charging it any time they can. You get uttering and publishing [bad checks] with the felony firearm, possession of heroin and felony firearm. The only time I've seen it not charged was, I had a case of a security guard who used a club against a guy. Of course, he also had a gun on him. The prosecutor knew that if the gun was charged that it might lead to an appeal, and he didn't want that kind of case making appellate law, so they didn't charge it.

Well, I think if there were a large number which were not being warranted, I think the police department would scream, because they, of course, have some interest in protecting their interest in a case. And I'm sure that we'd get some indication from them.... I know that there is some disagreement among the assistants [prosecutors] to the policy but I think for the most part, it is being adhered to. Since I usually see the ones that probably shouldn't have been charged, or at least borderline cases, they come up the pipeline for a decision as to whether we should change the policy or deviate from it in a given case. Generally we do not. I cannot think of one where we have allowed it.

Though the warranting prosecutors themselves maintained that they adhered to the policy in the overwhelming majority of cases and, indeed, accorded it the widest possible interpretation in unusual situations, they conceded that they might take an extra hard look at the facts in a small number of cases to determine if the gun charge could be avoided.

> Oh, you know, there are going to be cases where I'm going to be disinclined to do it [charge the Gun Law]. But then I see as my only, you know, as a practical matter my recourse then is to take an extra close look at the felony aspects of it, okay, now that's the only way that I see right now that I have discretion in the area of the firearm statute.

> In other words, insofar as our office is concerned, I will confess to you that there are times where I wouldn't want to recommend that particular second count because I feel that the equities and the ends of justice would be satisfied if that second count wasn't employed, and it's too harsh and too severe of a thing. However, our local individual policy is that we don't have any discretion in that area and that we must recommend that second count.... But let me say this to you, that where the equities come into play, I will search like hell to find a legal impediment which thereby permits me to deny the recommendation of the warrant. I may stretch it, okay? And most of the times you'll find that even the police officers are most compatible and cooperative in that area unless they're new and naive and just so narrow-minded that they can't see, but an experienced man, they pretty much get the feel of it. But mind you, we are talking about an isolated case, and I've already told you the rationale for the strictness of the policy in general.

It is impossible for us to gauge the number of cases in which the gun charge could have been warranted but was not. Nevertheless we can examine all armed robberies, felonious assaults, and other assaults prosecuted after January 1, 1977, and disposed by June 30, 1977, to determine whether the Gun Law was in fact charged in the warranted cases whenever it could have been, judged by information coded from the police reports. It is plain that in the overwhelming majority of cases the prosecutor did indeed charge the gun count. Furthermore, we have reexamined the cases in which it was not charged and no clear pattern of evasion appears.

In sum, with the exception of cases not warranted or warranted as misdemeanors and the handful of cases in which a felony was warranted but the gun count was not, it appears that the Prosecutor succeeded in proscribing plea bargaining by his subordinates. They "stuck to their guns," and defendants faced a mandatory two-year sentence in addition to their sentence on the primary felony. The following section examines the impact, if any, of the two innovations on the eventual disposition of felonious assaults, other assaults, and armed robberies.

Firearm Offenses: 1976 Versus 1977

The questions that we explore here are whether the Gun Law together with the Prosecutor's policy have increased the certainty of sentences delivered by the court and whether the increase in the severity of sentences is approximately two years. We will be examining only a subset of the cases we will eventually want to evaluate in estimating the impact of the law. Our analysis relies on two major comparative dimensions: (1) the type of offense, and (2) whether it was committed before or after the law went into effect. We compare three major felonies—armed robbery, felonious assault, and other assaults—in which the defendant or a co-defendant possessed a gun while committing the offense. Therefore, when we refer to robbery or assault in subsequent discussion, we will always be referring to those gun robberies or gun assaults unless we explicitly state otherwise.

In designating cases as representing one of these three offense types we ignore some of the complexities of the cases. We have used the following conventions to create the offense categories by abstracting what seems to be a reasonable set of common elements:

1. a case was designated an "armed robbery" if the defendant was arraigned on such a charge and there was no charge of murder or criminal sexual conduct;
2. a case was designated as a "felonious assault" if the defendant was arraigned on such a charge and there was no charge of another type of assault, armed robbery, criminal sexual conduct, or murder.
3. a case was designated as an "other assault" if the defendant was arraigned on a charge of assault with intent to commit murder, assault with intent to do great bodily harm, or assault with intent to commit armed robbery and there was no charge of murder, criminal sexual conduct, or armed robbery.

The category of offense in all subsequent discussions refers to original charge and not the charge on which the defendant was convicted.

The second major comparative dimension is the time period during which the offense was committed. In this paper we examine only the twelve-month period bracketing the intervention of the Gun Law—six months before and six months after January 1, 1977. We have divided all the cases in the sample into two time groups: Segment One consists of cases committed any time before January 1, 1977 and disposed of by the court during the twelve-month period; Segment Two consists of cases that were both committed and disposed of during the last six months of the study period.

Although there are many reasons why the first six months under the law might be atypical, most derive from the process of organizational adjustment to the law and are of substantive interest to us. They pose a problem to the interpretation of our data only in the sense that the behavior of the court may change over time. One possible difference between Segment One and Segment Two is problematic for the interpretation of our data because it derives from a constraint on Segment Two cases that is not shared by those in Segment One. Offenses in Segment Two must have been committed and disposed of by the court in the same six-month period. No such time constraint exists for Segment One cases; they could have been disposed of any time during the twelve-month study period and committed at any time prior to January 1, 1977. A consequence of this is that Segment Two cases, on the average, spend less time in the system. Other consequences of the difference in the sampling process are unknown. In the analysis that follows we will compare Segment One cases with Segment Two cases and interpret the difference as an effect of the Gun Law. This procedure will provide reasonable estimates if the segments are not systematically different with respect to factors that influence sentencing other than the law or variables associated with it. Because of the possible selectivity of cases in Segment Two, this assumption is made warily, and our conclusions remain subject to revision when cases that move through the system more slowly have been examined.

Since we are interested in the impact of the law on both the certainty and severity of punishment, we include cases in which the charges were dismissed or the defendant acquitted as well as those in which the defendant was convicted. This is a decision of some importance, which requires justification. The concept we want to measure is the expected value of the sanction. Such a concept clearly includes the probability of conviction as well as the severity of the sentence. Let us look at armed robberies, the prototype offense for the Gun Law. The typical armed robbery involves a predatory offense by a young male who uses a gun to threaten a victim and take property. It is the most frequent of the felony gun offenses that we examined and consumes more judicial resources than any other. If the sentences for armed robbery did not change as a consequence of the Gun Law, it would be fair to conclude that the law failed to achieve its explicit objectives.

More than a third of the armed robbery defendants processed by the court received no prison sentence at all in both segments and, though there is some variation between the segments in the components of this general disposition, there is little net change. The total who "walked" (received no prison time) in Segment One was 36 percent. In Segment Two, the proportion of armed robbery cases dismissed at or before the pretrial conference increased by 9 percentage points so that, despite a slight decrease in the other two categories, the proportion of the defendants who received no prison sentence went up slightly to 41 percent.

Since it is the increase in cases dismissed at or before pretrial conference that explains the decline in the probability of incarceration, it might be reasonable to attribute it to the disproportionate number of dismissals among cases that move through the system quickly. However, this interpretation loses some credibility because such a pattern is lacking in felonious assaults and is actually reversed in armed robberies committed without a gun.

Among the armed robbery defendants who are imprisoned there is a slight increase in the proportion of cases in which the sentence is five years or more but no dramatic increase in the proportion of sentences equalling or exceeding the two-year minimum. The strongest statement that can be made is that for every 100 robbery cases, an average of seven defendants who would have received a two- to five-year sentence in Segment One now receive a sentence of five years or more. We could increase this figure to 18 if we limited our comparison to defendants who were convicted, but this would ignore dismissals, and it is unlikely that these are ignored by potential offenders.

Of the offenses that we consider, felonious assault is furthest from the model Gun Law offense in terms of the characteristics of the offender and the crime. Although the presence of a gun certainly qualifies all of them as serious, many of these cases grow out of disputes among acquaintances or relatives and are, by conventional standards, less predatory than armed robberies and other assaults. This is reflected in the fact that the vast majority of convicted defendants do not receive time (more than 80 percent in both segments). Although the number of cases in Segment Two is small (only 39), it seems clear that there is little difference between the two segments in the proportion of defendants who receive no time. In particular, Segment Two does not display an increase in the proportion of the cases dismissed before the pretrial conference. There is an increase in the proportion of defendants who receive sentences of two years or more, which clearly seems to be an effect of the Gun Law, but again it is small. For every 100 defendants charged with felonious assault an average of 9 received a sentence of two years or more in Segment Two who would have received a less severe sentence in Segment One. If we keep in mind that all of these cases involved possession of a gun, it is evident that the law had not had much of an impact on the sentencing of felonious assault cases at the end of the first six months.

The category of other assaults occupies an intermediate position between armed robbery and felonious assault with respect to seriousness, which is reflected in the length of sentences and the proportion of cases dismissed. Dismissals at or before the pretrial conference increase, but this is offset by a decrease in convicted defendants who receive no prison sentence, so that the total proportion of defendants who "walk" is virtually the same in both segments. The number of cases in this category is somewhat larger than for felonious assaults, but it is still small enough (N=53 in Segment Two) to suggest caution. The proportion of defendants who receive a sentence of two years or more increased from 22 percent to 33 percent, the largest increase among the three offenses; an average of 11 defendants per hundred who would have received a lighter sentence in Segment One received a sentence of two years or more in Segment Two. Yet it is certainly not the dramatic increase in certainty and severity of punishment that some might have hoped for.

We expected the minimum mandatory sentence law and the ban on plea bargaining to have an impact on the process of case disposition as well as the outcome. One consequence that might be anticipated is a reduction in the proportion of defendants who plead guilty. The fact that cases in Segment Two have, on average, spent less time in the system probably results in an underestimate of the proportion of cases tried since these will generally take longer to complete. Such a bias probably explains why there are small reductions in the proportions of armed robberies and other assaults tried. Nevertheless, the proportion of trials for felonious assaults rose substantially.

If we distinguish between jury trials and bench trials we obtain a more detailed view of these changes. In felonious assaults and other assaults, but not armed robberies, the proportion of cases disposed of by bench trials is greater in Segment Two. In felonious assaults, but not other assaults and armed robberies, the proportion of jury trials was also greater in Segment Two. All of these trends stand in marked contrast to the uniform decrease in the proportion of trials in those felonious assaults, armed robberies, and other assaults that did not involve the use of a gun.

One possible reason for this apparent adjustment in the proportion of trials for assaults becomes evident when one asks what the relationship is between the mode of disposition (bench trial, jury trial, or no trial) and the severity of sentence. The data suggest that trials are associated with relatively light sanctions. Of the 68 assaults (felonious and other) in Segment Two, only 2 out of the 23 defendants tried received the mandatory sentence of two years or more, whereas 20 out of the 45 defendants whose cases were disposed of without a trial received that sentence.

In sum, the experience with cases completed during the six months after the intervention of the Gun Law indicates that there has been only a slight upward shift in the average sentence. Clearly there has been no massive increase in the number of cases that receive a sentence of two years or more. Furthermore, the only increase in the proportion of cases that go to trial is in felonious assaults, and these trials are associated with light sentences.

The System's Adaptive Posture: How to Manage Mandatory Sentences

Our review of the comparative disposition data was necessarily couched in very tentative language; as we have cautioned repeatedly there are several sources of bias in the Segment Two sample that make us reluctant to offer any definitive conclusions about the effects of the Gun Law on the distribution of outcomes. Nonetheless, the interview data suggest several dominant responses of the system to the double innovation, which are important to consider because they explain the outcomes of some of the cases we examined and indicate the capacity of the system to cope with reductions in discretion. These adaptive mechanisms are not unique to Detroit but can be expected wherever similar policy innovations are introduced.

Constitutional Challenges and the Question of Legislative Intent

It is beyond the scope of this paper to review systematically the lengthy list of constitutional issues and questions of legislative intent that have been raised about the Gun Law. But it is important to stress that the ambiguity of the law, coupled with the broad interpretation adopted by the prosecutor, led defense attorneys to make numerous claims of "unconstitutionality" and misapplication. Judges, passing upon such motions, could dismiss the gun count as unconstitutional or inappropriate, thus providing a "loophole" in the application of the Gun Law. Though their dismissals could be appealed (and the prosecutor's policy was to appeal them), the short-run effect was partially to undermine the law. Presumably, once the uncertainties are resolved, judicial flexibility in this area will be more narrowly circumscribed.

Waiver (Bench) Trials

If constitutional challenges and questions about legislative intent yielded some short-run relief from the reduction in discretion, waiver trials represent a more permanent mechanism for modifying the law. The waiver, or bench, trial is simply a "trial" in which the defendant waives his right to a jury and elects to go to "trial" before a judge alone. The judge's verdict (unlike his decision on a legal motion) is not readily attacked on appeal.

The waiver trial was employed, and will continue to be, to avoid the mandatory two-year sentence in cases where the judge felt that the "equities" did not warrant it. Such "trials" are attractive to the judge because he retains control over the fact finding process and because they do not entail a substantial expenditure of judicial time.

Q. A jury trial would take, on that case, a day or two?

A. A day, if you move the people.

Q. And a plea of guilty?

A. Fifteen minutes.

Q. And a waiver trial?

A. Half an hour. They won't make any opening arguments, both sides waive opening arguments, examination of witnesses is very brief, no tricks are done because there's no jury there. The whole thing just goes in rapidly and half the time they don't make any closing arguments ... and there's no time spent for jury selection which at a minimum takes an hour and a half or two hours. Every time you start with a jury you're talking about the better part of a morning or an afternoon to pick a jury.

Several types of waiver trial are employed in handling Gun Law cases. In one, the judge is alleged to give the defense attorney, prior to the trial, some explicit indication about the disposition of the gun charge. The following comments are illustrative (the first two are from prosecutors, the third from a defense attorney).

You get a lot of waiver trials. Not a whole lot, but you get a significant, I think, number of waiver trials, wherein, it's just one of those walk-through numbers—the judge finds the defendant is not guilty of the principal felony, in fact, he's guilty of a misdemeanor and since he becomes guilty of a misdemeanor, a felony firearm is naturally dismissed and the guy gets, you know, sixty days in the House [Detroit House of Corrections] or whatever. But it's just another way of subverting.... And it's a waiver, too, understand. I mean, it's all arranged really between the judge and the defense attorney beforehand.

Q. If a judge dismisses the gun count you'll appeal?

A. Right, if he dismisses before trial.

Q. But, if he takes it to trial on waiver...

A. And finds the guy not guilty on the gun charge?

Q. Right. I mean, is that a big thing for defense attorneys, a waiver?

A. No, in what terms?

Q. I mean in terms of preparation and...

A. Not if he knows in advance. First of all they're not going to take that kind of a chance without some kind of communication with the judge. But if he's gone to the judge, I mean what would happen if I were to draw a model of that case it would be as follows: the defense attorney would go to [the trial prosecutor] at pretrial and try to get him to dismiss the felony firearm charge. [The trial prosecutor] would say no, can't do it. Okay, go to the pretrial judge. The judge would put pressure on his trial prosecutor to dismiss the felony firearm. The trial prosecutor would say I can't do it. Then there would be a private communication between the defense attorney and the judge, waive the jury, I'll find the guy guilty of A and B [assault and battery], that will be a misdemeanor, the felony firearm charge drops by the wayside.

A. Waiver trials, that's the way he beat it [Gun Law]. The judge doesn't have to give a reason when he dismisses it, and the prosecutor can't appeal. I go talk to him and tell him it's a ridiculous case. I'll talk to the judge.

Q. With the prosecutor present?

A. I'll talk to the judge anytime. Fuck the prosecutor.

A second form of waiver trial is less explicit. In this model the defense attorney does not, or cannot, obtain explicit assurances from the judge but, based on the judge's prior sentencing behavior, he expects that the judge will deal reasonably with the gun charge or the underlying felony. He knows, for example, that the judge will be strongly disinclined to convict and impose the mandatory minimum sentence when the equities favor the defendant.

In quote equity type situations, [when there is a] a felony firearm [and] they waive the jury, the judges know what the story is. I mean sometimes they make an agreement beforehand. Hey listen, you waive the jury, I won't find them guilty of the F.A., or I won't find him guilty of the firearm but I won't make any promises as to what I'm gonna do with the felony. Or sometimes they just say "take your chances, you know, but I in particular think that the Gun Law shouldn't apply in this type of case, but you can do what you want."

Well, [the decision to opt for waiver trial] it's either something the defense attorney has spoken to the court about, they've gone out to lunch or something, and the defense attorney speaks to the court, and they have an understanding, or it's just an educated risk that the defense attorney evaluates the court, evaluates the case, and just hopes that it's one of those cases where he has the equities, where he's ready to gamble on the judge.

I got a case which is in front of [a judge]. The complainant, he lives upstairs, he and my client have been having words, my client he, he's taking out the garbage one night, and my guy, according to the complainant's testimony, takes a gun out of his back pocket, puts it at his side, never points at him, says, "Come on down here, I'll deal with you, you mother fucker." Now they charged F.A. off that. I think it's a questionable F.A. But they charged the gun. And the pretrial division is telling me this case, they'll take this case to trial. Now if that would have been assault and battery and I would have, because of my client's record, probably would have pled him to assault and battery. But you know, ninety days, and I'm sure he wouldn't have done any time. You know, but I can't do anything. If we take this case to trial, I mean, can you imagine wanting to put some guy in prison for two years on a case like that?

Q. What are you going to do with it?

A. I'm not sure.... I mean, it does make me think a little about waiving a jury. I mean there's definitely an effect that I know it's had on everybody here with a decent judge. I mean usually with a decent judge you still have, I mean you've got to have a good reason to waive a jury here because juries are good. And I think we do good jobs in front of juries. But that might be a good reason, you know, the chance, just the chance [of two years]. So you know, that is really one of the things we're coming up against.

We do not mean to suggest that waiver trials invariably provide a definite out for defense attorneys and their clients. Not all judges will make explicit prior agreements nor can all judges be counted on to work something out during the waiver trial. Some judges may view the two-year sentence as inappropriate in a particular case but believe that they cannot ignore the statute when a defendant is technically culpable. They are torn between their obligation to the law and their desire to individualize justice. These judges concede that they would consider every possible defense and require strong evidence of every element of the charge such as the presence of an operable firearm; but when the case is technically there, they feel trapped by the law and left with no option but to apply it. In the following excerpt a judge, who told us that he had not yet sentenced anyone to two years in an equity type of case because, during waiver trials, he had managed to find justifiable reasons to lower the felony or dismiss the gun charge, then speculated on the dilemma if no such reasons had been available.

It would've put me in a very difficult position and I guess what I'm saying is that one of the reasons I don't like it is that we all recognize as judges that we have to make accommodations that I regard as corrupted, I find that a very uncomfortable position to be in, one I don't want to be in. I know there are judges who will take waiver trials on felony firearms and find the person not guilty on the felony firearm even though the evidence is present of the felony firearm and I just will not be in that position. So I guess my answer to your question is, fortunately I haven't been in that position yet, I've always been able to find a way that comports with my sense of law. But my real point is, that like every other prosecutorial policy there should be discretion used and to the extent it's not used, it's bad, it has bad effects throughout the system, and has bad effects on the bench, has bad effects on individual prosecutors because they can't exercise their own discretion. And everybody is involved in a kind of conspiracy to undermine it without getting caught.

These comments indicate that some judges find limits in the use they can make of the waiver trial as a means to mitigate the inflexible policy. It may be these limits that explain the increase in jury trials for felonious assaults during Segment Two. Defense counsel, unable to count on some judges in the waiver trial, may gamble that the equities will play before the jury. This approach is riskier but perhaps worth the gamble in some situations.

But, notwithstanding these limits, the waiver trial has been an important adaptive mechanism in Detroit and, we believe, is likely to be employed in other jurisdictions facing similar policies. There is evidence in the literature that some jurisdictions rely on waiver "trials" to dispose of many cases. These "trials" resemble slow pleas of guilty far more than any standard conception of a trial. If Detroit, which historically relied on waiver trials less than some other jurisdictions, "discovered" waiver trials to cope with inflexible policies, then other jurisdictions are likely to make a similar discovery, and those that already rely on waiver trials would have even less difficulty adjusting. We will consider the implications of this resort to waiver trials in our concluding comments.

Sentence Bargaining and Sentence Adjustments

The fact that most of the interview comments about waiver trials focused on felonious assaults and other cases that raised issues of equity was a function neither of chance nor of our selectivity. Prior to the Gun Law, defendants in these cases typically received probation or a relatively mild sentence. In the overwhelming majority "time" (in prison) was not at issue (as we saw in the 1976 data); defendants walked in most cases. Thus the introduction of the mandatory minimum sentence threatened a radical departure from previous practice, and the waiver trial, along with various constitutional challenges, emerged as mechanisms employed to preserve the going rate.

With respect to more serious offenses, such as armed robberies and some of the other assaults, the Gun Law posed a different, and in some ways less complex, problem. Recall that in 1976, of the armed robbery defendants not screened out at the preliminary examination or pretrial stage, 73 percent received time. Let us assume that some of the other cases involved equity matters (first offenders, mitigating circumstances, etc.) and were handled in Segment Two much like cases of felonious assault. What we are left with is a court norm or going rate that imposes periods of imprisonment upon many of the remaining armed robbers.

Put slightly differently, it appears that defendants in these cases will plead in the expectation of incarceration (most "time" sentences followed guilty pleas) as long as the alternative clearly is a longer prison term after trial (see Heumann, 1978: 156–57; Church 1976: 396–400). That a mandatory two-year sentence in and of itself would drive defendants to demand jury trials is a simplistic hypothesis, ill-grounded in the literature and easily refuted by the data we have presented.

An alternative hypothesis would be that the probability of trial increases when defendants who would have pled to the old going rate learn that the ante is upped to the going rate plus two, thus narrowing by two years the difference between what they get by pleading and what they hope for at trial. Again, because our disposition data for Gun Law offenses only represent the first six months and some of the uncompleted cases probably went to trial thereafter, we cannot speak conclusively to this hypothesis. However, the interviews address this question, if only suggestively.

Essentially, the respondents agreed that the Gun Law would not lead to a substantial increase in the "going rates." Most respondents claimed that judges adjusted their prior going rate to take into account the two years added by the new law. These adjustments were made through sentence bargaining: as the prosecutor's input into the plea bargaining process was eliminated, judges took up the slack and increasingly made explicit sentence bargains with defense attorneys. And even those judges who did not actively enter into these agreements communicated, through their sentences, a willingness to adjust the time for the primary felony, thus implicitly sending out a message about the discount for a plea. The latter pattern gives the defendant and his attorney less assurance about the eventual outcome but still allows them to make a reasonably reliable guess. In serious cases, it is often precisely this reduction of uncertainty that appears to contribute to the defendant's willingness to plead (see Casper, 1972: 67, 87).

When judges simply subtract the two years for the gun charge from the sentence for the primary felony (the pattern reported most frequently) there is in fact a slight increase in the time defendants will serve because the two years are "hard time"—there can be no reduction for "good time" served. Some defense attorneys report that they mention this and urge the judge to reduce the sentence for the primary felony by more than two years to compensate for the loss of good time. The illustrative interview excerpts that follow convey the flavor of the sentence adjustment process (the first two are judges, followed by a defense attorney and a prosecutor).

> I have a feeling that I decide what the sentence is and then take the Gun Law into account later. Thus if I think that a man needs to go to prison for seven years, I'm more likely to make it five and two, five for the principal charge and the other two into the Gun Law. I'm not so certain that the Gun Law has thus enhanced the length of sentence for persons who were going to get two years or more in the first place.

> Yeah, first time armed robbery with a gun, if it's a street robbery, that's five years. If he pulls a gun out and points it at someone, give me your money,

that's five to fifteen, to ten. And as I indicated most defendants are not concerned about the maximum anyway. They're only concerned about the minimum.

Q. Now, if you had that same guy with the gun law?

A. Three and two. Yeah. So you're really back to this. Except, see, he has, if I give him five to fifteen on a straight armed robbery, you're only really talking about three years at the most. Whereas I give him five, three plus two, you're really talking about four years because he's got to do the two first, you see. Then he's probably got to do two more you see before he's up for parole.

Q. Have defense attorneys come to you and tried to get two and a half or something?

A. Oh yeah, they come to me with that, and it depends .... [Y]ou know, when you look at the facts in a case like that there is no question that a guy did in fact rob somebody, and he pulls up at a stop sign and jumps in and robs someone, he could get life, okay, for that crime. And you look at that and you say, "Well, he would have gotten four years. Now he'll get two years on the robbery and two years on the gun." By the time you balance your alternatives, you still might say, "Well, look, I think our chance of winning this case is remote and you get two years on the robbery, two years on the gun, you might as well, my advice to you would be to go ahead and take the cop." Because he has so much to lose.

I think the application of the felony firearm rule is a complete failure in this building. The judges use it in sentence bargaining. They're normally gonna give a guy seven and a half to fifteen, for example, and they give them five and a half to fifteen and two for the gun. So they get absolutely no more time for the gun. And if they were gonna get, on offenses where they were gonna get, two years let's say, let's say on an attempt with great bodily harm, the judge would normally have given two to ten, they've given probation on the felony and two years on the gun, so it comes out the same thing. And it happens all the time in this building. I've yet to hear of an instance where the judge looked at a case and said, "this guy deserves seven and a half to fifteen, that's what I'm giving him. And then I'm giving him two in addition to that because he has a gun." Never heard it yet.

Several respondents qualified this generalization that sentences were simply adjusted to comport with the old norms. They argued that in certain circumstances the Gun

Law did influence the time the defendant received, and such cases may partially explain the somewhat higher sentences on armed robberies and the other assaults in Segment Two. In particular, some felt that in the "less serious of the serious" armed robberies and assaults, the Gun Law marginally increased the sentence. For example, a defendant convicted of armed robbery in Segment One could receive as little as one year from some judges, two from others. In Segment Two the minimum would be three years (one year for the armed robbery, two for the Gun Law). It is possible that an increase at the bottom of the scale produces some "trickle-up" effect on more serious armed robberies: a judge who gave two years for armed robbery before, and now must give at least three, might raise the norm for more serious armed robberies from perhaps four years to five.

Unraveling these speculative propositions and obtaining a firm grasp of the extent of sentence recommendations and adjustments must await the collection of more data over a longer time. Those data, for example, will allow us to make comparisons among judges over time and determine whether an individual judge's going rate has been affected by the Gun Law. But it is clear, even now, that the Gun Law has caused neither a dramatic increase in the frequency of trial for serious cases nor a uniform two-year increase in sentence length. Instead, the judge has frequently supplanted the prosecutor as an actor in the bargaining process and has been able to continue sentencing defendants to a term of years consonant with his own going rate and with the defendant's (and defense attorney's) expectation of what constitutes a reasonable sentence.

Conclusions

What lessons can be learned about the implementation of mandatory sentencing when a prosecutor opts to abdicate his discretion? Was plea bargaining really abolished in Detroit? Does a mandatory sentencing statute ensure mandatory sentences? Can these hard and fast lines drawn by legislatures be translated into reality in the complex labyrinth of the criminal court?

These questions, of course, are central to the ongoing debate about plea bargaining and sentencing reform, and our responses to them are necessarily tentative. Nonetheless, we do urge caution in expecting any sweeping changes as a result of a proscription on plea bargaining, a mandatory sentencing statute, or the simultaneous introduction of both.

Was plea bargaining abolished in Detroit? The answer must be: "sort of." If by plea bargaining one means the prosecutor's reduction in charge in return for the defendant's plea of guilty, then the Prosecutor, by exercising constant vigilance over his subordinates, prevented such reductions where the Gun Law was charged and was reasonably successful in ensuring that the warranting prosecutors charged the Gun Law consistently. Though there is good reason to be generally skeptical about the efficacy of prosecutorial policies (see Alschuler, 1978: 575 n.73), a willingness to penalize subordinates who deviated, an ability to detect deviation, and an office accustomed to policies and organized bureaucratically combined to facilitate implementation of the Prosecutor's policy in Detroit. There was probably slippage at warranting and somewhat less at other stages. Furthermore, we cannot know whether assistant prosecutors were ever half-hearted in resisting a defense motion to quash the felony or the gun count, thus tacitly subverting the spirit of the policy.

But let us assume (as the data tentatively suggest) that these were rare and the policy was actually implemented. As noted earlier, other mechanisms came into play, which we feel constitute "functional equivalents" of prosecutorial plea bargaining. In serious cases (armed robberies, some of the assaults) sentence bargaining and sentence adjustments allowed defendants to plead with as much assurance about the outcome of their cases as they had before the innovations—and sometimes with more. Sentence bargaining, which had been less frequent in Detroit than in other jurisdictions, has become a common practice, partially as a result of the Gun Law. And sentence bargaining differs from charge bargaining (the traditional procedure in Detroit) in only one important respect: it is a far more important form of negotiation since defendants have an even better idea about outcome in advance of their pleas.

A comparable argument can be made about the "walk through" waiver trials employed in cases of felonious assault (and some other assaults) where the equities militated against a two-year sentence. The proceeding was perfunctory, resembling a guilty plea hearing more than a trial. The defense attorney had either reached an explicit agreement with the judge or was taking a calculated gamble that the latter would be disinclined to sentence the defendant to the mandatory two years and thus would search for an out. It is almost as if a guilty plea is prohibited in these cases because a two-year sentence is so far out of line with the going rate that the defendant simply cannot plead. And it is interesting that in Continental legal systems in which defendants literally are not allowed to plead, two observers have found what they call "the analogue of the guilty plea: the uncontested trial" (Goldstein & Marcus, 1977: 264–67). In these Gun Law equity cases we come full circle: the waiver trial is an analogue of the European trial, which itself is often an analogue of the American guilty plea. Call these procedures trials, if you like, but the functions they serve and the manner in which they are held resemble our plea bargaining processes (or the European trial) far more closely than they do a full-fledged trial.

By a mix of constitutional challenges, motions to quash the charge, sentence negotiations and adjustments, waiver trials, and other techniques, the system managed to digest the two policy innovations without a radical alteration in its disposition patterns. Court personnel suspected as much: time and again in the interviews they indicated that somehow the system would accommodate itself, that things would work themselves out without any major departures from past practice (the first speaker is a judge, the others both prosecutors).

What's really happening I think is that judges are bargaining down the armed robbery charge as a concession because the person has to do two straight years on the felony firearm. In those serious cases the two years has proven not to be too much, the system has accommodated itself to that. The cases in which I think it is too much, and my experience, what my experience has suggested to me is that there are instances in which the universal recommendation of felony firearm by the prosecutors is incorrect as a matter of policy, and these cases are putting pressure on the system and ultimately in my view will put a lot of pressure on the law. I think it's, assuming that you think the felony firearm is a good law, you jeopardize the law by running cases through the system that are inappropriate for felony firearm and that's become the real problem as far as I'm concerned as a judge.

Somehow, some way, those judges invent ways of bypassing that particular thing, and you can get into the mechanics with them. Believe me, for things that we come up with, there's always some way of circumventing it and I'm suggesting to you that no one wrongfully, unnecessarily for the most part, I mean we're dealing with imperfect creatures, gets screwed with two years when he shouldn't. Take it on faith if you can't take it on anything else. I'm telling you that it'll work itself out, believe me.

I've had judges call me and ask for a dispensation; when I say "no," and they may even go beyond me, and they get the same answer, and I check and find out that, you know what happened to the case, and I know they found a way around it. And, there's so many, we have so many fingers to put in the dike and they're just very inventive, some of them. And the word gets out. When one gets away with it, and the word gets out then it becomes part of a pattern.

There is a serious problem hinted at in these comments that transcends the Detroit case and is inherent in the introduction of mandatory sentencing and proscriptions on plea bargaining. Essentially these rigid policies force criminal court actors into making adjustments that are unstructured, ad hoc, sometimes contrary to the letter of the law, and sometimes unsuccessful. Most defendants may be accommodated, but some are not. A judge may not agree to a waiver trial arrangement, a prosecutor may refuse to acquiesce in a motion to quash, a judge may not negotiate the time on an armed robbery.

Policies, both no plea bargaining and mandatory sentences, champion orderliness, consistency, equal treatment. Ironically, they promote disorder, unequal and sometimes inequitable treatment, and even lawlessness. The movement to open up plea bargaining has been a healthy one for it has made public practices that previously were conducted in a climate of uncertainty about their legitimacy;

consistency is enhanced, and the product of these negotiations is increasingly made an explicit part of the court record. The introduction of the policies discussed in this paper moves the system a step backward—they promote the same piecemeal, ad hoc adjustments that have been the subject of so much criticism in the plea bargaining literature.

One problem with these policies, of course, is that they do not allow for exceptions. They are intended to reduce discretion by establishing general rules. But as several astute observers of the criminal justice system have noted, it is one thing to speak about policies for general categories of crime and quite another to confront the almost infinite variety of factual circumstances in particular cases (Alschuler, 1978: 556–58). The pressure to make exceptions is almost irresistible but they introduce the problem of unequal treatment and begin to undermine the policy itself. Exceptions in the criminal court have a way of quickly becoming expectations; one exception becomes a precedent to justify others (see Heumann, 1978: 157–62).

In its conception, the Prosecutor's ban on plea bargaining was designed to guard against this snowballing of exceptions.

> [W]e believe that the percentage of those cases which we would honestly like to get rid of in another way is so low that we're willing to take the heat on those few cases in order to preserve the concept and the viability of our principle that we want to get rid of guns and we want certainty of punishment.... Well, if we allow ... [the judge to make an exception] we have 25 other judges in the building who are going to want an exception in their given case, and there's no way that you can do it equitably.

> Because there are many prosecutors working here, and we're not sure what their judgment will be. And pretty soon, it's the easy way out, and you start giving this away and that, and before you know it, you wake up to the fact that now you've given all this statute away. And for the few cases where I may want to, where I, I am personally concerned about it and so on, I can live with those and I think that's the price we've got to pay. We're not talking about completely innocent people; we're talking about 85 percent guilty people getting 100 percent shot in the ass. If that's what we need to make this town habitable again that doesn't bother me.

But in practice, as we have seen, exceptions developed nonetheless. Judges and defense attorneys found a way to accommodate the cases to ensure that the court norms in 1977 did not deviate too much from those of 1976. And it is at least arguable that the open and covert behaviors adopted to accommodate some of the equity cases were expanded to include cases in which the claims of equity were borderline.

We are therefore pessimistic about effecting radical change in the criminal justice system. On one hand, we are arguing that if a policy is not rigidly conceived it is likely to be overwhelmed by the proliferation and expansion of exceptions. On the other hand, if the policy is rigid, the system will accommodate itself by developing other means to attain flexibility. In the first instance, at least the claims to exceptional treatment are visible and subject to some review; in the second, the court's actors are forced to rely on more piecemeal accommodations and their actions are less open to scrutiny. Neither approach ensures equal application of the law to all defendants guilty of a specific crime; both run the risk that some defendants will be unable to escape the application of the policy even when the equities are strongly on their side and will receive a sentence disproportionate to the gravity of the offense while the policy is being evaded in similar cases.

Perhaps we are unduly pessimistic. There may be some sort of middle ground between a rigid policy and one whose exceptions quickly become the norm. Presumptive sentences might be an example and so might a more structured plea bargaining process. A prosecutor could be required to explain why he is plea bargaining, just as a judge must explain deviations from a presumptive sentence. One of the assistant prosecutors we interviewed strongly favored the Prosecutor's policy but felt that it ought to allow exceptions in about 5 percent of the cases. The assistant prosecutor would take immediate responsibility for such deviations and communicate them in writing to a superior, who would bear ultimate responsibility. Guidelines for these exceptions could be developed over time and the ceiling on their number carefully guarded. Similarly, one could imagine a board of overseers, composed of prosecutors, defense attorneys, and judges, who administered the implementation of the innovations, collected the data on exceptions, and gradually articulated criteria for them. Such a scheme would increase the probability that the momentum of the reform was not lost while allowing for structured deviation. The result might be a more open, more equitable process by which "some with a gun get none, one, or two" in proceedings that were neither as whimsical as those without any guidelines for sentencing or plea bargaining nor as rigid as those governed by rules that purported to be absolute.

DISCUSSION QUESTIONS

1. Why is discretion so troubling within the criminal justice system? Is it equally troubling in civil justice? other forms of state decision-making? private decision-making? Should we seek to eliminate discretion? minimize it? shift it? Discretion in the criminal justice system sometimes is analogized to water in a water bed: compress it at one place and it pops up in another. Is this an apt metaphor? What is the attitude of prosecutors to limits on their discretion? How could they evade the attempt to

constrain their discretion? Are you persuaded by the authors that discretion did not reappear in prosecutorial decisions?

2. What are the politics underlying passage of something like the Gun Law? Does it make sense to view the presence of a gun as always warranting two years of imprisonment? How does this affect your thoughts about other proposals for rigid sentencing, including federal guidelines and minima and the "three-strikes and you're out" proposals?

3. The research design here is a quasi-experiment or interrupted time series. When is that appropriate? When is it possible? Can you suggest examples of other laws whose effect could be tested by such a method?

4. If prosecutors lost discretion, did sentences increase in severity? If not, where did discretion re-emerge? Are you surprised that the length of sentences increased only slightly, if at all?

5. What is a waiver trial? Why do judges and lawyers like it? Is this another instance of Alschuler's interpretation: as procedural safeguards become more effective, trials disappear entirely? Whose discretion increased? Is this a better place to locate discretion? a better procedure to exercise it? What are the differences between plea bargaining with the prosecutor and with the judge? explicit and implicit bargaining? What kinds of information and assurances do defendants (and their lawyers) obtain in each? How is this likely to affect their willingness to plead? Do prosecutors and judges differ in their attitudes toward constraints on their discretion? What discretion does the jury retain? Could this be restricted? Should it? Will any legal system produce a procedure by which the defendant declines to contest guilt and receives a sentence reduction in return? Is the tension inescapable between rule and standard, uniformity and individualization?

Norm Creation

10

The New Dutch and German Drug Laws: Social and Political Conditions for Criminalization and Decriminalization

Sebastian Scheerer

Introduction

The relation between social structure and change in substantive criminal law has attracted renewed interest among criminologists and social historians in Germany. In this paper, processes of criminalizing and decriminalizing drug use in Germany and the Netherlands are compared with regard to the political patterns followed, the actions taken by organized social groups, and the underlying structural variables influencing the content and direction of legal change. My central concern is the conditions for successful decriminalization processes.

From a functional perspective, the norms of a society can be seen as a specific subsystem incorporating basic expectations of that society about its members; the criminal law can be viewed as its moral core. Because of their normative quality these generalized expectations are for the most part impervious to disappointments: even if the norm is frequently broken and sanctions are rarely imposed, the expectation can remain largely unscathed. Sometimes, however, noncompliance with a norm is perceived as a threat to the identity of the social system (see Erikson, 1966: 68). This is most likely to occur in a context of structural strain (Smelser, 1962: 15–17, 290) generating violations of normative expectations that do not simply attempt to evade the law on a particular occasion but rather question the legitimacy of the norm itself. The drug users of the late 1960s, unlike most criminals (thieves, for instance), were not just trying to dodge the effects of the law but were attacking the norm as such.

Where deviance is directed against the very existence of a norm, public awareness of the inefficacy of law can endanger both the moral authority of those social groups or classes whose beliefs it symbolizes and the political authority of the agencies of social control. The issue becomes a central concern for social and political groups who are threatened by delegitimization. A legal system can adapt to such a challenge in two ways. One is to restore confidence in the existing norm-

Abridged from *Law & Society Review*, Volume 12:585 (1978).

ative order through ritual affirmations of the norm by means of increased penalties, purges, and witch hunts that eliminate the hard-core deviant while forcing others to conform to the conventional normative order. The second possibility is to accommodate the normative order to the challenging behavior. Such an adaptation requires the system to adjust its moral boundaries to incorporate the hitherto deviant behavior into the realm of normality while the behavior itself remains unchanged, at least as far as formal sanctions are concerned. All legal change falls in one or the other category.

Criminalization can be defined as the creation of new moral boundaries within a social system or the affirmation of existing ones, in an attempt to assimilate normative challenges. Decriminalization can be defined as the adjustment of moral boundaries to social change or, to retain the vocabulary borrowed from Piaget, as normative accommodation. The Federal Republic of Germany (hereafter referred to as Germany) and the Netherlands both witnessed a sudden increase in the use of cannabis (and later heroin) among youths, which became known as the "drug wave." Although the Netherlands fell prey to this innovative deviance somewhat earlier than did Germany, conditions of diffusion and public reaction were similar in most respects: representative surveys conducted in both countries showed attitudes toward all illegal psychoactive drugs that were equally puritan and strong public emotions in favor of a punitive legal response to cannabis use. Yet despite these similarities legislative responses are strikingly different: the normative system of the Netherlands accommodated to cannabis use (and partly even to heroin), but the German system reaffirmed existing moral boundaries by increasing prescribed penalties. A comparison of the two, therefore, should generate some hypotheses about the conditions underlying the legislative process.

The Dutch legislature amended the Opium Law in 1976 to decriminalize consumption of both hard and soft drugs while significantly increasing the sanctions for large-scale dealing in illicit hard drugs. On the other hand, the German legislature amended the Opium Law in 1971 to increase the penalties for soft and hard drug users and dealers. Whereas Dutch policy provides for the legal administration of methadone and, sometimes, heroin to addicts, German policy gives freedom from drugs the highest priority, subjecting doctors who supply addicts with methadone or other substitutes to prosecution, fines, and imprisonment. Felony charges for possession of marijuana or other drugs are common in Germany, whereas punitive sanctions for consumers exist only on paper in the Netherlands. The difference is experienced most acutely by Dutch youth, who are arrested and severely punished in Germany for acts they are, de facto, free to engage in just a few miles to the west in their own country. In fact, it has been reported that German courts like to hand out tough sentences to Dutch citizens reasoning that they must aid the Dutch people since their authorities are evidently unable to meet the obligation of the state to do so.

The criminological literature offers several explanations for these variations in legal response. The relativity of crime is constantly reaffirmed; the fact that what is considered proper in one society is a heinous crime in another has best been illustrated by Sutherland and Cressey (1974:15–16). There has been considerable research on the impact of economic development on crime, law, and sanctions by scholars such as Chambliss (1969), Hall (1952), and Rusche and Kirchheimer (1939). Others have pointed to the importance of governmental organizations (Becker, 1963; Dickson, 1968) and of norm-oriented collective behavior, often aroused by issues such as pornography (Zurcher et al., 1973). Finally, it is important to know the mechanisms of legislative politics (Heinz et al., 1969; Steiner & Gove, 1960) and consider the attitudes and idiosyncrasies of legislators (Blum & Funkhouser, 1965).

Yet despite all this research, progress toward a general theory of the emergence of criminal laws has been modest. Much ado has been made of the debate between consensus and conflict models, the former explaining legal change as a consequence of changing social consensus on norms, whereas the latter proclaims that law is both an expression of the interest of and a means of domination by a powerful group or class (see Quinney, 1969; Carson, 1974; Turk, 1976). Although the conflict perspective seems to provide a more fertile framework for analysis, the consensus model also has its merits as long as it is not seen as an adequate "theory" by itself but merely as one important aspect of legal change. Even for conflict theorists consensus plays an important part in the legitimation of interests and domination, which can be seen as the process by which rule is justified to the ruled and domination thereby transformed into (or based upon) differing degrees of consensus. This view, which refuses to see conflict and consensus as mutually exclusive "theories," is supported by most case studies on drug (Lindesmith, 1965; Bean, 1974) and other legislation (Sutherland, 1969). Not surprisingly, Galliher, McCartney and Baum (1977:81) had to borrow from both the conflict and consensus models to explain the success of the effort to decriminalize marijuana in Nebraska.

It therefore seems more fruitful to examine the relationships between social structure variables and historical patterns (such as the trend away from punishment and toward treatment and its economic and cultural foundations), as well as the roles of organized social groups (such as the strategies pursued by conservative and liberal parties to retain or regain power and changes in their attitudes). There has recently been renewed interest in the influence of macrosocial variables on the criminal law. As Sutherland has shown, this relationship is "vague and loose" at best, requiring consideration of the intermediate sphere between macrosocial trends and their concretion in politics (1969: 96). How this can be done has been shown by Zurcher and his associates (1973), who borrowed the "value-added framework" invented by Smelser (1962) for the analysis of norm-oriented movements. His framework is appropriate for describing and explaining criminal laws that emerge in response to strong public feelings and interests, but because it is derived from a theory of collective behavior it is incapable of analyzing instances of criminalization or decriminalization that occur without popular support.

These cases of lawmaking "from above" are by no means rare, as demonstrated by the decriminalization of marijuana. The vast majority of bills decriminalizing marijuana in the United States were passed in conservative, rural, Protestant states; even if the Nebraska bill was passed for reasons of efficiency, its effect in decriminalizing marijuana had to be carefully concealed from the eyes of a punitive public (Galliher et al., 1977: 81). In the Netherlands, a majority has long favored stricter punishment for users of marijuana and other drugs, and an opinion poll taken today would probably show that they still do:

> I think that one would find today a rather large majority still who would be opposed to liberalization of cannabis. I think there would be flat 65 percent against it. [Dutch Ministry of Public Health official]

Criminal legislation "from above" is directed not by public opinion but by the powerful. In legal democratic societies the powerful are organized social groups and the bureaucratic apparatus of government. It is their perception that determines where legislative action is needed. When they articulate their legislative interests the articulation alone is sufficient to create a political vacuum or a "policy deficit," which every government must fill with some activity if it has not completely lost interest in remaining in power. These groups exercise a high degree of control over the political process. They are seldom progressive and often morally conservative. But if public opinion is punitive and repressive, the morally conservative masters of policy deficits are the only ones who can successfully decriminalize. And the remarkable thing is that they do.

This is not to say that a few elitist groups are free to do whatever they want. But the variable upon which their actions depend is certainly not public opinion. Indeed, hardly any indicator of the direction of legal change is as unreliable as public opinion. States generally regarded as "liberal" have passed extremely "tough" laws (Cagliostro, 1974), and others with solidly conservative publics have "liberally" reduced penalties. The commonplace assumption that a given society has liberal laws because it is inhabited by a liberal public therefore seems unfounded. Decriminalization normally occurs in spite of a punitive and repressive public and not because it is welcomed by a community of liberal eggheads. My point is that the key to decriminalization is actually held by the moral conservatives, the "moral center" of society. Even if the initiative for decriminalization is taken by liberals, it will be the moral center that determines its success. Yet the powerful organizations of the moral conservatives are still not entirely free in choosing the direction of legal change. The decision to criminalize or decriminalize is dependent on the activities of organized social groups and the position of the government officials. Both of the latter are influenced by the political culture in which they are embedded, which in turn is a function of social structure. Because these relationships are not mechanical, but loose and vague, their explication cannot result in a deterministic model. We thus must be content with outlining a few conditions for successful criminalization and decriminalization.

A Political History of the German Reform of 1971: Linear Criminalization

Small groups favoring liberalization of the drug policy have been active in both Germany and the Netherlands. In Germany, however, the movement encountered rigid opposition from all potential political sponsors and never got off the ground. Although the literary works of Charles Baudelaire, Thomas de Quincey, Aldous Huxley, and Timothy Leary had been translated and had "turned on" quite a number of intellectual journalists, anarchists, students, and scientists, neither the publications nor their adherents had any influence on the lawmaking process. They did stimulate public debate, inspired some liberal journalists to take decriminalization seriously and even recommend it and attracted the sympathy of individual members of the Liberal and Social Democratic parties, but neither of the latter groups—the natural allies of such a reform—would endorse it. Without any sponsor for these more radical views, the German "reform" of the Opium Law was hardly more than a linear continuation of the conventional politics of drug prohibition.

Although the Social Democrats and the liberals formed a coalition government, the key to their stand against legalizing cannabis lies with the strong Christian Democratic opposition. The Christian Democrats (CDU/CSU) had ruled the country during the entire reconstruction period, from 1949 through 1966. That year, they had been forced to take in the Social Democrats (SPD) as a junior cabinet partner, one that was to oust them completely after the 1969 elections, when the SPD formed the government with the Liberal Party (FDP). With almost half of the popular vote behind it, the CDU/CSU used every chance to topple the government even before the next general election. Four important state elections scheduled for 1970 seemed to provide a good testing ground for the stability of the new socialist-liberal government. There appeared to be a great deal of public fear about and hostility toward drug use, which could be mobilized and directed against a "liberal" government that just sat there and looked on while the youth of the country was being corrupted by foreign criminals and noxious weeds. The moral "liberals" could do little to counteract this political strategy. Had they taken a strong stand in favor of liberalization, the dramatistic strategy of the opposition would instantly have succeeded, in view of the repressive nature of public opinion. To do nothing in the face of the opposition's credible proclamation of a policy deficit would also have led to defeat. The "liberals" therefore thought it wise to accept the definition of the situation advanced by the "conservatives" and outdo the opposition by simply passing a "tough" law.

To keep, or regain, the trust of conservative voters who gave the new government its fragile majority, the SPD proclaimed an emergency situation in drug use early in 1970. Laws are relatively easy to make and yet have enormous symbolic impact on the public, which sees its central concerns officially proclaimed. In the drawers of the Ministry of the Interior the government found a draft reform bill providing for stricter penalties. When the Ministry of Health had polished this bill and adapted it slightly to present needs, the government presented it as evidence of an ability to cope with the challenge of hostile and deviant life styles. As a consequence, the government's official commentary on the proposed law was rather sensational, portraying it as an instrument urgently needed to protect individual life, liberty, and even the basic functions of society itself. Political pressure from the moral conservatives proved so strong that even postponing action until a scientific inquiry could be made would have been regarded as a weakness. Therefore no commission was appointed. Nor were there attempts to learn from the findings of government commissions on marijuana in other countries. There were no hearings and no organized process of information gathering. Some legislators met privately with clergymen, social workers, and friends to discuss the dangers of cannabis. Others, like the health expert of the SPD, explained that they did not trust foreign reports, contending that personal experience offered more reliable evidence: "There are many pictures, photo series, from Algieria, Morocco, where you can see the physical decay after years of [cannabis] use." This expert had also met Rudolf Gelpke, the renowned orientalist and advocate of decriminalization, at a television debate. After the debate, the expert refused an offer to try cannabis in the hotel lounge with Gelpke—a wise decision, the expert later said, because, he insisted, Gelpke shortly thereafter lost weight, turned yellow, fell into total decay, and died the tragic death of a cannabis addict: "His end must have been terrible."

The government's bill confused the dangers of hard and soft drugs, proclaiming that the difference was immaterial since soft drugs would lead to hard drugs sooner or later. Criminalization of cannabis users was defended in Parliament on the ground that it was necessary to combat "people who possess no conscience and who profit from other people's misery." Drug dealers, it was said, were organized like foreign intelligence services (and paid by them). Children were being used at the lowest level of distribution: "Normally, they are already addicted and are being paid with so-called 'stuff,' so they are willing instruments in the hands of the gang leaders." A few legislators questioned the wisdom of the proposed policy during the committee sessions, warning that further repression of cannabis users would contribute to the development of a drug subculture and inhibit access to official aid and therapeutic institutions. But they could not resist the arguments of ministry officials, who asserted that cannabis involved a terrible risk for the structure of society itself.

Despite all this, the true moral conservatives held the better cards. The opposition simply copied the government's draft bill, adding even tougher sentences and a few vague clauses, and presented this as the only way to deal effectively with the drug scene. Of course, the opposition draft did not become law, but it did advance the political interests of the conservatives. For even though the legislature adopted the government proposal, the public did not seem particularly impressed by what it correctly perceived as an imitative law-and-order campaign. Asked in 1972 which party they trusted most to solve the drug problem, a sizable majority of Germans voiced their conviction that only the opposition would be able to do so.

A Political History of the Dutch Reform of 1976: Digressive Progression

Dutch groups favoring decriminalization were more fortunate than their German counterparts for they found a political sponsor in the Socialist Party (PvdA), or at least in its shadow Minister of Health, Mrs. Vorrink. This was not due to their numerical strength or organization since they, too, belonged to communes, unorganized networks, and intellectual groups, but to a political situation that allowed the progressives to take the offensive and not get caught trying to outdo the moral conservatives. As early as 1968, a conservative State Secretary of Health (the highest ranking civil servant in the department) appointed a committee to investigate better ways of detecting and approaching users and dealers of illegal drugs and instructed it to publicize the dangers of drug use. In 1970, the elderly head of the working group was succeeded by Mr. H. P. A. Baan, a brilliant and energetic neurologist who favored legal reform. He enlarged the working group to include several sociologists knowledgeable about the Dutch drug scene.

When the working group delivered its report to the government in 1972, its recommendations diverged considerably from the original intentions of the conservative State Secretary. Although he still believed that cannabis was even more dangerous than other drugs because of its stepping-stone effect, the report concluded that to

> make the overall policy pursued by the government credible, one would have to make a distinction between drugs which carry an unacceptable risk in the social sense and those whose risks are doubtful or perhaps acceptable.

The policies advocated by the report—classification of cannabis as a misdemeanor, imposition of sanctions upon addicts only to induce them to undergo treatment, construction of a network of services—ultimately became law, but its chances of success at the time of publication were minimal.

With the Socialist victory in late 1972, prospects for implementation improved. The new Minister of Health, Mrs. Vorrink, had chosen abortion and drug law reforms as her top priorities. But the new government was based on a coalition that included the (puritan) Antirevolutionary Party (AR) and the Catholic People's Party (KVP) of Mr. A.A.M. van Agt, later Prime Minister. Both coalition partners, and even the Calvinist wing of the Socialist Party (PvdA), were initially opposed to decriminalization, and nobody knew if they could be persuaded to change their minds. Nevertheless, the moral conservatives did not seek to blame the government (or the Socialists) for causing the drug problem by following too lenient a policy, and there was no attempt by any major political force to mobilize public opinion. In general politicization of the issue was lower in the Netherlands than in Germany. As the Socialists were not politically threatened with a conservative backlash, they could afford to take a progressive stand on the issue without risking too much voter support. This low level of politicization also prevented the "moral center" of Dutch society from using the issue as a self-serving sociopolitical symbol.

Nevertheless, until the new law was passed in 1976, the moral conservatives never lost their veto power, and some prominent political figures tried to exercise it. For instance, Ms. E. Veder-Smit, chairperson of the special legislative committee on drug policy and member of the antireform Liberal Party (VVD), sought to stiffen conservative opposition to the bill by means of a journey to Sweden in 1973. The committee was presented with the case against liberalizing the law on amphetamines and cannabis, endorsed by the Swedish government, which had adopted a strict prohibitionist policy on drugs. The committee chair, an experienced legislator and moral conservative, knew perfectly well that arguments carry less weight than party interests, but stated:

> I was opposed to the greater part of the draft law, and I hoped that colleagues in Parliament who were hesitating by intuition against that law could get arguments for their feelings.

But in the end this tactic failed. Members of Mr. van Agt's KVP, its principal target, were moved by the argument but ultimately voted for the reform bill, thereby saving it from failure. Expressing her disappointment with the lenient position eventually taken by the KVP, Ms. Veder-Smit commented:

> The Christian Democrats [KVP] showed what they always show in Dutch polities ... they say they are impressed, and that they will think it over. And then they decide on the basis of other arguments.

The committee was quite conscientious, gathering information from police and scientific sources. Experts from the World Health Organization were invited, and two professors of pharmacology testified on the dangerousness of drugs. The Amsterdam police stated their case, as did an American official, Mr. Robert L. Dupont, head of the Narcotics Special Action Office for Drug Abuse Policy, then located at the White House. Later, the committee held a public hearing, and many individuals and groups spoke, including the communes "I Ting" and "We smoke hashish, why not" from Amsterdam, who pleaded the case for radical decriminalization.

Compared with the German approach, this legislative process allowed a high level of scientific involvement. The repeated arguments by scientists for differentiating between drugs entailing risks that were acceptable or uncertain and others whose risks were definitely unacceptable made it more difficult for opponents of the bill to argue their case. But scientific arguments clearly were not the decisive factor in converting the conservatives. More important was the fact that the moral conservatives were members of a coalition that favored change and, it would be argued, were simply interested in preserving their position in government. Yet though this may have been a consideration, it also was not determinative: shortly before, van Agt's KVP and other elements of the moral center had killed the abortion reform bill, another "pet" project of the socialist Minister of Health, and had no regrets about it.

The real reasons, it seems, were changes in the drug scene. It was well known to the conservatives that only one out of every 140 marijuana users was apprehended by the police in 1970, that law enforcement had become completely incapable of administering the drug laws even before organized crime invaded the Netherlands with large-scale heroin transports after the killing of the French Connection in 1972. To cope with hard drugs the police had to concentrate all their resources on this problem. As Minister of Justice in the coalition government with the Socialists, Mr. van Agt had learned for himself the impossibility of prosecuting both kinds of drug trade with any chance of success.

But face saving is more important in politics than instrumental action, and to translate this insight into the politics of decriminalization is sometimes difficult for moral conservatives because of their constituents. In Nebraska, a conservative sponsor of the misdemeanor bill introduced "tough" bills immediately before sneaking in a decriminalization bill, in order that his conservative image might be left unscarred by the stigma of liberalism (Galliher et al., 1977: 78). The same diversionary tactics were necessary in Dutch politics, where decriminalization was linked with a trebling of penalties for hard drug trafficking and the promise of stricter prosecution of dealers. The bill's chances were further improved when Mrs. H. van Leeuwen of the staunchly conservative Antirevolutionary Party (AR) publicly declared that it was the Christian tradition to help addicts rather than punish them. As a health expert of the Socialist Party remarked, this statement legitimated the change of opinion within the ranks of the Catholic People's Party (KVP) of Mr. van Agt:

> It was a brand new idea of the Christians. The attitude of Hannie van Leeuwen opened a very frank debate of the problems. The Christian Historical Union had propagated very reactionary views. And then the Antirevolutionaries came with very progressive ones.... The Catholic People's Party [KVP] couldn't do much else, after the newspapers had written about the very Christian and moral attitude of Hannie van Leeuwen. The KVP really didn't have much of a choice.

To support a piece of progressive legislation and still appear to remain conservative, the KVP endorsed a few clauses that possessed great symbolic value. It supported an amendment proposed by the Liberal Party (VVD) aimed at curbing the activities of the son of the Socialist Minister of Health, who read the whole list of black market cannabis prices on the nationwide radio station, Hilversum 1, every Saturday at noon. This broadcast so enraged the anticannabis factions that they introduced article 3b into the draft bill imposing a four-year prison sentence for public advertisement of and propaganda for drugs. Having demonstrated its impeccable conservative credentials, the Catholic People's Party could afford to vote for the bill in the Second Chamber of Parliament and even save it from defeat in the First.

Some Determinants of the Making of a Symbolic Issue

The preceding case histories have demonstrated that conservatives hold the key to decriminalization when the public itself is generally conservative, since it lies in their hands to mobilize public opinion and trigger a legislative or electoral defeat of the moral liberals. Moral conservatives are free to decriminalize when the existing laws are ineffective, and diversionary strategies allow them to fulfill symbolically the conservative expectations of the public. But conservative support for decriminalization depends even more strongly on a quiescent state bureaucracy and on the willingness of organized social interest groups to refrain from demanding more punitive measures.

In Germany, the political voice of the moral center was forced to crusade for punitive measures by the pressure of a powerful medical association and a conservative bureaucratic staff. Soon after the drug wave began, the medical profession came to dominate public debate, issuing most of the expert statements, publications, and comments on the drug situation. Most of those active in the debate belonged to a moral crusade led by Dr. Dietrich Kleiner, a neurologist who became convinced that cannabis was an evil that had to be erased from the face of the earth when his son left home for Nepal to join the hippie movement during the mid-sixties. Dr. Kleiner dedicated himself to organizing symposia, distributing anticannabis pamphlets, and other activities, through all of which he succeeded in creating a consensus within his profession. He founded an information center, sponsored by the government, that sent leaflets to opinion leaders. Under his influence the Federal Medical Association issued a statement proclaiming the dangers of cannabis and denouncing those who engaged in decriminalization initiatives as dangerous individuals who wanted to belittle the dangers.

The views of doctors and other organized social groups met with strong support among law enforcement staff and organizations, who favored a punitive response to drug use. Law enforcement officers spontaneously retold the old myths about marijuana murders (Becker, 1963: 140–43) to the public, the medical profession, and government officials responsible for drafting the new narcotics law. Indeed, the staff of the Ministry of Health relied on no other source of information as heavily as it did on telephone conversations with the criminal police headquarters at Wiesbaden. Differences in the size and structure of police organizations in Germany and the Netherlands may well be responsible for the magnitude of the policy deficit articulated by each police organization. Whereas the Dutch police numbered only 25,000 officials, divided into many local forces and one national force, which belong to different ministries, all German state police forces have a large, common headquarters at their disposal, located at Wiesbaden, which belongs to and significantly affects the federal Ministry of the Interior. Today, the Ministry of the Interior acts more as an advocate for, than a political restraint upon, the vested interests of the police. A measure of the influence of law enforcement in the German legislative process is that the legislature heard no scientific testimony but did listen to police experts. When the latter met with legislators in closed session the only outsider admitted was the producer of a television show.

With powerful police and medical associations rallying moral support for their punitive views it would have been nearly impossible for the political conservatives to fail to dramatize the drug issue as they did. Even the Social Democrats were forced to make some response. As the ruling party, they influenced the mass media in an unprecedented way, spending millions of deutschemarks on a partly open, partly covert operation to "destabilize" liberal positions on the drug issue. Scientists were awarded research funds if they seemed likely to come to the desired conclusions, and more than one criminologist sang the tune composed by the interest groups and the agents of social control. Given the monolithic response of organized social groups, administrative organizations, moral conservatives, and hard-pressed liberals, including the mass media and scientists, public emotion was bound to be excited. It therefore came as no surprise when a public opinion survey conducted in June 1972 revealed a dramatic intensification of hostility toward drugs and their consumers.

As a result of the popular outrage thus mobilized letters poured into the Ministry of Health at an unprecedented rate, most of them advocating the free distribution of heroin to addicts—not, as might be presumed, to enable them to live an integrated social life, but to get rid of them quickly and save the taxpayers' money. Others advocated the revival of concentration camps, leading an Under-Secretary of Health to reconsider the government's campaign and denounce these attitudes as unacceptable in a humane society and obstructive of any attempt to understand the causes that had led to such massive deviant behavior.

In the Netherlands, events took a very different course. Because the organizations that sought to form policy toward drugs were preoccupied with the heroin wave, the potential for any moral crusades was left with the doctors and the churches, which play a critical part in Dutch politics. Some members of each group spoke both for and against liberalization, but the churches were largely neutralized by a militantly progressive wing within the lower strata of the clerical hierarchy. The doctors' association in the Netherlands is less coherently organized than it is in Germany and therefore less likely to be led into moral crusades by dedicated individuals. Furthermore, the government cleverly involved potential leaders of the medical opposition in the legitimation of official policies by commissioning them to conduct important research—a transparent strategy of neutralization through participation, but no less effective for the social control agencies were not forced to launch crusades and seek to manipulate opinion, as they were in Germany. Since even the most articulate groups abstained from identifying any policy deficit, the conservatives could afford not to politicize the issue, and even to favor decriminalization. Devoid of sponsors, initial public hostility toward drug users gradually declined at the same time that it was being whipped up in neighboring Germany.

Discussion

We return to the question whether underlying macrosocial variables explain the avoidance of moral panic in one country and the creation of public hostility toward deviance in the other. The German people are no more and no less likely to engage in moral hysteria than the Dutch, if left to themselves, as public opinion polls showed. But German social structure—with its high degree of cultural, ethnic, and religious homogeneity and its large, well-organized interest groups possessing institutionalized access to policy-making bodies—is more conducive to mass movements and public rituals of exclusion than is the more complex structure of Dutch society. One can find many successful moral "purges" of incipient deviance in German history and social life. German society is relatively high on formal control and low in its capacity to adapt to emerging social change; in relation to the Netherlands it would certainly have to be classified as a rather "passive" society in Etzioni's (1968) sense of the term. Unable to produce a new social consensus, social reaction instead excludes dissenting groups from social life.

The Dutch political and cultural scene contains much greater diversity in areas ranging from theory all the way to the differences in hairdos and lifestyles. A prominent Dutch bureaucrat, reflecting on the variables underlying legislative reform, stated:

> Looking at the German scene, as we see it, I have personally felt that perhaps there is a difference between a large country and a small one ... maintaining discipline in large countries is much more difficult than with a small population. Now, in looking at German attitudes, both in the Ministries of Health and that of the Interior, I felt that deviant behavior as such, behavior that differs from average behavior, is criticized much more heavily than it is in this country. If you do not belong to the group as such that is a criminal

offense in itself—almost. [In the Netherlands] you may have your problem. People tend to look at you and say—ah well, you have a problem, why don't you belong to the group? Without becoming aggressive about it and without seeing that if you don't want to belong to the group, we'll throw you out.

In fact, the "famous" Dutch tolerance is founded on a unique social phenomenon—"verzuiling"—the composition of the whole social system out of political, religious, and ethnic groups, each possessing its own mass media of communications (including television), schools, soccer clubs, and banks. For hundreds of years, Holland has absorbed refugees and minorities from France, Portugal, Germany, later from Hungary and China, and most recently from Uganda. Instead of assimilating them, Dutch society has largely ignored them, allowing each its own "column" or "subculture" within the whole. This diversity of groups holding views that were often dogmatic and irreconcilable contributed to the development of Dutch tolerance and pragmatism. It is often argued that in a heterogeneous society like that of the Netherlands, government is possible only through compromise, adaptability, and pragmatism—or, if these are universal requirements, that they are especially vital to such a political system. To seek to induce a moral panic about a new kind of deviant behavior is not a viable political strategy in a society where each idiosyncrasy has its own "column" and where the roof of the state rests upon the sum of all. "You almost never find someone trying to mobilize people in the streets by appealing to emotions" in the Netherlands, one official of the Ministry of Justice stated. In more general terms, a comparison of deviance and control in the Netherlands and Germany would show a significantly greater emphasis on formal legal control in Germany than in the Netherlands, which possesses one of the most lenient or "consensual" control systems in Europe.

Conclusion

The enactment of decriminalizing legislation tends to follow a different pattern from that of laws criminalizing behavior. The literature about the latter stresses the elements of "consensus" and "collective behavior," thus introducing a "democratic bias" into the explanation of criminal lawmaking. My research suggests that it would be equally misleading to attribute decriminalization to an increase in popular tolerance toward deviant behavior. More often, decriminalization is imposed on an adamantly punitive public through cooperation between moral liberals and moral conservatives. In the Dutch case, decriminalization was a response to a small, aggressive, expanding minority that not only belonged to the "respectable" classes but also self-confidently asserted the legitimacy and even the superiority of its behavior to conventional lifestyles. The efforts of this deviant collective to throw off the criminal label succeeded after they had found political sponsors among "moral liberals" who were in a position to prevent the creation of an adverse "policy deficit" by influential organized groups both within and outside the state bureaucracy (law enforcement officials, doctors, and scientists). Given the essentially conservative views of the public, the cooperation of moral conservatives was indispensable. Their veto power was based not so much on their formal political position as on their ability to sponsor organized social groups who could articulate policy deficits or trigger a moral crusade, thereby producing a legitimation crisis for the minority within the apparatus of social control that favored decriminalization. A low degree of politicization of the issue was therefore the most important prerequisite for successful decriminalization. By avoiding moral panic and preventing the issue from acquiring symbolic value, the instrumental advantages of decriminalization remained visible and dominant.

Comparison of the Dutch and German cases revealed the impact of underlying social structural variables upon the degree to which a moral issue is politicized and given symbolic significance by powerful groups. A very heterogeneous society like the Netherlands possesses a great ability to accommodate conventional norms to emerging behavioral and subcultural challenges, whereas a structurally more homogeneous society like Germany will tend to exclude and repress emerging groups who refuse to assimilate to the conventional normative order.

DISCUSSION QUESTIONS

1.   Can you think of other examples where deviance challenges the normative foundation of law? What does it mean for a social or political institution to lose legitimacy? Can you give instances of the two responses: repression or incorporation of the deviant? What other behaviors provoke such wide variations in state response? What is the difference between the consensus and conflict models of criminal legislation?

2.   Do changes in criminal law reflect shifts in public opinion or manipulation by organized interests and elites? Does public opinion ever favor decriminalization? Why is the public so conservative and punitive? Is it possible to generalize about the legislative process?

3.   If conservative parties always have the advantage on the "law and order" issue (as they do on foreign policy), how do liberal reforms ever succeed? Can you give other examples of "liberal" parties supporting "conservative" laws? Conservative parties supporting liberalization? What is the advantage of legislation over other forms of governmental response to "social problems"? Are there other examples of policy-making predicated on merely anecdotal evidence? Why isn't the process more scientific? To what extent does Scheerer's explanation turn on the role of key individu-

als, like H.P.A. Baan in the Netherlands or Dietrich Kleiner in Germany? Can they make a difference? Why was the drug issue less politicized in the Netherlands than in Germany? Why did the Netherlands pursue a liberal policy on drugs but not abortion? Does the Dutch experience suggest that political ideology is highly malleable and hence not predictive of action?

4. How do individuals, groups, the media, and government officials create a "moral panic" or "moral crusade"? How important are experts (such as doctors) or the structure of police forces? Are you surprised by the corruptibility of "scientists"?

5. What macrosocial variables explain why the moral panic succeeded in Germany and was avoided in the Netherlands? On the basis of those variables, what predictions would you make about its success in the United States? Has our experience borne out those predictions? Is Dutch tolerance a sufficient explanation? Can we explain it in terms of social structural variables? Could those be created in other countries?

6. Apply Scheerer's approach to other morally freighted legislation: abortion, homosexuality, pornography, immigration, welfare.

11

Worker Safety, Law, and Social Change: The Italian Case

Kitty Calavita

Introduction

Every workday seven Italian workers are killed in occupational accidents, and thirty contract debilitating industrial diseases. Since World War II, Italy has had one of the highest occupational accident rates in the European community. In 1970, in response to this "silent violence" and the worker protest it had provoked, the Italian government passed the Statuto dei Diritti dei Lavoratori (Workers' Rights Law), Article 9 of which gave workers the broad right to oversee and regulate occupational safety and health conditions directly at the shop level.

Reactions to this law, and to Article 9 in particular, were mixed and in fact polarized. It was heralded by most unionists and pro-union academics as a major victory for Italian workers, the culmination of years of daily battle in the factories and on the streets. Legal scholars called it "a major innovative tool" that would "open new horizons" and "the first truly incisive step" toward the realization of Italian workers' constitutional right to safety and health. Labor journalist Ricchi praised it as a "real legislative turning-point."

However, the law evoked precisely the opposite reaction from others. A journal of the extraparliamentary left claimed that the legislation was useless to workers and was in fact a "law for employers and union leaders." Pointing to textual deficiencies and implementation difficulties, some concluded that the law was an empty, symbolic gesture made by the Italian Parliament to satisfy increasingly militant workers. Social scientist Santaloni argued that this law, like much labor law in a capitalist society, served only as "public legitimation of the capitalist mode of production."

The purpose of this paper is twofold. At the descriptive level, it will show that Article 9 of the Italian Workers' Rights Law was neither a useless symbolic gesture nor a tool to "open new horizons" for labor. At the theoretical level, the paper will demonstrate that both of these interpretations were based on overly simplistic notions of law and the state. In particular: 1) they underplay the ongoing, dynamic nature of the class struggle, a struggle in which law is but one component; 2) they

Abridged from *Law & Society Review*, Volume 20:189 (1986).

overlook critical contradictions in both the Italian economy and political structure; and 3) they overstate the potential of the state and legal phenomena to effect real social change.

This overestimation of the potential of law and the state to trigger social change and the underemphasis on prevailing economic, political, and class contradictions are not unique to the observers of the Italian Workers' Rights Law. Rather, scholars in the sociology of law and theories of the state, while recognizing the importance of the economic and political environment to the formulation of state policy, nonetheless tend to reify the state and exaggerate its potential for impact (see, for example, Domhoff, 1978; Miliband, 1969; Poulantzas, 1969; Weinstein, 1968). In fact, whatever the differences among these theorists, they share a view of the capitalist state as a relatively monolithic actor self-consciously pursuing its own interests and those of the capitalist class it represents. This examination of the formulation of the Workers' Rights Law and its effect on safety and health conditions challenges a kind of legal determinism in which the state and state action are highlighted as the primary protagonists of social change.

The model of law that informs this study is dialectical. Law is seen not as the product of a monolithic state structure but rather as the outcome of contradictory political and economic forces. Furthermore, once formulated, the implementation, enforcement, and outcome of law are subject to a similar series of conflicts. In other words, law is but one component of a dialectical process that both precedes and follows it. This process is fired by contradictions not only in the economy but also in the state itself. Therefore, while economic and class contradictions limit the potential impact of state action, political contradictions (within the Italian party system, for example) limit the extent to which the state can realistically be viewed as a single actor pursuing monolithic interests.

This view of law follows the analytical tradition of Chambliss (1979), Whitt (1979), and others, who have argued that an understanding of laws and social policies demands the untangling of the dialectical process in which they are embedded. I suggest, furthermore, that legal phenomena are not necessarily the central ingredients in this process; rather, political and economic constraints and conflicts are often the major protagonists.

The Economic, Political, and Legal Context

The growth of the Italian economy after World War II was surpassed only by that of Japan. Between 1951 and 1971, Italy's growth rate approached 6 percent annually, with its gross national product (GNP) doubling between 1950 and 1962. Both productivity and capital investments rose dramatically, particularly in the boom years from 1958 to 1962. Although a number of factors explain what has been referred to as Italy's "economic miracle," the most important was the country's "competitive integration in the capitalist world economic system." With the general economic expansion and increase in world trade following World War II, capitalist countries were integrated in a complex and delicate balance of interrelationships. Italy's place in this world system and ultimately its "economic miracle" were based on a unique set of circumstances. In particular, Italy's "competitive integration" was dependent on the existence of a large supply of very low-wage labor, relative to other industrialized countries, which included a plentiful reserve brought up from the nation's undeveloped southern regions as the need arose. It has been pointed out that "Italian industry in the '60s had much in common with that of the third world, above all because it made use of such low-wage labor."

This "economic miracle" did not affect all geographic regions and economic sectors equally. In fact, a prominent feature of Italy's economy is its geographic and structural duality. Since its unification, Italy has been divided economically into a thriving capitalist north and a quasi-feudal, agrarian south. In part the consequence of location and in part the result of deliberate government and economic strategies, this uneven development is a distinguishing characteristic of Italian-style capitalism. Although the Italian government sponsored emergency measures in the 1960s and 1970s in an attempt to reverse the effects of decades of intentional underdevelopment in the south, the results were limited to the transfer of a few large factories.

This uneven development supplied northern industry with an important source of cheap labor with which to fuel its "economic miracle." Approximately six million people left the south between 1950 and 1975, most heading to factories in northern Italy or across the border. One Italian observer bluntly assessed the importance of both this cheap labor force and the uneven development, stating that "behind the so-called Italian 'miracle,' then, was a harsh reality of heavy sacrifices for the working class ... and for the south."

In addition to this geographic split, a pronounced structural division crosscuts the Italian economy. To a greater extent than in probably any other industrialized nation, Italy's economy is bifurcated into a monopolized primary sector in which a few large companies have achieved international prominence (Italy's Montedison and FIAT rank eighth and thirteenth in size, respectively, among non-United States world firms) and a larger secondary and underground sector of small, family-run businesses. This dichotomy and the predominance of low-cost, small enterprises not only contributed to Italy's economic growth in the immediate postwar period but has also had and continues to have major ramifications for the occupational safety and health of Italian workers in both sectors.

Side by side with these economic divisions is a political system that is at the same time both relatively unstable and firmly entrenched. In the thirty years between the end of fascism and 1973, Italy had thirty-five different cabinets with an average term of ten months, each ousted largely by votes of no-confidence from parliaments consisting of as many as nine political parties. Since none of these parties has ever achieved an absolute majority in a national election, every government in the post-fascist period has been dependent on precarious coalitions. When the conflicts among the interests and ideologies of these coalition and extracoalition parties surface, as they regularly do, the makeshift government falls.

While the transience of Italian governments is frequently noted, it should not be exaggerated. In fact, since World War II the It alian political system has been characterized by both a nominal change at least every year and an unusual stability of top personnel and majority parties. Thus while governments come and go, the major political parties are well established. The Christian Democrats (DC), supported by the leading economic forces of the country and by the Catholic Church, have enjoyed a dominance unrivaled by any other political party in the West. The Communist Party (PCI), supported by the working class and the largest national union, has consistently been the leading opposition party and the second party in votes polled. By 1972, it was the strongest communist party in Europe. Although the DC has always succeeded in excluding the PCI from government coalitions, the PCI—as the second-largest party in parliament—has played a crucial role in state policy.

The fact that the second-largest party in Italy has regularly been excluded from government coalitions has significantly contributed to the fragility and instability of these coalitions. Thus, while the transience of Italian governments should not be overstated, the political fragmentation and contradictions that underlie this game of "musical chairs" are significant. Their impact on party behavior in supporting legislation and the equivocal outcome of that legislation will be shown below.

Within this context of economic and political fragmentation, Italy's occupational safety and health laws have evolved by fits and starts. The Italian Constitution, framed in 1948, guarantees in Article 32 that "the Republic will protect health as a fundamental right of the individual and of the public interest"; Article 41 states that "the economic enterprise ... must not take place in a way that conflicts with social utility or threatens human safety"; and Article 35 promises that "the Republic oversees employment in its various forms." Article 2087 of the Civil Code makes employers "responsible for adopting all measures which ... are necessary to protect the physical integrity...of their employees."

The first specific legislation concerning occupational safety and health in modern Italy was a general law of February 12, 1955 (Law Number 51), which requested the government to establish standards with regard to industrial safety and health. Ironically, the practical effect of the standards that resulted was to restrict constitutional guarantees to the worker and maximize the opportunity for employer discretion. The two laws that still provide the foundation of occupational safety and health in Italy are representative.

In April 1955, Law Number 547 laid out in very general terms the obligation of employers to establish safe work environments, largely reiterating what was contained in the Civil Code. With this law, however, the mandate of the code was qualified. The new law was replete with references to what the employer should do when "technical reasons of production" or "inconvenience" did not permit the elimination of danger. The placement of "warning signs" and "other measures" are among the suggested alternatives (Articles 8 and 11).

The second cornerstone of Italian occupational safety and health legislation, Law Number 303, passed in March 1956, established a number of specific requirements, such as periodic medical examinations for workers in certain industries. Most of the law, however, was devoted to the promulgation of the general standards concerning dust, noise, ventilation, and the like, which are still used today. Again, however, these standards are so general as to be of little practical utility and provide the employer with the option to ignore them if they are deemed "inconvenient." For example, the law stated on one hand that "temperatures must be such as to avoid deleterious effects on workers' health," while on the other, temperature and humidity may be determined by "the exigencies of production" (Article 13). Articles 18 and 19 provide prime examples of such legislative hedging: Article 18 begins: "Substances used in the production process that might be dangerous to the health of workers must not accumulate in the work environment beyond the level that is strictly necessary for production purposes"; Article 19 then continues: "The employer should carry out, whenever possible, work that is dangerous or unhealthy in separate locations, so as not to expose more workers than necessary to the risks."

These two laws have been periodically followed by industry-specific norms, but these standards provide only general guidelines. As of 1984, Italy was one of the few industrialized countries without legally established maximum levels of exposure to toxic substances (MACs).

From 1955 to the early 1980s, the Italian Labor Ministry was largely responsible for the implementation of these safety and health laws. Regional and provincial inspectors under the labor minister's jurisdiction were authorized to conduct work-place inspections and denounce negligent employers. Given the nature of the standards, subjectivity and inspector discretion were inevitable. Furthermore, in spite of its vast responsibilities, the Labor Ministry's inspectorate was notoriously understaffed. In 1969, for example, only ninety-four provincial inspectors and ten regional inspectors comprised the entire field staff, and occupational safety and health constituted only a part of their job. The field inspection staff in Turin in 1973—responsible for overseeing 43,000 firms—was made up of nine inspectors, five engineers, and a doctor. There were approximately 90,000 reported industrial accidents a year in the city, yet these inspectors concluded only 637 field visits.

When penalties are imposed, they are minimal. The maximum fine through the mid-1970s was 300,000 lire per violation—approximately 400 dollars. Article 437 of the Penal Code, which provides for six months' to ten years' imprisonment for serious violations, was subject to "systematic non-use," being imposed only ten times between 1955 and 1967.

The National Agency for the Prevention of Accidents (ENPI) operated along with, and frequently overlapped, the labor inspectorate. The jurisdiction of ENPI was technically plant equipment and machinery as they affect worker safety; this category was so general, however, that ENPI was de facto authorized to oversee almost all aspects of worker safety. In addition, a major contradiction so flawed ENPI's bureaucratic structure that in 1974 the Italian labor minister called it the agency's "original sin." ENPI was a parastatal agency, for its budget was not derived directly from the state. Rather, it was financed in part by the national disability insurance agency (discussed below) and in part by employers themselves. This dual funding system had two major effects. First, since insurance premiums are based on industry risks, the insurance agency (and hence ENPI, which it funded) had some interest in maintaining high risk levels. Second, while ENPI's purpose was to *regulate* industry, half of its budget was provided by contracting out its services to the very employers it was to regulate.

The agency's mandate to regulate its own clients created enough scandals to validate labor's claim that "ENPI is an employer's institution." A court decision in Turin in 1973 revealed that in this industrial capital only about 10 percent of industries had ever been inspected by ENPI and that records of more than 13,000 violations had been deliberately buried in the agency's archives. As one ENPI employee explained to the court, "It's not a good idea ... to denounce an employer since he pays the bill and has demonstrated his faith in you by calling ENPI."

Interacting with these two inspection agencies, and seemingly contradicting the deterrent model on which they were based, is the National Institute of Insurance against Occupational Accidents and Illnesses (INAIL). A central component of Italian safety and health law is compulsory insurance, paid by employers, for employees engaged in certain high-risk work. Detailed tables list the types of work for which such insurance is required and for which payments will be made by INAIL in case of injury. However, the actual consequence of this insurance system is to indemnify employers against accidents and illnesses rather than to regulate them. While employers are required by law to establish safe and healthy working conditions, this thriving state agency informs them that they can (and must) buy insurance against their own transgressions.

In light of these ambiguous laws, understaffed bureaucracies, and contradictory enforcement ideologies, it should not be surprising that Italy's postwar economic boom was accompanied by a large number of worker deaths and injuries. In fact, in the thirty years following World War II, the number of industrial accidents and illnesses in Italy rose precipitously. In 1946, according to INAIL, 349,000 Italian workers were the victims of industrial accidents and 1,157 contracted disabling occupational illnesses. By 1970, the year of the Workers' Rights Law, the number of accidents had almost quadrupled to 1,340,000 and the number of illnesses had jumped to more than 50,000. This increase was not due solely to an increase in the size of the industrial work force. While the frequency of industrial accidents was 17.32 per 1,000 workers at risk in 1951 (the first year for which data are available), by 1970 the frequency had risen to 21.78. Over the same period, the rate of industrial illnesses increased from 0.13 per 1,000 workers to 0.81.

By the early 1970s, for every worker who received an old-age pension, another had already received worker disability compensation. In the decades following the war, industrial accidents and illnesses were so frequent that by the mid-1960s many Italian workers and their unions began to suspect that the "economic miracle" was being performed on their backs and with their blood.

The Workers' Movement for Occupational Safety and Health

After World War II, the strategy of Italian workers with regard to occupational safety and health was so-called monetization. Rather than demanding that risks be eliminated, workers focused on securing remuneration for high-risk jobs. Assuming the inevitability of industrial accidents and illnesses, workers attempted at least to receive compensation for the health that they "sold" along with their labor.

By the time of the Workers' Rights Law in 1970, monetization had been rejected with a vengeance, as Italian workers demanded the reorganization of the work place and confidently proclaimed that "Health is not for sale!" The origins of this ideological and strategic shift can be traced to the recession of 1964–65. As the economy slowed down and the "economic miracle" began to wane, layoffs and work reductions were common. Six hundred thousand metalworkers were either laid off or put on part-time schedules, 150,000 construction workers lost their jobs and 60,000 jobs disappeared in the textile industry. Industry and the government responded to defensive strikes against these cutbacks with "purges," which consisted primarily in laying off the strikers and union activists. It has been estimated that 50,000 workers were laid off in 1965 alone as a consequence of their strike activity.

In the face of these events, the three major Italian unions—the Confederazione Generale Italiana dei Lavoratori (CGIL), the Confederazione Italiana del Lavoro (CISL), and the Unione Italiana del Lavoro (UIL)—sought strength in unity and, although they remained distinct confederations, pledged to follow a course of solidarity. By 1966, with Italian workers ever more bitter, the major unions forced together by a common enemy, and the economy reviving, a new era in the class struggle began. The number of hours lost to strikes doubled in that year in spite of industry's strategy of laying off strikers.

United factory committees and factory councils were created at the shop level to represent workers directly and increasingly played a critical role in forcing the hand of employers and in forming union strategy. In part in response to the demands of these grass-roots groups, working conditions and safety and health became increasingly important issues on the union agenda.

With major national contracts set for renewal in 1968, 100,000 FIAT workers waged the largest strike in fourteen years and won a new contract that included reductions in the work pace and a change in the piece-rate system. Pirelli rubber workers, urged on by the "united grass-roots committees," reduced their work pace and refused to respond to employer counteroffensives. Eight hundred thousand construction workers throughout the country marched through the streets demanding an end to the "white homicides" (workplace fatalities); in Milan they carried forty-two white crosses in denunciation of the recent job-related deaths of forty-two of their colleagues.

Strikes continued to increase in number and intensity in 1969, as production was paralyzed in sector after sector. In that year's so-called hot autumn, workers were joined by students in factory sit-ins and work stoppages. FIAT, Pirelli, and most other major industries were the battlefields for almost daily confrontations as Italian industrialists faced for the first time an organized and intractable opponent.

Contracts achieved following the "hot autumn" gave workers substantial salary and benefit increases and featured as their centerpieces safety and health clauses. The chemical workers' contract of 1969 opened a new era as MACs were built into the agreement and workers were given the right to participate in safety and health research and in the implementation of standards. Similar victories among workers in the construction, rubber, and textile industries followed rapidly as an estimated 2.5 million workers reaped the benefits of the "hot autumn." Riding the wave of union successes and responding to grass-roots militancy on safety and health issues, the secretary of the CGIL began his speech at the union's annual congress in 1969 with this vow: "Every hour an Italian worker is killed and every two minutes there is a work accident.... The CGIL right now makes a solemn commitment to a vast, broad-based campaign for the defense of the factory worker."

A new workers' model of occupational safety and health evolved from and subsequently guided these struggles. With the conviction that "health is not for sale" replacing monetization as their strategy, Italian workers developed a distinctive methodology for the achievement of safety and health. This model included four items:

1.   Subjectivity. Rooted in a suspicion of scientists and experts derived from the workers' fruitless encounters with ENPI officials and company doctors, "subjectivity" asserted the unique capacity of the worker to experience and report symptoms of illness and workplace hazards by her- or himself.

2.   Nondelegation of authority. "Nondelegation" referred to the refusal to entrust to official authorities—labor inspectorates as well as union leaders—the job of workplace improvement. Not only are the workers themselves the only source of actual knowledge about working conditions (subjectivity), but it is they who must take the responsibility for combating them. As expressed by one unionist, "It is the delegation of authority—to the psychiatrist, to the doctor, to the labor inspector, to the judge, to the safety engineer, and to the union organization—that has produced these

results, that is, that has permitted the prevention system to function in the interests of the dominant classes."

3. Consensual validation. "Consensual validation," in a collective version of subjectivity, held that while individual workers experience the effects of hazardous conditions (subjectivity), groups of workers in similar production situations can, through regular assemblies in which symptoms are discussed, arrive at more adequate conclusions regarding the safety of the work environment than can traditional scientific instruments.

4. Homogeneous worker group. The "homogeneous worker group" was to be comprised of those workers who face similar production conditions and are therefore likely to experience similar symptoms. The group was to be small enough for workers to exchange information personally and large enough for conclusions to be drawn regarding the work environment. It was through the efforts of these homogeneous groups that consensual validation was to be achieved.

The form of the occupational safety and health component of the Workers' Rights Law, particularly its emphasis on direct worker participation in the struggle to improve working conditions and nondelegation of authority, was based in large part on this workers' model.

The Workers' Rights Law of 1970

While Italian workers were unable to reduce accident and illness rates in the late 1960s, they were more successful at the political level. As social scientist Greco said, "the institutional response to ["the hot autumn"] could not be other than flexible.... The Workers' Rights Law of 1970 symbolizes, at the legislative level, the changes taking place in society."

The first union rights law in Italy, the Workers' Rights Law of 1970 (Law Number 300) included thirty-two articles that addressed issues ranging from the right of workers to hold assemblies within the factory to the definition of illegal anti-union activity by employers. Article 9 gave workers substantial rights to control occupational safety and health conditions at the shop level. The law was passed on May 20, 1970, by overwhelming majorities in both the Senate and the House.

It is clear from a brief examination of the various workers' rights bills in this period and the debates surrounding them that 1) the law was a direct response to the workers' movement, 2) this response was not merely a symbolic one, and 3) the state itself and the political parties within it faced a number of irresolvable conflicts. The Workers' Rights Law was in part a response to these various conflicts.

Beginning in 1963, a number of workers' rights bills were introduced in the Italian Parliament, but none elicited any serious debate. Furthermore, none of these bills made any reference to worker control of safety and health conditions. The political situation in 1968 and 1969 transformed this parliamentary disinterest into almost frenetic legislative activity. Just as the workers' movement was exploding throughout Italy and much of Western Europe, a number of developments in Italian party politics enhanced the major parties' receptivity to a politics of reform. First, the election of 1968 confirmed a continuous shift to the left by Italian voters. While in 1958 the DC polled 42.2 percent of the national votes to the PCI's 22.6 percent, ten years later these two leading parties polled 39.1 percent and 26.9 percent, respectively. This increased electoral strength of the left, combined with the growing political influence of the unions, gave the Christian Democrats and their center-left coalition government little choice but to support a politics of reform.

At the same time, the newly strengthened PCI was initiating its strategy of progressive integration in the hope of achieving an official role in future government coalitions. As part of its attempt to demonstrate simultaneously its continued support for workers' causes and its new responsibility and willingness to compromise, the PCI joined the DC in calling for moderate reforms. Strengthened by the rapidly growing power of unions and recent electoral victories but limited by the need to compromise to exercise that power, the PCI came face-to-face with the "Catch-22" that has plagued it for more than a decade.

Immediately following the elections of 1968, each of the three major leftist forces in Parliament (the communist PCI and the socialist PSIUP and PSI) submitted their own workers' rights bills. The Communist bill was the first to be introduced and the only one to contain an occupational safety and health clause. Pointing to the "intensification of the exploitation of the physical and psychological powers of workers," the PCI argued for "more humane working hours and work pace, [and] greater protection of worker health and safety." Nonetheless, the PCI bill was far from revolutionary. Rather, its express purpose was to achieve for workers a greater role in the "exercise of legitimate power" in the interests of "a regulated democratic system."

In early 1969, as workers increased the pressure on both their employers and the government, the Italian labor minister established a Senate commission to investigate the need for a workers' rights law and to elicit worker and management input. In responding to the commission's surveys and during its hearings, workers expressed strong support for such a law. The subject of occupational safety and health was altogether neglected by the commission's surveys, however, which focused instead on such broad issues as the right of workers to hold assemblies and the right not to be fired for anti-union activity. Nevertheless, worker after worker broached the subject of safety and health independently and stressed the need for worker input. A FIAT worker and union activist summarized the opinion workers consistently expressed to the commission: "The union must have an effective control inside the factory particularly with regard to health and safety, which is a critical point.... These are the important things that interest the worker."

In June 1969, one year after the PCI initiative and subsequent to the Senate commission investigation, the DC presented its proposal for a workers' rights law. In spite of worker demands for a safety and health clause during commission hearings, the DC bill included no such provision. In fact, the DC's rationale for the proposal had little to do with the needs of workers. Rather, the party supported the law to prevent the promulgation of more dangerous "demagogic" legislation. Furthermore, the DC version of the law was designed to protect unions and collective bargaining against competition from the grass-roots workers' movement that was daily gaining momentum. Much as the Progressives in early twentieth-century America preferred to support the American Federation of Labor rather than risk the wrath of less predictable forces, the DC attempted to "normalize" and regulate labor relations: "It is best to recognize that the base of the building is to be found in the union and collective bargaining.... No alternative to the union can exist as an expression of the workers."

In response to the Senate commission's recommendations, the coalition government submitted a bill to the Senate in June 1969. The introduction to this bill states that it was "a precise response by the government to demands ... that are being presented in an ever more compelling way in the world of work." This bill also excluded any safety and health provision, postponing it "for later consideration." The commission quickly followed with its own bill, only slightly different from the government proposal. It also made no mention of worker control of safety and health and underscored the privileged position of established unions as compared to grass-roots groups.

The "hot autumn" of 1969 brought rapid, virtually uncontested changes in the Senate commission's bill. At the instigation of a group of Communist senators, the commission was persuaded to add a number of provisions to its bill, including the occupational safety and health clause of the earlier Communist bill. Thus, Article 6 read: "The workers, through their representatives, have the right to oversee the implementation of standards for the prevention of occupational accidents and illnesses and to engage both in research and in the establishment and application of any measures that will promote occupational health."

This provision elicited little discussion when the bill came before the Senate for a vote in December 1969. In fact, rather than contesting its inclusion, the senators added an amendment to liberalize this new article. The original wording implied that only union representatives had the right to meet with and advise workers on safety and health conditions in the factory. A group of Communist senators introduced an amendment to imply that any worker representative, not only those formally recognized as such, could enter the workplace to advise workers on safety and health. The Communist senators' argument was that in order to realize the potential of this article, outside experts must be allowed to enter the factory as worker representatives. In this form, the Senate bill was approved on December 11, 1969; a similar House bill passed with little debate on May 20, 1970.

The spokesmen of all major political forces in Parliament recognized the importance of the threat posed by the workers' movement in getting the legislation passed. A DC leader, in his concluding speech before the final vote, clarified his intention to support the measure: "This road must lead not to increasing battles in our country, but to a pacification." Others agreed: "The union battles now in progress, with their vehemence and their demands, have made clear the necessity for a serious reform measure." The labor minister voiced his concern that without such a reform, the political situation would worsen: "It is more probable than ever that, in the absence of reforms ... the crises that have emerged in some sectors of society ... will explode."

The political evolution of the Workers' Rights Law and its safety and health provision demonstrates a number of points. First, the law was a response to the increasingly threatening workers' movement. Although this legislation had been demanded by unions since 1952, it was not until Italian workers gained significant leverage in 1968 and 1969 that such a bill was seriously debated in Parliament. Furthermore, it was not until after the "hot autumn" of 1969 that the DC and their center-left government accepted the inclusion of a safety and health provision in the legislation.

Second, although the law was a response to working-class pressure and was often supported for its pacification potential, it did not follow the typical course of "symbolic law." A number of sociologists of law have argued that much occupational safety and health legislation is "symbolic" in that, while it is apparently a response to workers' demands, it is rendered meaningless in the legislative process (Calavita, 1983; Donnelly, 1982; Stearns, 1979). Whether the aim of legislators from the beginning is to create an impotent law with which to placate constituents, these sociologists have labeled as "symbolic" any law that appears to respond to political demands yet is so weakened in the amendment process or the implementation stage that the final product is an empty gesture.

However, the Workers' Rights Law and its safety and health clause took just the opposite course. In the amendment process following the "hot autumn," Communist senators were successful in strengthening the bill, not only adding the safety and health provision but also liberalizing it to ensure that it would not become meaningless. While earlier occupational safety and health laws in Italy had focused on employers' obligations in very general terms, often allowing for "extenuating circumstances," Article 9 gave workers both the right to improve the work environment and some of the tools with which to achieve this.

Third, the legislation was the product of a fragmented government, each part of which had specific interests and faced its own unique conflicts as well as the more general contradictions shared by all. The final form of the bill was the result of each sector of Parliament attempting to cope with the conflicts it faced and to hammer out the best possible political bargain within the context of these conflicts. This is particularly evident in the case of the PCI. As a Communist, working-class party in an advanced capitalist society, the PCI confronted two specific contradictions by the late 1960s. First, it inevitably experienced a gap between the working-class interests it represented and the reforms it could realistically expect to achieve within the capitalist context. This gap helps explain the party's support for an essentially reformist measure and its failure to introduce anything more progressive.

Compounding this dilemma is a political contradiction that continues to plague the PCI. It has often been noted that "the politics of the [Italian] Communist Party is dominated by the fear of losing—or not gaining enough—allies." Just as the PCI is strengthened by popular support and workers' victories and could thus convincingly bid for a position in the coalition government, it must moderate its political activity in the hopes of realizing this opportunity (so far unsuccessfully). At such times, the PCI is strong enough politically to take a leading role in pressing for the progressive changes that the working class expects of it but must simultaneously exercise self-restraint in its quest for governmental power.

Thus, Communist senators during the parliamentary discussions of the Workers' Rights Law praised the flexibility of Parliament and stressed the advantage of confrontations among different points of view. In his closing comments before the final vote, one PCI senator referred to the "vitality" of Parliament in constructing the law—"a vitality ... that was expressed in a kind of dialectic and confrontation." Another, in speaking of his success in persuading the Senate commission to strengthen the legislation, used the occasion to make an open plea for PCI participation in the government coalition: "Certainly there were differences of opinion and these will remain, but it must be recognized [that]...the commission has demonstrated how useful a different relationship between majority and opposition could be." Needing to show workers its courage in representing them and at the same time to prove to the DC its moderation and willingness to compromise, the PCI played an important role but nevertheless always a tentative one, in the formation and passage of the law. While the PCI was instrumental in liberalizing the bill after the fall of 1969, its express goal never went beyond the achievement of a "pluralist democracy," a "more adult, modern, and advanced democracy," a "regulated, democratic system."

The demand for this legislation was rooted in class contradictions in the Italian economic system, particularly the conflict between employers' drive to maximize profits and the safety and health of the workers who produce these profits. However, the form of the legislation was shaped by contradictions and tensions within the Italian state itself (for example, the long-standing exclusion of the Communist Party, the second-largest party in the country, from the coalition government) and within the political parties, particularly the PCI. On one hand, the PCI was to represent the interests of workers, and its growing political strength depended on this; on the other, it was not to alienate the DC and the capitalist interests the latter represented, and the PCI's participation in government depended on this. The outcome of these contradictions was a law that, in the area of safety and health, cautiously responded to workers' demands for control of the work environment, yet on the whole tended to limit the legitimacy of the spontaneous, grass-roots groups that increasingly characterized the Italian labor movement. The product of a struggle among contradictory political forces within the context of a capitalist economy and its class contradictions, the final version of the 1970 law resembled more a precarious balancing act than a symbolic sleight of hand.

Article 9 in Action

In Italy the early 1970s was a period of continued working-class strength and mobilization. Alfa Romeo, FIAT, Olivetti, and other major factories were the sites of regular sit-ins and strikes, which ultimately won the workers lucrative new contracts. Two Italian scholars declared: "At the level of actual achievements as well as at the level of the form of the struggle, the period 1970–74 must be considered an extension ... [and] consolidation of the victories and aspirations of 1969."

Armed with Article 9 and an increasingly sophisticated political consciousness, workers, factory councils and unions initiated several years of unprecedented occupational safety and health activity. Initially, conferences aimed at political consciousness-raising and communication among workers comprised a large part of the union effect. A national occupational safety and health conference sponsored by the three unions—CGIL, CISL, and UIL—drew thousands of workers and union activists in 1972, and its proceedings provide an important historical document of worker concerns and strategies in this period. Speaker after speaker at this conference in Rimini spoke of the need for "a new organization of production...[and] an end to socioeconomic exploitation."

Supported by Article 9, workers in factories throughout Italy named physicians and scientists as their "representatives" and set about the task of documenting and combating workplace hazards. The results of these investigations frequently formed the bases for contracts that, among other provisions, fixed maximum levels of exposure to toxic substances, abolished piece rates, and mandated more frequent work pauses.

Extensive research into the dangers of the work setting was often unnecessary. Olivetti workers in Turin in 1970 were well aware of the physical and psychological hazards of their work pace and, after months of bargaining and work stoppages, won the right to determine the pace of the assembly line based on the judgment of homogeneous groups of workers. In the early 1970s, FIAT automobile body-paint workers at the large Mirafiori plant, faced daily with the immediate physical risks of their assembly-line work, won an intense and prolonged battle with management for the establishment of work rotations and "assembly islands."

In 1972 workers were given a new weapon for these struggles when many regional governments created local Occupational Medicine Services (SMLs). The Rimini conference had concluded with workers calling for local public services that would be preventive in nature and work hand-in-hand with workers to reduce occupational health risks. The first SML was established in the "red" region of Emilia-Romagna, followed by those in Tuscany, Lombardy, and other regions throughout northern and central Italy. These services were seen by the predominantly communist-administered regions in which they were located as alternatives to the understaffed and employer-captured national agencies, and as such they tended to be run by personnel who were politically committed to the workers' struggle. While these local officials were frequently useful as the outside "representatives" to which Article 9 referred, they had no real enforcement authority. Consistent with the workers' principle of nondelegation, the legally ambiguous SMLs became outside consultants for the workers' investigations, upon which collective bargaining was based.

In the first half of the 1970s, accident rates declined only slowly, and illness rates continued to rise. As the secretary of the CGIL said, "We have undergone a massive counterattack." In fact, employer response to workers' offensives was both immediate and varied. Management's "concessions" were carefully calculated to involve neither mechanisms of control nor any substantial reorganization of production and were frequently accompanied by countermeasures designed to recoup expenditures or any potential loss of control. The experience of workers at FIAT's Mirafiori plant is exemplary. FIAT-Mirafiori, one of the largest factories in Italy, is noted for both the intensity of its workers' safety and health efforts and the scope of their victories. However, these victories were frequently either limited to the installation of mechanical devices (such as fans for increased air circulation) or—in the case of more radical changes—were restricted to a small number of workers involved in one circumscribed task. The establishment of "assembly islands" at Mirafiori, for example, widely recognized as a significant innovation involving the organization of production, affected only 250 of the 55,000 workers at this plant. Furthermore, FIAT workers' demands for "a new way of making the automobile" took an ironic twist as these assembly islands were counterbalanced by an increased hierarchy of control, more automation and the introduction of robots, and the increased parceling and subcontracting out of tasks. Factory councils told of a similar experience among body-paint workers and concluded that "the reduction of one group [of hazards] ... ends up opening the way for an increase in another type of hazard."

The consequence was not only that overall safety and health conditions did not significantly improve, but also that worker control was frequently reduced with these production changes. "FIAT was required by the workers' movement to 'change' the work environment, but they did it according to a plan that tended to cut the legs off the workers' movement.... Technical changes have been introduced by FIAT not so much to reduce health risks but to reduce the capacity of workers' battles to affect the production process."

Employers did not hesitate to take advantage of a contradiction facing workers in any capitalist society who demand radical changes in the organization of production. A fundamental contradiction exists between the employers' drive for maximum profits and the health and safety of the producers of those profits. This means, most obviously, that employers will often violate workers' interests in health and safety. But, conversely, it also means that factories in which workers effectively demand expensive production changes may experience profit reductions and ultimately, shutdowns. Italian employers, exploiting this contradiction, frequently met recalcitrant workers with the threat of closing the factory, which was predicated on profit considerations.

Related to this dilemma, Italian law allows the closing of plants or sections of plants as a last-resort sanction against employers who continually violate safety and health norms. Thus, workers' appeals to state officials often had negative consequences for the workers themselves. As the national secretary of the Italian steelworkers' union pointed out bitterly, recourse to the state after an accident in which a worker is injured could mean "one injured and fifty unemployed."

The most powerful of management's weapons was the "externalization" of dangerous tasks to smaller shops, the underground economy, or the less unionized south. As workers in Italy's largest factories demanded the reduction of health risks, management often responded by "cleaning up" the work environment by relocating the offending production unit outside the main factory's gates. This sometimes meant the dispersal of the dangerous work to small, less politically active plants, as in the case of Montedison di Castellanza; the transfer of operations to less unionized southern regions (one of FIAT's most successful strategies), the contracting out of dangerous work to underground entrepreneurs; or even, in the case of one firm, the contracting out of contested production tasks to small cooperatives of ex-employees, some of whom had been laid off with the department shutdown. One group of Italian scholars summarized FIAT's strategy:

> The factory revolts ... have taught FIAT management one elementary truth: Big plants like FIAT Mirafiori are no longer governable and therefore FIAT has established a new system. That is, plants are set up in the south, but they are set up in a particular way. FIAT is not setting up a "Mirafiori of the South," but rather many small establishments.

A union study of the FIAT experience concludes that "the objective result of our battles has been the export of hazards from situations of strength to situations of weakness."

This dispersal of health risks by management highlighted and played on a difficulty inherent in the workers' model of safety and health as well as in Article 9. Any approach to occupational safety and health that hinges entirely on workers' vigilance and control is dependent on both a strong workers' movement and a production process that brings these workers together. Subjectivity, nondelegation of authority, and consensual validation all presuppose a collective of workers, just as the implementation of Article 9 requires an attentive and strong bargaining unit of workers. These newly dispersed, isolated, and small production units, often located in the underground economy, were virtually immune from workers' safety and health activity and thus to all safety and health regulation. The very principle of non-delegation, which informed the workers' movement and on which Article 9 had been based, appeared to have backfired. As employers exported hazards to nonunion shops, the focus on control by the workers and away from reliance on the state meant that these shops were effectively insulated from safety and health intervention of any kind.

Confronted with employers' strategic maneuvers and the economic and structural contradictions on which many of these tactics depended, workers found that safety and health conditions were slow to improve. The occupational illness rate showed no improvement in the first half of the 1970s, while the incidence of industrial accidents was reduced slightly, most notably in 1972. The cynics who predicted that Article 9 would be meaningless to workers and the optimists who foresaw a dramatic turnaround in safety and health conditions were thus both wrong. They were wrong empirically, as this review of workers' partial victories and a look at the halting improvements in safety statistics document. But they were also wrong in the respective views of the law and the Italian state that were implicit in their interpretations of the law. As the last section demonstrated, the notion of a monolithic state upon which depictions of a symbolic law depended is inapplicable to the fragmented Italian political scene of the 1970s and is particularly inaccurate with regard to the enactment of the Workers' Rights Law. The present section demonstrates that the essentially pluralist model on which hopeful predictions of a turnaround were predicated overstated the potential of law to effect social change and overlooked the larger, ongoing battle into which the law was inserted and in which it was only one weapon.

The evidence from the second half of the 1970s confirms the importance of extralegal factors in understanding the occupational safety and health experience of Italian workers following the passage of Article 9. While the class contradiction and employers' opportunistic use of the economic dilemmas inherent in the safety and health struggle had imposed restraints on the powerful workers' movement in the early 1970s, a curious development occurred in the second half of the decade. As economic collapse weakened the Italian working class and precipitated a withdrawal of participation in safety and health issues, occupational accident statistics improved.

Economic Collapse and Worker Safety, 1975–80

In 1975 the Italian economy entered a serious depression. The GNP fell for the first time since the war, 3.7 percent in absolute terms. Overall productive activity declined more than 11 percent, and industrial investments plummeted by 25 percent. The rest of the decade showed only slight and inconsistent improvement. Industrial investments rose in 1976, but not enough to compensate for the 1975 decline, and fell again in 1977 and 1978. Unemployment increases accompanied the recession as the number of people employed remained approximately the same between 1974 and 1978 despite increases in the size of the labor market. Mass layoffs were common occurrences. According to one estimate, FIAT laid off 23,000 workers in one year.

Employers who had suffered the humiliation of the "hot autumn" and its aftermath were quick to turn economic crisis into political opportunity. Agnelli and other leaders of the Italian economy called for the liberation of Italian employers so that they would be free "to accumulate capital and labor as [they] judged most convenient." The Italian employers' association—Confindustria—spoke sardonically of the need for an employers' rights law. Addressing safety and health issues, the head of the Bank of Italy warned that "the real problem is not the quality of life in the factories, but the survival of the factories themselves."

Under the onslaught of economic crisis and worker layoffs, which was coupled with double-digit inflation (more than 20 percent by 1976), unions gave priority to unemployment and salary issues. The political sophistication of the early 1970s and the focus on the need for a radical reorganization of production that had spawned militance only a few years earlier now seemed to encourage fatalism. One legal scholar has offered the following explanation for this fatalism and the reduced worker interest in safety and health research: "The precise diagnosis of an illness is a waste if you know the cure is impossible."

With this new fatalism came a tentative return to the monetization approach to occupational safety and health, although now it was a monetization that reflected less a rolling back of workers' hard-won political awareness and more their desperation to secure at least minimal gain in an increasingly one-sided battle. While Italian workers had once proudly proclaimed, "Health is not for sale," they now said bitterly, "Yes, it's true that health is not for sale, but neither is it free." By the end of the 1970s, the safety and health movement had suffered setbacks so great that the CGIL sponsored a national seminar on how to revive the moribund movement.

The recession of the mid-1970s precipitated a "salvage mission" by the Italian government that aimed primarily to reduce the cost of labor in an attempt to revive the nation's economy. Central to this mission was a series of laws, passed between 1976 and 1979, known as the "crisis legislation." As part of this package, a number of court decisions reversed earlier court interpretations of Article 9, which had given outside experts access to the factories. In 1980, the federal court of appeals concluded that Parliament had intended the "representatives" referred to in Article 9 to mean only union representatives, thus denying factory access to workers' consultants and effectively emasculating the article.

Ironically, as the worst depression since World War II silenced the workers' movement and de facto nullified the Workers' Rights Law, occupational accident statistics in 1975 showed the greatest improvement in postwar history. Even controlling for the number of workers at risk—a crucial consideration during economic booms and busts and concomitant fluctuations in the size of the labor force—the 1975 accident rate registered unprecedented improvements. In the rest of the decade there were less pronounced but nevertheless continuous reductions in the accident rate, in spite of increasing barriers to both safety and health organization and the implementation of Article 9.

A number of explanations might be offered for this reduction in industrial accidents despite workers' increasing economic, political, and legal vulnerability. One might argue, for example, that the reduction reflects a time-lag in the statistics between workers' earlier demands and gradual changes in working conditions. Or it might be suggested that the local SMLs discussed above—which had proliferated by mid-decade—carried on the struggle when workers' power was eroded. It could even be argued that the seeming "improvement" was entirely spurious, reflecting instead the externalization of hazards to the underground economy where accidents are effectively concealed.

A close look at the statistical pattern forces one to reject all these interpretations. First, they suggest a continuous, gradual improvement, while most of the accident reduction in this period is attributable to an abrupt decline in one year—1975. Furthermore, a look at the regional patterns suggests that this reduction cannot be explained by SMLs, externalization, or earlier worker militance, for the decline was as pronounced in the southern regions without a strong workers' base, SMLs and the impetus for externalization as it was in the more unionized and politically left areas of northern and central Italy. In fact, in some southern regions, such as Calabria, Sardegna, and Puglia, the improvements were greater than those in the north. For example, the accident rate fell from 120 in 1974 in Calabria to 77.3 in 1975, a 30 percent decrease unrivaled by any northern or central region. These statistics are even more provocative if one remembers that northern employers frequently relocated their most hazardous production units to the south.

In attempting to explain these accident reductions during a period of worker vulnerability and attacks on Article 9, it will help to reexamine the class contradiction between employers' drive for maximum profits and workers' safety and health. This contradiction or tension is integrally linked to the logic of capital and the production of surplus value and is, therefore, endemic to any capitalist society. The particular ways in which this tension plays itself out depend on historically specific conditions, such as the relative power of labor, imbalances and dualities in the economy, and capital mobility. Two aspects of this contradiction have already been discussed: 1) In the most general sense, employers who seek to maximize profits by minimizing production costs will often violate workers' safety and health interests;

and 2) conversely, workers who effectively demand production changes may be threatened with a production unit shutdown based on profit considerations.

The drive for maximum profits may be antithetical to workers' safety and health interests in another way as well. During periods of economic boom and responsive markets, manufacturers seek to maximize their profits by increasing production. Given the short-term nature of economic fluctuations, this increase in production is not accompanied by a corresponding increase in personnel. Instead, it is based on a general intensification of production achieved with methods such as quickening the work pace, short-circuiting time-consuming safety precautions, and increasing overtime. Many scholars have noted the connection between production pressures and industrial accidents. Carson (1981), for example, describes the twelve-hour days of North Sea oil workers and explains the extraordinarily high death and injury rate on offshore oil rigs as the direct consequence of such productive intensity. Perrow (1984) examines "high-risk technologies" and argues that the high accident rate in these industries is at least in part determined by production pressures.

The argument here, however, is that productive intensity varies with economic fluctuations and, as the work pace decreases with economic recessions, so may worker accidents. Thus, just as employers could most easily afford to improve the work environment, the intensification of production to meet market demands increases the risk of accidents. Conversely, during periods of recession, dangerous overtime is reduced or eliminated, and productivity per worker is likely to fall. Ironically, as workers' bargaining power is eroded by their economic vulnerability in a recession, the accident rate may decline, not because of any major changes in the production process but rather because of a slackening of productive intensity.

An Italian study relates two indicators of economic activity—gross industrial investments and utilization of productive capacity—to the accident rate both in the economy as a whole and in specific industries from 1920 through 1972. Since 1920 the number of industrial accidents has been closely linked to industrial investments, a general indicator of economic activity. The percent of productive capacity utilized—an indicator of productive intensity—correlates closely with the incidence of industrial accidents in the metal, chemical, rubber, and paper industries during the twenty-year period of Italy's "economic miracle." The general conclusion to be drawn from the study is that economic booms consistently cause the accident rate to rise. It is only at moments of serious economic deterioration, for example, in 1965 and 1972, that the accident rate takes significant dips. Less severe economic declines, as in 1958, are accompanied by more subtle reductions in the accident rate. While recessions increase the pressure on employers to cut costs and hence conceivably to bypass costly safety precautions, the decline of productive intensity during recessions more than offsets the influence of this cost-reduction factor.

The statistics for Italy in the 1970s follow this long-standing pattern. As a whole, the decade saw an economic slowdown after the "miracle" of the 1950s and 1960s. It was a slowdown punctuated by economic crises beginning with the recession in

1972, followed by economic collapse in 1975 and, after a brief and tentative recovery, another recession-stagnation in 1977–78. It is precisely these recessionary years that account for most of the decline in industrial accidents during the decade. Some of this reduction is no doubt attributable to the concerted efforts of labor and their determined use of all the weapons at their disposal, including the Workers' Rights Law. However, the historical pattern, the overall improvement in accident rates in the 1970s, and the accelerated decline in the rates after the virtual defeat of labor all point to the powerful influence of independent economic forces on worker safety statistics.

While these economic forces are independent of legal and political efforts aimed at worker safety and health, they are by no means autonomous of the underlying relations of production. Rather, this study suggests that there is a fundamental contradiction between the drive for maximum profits and worker safety and that this contradiction manifested itself in at least two specific ways in Italy in the 1970s. First, the contradiction worked against labor's efforts in the early 1970s to ameliorate the work environment as employers responded with factory shutdowns and the dispersal of production units. Second, the inexorable drive to maximize profits during economic booms and the resulting intensification of production create an effective counterpressure to labor's efforts to reduce workplace accidents. This defines occupational safety and health as a unique labor issue, for with most other concerns (for example, wages and benefits), workers' bargaining power increases during economic booms when owners can most easily afford concessions. However, workers fighting for occupational safety and health are in a double bind. Not only do they confront the more general class contradiction faced by all workers but, given the intensification of production during times of prosperity, they are least likely to be able to realize their class interests with regard to safety and health just as their bargaining power increases. Thus was created the irony that Italian labor, armed with Article 9 and broad-based worker participation in the early 1970s, wrenched from management only a few partial victories and saw merely halting progress in safety conditions, whereas the greatest statistical improvements in occupational safety of the postwar period came at the height of workers' economic and political vulnerability in the second half of the decade.

This is not to suggest that the recession brought Italian workers qualitative improvements in their working conditions. The historical record suggests that the improvement in accident statistics during recessions is strictly temporary and that the accident rate will resume its upward trend as the economy recovers and productivity increases.

Conclusion

This study began as an attempt to understand the polarized interpretations of Article 9 of the Italian Workers' Rights Law. It was found that those who hailed the law as a turning point overlooked the potential of employers' strategies to stymie or counterbalance such legislative efforts and that those who claimed that it was merely symbolic oversimplified the nature of the Italian state. In each scenario law and the state are highlighted as the primary actors, while the playing out of fundamental economic and political contradictions is ignored.

The interpretation of Article 9 as a deliberate palliative to militant workers after the "hot autumn" of 1969 neglects the fact that the PCI used its electoral strength to liberalize the provision to ensure its utility to workers. More importantly, this view reifies the Italian state and overestimates its deliberateness and unity. The Italian state is in fact fragmented among a number of political parties that serve varying political, economic, and ideological interests. It may be true that capitalist governments, no matter what their political stripe, must not interfere with the smooth operation of the dominant economic system and thus ultimately serve the interests of the capitalist class. However, the Italian Communist Party occupies the unique position of being the second-largest party in electoral strength yet never having been allowed a part in postwar government coalitions. While it is part of the Italian state and therefore plays a role in shaping legislation, as an opposition party the PCI is not a partner in the capitalist government. It is the PCI's unique location in the Italian political system—electoral strength but governmental exclusion—that accounts for both its lead role in pressing for Article 9 and the political contradictions that restricted the parameters of that legislative effort as the party lobbied for political respectability. In other words, political contradictions within the Italian state itself both precluded the possibility of a purely symbolic Article 9 and curtailed its potential.

Although its supporters took the opposing view of Article 9, seeing it as the "first truly incisive step" toward occupational safety and health, their interpretation also was clouded by an exaggeration of the role of concerted state action and an underestimation of the dynamism of class and economic forces as exemplified by the myriad counterstrategies of employers. While Article 9 was considered by its advocates to be consistent with socialist principles of worker control, it confronted an economic reality not only of the private ownership of the means of production but also of uneven development.

A prolific tradition in the sociology of law attempts to explain the origin or outcome of given laws primarily by reference to the nature of the state that forges those laws (Freeman, 1978; Holloway & Picciotto, 1977; Miliband, 1969; Poulantzas, 1969; Trubek, 1977). Whatever the differences among the models proposed in these various studies, they—like the observers of the Italian Workers' Rights Law cited above—tend both to reify the state and to place the state and state action at the center of explanations of sociolegal development. In spite of the considerable contributions made by these theorists and their sensitivity to the role of economic interests and contradictions in the creation of public policy, it is a primary goal of their studies to determine the nature of a state through an analysis of the form and impact of the laws constructed by that state. By contrast, this study of the Italian Workers' Rights Law and the complex socioeconomic environment of which it was a part demonstrates the dangers inherent in any sociology of law methodology or angle of vision that assumes that the state and legal phenomena are the central protagonists.

A dialectical model of law and its economic and political context emerges from this study. It replaces a kind of implicit legal determinism with an emphasis on the role of economic, political, and class contradictions in the formulation of law and its impact. For example, with regard to Article 9, it was the class contradictions surrounding worker safety and health and the political contradictions within the Italian state that both forced a reform in safety and health legislation yet limited the scope of that reform. Furthermore, the playing out of fundamental economic contradictions, some of which are shared by all advanced capitalist democracies and some of which are peculiar to Italian-style capitalism, was far more important than state action in determining subsequent safety and health outcomes.

The pattern of safety statistics in the second half of the 1970s confirms the importance of this untangling of the "adventures of the dialectic" if one is to avoid mistaking the consequences of independent economic forces for state intent or the product of legal reform. Curiously, it was when workers' economic and political power began to wane in 1975 that safety statistics showed the most improvement. A close look at the pattern of these reductions in the accident rate, however, suggests that they were not the harvest of Article 9 but rather the temporary consequence of economic collapse and the attendant slowdown of production.

In documenting the various economic and political contradictions that influenced the creation and impact of the Italian Workers' Rights Law, this study challenges previous interpretations. But more importantly it demonstrates that research that places the state and law at the center of analysis risks misinterpreting the developments that may chronologically follow law but be only peripherally or indirectly related to state action.

DISCUSSION QUESTIONS

1. In what ways do scholars overestimate the importance of law and the autonomy of the state? In what ways do they underestimate it? How does a dialectical model of law avoid these errors?

2. How common are regulatory regimes, like the early Italian health and safety laws, that declare broad goals but are riddled with loopholes? How common is the conjunction of bold regulatory ambitions and inadequate resources to achieve them? Can you give other examples?

3.   Does insurance undercut safety? Do workers in other countries "monetize" their health and safety?

4.   What were the conditions for enactment of the Workers' Rights Law? How did health and safety emerge on the agenda of Italian labor? Why did it have the power to secure legislation? How important was the business cycle? Have American workers ever adopted the four elements of the Italian approach to health and safety?

5.   Contrast the politics of legislating about drugs (in Scheerer's article) with Italian worker health and safety. If conservative parties have an advantage with respect to law and order issues (and national security), do left parties have an advantage with respect to social welfare measures? Why did the DC support this law? Do you think the Workers' Rights Law was symbolic legislation? Can you give American examples of symbolic legislation? What were the internal contradictions of the DC and PCI? Do American parties suffer similar contradictions?

6.   How did capitalists respond to the law? Is there any solution to the inequality inherent in the mobility of capital and the relative immobility of labor? How has this structural inequality affected the American economy? regulatory efforts?

7.   Why do you think work accident rates improved despite workers' legal defeats? If you accept Calavita's interpretation, is there any way for workers to improve their health and safety?

Regulation

12

Organizational Compliance with Court-Ordered Reform

Sheldon Ekland-Olson and Steve J. Martin

Introduction

A revolution has taken place in the way prisons are administered in the United States. Prior to the early 1960s federal courts adhered almost exclusively to a "hands-off" policy. By 1983, three-fourths of the state prison systems were subject to some type of federal court order, and additional systems were embroiled in ongoing litigation (U.S. Department of Justice, 1983; Brakel, 1986).

Assessments of this prison reform movement have been mixed. A decade after it began, Orland (1975: 11) asserted that the movement was "nothing short of a legal revolution" that "may have prevented mass insurrection." By contrast, Engel and Rothman (1983: 105) concluded that "the overall effects of the reform movement have been the dissolution of the inmate social order and heightened violence." The link between prison reform and prison violence is only one of many issues that might be raised regarding what are clearly dramatic changes in the nation's prison systems. Unfortunately, with limited exceptions (e.g., Harris & Spiller, 1977; Marquart & Crouch, 1985; Ekland-Olson, 1986), few studies carefully assess the impact of court-ordered reforms aimed at prison conditions, and even fewer explore the social dynamics through which the effects of litigation take place. Particularly lacking is a careful examination of administrative responses to the shifting moral, legal, and practical demands brought about by reform-minded lawyers, writ-writing inmates, and activist judges. This article presents a detailed case study of administrative responses to litigated reform efforts directed at the Texas Department of Corrections (TDC) over a two-decade period. The major prison conditions case litigated in Texas, *Ruiz v. Estella,* is summarized in the Appendix.

Administrative Resistance to Early Reform Efforts

The boundary between an organization and its social environment is never entirely clear. Organizations, especially those that exhibit characteristics of "total institu-

---

Abridged from *Law & Society Review*, Volume 22:359 (1988).

tions," are constantly implementing strategies to regulate what Goffman (1961) referred to as the "semi-permeable membrane" separating the organization from its surroundings. In Texas, prison administrators reacted to would-be reformers by attempting to reduce the permeability of the system's boundaries through: (1) the control of information going into and out of the institutions, as well as the exchange of information within the inmate population; (2) political connections and influence in the broader community; (3) a judicial counterattack; and (4) the exercise of administrative prerogatives over housing assignments, visitation rights, work assignments, and disciplinary punishments.

The Struggle to Control Information

The effective litigation of prison conditions in Texas began in 1967. At the time, there were fourteen separate prison units in a narrow corridor running north and south of Huntsville in East Texas, housing 12–13,000 inmates. Prison administrators enjoyed almost total autonomy from external oversight and exercised tight authoritarian control over virtually every aspect of the prisoners' lives. This control was maintained in part through rigid restrictions on information entering and leaving the system. Prison administrators were practiced experts at implementing Weber's (1968: 1418) proposition that information control is a critical bureaucratic tool to protect the organization from outside supervision.

TDC staff routinely censored all prisoner correspondence leaving the prison, giving special attention to "false or debasing information about other inmates or prison officials and employees" (TDC, 1968: 13–14). In addition, there was an absolute ban on prisoners assisting other prisoners in the preparation of legal documents. Violators of these rules could expect to be removed to administrative segregation, where their activities could be more readily monitored. In addition, prison officials developed a standard routine for handling visiting outsiders. Inmates were, however, allowed some access to outside information through various newspapers as well as approved lists for mail and visitors.

In the 1960s the insulated nature of prison life was challenged when the national civil rights movement coalesced around the more narrowly defined rights of prisoners (Jacobs, 1980). The initial challenge in Texas came from a prodigious jailhouse lawyer, Fred Arispe Cruz, and a 57-year-old volunteer attorney, Frances Jalet, who arrived in Texas fresh from a short training course in poverty law at the University of Pennsylvania Law School, where she was funded by a fellowship from the Office of Equal Opportunity. These two individuals made contact by happenstance when Cruz read an article published in an Austin paper about the attorney and her position with a local legal aid office and subsequently wrote her requesting assistance. Together they, along with other inmates and legal counsel they contacted, established the foundation for litigated change in what was at the time a proud and seemingly invulnerable prison system.

When Jalet contacted prison officials about her visit with Fred Cruz, she was invited to meet first with the system's director, George Beto, and then to tour the Huntsville prison. On her first visit Jalet was duly impressed. In a letter to the director, thanking him for his cooperation, she wrote: "The white suits the men wear surprised me. Somehow I expected gray or tan, but white is better. And I could not resist making some purchases from the display of the prisoners' handwork." However, unlike most initially impressed outsiders, this attorney continued to solicit and receive information from inmates and became convinced that there was a darker side to prison life in Texas than that revealed by the prisoners' white uniforms and her conversations with the system's director.

As her suspicions rose and the issues of potential litigation expanded, Jalet sought help from her former law professor at the University of Pennsylvania, who in turn put her in contact with a staff attorney at the NAACP Legal Defense Fund office in New York City, William Bennett Turner. At the time, Turner was rapidly becoming a central figure in the national prisoners' rights litigation movement. It was through this interpersonal network, embedded in a wider arena of societal reform efforts, that the national civil rights movement and the more narrowly focused prisoners' rights movement began to coalesce around prison conditions in Texas.

One of the first issues these reformers attacked was the TDC's rule prohibiting mutual legal assistance among prisoners. Two of Jalet's clients, Fred Cruz and Ronald Novak, charged in *Novak v. Beto* [453 F.2d 661 (5th Cir. 1971)] that since mutual legal aid among prisoners was prohibited, the presence of a single full-time attorney and the limited availability of law libraries in the Texas prison system did not constitute a reasonable alternative for access to legal assistance as set forth in *Johnson v. Avery* [393 U.S. 483 (1969)].

The district court found otherwise. On appeal, however, the Fifth Circuit judges reversed this finding and held that the TDC had failed to carry its burden of proving the availability of reasonable alternatives to mutual aid among prisoners. Thus, one brick in the wall of information control was loosened. However, prison officials kept in place prohibitions against mutual assistance among litigation-minded inmates, arguing successfully that such assistance might lead to "unconscionable control" by legally skilled inmates.

The Use of Political Connections

While prison officials were largely successful in their early attempts to ward off the influence of outside reformers and litigious inmates, they were well aware that reform efforts posed a substantial threat to the stability of existing practices. With his ability to control the flow of information among inmates and the outside under fire, the prison director called upon political connections to restrict the damage. In particular, there is evidence [*Dreyer v. Jalet*, 349 F. Supp. 452, at 469 (S.D. Tex. 1972)] that the director applied pressure through contacts in Austin to have Jalet involuntarily transferred from her position with the Austin legal aid office to the

Texas Legal Services office in Dallas. When Jalet continued visiting TDC prisoners, director Beto called her Dallas supervisor, complaining that she was fomenting unrest in a number of prison units and in general was becoming a "thorn in his side." Thereafter, the Dallas supervisor issued a memorandum stating that Jalet should not counsel TDC inmates. With the memorandum in hand, Beto removed Jalet from the approved visitors list and in effect barred her from contacting her clients in late 1968. Shortly thereafter, Jalet filed suit against Beto and the director of the Dallas Legal Services office, whereupon she was fired on December 24, 1968.

However, Jalet was not without political connections of her own. She wrote to a professor at the University of Pennsylvania Law School stating that she "was terribly frustrated and unhappy" about being removed from the approved visitors list. She went on to note how she wanted to "lash out" at the director and the entire prison system but realized that she needed to proceed in the "most effective way." A short time later Jalet secured a position with a legal aid clinic at Texas Southern University in Houston, where she resumed her work with TDC prisoners. George Beto immediately contacted her superiors, but this time Jalet received support, which lasted until February 1970, when her fellowship funds ran out. Additional funds were secured to support her work, but her appointment was sidetracked, once again through the political connections of Beto.[1] Faced with this loss of funds, Jalet nevertheless continued her efforts to assist prisoners in the TDC.

A Judicial Counterattack

When it became clear that political pressure was not going to stop the assault on existing prison policy, prison officials along with three inmates came up with a litigation strategy of their own. In September 1971, four years after Jalet's arrival in Texas and very close to the time of widely publicized inmate and guard killings in California that were said to be the result of revolutionary activities, the three inmates filed a highly unusual lawsuit, *Dreyer v. Jalet* [349 F. Supp. 452 (S.D. Tex. 1972)], charging Jalet with indoctrinating prisoners with revolutionary ideals and encouraging violence in the TDC. Jalet counterclaimed that the suit had been instigated by prison officials by promising the inmate-plaintiffs benefits such as early parole.[2]

Ironically, the judicial counterattack by prison officials and coopted inmates in *Dreyer* resulted in extensive testimony on aspects of prison life that prison officials had been so careful to protect from public view. In the closing portions of the opinion, the court noted evidence on building tender and staff abuses, solitary confinement, censorship of prisoner mail, and restricted prisoner access to court. While the evidence was contradictory, the court found it "perfectly apparent" that neither the prisoners' nor the officials' version could be "summarily dismissed and forgotten." With this in mind, the court noted the need for increased scrutiny of prison conditions, policies, and practices.

With a lack of public awareness and an absence of independent outside checks on prison methods, it certainly cannot be denied that the opportunity, at least, has been present for a prison system to become a law unto itself. Once such a total institutionalization emerges, its very preservation depends upon the exercise of unrestrained administrative discretion to control every facet of the lives of its inmates. (*Dreyer*, at 488)

The Exercise of Administrative Prerogatives

Political pressure to oust Jalet from the Texas prison system resulted in expanded assistance for prisoners from a national pool of legal talent. A judicial counterattack, filed by inmates but encouraged by prison officials, ironically succeeded only in further opening the door of judicial scrutiny. Internal administrative policies remained as a last means of resisting outside interference and thus of maintaining the organizational status quo. Administrators had substantial discretion over who visited prisons, where prisoners were housed, what jobs prisoners were given, and what disciplinary measures were employed. The exercise of these administrative prerogatives to ward off outside reformers would also ultimately backfire.

Approximately one month after the prisoners filed suit against Jalet, Beto sent her a telegram stating that her frequent visits to the TDC made it impossible for him to guarantee the "tranquility within the institutions and the protection of the inmates." Effective October 14, 1971, he instructed all wardens to deny Jalet admission to TDC institutions and to terminate correspondence between her and "any inmate" within the Texas prison system.

This action served mainly to galvanize the legal community. There were immediate protests from such organizations as the NAACP and La Raza Unida, a politically active organization aimed at supporting the interests of Mexican-Americans. In addition, the Texas bar and the Texas Attorney General's office, both of which had been only marginally interested in the struggle between Beto and Jalet and her clients until this time, voiced their concern. In late October 1971, negotiations were held with an NAACP attorney and Beto's representative, which resulted in the partial restoration of Jalet's visitation rights in early November. However, in an attempt to monitor the activities of Jalet and her clients (who at the time numbered 27 inmates at a number of separate prison units), Beto compromised by transferring all prisoners identified as her clients to a single unit, just outside Huntsville, run by a warden known for his heavy reliance on several notorious inmate guards, or building tenders. There they were segregated in one location within the prison unit and assigned to work in the fields on the "8-hoe squad." A number of the original 27 were released from this squad to more desirable jobs, in which they were able to accumulate higher ratings for parole, when they agreed to sever their relationship with Jalet. Those who remained were confronted with direct threats and pressures as well as more subtle conditions of confinement.[3]

Shortly after the new 8-hoe squad was established, Jalet, along with 12 of the original 27 inmates, filed suit against George Beto for restricting attorney-client contact, depriving inmates of privileges, and subjecting them to conditions of confinement discriminatorily. The district court's decision left no doubt that the actions taken by Beto were unlawful and prompted by his "longstanding antagonism towards Mrs. Jalet's contact with TDC inmates ... taken primarily to discourage the prisoner-plaintiffs from exercising certain constitutional rights and to prevent Mrs. Jalet from representing inmates in civil litigation" [*Cruz v. Beto,* No. 71-H-1371, at 9 (S.D. Tex. 1971)]. The court found further that the unlawful intimidation and punishments were carried out in bad faith, held Beto personally liable, and, in an unprecedented action, awarded Jalet and her clients damages totaling just under $10,300. The appellate court affirmed this decision noting, "not even the broadest [administrative] discretion may be used to punish prisoners for the exercise of their constitutional rights to counsel and to gain access to courts" [*Cruz v. Beto,* 603 F.2d 1178, at 1185 (5th Cir. 1979)].

Summary

The 8-hoe squad, with its accompanying harassments and restrictions, was maintained from November 1971 through October 1972. George Beto resigned as director on September 1, 1972. The political, judicial, and administrative actions he had taken to restrict the flow of information into and out of the prison system and thereby to discourage litigation by Frances Jalet and her clients had resulted in expanded judicial scrutiny as well as a "writ-writers' consortium" backed by skilled outside legal talent. All of the major litigation that confronted Beto in his final years as director, as well as that naming Beto's successor, W. J. Estelle, as defendant, came from members of the 8-hoe squad and their attorneys.

It is impossible to tell whether the intensity of litigation efforts would have been the same had Beto and his wardens not reacted to Frances Jalet and her clients as they did. What is clear is that inmates targeted for repressive actions were responsible, with the assistance of legal counsel, for litigation that opened the prison to outside scrutiny and supervision that eventually brought broadscale changes to the TDC. No case was more important in this regard than the largest class action prisoners' rights suit in the history of American jurisprudence—*Ruiz v. Estelle.*

The Prison Reform Movement Coalesces in Texas

When W.J. Estelle took over as director of the TDC in 1972, the Texas prison system continued to enjoy a high degree of national credibility as well as autonomy from outside interference. At the same time, a firm footing had been established for the forces that eventually reshaped the way Texas prisons were run. In the early 1970s these judicial, social, and political reform efforts coalesced as never before.

Judicial Attention Turns to the Totality of Prison Conditions

The judicial forces were strengthened first by *Holt v. Sarver* [309 F. Supp. 211 (E.D. Ark. 1970); 442 F.2d 304 (8th Cir. 1971)] and then by *Gates v. Collier* [390 F. Supp. 482 (N.D. Miss. 1975)]. These cases, involving the Arkansas and Mississippi prison systems, respectively, were of general importance in that they moved beyond the constitutionality of individual policies or practices to attack the systemic nature of prison conditions. A comparison of the findings in these opinions with the testimony heard in *Dreyer* and *Cruz* revealed the possibility, which could not be "summarily dismissed and forgotten," that there were conditions in the Texas prisons similar to those found unconstitutional in Arkansas and Mississippi. In particular, it was alleged that Texas prisoners were used in positions of authority within the TDC and were frequently involved in the physical abuse and intimidation of other inmates, especially those active in prison conditions litigation.

Public scrutiny of the possible parallels was facilitated by *Guajardo v. McAdams* [349 F. Supp. 211 (S.D. Tex. 1972)] and later *Guajardo v. Estella* [580 F.2d 748 (5th Cir. 1978)], which mandated the relaxation of TDC rules restricting inmate correspondence. In response, prisoners sent more than a thousand letters to the media, the courts, legislators, and a variety of other interested parties. Much of this correspondence centered around alleged abuses by staff and inmate building tenders.

In June 1972 David Ruiz, a member of the 8-hoe squad, filed a handwritten petition raising issues strikingly similar to those litigated in *Gates*. In 1974 this petition was consolidated with seven others, including two from fellow 8-hoe squad inmates, into a class action suit aimed at the totality of conditions in the TDC. These petitions formed the basis for the revolutionary changes mandated in *Ruiz v. Estelle*.

Prison Activists Join Forces

Fred Cruz was released from prison the same month David Ruiz filed his petition. Immediately upon release, Cruz and Jalet, now married, joined forces with a newly formed prison reform organization, Citizens United for the Rehabilitation of Errants (CURE), in a concerted effort to lobby for prison reform. CURE had been started several months prior to Cruz's release by a former Catholic priest and a nun, Charles and Pauline Sullivan, who had become intimately acquainted with jail conditions as a result of their participation in the peace movement. After being arrested in both San Antonio and Washington during public protest demonstrations, the Sullivans decided to concentrate their attention on the reform of prison conditions because "no one else seemed interested in confronting the frustrating and depressing issue of poor conditions in local jails and state prisons."

At first CURE organized a low-cost bus service from San Antonio to Huntsville to transport families who wanted to visit relatives in prison. In the process, the Sullivans met and began corresponding with a number of the 8-hoe squad prisoners, including Fred Cruz. What started out as a bus service quickly turned into broad-based lobbying for prison reform. These efforts resulted in two important legislative actions taken in 1973.

Charles Sullivan and Fred Cruz worked with a San Antonio representative to prepare a bill outlawing the use of inmates in positions of authority within the TDC. In May 1973 this bill was passed [H.B. 1056, *Civil Statutes* 6184K-1 (1973)]. W.J. Estelle testified in its favor, arguing that it simply reflected existing policy. However, on the day the bill was passed, another client of Frances Jalet filed a civil rights suit that provided evidence in stark contrast to Estelle's claims [*Guajardo v. Hudgens*, 73-H-672 (S.D. Tex. 1973)].

In addition to the lobbying efforts of Cruz and the Sullivans, the findings in *Holt* and *Gates* regarding the abuses of inmates in administrative and disciplinary positions influenced the Texas legislature when it passed H.B. 1056 prohibiting such practices in the state's prison system. It is testimony to the insulated nature of prison life, the ability of prison administrators to protect their organizational boundaries, and the tenacity of informal arrangements between prison staff and inmates that the building tender system in Texas continued for almost a decade in the face of court cases and statutory provisions to the contrary.

The second major legislative action directly linked to the lobbying efforts of the coalition of prison reform activists was the establishment, in May 1973, of a special Texas House-Senate committee on prison reform, which in turn led to a citizen advisory group, chaired by Charles Sullivan. Two reports were released in December 1974, one from the joint committee and one from the citizens' advisory group. The findings were broad in scope and specific in detail. Together the two reports produced some 160 recommendations, which were submitted to the state's 1975 legislative session. Only one was acted upon directly. The 1975 legislature deleted the archaic language from a 1927 statute requiring that "White and Colored prisoners shall be segregated in separate living quarters, work, shops, and hospitals" and called for legislation prohibiting discrimination against prisoners based on race. Thus, while the committee reports were highly critical of TDC operations, the legislature as a whole, by not calling for more sweeping reforms, reaffirmed its faith in prison administrators and the insulated nature of their prerogatives. Although the legislative response to the committees' recommendations was hardly revolutionary, the reports were influential as lawyers and inmates continued to craft their systemic attack on the TDC. Eventually, conclusions similar to those of the joint committee were supported by testimony and mandated by the court in *Ruiz*.

Boundary Maintenance Through Denial and Defiance

Organizational compliance with the law, particularly in the context of ongoing reform, is not easy to assess. Court-defined constitutional requirements are not always self-evident when applied to particular situations. While issues are being litigated, administrators can always claim their organizations are in compliance. On the other hand, when clear and specific court orders are violated and statutory prohibitions are ignored, noncompliance is more evident. Our analysis of administrative defiance of the law is restricted to these latter instances.

We focus on the influence of three organizational properties that encouraged and facilitated law violations by prison personnel in the TDC: (1) The organizational culture of the Texas prison system developed and existed in isolation not only from the federal courts, but also from oversight by state officials. (2) Public pronouncements by the TDC leadership during and after the *Ruiz* trial created a moral climate in which court-ordered reforms could be readily defined by the prison staff as illegitimate. (3) Control structures within the prison were ineffective in their response to known violations of the law. This applied not only to court orders but also to violations of the state statute prohibiting the use of inmates in positions of supervisory authority. Together, these three factors gave rise to a prison system that operated in large measure as a law unto itself.

TDC: A Separate Moral Community

The Texas prison system in the mid-1970s was a graphic illustration of the general tendency in prisons [and other social collectivities closed to the outside (e.g., Weber, 1968: 1417–19; Simmel, 1950: 345–76; Suttles, 1972: 34–36)] to develop a unique moral order and a feeling of "us against them." Unlike most state prison systems, the top prison administrators in Texas are not located in the state capital. Instead, they are officed some two hundred miles from Austin in rural East Texas. This physical isolation made it difficult to maintain more than sporadic contacts between state legislators and prison officials. In addition, the prison system recruited most of its employees from the surrounding rural communities. The TDC constituted the major economic base for the communities in which it was located. Its employees received not only wages but also such side benefits as food, laundry, haircuts, and yard service. Thus, both the top officials and the rural guard force were highly dependent on the department for basic necessities and amenities. The parochial "good ole boy" existence was perpetuated by promotions from within. For example, in the 1960s all wardens had been promoted through the ranks. The self-contained nature of the TDC community naturally facilitated a feeling of "us," meaning anyone who worked for the TDC, and "them," meaning anyone who did not.

It was in this isolated arena that a separate moral order emerged among prison officials and staff. An officer's status in the community, sense of purpose, and perceptions of right and wrong were all dependent on approval from his fellow employees. The TDC operated as a culture within a culture. On one level there were strong feelings that states' rights should predominate and that Texans knew better than federal courts how to run their prisons. At a second level there was the belief that prison officials knew better how to run a prison than investigating legislators, meddlesome citizen groups, and federal judges. Right or wrong, these perceptions allowed prison officials to deny the legitimacy and normative appeal of legislative and judicial findings. This denial of legitimacy encouraged organizational policies and individual actions that were in noncompliance with the law.

Prison Leadership Challenges the Legitimacy of Court-Ordered Reforms

While *Ruiz* was being litigated between 1974 and 1979, prison administrators and their lawyers maintained that the struggle over control of the Texas prison system was not over legal principles but over contrasting philosophies about what a prison system should be and do. They charged Judge William Wayne Justice, who was overseeing the case, with abuse of judicial power and biased ignorance. They argued further that the judge's actions were jeopardizing the safety of both the staff and inmates within the TDC.

The court had no right to act, the TDC argued, because prison administrators had independently initiated a set of reforms that had brought the TDC from one of the worst to one of the best prison systems in the United States (TDC, 1977). Evidence showed that violence and escape rates compared favorably with any state or federal prison system. Inadequacies in medical treatment were acknowledged, but once again it was asserted that administrative actions were being taken to alleviate the problems. Thus, it was argued that the prison system could no longer be found constitutionally inadequate by the standard of "deliberate indifference" established in *Estelle v. Gamble* [429 U.S 97 (1976)]. Once the issue of the court's right to act became moot with the initiation of the *Ruiz* trial and Judge Justice's subsequent rulings, prison administrators challenged the legitimacy of the actions taken by sharply criticizing the judge's competence, personal philosophy, and ability to look at the facts in an unbiased manner.

Many of these challenges occurred in highly visible arenas. Director Estelle, in a speech before the Public Relations Society of America shortly after some inmate demonstrations near the beginning of the *Ruiz* trial, was quoted in the *Houston Post*: "I find little charity and less solace in bringing issues before a court that has no knowledge, direct or indirect, of what the real issues are and could care less that their personal social philosophy finding its way into so-called law, jeopardizes not only our inmates' safety, but the safety of prison staff as well." Later in the trial, the state's lead attorney was threatened with contempt when he charged in open court that Judge Justice had been biased against the TDC since the beginning of the trial. Thus, before and during the trial, relations between the court and the prison administrators and their counsel were characterized by a good deal of personal animosity and mistrust.

Similarly, in the months following Judge Justice's memorandum opinion, state officials, with Estelle in the vanguard, engaged in what was eventually characterized as a personal and unseemly campaign of vilification. Estelle was repeatedly quoted in the media attacking Justice's ruling: "It read like a cheap dime store novel. I think he overused the adjective aspect of his dictionary. It did not read like a legal opinion and it did not even make interesting reading as far as I'm concerned" (*Houston City*

Magazine, April 1982: 9). On another occasion, in a speech before the Texas Associated Press Broadcasters, Estelle suggested that since Judge Justice was "insulated from the real world," he should not try to run the Texas prison system, and that his decision evidenced a "crass, gross, almost incredible lack of literary skills." With imagery to which Texans would surely respond, Estelle noted in the same speech that "going into Justice's courtroom is like playing poker in a strange town without a clean deck" (*San Antonio Light*, February 21, 1982).

To the extent that the attribution of illegitimacy by an organization's leadership affects the commitment of lower-level personnel to legal standards (see, e.g., Brenner & Molander, 1977), it can be expected that such statements from the prison system's leadership set a moral climate in which the TDC staff could readily justify violations of court rulings. Whatever the influence of the leadership's pronouncements, there is evidence throughout the *Ruiz* proceedings that many court orders were being either totally ignored or routinely violated by some TDC staff.

Ineffective Responses to Violations of Court Orders

During the early phases of the *Ruiz* litigation, TDC officials were repeatedly charged with violations of protective orders designed to limit harassment of inmates involved in the suit. By July 1976 officials at one prison unit had been subjected to three court hearings at which evidence indicated repeated violations of court orders. These violations ranged from rather petty harassments (including not issuing underwear to inmates, restricting access to the law library to early morning hours in uncomfortable quarters, and subjecting the inmate-plaintiffs to numerous strip searches, including digital rectal exams, when such searches were not normally conducted) to more severe charges of brutality (including the use of Mace on inmates securely locked in their cells).

After one hearing, Judge Justice found for the inmate-plaintiffs on a number of very specific charges and issued a thirty-point set of orders regarding the handling of legal correspondence, cell searches, rectal searches, the use of Mace, and triple celling when open cells were available. On appeal, the state's attorneys did not question the factual findings, and the Fifth Circuit found that the named plaintiffs had been subjected to "intimidation, coercion, punishment and discrimination" [*Ruiz v. Estelle*, 550 F.2d 238 (5th Cir. 1977)].

Some seven months after this hearing, prison officials once again found themselves charged with similar violations. This time they agreed to remedy the problem by removing illegitimate disciplinary charges from the affected inmates' records. They also agreed that the officers involved would be reprimanded. However, the only disciplinary action taken was initiated at the insistence of the plaintiffs' attorneys and consisted of a written reprimand from Estelle to an assistant warden, which read in part, "I realize there was no more intent on your part than mine to violate any of the court's Order, I know we will renew efforts to see such violation does not occur again. Consider us both reprimanded by this document."

Rather than subjecting themselves to harsh criticism for repeated violations of court orders, the warden and assistant warden most directly involved seemed to enhance their standing with high-level administrators. The warden was promoted to assistant director and named warden of the year. The assistant warden was promoted to warden shortly thereafter. The newly appointed warden would be the subject of repeated accusations of brutality as evidence was gathered in the *Ruiz* trial in later years.

The anemic reaction to violations of court orders continued well into 1983. It was not until Judge Justice set up a special mastership with investigative powers that the administrative practice of nonresponse came to a halt. Once the practice was changed, six wardens were removed from their positions based on findings of brutality and fabrication of evidence. Over 200 disciplinary actions were taken against several assistant wardens and numerous ranking correctional officers. Two officers were eventually convicted of felony charges of brutality against inmates. Much of the change in policy came when charges of staff brutality and the continued illegal use of building tenders were made in the special master's monitor reports and confirmed by the TDC's own lawyers and staff members in the newly created internal affairs division.

Continued Violations of the Building Tender Law

The law prohibiting the use of inmates in positions with supervisory authority, H.B. 1056, was passed in mid-1973. From the beginning prison officials claimed that the bill simply reflected existing policy. From the bill's inception, however, inmates, their lawyers, and citizen activists charged quite the contrary. As judicial intrusion into the prison system increased, the accumulating evidence clearly indicated that inmates were used to supplement the guard force on numerous prison units, that these inmates were expected to supervise other inmates and keep order in the cell blocks, and that these supervisory inmates frequently engaged in the brutal treatment of other inmates. Further, it was shown that much of the building tender abuse was done with the knowledge and complicity of the prison staff.

As evidence continued to mount, prison officials maintained their denial of any wrongdoing, and failed to take remedial actions. It was not until independent investigations were launched by monitors employed by the special master's office and confirmed by the prison system's own lawyers that members of the state Board of Corrections confronted the director of TDC on the issue.

There was evidence that building tenders were involved either directly or indirectly in the deaths of several inmates. Two of these incidents occurred near the end of the *Ruiz* trial in October 1979. In one, an inmate was killed in an altercation with another less than a year after his testimony regarding a brutal beating he had allegedly received at the hands of building tenders. In the second, an inmate died after he was allegedly attacked by a group of building tenders upon returning from work in the fields. This inmate had been willing to testify in the *Ruiz* trial but was never called. Disciplinary records indicate that he was one of the inmates identified as a ringleader in the inmate disturbances that had accompanied the beginning of the trial. The inmate died shortly after the altercation on October 23, 1979. In April 1980 the inmate's parents filed a wrongful death suit against the prison warden and building major as well as one of the inmates involved. It was alleged that the attack had occurred with the knowledge and complicity of the prison officials and that the attacking inmate had been acting in his capacity as a convict guard. In April 1980 the suit was settled when prison administrators indicated they did not want the case to go to trial, due in part to the involvement of building tenders. The officials involved were never reprimanded or otherwise punished. The inmate's parents were awarded a little over $18,000.

In addition to evidence indicating building tender involvement in inmate deaths, there was evidence, confirmed by the TDC's own attorneys, that building tenders, armed with pipes, clubs and knives, were used by the prison staff to help quell a riot. When this evidence was combined with other information about similar abuses and relayed to the Board of Corrections, the wall of official denials finally broke. The fact that the denials had been effective for almost a decade following the passage of H.B. 1056 is certainly testimony to the isolated nature of prison life, the boundary maintenance skills of prison officials, and the fact that as late as 1982 the TDC remained a law largely unto itself.

Summary and General Observations

As litigated prison reform progressed in Texas, information control, external political pressure, informal intimidation, administrative rules, judicial counterattack, and finally denial and defiance were used to maintain existing policies, both formal and informal, within the numerous institutions of the Texas prison system. Much of this organizational defiance of legal standards was facilitated by the isolated nature of the TDC in rural East Texas, a style of leadership that denied the legitimacy of the court-ordered reforms, and an unresponsive administrative control structure.

In one sense, the process of prison reform is unique to each set of issues, lawyers, inmates, judges, state officials, prison administrators, and prison systems involved. Much of the empirical research to date, including our own, has emphasized this uniqueness. There are, however, more general questions. Litigated prison reform involves the rights of inmates to be free from cruel and unusual punishments. The process of defining these rights in the context of evolving standards of decency resembled in many ways other reform efforts, such as those surrounding mental hospital patients (e.g., Jones & Parlour, 1981; Rothman & Rothman, 1984). In each case the evolution of reforms involved a collision of power structures, both federal and state administrative and judicial systems, and human beings who try to function within them (Stickney, 1975). It is also useful to develop a general research agenda to guide future case studies and at the same time to explore patterns of variation in the litigation process and the overall impact of the prison reform movement (see, e.g., Handler, 1978; Jacobs, 1980). With the limitations of a single case study in mind, we conclude with some general observations.

Much of the reaction to prison reform efforts in Texas stemmed from the isolation of the prison system in both normative and structural terms. Geographically, TDC administrators were separated from the state capital by some two hundred miles. The prison system as a whole had achieved a high degree of self-sufficiency. Recruitment of prison guards was restricted largely to rural East Texas. Each of these factors meant that interaction with the broader community was restricted. It also meant that conditions were right for the development of a separate moral order and a symbolic attachment and loyalty to those who belonged to the TDC community.

All prison systems are isolated from the broader society, but the degree varies between systems and across time. Structurally, normatively, and symbolically, the TDC was more isolated in the late 1960s than it is in the late 1980s. Geographic remoteness and incestuous labor recruitment persist, but normative, economic, and symbolic isolation have diminished. The TDC of the late 1980s is also more likely to be in compliance with statutory law and less defiant of court orders.[4]

All lawsuits concerning prison conditions threaten administrative authority. Adjudication, by definition, relies on an outside authority higher than either of the parties. Suits are generally brought by those who occupy the lowest rungs in the hierarchy of authority within the prison. However, some adjudicated issues constitute a greater threat to the balance of power within prison than others. Use of force standards, the nature of disciplinary hearings, the use of inmates in positions of authority, and inmate access to courts are all issues with direct power implications. They were also the most strongly contested issues throughout the litigation process in Texas.

On questions more tangential to the distribution of power, such as the provision of certain medical services and the type of food served to prisoners, there was a greater tendency to negotiate settlement and to implement voluntary changes not required by the court. For example, once the District Court and the Fifth Circuit Court of Appeals had decided that the "bread and water" diet for inmates in solitary did not offend "evolving standards of decency" and was within the prison administrator's discretionary power [*Novak v. Beto* (453 F.2d 661, at 665 (5th Cir. 1974)], Director Beto voluntarily elected to abandon the practice.

Comparative studies of litigated institutional reform might well focus on the administrative implications of the specific issues being contested. The more the lawsuit is perceived as a threat to the organization's authority structure, the more intense the administrative resistance and the lower the voluntary implementation of reforms.

Finally, our observations suggest quite strongly that the contentious nature of relationships among the lawyers and primary actors in the case is linked to the eventual resistance to and implementation of reforms. We were repeatedly struck by evidence of overt animosity among the parties in *Ruiz*, animosity that eventually became the subject of litigation, threatened contempt citations, and discussions of criminal charges. The level of interpersonal tension among the primary actors may influence the litigation process, since contentious relationships are less likely to move toward negotiated settlement. Without negotiation, prison personnel perceive change as being externally imposed and will resist it, reducing staff morale. This is true not only for court-ordered reforms but also for changes imposed on staff by reform-minded correctional administrators (see, e.g., McCleery, 1961; Jacobs, 1977: 74–86; Barak-Glantz, 1985). Prison administrator and staff participation in the design and implementation of reforms enhances the likelihood of compliance and a smooth transition.

Notes

1. In a deposition taken for a later trial [*Cruz v. Beto*, 603 F.2d 1178 (5th Cir. 1979)] Jalet recalled the sequence of events.

> Well, he [Beto] was also in touch with the president of the university ... and with the vice president.... We had gotten a CLEPR grant, and then instead of that, my work there [Texas Southern University] was terminated... immediately following the Novak trial.... [A university official said] that the president of the university had told him that it was not in the best interest of the university to have me continue because they would lose their funding due to pressures from Austin.

2. As evidence for her counterclaim, Jalet's attorneys detailed the four years of animosity between Jalet and Beto. In addition, it was revealed that two of the inmate-plaintiffs were "building tenders," who functioned as agents of control for unit officials. The third plaintiff was a "trusty," the classification given to inmates with the greatest freedom in the prison environment. Through implication, Jalet's attorneys hoped to show that the inmate-plaintiffs had been coopted by prison officials. Evidence elicited at trial further underscored this possibility. One of the building tender plaintiffs did not even know Jalet and was unable to provide any evidence of a conspiracy. Other inmates, testifying for Jalet, indicated that this inmate had entered the suit, with the encouragement of prison officials, in order to ward off Jalet's attempts to have the building tender system dismantled. The second building tender plaintiff was paroled during the trial and disappeared just before he was to testify, forcing the plaintiff's attorney to rely on his deposition. The trusty plaintiff testified first for the plaintiffs and then reversed his testimony, stating that TDC officials had pressured him to file suit. In addition to the trial testimony, there is further evidence that prison officials were taking more than a passing interest in this case (see Martin & Ekland-Olson, 1987).

3. Six of these inmates had been in college programs prior to their assignment to the 8-hoe squad, four had been in the Alcoholics Anonymous program, and three had been in primary or secondary education programs. Once assigned to the squad their participation was

terminated. This, coupled with other restrictions, made it impossible for squad members to accumulate enough points for parole consideration. In addition, prisoners were assigned two to a cell, even though there were numerous vacant cells on the wing. This was done, contrary to established practice, so as to increase racial tensions among the inmates. A number of these prisoners who had heart and respiratory conditions as well as other handicaps were forced to do field labor, again contrary to policy. The squad as a whole was assigned to tasks (e.g., cleaning manure out of livestock areas) generally reserved as some sort of punishment. Eventually, the court characterized these conditions as "unusually discriminatorily harsh" [*Cruz v. Beto*, 453 F. Supp. 905, at 1180 (S.D. Tex. 1977)].

4. In January 1987 Judge Justice found that the Texas prison system was in blatant contempt of court and had "been habitually and inexcusably dilatory in fulfilling its obligations in respect to the relevant orders." Having thus found, Justice threatened to impose fines that could go as high as $800,000 per day. The state responded by appealing this ruling. Shortly after his election, Governor-elect William Clements met personally with Judge Justice to work out a resolution to the issues and thereby avoid the threatened fines.

APPENDIX. Major Stages in *Ruiz v. Estelle*

1972   In June, while a member of the 8-hoe squad, David Ruiz filed a handwritten petition in Judge William Wayne Justice's court in Tyler, Texas. Other inmates filed similar suits, raising issues about the Texas prison system similar to those decided in *Gates v. Collier* [390 F. Supp. 482 (N.D. Miss. 1975)].

1974   In April, Judge Justice consolidated eight separate inmate petitions into the class action suit, *Ruiz v. Estelle*. He also asked the U.S. Department of Justice to investigate the facts and participate with the full rights of a party. William Bennett Turner, a leading civil rights attorney with the NAACP Legal Defense Fund, was appointed counsel of record for the plaintiffs.

1975-77   The Fifth Circuit Court of Appeals denied the state's application to prevent the U.S. Department of Justice from intervening in the case. Judge Justice issued a series of protective orders for inmates being harassed for their involvement in prison reform efforts. Separate contempt hearings established a pattern of the abusive treatment of *Ruiz* "jailhouse lawyers." Plaintiffs and defendants in *Ruiz* began exchanging massive amounts of evidentiary documents in preparation for trial.

1978   On October 2, the *Ruiz* trial began in Houston. Plaintiffs organized their case around five issues: (1) physical security and the right of inmates to be free from assault and the fear of assault; (2) living and working conditions; (3) medical care; (4) summary punishments; and (5) access to courts.

1979   After calling some 150 witnesses, attorneys for the plaintiffs and the U.S. Department of Justice rested on May 2. Attorneys for the prison system completed their defense on August 30. Trial ended September 20.

1980   Judge Justice issued a memorandum opinion in December, which was organized around six major issues: (1) overcrowding, (2) security and supervision, (3) health care, (4) discipline, (5) access to court, and (6) other conditions of confinement, such as fire safety, sanitation, work safety, and hygiene.

1981   The consent decree was approved by Judge Justice in early March. Common ground was reached on issues of health care, work safety, use of chemical agents and administrative segregation, and diet for inmates in solitary confinement. Judge Justice issued a broad and extremely detailed final decree on April 20. He also established the office of the special master to oversee the implementation and resolution of disputed issues. Vincent Nathan was appointed special master. The state's attorneys filed a motion in June to suspend Judge Justice's sweeping orders. The building tender system became the subject of the first monitor's report from the special master's office.

1982   A court hearing on allegations involving building tender abuses was scheduled for March 15. State officials prepared a motion to dismiss the special master and consider having him and his staff investigated for criminal charges. Due to rising litigation costs and the TDC's potential vulnerability on the building tender issue, a state senator and Board of Corrections member called for a cease-fire and negotiated settlement in mid-March. By early April, an agreed settlement was reached on the most volatile issue, the building tender system. In May, the TDC closed its doors to further admissions. This prompted a special session of the legislature to appropriate $5 million for construction and staffing increases. In June, the Fifth Circuit affirmed the facts but narrowed the relief ordered by Judge Justice in *Ruiz*.

1983   The ninth monitor's report issued by the special master's office claimed that physical abuse of inmates continued to occur with "alarming frequency." These findings were documented in over 400 pages of appendices to the main report. W. J. Estelle announced his intention to resign shortly after the release of the ninth monitor's report and just prior to having to terminate his most senior warden. He cited as reasons his inability to secure funds from the legislature and his refusal to compromise further on court-ordered changes. His resignation was accepted in October.

1984   Large-scale turnover of high-level TDC officials took place. Approximately 200 disciplinary actions were eventually taken against TDC officers for use of force violations.

1985   A settlement agreement was reached in July on a wide range of issues, including crowding, visitation, staffing, construction, and classification of inmates.

1986   William Bennett Turner filed a contempt motion, charging the TDC with failure to implement major provisions of the 1985 agreement. On December 31, Judge Justice issued an opinion finding the TDC in contempt of court. He threatened fines as high as $24 million per month.

1987   Shortly before Governor-elect Clements took office, he met with Judge Justice in what Turner called an "unbelievably useful, productive exchange of views." Governor Clements addressed the state legislature and declared that the state had no choice but to comply with the court orders as soon as possible. Judge Justice personally visited the TDC units for the first time.

DISCUSSION QUESTIONS

1. Why is prison litigation necessary? What makes prison conditions so bad: personnel, inmate population, ideology? Why do other regulatory and reform efforts fail? What were the origins of the prisoners' rights movement? What resources do prisoners have available? How does the prisoners' rights movement differ from other social movements: e.g., civil rights, feminism, environmentalism? What kind of lawyers champion prisoners' rights and why? What is the role of other activists? What role does chance play in campaigns like these?

2. How did the prison department respond to challenges by prisoners and lawyers? What remedies did the latter have to resist these responses? How can litigation be used against prisoners' rights as well as on their behalf? Why did the attempt backfire? Are there other illustrations of the paradox that total power can undermine itself and powerlessness become a form of power?

3. What is the role of information in revealing and correcting abuses? the relationship between litigation and the media? both of these and legislation?

4. What structural attributes would make institutions more permeable to external review and regulation?

5. Under what circumstances can courts reform institutions like prisons (or mental hospitals, or schools)? Is the court's "legitimacy" placed at risk? What can a court do if the institution is utterly intransigent? What are the appropriate roles of courts and legislatures? Why was the legislation outlawing "building tenders" (inmates used to control and discipline other inmates) ineffective for a decade? What are the conditions for effective legislation? Is there an inverse relationship between the efficacy of external regulation and the importance of what is being regulated?

13

Penetrability of Administrative Systems: Political "Casework" and Immigration Inspections

Janet A. Gilboy

Administrative agencies are subject to a wide variety of devices to ensure that government power over individuals is adequately restrained. Among the mechanisms of control of agency action is "casework" by legislators and local politicians (Gormley, 1989: 45; Gilboy, 1988: 516–18). At the request of their constituents, politicians may contact government officials to obtain information or nudge or challenge an agency.

Casework is a popular activity. It is a type of divisible benefit politicians can extend at almost no cost, in contrast to taking a policy stand that may gain the support of some individuals but engender the dissatisfaction of others. Casework is particularly attractive to modern politicians since many other low-cost divisible benefits, such as various forms of patronage, are now illegal. Politicians also view casework as an important opportunity for gaining reelection support and devote much effort to servicing constituent requests.

There are two views of casework. On one hand, inquiries by members of Congress are thought to act as an "outside needling force" to ameliorate bureaucratic arrogance, delays, and mistakes. Moreover, casework can increase legislators' knowledge of agency functioning, which may be beneficial in restructuring agency programs or providing corrective legislation.

But legislator intervention may result in special deference to inquiries, particularly when the one initiating an inquiry is a powerful political actor on a substantive committee or appropriations subcommittee relating to agency business. Gormley (1989: 200) has described casework as "a thinly veiled request for special treatment for a favored constituent." Some believe that even legislators' routine inquiries may affect case handling, since agencies must guess at a legislator's intentions or extent of involvement in a particular case.

Decisions in response to casework are made by officials exercising considerable discretionary power within the dimly visible recesses of bureaucracy. To understand

Abridged from *Law & Society Review*, Volume 22:359 (1988).

the implications of casework, it is important to step inside administrative systems and attempt to grasp from within the concerns and activities of agency officials.

This article provides such a glimpse through a case study of the inner workings of one system—immigration inspections. Immigration and Naturalization Service (INS) inspectors work at ports of entry to the United States and are responsible for determining whether to allow foreign nationals to enter the country.

My purpose here is not to pass judgment on the desirability of casework or its merits relative to other mechanisms of control but instead to provide a picture of the potential effects of casework on administrative systems. I do this by extending the view beyond the typical point of politicians' casework contacts—usually higher-echelon administrators—to the organizational level of front-line officials. Appreciation of the work environment as known and understood by lower-level officials and the perceived risks and incentives operating in this context are central to understanding the implications of casework.

I first explore past approaches to the study of casework, identifying conceptual tendencies that have been barriers to our full appreciation of casework's consequences for official behavior. Next, I examine the INS's distinctive institutional context, which increases the susceptibility of front-line officials to outside pressures. I discuss the case-handling strategies of inspectors generated by their critical "background knowledge" (Emerson 1991; Emerson & Paley, 1992) of the organizational meaning and import of casework complaints, as well as the indirect effects of casework on agency routines and the exercise of discretion. Finally, using observations from other agency contexts, I describe several characteristics of the legal process and decision environment that allow accommodation to outsiders.

Limitations of Prior Research

Although a substantial literature discusses casework, it focuses largely on the activities of legislators and their staffs rather than the responses of agency officials. A few scholars have explored the effects of casework on organizational behavior, but this work provides only limited insights. Barriers to full appreciation of the effects of casework arise in large part from conceptualizing the subject abstractly rather than contextually. With few exceptions, such as Robert Emerson's (1969: 33-38) study of the juvenile court, existing research seeks to construct the gross effects of political intervention—that is, how often officials change their decisions as a result of casework, rather than inquiring how officials working in distinctive contexts with particular incentive systems respond to political intervention. As a result, radically different estimates of casework effects are reported. Realistically, efforts to construct some single estimate are doomed because administrative agencies are embedded in a variety of political-cultural environments that are likely to produce different agency responses to outside attempts to control or influence agency actions.

The literature also fails to grapple with the full range of casework effects. Studies inquiring about how often officials change their decisions focus largely on the consequences of direct legislator intervention while taking little account of indirect effects, such as subsequent anticipatory official behavior. Moreover, where indirect influences are explored, only positive effects are discussed, such as greater internal supervision and self-correction. The research also tends to discuss only the activities pursued by agencies in response to casework (e.g., changed decisions, rules, etc.). Yet official inaction is a plausible response to external pressures or threats.

The effects of casework are not reducible to instances of actual casework intervention, casework consequences are not all positive, and inaction constitutes a form of official response. More specifically, the focus on direct legislator intervention ignores important linkages between administrators and front-line officials. The decisions of front-line staff are fundamentally shaped by their understandings of how superiors have responded or are likely to respond in matters involving casework intervention. The anticipatory behavior emerging from such knowledge can magnify the effects of direct casework intervention (particularly where front-line officials anticipate that superiors will not back them up).

Recent theoretical work by Robert Emerson (1991; Emerson & Paley, 1992) suggests the core phenomenon at work. In organizational settings, decision-makers have considerable working knowledge of the likely organizational consequences of certain kinds of decisions. Legal actors draw on such knowledge in shaping their inquiry, interpreting facts, and classifying cases for purposes of disposing of them. Indeed, "the foreseeable interests and reactions of institutional agents at future processing points become increasing salient concerns in making some present decisions about a case" (Emerson & Paley, 1992). Empirical work by Emerson and Paley (1992) on complaint filing in a district attorney's office, Schuck (1972) on regulation by meat inspectors, and Lundman (1980) on police officer arrest practices suggests the involvement of background knowledge of the "downstream consequences" (Emerson & Paley, 1992: 14) of different decision options for present decisions. In the inspection setting, awareness of casework intervention gets built into this background knowledge, and the likely organizational fates and implications of different types of cases provide a "tentative frame" (ibid.) in which cases are initially viewed by front-line staff.

It is tempting to draw from this conceptualization simply a caveat to researchers to be aware of the role of background knowledge in officials' actions. But the conceptualization embodies more; the central concern differs depending on whether the focus is *actual casework* or work involving background knowledge and anticipation of possible *future casework*. Actual casework involves officials in direct contact with complainants. Research focuses on understanding the sources, variety, and escalation of such casework contacts. Attention turns to the official strategies for managing complaints and to strategies for containing the involvement of increasingly more powerful individuals.

In contrast, the official anticipating casework is not dealing with a complaint but considering if and when a case will evoke vocal opposition, particularly of the sort that will get the sympathetic attention of higher-ups. Research attention is directed to officials' background knowledge about the kinds of decisions generating complaints, the perceived concerns and practices of those who receive the complaints, and officials' assessments and use of this information in their work. Specifying and distinguishing the distinct concerns of different tiers of organizational decision-makers (and tensions between tiers) is of research interest.

Whether one explores actual or anticipated casework, research requires sensitivity to the distinct context in which officials labor. These work environments vary not only between but also within agencies. Scholz and Wei's study of OSHA (1986) provides clear data that agency behavior across 50 states varies by local political complexion. More generally, when officials act, their responses reflect not simply external pressures but also the spectrum of incentives operating on them as shaped by the tasks they perform (Wilson 1989: 88; Schuck 1983).

The Research Setting

Thousands of foreign nationals come to the United States each day seeking entry as tourists or for business. Decisions as to their admissibility (or excludability) are made by INS inspectors at ports of entry along our Mexican and Canadian borders and at international airports.

All individuals arriving at ports of entry go through a primary inspection in which entry documents (passports, visas, etc.) are examined (Gilboy, 1991). If the entry documentation meets the approval of the primary inspector, the alien is admitted to the country. If there is a question regarding a person's admissibility (such as inappropriate or questionable documentation), he or she is sent to secondary inspection.

Secondary inspection involves questioning individuals in greater depth about their documents and the purposes of their trip. After questioning, the individual may be admitted. If the inspector concludes, however, that the individual entering with a visa is not admissible, that individual typically is given the choice of going home or being detained and having his admissibility determined in an administrative exclusion hearing before a Department of Justice immigration judge. This article focuses on secondary inspections. Inspectors' decisions are thought to involve the exercise of considerable discretionary power delegated by Congress. Discretion exists in part because of the vagueness in the law specifying the particular grounds for exclusion (there are nine exclusion categories, including health, criminal and security reasons). This discretion is expanded because of case disposition choices as well as difficulties in fact finding. For instance, what type of evidence and how much is necessary to conclude that the foreign national is actually not coming to visit but instead intending to live and work illegally? Decisions on length of questioning, its tone (nonantagonistic or hostile), whether to search hand baggage and luggage, and whether to widen the inquiry by calling to verify information are left largely to the discretion of individual secondary inspectors.

I observed and interviewed officials for about 100 days at a U.S. international airport ("Metropolitan Port") and two weeks at a port of entry on the Mexican border ("Border Port"). Officials at Metropolitan Port report that politicians attempt to influence their decisions in four kinds of cases. These involve relatively nonserious immigration violators as compared to other would-be illegal entrants: criminal aliens, drug violators, terrorists, and fraudulent document users aided by organized crime rings. First, there are the domestic employment cases, which I emphasize here. These are individuals seeking to enter the country without proper visas to work as domestic employees such as child-care helpers, stable workers, gardeners, household cooks and cleaners. The most common group is "nannies" or au pair girls coming to do child care. Such employment would not be illegal if the families had gone through the proper agencies and paperwork, but these women enter the country with tourist visas or visa waivers that do not permit employment. Another set of cases involves abandonment of permanent resident status. These are lawful permanent resident (LPR) aliens who "abandoned" their residence by living outside the United States for more than a year without INS permission. One familiar situation involves cases in which naturalized U.S. citizens have obtained LPR status for their parents and have encouraged them to live in the U.S. Sometimes the elderly parents prefer to spend their last years residing in their native country. They return each year to the U.S. under the erroneous assumption that to "maintain" their resident status they need only make an annual reentry. A third set of cases concerns fiancées and intending immigrants. These are individuals seeking to enter without proper visas in order to join spouses living in the U.S. or marry U.S. citizens or permanent residents. These intending immigrants attempt to use tourist (nonimmigrant) visas rather than waiting for immigrant or fiancée visas. Finally, at the time of the research, outside intervention was perceived to be likely on behalf of nationals from a particular "favored" nation thought to have powerful local and national political representatives who would intervene if admissibility were challenged at the port of entry.

I focus on domestic employment cases to explore some effects of actual and anticipated intervention on agency case processing. Metropolitan Port conducts about a half-million inspections of foreign nationals a year. Most are admitted after primary inspection. Most of the 2 percent sent to secondary inspection ultimately are admitted. Referrals to secondary inspection occur for many reasons, including suspicion that the individual intends to live or work in the U.S. illegally, is using altered or fraudulent entry documents, or has a criminal background. My data indicate that "possible nanny" cases make up about 5 percent of the referrals to secondary inspection (Gilboy, 1991: 595, Table 2).

Agency Dependence on the Support of Politicians

Agencies commonly rely on three centers for political support: the community, the executive branch, and the legislature (Rourke, 1976: 43). Many agencies are in the fortunate position of having community interest groups whose concerns are compatible with the agency's formal goals (Wildavsky, 1971: 390). These agencies are able to command the intervention and support of their natural constituencies to obtain necessary resources and programs by relying not only on the self-interested action of these groups but also on the agency's power to dispense desired benefits and favors (Rourke, 1976: 47). Other agencies, such as the INS, have few natural allies. It cannot expect the undocumented alien population to support efforts to keep them out. Although several national groups support aspects of the INS mission (among them the Federation for American Immigration Reform and the Governors' Association), these either have narrow constituencies or are not consistently involved in defending or promoting the agency. American ambivalence toward aliens and immigration enforcement in particular further inhibits the emergence of vocal broad-based interest group support for the agency's policing efforts.

The INS also draws relatively little political support from the executive branch. It enjoys little institutional prestige among enforcement agencies within the Department of Justice (DOJ), having been characterized by the chairman of a DOJ task force as a "stepchild of the Justice Department" (Interpreter Releases, 1991: 519), and described (along with the Border Patrol) as "whipping boys and the laughing stocks of the executive branch ... underfunded, mismanaged, undermanned, inadequately supplied, riven by internal dissension, and politically manipulated" (Teitelbaum, 1980: 54). It "rarely receive[s] the benefit of the doubt in its many controversies" with other parts of the executive (Aleinikoff & Martin, 1991:102). Although the INS handles issues that are volatile, create problems for effective administration, and involve difficult policy trade-offs, most Attorneys General have disregarded them.

Although all agencies seek to maintain support from influential political institutions, particularly legislators who control fiscal resources, this is especially critical for agencies like the INS or Bureau of Prisons, which have few other sources of political support. Officials of such agencies may look for opportunities to provide favors and services to powerful individuals. District administrators also need local support for the agency's programs. No office wants to find itself in the situation of the San Francisco district after the city council declared the city a sanctuary for Central American refugees. An administrator wants to have credibility and working relations with legislators' offices, local community leaders, consuls general and other influentials. Many district offices, including Metropolitan Port, are located in states with powerful national legislators whose understandings of the INS presumably are drawn in part from contacts with the local office.

District offices must not only accommodate local politicians but also develop administrative practices and policies that protect the district and enhance its image by limiting the number of "needless" harmful or counterproductive encounters. Political casework tends to involve cases in which the public is indifferent or hostile to the "law-on-the-books." Certainly public opinion is not sympathetic to the tough handling of an 18-year-old Scandinavian coming to babysit for the summer, stringent application of fiancée visa rules to a woman arriving with joyful expectations of marrying a U.S. citizen, or withdrawal of permanent residence cards from elderly people living their last years outside of the country. The potential for external influence is likely to be greater when the agency views the matter as minor and the agency mission as unthreatened by compliance with demands. One administrator suggested that less aggressive enforcement of relatively minor segments of its regulatory program (specifically "au pair" cases) can help the district maintain the community support needed for more important activities.

The Context of Front-Line Inspection Work

Port officials confront asymmetric risks, which promote accommodation to outsiders. Three features of their decision environment are known and understood by officials: the high likelihood of political intervention in certain cases; the failure of superiors to back them when complaints occur; and the low risk of detection when exceptions are made. This knowledge of the foreseeable organizational and personal consequences of various decisions is a critical source of information, which officials draw on in their work (Emerson & Paley, 1992).

Predictable Intervention in Certain Cases

Prior casework provides port officials with background knowledge about the situations in which intervention is likely. Intervention is perceived as very likely in nanny and permanent resident cases but not in more serious cases. Those aiding or awaiting the entry of a fraudulent passport holder, for instance, are thought to be unlikely to call the port to inquire about why the person was not admitted. Even if legislators were contacted, politicians would be unwilling to intervene in such serious matters.

Port officials can readily describe the foreseeable "organizational futures" of various kinds of cases. (Numbers in brackets identify the official speaking.)

> [Nanny cases] are a real pain in the you-know-what. They're a lot of work and you get all the aggravation with them. You've gone around and around with them... you can always expect congressionals with them. [13]

These families want their nannies. They're wealthy and have influence. It makes it hard for us to do our job.... The follow-up replies consume a lot of time needlessly because we are enforcing the law the way Congress intended us to do. There's more work with nannies than with criminals! Then, too, someone who overstays [their authorized time in the United States], well, that's the end of that. You hardly ever get an inquiry about why we sent them back. On the nannies it's the opposite, hardly a time when we never get a response as to why we did send her back. So, it's just the aggravation and futility as far as trying to enforce the law. [11]

[Unlike fraudulent passport holders sent back,] if a person is coming to be a nanny or a person is coming to marry a permanent resident—you send them back, they will complain! [19]

[An inspector] had a [nanny] case not a long time ago. We were going to send her back [after documents were found and an admission of intent to work]. She had signed and was ready, then [supervisors] changed their minds and decided to let her in. There's too much pressure from outside, congressmen. [Q: A congressman called?] No, a big shot called the supervisors.... For supervisors, the pressure is on them too. If they make a wrong decision, then they [employers] call congressmen, and they call [the district director], and then back to us. So much politics involved, that's what it boils down to. [22]

Inspectors handling nanny cases assume they are dealing with wealthy, politically connected families "who will complain" themselves or through political representatives. During the secondary inspection telephone calls are likely from the girl's suspected employer, concerned that she was stopped and questioned. Callers may simply ask "what is happening," but on hearing that the girl is a suspected nanny they may demand that the port release her and threaten to enlist the help of legislators or her consul general. They may contact downtown administrators. Even if an "inadmissible nanny" is immediately removed from the port and returned home after withdrawing her application to enter the U.S., inspectors fear the case may not go away and brace themselves for a "congressional"—a letter of inquiry asking the agency to justify its actions.

Lack of Support by Superiors

The effects of casework intervention are mediated through the local INS organizational hierarchy of district administrators, port superiors, and inspectors. Although inspectors do not fully share agency orientations to political casework, they comply with them since they are not free to express their own preferences. Their behavior is constrained by direct supervision as well as apprehension of criticism and embarrassment for failing to fulfill expectations. Port inspectors have developed considerable familiarity with the orientations of their superiors.

> They are deathly afraid of—as far as supervisors—complaints from congressmen or any agency that allocates money. [18]

> The office downtown is very politically oriented. All you have to do is get a congressman on the case and they get in. [14]

> The Port Director sets port policy based on port experience, which means past trouble. Unfortunately they tend to be gun shy. It affects morale. [6]

Inspectors also have more particularized knowledge of the likely organizational consequences of decisions superiors may not support.

> [In fiancée cases] they don't want you to look hard even though you'd be right under the law. [Downtown administrators] say, "You could have handled it in a more positive way. The congressional was unnecessary." And the supervisor will get involved because they signed off.... If there is a hot issue, the higher-ups want to know the circumstances behind it. [The downtown office will] question it all down the line so they can get off the hot seat. Some officers at the airport would stand up [for you] to a certain degree but not downtown. And that's basically what counts. [19]

> [Speaking about a traveler from the favored nation:] We may defer his or her inspection to make it look good. The relative would then get up their barrage of attorneys and the [downtown inspector completing the secondary inspection] would admit. There's no point to it.... [Y]ou have this person who has the credit cards, the apartment lease, the check stubs in their baggage ... still we have them admitted as a visitor. They're [downtown administrators] trying to send a message indirectly, I would think. And, you're pretty naive not to take it seriously.... So why create problems for myself, other inspectors, and for the district? [11]

> [In lawful permanent resident cases] no judge is going to take away the card. And that is what you have to think about. Once you've had several cases like this and you've been burned, you are more careful. When you take a card away you're doing something pretty major to them. There may be complaints at the office downtown. You don't need that. [13]

[Speaking about nanny cases:] When it's a nanny case, the employer calls the congressman, and the congressman in turn calls the district director and the girls get in. There's nothing else that we can do. [30]

Most inspectors experience discomfort with with an institutional structure that undermines their ability to "do their job" of enforcing the law. They not only feel entitled to proceed but obligated to do so to prevent unfair treatment of persons similarly situated.

[Comparing fiancée cases at the port and overseas:] If you're coming to get married and it's a U.S. citizen and you have no return tickets and no intention of returning... [you] are an immigrant without an immigrant visa.... Port policy is, well, go ahead and let them in and given them some time to defer the inspection to the downtown office and let them determine what to do with them. But clearly within that time they are going to get married. So then they are going to become an adjustment case. They are clearly excludable [at the port]. What is the purpose of a K visa? Why penalize the person who has waited a year for their fiancée to [legally] come in and others just come in as B2 visitors [visitors for pleasure] with the intention of marrying? But it's port policy [to defer inspection]—it's in the interest of a port to do it. [19]

Tensions between inspectors and their port superiors are usually suppressed in their exchanges but surface in private derisive remarks about downtown superiors and cynical (often humorous) conversations. One inspector told another that before wasting any time on another secondary inspection he planned to ask what senators or other politicians the applicant knew!

Some potential tensions also are dissipated by the perceived de minimis nature of most of the cases that are the object of casework and bureaucratic accommodation. A few inspectors feel the law should not be enforced. Some rationalize admitting travellers by noting that they would eventually enter somehow. Or they observe that citizen children of lawful permanent residents living outside the country could always reapply for that status for their parents. Why "spin one's wheels" and create extra work for the government by seizing their cards and opening the door to casework. Resentment and resignation are widespread with respect to citizens of the favored nation.

Inspectors' disagreement with organizational policies and practices arises in part from their position within the organization: they do not have to worry personally about the consequences to the agency of offending politicians. Downtown administrators, in contrast, are usually subject to, and must deal with, legislators and other politicians. Although noncooperation is an expected consequence of lower-level staff disagreement with superiors' policies, inspectors have few resources with which to express their dissent. Formal compliance is ensured, in part, by port supervisors' review of inspectors; they must "sign off " on any case in which a foreign national is sent for an exclusion hearing or returned home after withdrawing his or her application to enter the U.S. At times inspectors have sought to express their dissatisfaction with port practices by using countermeasures to punish people they believe should not be admitted (e.g., limiting the period of stay in the U.S. of those "lying"), but port superiors have stopped such expansion of discretion whenever they detect it.

Moreover, whether an inspector's disagreement with organizational practices is minimal or substantial, compliance is encouraged through the threat of significant sanctions. Inspectors (and port superiors) clearly are concerned that downtown superiors will not back them up when inquiries come. As one supervisor observed, "I'd rather deal with a felon and have everyone's support [than] with a nanny or 407 [suspected abandonment of permanent resident status, where] no one's supportive." Downtown administrators are perceived as all too willing to believe or accommodate those complaining. Port superiors are quick to point out, however, that there is a larger agency-wide problem of nonsupport that affects even local district directors.

This sense of vulnerability was expressed by a port superior during a meeting to discuss a nanny case in which the suspected employer called the port:

> These cases are the kiss of death for us. She called and began to give me the names of people [in a wealthy nearby town] she knew. You begin to ask yourself, "Is it worth it?" [All inspectors were then warned to do a thorough Q & A—a question-and-answer interrogatory—so the port could use it in answering inquiries.] Especially the nanny cases, they all go to the front office [downtown district administrators] and it comes back to supervisors. They particularly like to put [supervisors] in a noose, and it goes on down the line [implying to lower-level inspectors], so it's important to do a good Q & A.

Port officials suggest their "credibility" will be questioned by downtown superiors if too many inquiries are received by the agency about their actions—a conclusion that officers believe has important implications for their performance evaluation, career advancement to other positions, and professional respect within the agency.

Proactive Policing: Low Risk of Detection Where Exceptions Are Made

Inspection work is predominately proactive rather than reactive. Inspectors identify most suspected illegal entrants themselves. Relatively few inadmissible foreign nationals are targeted by "tips" or complaints from the community or other government agencies. Suspected illegal entrants normally are identified through focused questioning of incoming travelers by primary inspectors and application of unwritten categories of suspicious persons. Young women who tell certain "stories" about why they are entering suggest arrangements to work for families without legal authorization. Such a "story" would prompt a primary inspector to send her to secondary inspection. Without complainants, however, there are no case-specific pressures for strict enforcement, and exceptions are unlikely to be detected.

Inspector Responses to Anticipated Casework

Given the pressures, constraints, and opportunities in the setting, how do inspectors behave? Inspectors' awareness of possible casework intervention has led to anticipatory strategies, among them protective documentation, higher thresholds for proceeding, a wait-and-see approach to cases, and enforcement inaction. In some instances these strategies were beneficial, allowing inspectors and port superiors to resist or rebuff undesired pressures or demands. In other instances, they resulted in compliance with external constraints.

The enforcement strategies observed were partly adaptations to perceived past problems. Indeed, a few cases of past intervention had an uncanny tendency to take on a life of their own in shaping inspectors' assessment of later cases, pushing them toward a more cautious and lenient approach to the processing of certain groups of suspected excludable foreign nationals.

Preparing Protective Documentation

Inspectors concerned with outside intervention naturally build a paper record to support their actions. If a suspected nanny is judged inadmissible and recommended for return home without an exclusion hearing, a question-and-answer interrogatory is prepared by the secondary inspector. How does she know the family? How many children of what ages were in the home? Was the woman of the house employed or in the home during the day?

Thoroughness is stressed. If "a case comes back" to the agency after the girl is removed from the country, port superiors want a document to answer inquiries. A good Q & A allows them to respond with the girl's stated intention to work for compensation. One port superior told an employer who denied the girl's illegal employment: "How could I make this all up about you?" In another case, a port superior reported that a foreign embassy appeared satisfied when told that the agency had the girl's statement.

The Q & A is used most commonly when inspectors expect outside intervention.

> Sometimes if they're nannies you can expect repercussions and you want to protect yourself. It depends on the situation [as to whether a Q & A is conducted], but with nannies we do it. It's good to take a Q & A that says that they told you that they were working here. It can come back to haunt you. [12]

Such documentation is not necessarily undertaken for its administrative or supervisory benefits in structuring discretion but rather as a protective device.

Raising the Standard for Proceeding

Another response is to raise the standard of evidence for agency action to eliminate all but the most blatant violations. Although this makes agency action easier to defend it also reduces the frequency of such action. Problems arise when inspectors are unable to find an employment contract or personal letter suggesting a girl's intentions to work as household help. An applicant may challenge admissions in a Q & A, claiming she misunderstood the interpreter, was tricked into saying she was employed by the family, and was coerced into signing the statement by the threat of confinement pending a hearing.

> [With nannies] it's always intimidation. But the biggest thing is the breakdown of communication. We say we had a translator from the airlines. They [the outside caller] start to challenge the competency of the translator. [11]

> The Service would detain a suspected [nanny] if we had a real good one. If she told us everything. If we had a real good Q & A. Because otherwise, the family calls and tells it differently and she was jailed too, and we look like the Gestapo. [13]

> I had a case, she told me she had been here several times working for families, the usual MO [modus operandi]. We got downtown [for a hearing], her story changed. She said we threatened her with detention, that she was confused. The judge let her in. [12]

Inspectors seemed increasingly reluctant to run the risk of reversal, acting only when they had virtually incontrovertible proof, such as an employer's letter.

> I could be the hard guy, talk softly and carry a big stick and get her to admit she is a nanny. But—the repercussions—it is not worth it. I've learned my lesson and so have the other inspectors. The people she is coming to see call the congressman, and it makes problems for me, and for the supervisors, and the port. But if I find something like a letter, they can scream all they want and I have the backing of my supervisors. If I just get it out of the mouth that they are a nanny, I have nothing. It is not substantiated. After ten minutes, one hour, they say that just to get out of the situation they said, "I am a nanny." ... I learned my lesson the hard way. All inspectors who did what I did had nothing but problems. [7]

Another inspector explained his decision not to question one girl further after finding no employment letter:

> It would take two hours to break her. I wouldn't be paid for that [it was 7 P.M. and he was to leave at 8 P.M.] and the supervisors wouldn't want that either. Nannies are not worth it.... [M]iddle-income families have a certain perspective, and they'll say, "What are you doing? What are you doing sending home an 18-year-old girl who's coming to babysit? You guys have something better to do?" ... You've got to face reality. If I send it downtown, what's going to happen? I've had good cases I've sent downtown. They will let them in. They feel it's in the special interest of the Service to let them in. I had a [European nation] girl who was coming to do an au pair job. I did the Q & A, and, yeah, she's was coming in, and, yeah, she was babysitting and doing cleaning and laundry and she was getting paid. The USC [U.S. citizen] was outside [in the airport lobby], and the next thing the girl wanted to go to the judge. So I sent it downtown.... She was admitted [by the agency].... Even if you have an ironclad case and it goes downtown, all you have to do is get people who call downtown and you get special interest and they are admitted. [19]

The standard for proceeding also rises in "407" cases—suspected abandonment of lawful permanent resident (LPR) status. Except in "clear-cut" cases that preclude discretionary action, there is a port policy that inspectors only take voluntarily relinquished LPR cards for fear of outcries by citizen sons and daughters.

> With a 407, within 10 minutes you know what the outcome is going to be. I'm not going to say you take advantage of the situation, but if the sons and daughters are professionals...you know you are going to hear from them. But if there are blue-collar parents or not educated, nothing is going to come of it. More or less that's the case. If an individual comes in and they say their son is in the passenger area...and the son turns out to be a professional—an engineer, doctor, lawyer—they're going to pursue it and you will lose. You're better off letting it go. You tell the son or daughter what is required of an LPR and that they need a reentry document, and do not do it again, and you give the card back. [11]

"Decisions Not to Decide"

Port officials sometimes take an approach that promotes the appearance of doing something but avoids the risks of full enforcement. Peter Schuck (1983: 75) characterizes this as a strategy to "substitute relatively riskless acts for relatively risky ones." By putting off a final decision on a case, officials have the option of backing down if outsiders intervene vigorously or proceeding if circumstances are advantageous. In one case a young woman indicated her intentions to work in a family's stable for room and board, was ruled inadmissible, and voluntarily returned home without an exclusion hearing. This produced a barrage of calls to the port from the suspected employer (a judge elsewhere in the U.S.) and a member of his family. Eventually the port and the overseas State Department office (also thought by some port officials to be under pressures from the suspected employer to issue another visa) were in contact. The State Department issued another visa, and she was admitted. An official familiar with the case provided this account:

> When she came in, she gave a Q & A that incriminated her. She said she was going to take care of the horse and get room and board for doing that. Where do you draw the line? She was to take care of the horse and she'd be able to ride. But he [the suspected employer] had enough financial resources to show that he had other people to take care of the stable and that she did not need to work. He does travel and may have just met her and invited her. But she was coming to work. You can only do what you have to do, you prepare a case the best you can, but you can't control those higher up than you.

Speculating on what would have happened had the port adamantly blocked entry, the official suggested that agency superiors were unlikely to back the port's actions.

> Technically it's a strong case, but some people have an ability to write letters all over the world and unfortunately some people higher up will acknowledge them. If they had contacted the [INS] Commissioner, they'd call us to say what's going on. There is a tendency [the official paused for a moment] let's say for them to believe them more than us.

The official suggested a less risky course of action: "deferring" the girl's inspection to a later date rather than finding her inadmissible and removing her after she withdrew her application to enter. (A deferral allows an applicant into the country, postponing the secondary inspection into admissibility.) If the violator rallied her forces, the agency could back down. If not, it could proceed with enforcement. In retrospect, the perceived power of the violator (through her suspected employer) suggested this more moderate action to the port superior. The case "came in one night and I signed it and probably I shouldn't have, given the trouble. She [the nanny] was going to see a judge and, it shouldn't affect your decision."

Fiancée cases are also illustrative. Those entering the country on tourist or business visas (or on the visa waiver program) with the intention of marrying a citizen or lawful permanent resident and remaining in the U.S. are excludable as immigrants without an immigrant visa. Fiancée K visas (obtained prior to entry) are available for those planning to marry, although they take effort and time to obtain.

Those arriving at the port intending to marry often are given deferred inspections at the downtown office.

Fiancée cases illustrate the agency's ability to "decide not to decide" and thereby preserve its discretion to overlook the violation by yielding control over a portion of its enforcement program to this politically represented sector of the public. If, as is typical, the couple marries before the downtown inspection, the agency recategorizes the case as adjustment-of-status, allowing the applicant to petition to become a permanent resident by virtue of marriage to a U.S. citizen.

Deferred inspection is employed when officials anticipate political intervention. Assessments of the political power of violators also are found in other settings. Lundman's study (1980: 196) of the police suggests that officials try to protect themselves from liability and avoid creating problems for their superiors by classifying arrests along a continuum from "safe to risky." Emerson's (1969: 35–36) study of juvenile court decisions reveals similar variability in judicial behavior depending on whether individuals have "effective voice in court affairs" through political or community sources.

"Decisions Not to Act"

When inspectors handle cases, they protect superiors by anticipating situations likely to lead to unhealthy confrontations or encounters. Overt decisions not to pursue nanny cases because of their potential political ramifications were rare. In one domestic employment case, for example, the secondary inspection revealed that the girl appeared to be coming to work for a European consulate. The inspector quickly terminated the interrogation, suggesting it would only lead to problems for the port: "Once she said she was coming to see the [European] consulate—hands off! [Q: You would get a call?] Not me, the supervisors would get it, a complaint." Agencies circumscribe their action in more subtle ways, as discussed in the next section, structuring decision-making so that front-line inspectors never encounter sensitive situations.

The Indirect Power of Casework: Anticipation of Intervention in Agency Routines

Decision-makers may consider certain types of agency initiatives to be unacceptable because of the reactions they may produce. External constraints promote this form of organization inaction. In their classic work on power in the community context, Bachrach and Baratz (1970) suggest that individuals may prevent certain potentially threatening issues from becoming part of the political process by establishing committees to defuse them or making certain appointments. Lukes (1974: 21–22) suggests further that potential issues may be suppressed by the *inactivity* of persons and groups whose interests may be at risk.

At Border Port and Metropolitan Port, I first glimpsed circumscribed agency activity in offhand remarks and grumblings from inspectors who saw evidence of evasion of the law but felt constrained from initiating enforcement efforts. Early one morning at the Mexican border, an immigration inspector complained to me about the widespread illegal use of border-crossing cards by Mexicans seeking to work as domestics. (Such cards only allow border-town residents to enter for 72 hours to shop and visit.) Pointing to a woman awaiting inspection, he asked, "Well, where do you think she's going? She says she's going to do some shopping!" Seeing another women in line carrying a handful of nylon shopping bags, the inspector remarked that workers often use the bags to make it look as if they are going shopping.

The inspector then raised the sore subject of lack of enforcement. The previous year the district office had mounted an unsuccessful "maid blitz." Several hundred border-card crossers each day were questioned by immigration inspectors. Mexican women seeking entry in the morning hours with border-crossing cards were sent inside the port for further questioning about their intentions. Those "going shopping" were allowed to proceed, but the INS exchanged their border-crossing cards for temporary passes giving them only a few hours to conduct their business and return to Mexico, at which time their cards would be returned.

This threatened to cut off a plentiful source of cheap domestic labor. The adjacent communities long had enjoyed a relatively open border. Americans had grown used to illegal Mexican maids, enjoying a level of domestic service available only to the wealthy in other cities. So widespread was the use of maids, even among the working class, that the local paper reported one developer saying it was difficult to sell a modestly priced home of 1,800 square feet without a maid's room.

The crackdown sparked a huge public outcry (on both sides of the border), which was extensively reported in the local newspapers. Shortly after it began, American merchants complained vociferously that it was hurting business because Mexicans feared losing their border-crossing cards. By the third day the enforcement actions triggered protests from other sectors, including human rights and religious groups in Mexico and farm worker, labor, and Hispanic groups in the U.S. Protests were staged at a nearby U.S. consulate and at the border-crossing point itself. The INS's enforcement activity also was brought to the attention of a local U.S. representative, who asked the district office for an explanation. No interest groups defended the agency.

By the end of the week, the enforcement effort was stopped. The district director apologized to American and Mexican businesses for not warning them in advance and promised to inform them if the program was resumed. It has not been. Two inspectors reflected on the experience.

There was a public backlash. There was an outcry on the U.S. side because the babysitter did not get there on time and parents did not go to work. So public pressure forced the Immigration Service to drop that. Because they were not getting to the places [they were working], people said it was not fair. They said no one in the U.S. was there to be babysitters. So, we stopped it. [41]

We had [a maid blitz] a year ago, or maybe it was two. As usual, the general public complained. And, as usual politics, and they stopped it. [42]

Resentment from inspectors who felt constrained to do nothing was also apparent at Metropolitan Port. Early in the research I heard inspectors complain about the special treatment of visitors from a particular nation. One port superior pointed out they do not "go by the book" with these cases because powerful local politicians and national legislators would call the INS. Such perceptions were reported to affect the primary inspector, who no longer referred problem cases for secondary questioning. A primary inspector, asked what he could do about the fact he believed they were entering illegally to work, responded:

Nothing. There's a feeling, it used to be desperation, now the feeling is "so what?" Usually the airplane is filled with 167 people.... You know everyone is telling you they have $25 and a ticket home and a visa. And you know 50% are going to get a job, and they're not going home. But there isn't a single thing you can do. They have a visa, someone is waiting for them [a citizen or lawful permanent resident]. They'll swear to it, that it's their cousin. There's not a thing you can do. If you really check one, you would find a reason to send them back or a lot of them. But it just doesn't happen.... If you take each and every one, and take the person outside, and question someone through with a trained questioner, then probably something can be done with them. But, 167 of them on a plane, it's hard to talk to everyone, it's hard, you need a translator....

I'm suggesting we do not have enough personnel with enough training. I'm also suggesting even if we could stop someone and [the person in the airport lobby is a citizen], they'd run to [local politician] and we'd get six or eight phone calls in here, and the next morning that person is gone.... If you were a USC here ten years, and you wanted your cousin and the INS said no, you would be furious.... You'd call [local politicians], the consulate, and pretty soon [the district director and the port director], and all of a sudden someone would be in ....

No one even says, "Why not secondary them?" because they're going to get in anyway. Why aggravate the passengers, yourself, and your co-workers because you've done something stupid. Because you know that they are going to get in.... [Q: Any group could call.] But another country does not have clout in this city like [this nationality]. [18]

These cases are difficult to prove. The entrants are unlikely to carry letters or contracts of employment showing their intent to work. Enforcement difficulties are exacerbated, however, by the perceived likelihood of successful intervention by politicians.

> It's the [nation's] congressmen. They call downtown and they want so-and-so admitted. And they get jobs and work in violation of their status. And the community as a whole puts pressure on the Service to admit them. It's pretty frustrating. [Q: Why is it so frustrating?] You can't enforce the law in this regard. It's like swimming up river against the current. [14]

The agency's restraint is produced not by continuing outside intervention in particular cases but by anticipation of the exercise of power and influence against the agency were it to act.

Implications of Casework for the Exercise of Discretion

The benefits of casework are described at length in the scholarly literature. Its contributions to the control and accountability of agencies, however, should not distract from its adverse effects. Ironically, legislative oversight can produce decision-making timidity, biases in agency treatment of individuals, and local political control over enforcement of national laws.

First, timidity is a potential by-product of officials' anticipation of casework. In making decisions to exclude, officials are more likely to be criticized for doing too much rather than too little (Gellhorn, 1966: 52–53). Timidity flourishes as much in the shadows of "anticipated" political intervention as in the light of actual legislator intercessions. Fear of criticism, sanctions, and the general desire to keep out of trouble with superiors encourages accommodation to outsiders through cautious and lenient handling of certain cases.

Second, external power can produce patterns of activity or inactivity that benefit some groups or individuals more than others (Bachrach & Baratz, 1970: 43–44). Agency interests are not identical with private interests, yet dependencies make agency pursuit of private goals more likely. By anticipating the likely response of individuals or their political representatives and modifying its behavior accordingly, the agency becomes an extension of those interests—a subsystem mirroring the existing mobilization of bias within the community.

In the cases involving nannies, fiancées, permanent residents, and favored-nation workers, individuals were able to exploit the highly discretionary legal area, absence of complainants, job concerns of lower-level agency workers, and public and institutional invisibility of enforcement decisions. As a result, the benefits and privileges of the system are denied to those outside the country: those denied or still awaiting visas legally permitting employment within the United States; those engaged in the slower process of seeking fiancée visas to enter and marry; or those painfully awaiting the day (months or years ahead) when their immigrant visa allows them to join relatives living in the United States. Those with the greatest stake in the fairness of the system are, by definition, not here or part of the political system. Indeed, they have no right to be here. They are not simply the "passive or silent" victims of government practices (Schuck 1983: 72). The very issue of exclusion denies them political influence because it does not allow them to raise the issue of equity—that some of those admitted should not have been.

Third, when local administrative officials respond to political pressures by accommodating their policies to actual or anticipated intervention, they may not serve broad public policy interests. Politicians represent narrow constituent bases. As their influence increases, central agency goals may decrease in importance (Kaufman, 1960: 80; Calavita, 1992). Such deviations from formal policy objectives are particularly troubling because casework effects have low visibility.

Enforcement in Context: The Asymmetry of Risks

The INS finds itself in a dilemma. On one hand, it is committed to enforcing immigration exclusion laws in a just and equitable manner; on the other, its institutional environment shapes its actions. While it seeks to be accountable and universalistic in handling cases, the need to retain and strengthen the support of legislators and local politicians produces lenient treatment of certain persons or groups. Casework intervention has a ripple effect beyond the point of agency contact. Drawing on their working knowledge, lower-level officials respond to reversals by superiors by taking steps to avoid them in the future (Emerson & Paley, 1992). Such anticipatory behavior enlarges accommodation to outside interests. In addition, through fundamental changes in legal norms—higher standards for action, routine reliance on dispositions malleable to political intervention, and official behavior adapted to violators' ostensible power—the stage is set for differential treatment of individuals and groups.

The agency's vulnerability to political pressure arises in part from the meager assistance it receives from other traditional sources of support. It has no natural constituency. Does this always expose an agency to influence from legislators or other political operatives? Such a conclusion probably oversimplifies and overstates the effects of casework intervention pressures on agency functioning. As James Q. Wilson recently wrote: "Government agencies are not billiard balls driven hither and yon by the impact of forces and interests. When bureaucrats are free to choose a course of action their choices will reflect the full array of incentives operating on them" (1989:88; see also Heinz et al., 1993: ch. 1). Indeed, several countervailing incentives may balance powerful pressures.

First, succumbing to external pressures may have such adverse consequences for institutional goals that it provokes an internal *culture* of stringent nonaccommodation. Administrative units that heavily rely on voluntary compliance for enforcement are illustrative. Kagan describes federal agency response to congressional inquiries on behalf of businesses seeking exceptions from the 1971 wage-price freeze. Those "congressionals" received VIP treatment (cases were brought to the top of the pile for accelerated dispositions), but there was no evidence that they substantially affected case outcomes (1978: 155). Although the implementing agencies had no natural constituency, they did have strong political support from the executive branch. Furthermore, their primary mode of enforcement was voluntary compliance, which could easily be disrupted by a scandal or favoritism (ibid.: 74-78). The INS, by contrast, does not rely on voluntary compliance for exclusion decision-making. It rather resembles agencies issuing permits, licenses, or benefits, whose applicants are less able to complain about government inequities. Therefore, it has less reason to worry about an accommmodative approach.

Second, in some law enforcement contexts, government officials fear exposure and criticism. The exceptions made by the INS are fairly invisible. Those aware of favorable outcomes (relatives, friends, and employers) desire the lenient treatment. In other settings where agencies might be particularly vulnerable to legislator interference (e.g., site judgments by the Environmental Protection Agency), competitors make it their business to learn about such concessions and complain if they are not given the same benefit (Kagan, 1978: 76). Moreover, opposing interest groups (such as the Sierra Club on environmental issues) make it riskier for legislators to get involved.

Agency officials thus operate in distinctive cultural- political environments that may provide varying incentives for and against accommodation. We need to study how officials working in diverse contexts respond to political intervention and the conditions that foster or discourage the penetrability of administrative systems.

DISCUSSION QUESTIONS

1. Our ambivalence about the appropriateness of legislators and politicians engaging in "casework" rests on a belief in the distinction between law and politics, between decisions according to rules and decisions shaped by political pressures. Is it possible to make such a distinction? What are the advantages and disadvantages of rules? of politics? of casework?

2.   What is the difference between an analytic focus on casework and a focus on the anticipation of casework? Why do officials exercise discretion? Would it be possible to eliminate discretion? desirable to do so?

3.   What are the potential sources of support for an agency: clients, community, executive, legislature? What are the sources of support for the INS? How does it enhance such support? In what other situations do regulatory agencies lack public support for their mission? What are the consequences of public indifference or hostility? When does enforcement generate organized protest? support?

4.   Why does political intervention vary inversely with the importance of the immigration matter? Is there really no political influence in momentous cases? Why do front-line staff and superiors approach cases differently?

5.   What is the difference between reactive and proactive enforcement? The relation of resources and personnel to the choice between these strategies? What steps do INS inspectors take to minimize the likelihood of political interference? reversal? reprimand? How does this resemble the relationship between police and courts? What is the difference between various kinds of evidence? How do job incentives (pay, hours, promotion) shape inspector behavior?

6.   Are you surprised by how explicitly inspectors acknowledge the effect of class on their decisions? Are there other regulatory settings where class plays an equally important role? Apart from inspector discretion, are the immigration laws themselves class biased? Why did the INS capitulate to political pressures, whereas the agencies enforcing the 1971 wage-price freeze did not?

Equality

14

Why the "Haves" Come Out Ahead: Speculations on the Limits of Legal Change

Marc Galanter

This essay attempts to discern some of the general features of a legal system like the American by drawing on (and rearranging) commonplaces and less than systematic gleanings from the literature. Our question, specifically, is, under what conditions can litigation be redistributive, taking litigation in the broadest sense of the presentation of claims to be decided by courts (or courtlike agencies) and the whole penumbra of threats, feints, and so forth surrounding such presentation?

For purposes of this analysis, let us think of the legal system as comprised of these elements:

A body of authoritative normative learning—RULES
A set of institutional facilities within which the normative learning is applied to specific cases—COURTS
A body of persons with specialized skill in the above—LAWYERS
Persons or groups with claims they might make to the courts in reference to the rules, etc.—PARTIES

Let us also make the following assumptions about the society and the legal system:

It is a society in which actors with different amounts of wealth and power are constantly in competitive or partially cooperative relationships in which they have opposing interests.

This society has a legal system in which a wide range of disputes and conflicts are settled by courtlike agencies, which purport to apply preexisting general norms impartially (that is, unaffected by the identity of the parties).

The rules and the procedures of these institutions are complex; wherever possible disputing units employ specialized intermediaries in dealing with them.

The rules applied by the courts are in part worked out in the process of adjudication (courts devise interstitial rules, combine diverse rules, and apply old rules to new situations). There is a living tradition of such rule-work and a

Abridged from *Law & Society Review*, Volume 9:95 (1975).

system of com munication such that the outcomes in some of the adjudicated cases affect the outcome in classes of future adjudicated cases.

Resources on the institutional side are insufficient for timely full-dress adjudication in every case, so that parties are permitted or even encouraged to forego bringing cases and to "settle" cases, that is, to bargain to a mutually acceptable outcome.

There are several levels of agencies, with "higher" agencies announcing (making, interpreting) rules and other "lower" agencies assigned the responsibility of enforcing (implementing, applying) these rules. (Although there is some overlap of function in both theory and practice, I shall treat them as distinct and refer to them as "peak" and "field level" agencies.)

Not all the rules propounded by "peak" agencies are effective at the "field level," due to imperfections in communication, shortages of resources, skill, understanding commitment and so forth. Effectiveness at the field level will be referred to as "penetration."

A Typology of Parties

Most analyses of the legal system start at the rules end and work down through institutional facilities to see what effect the rules have on the parties. I would like to reverse that procedure and look through the other end of the telescope. Let's think about the different kinds of parties and the effect these differences might have on the way the system works.

Because of differences in their size and resources and the state of the law, some of the actors in the society have many occasions to utilize the courts to make or defend claims; others do so only rarely. We might divide our actors into those claimants who have only occasional recourse to the courts (one-shotters or OS) and repeat players (RP) who are engaged in many similar litigations over time. The spouse in a divorce case, the auto-injury claimant, the criminal accused are OSs; the insurance company, the prosecutor, the finance company are RPs. Obviously this is an oversimplification; there are intermediate cases, such as the professional criminal. So we ought to think of OS-RP as a continuum rather than a dichotomous pair. Typically, the RP is a larger unit, and the stakes in any given case are smaller (relative to total worth). OSs are usually smaller units, and the stakes represented by the tangible outcome of the case may be high relative to total worth, as in the case of injury victim or the criminal accused. Or the OS may suffer from the opposite problem: his claims may be so small and unmanageable (the shortweighted consumer or the holder of performing rights) that the cost of enforcing them outruns any promise of benefit (Finklestein, 1954: 284–86).

Let us refine our notion of the RP into an "ideal type"—a unit that has had and anticipates repeated litigation, that has low stakes in the outcome of any one case, and that has the resources to pursue its long-run interests. An OS, on the other hand, is a unit whose claims are too large (relative to his size) or too small (relative to the cost of remedies) to be managed routinely and rationally.

We would expect an RP to play the litigation game differently from an OS. Let us consider some of his advantages:

(1) RPs, having done it before, have advance intelligence; they are able to structure the next transaction and build a record. It is the RP who writes the form contract, requires the security deposit, and the like.

(2) RPs develop expertise and have ready access to specialists. They enjoy economies of scale and have low start-up costs for any case.

(3) RPs have opportunities to develop facilitative informal relations with institutional incumbents.

(4) The RP must establish and maintain credibility as a combatant. His interest in his "bargaining reputation" serves as a resource to establish "commitment" to his bargaining positions. With no bargaining reputation to maintain, the OS has more difficulty in convincingly committing himself in bargaining.

(5) RPs can play the odds. The larger the matter at issue looms for the OS, the more likely he is to adopt a minimax strategy (minimize the probability of maximum loss). Assuming that the stakes are relatively smaller for RPs, they can adopt strategies calculated to maximize gain over a long series of cases, even where this involves the risk of maximum loss in some cases.

(6) RPs can play for rules as well as immediate gains. First, it pays an RP to expend resources in influencing the making of the relevant rules by such methods as lobbying (and his accumulated expertise enables him to do this persuasively).

(7) RPs can also play for rules in litigation itself, whereas an OS is unlikely to. That is, there is a difference in what they regard as a favorable outcome. Because his stakes in the immediate outcome are high and because by definition the OS is unconcerned with the outcome of similar litigation in the future, the OS will have little interest in the element of the outcome that might influence the disposition of the decision-maker next time around. For the RP, on the other hand, anything that will favorably influence the outcomes of future cases is a worthwhile result. The larger the stake for any player and the lower the probability of repeat play, the less likely that he will be concerned with the rules that govern future cases of the same kind. Consider two parents contesting the custody of their only child, the prizefighter vs. the IRS for tax arrears, the convict facing the death penalty. On the other hand, the player with small stakes in the present case and the prospect of a series of similar cases (the IRS, the

adoption agency, the prosecutor) may be more interested in the state of the law.

Thus, if we analyze the outcomes of a case into a tangible component and a rule component, we may expect that in case 1, OS will attempt to maximize tangible gain. But if RP is interested in maximizing his tangible gain in a series of cases 1...n, he may be willing to trade off tangible gain in any one case for rule gain (or to minimize rule loss). We assumed that the institutional facilities for litigation were overloaded and settlements were prevalent. We would then expect RPs to "settle" cases where they expected unfavorable rule outcomes. Since they expect to litigate again, RPs can select to adjudicate (or appeal) those cases they regard as most likely to produce favorable rules. On the other hand, OSs should be willing to trade off the possibility of making "good law" for tangible gain. Thus, we would expect the body of "precedent" cases—that is, cases capable of influencing the outcome of future cases—to be favorable to RPs.

Of course it is not suggested that the strategic configuration of the parties is the sole or major determinant of rule-development. Rule-development is shaped by a relatively autonomous learned tradition, by the impingement of intellectual currents from outside, by the preferences and prudences of the decision-makers. But courts are passive, and these factors operate only when the process is triggered by parties. The point here is merely to note the superior opportunities of the RP to trigger promising cases and prevent the triggering of unpromising ones. It is not incompatible with a course of rule-development favoring OSs (or, as indicated below, with OSs failing to get the benefit of those favorable new rules).

In stipulating that RPs can play for rules, I do not mean to imply that RPs pursue rule-gain as such. If we recall that not all rules penetrate (i.e. become effectively applied at the field level) we come to some additional advantages of RPs.

(8)   RPs, by virtue of experience and expertise, are more capable of discerning which rules are likely to "penetrate" and which are likely to remain merely symbolic commitments. RPs may be able to concentrate their resources on rule-changes that are likely to make a tangible difference. They can trade off symbolic defeats for tangible gains.

(9)   Since penetration depends in part on the resources of the parties (knowledge, attentiveness, expert services, money), RPs are more likely to be able to invest the matching resources necessary to secure the penetration of rules favorable to them.

It is not suggested that RPs are to be equated with "haves" (in terms of power, wealth and status) or OSs with "have-nots." In the American setting most RPs are larger, richer and more powerful than are most OSs, so these categories overlap, but there are obvious exceptions. RPs may be "have-nots" (alcoholic derelicts) or may act as champions of "have-nots" (as government does from time to time); OSs such as criminal defendants may be wealthy. What this analysis does is to define a position of advantage in the configuration of contending parties and indicate how those with other advantages tend to occupy this position of advantage and to have their other advantages reinforced and augmented thereby. This position of advantage is one of the ways in which a legal system formally neutral as between "haves" and "have-nots" may perpetuate and augment the advantages of the former.

We have postulated that OSs will be relatively indifferent to the rule-outcomes of particular cases. But one might expect the absolute level of interest in rule-outcomes to vary in different populations: in some there may be widespread and intense concern with securing vindication according to official rules, which overshadows interest in the tangible outcomes of disputes; in others rule outcomes may be a matter of relative indifference when compared to tangible outcomes. The level and distribution of such "rule mindedness" may affect the relative strategic position of OSs and RPs. For example, the more rule minded a population, the less we would expect an RP advantage in managing settlement policy.

But such rule mindedness or appetite for official vindication should be distinguished from both readiness to resort to official remedy systems in the first place and high valuation of official rules as symbolic objects. Quite apart from relative concern with rule-outcomes, we might expect populations to differ in their estimates of the propriety and gratification of litigating in the first place. Such attitudes may affect the strategic situation of the parties. For example, the greater the distaste for litigation in a population, the greater the barriers to OSs pressing or defending claims, and the greater the RP advantages, assuming that such sentiments would affect OSs, who are likely to be individuals, more than RPs, who are likely to be organizations.

It cannot be assumed that the observed variations in readiness to resort to official tribunals directly reflect a "rights consciousness" or appetite for vindication in terms of authoritative norms. Consider the assertion that the low rate of litigation in Japan flows from an undeveloped "sense of justiciable rights," with the implication that the higher rate in the United States flows from such rights consciousness. But the high rate of settlements and the low rate of appeals in the United States suggest it should not be regarded as having a population with great interest in securing moral victories through official vindication. Mayhew (1975) reports a survey in which a sample of Detroit area residents were asked how they had wanted to see their "most serious problem" settled. Only a tiny minority (0 percent of landlord-tenant problems, 2 percent of neighborhood problems, 4 percent of expensive purchase problems, 9 percent of public organization problems, 31 percent of discrimination problems) reported that they sought "justice" or vindication of their legal rights: "most answered that they sought resolution of their problems in some more or less expedient way."

Paradoxically, low valuation of rule-outcomes in particular cases may coexist with high valuation of rules as symbolic objects. Edelman (1967: ch. 2) distinguishes between remote, diffuse, unorganized publics, for whom rules are a source of symbolic gratification and organized, attentive publics directly concerned with the tangible results of their application. Public appetite for symbolic gratification by the promulgation of rules does not imply a corresponding private appetite for official vindication in terms of rules in particular cases. Attentive RPs, by contrast, may be more inclined to regard rules instrumentally as assets rather than as sources of symbolic gratification.

Figure 1

A Taxonomy of Litigation by Strategic Configuration of Parties

1. OS v. OS	2. RP v. OS
Parent v. Parent (Custody)	Prosecutor v. Accused
Spouse v. Spouse (Divorce)	Finance Co. v. Debtor
Family v. Family Member	Landlord v. Tenant
(Insanity Commitment)	I.R.S. v. Taxpayer
Family v. Family (Inheritance)	Condemnor v. Property Owner
Neighbor v. Neighbor	
Partner v. Partner	
3. OS v. RP	**4. RP v. RP**
Welfare Client v. Agency	Union v. Company
Auto Dealer v. Manufacturer	Movie Distributor v Censorship
Injury Victim v. Insurance	Board
Company	Developer v. Suburban
Tenant v. Landlord	Municipality
Purchaser v. Supplier	Regulatory Agency v. Firms of
Bankrupt Consumer v. Creditors	Regulated Industry
Defamed v. Publisher	

We may think of litigation as typically involving various combinations of OSs and RPs. We can then construct a matrix such as Figure 1 and fill in the boxes with some well-known if only approximate American examples. (We ignore for the moment that the terms OS and RP represent ends of a continuum rather than a dichotomous pair.)

On the basis of our incomplete and unsystematic examples, let us conjecture a bit about the content of these boxes:

Box 1: OS vs. OS

The most numerous occupants of this box are divorce and insanity hearings. Most (over 90 percent of divorces, for example) are uncontested. A large portion of these are really pseudo-litigation—a settlement worked out between the parties and ratified in the guise of adjudication. When we get real litigation in Box 1, it is often between parties who have some intimate tie with one another, fighting over some unsharable good, often with overtones of "spite" and "irrationality." Courts are resorted to where an ongoing relationship is ruptured; they have little to do with the routine patterning of activity. The law is invoked ad hoc and instrumentally by the parties. There may be a strong interest in vindication, but neither party is likely to have much interest in the long-term state of the law (for instance, custody or nuisance). There are few appeals, few test cases, little expenditure of resources on rule-development. Legal doctrine is likely to remain remote from everyday practice and popular attitudes.

Box 2: RP vs. OS

The great bulk of litigation is found in this box—indeed every really numerous kind except personal injury cases, insanity hearings, and divorces. The law is used for routine processing of claims by parties for whom the making of such claims is a regular business activity. Often the cases here take the form of stereotyped mass processing with little of the individuated attention of full-dress adjudication. Even greater numbers of cases are settled "informally," with settlement keyed to possible litigation outcome (discounted by risk, cost, delay).

The state of the law is of interest to the RP, though not to the OS defendants. Insofar as the law is favorable to the RP it is "followed" closely in practice (subject to discount for RP's transaction costs). Transactions are built to fit the rules by creditors, police, draft boards and other RPs. Rules favoring OSs may be less readily applicable, since OSs do not ordinarily plan the underlying transaction, or less meticulously observed in practice, since OSs are unlikely to be as ready or able as RPs to invest in insuring their penetration to the field level.

Box 3: OS vs. RP

All of these are rather infrequent except for personal injury cases, which are distinctive in that free entry to the arena is provided by the contingent fee. In auto injury claims, litigation is routinized and settlement is closely geared to possible litigation outcome. Outside the personal injury area, litigation in Box 3 is not routine. It usually represents the attempt of some OS to invoke external help for leverage against an organization with which he has been dealing but is now at the point of divorce (for example, the discharged employee or the cancelled franchisee).

The OS claimant generally has little interest in the state of the law; the RP defendant, however, is greatly interested.

Box 4: RP vs. RP

Let us consider the general case first and then several special cases. We might expect that there would be little litigation in Box 4, because, to the extent that two RPs play with each other repeatedly, the expectation of continued mutually beneficial interaction would give rise to informal bilateral controls. This seems borne out by studies of dealings among businessmen and in labor relations. Official agencies are invoked by unions trying to get established and by management trying to prevent them from getting established, more rarely in dealings between bargaining partners. Units with mutually beneficial relations do not adjust their differences in courts. Where they rely on third parties in dispute-resolution, it is likely to take a form (such as arbitration or a domestic tribunal) detached from official sanctions and applying domestic rather than official rules.

However, there are several special cases. First, there are those RPs who seek not furtherance of tangible interests but vindication of fundamental cultural commitments. An example would be the organizations that sponsor much church-state litigation. Where RPs are contending about value differences (who is right) rather than interest conflicts (who gets what) there is less tendency to settle and less basis for developing a private system of dispute settlement.

Second, government is a special kind of RP. Informal controls depend upon the ultimate sanction of withdrawal and refusal to continue beneficial relations. To the extent that withdrawal of future association is not possible in dealing with government, the scope of informal controls is correspondingly limited. The development of informal relations between regulatory agencies and regulated firms is well known. And the regulated may have sanctions other than withdrawal, for instance, political opposition. But the more inclusive the unit of government, the less effective the withdrawal sanction and the greater the likelihood that a party will attempt to invoke outside allies by litigation even while sustaining the ongoing relationship. This applies also to monopolies, units that share the government's relative immunity to withdrawal sanctions. RPs in monopolistic relationships will occasionally invoke formal controls to show prowess, give credibility to threats, and provide satisfactions for other audiences. Thus we would expect litigation by and against government to be more frequent than in other RP vs. RP situations. There is a second reason for expecting more litigation when government is a party. The notion of "gain" (policy as well as monetary) is often more contingent and problematic for governmental units than for other parties, such as businesses or organized interest groups. In some cases courts may, by proffering authoritative interpretations of public policy, redefine an agency's notion of gain. Hence government parties may be more willing to externalize decisions to the courts. And opponents may have more incentive to litigate against government in the hope of securing a shift in its goals.

A somewhat different special case is present where plaintiff and defendant are both RPs but do not deal with each other repeatedly (two insurance companies, for example.) In the government/monopoly case, the parties were so inextricably bound together that the force of informal controls was limited; here they are not sufficiently bound to each other to give informal controls their bite; there is nothing to withdraw from! The large one-time deal that falls through, the marginal enterprise—these are staple sources of litigation.

Where there is litigation in the RP vs. RP situation, we might expect that there would be heavy expenditure on rule-development, many appeals, and rapid elaboration of doctrine. Since the parties can invest to secure implementation of favorable rules, we would expect practice to be closely articulated to the resulting rules.

On the basis of these preliminary guesses, we can sketch a general profile of litigation and the factors associated with it. The great bulk of litigation is found in Box 2, much less in Box 3. Most of this is mass routine processing of disputes between parties who are strangers (not in mutually beneficial continuing relations) or divorced—and between whom there is a disparity in size. One party is a bureaucratically organized "professional" (in the sense of doing it for a living) who enjoys strategic advantages. Informal controls between the parties are tenuous or ineffective; their relationship is likely to be established and defined by official rules; in litigation, these rules are discounted by transaction costs and manipulated selectively to the advantage of the parties. In Boxes 1 and 4, by contrast, we have more infrequent but more individualized litigation between parties of the same general magnitude, among whom there are or were continuing multi-stranded relationships with attendant informal controls. Litigation appears when the relationship loses its future value, its "monopolistic" character deprives informal controls of sufficient leverage and the parties invoke outside allies to modify it, and the parties seek to vindicate conflicting values.

Lawyers

What happens when we introduce lawyers? Parties who have lawyers do better. Lawyers are themselves RPs. Does their presence equalize the parties, dispelling the advantage of the RP client? Or does the existence of lawyers amplify the advantage of the RP client? We might assume that RPs (tending to be larger units) who can buy legal services more steadily, in larger quantities, in bulk (by retainer) and at higher rates, would get services of better quality. They would have better information (especially where restrictions on information about legal services are present). Not only would the RP get more talent to begin with, but he would on the whole get greater continuity, better record-keeping, more anticipatory or preventive work, more experience and specialized skill in pertinent areas, and more control over counsel.

Figure 2
A Typology of Legal Specialists

Lawyer

	Specialized by Party	Specialized by Field and Party	Specialized by Field
RP	House Counsel or General Counsel for Bank, Insurance Co. etc. Corporation Counsel for Government Unit	Prosecutor Personal Injury Defendant Staff Counsel for NAACP Tax Labor/Management Collections	Patent
OS	"Poverty Lawyers" Legal Aid	Criminal Defense Personal Injury Plaintiff	Bankruptcy Divorce

Clients (RP / OS, left axis labels)

One might expect that just how much the legal services factor would accentuate the RP advantage would be related to the way in which the profession was organized. The more members of the profession were identified with their clients (i.e., the less they were held aloof from clients by their loyalty to courts or an autonomous guild) the more the imbalance would be accentuated. The more close and enduring the lawyer-client relationship, the more the primary loyalty of lawyers is to clients rather than to courts or guild, the more telling the advantages of accumulated expertise and guidance in overall strategy.

What about the specialization of the bar? Might we not expect the existence of specialization to offset RP advantages by providing the OS with a specialist who, in pursuit of his own career goals, would be interested in outcomes that would be advantageous to a whole class of OSs? Does the specialist become the functional equivalent of the RP? We may divide specialists into those specialized by field of law (patent, divorce, etc.), party represented (for example, house counsel), and both (personal injury plaintiff, criminal defense, labor). Divorce lawyers do not specialize in husbands or wives nor real-estate lawyers in buyers or sellers. But labor lawyers and tax lawyers and stockholder-derivative-suit lawyers specialize not only in the field of law but also by side. Such specialists may represent RPs or OSs. Figure 2 provides some well-known examples.

Most specializations cater to the needs of particular kinds of RPs. Those specialists who serve OSs have some distinctive features.

First, they tend to make up the "lower echelons" of the legal profession. Compared to those who provide services to RPs, lawyers in these specialties tend to be drawn from lower socioeconomic origins, have attended local, proprietary or part-time law schools, practice alone rather than in large firms, and possess low prestige within the profession.

Second, specialists who service OSs tend to have problems mobilizing a clientele (because of the low state of information among OSs) and encounter "ethical" barriers, imposed by the profession, that forbid solicitation, advertising, referral fees, advances to clients, and so forth.

Third, the episodic and isolated nature of the relationship with particular OS clients tends to elicit a stereotyped and uncreative brand of legal services. Carlin and Howard (1965: 385) observe:

> The quality of service rendered poorer clients is...affected by the non-repeat-ing character of the matters they typically bring to lawyers (such as divorce, criminal, personal injury): this combined with the small fees encourages a mass processing of cases. As a result, only a limited amount of time and interest is usually expended on any one case—there is little or no incentive to treat it except as an isolated piece of legal business. Moreover, there is ordinarily no desire to go much beyond the case as the client presents it, and such cases are only accepted when there is a clear-cut cause of action; i.e., when they fit into convenient legal categories and promise a fairly certain return.

Fourth, while they are themselves RPs, these specialists have problems in developing optimizing strategies. What might be good strategy for an insurance company lawyer or prosecutor—trading off some cases for gains on others—is branded as unethical when done by a criminal defense or personal injury plaintiff lawyer. It is not permissible for him to play his series of OSs as if they constituted a single RP.

Conversely, the demands of routine and orderly handling of a whole series of OSs may constrain the lawyer from maximizing advantage for any individual OS. Rosenthal (1974) shows that "for all but the largest [personal injury] claims an attorney loses money by thoroughly preparing a case and not settling it early."

For the lawyer who serves the transient clientele of OSs, his permanent "client" is the forum, the opposite party, or the intermediary who supplies clients. Consider, for example, the dependence of the criminal defense lawyer on maintaining cooperative relations with the various members of the "criminal court community." Similarly, Carlin (1962: 161–62) notes that among metropolitan individual practitioners whose clientele consists of OSs, there is a deformation of loyalty toward the intermediary.

> In the case of those lawyers specializing in personal injury, local tax, collections, criminal, and to some extent divorce work, the relationship with the client ... is generally mediated by a broker or business supplier who may be either another lawyer or a layman. In these fields of practice the lawyer is principally concerned with pleasing the broker or winning his approval, more so than he is with satisfying the individual client. The source of business generally counts for more than the client, especially where the client is unlikely to return or to send in other clients. The client is then expendable: he can be exploited to the full. Under these conditions, when a lawyer receives a client ... he has not so much gained a client as a piece of business, and his attitude is often that of handling a particular piece of merchandise or of developing a volume of a certain kind of merchandise.

The existence of a specialized bar on the OS side should overcome the gap in expertise, allow some economies of scale, provide for bargaining commitment and personal familiarity. But this is short of overcoming the fundamental strategic advantages of RPs—their capacity to structure the transaction, play the odds, and influence rule-development and enforcement policy.

Specialized lawyers may, by virtue of their identification with parties, become lobbyists, moral entrepreneurs, proponents of reforms on the parties' behalf. But lawyers have a cross-cutting interest in preserving complexity and mystique so that client contact with this area of law is rendered problematic. Lawyers should not be expected to be proponents of reforms that are optimum from the point of view of the clients taken alone. Rather, we would expect them to seek to optimize the clients' position without diminishing that of lawyers. Therefore, specialized lawyers have an interest in a framework that keeps recovery (or whatever) problematic at the same time that they favor changes that improve their clients' position within this framework. (Consider the lobbying efforts of personal injury plaintiffs and defense lawyers.) Considerations of interest are likely to be fused with ideological commitments: the lawyers' preference for complex and finely-tuned bodies of rules, adversary proceedings, individualized case-by-case decision-making. Just as the culture of the client population affects strategic position, so does the professional culture of the lawyers.

Institutional Facilities

We see then that the strategic advantages of the RP may be augmented by advantages in the distribution of legal services. Both are related to the advantages conferred by the basic features of the institutional facilities for the handling of claims: passivity and overload.

These institutions are passive, first, in the sense that Black (1973: 141) refers to as "reactive"—they must be mobilized by the claimant—giving advantage to the claimant with information, ability to surmount cost barriers, and skill to navigate restrictive procedural requirements. They are passive in a further sense that once in the door the burden is on each party to proceed with his case. The presiding official acts as umpire, while the development of the case, collection of evidence and presentation of proof are left to the initiative and resources of the parties. Parties are treated as if they were equally endowed with economic resources, investigative opportunities and legal skills. Where, as is usually the case, they are not, the broader the delegation to the parties, the greater the advantage conferred on the wealthier, more experienced and better organized party.

The advantages conferred by institutional passivity are accentuated by the chronic overload characterizing these institutions. Typically there are far more claims than there are institutional resources for full-dress adjudication of each. In several ways overload creates pressures on claimants to settle rather than to adjudicate:

(a)   by causing delay (thereby discounting the value of recovery);
(b)   by raising costs (of keeping the case alive);
(c)   by inducing institutional incumbents to place a high value on clearing dockets, discouraging full-dress adjudication in favor of bargaining, stereotyping and routine processing;
(d)   by inducing the forum to adopt restrictive rules to discourage litigation.

Thus, overload increases the cost and risk of adjudicating and shields existing rules from challenge, diminishing opportunities for rule-change. This tends to favor the beneficiaries of existing rules.

Second, by increasing the difficulty of challenging ongoing practice, overload also benefits those who reap advantage from the neglect (or systematic violation) of rules favoring their adversaries.

Third, overload tends to protect the possessor—the party who has the money or goods—against the claimant. For the most part, this amounts to favoring RPs over OSs, since RPs typically can structure transactions to put themselves in the possessor position.

Finally, the overload situation means that there are more commitments in the formal system than there are resources to honor them—more rights and rules "on the books" than can be vindicated or enforced. There are, then, questions of priorities in the allocation of resources. We would expect judges, police, administrators and other managers of limited institutional facilities to be responsive to the more organized, attentive and influential of their constituents. Again, these tend to be RPs.

Thus, overloaded and passive institutional facilities provide the setting in which the RP advantages in strategic position and legal services can have full play.

Rules

We assume here that rules tend to favor older, culturally dominant interests. This is not meant to imply that the rules are explicitly designed to favor these interests but rather that those groups that have become dominant have successfully articulated their operations to preexisting rules. To the extent that rules are evenhanded or favor the "have-nots," the limited resources for their implementation will be allocated so as to give greater effect to those rules that protect and promote the tangible interests of organized and influential groups. Furthermore, the requirements of due process, with their barriers or protections against precipitate action, naturally tend to protect the possessor or holder against the claimant. Finally, the rules are sufficiently complex and problematic (or capable of being problematic if sufficient resources are expended to make them so) that differences in the quantity and quality of legal services will affect capacity to derive advantages from the rules.

Thus, we arrive at Figure 3, which summarizes why the "haves" tend to come out ahead. It points to layers of advantages enjoyed by different (but largely overlapping) classes of "haves"—advantages that interlock, reinforcing and shielding one another.

Alternatives to the Official System

We have been discussing resort to the official system to put forward (or defend against) claims. Actually, resort to this system by claimants (or initiators) is one of several alternatives. Our analysis should consider the relationship of the characteristics of the total official litigation system to its use vis-à-vis the alternatives. These include at least the following:

(1) Inaction—"lumping it," not making a claim or complaint. This is done all the time by "claimants" who lack information or access or who knowingly decide gain is too low, cost too high (including psychic cost of litigating where such activity is repugnant). Costs are raised by lack of information or skill and also include risk. Inaction is also familiar on the part of official complainers (police, agencies, prosecutors) who have incomplete information about violations, limited resources, policies about de minimis, schedules of priorities, and so forth.

(2) "Exit"—withdrawal from a situation or relationship by moving, resigning, severing relations, finding new partners, etc. This is, of course, a very common

expedient in many kinds of trouble. Like "lumping it," it is an alternative to invocation of any kind of remedy system—although its presence as a sanction may be important to the working of other remedies. The use of "exit" options depends on the availability of alternative opportunities or partners (and information about them), the costs of withdrawal, transfer, relocation, development of new relationships, the pull of loyalty to previous arrangements—and on the availability and cost of other remedies.

Figure 3
Why the "Haves" Tend to Come Out Ahead

Element	Advantages	Enjoyed by
Parties	• Ability to structure transaction • Specialized expertise, economies of scale • Long-term strategy • Ability to play for rules • Bargaining credibility • Ability to invest in penetration	• Repeat players, large, professional[a]
Legal Services	• Skill, specialization, continuity	• Organized, professional,[a] wealthy
Institutional Facilities	• Passivity • Cost and delay barriers • Favorable priorities	• Wealthy, experienced, organized • Holders, possessors • Beneficiaries of existing rules • Organized, attentive
Rules	• Favorable rules • Due process barriers	• Older, culturally dominant • Holders, possessors

[a] in the simple sense of "doing it for a living"

(3) Resort to some unofficial control system—we are familiar with many instances in which disputes are handled outside the official litigation system. Here

we should distinguish those dispute settlement systems that are normatively and institutionally appended to the official system (such as settlement of auto injuries, handling of bad checks) from those that are relatively independent in norms and sanctions (such as businessmen settling disputes inter se, religious groups, gangs).

What we might call the "appended" settlement systems merge imperceptibly into the official litigation system. We might sort them out by the extent to which the official intervention approaches the adjudicatory mode. We find a continuum from situations where parties settle among themselves with an eye to the official rules and sanctions, through situations where official intervention is invoked, to those in which settlement is supervised and/or imposed by officials, to full-dress adjudication. All along this line the sanction is supplied by the official system (though not always in the manner prescribed in the "higher law"), and the norms or rules applied are a version of the official rules, although discounted for transaction costs and distorted by their selective use for the purposes of the parties.

From these "appended" systems of discounted and privatized official justice, we should distinguish those informal systems of "private justice" that invoke other norms and other sanctions. Such systems of dispute settlement are typical among people in continuing interaction, such as an organized group, a trade, or a university. In sorting out the various types according to the extent and the mode of intervention of third parties, we can distinguish two dimensions: the first is the degree to which the applicable norms are formally articulated, elaborated, and exposited, that is, the increasingly organized character of the norms. The second represents the degree to which initiative and binding authority are accorded to the third party, that is, the increasingly organized character of the sanctions.

Our distinction between "appended" and "private" remedy systems should not be taken as a sharp dichotomy but as pointing to a continuum along which we might range the various remedy systems. There is a clear distinction between appended systems like automobile injury or bad check settlements and private systems like the internal regulation of the Mafia (Cressey, 1969: chaps. 8–9; Ianni, 1972) or the Chinese community (Doo, 1973; Light, 1972: ch. 5). The internal regulatory aspects of universities, churches and groups of businessmen lie somewhere in between. It is as if we could visualize a scale stretching from the official remedy system through ones oriented to it through relatively independent systems based on similar values to independent systems based on disparate values.

Presumably it is not accidental that some human encounters are regulated frequently and influentially by the official and its appended systems, while others seem to generate controls that make resort to the official and its appended systems rare. Which human encounters are we likely to find regulated at the "official" end of our scale and which at the "private" end? It is submitted that location on our scale varies with factors we might sum up as the "density" of the relationship. That is, the more inclusive in life-space and temporal span a relationship between parties, the less likely it is that those parties will resort to the official system and more likely that the relationship will be regulated by some independent "private" system. This seems plausible because we would expect inclusive and enduring relationships to create the possibility of effective sanctions; and we would expect participants in such relationships to share a value consensus that provided standards for conduct and legitimized such sanctions in case of deviance.

The prevalence of private systems does not necessarily imply that they embody values or norms that are competing or opposed to those of the official system. Our analysis does not impute the plurality of remedy systems to cultural differences as such. It implies that the official system is utilized when there is a disparity between social structure and cultural norm. It is used, that is, where interaction and vulnerability create encounters and relationships that do not generate shared norms (they may be insufficiently shared or insufficiently specific) and/or do not give rise to group structures that permit sanctioning these norms.

We may surmise further that, on the whole, the official and appended systems flourish in connection with the disputes between parties of disparate size that give rise to the litigation in Boxes 2 and 3 of Figure 1. Private remedy systems, on the other hand, are more likely to handle disputes between parties of comparable size. The litigation in Boxes 1 and 4 of Figure 1, then, seems to represent in large measure the breakdown (or inhibited development) of private remedy systems. Indeed, the distribution of litigation generally forms a mirror image of the presence of private remedy systems. But the mirror is, for the various reasons discussed here, a distorting one.

From the vantage point of the "higher law," what we have called the official system may be visualized as the "upper" layers of a massive "legal" iceberg, something like this:

Adjudication
Litigation
Appended Settlement Systems
Private Settlement Systems
Exit Remedies/Self Help
Inaction ("lumping it")

The uneven and irregular layers are distinct, although they merge imperceptibly into one another.

As we proceed to discuss possible reforms of the official system, we will want to consider the kind of impact they will have on the whole iceberg. We will look at some of the connections and flows between layers mainly from the point of view of the construction of the iceberg itself but aware that flows and connections are also influenced by atmospheric (cultural) factors, such as appetite for vindication, psychic cost of litigation, lawyers' culture and the like.

Strategies for Reform

Our categorization of four layers of advantage (Figure 3) suggests a typology of strategies for "reform" (taken here to mean equalization—conferring relative advantage on those who did not enjoy it before). We then come to four types of equalizing reform:
(1)   rule-change
(2)   improvement in institutional facilities
(3)   improvement of legal services in quantity and quality
(4)   improvement of strategic position of have-not parties
I shall attempt to sketch some of the possible ramifications of change on each of these levels for other parts of the litigation system and then discuss the relationship between changes in the litigation system and the rest of our legal iceberg. Of course such reforms need not be enacted singly but may occur in various combinations. However, for our purposes we shall only discuss, first, each type taken in isolation and then, all taken together.

Rule-change

Obtaining favorable rule-changes is an expensive process. The various kinds of "have-nots" (Figure 3) have fewer resources to accomplish changes through legislation or administrative policy-making. The advantages of the organized, professional, wealthy and attentive in these forums are well known. Litigation, on the other hand, has a flavor of equality. The parties are "equal before the law" and the rules of the game do not permit them to deploy all of their resources in the conflict but require that they proceed within the limiting forms of the trial. Thus, litigation is a particularly tempting arena to "have-nots," including those seeking rule-change. Those who seek change through the courts tend to represent relatively isolated interests, unable to carry the day in more political forums.

Litigation may not, however, be a ready source of rule-change for "have-nots." Complexity, the need for high inputs of legal services and cost barriers (heightened by overloaded institutional facilities) make challenge to rules expensive. OS claimants, with high stakes in the tangible outcome, are unlikely to try to obtain rule-changes. By definition, a test case—litigation deliberately designed to procure rule-change—is an unthinkable undertaking for an OS. There are some departures from our ideal type: OSs who place a high value on vindication by official rules or whose peculiar strategic situation makes it in their interest to pursue rule victories. But generally the test case involves some organization that approximates an RP.

The architecture of courts severely restricts the scale and scope of changes they can introduce in the rules. Tradition and ideology limit the kinds of matters that come before them: not patterns of practice but individual instances, not "problems" but cases framed by the parties and strained through requirements of standing, case or controversy, jurisdiction, and so forth. Tradition and ideology also limit the kind of decision they can make. Thus, common law courts for example, give an all-or-none, once-and-for-all decision, which must be justified in terms of a limited (though flexible) corpus of rules and techniques. By tradition, courts cannot address problems by devising new regulatory or administrative machinery (and have no taxing and spending powers to support it); courts are limited to solutions compatible with the existing institutional framework. Thus, even the most favorably inclined court may not be able to make those rule-changes most useful to a class of "have-nots."

Rule-change may make use of the courts more attractive to "have-nots." Apart from increasing the possibility of favorable outcomes, it may stimulate organization, rally and encourage litigants. It may directly redistribute symbolic rewards to "have-nots" (or their champions). But tangible rewards do not always follow symbolic ones. Indeed, provision of symbolic rewards to "have-nots" (or crucial groups of their supporters) may decrease capacity and drive to secure redistribution of tangible benefits. Rule-changes secured from courts or other peak agencies do not penetrate automatically and costlessly to other levels of the system, as attested by the growing literature on impact. This may be especially true of rule-change secured by adjudication, for several reasons:

(1) Courts are not equipped to assess systematically the impact or penetration problem. Courts typically have no facilities for surveillance, monitoring, or securing systematic enforcement of their decrees. The task of monitoring is left to the parties.

(2) The built-in limits on applicability due to the piecemeal character of adjudication. Thus a Mobilization for Youth lawyer reflects:

> What is the ultimate value of winning a test case? In many ways a result cannot be clearcut...if the present welfare-residency laws are invalidated, it is quite possible that some other kind of welfare-residency law will spring up in their place. It is not very difficult to come up with a policy that is a little different, stated in different words, but which seeks to achieve the same basic objective. The results of test cases are not generally self-executing.... It is not enough to have a law invalidated or a policy declared void if the agency in question can come up with some variant of that policy, not very different in substance but sufficiently different to remove it from the effects of the court order. (Rothwax, 1969: 143)

(3) The artificial equalizing of parties in adjudication by insulation from the full play of political pressures—the "equality" of the parties, the exclusion of "irrelevant" material, the "independence" of judges—means that judicial outcomes are more likely to be at variance with the existing constellation of political forces than decisions arrived at in forums lacking such insulation. But resources that cannot be employed in the judicial process can reassert themselves at the implementation stage, especially where institutional overload requires another round of decision-

making (what resources will be deployed to implement which rules) and/or private expenditures to secure implementation. Even where "have-nots" secure favorable changes at the rule level, they may not have the resources to secure the penetration of these rules. The impotence of rule-change, whatever its source, is particularly pronounced when there is reliance on unsophisticated OSs to utilize favorable new rules.

Where rule-change promulgated at the peak of the system does have an impact on other levels, we should not assume any isomorphism. The effect on institutional facilities and the strategic position of the parties may be far different from what we would predict from the rule-change. Thus, Randall's (1968) study of movie censorship shows that liberalization of the rules did not make censorship boards more circumspect; instead, many closed down, and the old game between censorship boards and distributors was replaced by a new and rougher game between exhibitors and local government-private group coalitions.

Increase in Institutional Facilities

Imagine an increase in institutional facilities for processing claims such that there is timely full-dress adjudication of every claim put forward—no queue, no delay, no stereotyping. Decrease in delay would lower costs for claimants, taking away this advantage of possessor-defendants. Those relieved of the necessity of discounting recovery for delay would have more to spend on legal services. To the extent that settlement had been induced by delay (rather than insuring against the risk of unacceptable loss), claimants would be inclined to litigate more and settle less. More litigation without stereotyping would mean more contests, including more contesting of rules and more rule change. As discounts diminished, neither side could use settlement policy to prevent rule-loss. Such reforms would for the most part benefit OS claimants, but they would also improve the position of those RP claimants not already in the possessor position, such as the prosecutor where the accused is free on bail.

This assumes no change in the kind of institutional facilities. We have merely assumed a greater quantitative availability of courts of the relatively passive variety typical of (at least) common law systems. One may imagine institutions that had augmented authority to solicit and supervise litigation, conduct investigations, secure, assemble and present proof, enjoyed greater flexibility in devising outcomes (such as compromise or mediation), and had staff for monitoring compliance with their decrees. Greater institutional "activism" might be expected to reduce advantages of party expertise and of differences in the quality and quantity of legal services. Enhanced capacity for securing compliance might be expected to reduce advantages flowing from differences in ability to invest in enforcement. It is hardly necessary to point out that such reforms could be expected to encounter not only resistance from the beneficiaries of the present passive institutional style but also massive ideological opposition from legal professionals whose fundamental sense of legal propriety would be violated.

Increase in Legal Services

The reform envisaged here is an increase in quantity and quality of legal services to "have-nots" (including greater availability of information about these services). Presumably this would lower costs, remove the expertise advantage, produce more litigation with more favorable outcomes for "have-nots," perhaps with more appeals and more rule challenges, more new rules in their favor. (Public defender, legal aid, judicare, and prepayment plans approximate this in various fashions.) To the extent that OSs would still have to discount for delay and risk, their gains would be limited (and increase in litigation might mean even more delay). Under certain conditions,

increased legal services might use institutional overload as leverage on behalf of "have-nots." Our Mobilization for Youth attorney observes:

> [I]f the Welfare Department buys out an individual case, we are precluded from getting a principle of law changed, but if we give them one thousand cases to buy out, that law has been effectively changed whether or not the law as written is changed. The practice is changed; the administration is changed; the attitude to the client is changed. The value of a heavy case load is that it allows you to populate the legal process. It allows you to apply [un]remitting pressure on the agency you are dealing with. It creates a force that has to be dealt with, that has to be considered in terms of the decisions that are going to be made prospectively. It means that you are not somebody who will be gone tomorrow, not an isolated case, but a force in the community that will remain once this particular case has been decided. As a result...we have been able, for the first time to participate along with welfare recipients...in a rule-making process itself.... (Rothwax, 1969: 140–41)

The increase in quantity of legal services was accompanied here by increased coordination and organization on the "have-not" side, which brings us to our fourth level of reform.

Reorganization of Parties

The reform envisaged here is the organization of "have-not" parties (whose position approximates OSs) into coherent groups with the ability to act in a coordinated fashion, play long-run strategies, benefit from high-grade legal services, and so forth.

One can imagine various ways in which OSs might be aggregated into RPs. They include the membership association-bargaining agent (trade unions, tenant unions); the assignee-manager of fragmentary rights (performing rights associations like

ASCAP); (3) the interest group-sponsor (NAACP, ACLU, environmental action groups). All of these forms involve upgrading capacities for managing claims by gathering and utilizing information, achieving continuity and persistence, employing expertise, exercising bargaining skill and so forth. These advantages are combined with enhancement of the OS party's strategic position either by aggregating claims that are too small relative to the cost of remedies (consumers, breathers of polluted air, owners of performing rights); or by reducing claims to manageable size by collective action to dispel or share unacceptable risks (tenants, migrant workers). A weaker form of organization would be a clearing-house, which established a communication network among OSs. This would lower the costs of information and give RPs a stake in the effect OSs could have on their reputation. A minimal instance of this is represented by the "media ombudsman"—the "action line" type of newspaper column. Finally, there is governmentalization—utilizing the criminal law or the administrative process to make it the responsibility of a public officer to press claims that would be unmanageable in the hands of private grievants.

An organized group is not only better able to secure favorable rule changes, in courts and elsewhere, but also is better able to see that good rules are implemented. It can expend resources on surveillance, monitoring, threats, or litigation that would be uneconomic for an OS. Such new units would in effect be RPs. Their encounters with opposing RPs would move into Box 4 of Figure 1. Neither would enjoy the strategic advantages of RPs over OSs. One possible result, as we have noted in our discussion of the RP v. RP situation, is delegalization, that is, a movement away from the official system to a private system of dispute settlement; another would be more intense use of the official system.

Many aspects of "public interest law" can be seen as approximations of this reform. The class action is a device to raise the stakes for an RP, reducing his strategic position to that of an OS by making the stakes more than he can afford to play the odds on, while moving the claimants into a position in which they enjoy the RP advantages without having to undergo the outlay for organizing. Similarly, the "community organizing" aspect of public interest law can be seen as an effort to create a unit (tenants, consumers) that can play the RP game. Such a change in strategic position creates the possibility of a test-case strategy for getting rule-change. Thus, "public interest law" can be thought of as a combination of community organizing, class action and test-case strategies, along with increase in legal services.

Reform and the Rest of the Iceberg

The reforms of the official litigation system that we have imagined would, taken together, provide rules more favorable to the "have nots." Redress according to the official rules, undiscounted by delay, strategic disability, disparities of legal services and so forth, could be obtained whenever either party found it to his advantage. How might we expect such a utopian upgrading of the official machinery to affect the rest of our legal iceberg?

We would expect more use of the official system. Those who opted for inaction because of information or cost barriers and those who "settled" at discount rates in one of the "appended" systems would in many instances find it to their advantage to use the official system. The appended systems, insofar as they are built on the costs of resort to the official system, would either be abandoned or the outcomes produced would move to approximate closely those produced by adjudication.

On the other hand, our reforms would, by organizing OSs, create many situations in which both parties were organized to pursue their long-run interest in the litigation arena. In effect, many of the situations that occupied Boxes 2 and 3 of Figure 1 (RP v. OS, OS v. RP)—the great staple sources of litigation—would now be moved to Box 4 (RP v. RP). We observed earlier that RPs who anticipate continued dealings with one another tend to rely on informal bilateral controls. We might expect, then, that the official system would be abandoned in favor of private systems of dispute settlement.

Thus we would expect our reforms to produce a dual movement: the official and its appended systems would be "legalized," while the proliferation of private systems would "delegalize" many relationships. Which relationships would we expect to move which way? As a first approximation, we might expect that the less "inclusive" relationships currently handled by litigation or in the appended systems would undergo legalization, while relationships at the more inclusive end of the scale would be privatized. Relationships among strangers (casual, episodic, non-recurrent) would be legalized; more dense (recurrent, inclusive) relationships between parties would be candidates for the development of private systems.

Our earlier analysis suggests that the pattern might be more complex. First, for various reasons a class of OSs may be relatively incapable of being organized. Its size, relative to the size and distribution of potential benefits, may require disproportionately large inputs of coordination and organization. Its shared interest may be insufficiently respectable to be publicly acknowledged (for instance, shoplifters, homosexuals until very recently). Or recurrent OS roles may be staffed by shifting populations for whom the sides of the transaction are interchangeable (for instance, home buyers and sellers, negligent motorists and accident victims). Even where OSs are organizable, we recall that not all RP v. RP encounters lead to the development of private remedy systems. There are RPs engaged in value conflict; there are those relationships with a governmental or other monopoly aspect in which informal controls may falter; and finally there are those RPs whose encounters with one another are nonrecurring. In all of these we might expect legalization rather than privatization.

Whichever way the movement in any given instance, our reforms would entail changes in the distribution of power. RPs would no longer be able to wield their strategic advantages to invoke selectively the enforcement of favorable rules while securing large discounts (or complete shielding by cost and overload) where the rules favored their OS opponents.

Delegalization (by the proliferation of private remedy and bargaining systems) would permit many relationships to be regulated by norms and understandings that departed from the official rules. Such parochial remedy systems would be insulated from the impingement of the official rules by the commitment of the parties to their continuing relationship. Thus, delegalization would entail a kind of pluralism and decentralization. On the other hand, the "legalization" of the official and appended systems would amount to the collapse of species of pluralism and decentralization endemic in the kind of (unreformed) legal system we have postulated. The current prevalence of appended and private remedy systems reflects the inefficiency, cumbersomeness and costliness of using the official system. This character is a source and shield of a kind of decentralization and pluralism. It permits a selective application of the "higher law" in a way that gives effect at the operative level to parochial norms and concerns not fully recognized in the "higher law" (such as the right to exclude low status neighbors, or police dominance in encounters with citizens). If the insulation afforded by the costs of getting the "higher law" to prevail were eroded, many relationships would suddenly be exposed to the "higher law" rather than its parochial counterparts. We might expect this to generate new pressures for explicit recognition of these "subterranean" values or for explicit decentralization.

These conjectures about the shape of a "reformed" legal system suggest that we take another look at our unreformed system, with its pervasive disparity between authoritative norms and everyday operations. A modern legal system of the type we postulated is characterized structurally by institutional unity and culturally by normative universalism. The power to make, apply and change law is reserved to organs of the public, arranged in unified hierarchic relations, committed to uniform application of universalistic norms.

The higher reaches of American law, where the learned tradition is propounded, exhibits an unrelenting stress on the virtues of uniformity and universality and a pervasive distaste for particularism, compromise and discretion. Yet the cultural attachment to universalism is wedded to and perhaps even intensifies diversity and particularism at the operative level.

The unreformed features of the legal system then appear as a device for maintaining the partial dissociation of everyday practice from these authoritative institutional and normative commitments. Structurally, (by cost and institutional overload) and culturally (by ambiguity and normative overload) the unreformed system effects a massive covert delegation from the most authoritative rule-makers to field level officials (and their constituencies) responsive to norms and priorities different from those contained in the "higher law." By their selective application of rules in a context of parochial understandings and priorities, these field-level legal communities produce regulatory outcomes that could not be predicted by examination of the authoritative "higher law."

Thus, its unreformed character articulates the legal system to the discontinuities of culture and social structure: it provides a way of accommodating cultural heterogeneity and social diversity while propounding universalism and unity; of accommodating vast concentrations of private power while upholding the supremacy of public authority; of accommodating inequality in fact while establishing equality at law; of facilitating action by great collective combines while celebrating individualism. Thus, "unreform"—that is, ambiguity and overload of rules, overloaded and inefficient institutional facilities, disparities in the supply of legal services, and disparities in the strategic position of parties—is the foundation of the "dualism" of the legal system. It permits unification and universalism at the symbolic level and diversity and particularism at the operating level.

Implications for Reform: The Role of Lawyers

We have discussed the way in which the architecture of the legal system tends to confer interlocking advantages on overlapping groups, whom we have called the "haves." To what extent might reforms of the legal system dispel these advantages? Reforms will always be less total than the utopia envisioned above. Reformers will have limited resources to deploy and face the necessity of choosing which uses of those resources are most productive of equalizing change. What does our analysis suggest about strategies and priorities?

By itself, change in substantive rules is not likely to produce redistributive outcomes because the system is so constructed that such changes can be filtered out unless accompanied by changes at other levels. In a setting of overloaded institutional facilities, inadequate costly legal services, and unorganized parties, beneficiaries may lack the resources to secure implementation; or an RP may restructure the transaction to escape the thrust of the new rule. Favorable rules are not necessarily (and possibly not typically) in short supply to "have-nots"; certainly less so than any of the other resources needed to play the litigation game. Programs of equalizing reform focussed on rule-change can readily be absorbed without any change in power relations. The system has the capacity to change a great deal at the level of rules without corresponding changes in everyday patterns of practice or distribution of tangible advantages. Indeed rule-change may become a symbolic substitute for redistribution of advantages.

Substantive rule-change is most easily contained if produced by courts. That courts can sometimes be induced to propound rule changes that legislatures would not make points to the limitations as well as the possibilities of court-produced change. With their relative insulation from retaliation by antagonistic interests, courts may more easily propound new rules that depart from prevailing power relations. But such rules require even greater inputs of other resources for effective implementation. And courts have less capacity than other rule-makers to create institutional facilities and reallocate resources to secure implementation of new rules. Litigation, then, is unlikely to shape decisively the distribution of power in society. It may serve to secure or solidify symbolic commitments. It is vital tactically in securing temporary advantage or protection, providing leverage for organization and articulation of interests and conferring (or withholding) the mantle of legitimacy. The more divided the other holders of power, the greater the redistributive potential of this symbolic/tactical role.

Our analysis suggests that breaking the interlocked advantages of the "haves" requires attention not only to rules but also to institutional facilities, legal services and the organization of parties. It suggests that litigating and lobbying have to be complemented by interest organizing, provisions of services and invention of new forms of institutional facilities.

The thrust of our analysis is that changes at the level of parties are most likely to generate changes at other levels. If rules are the most abundant resource for reformers, parties capable of pursuing long-range strategies are the rarest. The presence of such parties can generate effective demand for high-grade legal services—continuous, expert, and oriented to the long run—and pressure for institutional reforms and favorable rules. This suggests that we can roughly surmise the relative strategic priority of various rule-changes. Rule changes that relate directly to the strategic position of the parties by facilitating organization, increasing the supply of legal services (which in turn articulate and organize common interests), and increasing the costs of opponents—for instance authorization of class action suits, award of attorneys fees and costs, award of provisional remedies—these are the most powerful fulcrums for change. The intensity of the opposition to class action legislation and autonomous reform-oriented legal services, such as California Rural Legal Assistance, indicates the "haves'" own estimation of the relative strategic impact of the several levels.

The contribution of the lawyer to redistributive social change, then, depends upon the organization and culture of the legal profession. We have surmised that court-produced substantive rule-change is unlikely in itself to be a determinative element in producing tangible redistribution of benefits. The leverage provided by litigation depends on its strategic combination with inputs at other levels. The question, then, is whether the organization of the profession permits lawyers to develop and employ skills at these other levels. The more that lawyers view themselves exclusively as courtroom advocates, the less their willingness to undertake new tasks and form enduring alliances with clients and operate in forums other than courts, the less likely they are to serve as agents of redistributive change. Paradoxically, those legal professions most open to accentuating the advantages of the "haves" (by allowing themselves to be "captured" by recurrent clients) may be most able to become (or have room for, more likely) agents of change, precisely because they provide more license for identification with clients and their "causes" and have a less strict definition of what are properly professional activities.

DISCUSSION QUESTIONS

1. Galanter urges that we explore the relation between law and equality by redirecting attention from rules to parties. Why? Can you apply his typology of one-shot and repeat-player parties to contexts outside the legal system? What are the advantages of being a repeat player? Who are the RPs and OSs? Do they have different objectives in litigation? If so, why? Do these categories coincide with other major social divisions?

2. Under what circumstances and in what configurations do one-shot and repeat-player litigants confront each other? What are the consequences for process and outcome?

3. How do lawyers alter this configuration? with what consequences? How do they differ among themselves? Can they equalize the party inequalities?

4. What characteristics of courts (and similar institutions) accentuate party inequalities?

5. What is the range of alternative responses to grievance and conflict? How do party inequalities play out in each? What explains the choice among these responses?

6. What suggestions for reform are suggested by Galanter's analysis of party inequality and advantage? Are they feasible? Would they be effective? Describe the politics of their implementation. What are the inherent limitations of courts as agents of equalization of power? How would you expect the "haves" to respond to Galanter's proposed reforms?

7. How would Galanter reduce the tensions between rule and discretion, formal and informal legal system, law on the books and law in action, monist and pluralist regulation?

15

Race and Prosecutorial Discretion in Homicide Cases

Michael L. Radelet and Glenn L. Pierce

Introduction

Like other people-processing organizations, prosecutors' offices must make decisions concerning the allocation of their limited resources to the large number of cases that are presented. These decisions include such choices as how thoroughly to investigate each case, whether or not to file formal charges, the number and severity of violations to allege, the rigor of prosecution, and whether and how much to plea bargain. Every case cannot be given top priority. While some potential evidence may be ignored or discounted in cases in which a plea bargain is desired, the evidence in cases deemed deserving of a maximum penalty will be thoroughly documented and buttressed in the attempt to present the strongest case possible.

The prosecutor's role is probably most important in criminal homicide cases. In these cases there is a wider range of sanctions available (typically, from probation to death) than for any other criminal offense. In addition, homicide cases often reflect a much broader spectrum of motivation and planning than do other types of serious criminal behavior. This requires the prosecutor and judge to make numerous distinctions among the population of homicide cases that come to their attention.

This paper focuses on prosecutorial decisions in Florida homicide cases. We are particularly interested in identifying those cases in which the prosecutor's assessment of the case is either more or less severe than its initial assessment by the investigating police department. At issue are 1) whether alterations in assessments of the seriousness of cases are associated with extralegal factors such as race, independently of legally relevant factors, and 2) whether such alterations affect the severity of sanctions that defendants receive. In particular, we examine how this exercise of prosecutorial discretion affects the likelihood of receiving a death sentence. We focus on the sentence of death not only because it is qualitatively different from other criminal sanctions but also because it is a penalty for which arbitrary or discriminatory behavior by prosecutors raises clear policy and constitutional issues.

Abridged from *Law & Society Review*, Volume 19:587 (1985).

Theoretical Background

Between 1930 and 1972, 54 percent of the 3,859 persons executed in the U.S. were black, including 89 percent of the 455 men executed for rape (U.S. Department of Justice, 1982). In part because of this racial disparity, most death penalty statutes then in existence were invalidated by the 1972 Supreme Court decision in *Furman v. Georgia* (408 U.S. 238). Led by Florida, the states then began to rewrite their capital punishment statutes (Ehrhardt & Levinson, 1973). By 1985, 37 states had active capital punishment laws, and 32 of these jurisdictions had at least one person awaiting execution. Nationally, 51.2 percent of the 1,590 death row inmates on October 1, 1985, were white (Legal Defense Fund, 1985). Between 1930 and 1972, 49.9 percent of the 3,334 executions for murder involved white offenders, so the proportion of whites among the population of those on death row in 1985 was virtually the same as the proportion of whites executed in the 42 years before *Furman.*

How does the criminal justice system select the small proportion of convicted murderers it sentences to death and the even smaller fraction who are eventually executed? If those convicted murderers who are sentenced to death cannot be distinguished from those not sentenced to death on the basis of legally relevant variables, then the process through which some are selected for execution can be said to be arbitrary. Should that arbitrariness parallel race, sex, or social class lines, independently of legally relevant variables, it can be said to be discriminatory as well. The most thorough discussion of the likelihood that the death penalty will be imposed in a capricious and discriminatory manner has been presented by Charles Black (1981). He argues that every decision point in the criminal justice process, from arrest through appeal to executive clemency, is characterized by inexact standards and wide discretion, leading to a high degree of arbitrariness in the determination of who is eventually executed. The decisions by the prosecutor of what charge to file, how rigorously to prosecute the case, and whether or not and how much to plea bargain occur at the beginning of the process. The quality of the defendant's lawyer, witnesses, and psychiatrist(s) (if the insanity defense is pled) will affect the probabilities of a guilty verdict and a death sentence. Given similar circumstances, the discovery of aggravating and mitigating factors in the sentencing phase of the trial varies widely (Mullin, 1980). In short, Black argues that because so many vague factors are used to evaluate the seriousness of an offense, the final determination of who are the worst murderers and who should be executed is necessarily capricious and significantly influenced by legally irrelevant variables.

Postsentencing

In a seminal study of 412 persons sentenced to death in Pennsylvania for first-degree murder between 1914 and 1958, Wolfgang et al. (1962) found that black offenders were significantly less likely than whites to have their death sentences commuted.

This remained true even after controlling for whether or not the homicide was classified as a felony murder. A second study of 660 death sentences handed down in North Carolina between 1909 and 1954 reported similar results: whites sentenced to death were significantly more likely than their black counterparts to have their death sentences commuted (Johnson, 1957). A more recent postsentencing study of the first 145 cases decided by the Florida Supreme Court under the post-*Furman* statute found, controlling for the type of defense attorney, that the number of victims, the trial jury's sentence recommendation (life or death), and the interaction between victim's sex and defendant's race all exerted significant effects in a regression equation predicting outcome (Radelet & Vandiver, 1983). Black defendants with female victims were the most likely group to have their death sentences affirmed.

Sentencing

Other studies have examined racial disparities at the sentencing stage. Research on pre-*Furman* statutes found that racial disparities were most pronounced in the punishment for rape (LaFree, 1980; Wolfgang & Riedel, 1973), but since 1977 rape that does not eventuate in homicide is no longer a capital offense [*Coker v. Georgia*, 433 U.S. 485 (1977)].

Several studies have found racial disparities in the post-*Furman* application of the death penalty in the United States, particularly with regard to the race of the victim. Riedel (1976), examining patterns of death sentencing under the statutes enacted shortly after *Furman*, found that the proportion of blacks among those condemned to death had increased rather than decreased. Bowers and Pierce (1980), using data from Georgia, Texas, Ohio, and Florida, found that the races of victims and defendants were significant factors in the imposition of the death penalty in all four states. The same pattern, although somewhat reduced in strength, was found when only those homicides with an accompanying felony were examined (an analysis not done for Ohio). Restricting his analysis to homicides in Florida involving strangers, Radelet (1981) found that 17.5 percent of the blacks accused of killing whites were sentenced to death, compared to 12.6 percent of the whites accused of killing whites and 5.8 percent of the blacks who allegedly killed blacks. Similar but less extreme differences were found when only those homicides between strangers that resulted in a first-degree murder indictment were examined, although the reduced sample size eliminated the statistical significance of the differences.

Two recent projects have extended this line of inquiry. First, in the most extensive social science study ever conducted on capital sentencing patterns, Baldus et al. (1983) found that blacks accused of killing whites in Georgia were more likely to be sentenced to death than were other defendants [see *McCleskey v. Kemp*, 753 F.2d 877 (1985)]. This difference remained after a consideration of the effects of over 200 control variables. Second, Gross and Mauro (1984) used the FBI's Supplemental Homicide Reports to examine sentencing patterns in eight states

(Arkansas, Florida, Georgia, Illinois, Mississippi, North Carolina, Oklahoma, and Virginia). They found "remarkably stable and consistent" discrimination, based on victim's race, in all the states. Again, these results held when several other factors that might affect sentencing decisions were statistically controlled.

Presentencing

Few studies have focused specifically on the possibility of pretrial racial disparities in decisions regarding homicide cases. Garfinkel (1949), studying potential capital cases from North Carolina between 1930 and 1940, found that both defendant's and victim's race correlated with the grand jury's decision to indict for first-degree murder (rather than other degrees of murder) and the prosecutor's decision not to reduce first-degree murder charges. Blacks accused of killing whites were the most harshly treated. More recently, Bowers (1984) found that the races of both defendants and victims affected the likelihood of prosecutors obtaining first-degree murder indictments. Similarly, in an analysis of the first 205 cases that were potentially eligible for the death penalty under South Carolina's current statute, Jacoby and Paternoster (1982) found that prosecutors were 3.2 times more likely to seek the death penalty for defendants charged with killing whites than for those charged with killing blacks, and prosecutors were four times more likely to seek the death penalty for blacks accused of killing whites than for blacks accused of killing other blacks. This analysis was expanded by Paternoster (1983) to include the first 316 cases eligible for the death penalty under the current South Carolina statute. The probability of a death request was again higher for defendants with white victims than for those with black victims, with the victim's race being a more powerful predictor than the race of the defendant. These patterns held after he controlled for whether or not the homicide involved multiple victims or occurred between strangers. Similar patterns were also found when additional control variables were added and only felony homicides from South Carolina were examined (Paternoster, 1984).

Radelet's (1981) study of Florida homicide cases from the mid-1970s found that after restricting the sample to homicides between strangers (death sentences are rarely given for homicides occurring within primary groups), persons accused of killing whites were significantly more likely than those accused of killing blacks to be indicted for first-degree murder. In fact, the correlation of race with this prosecutorial decision was stronger than at the sentencing stage (see also Foley & Powell, 1982; Bowers et al., 1984).

Finally, Bowers and Pierce (1980) presented preliminary evidence that further suggests prosecutors might be more rigorous in their treatment of cases involving black defendants and white victims. They compared police reports and court record summaries in 346 Florida homicide cases (1980: Table 9). According to their data, cases characterized by the police as involving no felony circumstances or only suspected felony circumstances were most likely to be characterized by the prosecutor as felony murder if the defendant was black and the victim white. This selective upgrading, they suggest, is a key reason for the high proportion of blacks with white victims among those sentenced to death. However, because of a large amount of missing data and the lack of multivariate controls, their findings on this point are more suggestive than definitive.

Research Issues

It is clear that studies focusing on only one point in the criminal justice process risk missing substantial racial disparities (cf. Berk, 1983; Klepper et al., 1983). As Thomson and Zingraff suggest:

> [P]opulations in the later stages of the judicial process may be homogeneous.... If, as the research indicates, discrimination is concentrated in the earlier decisionmaking stages, research which does not account for the processual nature of decision making or which analyzes populations at just the later decision points will tend to produce findings of no discrimination. (1981: 871)

Equally important is the possibility that some cases that initially do not appear to be among the most serious are first selected for harsh treatment and then characterized so as to *appear* similar to cases classified as most serious from the time they entered the criminal justice process. The ability of prosecutors or other criminal justice decision-makers to develop or minimize evidence in order to justify the results desired in particular cases may create an appearance of similarity among initially dissimilar cases that reach the later stages of the criminal justice system. If cases that *could* have gotten to that stage but did not are never seen or are otherwise unavailable for comparative analysis, such evidential manipulation will be particularly hard to spot. Most importantly, if the process of selectively developing or ignoring evidence in cases is related to extralegal factors, such as race, then this process will help create the illusion of even-handed justice at later stages in the criminal justice system. Studies are therefore needed that focus specifically on the process of case selection and the acquisition and development of evidence in the early stages of the criminal justice process (for a case example see Bedau, 1983).

To date, the little research on prosecutorial discretion at the pretrial stage has focused primarily on the indictment decision (Radelet, 1981; Paternoster, 1983; 1984; Bowers et al., 1984). To understand the implications of race for the death penalty, we must understand the process through which the pool of potential death penalty cases is narrowed.

The possibility of bias in the identification of potential death penalty cases could be assessed if a description of the criminal homicide that is both logically prior to and independent of the prosecutor's assessment were available. Police reports of criminal homicide, although they may have their own biases and deficiencies, are the only possibility. Data from such reports have been gathered for this paper. If a comparison of the police description of a homicide with the subsequent description of the same homicide in the court records reveals differences that parallel differences in the racial characteristics of defendants and victims, then evidence suggesting selective manipulation or amassing of evidence and racial bias would be found.

The study of disparities between police and court classifications of criminal homicides with respect to accompanying felonious circumstances is important for several reasons. First, it allows us to investigate (for at least a portion of the evidence) the possibility that racial or other extralegal factors affect the rigor with which the criminal justice system prosecutes homicide cases. Second, it is necessary under most post-*Furman* statutes for the court to find at least one aggravating circumstance in a criminal homicide case in order to sentence the defendant to death. An accompanying felony is probably the most commonly cited aggravating circumstance in death penalty cases today. Bowers and Pierce (1980), for example, found that 79 percent of the Florida death sentences they examined and 85 percent of their Georgia death sentences involved homicides accompanied by some other felony. Finally, the comparison between police and court determinations of felony circumstances surrounding homicides provides an opportunity to study one element in the much broader process of developing and constructing evidence in criminal cases, a topic important in its own right. We focus on one aspect of this process: the possible influence of race.

Analysis

The analysis proceeds in three stages. First, the Supplemental Homicide Reports (SHR) and court classifications of the homicide (felony, possible felony, and non-felony) are compared. They are then broken down by defendant/victim race. Finally, a series of loglinear models are generated to ascertain whether discrepancies between police and court findings of a felony circumstance are associated with sentencing outcomes and in particular with the probability of a death sentence.

Police versus Court Record Classifications of Criminal Homicides: Upgrading and Downgrading

Table 1 indicates that 174 cases (17.1 percent) had a classification in the court data different from the classification in the police (SHR) data. A total of 82 cases were "downgraded" from the initial SHR police classification to the description found in the court files (a felony becomes a possible or non-felony, or a possible felony becomes a non-felony, i.e., those cases below the diagonal), and 92 cases were "upgraded" (those cases above the diagonal). This upgrading and downgrading does not, however, involve formal charge manipulation, as when the police book someone for sale of marijuana but the prosecutor charges only possession. Rather, it is descriptive or behavioral. The prosecutor, so far as we can determine, presents the case to the court as if it were more or less serious with respect to accompanying felonies than the police originally perceived it to be.

Twelve of the 73 cases upgraded to a felony homicide in the court records (16.4 percent) eventually received a death sentence. In contrast, none of the 52 cases down-graded to non-felonious circumstances from the police to the court classification received a death sentence, and only one case that was downgraded from felonious circumstances to possible felonious circumstances did so.

Upgrading, Downgrading, and the Racial Characteristics of Victims and Defendants

In this section we examine whether the discrepancies observed in Table 1 between the finding of a felony circumstance in the court records of criminal homicide cases

Table 1

Court Record Classification of Homicide Cases by Initial Classification Found in Police Records (row proportions in parentheses)

Police Record Classification of Circumstances	Court Record Classification of Circumstances			
	Non-Felony	Possible Felony	Felony	Total
Non-Felony	585 (.906)	19 (.029)	43 (.065)	646 (1.000)
Poss. Felony	20 (.345)	7 (.121)	31 (.534)	58 (1.000)
Felony	52 (.166)	10 (.032)	251 (.802)	313 (1.000)
Total	657	36	324	1017 (1.000)

and the initial finding contained in the police SHR records are associated with the race of either the victim or the defendant. Of those cases classified as felonies from the police (SHR) data, 91.6 percent remain felonies in the court descriptions when a black kills a white (BkW), 77.7 percent when a white kills a white (WkW), 62.1 percent when a black kills a black (BkB), and 83.3 percent when a white kills a black (WkB). Thus, BkW are the most likely to remain classified as involving felony circumstances, and cases with black victims are the least likely. Similar patterns are evident among cases in which the circumstances are classified as a non-felony by the police. Here, 63.6 percent of the cases remain without the suggestion of an accompanying felony in the court data when a BkW, 86.4 percent when a WkW, 94.5 percent when a BkB, and 93.3 percent when a WkB. From these data it appears: 1) that the defendant's race does not make much difference in cases with black victims, 2) that cases with white victims are more likely to be upgraded than cases with black victims, and 3) that among cases with white victims, black defendants are more likely than white defendants to be upgraded and less likely to be downgraded.

The next question to be explored is whether this degree of upgrading and downgrading by defendant/victim race is statistically and substantively significant. If the marginal distributions for police classifications were the same for the four racial groups, we could ascertain the possible presence of race effects through a simple comparison of the court classifications for the four racial groups. However, there is not much potential for upgrading among the BkW category because nearly all are labeled as involving additional felonies at the police stage, whereas there is greater potential for upgrading among the WkW group. The statistical analysis must take these disparate distributions into account. This can be done by comparing court record descriptions of the four defendant/victim racial groups (BkW, WkW, BkB, and WkB), controlling for the initial police classification.

To begin, the row effects loglinear model, which posits an effect of race on court classifications, can be compared to a simple loglinear model in which the court classification of criminal homicides is treated as independent of racial group, controlling for the police classification. The independence model is the special case of the row effects model in which all the effect parameters are zero; that is, it is the model in which there are no differences in court classifications, if we control for police classifications, between the racial configurations.

The independence model fits poorly, with a chi-square of 73.75 and 18 degrees of freedom. The row effects model has only three more parameters than the independence model, but fits well, with a chi-square of 16.88 and 15 degrees of freedom. The difference in chi-squares of 73.75-16.88=56.87, based on df= 18-15=3, gives a test of the null hypothesis that court classification is independent of racial group, controlling for police classification. The chi-square is significant at the .001 level. Thus, there is extremely strong evidence that the court classification varies by the racial configuration of defendants and victims, controlling for police classification.

The largest difference between groups is found when comparing BkW and WkB. Here, when the police report that the homicide was not or was only possibly accompanied by a felony, the ratio of cases involving an upgrade of one level to cases in which the court and police classifications are the same is estimated to be 3.76 times higher for the BkW configuration than for the WkB configuration. Conversely, when the case circumstance is classified as Felony or Possible Felony by the police, the ratio of cases classified similarly by courts and police to cases downgraded one level is estimated to be 3.76 times higher for the BkW configuration than for the WkB configuration, indicating that the latter are more likely to be downgraded. We expect this comparison to show the greatest difference between pairs of racial configurations because it matches the group that should produce the most upgrading (BkW) (if race were operating) against the group that should produce the least amount of upgrading (WkB). Not surprisingly, the smallest and only nonsignificant difference between pairs of racial configurations among the six possible comparisons occurs between the two groups we would expect to produce the least (WkB) and second least (BkB) amount of upgrading. It is interesting to note that despite the low frequency of WkB homicides ($21/1017 = 2.06$ percent), the evidence strongly suggests that cases with this racial configuration are treated differently from either BkW or WkW cases. In sum, the results strongly indicate that given the initial police description, the court or prosecutorial description is most likely to be upgraded in cases with a BkW racial configuration, followed in order by WkW, and then BkB and WkB.

Consideration of Additional Correlates

Thus far, it has been demonstrated that given the prosecutor's police classification, the severity of the description of the felony circumstances of a homicide case is strongly associated with the race of both the defendant and the victim. But will the predictive impact of race be reduced when other possible correlates of upgrading and downgrading are considered? It is possible that while upgrading or downgrading may not be related to the actual factual circumstance of a particular case, these processes may nevertheless reflect a prosecutor's general perception concerning the overall seriousness of a given case. Thus, for instance, while no obvious accompanying felony may have occurred in a multiple murder case, the severity of such a crime would encourage a prosecutor to find evidence of some associated felony such as a robbery (e.g., a missing wallet). If this type of case more often involved white victims, then controlling for multiple victim homicide cases might reduce the association between the victim's race and upgrading and might explain why felony circumstance murders are especially likely to lead to death sentences. In order to address this issue, it is necessary to introduce possible indicators of the seriousness of the homicide cases (other than felony circumstances) to assess whether their effects qualify the apparent association between race and the upgrading or downgrading of cases.

Table 2 presents the probabilities of upgrading and downgrading across each of eight control variables that might affect or be proxies for factors affecting prosecutorial decisions to seek the death penalty. The 704 homicide cases listed in the police data without mention of accompanying felonies or with only their possibility noted are used as the denominator in determining the proportion of each category upgraded. The 313 cases listed in the police data as involving accompanying felonies are used as a base to calculate proportions downgraded. It can be seen that while the victim's sex has no effect on the probability of upgrading, those accused of killing males are more likely to be downgraded than those accused of

Table 2
Proportions of Cases Upgraded and Downgraded by Control Variables

Control Variable	Proportion of Cases Upgraded (N=92/704)	Attained Significance	Proportion of Cases Downgraded (N = 62/313)	Attained Significance
Victim's Sex		0.4529		.0196*
Male	72/528=.136		54/237 =.228	
Female	20/175=.114		8/76 =.105	
Def.'s Sex		.0116*		.3922
Male	83/574 =.145		8/129 =.062	
Female	60/296 =.203		2/17 =.118	
Relation		.0000*		.0000*
Family	4/167 =.024		4/9 =.444	
Stranger/Unk.	67/299 =.224		31/240 =.129	
Known	21/238 =.088		27/64 =.422	
Victim's Age		.9765		.4984
0–19	10/73 =.137		5/19 =.263	
Else	73/528 =.138		52/262 =.198	
Def.'s Age		.0000*		.1826
0–19	26/80 =.325		11/82 =.134	
Else	27/579 =.098		38/188 =.202	
No. Victims		.0327*		.2058
One	85/678 =.125		59/285 =.207	
Else	7/26 =.269		3/28 =.107	
No. Offenders		.0000*		.0000*
One	45/585 =.077		44/105 =.419	
Else	45/117 =.167		18/207 =.087	
Weapon		.0172*		.0031*
Gun	51/480 =.106		31/203 =.153	
Else	35/203 =.172		30/101 =.297	
Def./Vic. Race		.0000*		.0001*
WW	58/303 =.191		29/130 =.223	
WB	2/23 =.087		1/6 =.167	
BB	22/259 =.061		22/58 =.379	
BW	10/19 =.526		10/119 =.084	

Notes: Sample sizes for cross-classifications vary because of missing data.
For upgrading, we start with felony or possible felony in FBI data (N = 704).
For downgrading, we start with felony in FBI data (N = 313).
Probabilities computed on chi-square statistic. *$p \leq .05$

killing females. Prosecutors are apparently no more likely to construct felony circumstances that the police did not find when the victim is a woman, but they are less likely to overlook felony circumstances found by the police in such cases. Male defendants are more likely than females to be upgraded, but the defendant's sex has no significant effect on the probability of downgrading. Table 2 also reports the zero order relationship between upgrading and downgrading and the relationship between defendant and victim, the victim's age, the defendant's age, the number of victims, the number of offenders, whether a gun was used, and the racial configuration of defendant and victim. In most cases, the direction of effects is such that categories of variables that are more likely than average to be upgraded are less likely than average to be downgraded, and vice versa. Only gun usage is significantly related to both a lower probability of upgrading and a lower probability of downgrading. This may be because the use of a gun may, on the one hand, indicate premeditation and thus add to the perceived severity of a homicide case; on the other hand, since it inflicts a quick death, it may reduce the perceived heinousness of a homicide. Thus, prosecutors may be more likely to view gun cases as either clearly justifying or clearly not justifying the death penalty, and they may present the evidence accordingly.

Multivariate analysis can now be used to examine the significance of the relationship between victim/defendant racial characteristics and both upgrading and downgrading, controlling for the other possibly influential factors that appear in Table 2. We first examine the phenomenon of upgrading using logistic regression procedures and include as predictors all variables that showed a significant bivariate association with upgrading in Table 2. The analysis of upgrading reveals that seven of the ten predictive variables remain statistically significant in the final model. Only the number of victims, defendant's sex, and being white with a black victim (compared with being black with a black victim) do not show effects on upgrading in the final model. For downgrading, the defendant-victim relationship (stranger or family) and the categories WkB and WkW are not statistically significant. However, BkW homicide cases are 26 percent less likely than BkB cases to be downgraded, a difference that is statistically significant.

The Impact of Upgrading on Sentencing: The Question of Motivation

The preceding analysis suggests that the prosecutor's decision to characterize a case as a felony homicide is correlated with the races of the defendant and the victim. Moreover, the correlation between race and prosecutorial classification remains after we control for the initial classification found in police records, as well as for a variety of other apparently influential factors. However, the question remains whether the patterns observed in the selective development of felony circumstance evidence actually affect the likelihood of death sentences. If upgrading were motivated by a desire to seek the death penalty, upgraded cases might be more likely to receive the death penalty than cases consistently classified (by police and court) as involving an accompanying felony.

Table 3
The Probability of a Death Sentence among Consistently Classified versus Upgraded Felony Homicide Cases

	Consistently Classified	Upgraded Cases	Attained Significance
Probability of a Death Sentence	.151	.164	.7869
Total	(251)	(73)	

Table 3 compares the probability of receiving the death sentence in cases that have been upgraded to show an accompanying felony in the court records with the probability of the death sentence in cases consistently classified as involving an accompanying felony in both police and court records. The results in Table 3 suggest that the treatment of upgraded cases does not significantly differ from cases consistently classified as involving accompanying felonies. This analysis is highly misleading, however, because it fails to consider two major and mutually exclusive reasons why a prosecutor might decide to upgrade evidence in homicide cases: 1) to induce the defendant to plea bargain, and 2) to buttress a decision to seek a more severe sentence. Where the prosecutor has upgraded with an eye toward a more severe sentence, prosecutorial selectivity means that we expect a higher probability of a death sentence than felony circumstances alone would warrant. If such upgrading is associated with the race of the defendant or victim, it might reflect a prosecutorial decision to "go after" a defendant because of the racial configuration of the crime. Where the prosecutor has upgraded a case as an inducement to a plea bargain, we would expect an inverse relationship between the probability of a death sentence and upgrading, because the prosecutor is aiming at an expedited resolution of the case, without the ultimate sanction. These upgraded cases are presumably less deserving of death than the cases consistently classified as involving accompanying felonies because the former were not initially classified as involving felony circumstances. It is also possible that upgrading occurs without any end in view other than the desire to paint a full picture of the crime. The police may have misclassified the case to begin with or evidence of an accompanying felony may have been discovered only after the initial police report. In these circumstances we would expect no relationship between sentence severity and upgrading.

Table 4 reanalyzes the data in Table 3, controlling for whether a plea bargain was offered. Looking first at cases in which plea bargains are known to have been offered, we see that death sentences are less likely among upgraded cases than among consistently classified cases. This suggests that prosecutors upgrade some cases that are not truly death eligible to secure plea bargains. Moreover, defendants who are offered a plea and accept it are not at risk of receiving a death sentence. Thus, the pool of defendants eligible for a death sentence among cases in which a plea was offered includes only those who refused the bargain. Among the 168 cases with a court recorded felonious circumstance in which a plea was offered, 28 of 132 defendants in consistently classified cases refused the offered plea bargain, as did 1 of 36 defendants in upgraded cases. When we examine the probability of receiving a death sentence among the former, we find that 68.7 percent of the 28 defendants eventually were sentenced to death, a surprisingly high figure given the fact that the prosecutor in these cases, at least at some point, did not feel compelled to argue for a death sentence. This pattern suggests that refusal to accept an offered plea often evokes retaliation by the prosecutor.

Table 4
The Probability of a Death Sentence among Consistently Classified versus Upgraded Felony Homicide Cases by Plea Offered and Not Offered

	Consistently Classified	Upgraded Cases	Attained Significance
1. Plea Offered Defendant			
Probability of a Death Sentence	.144	.028	.0564
Total	(132)	(36)	
2. No Plea Offered or Unknown			
Probability of a Death Sentence	.160	.297	.0636
Total	(119)	(37)	

In sharp contrast, when we examine those cases in which no plea is known to have been offered to the defendant, the relationship, consistent with our expectations, changes directions. Cases in the upgraded category are about twice as likely as consistently classified cases to result in a death sentence. This difference approaches statistical significance ($p = .06$) despite the small sample size. Moreover, some of the upgraded cases reflect adjustments motivated not by the desire to build a case that will merit the death penalty but rather by the discovery of new evidence or the realization that the police were mistaken in their original classification. If these cases could be identified and eliminated, the relationship between the death penalty and upgrading in cases in which plea bargains are not offered would be even stronger if we are correct in our supposition that these cases are motivated by the desire to seek a more severe sentence. These results are also likely to underestimate the relation between upgrading and the prosecutor's desire to justify the death sentence because some cases in which the prosecutor seeks the death penalty, unidentifiable with our data, do not result in its eventual imposition by the judge.

Table 5

Death Sentence Probabilities among Consistently Classified versus Upgraded Felony Homicide Cases by Race of Victim for Defendants in Cases with No Evidence of Plea Offers

	Consistently Classified	Upgraded Cases	Attained Significance
1. Black Victim Homicides			
Probability of a Death Sentence	.053	.111	.5747
Total	(19)	(9)	
2. White Victim Homicides			
Probability of a Death Sentence	.180	.357	.0451
Total	(100)	(28)	

Table 5, which includes only cases in which no plea bargain is offered, tests the hypothesis that prosecutors are more likely *to selectively* upgrade cases to justify a death sentence when the victim is white. Consistent with this hypothesis we first note that upgrading in cases where no plea was offered is more likely when the victim is white; 18.3 percent of the 153 cases with white victims that are not classified by the police as involving felony circumstances are upgraded by the prosecutor, compared to 4.9 percent of the 184 cases with black victims that are eligible for upgrading. Second, we find that when victims are black, there is no significant difference between upgraded and consistently classified cases in the probability of a death sentence, but when victims are white, upgraded cases are twice as likely to result in a death sentence as those that have been consistently classified. Thus, upgrading cases to buttress a decision to seek the death sentence is most clearly a tactic prosecutors use when the victim is white. The evidence with respect to black victims is ambiguous on this point. Since few cases with black victims are classified by either the police or the prosecutor as involving accompanying felonies, statistical significance is hard to achieve. Although black victim cases in Table 5 have a death sentence probability that is less than one-third that of white victim cases, as with white victims upgrading makes the death sentence twice as likely.

Consideration of Additional Correlates

Finally, we examine the hypothesis that the observed effects of upgrading on the likelihood of a death sentence may arise from the impact of factors, other than race that happen to be associated with upgrading. For example, homicides involving multiple victims, multiple offenders, or those occurring between strangers may motivate prosecutors to pursue a death sentence. If these same types of factors are associated with or promote upgrading, we would expect that controlling for these factors would reduce the relationship between upgrading and the likelihood of a death sentence.

Upgrading remains a significant predictor of the imposition of the death penalty even when the effects of seven other possibly important variables are controlled. This predictor actually attains somewhat greater significance than it does in a model in which it alone is used to predict death sentences. Upgrading increases the probability of a death sentence by 22 percent. These results strongly support the proposition that upgrading evidence to reflect felony circumstances increases the probability of a death sentence in a way that cannot be explained by either the introduction of evidence of a felony or other possibly influential factors. It is the kind of pattern that would be expected if (1) upgrading cases were often done strategically by prosecutors in a special effort to secure the death penalty and (2) if such special prosecutorial efforts secured death sentences in cases that on the objective evidence would not have otherwise merited it. This does not necessarily suggest that the sentencing judge is responding to extralegal or improper factors in sentencing defendants in upgraded cases more severely than other felony murderers, for if upgrading is associated with a special prosecutorial effort to secure the death penalty, upgraded cases as presented to the court may appear more heinous than other murders that involve accompanying felonies. Rather, in deciding whether to upgrade, prosecutors appear to be influenced by the racial configuration of the crime over and above the effects of other more properly influential factors. If this analysis is correct and upgrading reflects a prosecutorial motivation to pursue more severe sentences for selected defendants, the operation of this process masks some of the extralegal influences on the selection of candidates for the death sentence and gives judicial decisions a greater appearance of propriety than is warranted.

Discussion and Conclusions

The above data show that between the time a police department classifies a homicide and the time the case is presented in court there can be significant changes in the characterization of the homicide. These changes, which relate ultimately to the imposition of the death penalty, are associated with both the defendant's and the victim's races and are not explained by factors such as the victim-offender relationship, number of offenders, or number of victims. Thus, race, in effect, functions as an implicit aggravating factor in homicide cases.

These results underscore the point that prosecutors have broad discretionary power, which affects how homicides are investigated and presented, whether defendants are allowed to plead guilty to noncapital offenses, whether death sentences are sought, and numerous other decisions concerning the processing of a case (Bentele, 1985: 609–16). Sentencing studies that take the prosecutor's case descriptions and the formal charges as objective and unbiased reflections of the seriousness of a crime are based therefore on a questionable foundation, which can lead to the underestimation of race effects on sentencing whenever race has affected earlier processing decisions. To understand the full effects of race (and other variables), the presentencing and precharging decisions that affect the prosecutor's construction of a case must be examined (cf. Klepper et al., 1983).

The argument that prosecutorial discretion in homicide cases works to the detriment of black offenders and those with white victims does not depend on a presumption of conscious racial discrimination by prosecutors. Myers and Hagan (1979) have provided what is perhaps the best discussion of the process. Drawing on their study of 980 felony cases arising during the mid-1970s, they argue that a process they call "strong case typification" occurs, in which prosecutorial resources are allocated "so as to maximize the ratio of convictions (and sometimes harsh sentences) to manpower invested" (1979: 440). They find that the strength of evidence in criminal cases (or the opportunity to construct strong evidence) is based in part on extralegal factors. As Myers and Hagan point out:

> [R]egardless of the race of the defendant, prosecutors may consider white victims more credible than black victims or their troubles more worthy of full prosecution. Whatever the reason, prosecutors at this stage demonstrate greater concern with the race of the victim, rather than of the defendant. (1979: 447)

Thus, the racial effects that we have observed are not unique to homicide cases. In an effort to be responsive to the community and perhaps protect perceived self-interests, prosecutors can use their discretion to allocate resources to the most publicly visible cases. Faced with heavy workloads and forced to make priority decisions (Carter, 1974), prosecutors may downgrade cases because they see no great returns from investing in the substantiation of possible aggravating factors. Conversely, once a case is in the public eye, upgrading may be seen by the prosecutor as politically expedient or as worth the extra effort necessary to justify the upgrade. In short, bureaucratic and political variables affect what in theory is a purely legal decision (Jacoby, 1979). If the murder of a white has a different effect on the bureaucratic and political situation from the murder of a black, as it would if murders with white victims are more publicized than murders with black victims, or perceived as more threatening by politically powerful groups, racism will enter the legal system through the prosecutor's office even if the prosecutor never explicitly attends to race.

This analysis indicates that whether a murder is described in a court record as involving an accompanying felony depends in part on the prosecutor's view of the appropriate penalty, which in some cases may be capricious or influenced by extra-legal considerations. Thus, even apparently concrete information may provide at best a vague standard for determining who from a group of murderers is appropriately sentenced to death.

The significance of the above findings is amplified when we realize that the selection of homicide defendants for death is the cumulative result of a series of decisions and evaluations. While at any one decision point race may have only a slight biasing impact, the cumulative product of bias at each point may mean that ultimately the defendant's and victim's races are major determinants of who is selected for execution. Moreover, discriminatory or arbitrary processes and decisions early in the criminal justice process (e.g., in the investigating and building of a case or in the charging decision) will mask evidence of discrimination at later stages. In this way, the criminal justice system, without the venal behavior of anyone, effectively "covers its tracks."

In sum, the question whether the processing of homicide defendants yields racially biased outcomes cannot be answered simply by examining the relationship between race and sentencing while controlling for legally relevant variables. The processual nature of the criminal justice system requires the examination of multiple decision points. The present analysis has focused on only one of the early decision points and has found that discretion, arbitrariness, and discrimination are present. The stage we examined, the decision on how to charge and present a case, has been assumed to be free from arbitrariness and bias by three justices of the U.S. Supreme Court, whose votes were crucial in reinstating the death penalty. In dismissing this possibility in *Gregg v. Georgia* [428 U.S. 153 (1976)], Justices White, Burger, and Rehnquist stated:

> Petitioner's argument that prosecutors behave in a standardless fashion in deciding which cases to try as capital felonies is unsupported by any facts. Petitioner simply asserts that since prosecutors have the power not to charge capital felonies they will exercise that power in a standardless fashion. This is untenable. Absent facts to the contrary it cannot be assumed that prosecutors will be motivated in their charging decision by factors other than the strength of their case and the likelihood that a jury would impose the death penalty if it convicts. (Ibid. at 226)

The analysis in this paper suggests that it is the Justices' view that is untenable. It appears that not only are prosecutors sometimes motivated to seek a death sentence for reasons that reflect the racial configuration of the crime but they do so in a way that greatly reduces the possibilities for discovering evidence of discrimination and arbitrariness when only later stages of the judicial process are examined. Moreover, if prosecutorial actions are discriminatory in their consequences, the most objective and unbiased decisions by the judge and jury can create only an image of justice. They will not correct previously embedded biases. As Justice Marshall noted in *Godfrey v. Georgia* [446 U.S. 420, at 442 (1980)], "the task of selecting in some objective way those persons who should be condemned to die is one that remains beyond the capacities of the criminal justice system."

DISCUSSION QUESTIONS

1.   At which points in the criminal process can racial bias occur? Where would you expect it to be greatest? least? What evidence would you examine to test racial bias? At each point where it might enter, how could it be reduced? How might racial bias infect the civil justice system?

2.   The authors are concerned with bias in low-visibility decisions during the criminal process. What other decisions are relatively invisible, contemporaneously or retrospectively? Are there other situations where different actors make judgments about the same crime, allowing the kind of comparison performed in this article? Are you surprised that victim race is a more significant variable than defendant race? that victim-defendant race pairs are the most significant variable?

3.   What other variables might confound this correlation? Have the authors tested all of them?

4.   Why might prosecutors be more severe than police on BkW homicides? Is the effect of racial bias at each decision likely to be cumulative?

5.   What would be necessary to eliminate racial bias in the criminal justice system?

6.   What are the implications of data documenting racial disparities for modern debates about capital punishment?

16

Structure and Practice of Familial-Based Justice in a Criminal Court

Kathleen Daly

Introduction

A variety of theories have been advanced to explain gender differences in criminal court outcomes. They include court paternalism (e.g., Nagel & Weitzman, 1971; Moulds, 1980; Curran, 1983), gender differences in informal social control (Hagan et al., 1979; Kruttschnitt, 1982; 1984), sociostructural "typescripts" by which men exercise institutional hegemony by maintaining women's familial labor (Harris, 1977), and multifactor explanations that include court chivalry, attributions of male and female criminality, and the practical problems of jailing women with children (Simon, 1975; Steffensmeier, 1980). Each attempts to explain a body of statistical evidence showing that women are sentenced more leniently than men (see Nagel & Hagan, 1983; Parisi, 1982; Chesney-Lind, 1986).

These theories all evince a common problem: none has been grounded in a systematic study of the decision-making processes of court officials. For example, those who have found significant sex effects favoring women say these differences arise from "court paternalism." Yet how do we know that paternalism structures court officials' reactions to men and women? How do we know that other interpretations of officials' reasoning are more accurate? Although sentencing studies may reveal more lenient outcomes for women, they tell us little about how court officials arrive at these decisions.

Concerned with the paucity of qualitative evidence on how gender enters into the "commonsense reasoning practices" and "conceptions of justice" (Feeley, 1979: 284; Maynard, 1982: 347) of court personnel, I observed court proceedings and interviewed court officials (prosecutors, defense attorneys, probation officers, and judges) in a Springfield, Massachusetts courthouse from October 1981 through January 1982. Reported here are the results from my interviews with 35 officials concerning their considerations in sentencing men and women. The interviews reveal a pattern of responses not adequately explained by existing theory but consistent with a model I call familial paternalism. Before illustrating how this fam-

Abridged from *Law & Society Review*, Volume 21:267 (1987).

ilial-based logic is used in the adjudication process and how it affects the court's response to men and women, I shall review extant theory.

Theoretical Review

Paternalism

The most frequent explanation in the literature is that judges and other court officials try to protect women, as the "weaker sex," from the stigma of a criminal record or the harshness of jail. Precisely why such a notion might arise in the criminal courts and how officials justify this gender-based disparity have not, however, received empirical attention. Typically, researchers either interpret statistics indicating that women are favored as evidence of judicial paternalistic attitudes (e.g., Nagel & Weitzman, 1971; Moulds, 1980; Curran, 1983) or conclude that "widespread conviction" (Martin, 1934: 58) and "popular beliefs" (Baab & Furgeson, 1967: 497) offer convincing proof. Feminist critiques of the paternalism thesis include Klein's (1973) argument that only a few women before the court (white and middle class) may be subject to court protection, Moulds's (1980) concern that the protection of women as the "weaker sex" reflects unequal power relations between men and women, and Chesney-Lind's (1978) and Edwards's (1984) conclusions that paternalistic treatment can promote harsher outcomes for women.

Although scholars continue to debate whether paternalism generates more lenient or harsher treatment of women (Nagel & Hagan, 1983: 115), the concept is so entrenched in the literature that few have raised the more fundamental and more critical question: do court officials use paternalistic reasoning, that is, are they in fact concerned with protecting women?

Multifactor Explanations

Simon (1975) and Steffensmeier (1980) identify several factors in addition to paternalism that bear on gender differences in court outcomes. Both emphasize the difficulty judges have in jailing women with children. Steffensmeier also suggests that court officials hold differing gender-based conceptions of the seriousness of criminality (men are perceived as more dangerous) and the potential for reform (women are viewed as more easily directed to law-abiding behavior). In addition to assessing the merits of the paternalism thesis, another aim of my interviews was to determine whether judges find it difficult to jail women with children and, if so, why. I also wanted to see if court personnel believed that women had greater potential for reform than men.

Social Control Arguments

Kruttschnitt (1982; 1984) and (Kruttschnitt & Green, 1984) use social control arguments to explain gender differences in the treatment of defendants, and Hagan et al. (1979) use them to explain gender differences in juvenile offending rates. Their arguments center on the impact of an inverse relationship between informal and formal social controls for the criminal involvement, arrest, and sanctioning of men and women.

As applied to criminal court practices, a social control explanation takes the following form: The more tied a person is to others (e.g., family members), the more that person is subject to informal social control; thus, the chances for future law-abiding behavior are greater, and the need for formal social control (especially penal sanctions) is reduced. To explain gender differences in criminal court outcomes, Kruttschnitt (1982: 496–98) and Kruttschnitt and Green (1984: 542–43) suggest that the differences in the amount of informal (i.e., familial) social control in the lives of men and women promote differences in the degree to which they will be subject to formal control. Further, they argue that informal social control is greater in women's than men's lives because women are more likely to be economically dependent on others (e.g., a spouse or the state). Harris (1977), by contrast, theorizes that women are less likely to be incarcerated than men not because women are more dependent on others, but because men have an interest in maintaining women's familial labor in the home.

Does social control reasoning operate in criminal court decision making? Does it explain differences in the court's treatment of men and women? I explore these questions, together with the different ways in which Kruttschnitt and Harris explain why women are less likely subject to jail time than men. Does leniency arise because women are more likely than men to be dependent on others, or because men are dependent on women's familial labor?

Analysis of Interviews

To understand the context of the interview responses, it is important to know the ways in which court officials oriented themselves to the questions. Two predictable response sets emerged when I asked them what they considered in sentencing. All immediately focused on the "in-out" decision, and all emphasized case individualization.

All interpreted "the sentencing decision" to mean whether a defendant should receive jail time or probation. Thus, when contemplating the exercise of discretionary power, they reflected on the decision that poses dilemmas for them and has the greatest consequences for defendants. Wheeler et al. (1982) suggest that the in-out decision is the "first and hardest" for federal judges, and this holds true for these state court officials as well. The interview analysis focuses on their considerations for this particular decision, although the same types of concerns are evident for the pretrial release decision.

Case individualization was stressed by all court personnel, reflecting their emphasis on rehabilitation as a primary aim of punishment. Indeed, initial reactions to the question "What factors are important to you in sentencing?" were radically individualistic and included responses such as, "Each case is unique," "Every crime has a different set of facts," or "Defendants are all individual human beings so it is hard to say." But as Maynard (1982) and Mann et al. (1980) show, case individualization is patterned, even if specific selected elements of the defendant's biography and the incident are complexly interwoven. Springfield court personnel repeatedly mentioned three factors in characterizing cases: the defendant's prior record; the specific aspects of the incident, including the circumstances that gave rise to it and the defendant's motivation; and the defendant's work and family situation.

Work, Family, and Differential Treatment

Court officials consistently drew on the categories of work and family in explaining why some defendants deserved leniency. One theme is that defendants who provide economic support or care for others deserve more lenient treatment than those without such responsibilities. I shall refer to these defendants as "familied" and "nonfamilied," respectively. When identifying the factors important in sentencing, one judge said:

> Is he or she employed and what is the employment history? If you have a defendant who has worked at the same job for 5 years, has a wife and 2 children, I would be less inclined to put him in jail than one who is not working and who doesn't have a wife. Otherwise, you may be short-changing the pound of flesh. You have got to think of the good for society. You try to balance equities.

Leniency toward the familied defendants is thus justified on the grounds that these defendants are more stable and have more to lose by getting into trouble again. As one prosecutor put it:

> I look at it this way. People with family responsibilities are being given a break. You can't say that singles are being treated more harshly; it's that people with dependents are being treated more leniently. There's the maxim: "There's more stability in these defendants because they have a family." The fact of being hit with incarceration, the kids being taken away from you, losing a job—the chances are more likely that they won't get in trouble again.

The prosecutor's comment reveals a second theme: leniency toward familied defendants is legitimate and just because these defendants have more informal social control in their lives and have a greater stake in normative social adulthood. Although such social control reasoning is apparent in the court's calculus of those thought to be deserving of leniency, court officials typically justify leniency in other ways. They would repeatedly refer to the negative consequences for families and society if familied defendants were jailed. When the judge above says, "You have got to think of the good for society," he is concerned with the potential social cost of a broken family. And, as the defense attorney argues below, when familied defendants are jailed, the defendant's dependents are also punished. This attorney likes to "stress the family situation" in defense summations because if the defendant is

> supporting the household and a couple of kids, you are trying to show the judge that he will be hurting other people. He should pay for it, but not other people.... Who is going to pay the price if we send them away? Does he pay the price, or does the family? Do the kids pay the price?

This concern with the negative consequences of jailing familied defendants anticipates a third theme: familied women deserve greater leniency than familied men. This probation officer alludes to the "special consequences for the family unit" if women with children are jailed:

> I am looking for support. Are there small children that would be better with parents? Will they need social services? Is the person employable? Is he supportive of the family? Will the incident happen again with the same family situation? For women with children, there may be special consequences for the family unit. I'm afraid to continue the defendant's problems if children are there.

The most succinct statement about what influences sentencing was made by another probation officer, who said simply, "prior record and the intangibles." If, as all court officials said, prior record and the nature of the offense strongly inform their sentencing decisions, "the intangibles" hinge on how much informal social control features in defendants' lives, whether defendants are responsible for the welfare of others, and whether society or families can or should pay the costs that result from removing the sources of the families' economic support or care.

Family and Social Control

The general proposition of an inverse relationship between informal and formal social control rings true in the way Springfield court personnel describe their decision-making. A defendant's particular familial situation is a diagnostic tool which allows the court officials to weigh an appropriate sanction. However, positing this informal-formal social control relation begs the question, Why and how is this diagnosis made?

For example, why is "being embedded in a family" or having "strong family ties" salient to the court? Although a complete answer to this question is beyond the scope of this paper, I highlight two related causes. First, the state does not have the resources to impose penal sanctions or intensive probation on all those found guilty; second, the state must therefore rely on others—family members or perhaps employers—to inculcate law-abiding behavior. Using the family to do the state's work can be rationalized as a more humane method of rehabilitation; as a defense attorney stated, "There is no way a state can do what a family can do better." This rationalization, however, stems from the inability of the state to implement prescribed sanctions or, perhaps alternatively, to devise less punitive sanctions.

How court officials apply social control reasoning is contingent on the nature of a defendant's familial situation. The strength and locus of informal social control vary depending upon whether the defendant has dependents or is dependent on others. As one prosecutor said:

> The characteristics that are important are: Responsibilities—who are the people dependent on the defendant? Family contact—do they have concern from parents or siblings? If concern is shown, then the defendant will be on double probation.... The responsibilities of family is what is important for female defendants: Will the children be the victims? Other family ties are very important, and family support is important: Will someone be at home to keep an eye on the defendant?

For familied defendants, the locus of social control comes from family members who are dependent on the defendant; but for nonfamilied defendants, social control emanates from those upon whom the defendant is dependent, or as the prosecutor suggests, "someone [who will] be at home to keep an eye on the defendant."

1. Nonfamilied defendants. Judges spoke of the positive impression created by the presence of "concerned" family members of defendants in the courtroom. They felt it was easier to be lenient toward such defendants because of the expectation that kin could provide daily supervision and rehabilitation (in essence, "familial probation"), which the state could not. As one judge expressed it: "Many kids feel parents give worse punishment than the court." Another judge was quite specific in describing the kind of family relation he could count on to provide informal social control for the nonfamilied man: "Sometimes you see him with his mother present, and you may say to yourself that he has been conning her for 25 years and *this* is a con. The family I like to see for men is their father or uncle, an older responsible male." In a string of characteristics describing a "17-year-old male in need of maximum [rather than minimum or moderate] probation supervision," a probation officer recited the following: "10th grader, unemployed, from a broken home, living with an elderly grandma, no means of support...." Thus, mothers and "elderly grandmas" may not be considered effective sources of informal social control in the lives of nonfamilied men. Whether the same notion obtains for nonfamilied women is uncertain because court officials rarely spoke of differences in informal social controls between nonfamilied men and women.

The salient factors that may differentiate treatment among the nonfamilied men and women are the presence of an active familial authority figure in the household and the defendant's employment–job training–educational situation. I say "may differentiate" because court personnel routinely learn that nonfamilied men and women are "living with parents" or "trying to get a job," but they are not convinced this translates into informal social control. Indeed, one judge said:

> Such things as, "He has a part-time job and lives at home with his mother and father, and he's 19 years old, etc., etc.," doesn't interest me. But if you tell me that this guy works for a children's group or other sort of helping group, that would have an effect.

What would impress this judge is whether the nonfamilied defendant is helping others. With familied defendants, however, it is evident that they are in some way helping others via their economic support or caretaking labor.

2. Familied defendants. It is assumed by court officials that familied defendants have greater informal social control in their lives than nonfamilied defendants. In the words of one judge, familied defendants are "already conforming" and "showing some responsibility."

> I am more loath to incarcerate the family man and woman. It is harder to send someone off to jail who has family responsibilities. They are already conforming to society and the norms that we have at this time in society. They are showing some responsibility.

In their summations before sentencing, defense attorneys said they like to impress upon the court that their clients "have a lot of family support" or "care for others." Recalling the pretrial advice given to a male client, a defense attorney said:

> I told my guy to get married, have a kid, settle down. You usually know what the judges want. I could say to the judge, "Look, this kid has been trying, so give him a break." If he were single and unemployed, he'd be in jail now.

If getting married and settling down is "what the judges want," does this imply that the court is rewarding familied defendants for conforming to norms of social adulthood—for being "good" fathers, husbands, wives, or mothers? In part, yes. However, court officials gave another set of reasons for being lenient to familied defendants: They pointed to the differing social and economic consequences of jailing familied and nonfamilied defendants, which I call the social costs of punishment.

Familied Defendants and the Social Costs of Punishment

The following comments reveal judicial concern with the consequences of sentencing for families and society. Note how each judge wants to learn what the defendant is doing for others; once they obtain this information, they try to predict the impact of their sentences.

> If a woman has children, that affects me. The kind we usually get has two children. If she is supporting them and if she is doing a crime for the benefit of others, compared to drugs, then that counts positively. For women, if a

woman has children, but she in fact has no child care responsibilities, that won't impress me.

Now you look at the record, Is this the first time? What were the circumstances? What are the defendant's living conditions? Is the defendant supporting children or family members? What effect will the disposition have on other family members? Are they a breadwinner? Are you taking a father or a mother away from a family? Are you punishing a victim? Is the society in danger?

Judges are concerned with fitting the punishment not only to the crime and the defendant's background but also to those to whom the defendant might be tied. The second judge just quoted asks if the sentence might be "punishing a victim" and if jail is necessary because "society [is] in danger." The first judge is not impressed by the mere fact that a woman has children unless she is caring for them. This judge also said, "If [the sentence] has a side effect on innocent people, you have to take it into account. If it's not a violent crime, then leniency is called for. You don't hurt a group because of just one guy." Court officials face a set of constraints in sanctioning familied defendants that are not present for nonfamilied defendants. By removing economic or caretaking responsibilities from families, they may cause the dissolution of these fragile units of social order. Moreover, they may punish victims or other innocents—those dependent on the defendant—in the process.

1. Family and gender divisions. Court personnel assume gender divisions in the work and family responsibilities of familied men and women. In fact, such assumptions are so ingrained that one judge, when asked about these differing responsibilities, replied impatiently:

Male and female, mother and father. Are you following through on that responsibility? There are different responsibilities depending on whether you are male or female.... The responsibilities they assume when they bring children into the world are different. Are they fulfilling those responsibilities? For men, I want to know: Is he holding the home together as best he can? Does he contribute to the support of the family? A woman has a different function. Is she fulfilling her obligations as a mother?

Differences in the expected responsibilities of familied men and women, combined with the family profiles of defendants, foster discrepancies in the treatment of familied men and familied women. As one probation officer said, "The treatment of males and females balances out. If the guy is working, you try to help him keep his job; and with a female, you try to keep her with the kids." Although this official believes that the treatment of male and female defendants "balances out," note his asymmetrical reasoning: being a male is qualified by "if the guy is working," while being a female contains the unqualified assumption that she has children.

The presumed gender divisions in work and family life can make it difficult, one lawyer said, to persuade the court that familied men do care for their children. Coming directly from bail arguments to the interview, this lawyer recounted with exasperation his inability to secure pretrial release of his client, who was caring for his children while his wife was about to be hospitalized:

> The man was charged with A & B [assault and battery]. He has a wife going into the hospital, and he has two kids. They wanted $1,000 bail. There is no prior, and there doesn't seem to be any reason for the high bail. There is a presumption that he is going to leave town. How can he leave, with a wife and two children? He's not going anywhere. If it were a woman, she would have been ROR'd [released on recognizance].

2. Familied men and women. Three features of the differential response to men and women can be analytically distinguished, although they overlap in the minds of court personnel:

a. Women are more likely to have dependent children than men.
b. Familied women fulfill their familial obligations more responsibly than familied men.
c. Child care is more important than breadwinning in the maintenance of families.

With respect to the first, more familied women than familied men appear in court; indeed, court officials characterized most female defendants as having children. Although this typification is not wholly inaccurate, it activates a reasoning pattern, exemplified by the above statement from the probation officer, that conceptualizes the differential treatment of men and women as the response to all men and familied women.

Among the familied men and women, court officials see more "good" mothers than "good" fathers. Although many familied men are biological fathers, they may not be providing economically for families. Furthermore, from the court's viewpoint, men's affective support for families is not sufficient to define social fatherhood, which rests on being a breadwinner. Familied women, in contrast, are viewed as fulfilling their familial responsibilities more often, as a probation officer expressed.

> If a female is a mother of a child, we overlook certain weaknesses she may have in a lot of areas. A lot of girls get jammed up in serious offenses, but if she is a good mother of small children, this is very, very important. It has a neutralizing effect on seriousness. You do more harm to the community by locking them up. A lot of female defendants are good mothers, but not many male defendants are good fathers. For male defendants, we see them after they have failed in school and in the marketplace. In every area, including family, he is a total failure. You check probate, and you know he is not doing his duty as a father—though they often cry about how they have to support kids.

Note the officer's concern that greater harm will accrue to the community by jailing mothers. Mann et al. (1980) discovered similar concerns in their analysis of judicial considerations in sentencing male white-collar offenders; but unlike these defendants, male common crime defendants have "failed in school and in the marketplace" and are less likely to be "good" fathers. Indeed, some court officials acknowledged that minority group men may have more difficulty presenting themselves as "good family men" because this status is contingent on having a job; according to a judge, "A person with a job and supporting a family is less likely to go to jail than someone who isn't. Having a job is a negative factor to putting someone in jail. Of course, this works against minority groups who have more difficulty getting employed."

Finally, differences emerge in the treatment of familied men and women because child care is considered more essential than economic support in maintaining families. This attitude is revealed by a defense attorney's description of how a defendant's familial relations evoke the "same reaction" but have a "different impact" for the familied man and woman: "The [court's] reaction is the same if the man has a family. It helps, but the impact is different than if it's a mother." Judges do have difficulty jailing a woman with children, and they also find this more difficult than jailing a familied man. When I asked judges if they considered different factors when sentencing men and women, they replied that women may have an advantage as a consequence not of sex but of differences in men's and women's work for families.

> Family responsibility is something you have to recognize. It weighs against incarceration or the difference between a long versus a short incarceration. Women are more likely to have kids and dependents than men. It is more difficult to send a woman with a kid to prison than a man. But if the man was taking care of a child, it would be the same thing, but this has never happened to me in the court.

As this and other judges report, familied men would be treated like familied women if they were caring for children.

Women's care for children is often cited in the literature as a reason for their more lenient sentences (e.g., Simon, 1975; Steffensmeier, 1980). However, it is not self-evident why judges and other court officials believe that child care is more important than economic support for maintaining families. Without this distinction, familied men and women might be treated equally. Like gender divisions in work and family life, the privileging of child care over economic support is simply assumed by court officials, and few tried to explain the basis of this presupposition. One judge, however, provides a clue.

> For [the woman with children], it is a twofold consideration. First, financial, by putting the mother in jail, are we going to throw the children on society as a burden? No, we're not going to do that. Second, for the female

defendants, how much do the children need the mother, or the aunt, or the grandmother?

The judicial reference to financial reasons suggests that there are different economic consequences to the state of removing breadwinning and child-care responsibilities from families. Father surrogates exist in the form of welfare benefits and other state supports (for example, Aid to Families with Dependent Children, housing allowances, and foodstamps), but mother surrogates in the form of foster or institutional care of children are more rare and expensive and less satisfactory. Thus, the loss of breadwinning is replaced by state supports more easily than the loss of parental care. This asymmetry is at the heart of the "practicality problem." To extend Harris (1977), both men's and the state's interests are jeopardized by removing women's familial labor.

The consequences of gender divisions in work and family life take an ironic twist in the criminal courts. The differential value placed on men's and women's labor in the wider society, where women's unpaid familial labor has "no price" and is not socially recognized as work, is reversed in the context of contemplating its removal from families. Maternal labor, based on a model of personalized motherhood, becomes socially recognized as invaluable, priceless, and irreplaceable while breadwinning does not.

Female versus Familial Paternalism

The interviews show that although a form of paternalism exists in the court, it does not center on the protection of women. Rather, its ideological emphasis is on protecting the social institution of the family, specifically: (1) keeping families together, (2) maintaining familied defendants' labor for families, and especially women's caretaking labor, and (3) protecting those dependent on a defendant's economic support or care. These results challenge the commonly held notion that the court protects women (female paternalism) and reveal instead that the real object of judicial protection is families (familial paternalism). This distinction between female and familial paternalism is illustrated by the following judicial discussion of whether a woman who cared for children should be jailed.

> A lot will depend on what will happen to the children. Chances are that if there is no one to take care of the children, I won't punish the children. I feel no sympathy toward her, but I do feel that the children are entitled to sympathy.

In extending sympathy toward children and trying to keep families together, court officials respond to both men and women using a familial paternalistic logic. While familied defendants are generally thought to deserve greater leniency than nonfamilied defendants, familied women may be treated more leniently than familied men for two reasons: (1) gender divisions of labor define women, not men, as the primary caregivers; and (2) the court attaches more importance to caregiving than breadwinning in maintaining family life. Thus, those engaged in caregiving (predominantly women) are thought to be most deserving of leniency.

Although court officials' reasoning is infused with familial paternalism, they frequently conflate "female" and "being familied" by assuming that all women have children. This conflation may explain a contradiction that emerges from the interviews of the nonjudicial court workers. On the one hand, they make their decisions along familial paternalistic lines, but on the other, they say that women are sentenced more leniently than men because of judicial female paternalism.

Of the 24 prosecutors, defense lawyers, and probation officers, 20 agreed that "judges are more lenient to women than men," 14 attributing this to "sexism ... paternalistic attitudes" or a view of women as "the weaker sex." Thus, the courthouse lore is that judges engage in female paternalism.

Do judges actually use female paternalistic reasoning, or are these perceptions inaccurate? I asked them to comment on the following statement (adapted from Simon, 1975: 49).

> Judges treat female defendants more kindly or protectively than they do male defendants because female defendants remind them of their daughters, or wives and sisters—women close to them. Or just in general, judges find it hard to be as tough on a woman as a man.

Their reaction was mixed. Although most judges said it did not apply to them, three believed it might have some applicability to their decision-making. Thus, although judicial thinking is not completely devoid of female paternalism, the processes structuring an apparent judicial leniency toward women are rooted in a family-based paternalism that is practiced by all court workers.

Qualifying Concerns

Some caveats about familial paternalistic practices are in order to present a balanced and fair view of its expression and impact.

1. "Hiding behind the children" and "bad mothers." Women's caregiving may militate against but certainly does not prevent incarceration. Both the quality and indispensability of maternal care were considered by Springfield court personnel in a manner similar to the diagnosis of men as "good" or "bad" fathers. Of all court officials, prosecutors were most likely to question whether familied women were "good" mothers. They were skeptical of defense attorneys who "used the mother situation," criticizing it as a means for female defendants to "hide behind the children."

> Women can use children as an excuse. There are a lot of women who are not good mothers. If I could prove that she was a lousy mother, then I would prove it. You have to think of the welfare of the children.

Defense lawyers do use the tactic of women with children to prevent incarceration of the defendant or holding before trial. But in some cases, it is really just a tactic. For example, I saw a woman brought in for stealing hubcaps at 3 A.M. with her boyfriend. Her lawyer said she needed to care for a 1-month old baby at home. Well, I really wondered why she was out at 3 A.M. if she had to care for an infant.

The standards for being classified as a "good" mother were never made explicit but rather couched in vague terms of "taking responsibility" for the welfare of children, much in the same way that the criteria for being a "good" father rested on notions of "taking responsibility" for the economic welfare of the family unit. Thus, having children is necessary but not sufficient for social motherhood for female defendants in the same way that having a family is not sufficient for social fatherhood for male defendants.

2. Gender, family responsibilities, and offenses charged. The interviews reveal that these elements interact in different ways. First, the offense and the defendant's prior record can eclipse both gender and familial relations in determining sentencing (or pretrial release) decisions. Court personnel said that familied defendants were as likely to be jailed as nonfamilied defendants if previously convicted of serious or violent offenses (e.g., murder, sexual assault, major drug dealing, and robbery). However, sentence length and type (e.g., weekend sentences) may vary by the familial situation of those incarcerated.

Second, some offenses indicate that familied men and women may be "bad" parents and thus not deserving of court mercy. The offense provoking the strongest reaction against familied men and women was sexual abuse of children. Concern was frequently voiced for this type of familial violence but not for spouse abuse—a predictable but still troubling finding.

Familied women charged with prostitution are a priori considered "bad" mothers as prosecutors rhetorically ask, "Who's taking care of the children while she's out at night?" These women are as likely to be jailed as nonfamilied women. Springfield court personnel disagreed, however, over how these cases should be handled. A probation officer and defense lawyer described the visceral reaction of judges by saying, respectively, "Some judges hate prostitutes," and "They treat prostitutes ridiculously." Three judges said they thought of prostitutes more as victims than offenders and stressed that they viewed prostitution less seriously than other judges did.

Finally, a defendant's familial situation can interact with the motivation for criminal involvement and affect the degree of blameworthiness attributed to a defendant's behavior. For example, in a sentencing vignette given to judges, which involved a person convicted of larceny, one judge wanted to know, "Was there a need for the family or not?," while another said, "If it's stealing milk for the children, I wouldn't send the person to jail." Their responses suggest that leniency may be granted to those who commit crimes intended to help family members, that is, those motivated by need rather than self-interest or greed. Familied defendants may more often conform to this "Robin Hood" image, particularly for property-related offenses.

3. Punishment and potential for reform. Perceptions of the reform potential of men and women, independent of their familial situation, may be another basis for differential treatment. Some probation officers thought that women—both familied and nonfamilied—were "more easily reformed than men" and that men didn't "want to help themselves," one even saying that "females are easier to intimidate. I guarantee her jail if she is not clean. Females are impressed with this more than males." Thus, Steffensmeier's (1980) ideas on the reform potential of men and women receive some support from these interviews, although this "potential" is related to job segregation by sex. For example, when describing the relative success of men and women on probation, a probation officer reported, "It's easier for women to find jobs," adding that the reason is that men have a "masculine image" to protect and thus "are hesitant to go into the Skills Center if they can't get a masculine job. They will drive a regular bus, but not a school bus." It is in fact no easier for women to find paid jobs, but so-called feminine jobs, which often pay less, are not acceptable to men.

In contrast to the three other groups of court workers, probation officers more often spoke of a gender-based substantive justice that was independent of a woman's familial situation. The logic of this substantive justice is that the "equal punishment" of men and women is not necessary to achieve "equal outcomes" (i.e., identical rehabilitation or deterrent effects). We need additional research to determine the distribution and extent of this reasoning pattern; perhaps this type of thinking is more common among court workers and jurisdictions taking a forward-looking (rehabilitation) rather than backward-looking (retribution or "just deserts") stance in sanctioning.

Summary

Family-based conceptions of justice dominate the reasoning of Springfield court officials when they describe and justify their sanctioning decisions. The court's interest in protecting family life and those dependent on the defendant promote two axes of variation in treatment—between familied and nonfamilied defendants and between familied men and familied women. Court officials think of this differential treatment not as discrimination but rather as legitimate and pragmatic justice. Because of their concern with the *consequences* of their sanctioning decisions for families and society, they rationalize leniency for familied defendants in the following way: if familied men or women are jailed, social disorder may increase, bonds of economic and affective responsibilities to others may be severed, and victims, particularly children, may be punished. Differences in the treatment of familied men and women arise because familied women are thought to be "more responsible" than familied men and child care is considered more important than economic support to maintain family life.

The ideological emphasis given to defendants' familial relations by Springfield court officials has also been documented by Eaton (1983; 1984; 1985) for an English lower court. While I agree with Eaton that traditional and gendered conceptions of work and family life are reproduced in criminal court decision-making, I would add that this ideological stance also appears to be structured by economic considerations. The state pays both economically and socially for imposing equal punishments on defendants whose obligations for the care and economic support of others are unequal and differ by gender. For example, more families may be placed on welfare (see Maynard, 1982), and foster care for children may be required (see Daly, 1989a). These economic costs form part of the decision-making calculus in court workers' conceptions of justice.

Based on the interviews, Kruttschnitt's (1982; 1984; Kruttschnitt & Green, 1984) social control arguments need to be modified. With respect to the locus of social control, the presence of dependents is what court officials consider, for as a prosecutor said, "As long as there are dependents in the picture, they will help men as well as women." Being dependent on others is less important to court workers and primarily affects the treatment of nonfamilied defendants. In jailing familied men and women, the differing social costs arising from separating them from their families seems to be more significant than differences in informal social control.

I have described the kinds of decision-making processes that promote gender differences in criminal court outcomes, but the skeptical reader may require more statistical evidence. I have conducted multivariate analyses of court outcomes in two other states—a lower court in New York City and an upper court in Seattle—to test hypotheses on the differential treatment of familied and nonfamilied defendants and of familied men and women in sentencing and other court decisions (Daly, 1983; 1987). Both showed strong family effects militating against pretrial detention and jail sentences. In addition, I found family effects in nonjail sentencing outcomes, suggesting that familial paternalism may spill over to other court decision-making contexts. Thus, although the familial paternalistic logic is most vividly revealed in the in-out decision, it may also be applied in other, less momentous contexts. Future research might investigate this possibility and, more generally, whether the kinds of family-based reasoning patterns employed by Springfield court officials exist elsewhere. The statistical analyses suggest that such patterns are not confined to just one medium-sized city courthouse in one state.

For too long theories of gender differences in the criminal court sanctioning process have suffered from a lack of empirical attention to the ways in which court officials construct justice and rationalize their decisions. Rather than continuing to speculate and make inferences about their reasoning processes from analyses of large court datasets, we may do better by observing and interpreting these processes firsthand.

DISCUSSION QUESTIONS

1.   In what ways would you expect gender bias in the legal system to differ from race and class bias? How do the sources of bias differ?

2.   What are the relative advantages of quantitative and qualitative research into bias?

3.   What are the different explanations for gender bias in the criminal process? Which do you find most convincing? Did the article change your preconceptions of the nature of gender bias? Where else might "familial paternalism" affect legal decisions?

4.   Do you find it objectionable that judges consider the defendant's work and family situation in sentencing? Does it logically imply greater leniency for women? Would you prefer a sentencing regime that entrusted judges with less discretion? Do these male judges focus more on rights or on relations, in Gilligan's typology of moral reasoning?

5.   The Federal Sentencing Guidelines instruct officials generally to disregard previous employment record and family ties and responsibilities in order to reduce class, race, and gender disparities. Would a policy designed to treat defendants "more equally" lead to unjust sentences in individual cases?

6.   Which kind of bias is more difficult to eradicate from the criminal justice system: class, race, or gender? What happens when these forms of bias interact? Are there parallels between the leniency toward convicted women and protective legislation (labor law, statutory rape)?

Ideology and Consciousness

17

The Uses of History: Language, Ideology, and Law in the United States and South Africa

Elizabeth Mertz

Introduction

This paper examines the official language in which the governments of South Africa and the United States changed indigenous peoples' rights to land. The process relied on images of history in the language of the law to impose social ideologies on social life. The rhetorical transformation accomplishes more than a semantic change; the language of the law is powerful, and when it appropriates history in a particular way, it also affects and changes social structures and entitlements. Thus an analysis of linguistic mediation can provide important insights into the uses of history in social change.

Ideology and History

An ideology of history emerges in the legal and political texts of South Africa and the United States, but it is not a preexisting ideology mechanically expressed through language. Rather, legal language and ideology are intimately intertwined in a creative process that has drawn increasing scholarly attention (Brigham, 1978; Mertz & Weissbourd, 1985). Thus we capture ideology in the making as we examine the language in which courts and legislators speak of history, land, and people. At the same time, we see the impact of existing social structures and power in the language of the law. My approach to language and social praxis combines recent developments in anthropological linguistics and semiotics (see Silverstein, 1976; 1979; Mertz, 1985) with the concern for cultural content found in the work of Sarat and Felstiner (1986), and a focus on the social grounding of language characteristic of social theorists such as Bourdieu (1977). In its emphasis on the uses of history in legal ideology, my analysis continues some of the earlier concerns of Charles Miller (1969; re history and ideology more generally, see Moore, 1978; Sahlins, 1981).

Abridged from *Law & Society Review*, Volume 22:661 (1988).

The approach taken here views language as a key mediator in human interaction, and as socially grounded. In both respects, language is ideological. As work by linguists and semioticians has demonstrated, language filters and channels the stories speakers tell (see Mertz & Parmentier, 1985). Language is also the medium through which much of our social interaction is accomplished. Thus language is socially grounded, structuring and being structured by social context. In studying legal texts, we see the dynamic translation and creation of social relations as they are explained—an explanation that speaks of history and justifies social change.

Comparing South Africa and the United States

In comparing the uses of history in legal and political narratives from South Africa and the United States, we can begin to analyze the impact of differences in social histories, in legal systems, and in the language of the law, upon this complex interaction. Differences are immediately apparent in the kinds of texts with which we must work. South Africa has a system of "legislative supremacy," in which the courts may not overrule legislative enactments. Thus in South Africa we must look to the statutes, and to the legislative debates and governmental justifications behind their enactment, to understand the legal transformation of indigenous people's property rights. For instance, the case law that followed the "native" land statutes did not affect basic entitlements but merely clarified relatively minor semantic questions. By contrast, the United States Supreme Court has the power to void statutes if it decides they conflict with fundamental constitutional guarantees. The language of United States case law speaks authoritatively of history and social change, from John Marshall's Court to the most recent treaty cases. The legal narratives of South Africa and the United States thus have different institutional sources and fit into different systems of law. They also result in distinctive histories of indigenous peoples and differing assessments of the import of those histories, as the legal texts reflect and forge very different social structures.

At the same time, there remains a striking point of comparison; both South Africa and the United States have consigned their indigenous peoples to limited geographical areas, officially redefining the history and rights to land of people who once occupied entire nations. Through this point of comparison, we can isolate differences to understand better the ideological framing and definition of indigenous peoples' rights to land in the language of the law. The history generated in the American case has sometimes recognized that violence and unequal power led to the reservation system, and liberal canons of interpretation as well as reaffirmation of rights off reservation land have resulted from this recognition. This is an ideological difference, discernible in legal and political language, that has given radically different meaning to United States and South African laws encouraging separation of indigenous and "white" cultures. In the ideology is a justification for the distribututation of land and power; in the shape of the language used is a structure of social relations.

South African "Homelands"

The battle over history in South Africa has in many ways been stark and unsubtle. Quite simply, "white" South Africans have rewritten the story of South Africa's past, which they begin with the Europeans' arrival in South Africa. They have emptied the South African past of human occupants before colonial times (Modman, 1976: 1):

> Three and a quarter centuries ago the whites entered South Africa from the south at Table Bay.... It was a Dutch-speaking stream which for more than a century made no significant contact with Blacks. Only in about 1770 was it stopped ... by a Black stream moving southwards.

This quote comes from one of a series of official publications generated by South African government departments or institutes. The goal of these publications is to represent the history of white domination and current policies—for example, the homelands policy and apartheid—in benign terms (see RSA, 1973; 1976; 1980; 1983; 1987; Malan & Hattinger, 1976; see also textbooks reported in Thompson, 1985: 200–02).

The "white" South African ideology of history has varied through time. Early histories, like later ones, denied indigenous South Africans their past achievements—indeed, even their presence—but these texts more often focused on the generally "inferior" character of nonwhite races than on precolonial history. Thompson (1985) has noted a change in modern texts; they stress internal ethnic divisions among African peoples, and spend more time than did the older histories on elaborate chronologies designed to demonstrate that blacks were not prior occupants of the land.

Thompson views this shift as an attempt to justify South Africa's emerging "homelands" policy, in an international scene in which barefaced racist explanations relying on inherent superiority or inferiority were no longer acceptable. He also views the shift as a result of a general change in concerns following South African independence (ibid. 41).

> Race had always been a vital factor in the Afrikaner mythology. However, until the Second World War it took second place to the imperial element.... Nearly all white South Africans ... assumed that any sensible, civilized person knew that Africans were a culturally inferior race...an assumption that corresponded with the global distribution of power.

After the war, Thompson argues, racial issues moved to the fore, as African workers migrated to urban areas and participated in growing numbers in the nation's burgeoning industrial development (ibid. 43). The change in historical ideology of that time corresponds with the rise of the infamous "homelands" policy, which completed the sad process by which indigenous South Africans were stripped of their rights to most of their land.

In one sense, this seemed to be a different approach, a marked change. Yet in another sense, the postwar ideology and law merely continued earlier efforts to rob Africans of their history and property rights at the same time. We can follow that movement through contemporaneous accounts and legal developments.

History as "Civilization"

The ideology of history in early accounts is recounted in a story about "civilization," one that serves as justification for the disenfranchisement of South Africa's indigenous people (Bryce, 1897: 86, 96):

> The native races seem to have made no progress for centuries...the feebleness of savage man intensifies one's sense of the overmastering strength of nature.... The people were—and indeed still are—passionately attached to their old customs.... Their minds are mostly too childish to recollect and draw the necessary inferences from previous defeats.

This use of an evolutionary scale, the highest, most modern point of which is occupied by whites, is typical of European social thought of the time (see Chase, 1977; Gould, 1981; Stocking, 1968). This scheme distorts the time frame within which indigenous peoples' history is to be told; if they represent an "earlier" stage in evolution, then, although they live in the present, their past cannot be as developed as that of people representing "higher" stages. When used to represent an earlier stage in the development that led to European "civilization," indigenous South Africans are made to embody someone else's past in objectified form. The corollary of this vision of history is that indigenous South Africans lack a past of their own.

And, indeed, early South African historians linked their descriptions of the indigenous African population as "backward" or "primitive" to a denial of developed history; a number of these accounts concluded that such "backward" people could not possibly have produced the elaborate stone monuments discovered in Zimbabwe (Bryce, 1897: 80–81; Theal, 1912: 418). The ahistorical past to which early historians consigned Africans is perhaps best illustrated by the frequent analogy to children; like children, indigenous people represent an earlier ontogenetic stage and, precisely for that reason, lack any history of their own.

These historical narratives provide a backdrop to deliberations at the National Convention of 1908, at which the South Africa Act, "An Act to Constitute the Union of South Africa," was drafted. A key issue at the Convention was the extension of the franchise to "non-whites" living in South Africa. Representatives from the Cape Colony, which had extended the franchise to members of all races, were committed to defending an open franchise policy (Walton, 1912: 120–32). In the debate that followed, representatives argued the merits of universal suffrage. The evolutionist account of racial superiority that emerges in the debate encapsulates its conception of history in discussions of the notion of "civilization," discussions with direct and dramatic political consequences for indigenous South Africans. Sir Percy Fitzpatrick declared:

> few would contend that [civilization] consisted only of a surface education and of the signs of improvement such as those they readily welcomed among the Native peoples. Civilization went a great deal further ... and the white man gave as security the traditions of his race of many centuries of civilization. (Walton, 1912: 122)

In a similar vein, Sir Frederick Moor told the convention:

> the white and black races in South Africa could never be amalgamated. The history of the world proved that the black man was incapable of civilization and the evidences were to be found throughout South Africa today. (Ibid. 123)

Here the claims of history are encompassed in the concept of civilization; to be civilized is to have a past that has left tangible traces, a past that can be tracked through successive stages culminating in civilization. Indigenous South Africans lacked this tangible history; they were "uncivilized." In this collapse of temporal and cultural categories, Africans are robbed of their history and of the franchise, setting the scene for the Native Lands Act No. 27 of 1913, which followed four years later and revoked their rights to land throughout most of the country.

Interestingly, the language of the South Africa Act gives no rationale for its provision barring "natives" from Parliament or from voting; it merely lists, in a matter-of-fact fashion, "European male adult" as a requirement in provisions dealing with these matters. This declarative style represents a highly debatable position as fact, as not requiring an explanation. And the language of the debates behind the Act shows us why this is so; for the faction whose position won out, the only necessary explanation lay in the categories themselves. Once someone is classified as "native" or "civilized" (and, note also, as male or as female), ability and right to self-govern followed naturally. A rhetoric that characterizes people by their "stage" in history won over a rhetoric of rights and justice at the Assembly; the crude, unsupported imposition of categories translated this victory into law. In these early narratives the "white" South Africans deny Africans a developing past, a history, as they deny them legal rights as citizens in their own land. We see that in the "white" ideology, a history, defined in written records, is a key feature of "civilization," and only civilized people may be citizens, with rights to own land and determine their own political fate. This is a relatively subtle use of history in comparison with later South African debates; here the issue is not whether Africans can lay claim to land because they occupied it first but rather whether Africans can have any of the rights belonging to citizens of a "civilized" state. A refusal to recognize indigenous history is part of an attempt to classify the people without a history as inherently excludable from political rights and participation. Length of occupation becomes less relevant as long as the prior occupation can be treated as in some sense timeless or ahistorical.

The Cape Colony representatives who sought to guarantee Africans' political rights recognized this; they did not argue prior occupation of land but rather abstract political ideals. Mr. Sauer, for example,

> declared himself in favour of equal rights and he was one of those who believed that a great principle never yet shown to have failed in the history of the world would be a safe principle in South Africa to adopt at this great moment of her life. He could not accept Sir Frederick Moor's plan because he did not believe it would lead to peace, and permanent peace could never be founded upon injustice.... We could not govern the natives fairly and justly unless they were represented by their own elected representatives.... (Ibid. 126–28)

These arguments were not persuasive; the "compromise" that emerged from the Convention granted voting rights only to indigenous people who could vote at the time of the Union (the Cape Colony being the only area where Africans had had the franchise), with the proviso that Parliament could change the arrangement at a later date by a two-thirds vote. The South Africa Act also permitted only Europeans to be elected to Parliament.

Formal restrictions on land use emerged the same year, when the Transvaal Gold Law (No. 35 of 1908) barred "coloured persons" from land in mining districts (see Rousseau, 1960: 5). In 1913 Parliament passed the Natives Land Act (No. 27 of 1913), which declared:

> From and after the commencement of this Act, land outside the scheduled native areas shall ... be subject to the following provisions, that is to say:—Except with the approval of the Governor-General—(a) a native shall not enter into any agreement or transaction for the purchase, hire, or other

acquisition from a person other than a native, of any such land or of any right thereto, interest therein, or servitude thereover....

Europeans were also forbidden to purchase land from "natives." The Act also limited alienability of land within "native" areas. The Natives Land Act took an ostensibly protective arrangement, in which "native" areas had been those especially reserved for indigenous peoples, and changed it so that protected areas were now the only areas in which Africans could own land. These arrangements were modified in subsequent acts, most of which provided for the sale or transfer of designated reserves to Europeans or the government.

The language of all of these property-shifting statutes is formal and declarative and gives no reason or justification. It was apparently self-evident that this "uncivilized" people, this people without written history or European culture, could lose its land by fiat—through imposition of the written word. The power behind the imposition of law was evident in its summary treatment of indigenous peoples' history and rights—indeed, in its complete exclusion of their voices and stories. Here denial of history "makes sense" of the denial of rights in land.

"Protection" and Prior Occupation

By the 1930s there had already been a shift in the language used to describe Africans in South African accounts, and there had been a change in the framing of statutory language as well. An official of the Department of Native Affairs explained its purpose (Rogers, 1933: 17–18):

> The essential function of the Native Affairs Department is to assist, guide, protect and generally to subserve the interests of a large, undeveloped and, for the most part, inarticulate Native population, which is rapidly emerging from barbarism and is in the process faced with the necessity of accommodating itself to a novel and highly complex environment.

The evolutionist image is still strong here, and Africans are still characterized as primitive and inferior, but there is also an attempt to justify land policies as benefiting blacks. This slight shift away from unabashed supremacist language and declarative statutory structure can also be seen in the Native Trust and Land Act (No. 18 of 1936).

> A corporate body, to be called the South African Native Trust ... is hereby constituted.... The Trust shall, in a manner not inconsistent with the provisions of this Act, be administered for the settlement, support, benefit, and material and moral welfare of the natives of the Union.

The Act evinces much more concern for "natives" than did the Native Land Act of 1913, but at the same time it bars unregistered Africans from white rural areas and limits their overall mobility (see also Greenberg, 1980: 83). Here the characterization of indigenous peoples as "uncivilized" is not employed to justify outright denial of rights or land on the basis of raw claims to superiority. Instead it serves as an explanation of why European control over "native" lands and prerogatives is in the Africans' own interest: as "uncivilized" people, they need the guidance and protection of European supervision.

From the Act of 1913 through the Act of 1936, then, there was a steady move to segregate Africans in designated areas and to remove their rights to land in "white" areas, which constituted most of the country. Greenberg notes the utility of these measures in maintaining a rural labor force "though it had lost its grazing and cultivation rights and depended primarily upon wage labor" (1980: 86). The laws gave "white" landowners increased power over African land and labor during a critical transition from labor tenancy to wage labor. And, astonishingly, this separation of Africans from their land was accomplished in a rhetoric of increasing altruism.

After World War II, both economic and ideological changes again affected the uses of history in efforts to take rights to land from the African population. Economically, this was the period during which South Africa made the transition to capitalism (ibid. 105). Ideologically, the government rested its new "homeland" policy on an account of South African history that stressed differences among African groups and a recent date for the migration of Africans into South Africa (Thompson, 1985: 198–200). This crude attempt to rob Africans of their past, and of their common claim to the land, accompanied the rise of the "apartheid" policy under the Nationalist regime, which

> clearly and explicitly established that the only place where any African could hope to enjoy most of the political and civil rights accorded to white citizens was in a homeland. The fact that many urban Africans had been born outside these areas or had weak or nonexistent ties to them did not exempt them from a kind of resident alien status. (Fredrickson, 1981: 245)

Fredrickson paints attempts by the South African government to give these homelands "independent" national status as a natural outgrowth of the "resident alien status" conferred on so many Africans in their own land (see the Native Homelands Citizenship Act, No. 26 of 1970, and the Transkei Constitution Act, No. 48 of 1963). This disenfranchisement not only continues European control of land, political system, and the labor force, but it also divides the Africans into discrete groups, undermining unity among African workers.

How does the "official story" explain this unjust system?

The Government of the RSA (Republic of South Africa) is intensely aware of the special problems which are created by an historical heritage which has placed the White nation in a position of trusteeship over various underdeveloped Bantu peoples.... In an artificially integrated unified state, the Bantu would, as a result of their enormous backlog in comparison with the Whites (in terms of economic, technical and political-administrative development), be doomed to become a backward proletariate.... However, by creating for each Bantu people the opportunity to grow into an independent nation in a geopolitically acknowledged sphere of influence, i.e., in its own historical homeland, the possibility that the divergent interests of the groups concerned will lead to a continual political struggle for power is obviated. (RSA, 1973: 15)

With an Orwellian brand of double-speak, the government here appropriates an enlightened vocabulary—"proletariate," "independent nation"—in an effort to convince the reader that the substance of the program described matches the form of the language used to describe it. The complete political disenfranchisement of Africans since the inception of the Republic of South Africa is glossed over in the phrase "Whites' political leadership," as if somehow in an open and fair competition "whites" had won out, as if there had ever been any opportunity at all in the existing political framework for Africans to lead politically. The lack of African political power is represented as a failure, as a predictable component of a generally backward state, rather than as a necessary, indeed mandatory, part of the political system originated and maintained in force by "whites." The exile and forcible removal of Africans to unfamiliar areas of the country is portrayed as a benevolent assurance of independence to people in their own "historical homelands"; the accompanying limits on mobility and acquisition of land outside the homelands constitute an "opportunity"; subjugation is empowering; and poverty-stricken, undeveloped areas are "historic homelands."

Here the South African government's approach to text is authoritarian (see White, 1990). Complex and ambiguous situations are glossed authoritatively in single words; difficult political decisions and situations are expressed as simple and straightforward. Problems are not even acknowledged; instead, declarative and assertive language is used to describe the setting as the government wishes it to be seen. This is very much a monologic voice; multiple voices and perspectives, indeed, questioning of any kind, are not permitted. Language expressing doubts or indexing controversies is not to be found.

A similar match between authoritative, unreasoned narrative and a crude appropriation of African land and rights is found in government treatment of history.

When one considers that the White [South African] community forms one of the oldest European nations outside Europe, it is indeed naive to regard

> it as a community of settlers.... According to generally accepted historical and demographic criteria, the whites exist as an integral part of the socio-political structure of the African continent. The Whites regard themselves as a permanently established African nation in a geopolitically clearly described fatherland. They link this claim with three historical realities: purposeful and uninterrupted residence and occupation; effective and sustained economic development; and effective political and administrative control within clearly demarcated boundaries. (RSA, 1973: 9)

There is nowhere any comparable story of the history of African groups in this text; it casually mentions that the African groups fell under "the political sphere of influence of the Whites during the 19th century" and that this occurred through a "unique combination" of events (ibid. 5). Other texts go further, asserting that indigenous South Africans were not actually indigenous: "For over a century the two races occupied various regions of the country without really coming into contact with one another" (RSA, 1976a: 1). The land Europeans occupied was simply empty before they arrived. Here again is a rhetoric that deals with controversy, ambiguity, or difficult ethical issues by erasing them, by leaving them out of the text. "According to generally accepted historical and demographic criteria," the writers assure us, whites have a strong claim to South African land. The text's authors attempt to represent a normative claim as objectively measurable; a deeply controversial issue has already been determined, the author tells us, by scientifically legitimated criteria. Subjective judgments become objectively determined; open questions are closed; difficult issues are not even acknowledged to be remotely problematic.

This is the deceptive, authoritative language in which indigenous South Africans were robbed of their rights to land and to political self-determination, at the same time losing their history. And a government that seeks to appease international public opinion through propaganda of this sort continues to paint an optimistic, positive view of the current situation, still failing to perceive that among the crimes of which it stands accused is depriving a people of their history.

American "Reservations"

The United States initially paid somewhat more attention to legal rationales and authoritative grounds for European claims to particular territories. The Europeans who settled North America relied on treaties with the indigenous people to a much greater extent than did the South African settlers, on the premise that the "aborigines" had rights to the land they occupied (Cohen, 1947; 1971). An influential legal thinker of the time, Franciscus de Victoria, established this principle:

the aborigines undoubtedly had true dominion in both public and private matters, just like Christians, and ... neither their princes nor private persons could be despoiled of their property on the ground of their not being true owners. (Quoted in Getches et al., 1979: 30)

These treaties are still the subject of litigation, and modern courts take quite seriously the obligation to ascertain the intent of the original parties. An early concern about the grounds on which property rights could be claimed was translated into a practice of land transfer that allowed Native Americans some redress for grievances in later times [see, e.g. *U.S. v. Washington*, 384 F. Supp. 312 (W.D. Wash. 1974), affd, 520 F.2d 676 (9th Cir. 1975), cert. denied, 423 U.S. 1086 (1976)]. This practice was also characterized by at least some recognition of Native American history, a recognition that continued in later judicial opinions on the subject.

The strongest similarities between the Native American and South African situations can be found in statutory law. It was through statutes such as the Indian Removal Act [25 U.S.C. §174 (1830)] that Native Americans were summarily stripped of rights to land and forced to relocate in ever-smaller areas to the west. A number of statutes affected the Native American population, including the Indian Removal Act of 1830, the General Allotment Act of 1887 [25 U.S.C. §331 (1970)], the Indian Reorganization Act of 1934 (25 U.S.C. §461), and the Indian Civil Rights Act of 1968 [25 U.S.C. §§132-33 (1970)]. These statutes, along with executive orders to remove indigenous Americans from their homes, destroyed Native American communities. They also played a role not only in reshaping patterns of land use and ownership but also in the decimation of the people themselves during the process of forced relocation. Despite early confrontations in which numerous indigenous South Africans were killed, the indigenous people of South Africa remained numerically strong; Native Americans, by contrast, were reduced to very small numbers at an early date. Thus, while indigenous Americans were allowed more claim to their history than were South Africans, the danger to a white majority in allowing this claim was considerably less when most of the indigenous people had been eliminated.

Whereas statutes were decisive in determining indigenous South African land entitlements, Native American entitlements also were shaped by judicial opinions, which relied not only on statutes but also on the Constitution, international law, and treaties. Here official interpretation broadened the application of the texts, allowing the interplay of history and land entitlements to emerge clearly in the case law. We turn now to one key string of cases in which the contemporary position of Native Americans was largely determined.

The Marshall Decisions

In the early nineteenth century, Chief Justice Marshall wrote a series of opinions clarifying the relationship between native Americans, the states, and the federal government. In one of the first cases, Marshall held that title to land conveyed by tribal chiefs was valid; to reach this holding, he had to uphold "the power of Indians to give, and of private individuals to receive" such a title [*Johnson v. McIntosh*, 21 U.S. (8 Wheat.) 543 (1823)]. The opinion is a fascinating historical account, woven with the aim of establishing a "middle" road between denying Native Americans any claim to the land and granting them absolute ownership (Cohen, 1947: 48). Here Marshall attempts to sort out the relative claims of prior possessors and discoverers.

> This principle [upon which the European explorers agreed] was, that discovery gave title to the government by whose subjects, or by whose authority, it was made, against all other European governments, which title might be consummated by possession....
>
> In the establishment [of relations between discoverers and natives], the rights of the original inhabitants were, in no instance, entirely disregarded.... They were admitted to be the rightful occupants of the soil, with a legal as well as just claim to retain possession of it ... but their rights to complete sovereignty, as independent nations, were necessarily diminished, and their power to dispose of the soil at their own will ... was denied by the original fundamental principle, that discovery gave exclusive title to those who made it. (21 U.S. 543, at 573–74)

Marshall's writing is not devoid of the kind of supremacist language found in the early South African texts; he speaks of the "discoverers'" right as accruing to any "Christian" people, "notwithstanding the occupancy of the natives, who were heathens"—and he describes the indigenous people as "fierce savages," in whose hands the country would remain an undeveloped "wilderness."

At the same time, in contrast with almost any official South African account, Marshall speaks with some sympathy of "the painful sense of being separated from their ancient connexions" that faced Native Americans, acknowledging their prior claim to the land and their deeply-rooted history there. In order to ease that pain and ensure that "the conquered shall not be wantonly oppressed," Marshall urges that their rights to property remain "unimpaired." By contrast with the South African narratives, Marshall does not hesitate to admit the dubious character of the European claim, "acquired and maintained by force." While still subscribing to a weak variety of the supremacist argument used in South Africa (Europeans can take over land because they are advanced Christians), Marshall balances this grant of authority with the concession that the original inhabitants retain possessory rights.

There is an isometry here between the historical narrative told in the text and the balancing of legal rights Marshall hopes to achieve: Marshall tells both the story of innocent original inhabitants robbed of their land by force and the tale of fierce warring savages destined never to rise out of the wilderness. He paints a picture of Christian people come to develop an orderly and peaceful society and of brutal conquerors who wrest the natives' ancestral home from them. Legally, he tells us of the rights of the conquerors yet stresses that the conquerors recognized the prior claim of indigenous North American peoples. Thus the history he forges yields the legal balance of rights to land with which the opinion concludes. This balancing carries through to even more minute aspects of the text's linguistic structure. The text is at every point balanced; Marshall never moves the reader very far in any direction without immediately providing a counterweight.

Eight years after the Johnson case, Marshall again addressed the problem of indigenous peoples' rights to land. The cases arose under explosive political circumstances, which questioned the relative power of the states and the federal government, judiciary and executive. In the first of these, the Cherokees brought an original action in the Supreme Court, asking for injunctive relief against Georgia, which had passed statutes that sought to "annihilate the Cherokees as a political society, and to seize, for [its own use] the lands of the nation" [*Cherokee Nation v. Georgia*, 30 U.S. (5 Pet.) 1, 15 (1831)].

Marshall's opinion attempts a balance similar to that in the *Johnson* case; it is a complicated narrative replete with double-voicing, in which the apparent meaning of the text is undercut by a second "voice" or undertone and by other subtle cues undermining the ostensible message. Marshall actually holds against the Cherokee, on the basis that the Court lacks jurisdiction to hear the case. And yet, in classic Marshallian fashion, this holding is undermined by dicta that recognized Cherokee possessory rights and imposed a fiduciary standard on the government.

As in the Johnson opinion, Marshall's rhetoric in *Cherokee Nation*, and his appeal to history, mirror the opinion's legal impact, which appears to defer to the state at the same time as it dictates policy. Thus his initial discussion begins, "If courts were permitted to indulge their sympathies, a case better calculated to excite them can scarcely be imagined" (30 U.S. 1, at 15). He proceeds to describe the gradual downfall of Native Americans, who had once been "numerous, powerful, and truly independent" but who had gradually lost more and more land "by successive treaties, each of which contains a solemn guarantee of the residue" (ibid.). Marshall follows this emotional passage with a terse paragraph: "Before we can look into the merits of the case, a preliminary inquiry presents itself. Has this court jurisdiction of the cause?" Here we see Marshall removing himself as an agent as he moves to consider the technical procedural issue on which he hangs his decision. Again he contrasts a subjective and emotional state—indulging in sympathy—to which he as human actor might be drawn, with the objective and removed courts that must operate free of emotion. The distasteful outcome of the case is not Marshall's choice; he is merely addressing the unpleasant but necessary questions that "present themselves." Marshall does not present himself as an actor in the system shaping results; instead, he highlights the conflict of roles—human person with emotional reactions, legal persona following the dictates of law—as he in effect disowns responsibility for the legal outcome. This disaffiliation heightens the dual message sent by the opinion to Georgia: that he does not fully endorse the outcome he reaches cannot help but weaken the opinion's force.

The following year, Marshall brings to fruition the seed sown in the *Cherokee Nation* dictum, insisting that under treaties made with the Cherokees the United States had "assum[ed] the duty of protection" hinted at in his use of the guardian-ward metaphor in the earlier case *[Worcester v. Georgia*, 31 U.S. (6 Pet.) 515, 556 (1832)]. This time the challenge to the Georgia statutes came from two missionaries arrested in Cherokee territory for violating Georgia law. Marshall proceeds to sift through history, the law of nations, and the Constitution, to reach the conclusion that the statutes were unconstitutional. He uses an historical story to support his holding that tribes are to be viewed as independent entities with special status.

The Indian nations had always been considered as distinct, independent political communities, retaining their original natural rights, as the undisputed possessors of the soil, from time immemorial, with the single exception of that imposed by irresistible power.... (31 U.S. 515, at 559)

As in all of these key decisions, Marshall does not hesitate to give full recognition to Native Americans' prior claim to the land—to their history.

This provides a contrast with the South African case, in which prior possession and legitimate claim to land are denied along with indigenous history. Marshall writes a rueful history that insists on the conquerors' rights while at the same time admitting and giving some legal force to indigenous peoples' history and claims to land. Marshall was unable to stop the removal of the Cherokees from their land, because in the end all he had done was to reserve to the federal government the right to accomplish the decimation attempted by the state of Georgia. But in insisting on some measure of sovereign rights to land for Native Americans, and on a trust relationship between them and the federal government, Marshall set the stage for later Native American court victories.

Nonetheless, it should be stressed again that although there is a more overt recognition of history in later United States legal texts than can be found in the "official" South Africa story, there are a number of similarities. For example, early American settlers had their own version of the South African "empty lands" story, as in John Winthrop's contention that "almost all of the land in North America was vacuum domicilium because the Indians had not used it for agriculture" (Fredrickson, 1981: 35). This argument became a key rationale for dispossessing Native

Americans of their land, although dispossession of the coastal groups to which Fredrickson refers was accomplished "through legitimate purchase, fraud, treaties in which coercion was often involved, and land settlements resulting from wars" rather than through outright statutory seizure (ibid.). Thus even where there was an attempt to generate a story such as the one that has dominated South African accounts, North American settlers conceded prior presence in the area. This concession, however, did not stop the decimation of the indigenous population in North America nor the process by which Native Americans were robbed of their land.

Removal and the Statutory History

The American statutory framework for dealing with Indian lands offers some interesting parallels with early South African statutes. For example, just as early South African statutes ostensibly aimed at protecting indigenous people, so a United States statute passed in 1790 forbade the purchase of Indian land except by government treaty (1 Stat. 137, 25 U.S.C. §177) .

Under the infamous Indian Removal Act [4 Stat. 411, 25 U.S.C. §174 (1830)], President Andrew Jackson authorized the removal of many Southeast Native Americans, whose trek west became known as the "Trail of Tears" (cf. McNickle, 1975). Like the South African Native Land Act, this statute confined indigenous peoples' rights to land to a limited geographic area, which was progressively contracted. The laws authorizing these changes were not challenged in court, so that by the time the Supreme Court again dealt with indigenous peoples' property rights, a drastic change had occurred (Chambers, 1975: 1218). The concern with indigenous history and land rights initially evinced by the courts had little effect on the crucial process by which land was fundamentally reallocated and taken away from Native Americans. As in South Africa, the actual deprivation of land was accomplished through curt, declarative statutory language, which paid little heed to these concerns.

However, the broad outlines of subsequent American statutory development diverge from those in South Africa. In the late 1880s Congress passed the General Allotment Act [ch. 119 §1, 24 Stat. 228, as amended at 25 U.S.C. §331 (1970)], whose goal was to encourage assimilation by permitting individual Indian ownership of parcels of reservation land that had previously been communally owned by the tribe. A number of tribes objected to the allotment scheme because it undermined tribal integrity. The assimilationist policy was reversed in the Indian Reorganization Act of 1934 (25 U.S.C. §461), which returned power over Indian reservation land to the tribes and forbade its alienation. Where a move toward a more separatist homelands policy in South Africa had negative effects on the black majority, here a retreat from assimilationist policies was viewed for the most part as empowering for Native Americans (cf. *Michigan Law Review,* 1972). This is not surprising, given that the white majority in the United States could assimilate the Native American population without a significant loss of political or economic power, whereas the white minority of South Africa could not.

The statutory framework, then, granted little importance to indigenous peoples' history or claims to land until the 1930s. The case-law framework developed somewhat differently.

Of Treaties and Rights to Land

A number of recent cases have dealt with the problem of interpreting treaties that determine rights to land. If history has always played a major role in judicial decisions regarding Native Americans, it is in the treaty decisions that this role becomes most decisive. The courts committed themselves to a reading that construes treaties "in the sense in which the Indians understood them and 'in a spirit which generously recognizes the full obligation of this nation to protect the interests of a dependent people'" [*Choctaw Nation v. United States*, 318 U.S. 423, 432 (1942)]. As Charles Miller notes (1969: 24):

> This generous recognition of the full obligation to protect the interests of a dependent nation may sound strange, condescending, or even hypocritical in the face of the military force, political expediency, and social neglect which have bulked large in the history of the white man's relations with the Indians. But it has been white man's law that has provided the chief source of security for the Indians, and beyond an appeal to conscience and legal documents the best evidence in most Indian cases is the testimony of history, especially the use, possession, practices, and expectations concerning the lands.

Native Americans have won a number of encouraging court battles over treaty rights, turning the "white man's" ideology of history to their advantage.

The carefully crafted language of the Marshall opinions had great significance for later interpretations of treaties in court decisions. Building from the Marshallian notion that the federal government stood in a trust relation with Native Americans, later decisions showed considerable deference in interpreting the language of treaties.

> The unequal bargaining position of the tribes and the recognition of the trust relationship have led to the development of canons of construction designed to rectify the inequality.... Three primary rules have been developed: ambiguous expressions must be resolved in favor of the Indian parties concerned; Indian treaties must be interpreted as the Indians themselves

would have understood them; and Indian treaties must be liberally construed in favor of the Indians. (Wilkinson & Volkman, 1975: 617)

In the opinions following these canons, the use of history emerges full-blown, with much of the text of the opinion constituting a story of the history of the tribe and treaty in question. The telling of this story is a charter for the interpretation to be accomplished in the opinion; from the history will flow the result. Although the victories thus won may pale by comparison with past injustice, they also contrast with South African attempts to deny history altogether.

A number of early decisions established the canons described by Wilkinson and Volkman, although it should be noted that treaties have not always been accorded this measure of respect [cf. *Lone Wolf v. Hitchcock*, 187 U.S. 553 (1903); *Seneca Nation of Indians v. Brocker*, 262 F.2d 27 (1959)]. However, liberal canons of construction have remained critical through recent decisions, maintaining the approach indicated by Marshall and early treaty-construction cases (cf. Chambers, 1975). In two such early cases, the Supreme Court established the "reserved rights" doctrine, under which all rights not explicitly surrendered by treaties were reserved to the tribes [*United States v. Winans*, 198 U.S. 371 (1905); *Winters v. United States*, 207 U.S. 564 (1908)]. In *Winans* the Court explains why an examination of historical circumstances is to be crucial in construing treaties.

> [W]e will construe a treaty ... as "that unlettered people" understood it, and "as justice and reason demand in all cases where power is exerted by the strong over those to whom they owe care and protection," and counterpoise the inequality "by the superior justice which looks only to the substance of the right without regard to technical rules." How the treaty in question was understood may be gathered from the circumstances. (198 U.S. 371, at 380–81)

The opinion proceeds to develop the "reserved rights" doctrine through an analysis of the historical circumstances surrounding the treaty-making. The history was used to establish intent, and the treaty was then construed to give effect to that intent. From Marshall's earlier insistence on a trust relationship comes a doctrine for interpreting the language of treaties, a linguistic canon of deference to the protected people; careful consideration of their history is to guide such deference.

One of the most famous American decisions is *United States v. Washington* [384 F. Supp. 312 (W.D. Wash. 1974), aff'd, 520 F.2d 676 (9th Cir. 1975), cert. denied, 423 U.S. 1086 (1976)]. In this case, Judge Boldt took as his task the interpretation of treaties whose terms read: "The right of taking fish, at all usual and accustomed grounds and stations, is further secured to said Indians, in common with all citizens of the Territory...." (384 F. Supp. 312, 356). The decision turned on the meaning of the terms "in common with," which the state contended simply indicated that Native American fisherfolk were subject to the same regulations as any other citizens.

Judge Boldt engaged in a painstaking review of the settlement patterns and indigenous culture at the time of the treaties, dealing at length with the significance of salmon in the economic and religious life of the tribes. He also carefully examined the treaty-making process, in an effort to clarify how the Indians themselves would have understood the agreement achieved. A particularly crucial consideration was the way in which treaty terms could have been translated into indigenous languages.

> Since ... the vast majority of Indians at the treaty councils did not speak or understand English, the treaty provisions ... were interpreted ... to the Indians in the Chinook jargon and then translated into native languages by Indian interpreters.... There is no record of the Chinook jargon phrase that was actually used in the treaty negotiations to interpret the provision.... A dictionary of the Chinook jargon ... indicates that the jargon contains no words or expressions that would describe any limiting interpretation on the right of taking fish. (384 F. Supp. 312, 356)

The judge then looked to English language dictionaries of the time for an understanding of the words as English-speakers would have used them.

> By dictionary definition and as intended and used in the Indian treaties and in this decision "in common with" means sharing equally the opportunity to take fish at "usual and accustomed grounds and stations"; therefore, nontreaty fishermen shall have the opportunity to take up to 50% of the harvestable number of fish that may be taken by all fishermen at usual and accustomed grounds and ... treaty right fishermen shall have the opportunity to take up to the same percentage of harvestable fish. (384 F. Supp. 312, 342)

In the story of an indigenous people's past cultural understanding and language lies the key to current property rights; the semantics of treaty language, viewed through the filter of a linguistic and cultural history, are translated directly into current power. The linguistic history tells us that "equality" was envisioned; thus 50 percent of the fish belong to descendants of the treaty-makers.

History has emerged as the template for legal rights, and the telling of the historical tale constitutes a legal rationale with direct consequences for power over property. The resulting decision was hailed as an encouraging success by Native Americans (see Cohen, 1986: 177–78). Much the same interpretive process can be seen in other decisions that resolved contests over land and resources by careful analysis of treaty terms in historical context [see, e.g., *State v. Tinno*, 94 Idaho 759,

497 P.2d 1386 (1972)]. In constructing linguistic histories, the courts have given treaties expansive readings. And in retelling and confirming indigenous histories, they have restored control over resources and land. Here history, language, and legal rights flow together, at once recognized and reconfirmed in one another.

Conclusion

There are certainly similarities between the two cases. Both the United States and South Africa established limited geographical areas for indigenous populations. Both used history to guide their policies regarding those populations. However, there are also differences in their uses of history. The South African government, from earliest settlement, managed indigenous people by denying them their history and rights in land. The United States conducted a policy of removal and genocide as it established the reservation system; however, it also gave some weight to Native Americans' prior occupation and history in legal narratives, an admission that endowed indigenous people with limited legal power to determine the fate of their land in later years.

Scholars have noted that, although the United States has accorded legal protection to indigenous peoples and African Americans, white Americans have little claim to moral superiority over white South Africans; the European population in North America has not since its earliest history faced the demographic odds confronting whites in South Africa. Fredrickson contrasts the two histories (1981: 246–47):

> Assume for a moment that the American Indian population had not been decimated and that the number of European colonists and immigrants had been much less than was actually the case—creating a situation where the Indians, although conquered, remained a substantial majority of the total population of the United States. After the whites had seized the regions with the most fertile land and exploitable resources, the indigenes were consigned to a fraction of their original domain. All one has to envision here are greatly enlarged versions of the current Indian reservations. Then suppose further that Indians were denied citizenship rights in the rest of the country but nevertheless constituted the main labor force.

Fredrickson hypothesizes that under these circumstances, measures such as those taken in South Africa would become necessary for the white minority to retain control. In such a situation, the shift away from acculturationist policies toward recognition of tribal autonomy, which occurred in the United States during the 1930s, might take on much more sinister dimensions.

Although the surviving Native Americans arguably have greater political power than indigenous people in South Africa because they can vote, their current socioeconomic position does not approach equality with that of American whites (see Rosen, 1978: 1–2), and they have become such a small percentage of the population that their aggregate political power is minimal. Their current minority status reflects a history of genocide in the United States, which demonstrates anything but respect for indigenous people. Indeed, indigenous people in America may have kept their history—in an attenuated form—precisely because a large number of them were denied their future.

Thus, while differences in ideology have important consequences in both countries, we must note that whether by treaty, statute, or war, indigenous peoples in both lands were dispossessed and relocated, in a relentless process that eliminated rich cultures and histories. The government-created history of South African laws and treatises extols the virtues of the homelands policy, creating a fictional past in which people are given roots in homes they have never seen. Although the ideologies differ, history served a similar end in both cases. That the dispossession may have been viewed in other ways, that it decimated one people and left the other enslaved, are differences that cannot obscure a shared history of oppression.

Ideology, then, is not distinct from economic and social change; "ideas" do not have any priority in shaping social change. Rather, the history in legal discourse forms a social ideology that is an integral part of ongoing economic and social restructuring. In its appropriation of history, legal language is at once a conceptual framework and a powerful social praxis that maps and expresses a social "taking" of the most tangible sort, for in the history lie rights to land. Yet, in granting a people their history, law also limits such "takings." This limit is at once in language and in social practice.

DISCUSSION QUESTIONS

1. How does Mertz use the concept "ideology"? If legal language is one constituent of social ideology, what are others? How do these ingredients differ? What are the varied contexts in which law constructs social ideology? How do these differ between the United States and South Africa? What are the similarities and differences in the ways in which those two countries have treated indigenous peoples?

2. What is the relationship between ideology and audience? Who are the audiences for legal ideology? Why does history play so central a role in ideology? What is the relation between versions of history and legal entitlements? Why did the versions of history change over time? What are the various ways in which law justifies state power?

3.   What difference does it make that the South African Parliament was supreme, whereas American courts review the legality of legislative and executive actions? Which system is more protective of the rights of subordinated peoples? How do American judicial decisions use history to justify and shape their conclusions? How do judges present outcomes they find distasteful? Did Marshall's more nuanced view of history protect Native American land rights in the end? Did Native Americans have more to say about the content of their treaties with whites than Africans did about the content of the white government that ruled them?

4.   What other legal policies are justified by reference to history? How do people gain control over their own history?

18

Lay Expectations of the Civil Justice System

William M. O'Barr and John M. Conley

Background and Purpose

In their landmark study of procedural justice, Thibaut and Walker (1975) argued that the process used in resolving a dispute strongly influences the disputants' level of satisfaction with the resolution. In a series of laboratory experiments, they showed that disputants' judgments about procedural fairness have an effect on the satisfaction that transcends the outcome of disputes or the likelihood that particular procedures will be advantageous to individual disputants. Their work ultimately led many researchers concerned with fairness and consumer satisfaction to reevaluate the traditional focus on the fairness of outcomes ("distributive fairness") and concentrate instead on the significance of procedure.

Thibaut and Walker's theory of procedural justice has spawned a large and growing literature. A number of researchers have confirmed the basic procedural justice hypothesis with studies of such diverse subjects as criminal defendants, parties to alternative dispute resolution proceedings (Adler et al., 1983), citizens dealing with the police (Tyler & Folger, 1980), citizens evaluating the government benefits they receive against the taxes they pay (Tyler & Caine, 1981; Tyler et al., 1985b), and workers evaluating their employers' decision-making procedures (e.g., Alexander & Ruderman, 1989). Much current procedural justice research focuses on why procedural fairness is so important. Thibaut and Walker originally hypothesized that litigants prefer adversary procedures to inquisitorial ones because the former allow the litigants to maintain control over the process of presenting evidence. They later argued (1978) that such process control is important to litigants because they see it as promoting equitable, if not necessarily favorable, outcomes. Subsequent researchers have suggested that litigants value process control because they view it as either a means of controlling outcome (Brett & Goldberg, 1983) or a guarantee of the opportunity for self-expression (Tyler et al., 1985a). More recent work has concerned itself with the psychological processes that occasion preference for one procedure over another.

Abridged from *Law & Society Review*, Volume 22:137 (1988).

Both the work of Thibaut and Walker and the diverse research it has inspired share the goal of theoretical development through laboratory experimentation designed to explicate structural and/or psychological determinants of litigants' preferences. We have been greatly influenced by this body of work, but our disciplinary background leads us to ask somewhat different questions about procedural justice and the contexts in which it works. As anthropologists we ask about the ethnographic reality of process concerns for everyday litigants who encounter the civil justice system in practical as opposed to laboratory situations. We would have perhaps never formulated such questions without the stimulus of the insights that have come from laboratory research on procedural justice. In turn, we hope that an ethnographic understanding of lay expectations and concerns will make its way into the experimental research effort.

In addition to its relation to the study of procedural justice, the investigation of litigant perceptions of justice is significant in its own right, because it offers an opportunity to understand the theories of law that litigants themselves hold. Felstiner and Sarat (1986) have demonstrated that the examination of the dialogue between lawyers and their clients in divorce cases can reveal the theories that lawyers use to transform their clients' problems into legally sufficient claims that articulate with the law. Our investigation of the talk of small claims litigants reveals an equally interesting set of insights into the legal process, since the theories of both legal professionals and lay persons interact in the functioning of the legal system.

We interviewed small claims plaintiffs before and after the trial of their cases. Despite the diversity of the plaintiffs' backgrounds and claims, three themes run consistently through their comments. First, litigants are deeply concerned with legal process. By contrast, they seem to have little concern with substance. They tend to view the facts at issue as straightforward and assume that they will be readily understood by the court.

Second, litigants fail to appreciate the purely adversarial nature of civil litigation. In reality, civil litigants (with the aid of a lawyer in more formal courts) must conceive their own case, assemble their own evidence, find and prepare their own witnesses, and present their own case in court, with a passive judicial system providing little assistance. The criminal justice system, by contrast, has an important inquisitorial component: A victim or complaining witness goes to the police, who investigate; if a defendant is charged, the prosecution is in the hands of the authorities, with the victim often acting as a passive observer. As the texts we analyze indicate, many of the litigants in our study come to civil court with a model of procedure more appropriate to the criminal justice system. Moreover, at this point in the process most litigants have little or no awareness that they will encounter—and thus be required to overcome—another substantially different perspective or version of their case.

The third pervasive theme is the misapprehension of the remedial authority of the civil courts. The civil system can compensate but rarely punishes, whereas the criminal system punishes but rarely compensates. Thus, the civil system has no practical authority over an impecunious defendant. Our data indicate, however, that this basic distinction is lost on many litigants, some of whom base their very decision to go to small claims court on an overestimation of the remedial power of civil courts.

Data and Analysis

We will present five of the 45 cases we studied to determine what they show about lay perceptions of law and legal procedure. For each case, we present a summary of the facts and include relevant excerpts from the interviews.

Case 1: "$100 Worth of Drunk." The plaintiff, Edward Atkin, is a businessman in his twenties. He owns a large motorcycle, which was parked at the curb outside his house on the night in question. The defendant is an otherwise unidentified woman. Atkin was awakened late at night by his neighbor, who told him that a woman had just "dumped" the motorcycle. According to the neighbor's account, which was based largely on reconstruction and inference, a battered and obviously drunk woman appeared at his door looking for help in finding her own motorcycle. She apparently had just fallen off her bike, which skidded off down the street while she tumbled away in the opposite direction. The neighbor looked up and down the street, and the only motorcycle he saw was Atkin's, which he pointed out to the woman. The neighbor then either saw or heard Atkin's bike fall, and went to his house to tell him. When Atkin went out into the street, the woman was gone, but her bike was lying in the street. Apparently assuming that she would return in the morning, he went back to bed.

The next morning, Atkin waited for the woman for some time and then called the police to report the accident. His understanding was that the police then "picked her up." In any event, some time thereafter she came to his house to discuss the accident. The details are unclear, but it appears that Atkin took the bike to a repair shop. An initial assessment revealed that the forks were bent, in addition to minor damage to the blinkers and gas tank. The repair estimate for the forks alone was $100, and the woman paid Atkin that amount. According to Atkin, she gave him a receipt for that amount (perhaps she tendered a receipt that he signed and returned). However, while repairing the forks, the shop discovered more extensive structural damage, which would cost several hundred dollars to repair. At this point, the woman—with whom Atkin apparently was in regular communication—balked. Her "attitude," according to Atkin, was that she "couldn't have been more than $100 worth of drunk." When she refused to accept responsibility for the additional damage, Atkin sued, seeking the cost of the repairs to the frame as well as the cost of fixing the blinkers and gas tank, which he had been prepared to forget at the time of the $100 agreement. On the trial date, he went to court with his wife and three witnesses—his neighbor, a mechanic, and a friend who could testify about the bike's condition. The woman did not appear. In a five-minute proceeding, he and the friend testified, and the judge gave him a default judgment. Later, the woman applied to the court for relief from the default judgment. Atkin had to appear at another hearing, at which the judge confirmed the original judgment. When interviewed after the trial, Atkin was in the process of collecting the judgment by garnishing the woman's paycheck.

Edward Atkin is a middle-class businessman. Additionally, he has had experience with small claims court. On one prior occasion, he filed a complaint, the sheriff served the papers, and the defendant accepted responsibility and settled. Atkin's conduct during the present dispute and his interview comments suggest that his background and this previous small claims experience have led him to a reasonably accurate understanding of the civil justice system.

Consider first his conduct. After hearing the story of the drunken woman from his neighbor, his immediate objective was to "talk to her and see if she wanted to settle everything out of court." Toward this end, he left a note on her abandoned bike and waited on his front porch the next morning to see if she would appear. His first thought was compensation, a civil remedy; appropriately, he did not call the police but waited to see if a settlement were possible.

When the woman did not appear, he finally called the police. He believes (the source of his belief is unclear) that "the police went to her house, picked her up, and cited her for reckless driving." In any event, about a month later she finally appeared, and the parties began negotiating. The negotiations broke down over the extent of the damage for which the woman would assume responsibility, and Atkin filed a small claims action. Significantly, throughout the negotiation, he never spoke to the police—indeed, when the interviewer raised the topic, he responded that he might call them the next day, since he had not spoken with them for months. The most obvious interpretation of this course of conduct is that his objective was compensation rather than punishment and that he understands that one can achieve compensation through either direct negotiation or the civil justice system. Accordingly, he used the police for the limited purpose of flushing out the wrongdoer and then dealt with her himself. When he was unable to achieve his objective, he went not to the police but to the civil courts.

Atkin's conduct also reflects a general understanding of the burden placed on him by the adversarial system. On the trial date, he appeared in court with three witnesses and "all these receipts and all my stuff." After he obtained a default judgment, he took the initiative and garnished the woman's paycheck.

Atkin's stated understanding of the nature of civil justice is consistent with his conduct. After dismissing (perhaps erroneously) the idea of pursuing the woman's insurance company, he describes clearly the alternatives of instigating a criminal prosecution and seeking a civil remedy. (Except where otherwise noted, the texts are drawn from pretrial interviews; Q and Q2 refer to the male and female interviewers.)

Q2:	Does she have insurance that would cover it?
Q:	What about um...?
Atkin:	What kind of insurance?
Q2:	Well, don't for bikes you have to have something like—insurance?
Atkin:	Well, she didn't really hit it with her bike though.
Q2:	Oh, I see.
Atkin:	See, she got off it.
Q2:	That's right, yeah, that makes sense.
Atkin:	She got off. It's, it's, it's, uh...
Q:	I'd try and make a claim. [In a joking manner:] I'd, I'd roll the other bike under it, you know. I'd...
All:	[laughter]
Atkin:	No, but all I could do, you know, is cite her for, uh, destruction of personal property...
Q:	Yeah.
Q2:	Yeah.
Atkin:	...and, what I'm doing now.
Q2:	Yeah.

On the basis of this evidence, one might well conclude that Atkin has a thorough and accurate understanding of the role of the civil justice system. One might further conclude that his understanding is quite predictable, given his business background and prior legal experience. There is additional evidence, however, suggesting that the proper interpretation is somewhat more complicated. Near the end of the pretrial interview, he talks about his plans for trying the case.

Q:	Do you have it mapped out, have you practiced in front of the mirror, you know, how you're gonna handle the court case, or, you know, pictures and drawings or [laughter]?
Atkin:	Well, no.
Q:	Today we saw one [a case] with a diagram and a model truck...
Atkin:	[laughter] Did you?
Q:	...demonstrating how an accident could not have possibly happened.
Atkin:	[laughter] No, well, I don't. I don't, you know. I'm not totally unprepared, but I haven't rehearsed either. You know I've got uh, I'm gonna have my neighbor come in.
Q2:	Uh huh.
Atkin:	And he can tell his story. Uh, I'm gonna have the mechanic come in; he can tell his story. You know, can this actually happen by a bike being tipped over. He can tell them that it can happen.

Q2:	Right.
Atkin:	Which obvious—, obviously it can happen.
Q2:	Did he know your bike before? I mean...
Atkin:	No, I've got a friend, that's the best I can do as far as that goes, I've got a friend coming in that, uh, knows the bike was in min—, mint condition.
Q2:	Right.
Atkin:	So I don't know what more I can do, much else I can do, you know.
Q:	Yeah.
Q2:	If you get that, that's, you know, that's a lot.
Atkin:	And then I'll just ask, answer the referee's questions or judge's questions or whatever.
Q:	Yeah.
Atkin:	I dunno. What can I rehearse?

These remarks suggest that in spite of his background and experience, Atkin has brought to this case some mistaken assumptions about the burden the civil justice system will place on him to produce evidence and prove facts. With the trial a week away, he has not prepared his own testimony, relying instead on an anticipated interrogation by the judge to elicit the facts—a rare occurrence in the small claims courts we have observed. Moreover, he seems not to consider seriously the possibility that the defendant will present a vigorous case of her own, saying, "I don't see how I can go wrong unless she does skip town." (There are in fact a number of plausible defenses she might have presented, including denying that her actions caused the damage to the bike and contending that their $100 arrangement was a final settlement.) Additionally, the interviewers met the neighbor shortly after talking to Atkin and learned that he had not yet contacted this critical witness to insure his appearance and confirm the content of his testimony. Thus, even this relatively sophisticated litigant seems to view the civil court as more active and inquisitorial than it is in reality and to underestimate his own role in prosecuting his case. We cannot assess the effect of this misunderstanding since Atkin won his case by default.

Case 2: "The Thirteen-Hour Day." The plaintiff, Harvey Johnson, is a middle-aged man. The defendant owns a lawn care business. Johnson agreed to work for the defendant cutting lawns. The defendant agreed to pay him $35 per day, which Johnson assumed referred to an eight-hour work day. The first day, the defendant picked him up early in the morning, drove him from house to house, and brought him home at the end of a thirteen-hour day. He paid Johnson $35. The next day, they started early in the morning and worked nine hours. At that point, Johnson said he refused to work until eight at night again, and the man responded, "We're gonna be here as late as we were yesterday." Johnson quit on the spot and demanded to be paid for his hours, but the defendant refused. Johnson took the bus home from the house where they were working.

Johnson then went to the State Labor Board. According to Johnson, they advised him that he was entitled to be paid an hourly wage for all the time he had worked, with time-and-a-half for any hours in excess of eight in a given day. They also told him that they could not collect his money for him, so he should go to small claims court. In filing his suit, he has made detailed calculations of the amount owed him. He began by dividing eight into $35 to get an hourly rate of $4.38. He is claiming two eight-hour days at this rate, plus six hours overtime (five the first day, one the second) at time-and-a-half, for a total of $111.62 (the arithmetic appears to be off by about a dollar). The court records show that Johnson was unable to get service and dropped the case. We were unable to locate him for a post-trial interview.

The evidence from Case 2 is quite different from what we observed in Case 1. The plaintiff, Johnson, seems to have a profound misunderstanding of the adversarial nature of civil justice and to have experienced dissatisfaction from the very first time the system frustrated his expectations. As the interview progresses, he reveals that his expectations may be derived from his previous dealings with the law. The different legal experiences of Johnson and Edward Atkin, the plaintiff in Case 1, may explain the different attitudes and expectations that they bring to small claims court.

As Johnson states below, he has brought the case because of a failure on the part of "the state," which "couldn't catch up with" the defendant and told Johnson to try small claims court. In so doing, the State Labor Board was effectively admitting that its inquisitorial undertaking had failed and suggesting that Johnson try his luck with the adversarial system.

> Johnson: I went by and asked him for my money a few days later. He said that he didn't owe me anything. So, I've been watching uh, Judge Wapner.
>
> Q: [laughter]
>
> Johnson: He said, "If you have a case..."
>
> Q: "The People's Court?"
>
> Johnson: Yeah, "People's Court." And uh, so I decided to bring him to court. Well, I took him to the state but the state can't catch up with him. He keeps his equipment in one place and he lives in another place.
>
> Q: Uh huh.
>
> Johnson: And it's hard to catch up, the state couldn't catch up with him 'cause they told me to bring it to sm—, small claims court. But the problem that I think I'm going to have is serving the papers, serving him.

Although he had learned something about small claims court from watching "The People's Court" on television, Johnson was unpleasantly surprised by the litigant-driven, adversarial process he confronted. In particular, his responsibility for serving the summons on the elusive defendant runs contrary to his view of how "the law" should function.

> Johnson: And, well, I probably know several guys that I could get to go around and just catch him, and give him the papers, but, uh, it's all left up to me.
> Q: Right.
> Johnson: And um, I thought the law was supposed to be, you know, if you have a case against someone, hey, I think the law, the deputy sheriff should be able anytime up until midnight, anytime, to serve papers.

The reason for Johnson's dissatisfaction with the passive system is itself interesting. As he acknowledges, he knows "several guys" who might be able to find the defendant. Nonetheless, he states below that he is reluctant to see the defendant until the court date, for he wants their ultimate confrontation to be mediated by the state.

> Johnson: I'll just have to get someone early in the morning or late at night and just wait on him...
> Q: Yeah.
> Johnson: ... to serve the papers. That's the problem, that's the thing I don't like. See, I don't want, I don't want—he knows what I'm doing to him. See, I don't want to have the, I, I don't want to be seeing him until court.

In the next text Johnson discloses the source of his reluctance to confront the defendant—his bad feelings toward him—and makes the point that this is the only grievance he has thus far with the small claims process.

> Johnson: And I, I don't, I don't, that's, the only thing that I don't like about the courts to start with, is serving him the papers.
> Q: Have you ever uh....
> Johnson: See, I don't, I don't feel good towards him at all.

In some respects, Johnson's expectations reflect a model of the small claims process that would be more appropriate for the criminal system. He believes that "the law" should seek out and serve the defendant while the plaintiff remains anonymously in the background until the trial. Later in the interview, he suggests the source of these expectations.

Q: Have you ever uh, you know, gone to a court before like that?
Johnson: No, not to claims, not to small claims, not suing anybody.
Q: Uh huh.
Johnson: When I've ever been to court, I've always been behind the gun in the courtroom, DUIs, disturbing, and things like that, I've always been behind the gun.

Thus, even though Johnson has been influenced to some extent by "The People's Court," his only previous personal experience with the legal system has been as a criminal defendant. He has probably seen the active, inquisitorial arm of "the law" at work. He expects the same when he is the complaining party and is dissatisfied with the civil justice system when it fails to perform up to his expectations. Since Johnson was ultimately forced to drop his case because of a feature of the system he has specifically complained about (lack of assistance in serving process), it is regrettable that we were unable to question him again about his reactions. Had his case gone to trial, it also would have been interesting to see whether he experienced similar dissatisfaction with such other manifestations of the adversarial system as the burden to produce evidence and to present an affirmative case.

Case 3: "Harassment at the Grocery Store." Plaintiff Lorna Terry, a young woman, sued the owner of a grocery store where she had worked for several days. The owner fired her (this is Terry's version—she said that the owner claims that she quit) and then refused to give her a paycheck. She went to the Colorado Labor Board, where she obtained a "demand notice" calling on the owner to pay her immediately or face a penalty of ten extra days' pay. She served a copy of the notice on the owner, but he still refused to pay her. On the advice of the Labor Board, she filed suit for the overdue pay plus the penalty. Late in the pretrial interview, Terry volunteered that "there's more to this story than what I'm tellin' you, it's a lot more." She then mentioned unspecified "harassments" as well as problems with bill collectors in the store. She believed that the store was on the verge of bankruptcy, even though the owner had money in other companies. She was confident that she would get paid, however, since her claim was "registered in the court already." Terry appeared for the trial with her father and her friend Charles, but the defendant did not show up. After a brief informal discussion with the judge, she was awarded a default judgment for $43.85, which she understands to represent ten percent of the amount she claimed. In a posttrial interview, she expressed complete satisfaction with the outcome and the small claims process.

Lorna Terry, the plaintiff, has no apparent prior experience with the law. Nonetheless, she has some accurate ideas about the legal system. For example, she is aware of the principle that a judgment gives its holder priority over many other creditors if the defendant goes bankrupt.

> Terry: If he goes bankrupt, I'm still gettin' mine. 'Cause I have mine's registered in court, already. Either way he goes, I'm gettin' mine's. Now I, I feel for the people that's still workin' for him and then try to file after he bankrupts. They don't get nothin'.

Like many other litigants, however, she attributes to the civil court far more power than it actually has. In the next text she considers the question of what will happen if the defendant fails to appear for trial:

> Q: I'll be interested to see what that guy's gonna say if he shows up.
> Terry: Oh, he, he, no he's gonna show up. Like [the clerk] told me, he's got to show up....
> Q: Uh huh.
> Q2: ... if he's served, he's got to show up.
> Q: Uh huh.
> Q2: And if he doesn't, like....
>   [inaudible]
> Terry: ... if he doesn't, better, okay, I will win like this [indicating paper] says.
> Charles: We'll have a warrant out for his arrest if he doesn't show up.
> Q2: Well, you can just get the money, I guess, you know.
> Terry: Okay, it says, "If you do not appear justi—," um, excuse me. "If you do not appear judgment will be made against you for the amount of the plaintiff's claim plus costs of this suit."

In Terry's view, "he's got to show up"; if he does not, she claims two consequences will ensue. First, perhaps informed by the summons that she later quotes, she concludes that "I will win...." Second, according to her companion, the defendant will find "a warrant out for his arrest." The first point is accurate in the limited sense that the court will issue a default judgment—a piece of paper—against an absent defendant. The second point is patently inaccurate, of course, which suggests that Terry did not mean "win" in the limited technical sense but had something more final and meaningful in mind. It is tempting to speculate that her slip in reading from the summons form ("If you do not appear justi—") is more than inadvertent and in fact reflects her view of the court's authority.

The evidence in the next text (from the pretrial interview) is consistent with this interpretation. Here Terry expresses her belief that if the defendant fails to appear for trial, "the government" will compensate her, and the defendant will be left to deal with the government—surely something he will want to avoid:

Terry: Yeah, and then he don't want the government to pay me 'cause he has to pay the government and if he pay the government, he's through. When he don't pay the government, he's through.

Once again, her view seems to be that the civil justice system is an omnipotent, self-directed authority which will recognize the justice of her cause and do whatever is necessary to protect her position.

In an objective sense, the court failed to meet Terry's expectations when it awarded her only $43.85. However, she made it clear in the posttrial interview that she sees considerable value in the outcome. From a purely economic perspective, she recognizes that her victory was insignificant: "If I got to chase him down just for $43, I don't want to." Nonetheless, maintaining her original belief in the power of the system and the documents it generates, she views the judgment as money in the bank: "Now if I needed that $43, I'll take it to him." Moreover, perhaps motivated by the same belief, she concludes that she has achieved something even more important: "Yeah, it came out great.... At least he knows he can't run over nobody else." Throughout the interview, she reiterated that her experience had been a positive one—thanks to the judge's sense of humor, the trial was "really funny"—and that she was satisfied with the system and would use it again. Thus, the very misconceptions about the system that set her up for possible disappointment ultimately shielded her from it by leading her to overestimate the practical and legal significance of what she had accomplished. Terry's reactions also demonstrate the fallacy of assessing the adequacy of the judicial system solely in rational, economic terms.

Case 4: "The Former Friends." The plaintiffs, Mr. and Mrs. Winner, are a couple in their twenties. They sued "some old friends" who failed to repay a loan. The story is unclear, but it appears that the defendants have a recent history of moving around the country, living with friends and borrowing money. They were living in Arkansas until the Winners offered to help them find jobs if they moved to Denver. The defendants came and lived with the Winners until, as they put it, "We kicked them out.... We starved them to death." Then Mr. Winner inherited some money, and he and his wife lent or gave the defendants $390. After a couple of months passed without repayment, the Winners prepared some type of loan document that the defendants signed, although they admitted while signing that they could not repay the money. The document apparently required the defendants to make a $50 payment by June 17. On June 24, having heard nothing from the defendants, the Winners sued. They sought the $390, plus $110 for their expenses in bringing the suit. According to Mr. Winner, the purpose of claiming the additional damages was to "make it hurt." The defendants did not appear for trial, and the Winners received a default judgment for $400. Although they located the defendants, they were unable to collect their money. The Winners thought the trial itself was fair and were pleased that they had damaged the defendants' credit rating but concluded that the whole small claims process was "a waste of our time." In particular, they felt that "there should be some way that the city or the court or somebody should be able to get our money for us."

The Winners claim to have considerable knowledge of the small claims process, derived largely from watching "The People's Court."

Q2:	How'd you know to do, do small claims? How'd you think of it?
Mrs. Winner:	I don't know. We just told them, you know, if they didn't pay us, we'd take them to court.
Q2:	Uh huh.
Mrs. Winner:	We watch Judge Wapner on TV.
Q2:	Oh yeah. People, a lot of people find out about, you know, small claims, you know, through that.
Mr. Winner:	Yeah.
Q2:	'Cause if not, you really wouldn't know where, what to do, I guess.
Mrs. Winner:	That's right, that's right. And we wouldn't know to, um, you know, charge them for lost wages and stuff....

The plaintiffs are also aware of the significance the law attaches to written contracts, particularly those sworn to before a notary. Thus, when their ex-friends failed to repay the loan, the Winners made them sign a sworn document and advised them of the potential legal consequences of continued failure to repay.

Mr. Winner:	They're some old friends of ours. And it took them a couple of months to finally make payment arrangements with us so I wrote up a contract and they signed it in front of a notary and everything, to pay me $50 a month and, uh, by the 17th of this month and they haven't done so.
Q2:	Uh huh.
Mr. Winner:	And I told them I'd take them to court, no hesitations. And they've done this...
Q2:	Sure.
Mr. Winner:	...they've done this to people before.

As is evident from the next text, however, the Winners are aware that the defendants simply do not have the money they owe (recall that the defendants so admitted when they signed the loan document):

Mrs. Winner:	She didn't think we would do it, I don't think.

Q2:	Oh yeah? So, um, do you think she, they have it?
Mrs. Winner:	No.
Mr. Winner:	They don't have it.
Q2:	Yeah, so....
Mrs. Winner:	They're gonna have to go to court, ah ha ha.

The obvious question is why these plaintiffs, sophisticated in some respects about law and procedure, are wasting time and money on the pursuit of debtors who will be unable to pay a judgment ("judgment-proof" defendants, in lawyers' jargon). The previous text provides one clue. Mrs. Winner says, in a mocking tone, "They're gonna have to go to court, ah ha ha," suggesting that she and her husband may intend to punish the defendants with the inconvenience and humiliation of a court appearance. Later in the pretrial interview, however, the Winners provide evidence for a different interpretation:

Mr. Winner:	You know, I figured I can go up for $390 but I'm losing time from work. I gotta pay these fees and....
Q2:	Sure.
Mrs. Winner:	... gas to get down here and everything else.
Q2:	Yeah, yeah.
Mr. Winner:	I'm gonna make it hurt.
Q2:	Mmhm.
Mrs. Winner:	[laughter]
Mr. Winner:	Feels good.
Q2:	Yeah. Well, I understand. Probably can use some money.
Mr. Winner:	Yeah, we sure could.

In this text Mr. Winner says, in reference to his inflated damage calculations, "I'm gonna make it hurt." The clear implication is that the increased damages will inflict more pain on the defendants, although they lack the resources to pay even the $390 loan. Mrs. Winner then concludes the interview by responding to the statement that they "probably can use some money" with "yeah, we sure could," suggesting some measure of economic motivation in bringing the case.

To the extent that the Winners' motivation is indeed economic, it rests on an erroneous assumption about the power of a civil court. In fact, the court merely furnishes a piece of paper called a judgment and then provides a mechanism for the successful plaintiff to collect it against the assets of a defendant who will not pay voluntarily. If the defendant refuses to pay and has no unencumbered property that can be sold off, the plaintiff is out of luck. The Winners seem to assume, however, that the court will somehow force the defendants to produce money they do not have or perhaps will punish them for their penury. They thus attribute to the court some of the power of the American criminal system or of some hypothetical inquisition.

The Winners' erroneous expectations contribute to their ultimate dissatisfaction with the process. In a posttrial interview, Mrs. Winner described the trial itself as being "real fair" and "real easy with them not being there," and she did not complain about the amount of the judgment. However, she became increasingly vitriolic when discussing her belief that "the court should be able to go after them." She progressed from stating that "we're pretty unhappy with the overall system" to "it just stinks," observing that her husband "was pretty pissed off about the whole thing." It is significant that for these litigants, dissatisfaction has arisen not because they "lost" in a normative sense nor because the system failed to perform up to its capabilities, but because it lacked capabilities that they had erroneously attributed to it.

Case 5. "The Man on the Street." The plaintiff, James Parker, is a middle-aged man. He is suing a landlord who locked him out of his apartment and seized his personal possessions, all because Parker owed $35. At the time of the interview, he had been living on the street for two weeks. He went to the police immediately after the eviction, but they told him they could not get involved because it was a civil matter. He is seeking recovery of his possessions as well as damages for being forced to live on the street. The police told him that the landlord has a reputation for doing this, and Parker has decided that he will pursue the suit even if the landlord returns his possessions and lets him back in, because "somebody's got to take a stand against him." Parker's name does not appear in the court records, indicating that he never completed the process of filing his complaint. We were unable to locate him for a follow-up interview.

This case is particularly interesting. The plaintiff, James Parker, is a street person in fact and appearance. On this basis alone, one might predict that he would be particularly susceptible to the misconceptions about civil justice, which the other four plaintiffs share to a greater or lesser extent. In reality, however, his understanding of the nature and respective roles of the civil and criminal systems is remarkably accurate.

At the beginning of the interview, Parker expresses confidence in his legal acumen:

Q:	So how did you, you know, how did you hear to uh, come on down here?
Parker:	Uh, well, I have some basic knowledge of law. I know I have rights.
Q2:	Sure, sure.
Parker:	You can't lock people outside their apartments
Q2:	Right.
Parker:	...because they owe you $35.

Immediately thereafter he makes two specific points that seem to justify this self-confidence. First, he acknowledges that the court will decide whether he really owes the $35 in allegedly overdue rent and that the decision could go against him, notwithstanding the rectitude of his position. Second, he suggests that if the landlord broke the law by locking him out, he may be entitled to damages, which will be somehow related to the two weeks he has been on the street:

> Parker: I'm willing to pay that [$35], but I refuse to pay it until such time 'til we bring it into court. And if he's due that $35, the judge will tell me to pay him that $35.
>
> Q: Yeah.
> Parker: But, due to the fact he's in violation of the law and I've been living on the streets for two weeks, common sense tells me that he owes me, eh heh, quite a bit as a matter of fact.

Parker thus recognizes two important legal principles: that the outcomes of legal disputes do not always comport with one's sense of natural justice, and that civil courts must usually reduce human problems to matters of dollars and cents.

Later in the interview, he displays an appreciation for the division of responsibility between the civil and criminal systems:

> Q2:   Have you ever seen him, like dealt with him?
> Parker: No, I, after he locked me out the police informed me that there is nothing they could do about it because of some, well, it's a civil matter....
>
> Q: Sure.
> Parker: ... and they are not gonna get involved with that, but they'll, they're aware of the situation.
>
> Q2:   Okay.
> Q: Yeah.
> Parker: And, uh, apparently he has a reputation for doing this.
>   [eight lines of detail omitted]
> Q: They didn't know about the small claims court?
> Parker: No, um, you can't expect law enforcement officers to know the law.
> All: [laughter]

When the landlord locked him out, Parker went to the police, although he understood when they told him there was nothing they could do "because it's a civil matter." Then, despite getting no advice from the laughably ignorant police officers, he determined that the civil small claims court was the place to seek relief.

Some contrary evidence is found in the next text. After hearing that his court date is likely to be several weeks away, Parker expresses his belief that the landlord will be forced to return his property sometime sooner.

Q: ...I don't, you know, I think, you know, my impression of what we were seeing yesterday [is] that I think it [Parker's court date] would be a matter, you know, of four, five weeks.

Parker: Yeah.

Q: I mean, it's like, you know, it's not like huge....

Q2: It's pretty fast considering, but, you know....

Q: ... but it's not like days, so, uh....

Parker: Yeah.

Q: So, uh....

Parker: Well, before the court action, that may be true, but, uh, I still think that, uh, he's required to return my personal property before four or five weeks.

Parker's last statement contrasts with his earlier recognition that it will be up to the judge at trial to decide whether he owes the $35 and is entitled to damages for the landlord's violation of the law. Here he implies that some legal authority, presumably acting on its own initiative, will come forward and compel the landlord to return his property even before the judge has acted. The uncertain basis of his faith is suggested by the lack of a responsible agent in the phrase, "I still think ... he's required...."

It is also instructive to note those areas in which Parker is unwilling to trust his own legal expertise. In the next text, taken from the beginning of the interview, he raises two specific questions concerning the timing of the service and the scheduling of the hearing. Near the end of the interview, he says, with reference to the complaint form, "I'm gonna try to find a lawyer to help me fill these out properly."

Parker: I was telling the lady outside [the assistant clerk] that I have a lot of questions, because I'm going into this [legal action] blindly.

Q: Sure.

Parker: Of course, there's a $9 filing fee.

Q: Yeah.

Parker: Okay, and I need to...

Q: They've got that in the big letters.

Parker: Yeah. They make sure you understand that. I need to find out once this summons is filed, how long will it be before it's served to the landlord, which is one question I got.

Q: Uh huh.

Parker: Another question is after you serve the summons, how long before the court date will be established for him to appear in court?

All of Parker's expressed concerns relate to court procedure. He does not ask the interviewers any questions about the substance of the case or the landlord's possible defenses, nor does he suggest that he will need a lawyer's help on such issues. Thus, his remark about "going into this blindly" seems to refer only to procedural details; he appears to trust his "basic knowledge of law" on those larger issues that will determine the outcome of the case. The interesting question is why his legal sophistication does not extend to an appreciation of the difficulties he may encounter in proving his case. The answer may lie in his failure to comprehend the ramifications of an adversary system; in particular, even though Parker understands that lawyers are sometimes necessary, he does not think he will need one to win his case because it has not occurred to him that the landlord will present his own, very different interpretations of the facts and the law. In Parker's view, facts are facts and law is law; he does not appreciate that in an adversary system, facts and law are what the parties make of them.

James Parker is in some respects the most complex of the five plaintiffs we have analyzed. Although a street person, he understands the distinction between civil and criminal law and the functions of civil courts. Despite this understanding, however, he has a vague faith in the power of the court to go beyond its procedural limitations and do what justice requires. Additionally, while concerned about the perils of procedural error, he seems oblivious to the complexities of proving a case, perhaps because he misperceives the adversarial process. Once again, the recurrent themes are the overestimation of the power and initiative of the civil court and the underestimation of the individual litigant's burden in the adversary system.

Conclusion

As these five cases illustrate, our ethnographic study of small claims litigants reveals that lay people come to court with expectations about the civil justice system that vary substantially. Three issues are particularly prominent in our interview data. First, many litigants do not seem to comprehend the burden that the adversary system imposes on them. Their comments indicate that they are unprepared to deal with such specific issues as their obligation to locate the defendant, find and prepare the witnesses, and make an affirmative presentation. Second, several litigants expressed a serious misunderstanding of the remedial power of the civil courts, believing that the government would pay them if the defendant failed to appear or would somehow "punish" a defendant who could not pay a judgment. Third, these misunderstandings may contribute to litigant dissatisfaction with the small claims process. Sometimes, as in the case of the Winners, the system's failure to live up to an unrealistic expectation may be a direct source of dissatisfaction. However, the Terry case suggests that similar misunderstandings may prevent some litigants from realizing that the system has failed them.

The unifying theme in the interview data is an overestimation of the power and initiative of the civil court. Litigants often see the court as an inquisitorial authority that will recognize the justice of their position and find and punish the wrongdoer, rather than as a largely passive tribunal that renders judgment on the basis of the facts brought before it. Many litigants thus come to the civil court with a model of justice that better fits the criminal system. Understandably, the one plaintiff who had experience with the criminal system had such a model; however, each of the litigants we considered—and numerous other litigants they represent—shared similar misunderstandings to some extent, irrespective of legal experience or business background.

We do not claim, of course, to have made a statistical showing of a pervasive misconception of the role of civil justice. We do believe, however, that the recurrence of this theme in the unstructured comments of litigants from diverse backgrounds is striking and significant in two important respects.

First, our findings suggest some new issues that complement the general understandings of process emerging from nearly two decades of social psychological investigations of procedural justice. Specifically, we find that process is at least as important in the minds of litigants as the substantive issues in their cases. We also find that lay conceptions of process are at variance, often considerable variance, with the realities of the legal process as it is practiced in many small claims courts. We would hope that researchers who focus on procedure would consider the potential relevance to their theoretical agenda of the assumptions and folk beliefs that lay people bring to the legal process.

Second, the observation of a discontinuity between lay culture and a powerful institution such as the law is significant in its own right. Traditionally, legal scholarship has examined legal issues from the perspective of those who make and practice law. More recently, social scientists, including procedural justice researchers, have begun to focus on the reactions and attitudes of consumers of justice. Even this research, however, poses questions that the law has defined as important. Accordingly, it assumes, at least implicitly, that lay and legally trained people think about disputes in similar ways. In our present research, we have been repeatedly reminded of the importance of examining legal issues from the perspective of the consumer. In addition to the findings reported here, we have learned, for example, that lay people have ideas about causation, proof, and the structure of adequate accounts that differ markedly from those of the law (O'Barr & Conley, 1985; Conley & O'Barr, 1990). This accumulating evidence of fundamental differences in reasoning and communication between lay and legal cultures should be of interest to those who study the cultural background of law as well as those who seek to reform the legal process.

Our findings also make a larger point about the role of ethnography in social science research about legal problems. In the design of experimental studies, some issues can be identified a priori. However, as we learned in our initial studies of law and language (Conley et al., 1978; O'Barr, 1982), other issues, less obvious but equally important, emerge only after lengthy observation of the system being studied. Thus, just as ethnographers should enlist the aid of quantitative specialists before making claims about the frequency or distribution of the behavior they observe, those who do quantitative analysis should acknowledge the role of open-ended ethnographic observation in identifying issues worthy of study.

DISCUSSION QUESTIONS

1. How do outcome and process interact in their effect on disputant judgments of fairness? Which is more important? Why do you think disputants value process?

2. What are the relative advantages of experimental psychology and anthropological participant-observation in studying disputant attitudes toward process?

3. Did you share some of the preconceptions of small claims plaintiffs about civil litigation? Why do lay litigants confuse civil and criminal justice?

4. Who uses small claims courts? How do they differ from the general population? How do prior experiences influence subsequent expectations? How else do litigants form their expectations? Could legal institutions fulfill litigant expectations? Should they? Which litigants use small claims courts? For what purposes?

5. What did litigants want from the court? Is the court equipped to provide it? Are these litigants typical? of all courts? small claims courts? If not, What makes them distinctive? Consider the differences among litigants: Did they all want the same thing from the court? How did their knowledge and expectations vary?

Legal
Profession

19

Law and Social Relations: Vocabularies of Motive in Lawyer/Client Interaction

Austin Sarat and William L. F. Felstiner

Introduction

C. Wright Mills (1940: 910) noted long ago the centrality and significance of what he called "motive mongering" in human interaction. By "motive mongering" Mills meant the frequency with which individuals impute motives in the effort to construct shared interpretations of action: "motives are the terms with which interpretation of conduct by social actors proceeds" (1940: 904; see also Weber, 1947: 98–99). For Mills (1940: 904) examination of what he labeled "vocabularies of motive" linked the study of linguistic behavior with social structure; it related the attribution of motives to the interests, patterns of power and social positions that give rise to particular ways of talking about social relations and explaining human action. Mills (1940: 908) believed that a close study of the interpretation and understanding of action is important because such interpretations and understandings are "significant determinants of conduct."

Mills was particularly interested in the development of vocabularies of motive in different social situations. The creation of a vocabulary of motive was, in his view, a social act; thus "different situations have different vocabularies of motive appropriate to their respective behaviors" (Mills, 1940: 906). For Mills, an important part of the task of the sociologist is to investigate particular groups or situations to uncover the vocabulary of motives that a group makes available to its members or that particular situations seem to legitimate.

While Mills called attention to the strong connection between interpretive activities and social structure, he tended to ignore the processes of interaction through which vocabularies of motive emerge. Thus his perspective seems somewhat mechanistic and deterministic. Others, however, have focused on the ways in which meanings emerge in social life (see, e.g., Berger & Luckman, 1966; Goffman, 1959; Scheff, 1966). Most often those who study that process describe it as one of negotiation (Scheff, 1966: 128).

Abridged from *Law & Society Review*, Volume 22:737 (1988).

Social interactions are treated as a process of exchange in which participants create shared understandings and interpretations through a series of proposals and counterproposals, sometimes explicit but most often implicit in their interaction. Thus the vocabulary of motive that a group legitimates is itself the result of a group process. Furthermore, the idea of negotiating reality suggests that social interaction requires agreement and closure. Those who use that idea argue that while social interaction may be conflictual and associated with inequalities of power, it generally proceeds until a shared agreement is reached (see Scheff, 1966; Sudnow, 1965). Others, however, suggest that vocabularies of motive may be imposed without anything that could remotely be labeled a negotiation process (see Foucault, 1977) or that social interaction can proceed without agreement on interpretation, meaning or vocabularies of motive (see, e.g., Mishler, 1985). In this view, social interaction involves a series of continuing struggles between different ways of seeing the world, and interaction is more open and incomplete than is sometimes captured by images of a negotiated reality (Yngvesson, 1985b).

This paper examines vocabularies of motive in the interactions of lawyers and clients. We have chosen to focus on these interactions because they are increasingly recognized as important in giving content to a wide variety of legal phenomena (see Felstiner et al., 1981; Cain, 1979; Macaulay, 1979; 1984; Blumberg, 1967; Mann, 1985; Hosticka, 1979; Rosenthal, 1974). Some scholars now argue that lawyer/client interaction is a critical site for the creation of "law in action," that "backstage" (Goffman, 1959) discourse provides a better understanding of what law really is than the official productions of legislation and judicial decisions. Thus Shapiro (1981: 1201) asserts that "law is not what judges say in the reports but what lawyers say—to one another and to clients in their offices...."

Shapiro's argument suggests that law exists in, and ought to be examined as part of, specific social relationships with particular histories and patterns of interaction and power. But law is not just occasionally relevant to society. Rather it is an important component of many transactions and events comprising social life (see Sarat & Silbey, 1988). And law not only lives in social practices, it also is a specific type of social practice. From this perspective, lawyer/client interaction is a social relationship that is important not only as a context for the study of law but also as an example of social construction and legal operation under conditions of unequal power generated by unequal knowledge and experience. In addition, the interplay of vocabularies of motive provides one component of the working ideology of the lawyer's office, one field in which to study the negotiation or imposition of a common view of the social world or the persistence of conflicting perspectives.

Investigation of the way lawyers and clients use vocabularies of motive requires attention to norms and orientations of ordinary citizens and legal professionals. Clients bring to their interactions with lawyers what Schutz (1962) called a "natural attitude" or an "attitude of everyday life." In this attitude the way the world appears is accepted as the way the world really is. The self is perceived to be at the center of society and events are interpreted in terms of their impact on the self. Lawyers, by contrast, might be expected to think of motives and actions in what Habermas (1970: 65) called "rational-purposive" terms in which technical rules and a problem-solving orientation are more important than emotional reactions and justifications of self. In the combination and confrontation of these views, law is given social meaning, and it, in turn, provides new perspectives on social relations and social behavior.

The construction of vocabularies of motive in lawyers' offices connects ideas, beliefs, experiences, and interests. As lawyers and clients together define how people behave and explain why they behave as they do, as they try to make sense of life events, they give shape and content to such behavior and events. What lawyers tell their clients about social relations, how they respond to client questions concerning the behavior of other people, structures, at least in part, the way in which clients "experience and perceive their relations with others" (Hunt, 1985: 15). At the same time, client interpretations and assessments of social relations channel the efforts of lawyers to carry out their professional tasks and to control the instrumental aspects of their interaction with clients. Thus, maintaining their own interpretive scheme, or using a different vocabulary of motive, is one way in which clients can resist the exercise of professional power.

This paper parallels a distinctive movement in legal scholarship in which doctrine is analyzed to identify the worldviews that it reflects (Unger, 1975) and to describe the way it gives meaning to the social relations of liberal society (Kelman, 1987). Thus, critical scholars have investigated the nature of legal consciousness reflected in legal doctrine and the way that such ideas about the law provide a foundation for the social world (Kennedy, 1980; Gabel, 1980; Klare, 1981; Gordon, 1982; Freeman, 1978). For those who engage in the critique of legal thought, the ideas encoded in legal doctrine "can be said to 'constitute' society" (Trubek, 1984: 589).

Because critical scholarship has in effect equated law and society, it has abstracted the meaning-making power of law from the social relations in which such power is exercised. Others, however, have studied the images of social life favored by law in concrete social relations and particular social practices. Recent work on dispute handling in lower courts, for example, has described the images of social relations that are produced by actors in those settings. Silbey and Merry (1986: 5) argue that proceedings in lower courts involve "active struggles over the construction of social meanings" as participants attempt to explain the behavior of those in trouble. Power in these settings is a function of the ability of different actors to determine what counts as an acceptable account, explanation, or interpretation of social behavior.

Yngvesson (1985a; 1988) has described the interaction between court and community in one small Massachusetts town in similar terms. She has examined interactions between complainants and court clerks in show-cause hearings. Her research describes the way social relationships are portrayed in those hearings and

406 *Sarat and Felstiner*

the struggle between complainants and clerks over the interpretations given to the behavior and conditions that occasion those proceedings. Thus, the hearings provide "arenas where law is used to shape community" (1987: 4). As clerks and complainants discuss the events and behavior involved in legal disputes, clerks seek to influence complainants' understandings of behavior by constructing "images of the virtuous citizen, the good neighbor, the responsible parent, the responsive and obedient child" (1987: 5). Yngvesson argues that clerks "draw on their knowledge of the local community and on middle class values, understandings that were held out as ideals to those before ... [them], to ... mobilize consent for ... agreement[s] that ... [keep matters] out of court but within ... [their] control" (1987: 24–25). She shows how meaning-making activity in the court serves the interest of particular segments of the community and of the legal officials whose interpretations come to dominate the proceedings. A vocabulary of motive is produced in this setting that is recognizable, and acceptable, to particular segments of the community. In the end, this vocabulary serves to protect the court from extended involvement in what court officials believe to be minor neighborhood disputes while simultaneously advancing their interest in a particular version of order.

The Data

We observed and tape recorded 115 lawyer/client conferences from one side of 40 divorce cases over 33 months in two sites, one in Massachusetts and one in California. Lawyer and client sometimes negotiate agreed interpretations of behavior. Agreement is more often reached when the discussion of motive concerns behavior during the divorce than when the focus is on behavior during the marriage. Moreover, in general, lawyers are more likely to secure "acceptance" of their interpretations than are clients. Clients focus their interpretive energy on efforts to construct an explanation of the past and of their marriage's failure. Lawyers avoid responding to these interpretations because they do not consider that who did what to whom in the marriage is relevant to the legal task of dissolving it. In this domain clients largely talk past their lawyers (see Griffiths, 1986; Sarat & Felstiner, 1986), and interpretive activity proceeds without the generation and ratification of a shared understanding of reality. Lawyers are rarely derailed from their effort to focus on the business of securing the legal divorce and negotiating agreements about property and children.

The interaction changes when interpretive activity moves to the present and future and to behavior involved in the legal process; lawyers become more active in constructing vocabularies of motive when interpretive activity is linked to the rational-purposive goals of legal work. In this domain lawyers are able to mobilize their experience, expertise, and authority in support of their own vocabulary of motive and to use that vocabulary, in turn, to reinforce their authority. Because decisions must be made that directly affect their lives, clients must respond to lawyer interpretations even though they have little experience, expertise, or authority in the legal process. The usual result is closure on an interpretation of behavior embodying the lawyer's vocabulary of motive.

The Domain of the Past: Explaining the Failed Marriage

Much of the conversation between lawyer and client in divorce cases involves a reconstruction of the past in the form of descriptions of the behavior of the parties within the marriage. Lawyers are regularly confronted with clients insistent on providing some account (see Scott & Lyman, 1968) of why their marriage failed. In these accounts clients focus on the character and personality dispositions of their spouse and emphasize their spouse's most objectionable traits and personal defects. As Vaughan (1986: 28–29) observes, this focus emerges early in the process of "uncoupling" and continues throughout it. While a few clients have little to say about what occurred during the marriage, most of those we observed devote considerable time to that activity, generally on their own initiative and in the face of an unresponsive lawyer. In so doing they stress personal and intentional explanations of their spouses' behavior (see Coates & Penrod, 1981: 664).

Clients' stories concerning the breakup of the marriage generally begin with a description of some disturbing spousal behavior and locate the source of that behavior within the allegedly offending actor. For example, a 40-year-old mother of three children in Massachusetts explained why her marriage failed.

Client: There was harassment and verbal degradation. No interest at all in my furthering my education. None whatsoever. Sexual harassment. If there was ever any time when I did not want or need sex, I was subject to, you know, these long verbal whip-lashings. Then the Bible would be put out on the counter with passages underlined as to what a poor wife I was. Just constant harassment from him.

Lawyer: Mmn uh.

Client: There was ... what I was remembering the other day, and I had forgotten. When he undertook to lecturing me and I'd say, "I don't want to hear this. I don't have time right now," I could lock myself in the bathroom and he would break in. And I was just to listen, whether I wanted to or not. And he would lecture me for hours. Literally hours.... There was no escaping him, short of getting in a car and driving away. But then he would stand outside in the driveway and yell, anyhow. *The man was not well* (emphasis added).

Lawyer: Okay. Now how about any courses you took?

This lawyer does not respond to his client's attribution of blame or characterization of her husband; no negotiation of reality occurs. The "okay" seems to reflect the end of his patience with her description, and he abruptly changes the subject.

Another client explained the failure of his short and stormy marriage to a woman much younger than himself by focusing on the habitual untruthfulness of his spouse. In the midst of a discussion about the wife's previous testimony in court, the client said that he did not believe it and explained how the marriage ended.

Client: After she lied to me about the death of her parents in a car-train accident. Okay? And after she lied to me about where she went to school. And after she lied to me about the fact that she was the only child.... She's lived a secretive life, as far as I'm concerned, all this time....

Lawyer: Hmm.

Client: So everything she told me about her background was a lie. I can't believe anything she says. I mean, it would be news to me if she says anything truthful while I'm sitting there in the courtroom. It would be news to me. I couldn't verify it for you. Because all this time I have been under the impression that she had no parents, no siblings, that she was a graduate of Radcliffe College. I mean, I had no reason.... When you marry somebody, you don't check these things out. You know, call Radcliffe and find out if somebody.... She gave me an alias for her maiden name. Collins is the one that she said in the.... She gave me an alias. She gave me a French name. She said her parents were French Canadian....

Lawyer: Hmm.

Client: It was ... we won't get any more information from her.

Lawyer: The only real way to find out anything would be to hire a private detective.

This lawyer appears to accept the client's characterization of his spouse while avoiding, as most lawyers do, comment on the reasons for the marriage breakup. He focuses on the problem of how to get information about her present circumstances and finances.

On a few occasions lawyers did participate in the construction of accounts about the failed marriage. In each instance they joined with, and reinforced, the view that the failure of the marriage should not be blamed on their client. One California lawyer resisted his client's willingness to accept responsibility for the failure of the marriage.

Lawyer:	If there was a failure I just don't think it is fair to attribute it to anything you have done. I mean you walked a country mile to try to make it work out well. You were married to a person who has any number of problems.
Client:	Well, I will have to ... I know that ... but ... confronting the alternatives as they presently exist—that's a very difficult thing ... there seems much about this situation that I've got to do but I don't like to do. But I don't see any other way out. I guess this is when it gets tough.
Lawyer:	All right.

This lawyer, like the few others who play blame the spouse, does so to support his client's decision to continue to seek a divorce in the face of her own growing ambivalence.

The instrumental character of lawyers' participation in such reconstructions of the past is further illustrated in the following exchange between a female lawyer and her 50-year-old, poorly educated, female client.

Client:	He keeps saying ... he'd like to get it together.
Lawyer:	But Bob really hasn't changed his behavior. You see what you are telling me about the pattern of living ... is what you told me about the pattern of living during your marriage.... And that kind of thing. It's the same way it's been throughout the marriage. He could probably live with this a great deal longer than you could. You have to own up to that, Carolyn. You made a decision when you came to me a while ago that that's not how you want it. So it's ... I don't think you should keep saying to me that if he wanted to get it together you would. Because if I understand what you said to me way back then ... that's not the way you want to live. And he could live like this indefinitely. I guarantee you that. I don't see any strain on him. The only strain that Bob is now enduring is the possibility that you are going to go through with this divorce. But his lifestyle hasn't changed ... he's got you in the same position he had you in throughout the marriage. And that is not going to change unless we go through the divorce. The moment that you ever showed him a glimmer or a possibility that you were going to be a free woman in your own words ... that's when he initiated a divorce. He just can't deal with that. You have to accept that. Your relationship is going to be the way your marriage always was ... or you're going to have to go through a divorce and have the kinds of things you want. And that's the bottom line.

Client: I mean ... I'm willing to sacrifice myself ... to live in hell, more
or less, for the kids ... but that's not right either....

The client's reference to living in "hell" suggests that she accepts the lawyer's characterization. Yet, as her case progressed, such exchanges of doubt and reassurance occurred frequently. When lawyers use the language of blame it is to remind clients why the divorce is either desirable or inevitable and ought to be pursued, an end result in which they have an obvious interest.

When discussion turns to the client's conduct in, or reasons for leaving, the marriage, the vocabulary of motive and style of explanation change dramatically. In interpreting their own actions clients shift from explanations based on personal dispositions and character traits to circumstances and situations. They emphasize their innocence, vulnerability, and injury. They suggest that any undesirable conduct on their part was the product of provocation or duress. The meanings they attach to their own behavior are consistent with their attempt to blame their spouses and to present their own actions as reasonable and justifiable responses to circumstances not of their making. Lawyers do not generally challenge their client's attempts at exculpation, nor do they validate them.

An example of such a client self-portrait is provided in the following exchange:

Lawyer: You know that she's really pushing to get this divorce going.
Client: I know she doesn't want to have any connection to me. She
hates to even have me there to say hello....
Lawyer: That will calm down eventually....
Client: Well, what makes me mad is that I'm the injured party. She's
acting like I am running out on her.
Lawyer: She's hurting a little bit ... and she thinks that if it gets into court
the pain is going to stop.

This dialogue is unusual only in the directness with which the client asserts that he "is the injured party." Claims of this type are tacit in many cases even when the client initiates the divorce (see Griffiths, 1986: 154).

Clients also portray themselves as victims to excuse their own marital misconduct. In the following exchange, taken from a Massachusetts case in which a deeply religious woman was asked by her lawyer to explain why she physically assaulted her husband, the client focuses on her husband's provocative actions rather than her own anger.

Client: They're going to bring up the time that I physically attacked
him. Can we beat them to the punch and get that in so I can
explain why I attacked him?

Lawyer:	Is that where you attacked him with the loaf of bread?
Client:	No.... This time.... Remember that day when I had the tubal ligation?
Lawyer:	Give me that whole story again.
Client:	Okay, I had gone in to have a tubal ligation.
Lawyer:	Yeah. I know that he got very upset, but I don't remember all of the circumstances afterwards.
Client:	He found out about it from my girl friend, subjected her to a severe tongue lashing, accused her of helping me.... You know. Called me all kinds of filthy names. I was obviously having a tubal ligation so that I could go out and, you know, run around and sleep around.
Lawyer:	Yeah.... It's probably hearsay. You know? They're probably going to object to it, all that stuff you just said ... about his conversation with your friend, and everything else. That's hearsay. Okay?
Client:	And then on the Saturday morning, which was several days afterwards, because I went in on a Wednesday.... Thursday. Wednesday. I was getting ready to go grocery shopping, and he.... We got into an argument about something, and then he started calling me dirty names. And something....
Lawyer:	Like what?
Client:	Oh, what was it? He called me "filth." That was the word that got me. "Filth." And something just went "boing." "Boing." My spring came undone. And I just.... I attacked him. I just went for him for maybe five minutes, yelled and screamed and kicked and slapped and scratched and did whatever I could. I wasn't even aware at the time that I was doing it. I didn't even realize I was the one screaming. It was Lottie who told me later that I was the one who was screaming. But I just lost it. He made me so angry. His reaction to this was so.... It was so senseless. The reason I had it done was because I wanted it done while I was covered by health insurance. I knew we were.... A divorce was coming up. And I knew I wouldn't have the health insurance any more. And to have it done under the insurance did not cost me anything. Because I didn't want to get pregnant again.
Lawyer:	I don't know if I want to bring it up first, because if we bring it up then they have to bring it up and what if they had chosen not to....

The client interprets her own misbehavior as a kind of temporary insanity and goes on, as if she has internalized the need to justify her decision to undergo the tubal ligation, to explain how that decision was itself a product of external circumstances. The lawyer's response is to remind his client of evidentiary problems and suggest that it may be better not to bring up her attack on her husband. He focuses on the tactical problem while ignoring everything that his client said concerning the reasons for the attack and her characterizations of her own behavior.

A few lawyers do not ignore such characterizations and, instead, validate the client's interpretation. This occurs in the following California case in which the client explained her decision to seek a divorce and described why her husband had hired a "tough" lawyer,

Client:	I think that's exactly what happened. It's very hard for him. He can't make a decision. He needs to be pushed into it. He would never have left if I didn't throw him out. Never. He would have gone on, because life was very comfortable for him. I mean, it was just fine, and he was totally amazed that I would do it. He didn't know I was discontent. After I go through this whole spiel about how I felt and what I thought, his answer to me was, I didn't know you were discontent. My world was coming down around my ears, and that was his choice of words, because he couldn't, he really sees himself as a wonderful person. He does. You know, kind and he sees himself as this wonderful person.
Lawyer:	Some of us like to have an opinion of ourselves. At least some of the time.
Client:	Well, you see, I made him this wonderful person. I told him how wonderful he was, while I was hiding behind this thing I built up for myself—this smiling, gentle lady—when I was seething, until I couldn't bear it anymore.
Lawyer:	So you helped create this Frankenstein.
Client:	Of course ... but now he's got someone else to tell him how wonderful he is.
Lawyer:	Well, why not keep a good thing going? Just change the....

This client, like many others, attaches the conversation about the failed marriage to another discussion (the husband's choice of lawyer). Her lawyer, unlike most others we observed, joins in the conversation about the failed marriage and accepts her interpretation. Together they create the "Frankenstein" portrait of the self-indulgent, spoiled husband and, in so doing, reach tacit agreement on the client's self-portrait as a long-suffering martyr.

Throughout their meetings with their lawyers the question of marriage failure remains very much alive in the minds of clients. They talk about the marriage in terms of guilt (their spouse's) and innocence (their own). This pattern is as observable in California, where there is a pure no-fault system, as it is in Massachusetts, where fault and no-fault options exist side by side. Even though law reform makes such questions legally irrelevant, clients continue to think in fault terms and to attribute blame to their spouses. Clients use a vocabulary of personal responsibility to interpret the failed marriage, and they seem to want their lawyers to accept and use a similar vocabulary (cf. Weitzman, 1985: 24–25). Most lawyers resist by avoiding discussion of who did what to whom during the marriage. They focus, when they are confronted with such an issue, on questions of tactics in the legal process of divorce. Client and lawyer are like performer and bored, but dutiful, audience—the lawyer will not interrupt the aria, but she will not applaud much either for fear of an encore. Lawyers generally join with, and validate, the client's vocabulary of blame only to reassure wavering clients of the correctness of their decision to secure a divorce.

The Domain of the Present: Explaining Problems and Justifying Demands in the Legal Process of Divorce

A somewhat different pattern emerges when discussion shifts to the legal process and present problems. Yet, the vocabulary of blame continues to play a prominent part in client thinking. Problems in negotiations are regularly interpreted by clients as originating in their spouse's blameworthy conduct and character. Lawyers, however, are much more active participants in these conversations and are frequently quite direct in challenging client characterizations and explanations. Take, for example, the following discussion of whether a college professor with several children would be willing to transfer title to one of the family motor vehicles to a client who had temporary custody of their children.

Lawyer:	Have you discussed any more about getting rid of the van and getting yourself another vehicle?
Client:	Yes, I did. I talked it over with him, and asked if he would be willing to release the van if I were to find a car.
Lawyer:	Yeah.
Client:	And he said, if he thought it was ... I don't remember the wording now, but a fair deal, or a decent deal, or something. And I said, "Well, why should you.... If I'm going to be making the car payments, what does it have to do with you? All I want from you is to release the van." He still wants that control.
Lawyer:	He's looking at everything as dollar signs for him ... pretty typical reaction.... He's going to be defensive on all those things. Have you been looking for vehicles?

The client's emphasis on "still" wanting control suggests that the husband's reluctance to transfer title is continuous with his behavior during the marriage. Her lawyer, on the other hand, suggests that his behavior was "typical" of people during divorce and, in so doing, resists his client's attribution of her husband's behavior to some flaw in his character. However, rather than trying to reach a shared position on why the husband refuses to shift title, the lawyer changes the subject to what his client is going to do about transportation for herself.

Similar patterns occurred in many other cases. In one a young man provides the following explanation of why he and his spouse have been unable to reach a negotiated agreement.

Lawyer: What would happen if the two of you sat down and started talking?

Client: Well, you know, anytime we've ever had discussions, the discussions always turn into arguments, is basically what it boils down to. And, you know, there are a number of other things besides the getting a job issue that I feel are, you know, inequitable in our relationship. And though she might.... You know, on the rare occasion that she actually listens, she's not a good listener. When she actually listens and senses that she'd better change her ways, that may last for a week or something before it's back to the same old thing. And she's tied up with her hobbies and hoping all.... You know, it's like.... We were really broke this winter, and I tried to discuss it with her. She said I should go see a financial counselor. She one evening said, "Well, when I get my inheritance I should share that with you." And I said, "Well, that would help." But then she'd just start ranting and raving, as if I had the nerve to consider that any of her inheritance would be mine. So she doesn't mean it when.... If she does ever make a concession. And it's very temporary and fleeting.

Lawyer: Maybe she'd make a stronger commitment to ... a counselor that can listen to your two points of view....

Reaching an agreement is, in the client's view, impossible because his wife rarely listens and never lives up to the concessions she makes. The client locates cause in character and uses a language of fault and blame. Other clients provide comparable explanations for the unwillingness of their former spouses to divide personal property reasonably or assume responsibility for their own postdivorce financial well-being. However, this lawyer, like most others, resists the characterological explanation and suggests that the problem is circumstantial. For him, the negotiation issue is not a matter of blame but rather a problem of finding the right vehicle to facilitate communication.

In a few instances, however, lawyers do endorse their clients' analyses of personality as they talk about particular problems in the divorce process. For example, one California client inquired about his lawyer's view of the fairness of their offer of spousal support, and the lawyer responded by reminding him of his wife's "aggressive and dominant tendencies."

Lawyer: On a long-term basis we are talking about a woman who is a gifted artist, who is certainly commercially acceptable in the sense that she can go out and sell a substantial number of paintings.... She can earn income at a desirable profession of hers....

Client: I think she told me today she was going to work. That she had to go to work. So I presume it was that.

Lawyer: That's up in the air at the moment as to whether she's going to continue to wait tables or not.

Client: Yeah.

Lawyer: Apparently she found out how little she's earning by doing that.... It's a desperate maneuver on her part. I have the feeling that she is aggressive and dominant as she tries to become ... is really getting uptight.

Client: Well, she always gets very paranoid about financial matters.

Another lawyer answered his client's question about the lack of a response to their long-standing offer concerning the division of marital property.

Lawyer: I hear that she [the spouse's lawyer] doesn't communicate with her much at all. It is hard to get a hold of her. She doesn't respond to letters; she doesn't answer letters and she changes her position all the time.

Client: Yeah. Really. I lived with it for a long time. I know.

Lawyer: Yeah, see what's fascinating is that people don't change their basic behavior patterns once they begin a divorce. They really don't. They really don't.

This lawyer's insistence on the continuity and stability of "basic behavior patterns" is unusual: most lawyers rely almost exclusively on situational explanations. But whatever the attribution, lawyers speculate about social behavior only when it appears relevant to legal activity.

When they do engage in such speculation, lawyers often deploy a stage theory to interpret and explain why the opposing spouse behaves as she does during the divorce. They suggest that most divorces produce intransigence and hostility at the beginning, followed by a period of emotional confusion and then a gradual return to rationality. They emphasize the importance of understanding problems in light of the different behavior and moods associated with each stage. One Massachusetts lawyer answered her client's question about why his wife got so upset when he purchased some new clothes.

Lawyer:	You are in the stage of divorce where she is promised and she thinks she can deliver ... you on to the street with one pair of jockey shorts ... nothing else ... that's the stage you're in.
Client:	I think that's what she thinks.
Lawyer:	Yes ... everyone thinks that in the beginning. I almost get worried when a person comes in and says ... my wife has just said that she's going to give me everything. I think it's normal for her to say ... I'll leave you on Main Street bare-assed ... when they don't do that then I know the normal process isn't happening. It won't happen.
Client:	Okay.

In her explanation she describes the behavior of the spouse as common, as reflecting what "everyone thinks," and she links that behavior explicitly to the stages of a "normal process."

In other cases lawyers were somewhat less explicit in establishing such linkages. Many use rhetoric such as that employed by the following lawyer to describe the opposing spouse's position on custody as a reaction to the beginning of the divorce process itself.

Lawyer:	Is it likely that the two of you would disagree on anything ... in terms of your relationship with your kids....
Client: ...	No, I don't think so.
Lawyer:	I think what you have, parents who have been relatively, consistently agreeable in regard to their kids and then they first get into a divorce situation. Sometimes unfortunately they can get their heels stuck in cement on something that just doesn't, it doesn't compute in view of their past experience. I mean all of a sudden they can't agree about anything when they've always agreed.

Clients, unlike their lawyers, employ circumstantial explanations selectively; in discussions of the divorce process they use such explanations to justify their own claims to particular assets or a particular division of property. Such an explanation is provided by a young, working-class female who was seeking a share of the equity in a house that her husband had constructed and in which she refused to live. Her lawyer asked her whether she had made any contribution to the construction of the house.

Client: I was working nights at the Hideout, regularly from 6 to 1 at night, and I just had Gail, and so I'd go home. I didn't want to get up in the morning and build a house. It was winter. Who wants to build a house in the middle of winter, December, January.

Lawyer: I just wanted to know whether there was anything to what he said about your never wanting to build the house.

Client: Well, no, I didn't really, I wanted the house, but I didn't want the house at my mother-in-law's—next door.

Lawyer: So that's what made you....

Client: Oh yeah, it didn't really....

Lawyer: Less involved with the project.

Client: Plus he wasn't building the house that I wanted him to. He was just building this little house, and I wanted a bigger house. It was just a little house, no garage, you know what I mean, so it was like, yeah, it was nice, he was building a house, but it was no—because it was going to be next to my mother-in-law. At the time my mother-in-law didn't even like, didn't even speak to me, and I'm going to live next door.

Lawyer: Self preservation....

The client's explanation for her refusal to contribute has several dimensions. First she talks about her work and her need to stay home with the children. Next she focuses on the fact that the house was being built next to her in-laws. Then she briefly suggests that the house was not to her liking before returning to its proximity to her husband's relatives. In this, as in other cases, the client explains and justifies her behavior largely by reference to circumstances beyond her control. Client and lawyer construct a mutually acceptable circumstantial explanation for what seems, initially, to be an unjustifiable negotiating position. The structure of their dialogue reflects a movement toward closure on an explanation that the lawyer accepts as legally defensible and strategically useful.

In talking about the legal process as well as about failed marriages clients frame a narrative of fault, blame, and excuse. The behavior of the spouse during the divorce process is portrayed as the product of permanent character traits and personality dispositions. Yet, when their own conduct is at issue, client self-portraits emphasize circumstance, situation, or the provocations and injuries inflicted by the spouse.

Lawyers take a more active role in constructing interpretations of problems in the legal process of divorce and justifications for client demands than when the client talks about the failure of their marriage. Where the reality to be negotiated focuses on the present and is relevant to the task at hand rather than on marital history, lawyers tend to join with, rather than ignore, their clients in constructing interpretations. Yet they rarely embrace a vocabulary that attributes action to fixed character traits or speaks in terms of fault and blame. Instead, they emphasize circumstantial factors in explaining the conduct of the spouse as well as that of the client.

The Domain of the Future: Giving Advice, Planning Strategy

Lawyers are most actively engaged in constructing vocabularies of motive when advising their clients about the strategy and tactics of the legal process itself. In so doing they signal clients that people in the throes of a divorce are vulnerable to stress and emotion. They suggest that clients ought to be suspicious of their own judgment; and, by implying that such judgment is likely to be unreliable, lawyers suggest the importance of depending on them for sound guidance (Sarat & Felstiner, 1986).

The warning that divorce clouds judgment provides the backdrop for many discussions of strategy and tactics. In one California case, the lawyer alerted his well-educated client to the danger that her emotions might get in the way of a satisfactory property settlement and advised her of the need to bring them under control.

Lawyer: I mean, people have a very, very hard time of separating whatever it is—so I think for shorthand, we call it the emotional aspect of the case from the financial aspect of the case. But if there is going to be a settlement, that's kind of what has to happen, or the emotional aspect of the case gets resolved and then the financial thing becomes a matter of dollars and cents and the client decides, I'm tired and I don't want to fight over the last $500 or the last $100....

Client: I mean, I don't want to fight and I do want to fight, right? That's exactly what it comes down to.

Lawyer: Yea, you're ambiguous.

Client: Oh, boy, am I ever. And I have to live with it.

Lawyer: That's right. I'd say the ambiguity goes even deeper than the issue of fighting and not fighting. It's how.... The ambiguity is what Irene talked about and that is—it's the real hard one—it's terminating the entire relationship. You do and you don't, and the termination.... I mean, you're angry; you're pissed off. You've said that. And are you ready to call a halt to the anger and I'm not so sure that that's humanly possible. Can your

	rational mind say, okay, Jane, there has been enough anger expended on this; it is time to get on with your life. If you are able to do that, great. But I don't know.
Client:	Well, obviously some of me is and some of me isn't.

While in this case the divorce and the emotions associated with it seem to be fueling the client's desire to fight, in many other cases lawyers caution their clients against being too trusting, too ready to make concessions or too impatient. They warn clients that the divorce process is long and tiring; they caution against the failing courage that springs from the need to make hard choices (see Kressel, 1985). Clients, eager to blame their spouses for problems in the marriage and for difficulties encountered in the divorce process, end up worrying about being too tough or unfair; many are overcome with second thoughts. In response, lawyers interpret those emotions as a natural, and frequent, reaction during a divorce.

Lawyers compare their clients' feelings or actions with what is "common" or with what they have seen in other cases. In this way lawyers employ a vocabulary of motive based on some idea of "normal divorce" (cf. Sudnow, 1965). In the following exchange concerning the difficulty of actually filing for divorce, the lawyer constructs such a norm through a variety of rhetorical devices.

Client:	I think he's exhausted and I think he understands that there is no hope. He kept on saying to me, "you don't want me anymore, do you...." I said.... "that's not what I am saying. I'm saying we are better off separated...."
Lawyer:	Yeah. I think it's, I may be wrong, but I suspect it's a very hard thing for you to file this petition. It's been a very hard thing for you to file this petition and I think it may be still difficult. Even when you are the one who wants the dissolution, sometimes it's really really hard to do that. I know. I have another client who has been separated for a couple of years and it's coming down now where it's a matter of actually getting the divorce and he's been the one who separated, his wife has been hysterical about the divorce, but he wanted it and now when it's coming down to the time he tells me, I feel so bad about this. And it's very natural. I mean people feel that way. But I think that you are going to be spinning your wheels with this until you decide, until you feel comfortable that you really want to file the petition and do it.
Client:	See I don't want him in my life, but filing the petition to me is just something that I think is gross, I don't know why.
Lawyer:	I can tell that....
Client:	It's just not....

Lawyer: That you have been really having a hard time doing that.

This lawyer validates his client's expression of difficulty but moves quickly from a focus on this client's difficulty to the general level; he locates her feelings in a general statement "sometimes it's really really hard to do that." The client is assured that her reactions fit a typical pattern, one that the lawyer has seen before. In describing her hesitancy as a reaction to making what seems like an irrevocable decision, the lawyer displays confidence in his own interpretation. "I know," he says, and he bases his knowledge on a comparison of this client's feelings with those of another client. He uses the term "natural" and folk wisdom, "people feel that way," to establish both his expertise in understanding her reactions and the extent to which those reactions arise out of the divorce process itself. After a long time spent figuring out how to have the papers served in the least upsetting way, the divorce petition was filed.

A similar focus on the divorce itself as an explanation for behavior and a similar use of the rhetoric of comparison and generalization in constructing particular explanations occurs as lawyers advise their clients about offers and demands concerning property, support, and child custody. In the following case a relatively inexperienced woman lawyer urges her client to ask for more support than the client feels is appropriate and explains that the client's reticence arises from guilt, which many "women feel" during the divorce.

Lawyer: You've got, and it's going to be up to you whether you think it will really hurt him or that he will be really impoverished by this or something and that he can't make it, but don't forget he's going to be left with a $50,000 house when it's all over.

Client: I know.

Lawyer: Or more. And what are you going to do. You'll have freedom. A lot of women feel that way at the time and they say, so what, you know. Do you feel guilty? Do you?

Client: I feel bad for him, I feel sorry that I hurt him or whatever, you know. You know and I don't want to screw up my ... and I'm sick of fighting.

Lawyer: How old are you?

Client: Thirty-two.

Lawyer: You have 40, 50, 60 years to say, "Gee whiz, why didn't I want to screw him?"

Client: Yeah, I know ... let's just get it over with.

This lawyer argues that the client's feelings, though temporary, still are extremely consequential and suggests that if her client acts on those feelings she will, in the long run, regret it. The client, in turn, accepts the lawyer's explanation for her reluctance to bargain and acquiesces in the lawyer's strategic advice.

Another example of talk concerning short-term feelings and their long-term consequences occurred in a California case in which support was again the subject of discussion.

Lawyer:	Well, taking spousal support out of the house payment is not being dishonest. You know, the main person we have to protect is you, because....
Client:	I know. [laughs]
Lawyer:	You know, as I have told you, whatever you take out of this marriage has got to last you the rest of your life. Prince Charming just has not been known, you know, to come along and sweep up my clients.
Client:	There's a lot of frogs out there, though.
Lawyer:	A lot of toads, even more than frogs. Not only that, but if they sweep you up and take you to the castle it's because they want you to sweep it up. So you can't count on him coming along and saying, "Oh, you need money you sweet little darling. Let me help you."
Client:	Right.
Lawyer:	You know, "Let me make your house payment for you." You know, "Let me pay off your house so you have it free and clear." They just are not beating the bushes out there.
Client:	I don't know how you work that out, you know. I mean, how do we....
Lawyer:	Hold out a little bit longer and don't just agree to, you know, giving him Grandma's undershorts and everything else, simply to get rid of him and be done with it.
Client:	Well, I'm a pushover. [laughs]
Lawyer:	At this point I've got a lot of people like you coming in here signing things I can't believe.
Client:	I've been a pushover all my life. That's my whole problem.
Lawyer:	Yes. And you have to toughen up and realize you're number one, now.
Client:	I'm trying. I'm trying. [laughs]
Lawyer:	Well, I mean if you stop and think, the rest of your life's out there.
Client:	I know. I've really tried to be nice about it, you know.
Lawyer:	Yeah. But you can only be nice so far. We've got to take care of you the rest of your life. And too many people have.... You know. "Too soon old and too late smart." And they have lived

to regret the fact that they wanted to get along with their ex-husband. If getting along with him means you live at poverty level and he lives on easy street, how long are you going to get along with him anyway, before you start resenting it?

Client: Not very long, I'm afraid. I'm afraid that's very true.

Lawyer: Right. Right. So in order to get along.... And he's going to resent it to some extent, but he's also going to, you know, respect the fact that you did stick up for your rights.

Client: Yeah.

Lawyer: He ain't going to like it.

Client: Oh no.

Lawyer: But because the two of you, if you don't get along with him because he's got too much and you don't have anything and you've got sufficient and he's having to give you a little of it, which do you think I'd vote for?

Client: Well, the sufficient.

Lawyer: That's what we need.

Client: Okay, I'll go back ... and tell him. This ought to ruin his whole Christmas.

In this case the lawyer emphasizes the consequences of the client's decision by repeated use of the phrase "the rest of your life." She interprets the client's feelings by referring to the experience of her "clients" in relation to "Prince Charming" and suggests that this client's willingness to give in just to "get rid" of her husband is similar to "a lot of people like you." She, like many other lawyers, employs folk wisdom ("Too soon old, and too late smart") to interpret her client's actions and to suggest more appropriate ways of behaving. In so doing she mobilizes interpretations from Schutz's (1962) "attitude of everyday life" to support her own rational purposive objectives. Here as elsewhere the lawyer is able to "sell" both her interpretation and her advice. Closure is reached; a successful negotiation of reality is consummated.

The tendency of lawyers to interpret client objectives as short-sighted, to urge them not to act on the basis of those desires, and to emphasize their legal experience as a source of expertise is further illustrated in discussions of visitation and child custody.

Lawyer The biggest mistake anybody can make in these situations in the initial stages is saying we'll let it go. That is the completely wrong idea and the reason it's wrong is that there has to be some kind of a pattern set up so that everybody gets comfortable with it. You can't get your life settled if you never know if [the] kids are going to be home or not. You know, it would really wreak havoc with you, and the same thing goes for the kids, they almost know they can push you around at that point.... I would say if we're going to go that way we should definitely state what nights they're going to stay with Mark and what nights they're going to stay with you and really set up a detailed program. Otherwise, it's just going to be havoc....

Client: It seems so hopeless to do that.

Lawyer: No it's not. I prefer to have very strict rules set up. I've seen too many cases where they say the visitation parent can come anytime they want and so on. That does not work out well.

Client: I will not get into that.... I'm not going to have a piece of paper saying my kids can be with me Monday, Wednesday, Friday and with ... Tuesday, Thursday, Saturday.... If John wants to spend the night he'll call, Mark will say sure and he'll come and pick him up ... like last night he stopped by the house ... I don't mind....

Lawyer: I've had a case, several cases, where the visitation parent would just show up anytime and where it was up to the custodial parent [and] she would just say I don't think this is an appropriate time. One time the guy showed up at 10 o'clock in the evening. We're talking about children around 10 years old. She was saying I just don't think this is an appropriate time. He was saying well I have reasonable visitation which means anytime, and they wind up back in court. Whereas if they had had a structured program, he would know when he could be there and not be there, etc. And the other reason, visitation gives her the discretion but that's the way most, most often happens, that's why I favor, in the beginning, that kind of a program, not everybody wants it. As I said I'm not gonna tell you that you have to take that, that's just my viewpoint. What I see is problems that can crop up and why we have those kinds of agreements.

Client: I want them to be with him whenever they want to ... if they decide they don't want to go with him I want them to go up to him and say I don't want to go with you dad. I don't think he would....

Lawyer: Well, just consider what I've said. Stop and think about it. Sit down in your living room or whatever and strongly consider what I've said and then give me your decision ... be logical about it, objective about it ... and ... I've seen people spend a lot of money trying to figure out what is reasonable visitation.

A later conversation about custody between this same lawyer and client replays similar concerns:

Client: I don't want to get involved in all these little nitty gritties.... I can't do it. I'm not up to it yet.

Lawyer: I disagree with you on the fact that ... I think you are playing with a real bomb. If you were to do it afterwards.... Let's say you gave custody to Mark of John and Max and Joel without having those little nitty gritties as you say worked out. I think you would be in a very poor position, because the person who has physical custody of the kids you know has the ace in the hole. And what I don't want to see is ... I don't want to see you behind the ball. I want to be sure that if a situation comes up that would hurt you, hopefully you've covered that and we've resolved that, so that you don't have to go back into court. Because it is really.... If he got ... you know he would leave in the middle of the night, you know, with the kids. And you could say "Well, I trust this guy" and everything else. See if you guys could really trust one another, or were really getting along, we wouldn't be sitting in front of Judge Sokol for this.

Throughout these conversations the lawyer portrays the client's reluctance to get involved in negotiating specific legal agreements as a misplaced reaction to the divorce process itself, as a mistake commonly made "in these situations." He refers to the divorce as "a very dangerous time period." He invokes his experience in "too many cases," and he describes another case, in which the client's unwillingness to be specific created "havoc," as a tactic to get her to reconsider. The client is urged to be "logical" and "objective." Through this advice the lawyer indicates that the client's expressed desires are neither logical nor objective and that client behavior during divorce is emotional and irrational. This lawyer ends by cautioning his client about an inclination to trust her husband, which the lawyer himself attributes to her; he tries to frighten her out of this posture by conjuring up an image of the husband sneaking off in the night with the children. In the end she agrees that she cannot really trust her husband, that she has to be careful about her own desire to get things over with and that they should go with "what we had approached them with originally. Me in the house with custody of the kids."

The focus on the temporary emotionalism that surrounds divorce is a continuing theme as lawyers give tactical advice to clients (see O'Gorman, 1963; Erlanger et al., 1987; Kressel et al., 1983). In one Massachusetts case, an experienced male lawyer focuses on the transient nature of hard feelings in a discussion with an older woman client whose husband has filed for a divorce after a long marriage.

Client: I think maybe it is just because of the way he's been I'm just on my guard all the time ... everything I do.

Lawyer: Don't be. He's angry, probably paying more than he thought he's going to pay.

Client: Considering....

Lawyer: Yeah. He was telling you how things were going to be before and he was wrong. Just don't let him get to you. Very often what happens after some time and the emotional aspects drop out you wind up having a better relationship than you had.

Client: I don't really feel that we're going to be friends again but I feel that we should at least be able to be civilized with one another.

Lawyer: You really can't. So many people that just are ready to go for the throat and after some years ... they start remembering the better times....

Client: My feeling now is that's over ... time to just go on.

Lawyer: You just can't find rationality though. Emotions get involved with that ... no matter who he is ... it just takes time.

This lawyer argues that his client's desire for a civilized relationship with her spouse cannot be attained during the divorce. Such a goal may only be realized after the divorce is over and "the emotional aspects drop out." He, like most of the other lawyers we observed, compares the emotionalism of divorce with a rationality that is put aside during that process.

This juxtaposition of emotion and rationality, this image of the divorce process itself as leading people to act in ways that they would not otherwise act, is prevalent as lawyer and client make decisions concerning the timing and substance of offers, demands and proposed agreements. One Massachusetts lawyer, for example, advised her client to postpone trying to reach an agreement with his wife.

She's too caught up in her own anger to really think straight. I wouldn't want to come up with an agreement now ... that six months from now she's going to go on and try to modify. I'd rather have her settle down again and on the basis of rationality work something out.

And a California lawyer suggests that an offer must be timed to coincide with one of the wife's emotional peaks.

Lawyer: Now, let me tell you what's coming up in the next two months. We've got the holidays coming up. Okay? And oftentimes you find people having tough times dealing with divorce cases around the holidays. My sense is we ought to get on it quickly, so that she isn't sitting there at her Thanksgiving table.... All of a sudden, even families who have had terrible times become the

Waltons at Thanksgiving, and everybody is a little bit ... I mean, holidays are classically depressing, even if you have your entire family.

Client: I agree.

Lawyer: So what I'm saying is, I think we ought to get on it, and get an offer over there, so that she has it long before Thanksgiving.... In other words, you want her to receive this offer at a time when she feels the best she's going to feel about you. Okay? If she gets it at a time that she feels the worst she's going to feel about you, don't care what's on the piece of paper, she's going to reject it.

Client: I'll do what I can.

This lawyer makes explicit the link between the explanation of behavior and the services that lawyers can provide. Interpreting behavior as responsive to circumstances and, therefore, contingent rather than rooted in intractable personality dispositions, lawyers suggest that their own sense of timing may be decisive. In so doing they increase the apparent value of the service they provide. As this same lawyer put it:

Your problems are pretty much accounting problems, not legal problems. The problems that you and I deal with are the psychological packaging of this thing, so it doesn't get your wife off chart.

Unlike clients who shift vocabularies when they move from their spouses' behavior to their own, lawyers deploy situational explanations in most contexts. They consistently use the effect of the divorce itself to explain behavior. In this way they construct an image of human behavior as adaptive and adaptable; they suggest that strategic thinking is as important in the realm of social behavior as it is in the planning and execution of legal maneuvers.

Conclusion

Close examination of lawyers' vocabularies of motive reveals that they overwhelmingly interpret conduct in situational or circumstantial terms. They rely on those explanations as they interpret their own actions and those of their clients and clients' spouses. Clients, on the other hand, attribute quite different meanings to social conduct. While they describe their own behavior in situational terms, they use dispositional or character terms to describe their spouses.

The vocabularies of motive used by clients in divorce cases excuse and justify their conduct and place blame for the failure of their marriage, as well as for problems in the legal process of divorce, squarely on their spouses. Client interpretations of behavior may save face and evoke sympathy. For most clients the divorce lawyer is a stranger whose loyalty cannot automatically be assumed and must to some extent be earned. By projecting blame on their spouses, clients work to reinforce that loyalty, to penetrate the objectivity and reduce the social distance built into the traditional professional relationship. Their vocabulary serves to add sympathy to fees as a basis on which their lawyers' energies can be commanded. The emphasis on fault and blame thus has an instrumental function in lawyer/client relations as well as providing psychological distance from a failed marriage and contentious divorce proceedings.

This emphasis poses an awkward choice for lawyers. If they were to join with clients in the project of reconstructing the marriage failure and the moral standing of spouses, they would be dragged into a domain that is, in principle, irrelevant to no-fault divorce, wastes their time, and is in fact beyond their expertise. On the other hand, if they directly challenge client characterizations, or dismiss them as legally irrelevant, they risk alienating their clients or deepening client mistrust. Thus, most of the time lawyers remain silent in the face of client attacks on their spouses. They refuse to explore the past and to participate in the construction of a shared version of the social history of the marriage. When they do interpret behavior they limit themselves to conduct that is directly relevant to the legal process of divorce, and they stress circumstances and situations that produce common responses rather than intentions or dispositions unique to particular individuals. In this way they deflect what is, for many clients, a strong desire to achieve some moral vindication, even in a no-fault world (Merry & Silbey, 1984). As Griffiths (1986: 155) argues:

> This contrast suggests that lawyers and clients are in effect largely occupied with two different divorces: lawyers with a legal divorce, clients with a social and emotional divorce. The lawyers orient themselves toward legal norms and institutional practices, the clients toward the social norms of their environment. Clients go to lawyers because it is otherwise impossible to secure a divorce, not because they want to invoke the legal system as a regulatory and conflict-resolving institution. That the law concerns itself with the substance of their relationship is an adventitious circumstance for most divorcing couples....

Lawyers and clients in our sample did negotiate about the meaning of the spouse's behavior during the divorce and its effects on strategies and tactics. In this domain the asymmetry in power between lawyers and clients is most apparent. By limiting interpretive activity to their area of expertise, lawyers are able to explain the social world through the lenses of the legal process. They are able to structure conversation to fit their rational-purposive ideology and to limit the impact of their clients' egocentric views of social life.

Just as the reliance of lawyers on situational explanations and their emphasis on the divorce itself as the most relevant situation in explaining behavior validates their implicit claim to expertise and authority, so the focus on divorce and its explanatory power brings more of the client's social world within the lawyer's claim to competence. Lawyers can have little insight into the dispositions or character of people with whom they have had little contact; legal training provides no readily recognizable psychological expertise (see Simon, 1980). However, knowledge of the divorce process and experience in dealing with people as they experience it is precisely what divorce lawyers are supposed to be able to provide. Lawyers' explanations put a premium on their own strategic judgment, and on deft manipulation of the legal process to minimize the effect on the divorce of the negative behavioral consequences often associated with marriage failure. Thus, the lawyer's construction of meaning justifies his authority and invites client dependence (Sarat & Felstiner, 1986; Kressel, 1985).

At the same time, lawyers' refusal to engage with client efforts to give meaning to the past is not without consequences. It often means that clients end up dissatisfied with lawyers who, they believe, do not understand or empathize with them. Furthermore, the legal construction of social relations may go far in explaining how contentious and difficult the settlement process becomes (see Erlanger et al., 1987; MacDougall, 1984; Mnookin, 1984). Because agreements often require continuing exchanges between the spouses, whether any proposed agreement has a reasonable chance of working, perhaps even whether it can be negotiated at all, depends on the way the divorcing parties view each other. Thus, lawyers' reactions to client vocabularies of motive have a direct effect on disposition prospects and consequences. If the lawyer does not challenge client attributions of fault and blame, unexamined, uncontradicted characterizations may make it more difficult to persuade clients to rely on future promises of the spouse whose allegedly hostile prior behavior remains salient. Our data suggest lawyers believe that behavior is more influenced by situation than by personality. However, to insist on that belief in the face of their clients' more personalistic construction of social relations may threaten their relationship; yet to ignore it may threaten their ability to help secure a negotiated or stable outcome.

The vocabularies of motive used in lawyer/client interaction in divorce respond to the distinctive characteristics of that social relationship. Lawyers deploy the resources of professional position; they emphasize their experience and the expertise that experience provides as they try to limit involvement in the client's social world. While this limitation gives power to lawyers' interpretations of the social world, it cannot guarantee acquiescent clients. By repeatedly expanding the conversational agenda, clients resist their lawyers' efforts to limit the scope of social life relevant to their interaction. They manipulate attributions of blame and victimization to counter professional authority and claims to expertise on which lawyers rely. Thus, in divorce as elsewhere, law and the images of social life with which it is associated are deeply embedded in a conflicted and unequal social relationship.

DISCUSSION QUESTIONS

1. Are understandings of motive negotiated or imposed? Is the result consensus or disagreement? Are lawyers more important than judges in structuring law-in-action?

2. Divorce involves a reconstruction of the past to determine the future; is this true of all litigation? all legal interaction? Does divorce have distinctive characteristics? Why are clients obsessed with what happened? Why are lawyers indifferent? When lawyers engage clients about their feelings, why do they favor divorce as the solution? What are the differences between the explanations clients give for their spouse's behavior and their own?

3. When clients tell their stories to their lawyers, what responses are they seeking? What responses are they getting? Why are the two so divergent? Do lawyers treat male and female clients differently? Would you expect male and female lawyers to behave differently? Is there an inevitable tension between the roles of lawyer as counsellor and advocate?

4. How does the power to shape and characterize the narrative shift as the temporal focus changes from past to present to future? How does the "knowledge" of client and lawyer differ, and what power does each derive from such knowledge? Why do lawyers appear to push their clients to seek a superior financial settlement and clear custodial arrangements? Is it only male lawyers who do this with female clients? What rhetorical devices do lawyers use to persuade their clients? How do the images of client and lawyer differ about the divorce process and post-divorce situation? How do their interpretations of behavior differ?

References

ABEL, Richard L. (1973) "Law Books and Books About Law," 26 *Stanford Law Review* 175.

_____ (1981) "Conservative Conflict and the Reproduction of Capitalism: The Role of Informal Justice," 9 *International Journal of the Sociology of Law* 245.

_____ ed. (1982a) *The Politics of Informal Justice*, 2 vols. New York: Academic Press.

_____ (1982b) "A Socialist Approach to Risk," 41 *Maryland Law Review* 695.

ADLER, J.W., D.R. HENSLER, and C.E. NELSON (1983) *Simple Justice*. Santa Monica, Calif: Rand.

AKERS, Ronald L., Marvin D. KROHN, Lonn LANZA-KADUCE and Marcia RODOSEVICH (1979) "Social Learning and Deviant Behavior: A Specific Test of a General Theory," 44 *American Sociological Review* 636.

ALEINIKOFF, Thomas Alexander and David A. MARTIN (1991) *Immigration: Process and Policy* (2d ed.). St. Paul, Minn: West Publishing Co.

ALEXANDER, S. and M. RUDERMAN (1989) "The Role of Procedural and Distributive Justice in Organizational Behavior," 3 *Social Justice Research*.

ALSCHULER, Albert W. (1975) "The Defense Attorney's Role in Plea Bargaining," 84 *Yale Law Journal* 1179.

_____ (1978) "Sentencing Reform and Prosecutorial Power: A Critique of Recent Proposals for 'Fixed' and 'Presumptive' Sentencing," 126 *University of Pennsylvania Law Review* 550.

AMERICAN BAR ASSOCIATION. PROJECT ON MINIMUM STANDARDS FOR CRIMINAL JUSTICE (1967) *Standards Relating to Pleas of Guilty*. New York: Institute for Judicial Administration.

AMERICAN LAW INSTITUTE (1934) *A Study of the Business of the Federal Courts, Part 1*. Philadelphia: American Law Institute.

ANDERSON, Linda S., Theodore G. CHIRICOS and Gordon P. WALDO (1977) "Formal and Informal Sanctions: A Comparison of Deterrent Effects," 25 *Social Problems* 103.

ARCHBOLD, John Frederick (1824) *Pleading and Evidence in Criminal Cases* (1st American Edition).

ARNAUD, André-Jean, ed. (1988) *Dictionnaire Encyclopédique de Théorie et de Sociologie du Droit*. Paris: Librairie Générale de Droit et de Jurisprudence; Brussels: E. Story-Scientia.

AUBERT, Vilhelm (1983) *In Search of Law: Sociological Approaches to Law;* Totowa, N.J.: Barnes & Noble.

BAAB, George W. and William FURGESON (1967) "Texas Sentencing Practices: A Statistical Study," 45 *Texas Law Review* 471.

BACHOFEN, Johann Jakob (1861) *Das Mutterrecht*. Stuttgart: Krais & Hoffman.

BACHRACH, Peter, and Morton S. BARATZ (1970) *Power and Poverty: Theory and Practice*. New York: Oxford University Press.

BAKER, Newman F. (1933) "The Prosecutor—Initiation of Prosecution," 23 *Journal of Criminal Law and Criminology* 770.

BAKWIN, Harry (1945) "Pseudodoxia Pediatrics," 232 *New England Journal of Medicine* 691.

BALDUS, David C., George WOODWORTH and Charles PULASKI (1983) "Discrimination in Georgia's Capital Charging and Sentencing System: A Preliminary Report." Unpublished report submitted by petitioner in *McCleskey v. Kemp*, 753 F.2nd 877 (1985).

BARAK-GLANTZ, Israel L. (1985) "The Anatomy of Another Prison Riot," in M. Braswell, S. Dillingham, and R. Montgomery, Jr. (eds.), *Prison Violence in America*. Cincinnati: Anderson Publishing Co.

BEAN, Frank D. and Robert G. CUSHING (1971) "Criminal Homicide, Punishment, and Deterrence: Methodological and Substantive Reconsiderations," 52 *Social Science Quarterly* 277.

BEAN, Philip (1974) *The Social Control of Drugs*. London: Martin Robertson.

BECKER, Howard S. (1963) *Outsiders: Studies in the Sociology of Deviance*. New York: Free Press.

BEDAU, Hugo Adam (1983) "Witness to a Persecution: The Death Penalty and the Dawson Five," 8 *Black Law Journal* 7.

BENTELE, Ursula (1985) "The Death Penalty in Georgia: Still Arbitrary," 62 *Washington University Law Quarterly* 573.

BENTHAM, Jeremy (1827) *Rationale of Judicial Evidence*. London: John Bowring.

BERGER, Peter and Thomas LUCKMAN (1966) *The Social Construction of Reality*. Garden City, N.Y.: Doubleday.

BERK, Richard (1983) "An Introduction to Sample Selection Bias in Sociological Data," 48 *American Sociological Review* 386.

BERMAN, Daniel M. (1978) *Death on the Job: Occupational Safety and Health Struggles in the United States*. New York: Monthly Review Press.

BIANCHI, Herman (1975) "Social Control and Deviance in the Netherlands," in H. Bianchi, M. Simondi, and I. Taylor (eds.), *Deviance and Control in Europe*. New York: John Wiley.

BICKMAN, Leonard (1976) "Attitude Toward an Authority and the Reporting of a Crime," 39 *Sociometry* 76.

BITTNER, Egon (1967) "The Police on Skid-Row: A Study of Peace-Keeping," 32 *American Sociological Review* 699.

BLACK, Charles L., Jr. (1981) *Capital Punishment—The Inevitability of Caprice and Mistake* (2nd Ed.). New York: W.W. Norton and Co.

BLACK, Donald (1970) "Production of Crime Rates," 35 *American Sociological Review* 733.

_____ (1973a) "The Mobilization of Law," 2 *Journal of Legal Studies* 125.

_____ (1973b) "The Boundaries of Legal Sociology," in D. Black and M. Mileski (eds.), *The Social Organization of Law*. New York: Seminar Press.

_____ (1976) *The Behavior of Law*. New York: Academic Press.

_____ (1989). *Sociological Justice*. New York: Oxford University Press.

BLACK, Donald and M.P. BAUMGARTNER (1983) "Toward a Theory of the Third Party," in K. Boyum and L. Mather (eds.), *Empirical Theories About Courts*. New York: Longman.

BLACKSTONE, William (1765–69) *Commentaries on the Laws of England*.

BLANKENBURG, Erhard, Günther SCHMID and Hubert P. TREIBER (1976) "Legitimitäts- und Implementierungsprobleme 'aktiver Arbeitsmarkt-politik,'" in R. Ebbinghaus (ed.), *Bürgerlicher Staat und Politische Legitimation*. Frankfurt: Suhrkamp.

BLOOR, Michael (1976) "Bishop Berkeley and the Adenotonsillectomy Enigma: An Exploration of Variation in the Social Construction of Medical Disposals," 10 *Sociology* 43.

BLUM, Richard H. and Mary Lou FUNKHOUSER (1965) "Legislators on Social Scientists and a Social Issue: A Report and Commentary on Some Discussions with Lawmakers about Drug Abuse," 1 *Journal of Applied Behavioral Science* 84

BLUMBERG, Abraham (1967) "The Practice of Law as a Confidence Game," 1 *Law & Society Review* 15.

BOHANNAN, Paul, ed. (1967) *Law and Warfare*. Garden City, N.Y.: Natural History Press.

BORTNER, M.A. (1982) *Inside a Juvenile Court: The Tarnished Ideal of Individualized Justice*. New York: New York University Press.

BOURDIEU, Pierre (1977) *Outline of a Theory of Practice*. Cambridge: Cambridge University Press.

BOWERS, William J. (1983) "The Pervasiveness of Arbitrariness and Discrimination under Post-*Furman* Capital Statutes," 74 *Journal of Criminal Law and Crminology* 1067.

BOWERS, William J. and Glenn L. PIERCE (1975) "The Illusion of Deterrence in Isaac Ehrlich's Research on Capital Punishment," 85 *Yale Law Journal* 187.

_____ (1980) "Arbitrariness and Discrimination under Post-*Furman* Capital Statutes," 26 *Crime and Delinquency* 563.

BOWERS, William J., with Glenn L. PIERCE and John F. McDEVITT (1984) *Legal Homicide: Death as Punishment in America, 1864–1982.* Boston: Northeastern University Press.

BRADY, James P. (1981) "Sorting Out the Exile's Confusion: Or a Dialogue on Popular Justice," 5 *Contemporary Crises* 31.

BRAKEL, Samuel (1986) "Prison Reform Litigation: Has the Revolution Gone Too Far?" 70 *Judicature* 5.

BRENNER, Steven N. and Earl A. MOLANDER (1977) "Is the Ethics of Business Changing?" 55 *Harvard Business Review* 57.

BRESSLER, Fenton S. (1965) *Reprieve: A Study of a System.* London: Harrap.

BRETT, J.M. and S.B. GOLDBERG (1983) "Grievance Mediation in the Coal Industry: A Field Experiment," 37 *Industrial and Labor Relations Review* 49.

BRICKEY, Stephen L. and Dan E. MILLER (1975) "Bureaucratic Due Process: An Ethnography of a Traffic Court," 22 *Social Problems* 688.

BRIFFAULT, Robert (1927) *The Mothers: a study of the origins of sentiments and institutions* (3 vols.). New York: Macmillan.

BRIGHAM, John (1978) *Constitutional Language: An Interpretation of Judicial Decision.* Westport, Conn.: Greenwood Press.

BRYCE, James (1897) *Impressions of South Africa.* London: Macmillan.

CAGLIOSTRO, Anthony (1974) "New York's New Drug Laws—An Analysis," 4 *Journal of Drug Issues* 117.

CAIN, Maureen (1979) "The General Practice Lawyer and the Client," 7 *International Journal of the Sociology of Law* 331.

CAIN, Maureen and Alan HUNT (1979) *Marx and Engels on Law.* New York: Academic Press.

CAIRNS, Huntington (1931) "Law and Anthropology," in Victor F. Calverton (ed.), *The Making of Man: An Outline of Anthropology.* New York: Modern Library.

CALAVITA, Kitty (1983) "The Demise of the Occupational Safety and Health Administration: A Case Study in Symbolic Action," 30 *Social Problems* 437.

_____ (1992) *Inside the State: The Bracero Program, Immigration and the I.N.S.* New York: Routledge.

CAMERON, Mary (1964) *The Booster and the Snitch.* New York: Free Press.

CAPPELLETTI, Mauro and Bryant GARTH, eds. (1978) *Access to Justice: A World Survey,* 4 vols. Milan: Giuffré; Alphen aan den Rijn: Sijthoff..

CARLIN, Jerome E. (1962) *Lawyers on Their Own: A Study of Individual Practitioners in Chicago.* New Brunswick, N.J.: Rutgers University Press.

CARLIN, Jerome E. and Jan HOWARD (1965) "Legal Representation and Class Justice," 12 *UCLA Law Review* 381.

CARSON, W.G. (1974) "The Sociology of Crime and the Emergence of Criminal Laws: A Review of Some Excursions into the Sociology of Law," in P. Rock and M. McIntosh (eds.), *Deviance and Social Control.* London: Tavistock.

_____ (1981) *The Other Price of Britain's Oil: Safety and Control in the North Sea.* Oxford: Martin Robertson.

CARTER, Leif H. (1974) *The Limits of Order.* Lexington, Mass.: Lexington Books.

CASPER, Jonathan (1972) *American Criminal Justice: The Defendant's Perspective.* Englewood Cliffs, N.J.: Prentice-Hall.

CHAMBERS, Reid P. (1975) "Judicial Enforcement of the Federal Trust Responsibility to Indians," 27 *Stanford Law Review* 1213.

CHAMBLISS, William (1969) "A Sociological Analysis of the Law of Vagrancy," in R. Quinney (ed.), *Crime and Justice in Society.* Boston: Little Brown.

_____. (1979) "On Lawmaking," 6 *British Journal of Law and Society* 149.

CHAMBLISS, William and Robert SEIDMAN (1982) *Law, Order, and Power* (2d ed.). Reading, Mass.: Addison-Wesley.

CHASE, Anthony (1977) *The Legacy of Malthus.* New York: Knopf.

CHESNEY-LIND, Meda (1977) "Judicial Paternalism and the Female Status Offender: Training Women to Know Their Place," 23 *Crime and Delinquency* 121.

_____ (1978) "Young Women in the Arms of the Law" and "Chivalry Re-Examined: Women and the Criminal Justice System," in L. Bowker (ed.), *Women, Crime, and the Criminal Justice System.* Lexington, Mass.: Lexington Books.

_____ (1986) "Female Offenders: Paternalism Re-Examined." Unpublished. Youth Development and Research Center, University of Hawaii, Honolulu.

CHRISTIE, Nils (1977) "Conflicts as Property," 17 *British Journal of Criminology* 1.

CHURCH, Thomas W., Jr. (1976) "Plea Bargaining, Concessions, and the Courts: Analysis of a Quasi-Experiment," 10 *Law & Society Review* 377.

COATES, Dan and Steven PENROD (1981) "Social Psychology and the Emergence of Disputes," 15 *Law & Society Review* 655.

COCKBURN, James S. (1975) "Early-Modern Assize Records as Historical Evidence," 5 *Journal of the Society of Archivists* 215.

_____ (1978) "Trial By the Book? Fact and Theory in the Criminal Process, 1558–1625," in J. H. Baker (ed.), *Legal Records and the Historian.* London: Royal Historical Society.

COHEN, Fay G. (1986) *Treaties on Trial: The Continuing Controversy over Northwest Indian Fishing Rights.* Seattle: University of Washington Press.

COHEN, Felix. (1947) "Original Indian Title," 32 *Minnesota Law Review* 28.

_____ (1971) *Handbook on Federal Indian Law.* Albuquerque: University of New Mexico Press.

COHEN, Julius, Reginald A. ROBSON and Alan BATES (1958). *Parental Authority: The Community and the Law.* New Brunswick, N.J.: Rutgers University Press.

COHEN, Lawrence and Rodney STARK (1974) "Discriminatory Labelling and the Five Finger Discount—An Empirical Analysis of Differential Shoplifting Dispositions," 11 *Journal of Research in Crime and Delinquency* 25.

COLE, George F. (1970) "The Decision to Prosecute," 4 *Law & Society Review* 331.

COLLIER, Jane (1973) *Law and Social Change in Zinacantan.* Stanford: Stanford University Press.

_____ (1975) "Legal Processes," 4 *Annual Review of Anthropology.*

COLLINS, Hugh (1982) *Marxism and Law.* Oxford: Oxford University Press.

COLSON, Elizabeth (1974) *Tradition and Contract: The Problem of Order.* Chicago: Aldine.

CONLEY, John M. and William M. O'BARR (1990) *Rules Versus Relationships: The Ethnography of Legal Discourse.* Chicago: University of Chicago Press.

CONLEY, John M., William M. O'BARR and E.A. LIND (1978) "The Power of Language: Presentational Style in the Courtroom," 1978 *Duke Law Journal* 1375.

COOK, Philip J. (1980) "Research in Criminal Deterrence: Laying the Groundwork for the Second Decade," in N. Morris and M. Tonry (eds.), 2 *Crime and Justice: An Annual Review of Research.* Chicago: University of Chicago Press.

COTTERRELL, Roger (1984). T*he Sociology of Law: an introduction.* London: Butterworths.

COTTU, Charles (1822) *On the Administration of Criminal Justice in England.* Boston: Little, Brown.

CRESSEY, Donald R. (1969) *Theft of the Nation: The Structure and Operations of Organized Crime in America.* New York: Harper & Row.

CURRAN, Debra A. (1983) "Judicial Discretion and Defendant's Sex," 21 *Criminology* 41.

CURRIE, Elliott P. (1968) "Crimes without Criminals: Witchcraft and its Control in Renaissance Europe," 3 *Law & Society Review* 7.

DALY, Kathleen (1983) *Order in the Court: Gender and Justice.* Ph.D. dissertation, Department of Sociology, University of Massachusetts-Amherst.

_____ (1987) "Discrimination in the Criminal Courts: Family, Gender, and the Problem of Equal Treatment," 66 *Social Forces.*

_____ (1989a) "Rethinking Judicial Paternalism: Gender, Work-Family Relations, and Sentencing," 3 *Gender & Society* 9.

_____ (1989b) "Neither Conflict nor Labeling nor Paternalism Will Suffice: Intersections in Race, Ethnicity, Gender, and Family in Criminal Court Decisions," 35 *Crime & Delinquency* 136.

_____ (1989c) "Criminal Justice Ideologies and Practices in Different Voices: Some Feminist Questions About Justice," 17 *International Journal of the Sociology of Law* 1.

_____ (1994) *Gender, Crime, and Punishment*. New Haven: Yale University Press.

DANET, Brenda, K. B. HOFFMAN, and N. C. KERMISH (1980) "Obstacles to the Study of Lawyer-Client Interaction," 14 *Law & Society Review* 905.

DANIELS, Arlene K. (1970) "The Social Construction of Military Psychiatric Diagnoses," in H. Dreitzel (ed.), 2 *Recent Sociology: Patterns of Communicative Behavior*. New York: Macmillan.

DANZIG, Richard (1973) "Toward the Creation of a Complementary Decentralized System of Criminal Justice," 26 *Stanford Law Review* 1.

DANZIG, Richard and Michael J. LOWY (1975) "Everyday Disputes and Mediation in the United States: A Reply to Professor Felstiner," 9 *Law & Society Review* 675.

DICKSON, Donald T. (1968) "Bureaucracy and Morality: An Organizational Perspective on a Moral Crusade," 16 *Social Problems* 143.

DOMHOFF, William (1978) *The Powers That Be*. New York: Random House.

DONNELLY, Patrick (1982) "The Origins of the Occupational Safety and Health Act of 1970," 30 *Social Problems* 13.

DOO, Leigh-Wai (1973) "Dispute Settlement in Chinese-American Communities," 21 *American Journal of Comparative Law* 627.

DURKHEIM, Emile (1964) *The Division of Labor in Society*. New York: Free Press.

_____ (1973). "Two Laws of Penal Evolution," 2 *Economy and Society* 285.

EATON, Mary (1984) *Familial Ideology and Summary Justice: Women Defendants before a Suburban Magistrate's Court*. Ph.D. dissertation, Department of Sociology, University of London.

_____ (1983) "Mitigating Circumstances: Familiar Rhetoric," 11 *International Journal of the Sociology of Law* 385.

_____ (1985) "Documenting the Defendant: Placing Women in Social Inquiry Reports," in J. Brophy and C. Smart (eds.), *Women-in-Law: Explorations in Law, Family, and Sexuality*. Boston: Routledge and Kegan Paul.

ECKHOFF, Torstein (1960) "Sociology of Law in Scandinavia," 4 *Scandinavian Studies in Law* 29.

_____ (1966) "The Mediator, the Judge and the Administrator in Conflict Resolution," 10 *Acta Sociologia* 148.

EDELMAN, Murray (1967) *The Symbolic Uses of Politics*. Urbana.: University of Illinois Press.

EDWARDS, Susan S.M. (1984) *Women on Trial*. Manchester: Manchester University Press.

EHRHARDT, Charles W. and L. Harold LEVINSON (1973) "Florida's Legislative Response to *Furman*: An Exercise in Futility?" 64 *Journal of Criminal Law and Criminology* 10.

EHRLICH, Eugen (1916) "Montesquieu and Sociological Jurisprudence," 29 *Harvard Law Review* 582.

_____ (1922) "The Sociology of Law," 36 *Harvard Law Review* 130.

_____ (1936) *Fundamental Principles of the Sociology of Law* (Walter L. Moll trans.). Cambridge, Mass.: Harvard University Press.

EHRLICH, Isaac (1975) "The Deterrent Effect of Capital Punishment: A Question of Life and Death," 65 *American Economic Review* 397.

EISENSTEIN, James and Herbert JACOB (1877) *Felony Justice: An Organizational Analysis of Criminal Courts*. Boston: Little Brown.

EKLAND-OLSON, Sheldon (1982) "Deviance, Social Control and Social Networks," in S. Spitzer and R. Simon (eds.), 4 *Research in Law, Deviance and Social Control*. Greenwich, Conn.: JAI Press Inc.

_____ (1984) "Social Control and Relational Disturbance: A Microstructural Paradigm," in D. Black (ed.), *Toward a General Theory of Social Control*. Vol. 2. New York: Academic Press.

_____ (1986) "Crowding, Social Control, and Prison Violence: Evidence from the Post-*Ruiz* Years in Texas," 20 *Law & Society Review* 389.

EMERSON, Robert M. (1969) *Judging Delinquents: Context and Process in Juvenile Court.* Chicago: Aldine.

_____ (1974) "Role Determinants in Juvenile Court," in D. Glaser (ed.), *Handbook of Criminology.* Chicago: Rand McNally.

_____ (1981) "On Last Resorts," 87 *American Journal of Sociology* 1.

_____ (1991) "Case Processing and Interorganizational Knowledge: Detecting the 'Real Reasons' for Referrals," 38 *Social Problems* 198.

EMERSON, Robert M. and Melvin POLLNER (1976) "Dirty Work Designations: Their Features and Consequences in a Psychiatric Setting," 23 *Social Problems* 243.

EMERSON, Robert M. and Blair PALEY (1992) "Organizational Horizons and Complaint-Filing," in Keith Hawkins (ed.), *The Uses of Discretion.* New York: Oxford University Press.

ENGEL, David M. (1980) "Legal Pluralism in an American Community: Perspectives on a Civil Trial Court," 1980 *American Bar Foundation Research Journal* 425.

ENGEL, Kathleen and Stanley ROTHMAN (1983) "Prison Violence and the Paradox of Reform," 73 *The Public Interest* 91.

ENGELS, F. (1902) *The Origin of the Family, Private Property and the State* (Ernest Untermann trans.). Chicago: Charles H. Kerr.

ERICKSON, Maynard L. and Jack P. GIBBS (1979) "On the Perceived Severity of Legal Penalties," 70 *Journal of Criminal Law and Criminology* 102.

ERICKSON, Maynard L., Jack P. GIBBS and Gary F. JENSEN (1977) "The Deterrence Doctrine and the Perceived Certainty of Legal Punishments," 42 *American Sociological Review* 305.

ERIKSON, Kai T. (1966) *Wayward Puritans: A Study in the Sociology of Deviance.* New York: John Wiley.

ERLANGER, Howard, Elizabeth CHAMBLISS, and Marygold MELLI (1987) "Participation and Flexibility in Informal Processes: Cautions from the Divorce Context," 21 *Law & Society Review* 585.

ETZIONI, Amitai (1968) *The Active Society. A Theory of Societal and Political Processes.* New York: Free Press.

EVAN, William M., ed. (1980) *The Sociology of Law: A Social-Structural Perspective.* New York: Free Press.

EVAN, William M. (1990) *Social Structure and the Law: Theoretical and Empirical Perspectives.* Newbury Park, Calif.: Sage.

FEELEY, Malcolm M. (1979) The *Process Is the Punishment: Handling Cases in a Lower Criminal Court.* New York: Russell Sage.

FEEST, Johannes and Erhard BLANKENBURG (1972) *Die Definitionsmacht der Polizei.* Düsseldorf: Westdeutscher Verlag.

FELD, Scott L. (1981) "The Focused Organization of Social Ties," 86 *American Journal of Sociology* 1015.

FELSTINER, William L. F. (1974) "Influences of Social Organization on Dispute Processing," 9 *Law & Society Review* 63.

_____ (1975) "Avoidance as Dispute Processing: An Elaboration," 9 *Law & Society Review* 695.

FELSTINER, William L.F. and Austin SARAT (1986) "Law and Strategy in the Divorce Lawyer's Office," 20 *Law & Society Review* 93.

FELSTINER, Wiliam L.F., Richard L. ABEL and Austin SARAT (1980–81) "The Emergence and Transformation of Disputes: Naming, Blaming, Claiming...," 15 *Law & Society Review* 631.

FERDINAND, Theodore T. (1973) "Criminality, the Courts, and the Constabulary in Boston: 1703–1967" (unpublished).

FERRARI, Vincenzo, ed. (1990) *Developing Sociology of Law: A World-Wide Documentary Enquiry.* Milan: Dott. A Giuffré.

FINKELSTEIN, Herman (1965) "The Composer and the Public Interest—Regulation of Performing Rights Societies," 19 *Law and Contemporary Problems* 275.

FISHER, Eric (1975) "Community Courts: An Alternative to Conventional Criminal Adjudication," 24 *American University Law Review* 1253.

FISHER, William H., III, Morton J. HORWITZ and Thomas A. REED, eds. (1993) *American Legal Realism*. New York: Oxford University Press.

FITZPATRICK, Peter (1983a) "Law, Plurality and Underdevelopment," in D. Sugarman (ed.), *Legality, Ideology and the State*. London: Academic Press.

_____ (1983b) "Marxism and Legal Pluralism," 1 *Australian Journal of Law and Society* 45.

_____ (1984) "Law and Societies," 22 *Osgoode Hall Law Journal* 115.

FOLEY, Linda A. and Richard S. POWELL (1982) "The Discretion of Prosecutors, Judges, and Juries in Capital Cases," 7 *Criminal Justice Review* 16.

FOOTE, Caleb (1972) "The Sentencing Function," in *Annual Chief Justice Warren Conference on Advocacy in the United States, A Program for Prison Reform: The Final Report*. Cambridge, Mass: The Roscoe Pound-American Trial Lawyers Foundation.

FOSDICK, Raymond (1922) "Police Administration," in Roscoe Pound and Felix Frankfurter (eds.), *Criminal Justice in Cleveland: Reports of the Administration of Criminal Justice in Cleveland, Ohio*. Cleveland: Cleveland Foundation.

FOUCAULT, Michel (1977) *Discipline and Punish* (trans. A. Sheridan). New York: Random House.

FRANKLIN, Julian H. (1963) *Jean Bodin and the Sixteenth-Century Revolution in the Methodology of Law and History*. New York: Columbia University Press.

FREDRICKSON, George (1981) *White Supremacy*. Oxford: Oxford University Press.

FREEMAN, Alan D. (1978) "Legitimizing Racial Discrimination through Anti-Discrimination Law: A Critical Review of Supreme Court Doctrine," 62 *Minnesota Law Review* 1049.

FREIDSON, Eliot (1970) *Profession of Medicine: A Study of the Sociology of Applied Knowledge*. New York: Harper & Row.

FRIEDMAN, Lawrence M. (1977) *Law and Society: An Introduction*. Englewood Cliffs, N.J.: Prentice-Hall.

_____ (1979) "Plea Bargaining in Historical Perspective," 13 *Law & Society Review* 247.

FRIEDMAN, Lawrence M. and Stewart MACAULAY, eds. (1977) *Law and the Behavioral Sciences* (2d ed.). Indianapolis: Bobbs-Merrill.

FRIEDMAN, Lawrence M. and Robert V. PERCIVAL (1976) "A Tale of Two Courts: Litigation in Alameda and San Benito Counties," 10 *Law & Society Review* 267.

FULLER, Hugh Nelson (1931) *Criminal Justice in Virginia*. Charlottesville: University of Virginia Institute for Research in the Social Sciences.

FULLER, Lon L. (1969) "Human Interaction and the Law," 14 *American Journal of Jurisprudence* 1.

GABEL, Peter (1980) "Reification in Legal Reasoning," 3 *Research in Law and Sociology* 25.

GALANTER, Marc (1974) "Why the 'Haves' Come Out Ahead: Speculations on the Limits of Legal Change," 9 *Law & Society Review* 95.

_____ (1983) "Reading the Landscape of Disputes: What We Know and Don't Know (And Think We Know) About Our Allegedly Contentious and Litigious Society," 31 *UCLA Law Review* 4.

GALLIHER, John F., James L. McCARTNEY and Barbara E. BAUM (1977) "Nebraska's Marijuana Law: A Case of Unexpected Legislative Innovation," in J.F. Galliher and J.L. McCartney (eds.), *Criminology: Power, Crime and Criminal Law*. Homewood, Ill.: Dorsey Press.

GARDNER, A. (1930) *Canfield: The True Story of the Greatest Gambler*. New York: Doubleday.

GARFINKEL, Harold (1949) "Research Note on Inter- and Intra-Racial Homicides," 27 *Social Forces* 369.

_____ (1967) *Studies in Ethnomethodology*. Englewood Cliffs, N.J.: Prentice-Hall.

GEERKEN, Michael R. and Walter R. GOVE (1975) "Deterrence: Some Theoretical Considerations," 9 *Law & Society Review* 497.

GEIS, Gilbert (1972) "Criminal Penalties for Corporate Criminals," 8 *Criminal Law Bulletin* 377.

GELFAND, Donna, Donald HARTMANN, Patrice WALDER, and Brent PAGE (1973) "Who Reports Shoplifters? A Field-experimental Study," 25 *Journal of Personality and Social Psychology* 276.

GELLHORN, Walter (1966) *When Americans Complain: Governmental Grievance Procedures.* Cambridge, Mass.: Harvard University Press.

GEORGIA DEPARTMENT OF PUBLIC WELFARE (1924) "Crime and the Georgia Courts," 16 *Journal of the American Institute of Criminal Law and Criminology* 169.

GETCHES, David, Daniel ROSENFELT and Charles WILKINSON (1979) *Federal Indian Law.* St. Paul: West.

GIBBS, Jack P. (1968) "Crime, Punishment and Deterrence," 48 *Social Science Quarterly* 515.

_____ (1975) *Crime, Punishment and Deterrence.* New York: Elsevier.

GIBBS, James L. (1963) "The Kpelle Moot," 33 *Africa 1.*

GIDDENS, Anthony (1979) *Central Problems in Social Theory: Action, Structure and Contradiction in Social Analysis.* London: Macmillan.

_____ (1982) *Profiles and Critiques in Social Theory.* London: Macmillan.

_____ (1984) *The Constitution of Society.* Cambridge: Polity Press.

GILBOY, Janet A. (1988) "Administrative Review in a System of Conflicting Values," 13 *Law & Social Inquiry* 515.

_____ (1991) "Deciding Who Gets In: Decisionmaking by Immigration Inspectors," 25 *Law & Society Review* 571.

GINSBERG, Morris (1953) *On the Diversity of Morals.* London: Royal Anthropological Institute of Great Britain and Ireland.

GLUCKMAN, Max (1963) "Gossip and Scandal," 3 *Current Anthropology* 307.

GOFFMAN, Erving (1959) *The Presentation of Self in Everyday Life.* Garden City, N.Y.: Doubleday.

_____ (1961) *Asylums: Essays on the Social Situation of Mental Patients and Other Inmates.* New York: Anchor Books.

GOLD, David, Clarence LO, and Erik Olin WRIGHT (1975) "Recent Developments in Marxist Theories of the Capitalist State," 27 *Monthly Review* 36.

GOLDSTEIN, Abraham and Marvin MARCUS (1977) "The Myth of Judicial Supervision in Three 'Inquisitorial' Systems: France, Italy, and Germany," 87 *Yale Law Journal* 240.

GORDON, Robert (1982) "New Developments in Legal Theory," in David Kairys (ed.), *The Politics of Law.* New York: Pantheon.

GÓRECKI, Jan (ed.). (1975) *Sociology and Jurisprudence of Leon Petrażycki.* Urbana: University of Illinois Press.

GORMLEY, William T., Jr. (1989) *Taming the Bureaucracy: Muscles, Prayers and Other Strategies.* Princeton, N.J.: Princeton University Press.

GOULD, Stephen (1981) *The Mismeasure of Man.* New York: Norton.

GRANOVETTER, Mark S. (1973) "The Strength of Weak Ties," 78 *American Journal of Sociology* 1360.

GRASMICK, Harold G. and Donald E. GREEN (1981) "Deterrence and the Morally Committed," 22 *Sociological Quarterly* 1.

GREENBERG, David F. and Ronald C. KESSLER (1982) "The Effects of Arrests on Crime: A Multivariate Panel Analysis," 60 *Social Forces* 771.

GREENBERG, Stanley (1980) *Race and State in Capitalist Development.* New Haven: Yale University Press.

GREENHOUSE, Carol J. (1982) "Nature is to Culture as Praying Is to Suing: Legal Pluralism in an American Suburb," 20 *Journal of Legal Pluralism* 17.

GRIFFITHS, John (1986) "What Do Dutch Lawyers Actually Do in Divorce Cases?" 20 *Law & Society Review* 135.

GRIMSHAW, A. (1990) *Conflict Talk: Sociolinguistic Investigations of Arguments in Conversations.* New York: Cambridge University Press.

GROSS, Samuel R. and Robert MAURO (1984) "Patterns of Death: An Analysis of Racial Disparities in Criminal Sentencing and Homicide Victimization," 37 *Stanford Law Review* 27.

GULLIVER, P.H. (1969) "Introduction" and "Dispute Settlement Without Courts: The Ndendeuli of Southern Tanzania," in L. Nader (ed.), *Law in Culture and Society*. Chicago: Aldine.

HABERMAS, Jürgen (1970) *Toward a Rational Society* (trans. J. Shapiro). Boston: Beacon Press.

HAGAN, John, John H. SIMPSON and A.R. GILLIS (1979) "The Sexual Stratification of Social Control: A Gender-Based Perspective on Crime and Delinquency," 30 *British Journal of Sociology* 25.

HALE, Matthew (1736) 2 *The History of the Pleas of the Crown* (S. Emlyn, ed.). London: Nutt; 1st American ed. (1847) Philadelphia: R.H. Small.

HALEY, John (1978) "The Myth of the Reluctant Litigant," 4 *Journal of Japanese Studies* 359.

_____ (1982a) "Sheathing the Sword of Justice in Japan: An Essay in Law Without Sanctions," 8 *Journal of Japanese Studies* 265.

_____ (1982b) "The Politics of Informal Justice: The Japanese Experience, 1922–1942," in Richard L. Abel (ed.), *The Politics of Informal Justice, Vol. 2: Comparative Studies*. New York: Academic Press.

HALL, Jerome (1952) *Theft, Law, and Society*. Indianapolis: Bobbs-Merrill.

HALLER, Mark H. (1970) "Urban Crime and Criminal Justice: The Chicago Case," 57 *Journal of American History* 619.

HAMILTON, Lee and Joseph SANDERS (1988) "Punishment and the Individual in the United States and Japan," 22 *Law & Society Review* 301.

HANDLER, Joel F. (1978) *Social Movements and the Legal System: A Theory of Law Reform and Social Change*. New York: Academic Press.

HARNO, Albert J. (1928) "The Workings of the Parole Board and Its Relation to the Courts," 19 *Journal of the American Institute of Criminal Law and Criminology*, app. at 83.

HARRIS, Anthony R. (1977) "Sex and Theories of Deviance: Toward a Functional Theory of Deviant Type-Scripts," 42 *American Sociological Review* 3.

HARRIS, M. Kay and D.P. SPILLER, Jr. (1977) *After Decision: Implementation of Judicial Decrees in Correctional Settings*. Washington D.C.: U.S. Department of Justice, Law Enforcement Assistance Administration.

HAZELRIGG, Lawrence E. (1969) "A Reexamination of Simmel's 'The Secret and the Secret Society': Nine Propositions," 47 *Social Forces* 323.

HEINZ, John P., Robert W. GETTLEMAN and Morris A. SEESKIN (1969) "Legislative Politics and the Criminal Law," 64 *Northwestern University Law Review* 277.

HEINZ, John P., Edward O. LAUMANN, Robert L. NELSON and Robert H. SALISBURY (1993) *The Hollow Core: Private Interests in National Policy Making*. Cambridge, Mass.: Harvard University Press.

HENRY, Stuart (1983) *Private Justice: Towards Integrated Theorizing in the Sociology of Law*. London: Routledge & Kegan Paul.

HEUMANN, Milton (1978) *Plea Bargaining: The Experiences of Prosecutors, Judges and Defense Attorneys*. Chicago: University of Chicago Press.

HINDLEGANG, Michael J. (1974) "Decisions of Shoplifting Victims to Invoke the Criminal Justice Process," 21 *Social Problems* 580.

HIRST, Paul Q. (1972) "Marx and Engels on Law, Crime, and Morality," 1 *Economy and Society* 28.

HOBHOUSE, L.T. (1915) *Morals in Evolution*. New York: H. Holt & Co.

HOEBEL, E. Adamson (1954). *The Law of Primitive Man: A Study in Comparative Legal Dynamics*. Cambridge, Mass.: Harvard University Press.

HOLLOWAY J. and S. PICCIOTTO (1977) "Capital, Crisis and the State," 3 *Capital and Class* 76.

HOROWITZ, Donald (1977) *The Courts and Social Policy*. Washington, D.C.: Brookings Institution.

HOSTICKA, Carl (1979) "We Don't Care about What Happened, We Only Care about What Is Going to Happen," 26 *Social Problems* 599.

HUGHES, Everett C. (1971) *The Sociological Eye: Selected Papers*. Chicago: Aldine.

HUNNISETT, R. (1961) *The Medieval Coroner.* Cambridge: Cambridge University Press.

HUNT, Alan (1978) *The Sociological Movement in Law.* London: Macmillan.

_____ (1985) "The Ideology of Law: Advances and Problems in Recent Applications of the Concept of Ideology to the Analysis of Law," 19 *Law & Society Review* 11.

IANNI, Francis A.J. (1972) *A Family Business: Kinship and Control in Organized Crime.* New York: Russell Sage Foundation and Basic Books.

ILLINOIS ASSOCIATION FOR CRIMINAL JUSTICE (1929) *The Illinois Crime Survey.* Chicago: Illinois Association for Criminal Justice.

INTERPRETER RELEASES (1991) "Congress Probes INS Management amid Proposed Reorganization," 68 *Interpreter Releases* 517 (May 6).

IOWA LAW REVIEW (1975) "The Elimination of Plea Bargaining in Black Hawk County: A Case Study," 61 *Iowa Law Review* 1053.

JACOBS, James (1977) *Stateville: The Penitentiary in Mass Society.* Chicago: University of Chicago Press.

_____ (1980) "The Prisoners' Rights Movement," in N. Morris and M. Tonry (eds.), *2 Crime and Justice: An Annual Review of Research.* Chicago: University of Chicago Press.

JACOBY, Joan E. (1979) "The Charging Policies of Prosecutors," in W.F. McDonald (ed.), *The Prosecutors.* Beverly Hills: Sage Publications.

JACOBY, Joseph E. and Raymond PATERNOSTER (1982) "Sentencing Disparity and Jury Packing: Further Challenges to the Death Penalty," 73 *Journal of Criminal Law and Criminology* 379.

JOHNSON, Elmer H. (1957) "Selective Factors in Capital Punishment," 36 *Social Forces* 165.

JONES, L. Ralph and Richard R. PARLOUR (eds.) (1981) *Wyatt v Stickney: Retrospect and Prospect.* New York: Grune & Stratton.

JONES, Schuyler (1974) *Men of Influence in Nuristan: A Study of Social Control and Dispute Settlement in Waigal Valley, Afghanistan.* New York: Seminar Press.

KAGAN, Robert A. (1978) *Regulatory Justice: Implementing a Wage-Price Freeze.* New York: Russell Sage Foundation.

KALMAN, Laura (1986) *Legal Realism at Yale, 1927–1960.* Chapel Hill: University of North Carolina Press.

KALVEN, Harry, Jr., and Hans ZEISEL (1966) *The American Jury.* Chicago: University of Chicago Press.

KAMENKA, Eugene and Alice Ehr-Soon TAY (1975) "Beyond Bourgeois Individualism: The Contemporary Crisis in Law and Legal Ideology," in E. Kamenka and R.S. Neale (eds.), *Feudalism, Capitalism and Beyond.* London: Edward Arnold.

_____ (1978) "Socialism, Anarchism and Law," in E. Kamenka, R. Brown and A. Tay (eds.), *Law and Society: The Crisis in Legal Ideas.* London: Edward Arnold.

KANTOROWICZ, Hermann (1937) "Savigny and the Historical School of Law," 53 *Law Quarterly Review* 334.

KATO, Masanobu (1987) "The Role of Law and Lawyers in Japan and the United States," 1987 *Brigham Young University Law Review* 627.

KAUFMAN, Herbert (1960) *The Forest Ranger: A Study in Administrative Behavior.* Baltimore, Md.: Johns Hopkins University Press.

KAWASHIMA, Takeyoshi (1963) "Dispute Resolution in Contemporary Japan," in Arthur von Mehren (ed.), *Law in Japan: The Legal Order of a Changing Society.* Cambridge, Mass.: Harvard University Press.

KELMAN, Mark (1987) *A Guide to Critical Legal Studies.* Cambridge: Harvard University Press.

KENNEDY, Duncan (1980) "Toward an Historical Understanding of Legal Consciousness," 3 *Research in Law and Sociology* 3.

KIDDER, Robert L. (1983) *Connecting Law and Society: An Introduction to Research and Theory.* Englewood Cliffs, N.J.: Prentice-Hall.

KLARE, Karl (1981) "Labor Law as Ideology," 4 *Industrial Relations Law Journal* 450.

KLEIN, Dorie (1973) "The Etiology of Female Crime: A Review of the Literature," 8 *Issues in Criminology* 3.

KLEPPER, Steven, Daniel NAGIN and Luke-Jon TIERNEY (1983) "Discrimination in the Criminal Justice System: A Critical Appraisal of the Literature," in A. Blumstein, J. Cohen, S.E. Martin and M.H. Tonry (eds.), *Research on Sentencing: The Search for Reform, vol. 2.* Washington, D.C.: National Academy Press.

KLUCKHOHN, Clyde (1960) "The Moral Order in the Expanding Society," in Kraeling and Adams, eds., *City Invincible*. Chicago: University of Chicago Press.

KRESSEL, Kenneth, A. HOCHBERG, and T. S. METH (1983) "A Provisional Typology of Lawyer Attitudes Towards Divorce Practice," 7 *Law and Human Behavior* 31.

KRESSEL, Kenneth (1985) *The Process of Divorce*. New York: Basic Books.

KRONMAN, Anthony T. (1983) *Max Weber*. Stanford: Stanford University Press.

KRUTTSCHNITT, Candace (1982) "Women, Crime, and Dependency," 19 *Criminology* 495.

_____ (1984) "Sex and Criminal Court Dispositions: The Unresolved Controversy," 21 *Journal of Research in Crime and Delinquency* 213.

KRUTTSCHNITT, Candace and Donald GREEN (1984) "The Sex-Sanctioning Issue: Is It History?" 49 *American Sociological Review* 541.

LaFREE, Gary D. (1980) "The Effects of Social Stratification by Race on Official Reactions to Rape," 45 *American Sociological Review* 842.

LANGBEIN, John H. (1974) *Prosecuting Crime in the Renaissance: England, Germany, France.* Cambridge, Mass.: Harvard University Press.

_____ (1977a) *Torture and the Law of Proof: Europe and England in the Ancien Régime*. Chicago: University of Chicago Press.

_____ (1977b) *Comparative Criminal Procedure: Germany*. St. Paul: West Publishing Company.

_____ (1978a) "The Criminal Trial before the Lawyers," 45 *University of Chicago Law Review* 263.

_____ (1978b) "Torture and Plea Bargaining," 46 *University of Chicago Law Review* 3.

LEGAL DEFENSE FUND (1985) *Death Row, U.S.A.* (October 1). New York: NAACP Legal Defense and Education Fund, Inc.

LEMPERT, Richard (1982) "Organizing for Deterrence: Lessons from a Study of Child Support," 16 *Law & Society Review* 513.

LEMPERT, Richard and Joseph SANDERS (1986) *An Invitation to Law and Social Science: Desert, Disputes, and Distribution.* Philadelphia: University of Pennsylvania Press.

LESIEUR, Henry (1976) *The Case: Career of the Compulsive Gambler*. Garden City, N.Y.: Anchor Books.

LEVIN Martin (1977) *Urban Politics and the Criminal Courts*. Chicago: University of Chicago Press.

LEVY, Gerald E. (1970) *Ghetto School: Class Warfare in an Elementary School*. New York: Pegasus.

LIGHT, Ivan H. (1972) *Ethnic Enterprise in America: Business and Welfare Among Chinese, Japanese and Blacks*. Berkeley: University of California Press.

LIND, E. Allen and Tom R. TYLER (1988) *The Social Psychology of Procedural Justice*. New York: Plenum.

LINDESMITH, Alfred R. (1965) *The Addict and the Law*. Bloomington: Indiana University Press.

LIPSKY, Michael (1980) *Street-Level Bureaucracy: Dilemmas of the Individual in Public Services.* New York: Russell Sage.

LIPSON, Leon and Stanton WHEELER, eds. (1986) *Law and the Social Sciences.* New York: Russell Sage.

LOFLAND, John and Rodney STARK (1965) "Becoming a World-Saver: A Theory of Conversion to a Deviant Perspective," 30 *American Sociological Review* 862.

LOGAN, Charles H. (1975) "Arrest Rates and Deterrence," 56 *Social Science Quarterly* 376.

LONGMIRE, Dennis R. (1981) "A Popular Justice System: Radical Alternative to the Traditional Criminal Justice System," 5 *Contemporary Crises* 15.

LOWIE, Robert H. (1927) *Origin of the State.* New York: Harcourt Brace.

LOWY, Michael J. (1978) "A Good Name Is Worth More than Money: Strategies of Court Use in Urban Ghana," in L. Nader and H.F. Todd Jr. (eds.), *The Disputing Process—Law in Ten Societies.* New York: Columbia University Press.

LUKES, Steven (1974) *Power: A Radical View.* London: Macmillan.

LUKES, Steven and Andrew SCULL, eds. (1983) *Durkheim and the Law.* New York: St Martin's Press.

LUNDMAN, Richard J. (1980) "Routine Police Arrest Practices: A Commonweal Perspective," in R.J. Lundman (ed.), *Police Behavior: A Sociological Perspective.* New York: Oxford University Press.

MACAULAY, Stewart (1979) "Lawyers and Consumer Protection Laws," 14 *Law & Society Review* 115.

_____ (1984) "Law and the Behavioral Sciences," 6 *Law & Policy* 149.

MacDOUGALL, Donald (1984) "Negotiated Settlement of Family Disputes," in John Eekelaar and Sanford N. Katz (eds.), *The Resolution of Family Conflict.* Toronto: Butterworths.

MAINE, Henry Sumner (1861) *Ancient Law.* New York: H. Holt.

MALAN, T. and P.S. HATTINGER (eds.) (1976) *Black Homelands in South Africa.* Pretoria: Institute of South Africa.

MALINOWSKI, Bronislaw (1926a) *Crime and Custom in Savage Society.* New York: Harcourt Brace.

_____ (1926b) "Primitive Law and Order," 117 *Nature* 9 (Supplement).

MANN, Kenneth (1985) *Defending White Collar Criminals.* New Haven: Yale University Press.

MANN, Kenneth, Stanton WHEELER and Austin SARAT (1980) "Sentencing the White-Collar Offender," 17 *American Criminal Law Review* 479.

MARQUART, James W. and Ben M. CROUCH (1985) "Judicial Reform and Prisoner Control: The Impact of *Ruiz v. Estelle* on a Texas Penitentiary," 19 *Law & Society Review* 557.

MARTIN, Roscoe (1934) *The Defendant and Criminal Justice.* Austin: University of Texas, Bureau of Research in the Social Sciences (Bulletin No. 3437).

MARTIN, Steve J. and Sheldon EKLAND-OLSON (1987) *Texas Prisons: The Walls Came Tumbling Down.* Austin: Texas Monthly Press.

MATHER, Lynn and Barbara YNGVESSON (1980–81) "Language, Audience, and the Transformation of Disputes," 15 *Law & Society Review* 775.

MAYHEW, Leon H. (1975) "Institutions of Representation: Civil Justice and the Public," 9 *Law & Society Review* 401.

MAYNARD, Douglas W. (1982) "Defendant Attributes in Plea Bargaining: Notes on the Modeling of Sentencing Decisions," 29 *Social Problems* 347.

McCLEARY, Richard (1975) "How Structural Variables Constrain the Parole Officer's Use of Discretionary Powers," 23 *Social Problems* 209.

_____ (1977) "How Parole Officers Use Records," 24 *Social Problems* 576.

_____ (1978) *Dangerous Men: The Sociology of Parole.* Beverly Hills: Sage.

McCLEARY, Richard, Michael J. O'NEIL, Thomas EPPERLEIN, Constance JONES and Ronald H. GRAY (1981) "Effects of Legal Education and Work Experience on Perceptions of Crime Seriousness," 28 *Social Problems* 276.

McCLEERY, Richard H. (1961) "The Governmental Process and Informal Social Control," in D.R. Cressey (ed.), *The Prison: Studies in Institutional Organization and Change.* New York: Holt, Rinehart and Winston.

McCORMICK, Charles (1954) *Evidence.* St. Paul: West Publishing Co.

McINTOSH, Wayne (1980–81) "150 Years of Litigation and Dispute Settlement: A Court Tale," 15 *Law & Society Review* 823.

McINTYRE, Lisa J. (1994) *Law in the Sociological Enterprise: A Reconstruction.* Boulder, Colo.: Westview Press.

McNICKLE, D'Arcy (1975) *They Came Here First.* New York: Harper and Row.

MEIER, Robert F. and Weldon T. JOHNSON (1977) "Deterrence as Social Control: The Legal and Extralegal Production of Conformity," 42 *American Sociological Review* 292.

MENDEL, Werner M. and Samuel RAPPORT (1973) "Determinants of the Decision for Psychiatric Hospitalization," in R. Price and B. Denner (eds.), *The Making of a Mental Patient.* New York: Holt, Rinehart and Winston.

MERRY, Sally and Susan SILBEY (1984) "What Do Plaintiffs Want?" 9 *Justice System Journal* 151.

MERTZ, Elizabeth (1985) "Beyond Symbolic Anthropology: Introducing Semiotic Mediation," in Elizabeth MERTZ and Richard PARMENTIER (eds.), *Semiotic Mediation.* New York: Academic Press.

MERTZ, Elizabeth and Bernard WEISSBOURD (1985) "Legal Ideology and Linguistic Theory: Variability and Its Limits," in Elizabeth MERTZ and Richard PARMENTIER (eds.), *Semiotic Mediation.* New York: Academic Press.

MERTZ, Elizabeth and Richard PARMENTIER, eds. (1985) *Semiotic Mediation.* New York: Academic Press.

MICHAEL, Jerome and Herbert WECHSLER (1940) *Criminal Law and Its Administration.* Chicago: Foundation Press.

MICHIGAN LAW REVIEW (1972) "Tribal Self-Government and the Indian Reorganization Act of 1934," 70 *Michigan Law Review* 955.

MILIBAND, Ralph (1969) *The State in Capitalist Society.* New York: Basic Books.

MILLER, Charles (1969) *The Supreme Court and the Uses of History.* Cambridge: Harvard University Press.

MILLER, Justin (1927) "The Compromise of Criminal Cases," 1 *Southern California Law Review* 1.

MILLS, C. Wright (1940) "Situated Actions and Vocabularies of Motive," 5 *American Sociological Review* 904.

MISHLER, Elliot (1985) *The Discourse of Medicine.* Norwood., N.J.: Ablex Publications.

MISSOURI ASSOCIATION FOR CRIMINAL JUSTICE SURVEY COMMITTEE (1926) *The Missouri Crime Survey.* St. Louis: Missouri Association for Criminal Justice; New York: Macmillan.

MIYAZAWA, Setsuo (1985) "Taking Kawashima Seriously: A Review of Japanese Research on Japanese Legal Consciousness and Disputing Behavior," 21 *Law & Society Review* 219.

MNOOKIN, Robert (1984) "Divorce Bargaining: The Limits of Private Ordering," in John Eekelaar and Sanford N. Katz (eds.), *The Resolution of Family Conflict.* Toronto: Butterworths.

MODMAN, J.H. (1976) "Historical Perspective: The Process of Occupation," in T. MALAN and P.S. HATTINGER (eds.), *Black Homelands in South Africa.* Pretoria: Institute of South Africa.

MOLEY, Raymond (1929) *Politics and Criminal Prosecution.* New York: Minton, Balch.

MOLEY, Raymond (1928) "The Vanishing Jury," 2 *Southern California Law Review* 97.

MONTESQUIEU, Charles de Secondat, baron de (1756) *The Spirit of Laws.* London: J. Nourse & P. Vaillant.

MOORE, Sally Falk (1969) "Law and Anthropology," 6 *Biennial Review of Anthropology* 252.

_____ (1978) *Law as Process.* London: Routledge and Kegan Paul.

MOORE, Underhill and C.C. CALLAHAN (1944) "Law and Learning Theory: A Study in Legal Control," 53 *Yale Law Journal* 1.

MORGAN, Lewis Henry (1877) *Ancient Society: or Researches in the Lines of Human Progress from Savagery Through Barbarism to Civilization.* New York: H. Holt.

MOULDS, Elizabeth F. (1980) "Chivalry and Paternalism: Disparities of Treatment in the Criminal Justice System," in S. Datesman and F. Scarpitti (eds.), *Women, Crime and Justice.* New York: Oxford University Press.

MULLIN, Courtney (1980) "The Jury System in Death Penalty Cases: A Symbolic Gesture," 43 *Law and Contemporary Problems* 137.

MYERS Martha A. and John HAGAN (1979) "Private and Public Trouble: Prosecutors and the Allocation of Court Resources," 26 *Social Problems* 439.

NADER, Laura (1965) "Choices in Legal Procedure: Shia Moslem and Mexican Zapotec," 67 *American Anthropologist* 394.

_____ (1969) "Styles of Court Procedure: To Make the Balance," in L. Nader (ed.), *Law in Culture and Society*. Chicago: Aldine.

NADER, Laura and Harry F. TODD, Jr. (1978) "Introduction: The Dispute Process — Law in Ten Societies," in L. Nader and H. Todd, Jr. (eds.), The *Disputing Process — Law in Ten Societies*. New York: Columbia University Press.

NAGEL, Ilene and John HAGAN (1983) "Gender and Crime: Offense Patterns and Criminal Court Sanctions," in M. Tonry and N. Morris (eds.), *Crime and Justice: An Annual Review of Research*. Chicago: University of Chicago Press.

NAGEL, Stuart S. (1962) "Culture Patterns and Judicial Systems," 16 *Vanderbilt Law Review* 147 (1962).

NAGEL, Stuart and Lenore WEITZMAN (1971) "Women as Litigants," 23 *Hastings Law Journal* 171.

NATIONAL ADVISORY COMMISSION ON CRIMINAL JUSTICE STANDARDS AND GOALS (1973) *Courts*. Washington, D.C.: Government Printing Office.

NATIONAL CENTER FOR STATE COURTS (1982) *State Court Caseload Statistics. Annual Report, 1977*. Charlottesville, Va.: NCSC.

NATIONAL COMMISSION ON LAW OBSERVANCE AND ENFORCEMENT (1931a) *Report on Crime and the Foreign Born*. Washington, D.C.: Government Printing Office.

NATIONAL COMMISSION ON LAW OBSERVANCE AND ENFORCEMENT (1931b) *Report on Prosecution*. Washington, D.C.: Government Printing Office.

NATIONAL COMMISSION ON LAW OBSERVANCE AND ENFORCEMENT (1931c) *Report on the Enforcement of the Prohibition Laws of the United States*. Washington, D.C.: Government Printing Office.

NELKEN, David (1982) "Is There a Crisis in Law and Legal Ideology?" 9 *Journal of Law and Society* 177.

NEW YORK STATE CRIME COMMISSION (1927) *Report to the Commission of the Sub-Committee on Statistics*. New York: New York State Crime Commission.

O'BARR William M. (1982) *Linguistic Evidence: Language, Power and Strategy in the Courtroom*. New York: Academic Press.

O'GORMAN, Hubert (1963) *Lawyers and Matrimonial Cases*. New York: Free Press.

O'MALLEY, Pat (1983) *Law, Capitalism, and Democracy: A Sociology of Australian Legal Order*. Sydney: George Allen & Unwin.

ORLAND, Leonard (1975) *Prisons: Houses of Darkness*. New York: Free Press.

PARDUCCI, Allen (1968) "The Relativism of Absolute Judgments," 219 *Scientific American* 84 (December).

PARISI, Nicolette (1982) "Are Females Treated Differently? A Review of the Theories and Evidence on Sentencing and Parole Decisions," in N. Rafter and E. Stanko (eds.), *Judge, Lawyer, Victim, Thief*. Boston: Northeastern University Press.

PARSONS, Talcott (1966) *Societies: Evolutionary and Comparative Perspectives*. Englewood Cliffs, N.J.: Prentice-Hall.

PATERNOSTER, Raymond (1983) "Race of Victim and Location of Crime: The Decision to Seek the Death Penalty in South Carolina," 74 *Journal of Criminal Law and Criminology* 754.

_____ (1984) "Prosecutorial Discretion in Requesting the Death Penalty: A Case of Victim-Based Racial Discrimination," 18 *Law & Society Review* 437.

PERROW, Charles (1984) *Normal Accidents: Living with High-Risk Technologies*. New York: Basic Books.

PETERSON, David M. (1971) "Informal Norms and Police Practice: The Traffic Ticket Quota System," 55 *Sociology and Social Research* 354.

PHILLIPS, Paul (1980) *Marx and Engels on Law and Laws*. Oxford: Martin Robertson.

POLLNER, Melvin (1979) "Explicative Transactions: Making and Managing Meaning in Traffic Court," in G. Psathas (ed.), *Everyday Language: Studies in Ethnomethodology.* New York: Irvington.

POPITZ, Heinrich (1968) "Über die Präventivwirkung des Nichtwissens," 350 *Recht und Staat in Geschichte und Gegenwart.* Tübingen: C. B. Mohr.

POULANTZAS, Nicos (1969) "The Problem of the Capitalist State," 58 *New Left Review* 67.

POUND, Roscoe (1923) *Interpretations of Legal History.* New York: Macmillan.

_____ (1930) *Criminal Justice in America.* New York: Henry Holt.

PRESIDENT'S COMMISSION ON CRIME IN THE DISTRICT OF COLUMBIA (1966) *Report.* Washington, D.C.: Government Printing Office.

PRESIDENT'S COMMISSION ON LAW ENFORCEMENT AND ADMINISTRATION OF JUSTICE (1967) *The Challenge of Crime in a Free Society.* Washington, D.C.: Government Printing Office.

PRUS, Robert C. and J. STRATTON (1976) "Parole Revocation Decisionmaking: Private Typings and Official Designations," 40 *Federal Probation* 48 (March).

QUINNEY, Richard (1969) "Introduction: Toward a Sociology of Criminal Law," in R. Quinney (ed.), *Crime and Justice in Society.* Boston: Little Brown.

RADCLIFFE-BROWN, A.R. (1933) "Law, Primitive," 9 *Encyclopaedia of the Social Sciences* 202.

_____ (1934) "Sanction, Social," 13 *Encyclopaedia of the Social Sciences* 531.

_____ (1952) *Structure and Function in Primitive Society.* Glencoe, Ill.: Free Press.

RADELET, Michael L. (1981) "Racial Characteristics and the Imposition of the Death Penalty," 46 *American Sociological Review* 918.

RADELET, Michael L. and Margaret VANDIVER (1983) "The Florida Supreme Court and Death Penalty Appeals," 74 *Journal of Criminal Law and Criminology* 913.

RADZINOWICZ, Leon (1956) 2 *A History of English Criminal Law.* London: Stevens.

RAMSEYER, J. Mark (1985) "The Costs of the Consensual Myth: Antitrust Enforcement and Institutional Barriers to Litigation in Japan," 94 *Yale Law Journal* 504.

_____ (1988) "Reluctant Litigant Revisited: Rationality and Disputes in Japan," 14 *Journal of Japanese Studies* 111.

RANDALL, Richard S. (1968) *Censorship of the Movies: Social and Political Control of a Mass Medium.* Madison: University of Wisconsin Press.

REDFIELD, Robert (1964) "Primitive Law," 33 *University of Cincinnati Law Review* 1.

REPUBLIC OF SOUTH AFRICA (RSA) (1973) *Homelands: The Role of the Corporations.* Pretoria: Government Printer.

_____ (1976) *Official Yearbook of the Republic of South Africa.* Pretoria: Government Printer.

_____ (1980) *South African Digest (July 25).* Pretoria: Government Printer.

_____ (1983) *Official Yearbook of the Republic of South Africa.* Pretoria: Government Printer.

_____ (1987) *Official Yearbook of the Republic of South Africa.* Pretoria: Government Printer.

RHEINSTEIN, Max (1954) *Max Weber on Law in Economy and Society* (Edward Shils and Max Rheinstein trans.). Cambridge, Mass.: Harvard University Press.

_____ (1960) "Process and Change in the Cultural Spectrum Coincident with Expansion: Government and Law," in Kraeling and Adams, eds., *City Invincible.* Chicago: University of Chicago Press.

RIEDEL, Marc (1976) "Discrimination in the Imposition of the Death Penalty: A Comparison of Offenders Sentenced to Die Pre-*Furman* and Post-*Furman*," 49 *Temple Law Quarterly* 261.

RIVERS, W.H.R. (1968) *Kinship and Social Organization.* New York: Humanities Press (first published 1914).

ROBERTS, Simon A. (1979) *Order and Dispute: An Introduction to Legal Anthropology.* Harmondsworth: Penguin.

ROBSON, W.A. (1935) *Civilization and the Growth of Law.* London: Macmillan.

ROGERS, Howard (1933) *Native Administration in the Union of South Africa.* New York: Negro University Press.

ROSCH, Joel (1987) "Institutionalizing Mediation: The Evolution of the Civil Liberties Bureau in Japan," 21 *Law & Society Review* 243.

ROSE, Arnold M. and Arthur E. PRESS (1955) "Does the Punishment Fit the Crime? A Study in Social Evaluation," 61 *American Journal of Sociology* 246.

ROSEN, Lawrence (1978) *American Indians and the Law*. New Brunswick, N.J.: Transaction Books.

ROSENTHAL, Douglas (1974) *Lawyer and Client: Who's In Charge?* New York: Russell Sage.

ROSETT, Arthur and Donald R. CRESSEY (1976) *Justice by Consent: Plea Bargains in the American Courthouse*. Philadelphia: Lippincott.

ROSHIER, Bob and Harvey TEFF (1980) *Law and Society in England*. London: Tavistock.

ROSNER, Menahem (1973) "Direct Democracy in the Kibbutz," in Rosabeth Kanter (ed.), *Communes: Creating and Managing the Collective Life*. New York: Harper.

ROSS, H. Laurence (1970) *Settled Out of Court*. Chicago: Aldine Publishing Co.

ROTHMAN, David J. and Sheila M. ROTHMAN (1984) *The Willowbrook Wars*. New York: Harper & Row.

ROTHWAX, Harold J. (1969) "The Law as an Instrument of Social Change," in Harold H. Weissman (ed.), *Justice and the Law in the Mobilization for Youth Experience*. New York: New York Association Press.

ROURKE, Francis E. (1976) *Bureaucracy, Politics and Public Policy* (2d ed.). Boston: Little Brown.

ROUSSEAU, F.P. (1960) *Handbook on the Group Areas Act*. Cape Town: Juta.

RUBINSTEIN, Jonathan (1973) *City Police*. New York: Farrar, Straus and Giroux.

RUSCHE, Georg and Otto KIRCHHEIMER (1939) *Punishment and Social Structure*. New York: Columbia University Press.

SACKVILLE-WEST, Vita (1936) *Saint Joan of Arc*. Toronto: Doubleday.

SAHLINS, Marshall (1981) *Historical Metaphors and Mythical Realities: Structures in the Early History of the Sandwich Islands Kingdom*. Ann Arbor: University of Michigan Press.

SAN FRANCISCO COMMITTEE ON CRIME (1970) *A Report on the Criminal Courts of San Francisco, Part I: The Superior Court Backlog — Consequences and Remedies*. San Francisco: San Francisco Committee on Crime.

SANDERS, William B. (1977) *Detective Work: A Study of Criminal Investigations*. New York: Free Press.

SANTOS, Boaventura de Sousa (1980) "Law and Community: The Changing Nature of State Power in Late Capitalism," 8 *International Journal of the Sociology of Law* 379.

SARAT, Austin (1977) "Studying American Legal Culture: An Assessment of Survey Evidence," 11 *Law & Society Review* 427.

_____ (1978) "Understanding Trial Courts: A Critique of Social Science Approaches," 61 *Judicature* 318.

SARAT, Austin and William FELSTINER (1986) "Law and Strategy in the Divorce Lawyer's Office," 20 *Law & Society Review* 93.

SARAT, Austin and Susay SILBEY (1988) "The Pull of the Policy Audience," 10 *Law & Policy* 97.

SAVIGNY, Frederick Charles von (1831) *Of the Vocation of Our Age for Legislation and Jurisprudence* (Abraham Hayward trans.) London: Littlewood.

SCHEFF, Thomas (1966) *Being Mentally Ill*. Chicago: Aldine Publishing.

SCHOLZ, John T. and Feng Heng WEI (1986) "Regulatory Enforcement in a Federalist System," 80 *American Political Science Review* 1249.

SCHUBERT, Glendon (1960) *Constitutional Politics: The Political Behavior of Supreme Court Justices and the Constitutional Policies That They Make*. New York: Holt, Rinehart and Winston.

_____, ed. (1963) *Judicial Decision-Making*. Glencoe, Ill.: Free Press.

_____, ed. (1964) *Judicial Behavior: A Reader in Theory and Research*. Chicago: Rand McNally.

_____ (1965) *Judicial Policy-Making: The Political Role of the Court*. Chicago: Scott, Foresman.

SCHUCK, Peter H. (1972) "The Curious Case of the Indicted Meat Inspectors," *Harpers Magazine* 81 (Sept.).

_____ (1983) *Suing Government: Citizen Remedies for Official Wrongs*. New Haven, Conn.: Yale University Press.

SCHUR, Edwin M. (1971) *Labeling Deviant Behavior: Its Sociological Implications*. New York: Harper and Row.

SCHUTZ, Alfred (1962) *Collected Papers, vol. 1: The Problem of Social Reality*. The Hague: Martinus Nijhoff.

SCHWARTZ, Richard (1954) "Social Factors in the Development of Legal Control: A Case Study of Two Israeli Settlements," 63 *Yale Law Journal* 471.

_____ (1957) "Democracy and Collectivism in the Kibbutz," 5 *Social Problems* 137.

SCHWARTZ, Richard D. and James C. MILLER (1964) "Legal Evolution and Societal Complexity," 70 *American Journal of Sociology* 159.

SCOTT, Marvin and Stanford LYMAN (1968) "Accounts," 33 *American Sociological Review* 46.

SEIDMAN, David and Michael COUZENS (1974) "Getting the Crime Rate Down: Political Pressure and Crime Reporting," 8 *Law & Society Review* 457.

SHAPIRO, Allen E. (1976) "Law in the Kibbutz: A Reappraisal," 10 *Law & Society Review* 415.

SHAPIRO, Martin (1981) "On the Regrettable Decline of Law French, or Shapiro Jettet le Brickbat," 90 *Yale Law Journal* 1198.

SILBEY, Susan and Sally MERRY (1986) "Interpretive Processes in Mediation and Court" (unpublished).

SILVERSTEIN, Michael (1976) "Shifters, Linguistic Categories, and Cultural Description," in K. Basso and H. Selby (eds.), *Meaning in Anthropology*. Albuquerque: University of New Mexico Press.

_____ (1979) "Language Structure and Linguistic Ideology," in P. Clyne, W. Hanks, and C. Hofbauer (eds.), *The Elements: A Parasession on Language Units and Levels*. Chicago: Chicago Linguistic Society.

SIMMEL, Georg (1950) "The Secret Society," in *The Sociology of Georg Simmel* (K.H. Wolff trans. and ed.). Glencoe, Ill.: Free Press.

_____ (1971) "The Stranger" (first published 1909), in D. Levine (ed.), *On Individuality and Social Forms: Selected Writings*. Chicago: University of Chicago Press.

SIMON, Rita J. (1975) *Women and Crime*. Lexington, Mass.: Lexington Books.

SIMON, William (1980) "Homo Psychologicus: Notes on a New Legal Formalism," 32 *Stanford Law Review* 487.

SKOLNICK, Jerome H. (1966) *Justice Without Trial: Law Enforcement in a Democratic Society*. New York: Wiley.

SMELSER, Neil J. (1962) *Theory of Collective Behavior*. New York: Free Press.

SNOW, David A. and Cynthia L. Phillips (1980) "The Lofland-Stark Conversion Model: A Critical Reassessment," 27 *Social Problems* 430.

SOROKIN, Pitirim A. (1937) *Social and Cultural Dynamics, vol. 2: Fluctuations of Systems of Truth, Ethics and Law*. Cincinnati: American Book Co.

SPENCE, Jack (1978) "Institutionalizing Neighborhood Courts: Two Chilean Experiences," 13 *Law & Society Review* 139.

STARR, June (1978) "Turkish Village Disputing Behavior," in L. Nader and H.F. Todd, Jr. (eds.), *The Disputing Process — Law in Ten Societies*. New York: Columbia University Press.

STATSKY, William P. (1974) "Community Courts: Decentralizing Juvenile Jurisprudence," 3 *Capital University Law Review* 1.

STEARNS, Lisa (1979) "Fact and Fiction of a Model Enforcement Bureaucracy: The Labour Inspectorate of Sweden," 6 *British Journal of Law and Society* 1.

STEFFENSMEIER, Darrell (1980) "Assessing the Impact of the Women's Movement on Sex-Based Differences in the Handling of Adult Criminal Defendants," 26 *Crime and Delinquency* 344.

STEFFENSMEIER, Darrell J. and Robert M. TERRY (1973) "Deviance and Respectability: An Observational Study of Reactions to Shoplifting," 51 *Social Forces* 417.

STEINER, Gilbert Y. and Samuel K. GOVE (1960) *Legislative Politics in Illinois.* Urbana: University of Illinois Press.

STICKNEY, S.B. (1974) "*Wyatt v. Stickney*: The Right to Treatment," 4 *Psychiatric Annals* 32.

STOCKING, George (1968) *Race, Culture and Evolution.* New York: Free Press.

STUDT, Elliot (1972) *Surveillance and Service in Parole: A Report of the Parole Action Study.* Los Angeles: Institute of Government and Public Affairs, UCLA.

SUDNOW, David (1965) "Normal Crimes: Sociological Features of the Penal Code in a Public Defender Office," 12 *Social Problems* 255.

_____ (1967) *Passing-On: The Social Organization of Dying.* Englewood Cliffs, N.J.: Prentice-Hall.

SUMNER, William Graham (1907) *Folkways: A Study of the Sociological Importance of Usages, Manners, Customs, Mores and Morals.* Boston: Ginn & Co.

SUTHERLAND, Edwin H. (1969) "The Diffusion of Sexual Psychopath Laws," in R. Quinney (ed.), *Crime and Justice in Society.* Boston: Little Brown.

SUTHERLAND, Edwin H. and Donald R. CRESSEY (1974) *Criminology* (9th ed.). Philadelphia: Lippincott.

SUTTLES, Gerald D. (1972) *The Social Construction of Communities.* Chicago: University of Chicago Press.

TAPP, June Louin and Felice J. LEVINE, eds. (1978) *Law, Justice and the Individual in Society: Psychological and Legal Issues.* New York: Holt, Rinehart and Winston.

TEITELBAUM, Michael S. (1980) "Right versus Right: Immigration and Refugee Policy in the United States," 59 *Foreign Affairs* 21.

TEXAS DEPARTMENT OF CORRECTIONS (1968) *Rules and Regulations of the Texas Department of Corrections.* Hunstville: Texas Department of Corrections.

_____ (1977) *Texas Department of Corrections: 30 Years of Progress.* Huntsville: Texas Department of Corrections.

THEAL, George (1912) *History of South Africa,* vol. 1. London: S. Sonnenschein.

THIBAUT, J. and L. WALKER (1975) *Procedural Justice.* Hillsdale, N.J.: Erlbaum.

_____ (1978) "A Theory of Procedure," 66 *California Law Review* 541.

THOMPSON, Leonard (1985) *The Political Mythology of Apartheid.* New Haven: Yale University Press.

THOMSON, Randall J. and Matthew T. ZINGRAFF (1981) "Detecting Sentencing Disparity: Some Problems and Evidence," 86 *American Journal of Sociology* 869.

TITTLE, Charles R. (1977) "Sanction Fear and the Maintenance of Social Order," 55 *Social Forces* 579.

_____ (1980) *Sanctions and Social Deviance: The Question of Deterrence.* New York: Praeger.

TODD, Harry F., Jr. (1978) "Litigious Marginals: Character and Disputing in a Bavarian Village," in L. Nader and H.F. Todd, Jr. (eds.), *The Disputing Process — Law in Ten Societies.* New York: Columbia University Press.

TÖNNIES, Ferdinand (1963) *Community and Society* (Charles H. Loomis trans. and ed.). New York: Harper & Row (first published 1887).

TRAIN, Arthur (1924) *The Prisoner at the Bar* (3rd ed.). New York: Charles Scribner's Sons.

TRUBEK, David M. (1972) "Max Weber on Law and the Rise of Capitalism," 1972 *Wisconsin Law Review* 720.

_____ (1977) "Complexity and Contradiction in the Legal Order: Balbus and the Challenge of Critical Social Thought about Law," 11 *Law & Society Review* 529.

_____ (1984) "Where the Action Is: Critical Legal Studies and Empiricism," 36 *Stanford Law Review* 575.

TURK, Austin T. (1976) "Law as a Weapon in Social Conflict," 23 *Social Problems* 276.

TWINING, William L. (1985) *Karl Llewellyn and the Realist Movement.* Norman: University of Oklahoma Press.

TYLER, T.R. and R. FOLGER (1980) "Distributional and Procedural Aspects of Satisfaction with Citizen-Police Encounters," 1 *Basic and Applied Psychology* 281.

TYLER, T.R. and A. CAINE (1981) "The Influence of Outcomes and Procedures on Satisfaction with Formal Leaders," 41 *Journal of Personality and Social Psychology* 642.

TYLER, T.R., K. RASINSKI and K. McGRAW (1985) "The Influence of Perceived Injustice on the Endorsement of Political Leaders," 15 *Journal of Applied Social Psychology* 700.

TYLER, T.R., K. RASINSKI and N. SPODICK (1985) "The Influence of Voice on Satisfaction with Leaders: Exploring the Meaning of Process Control," 48 *Journal of Personality and Social Psychology* 72

TYLOR, E.B. (1865) *Researches into the Early History of Mankind and the Development of Civilization.* London: J. Murray.

U.S. DEPARTMENT OF JUSTICE (1982) *Capital Punishment, 1981.* Washington, D.C.: Department of Justice National Prisoner Statistics (NCJ-78600).

U.S. DEPARTMENT OF JUSTICE, BUREAU OF JUSTICE STATISTICS (1983) *Report to the Nation on Crime and Justice: The Data* (Bulletin NCJ-87068). Washington, D.C.: U.S. Department of Justice.

UPHAM, Frank (1987) *Law and Social Change in Postwar Japan.* Cambridge, Mass.: Harvard University Press.

VAUGHAN, Diane (1986) *Uncoupling.* New York: Oxford University Press.

VERA INSTITUTE OF JUSTICE (1977) *Felony Arrests: Their Prosecution and Disposition in New York City's Courts.* New York: Vera Institute.

VERSELE, Severin-Carolos (1969) "Public Participation in the Administration of Criminal Justice," 27 *International Review of Criminal Policy* 9.

VINOGRADOFF, Paul (1920) *Outlines of Historical Jurisprudence* (2 vols.). New York: Oxford University Press.

WAEGEL, William B. (1981) "Case Routinization in Investigative Police Work," 28 *Social Problems* 263.

WAGATSUMA, Hiroshi and Arthur ROSETT (1986) "The Implications of Apology: Law and Culture in Japan and the United States," 20 *Law & Society Review* 461.

WALDO, Gordon P. and Theodore G. CHIRICOS (1972) "Perceived Penal Sanction and Self-Reported Criminality: A Neglected Approach to Deterrence Research," 19 *Social Problems* 522.

WALTON, Edgar (1912) *The Inner History of the National Convention of South Africa.* Westport, Conn.: Negro Universities Press.

WEBER, Max (1947) *The Theory of Social and Economic Organization* (trans. Talcott Parsons and A.M. Henderson). Glencoe, Ill.: Free Press.

_____ (1978) *Economy and Society: An Outline of Interpretive Sociology* (Guenther Roth and Claus Wittich trans.). Berkeley: University of California Press.

WEINSTEIN James (1968) *The Corporate Ideal in the Liberal State.* Boston: Beacon Press.

WEISBROD, Carol (1980) *The Boundaries of Utopia.* New York: Pantheon.

WESTERMARCK, Edward (1906) *The Origin and Development of the Moral Ideas* (2 vols.) New York: Macmillan.

WHARTON, Francis (1912) *Evidence in Criminal Issues* (10th ed.). Philadelphia: May & Brother.

WHEELER, Stanton, David WEISBURG and Nancy BODE (1982) "Sentencing the White-Collar Offender: Rhetoric and Reality," 47 *American Sociological Review* 641.

WHELAN, Christopher J. (1981) "Informalising Judicial Procedures," in S. Henry (ed.), *Informal Institutions.* New York: St. Martin's Press.

WHITE, James Boyd (1990) *Justice as Translation.* Chicago: University of Chicago Press.

WHITT, J. Allen (1979) "Toward a Class-Dialectical Model of Power: An Empirical Assessment of Three Competing Models of Political Power," 44 *American Sociological Review* 81.

WILDAVSKY, Aaron (1971) "Budgetary Strategies of Administrative Agencies," in R.E. Wolfinger (ed.), *Readings on Congress.* Englewood Cliffs, N.J.: Prentice-Hall.

WILKINSON, Charles F. and John M. Volkman (1975) "Judicial Review of Indian Treaty Abrogation: 'As Long as Water Flows or Grass Grows upon the Earth—' How Long a Time Is That?" 73 *California Law Review* 601.

WILSON, James Q. (1975) *Thinking about Crime.* New York: Basic Books.

_____ (1989) *Bureaucracy: What Government Agencies Do and Why They Do It.* New York: Basic Books.

WOLFGANG, Marvin E., Arlene KELLY and Hans C. NOLDE (1962) "Comparisons of Executed and Commuted among Admissions to Death Row," 53 *Journal of Criminal Law, Criminology, and Police Science* 301.

WOLFGANG, Marvin E. and Marc REIDEL (1973) "Race, Judicial Discretion, and the Death Penalty," 53 *Annals of the American Academy of Political and Social Science* 301.

YAMAGUCHI, Masao (1977) "Kingship, Theatricality, and Marginal Reality in Japan," in R. Jain (ed.), *Text and Context: The Social Anthropology of Tradition.* Philadelphia: Institute for the Study of Human Issues.

YNGVESSON, Barbara (1976) "Responses to Grievance Behavior: Extended Cases in a Fishing Community," 3 *American Ethnologist* 353.

_____ (1985a) "Legal Ideology and Community Justice in the Clerk's Office," 9 *Legal Studies Forum* 71.

_____ (1985b) "Re-examining Continuing Relations and the Law," 1985 *Wisconsin Law Review* 623.

_____ (1988) "Making Law at the Doorway: The Clerk, the Court, and the Construction of Community in a New England Town," 22 *Law & Society Review* 409.

YNGVESSON, Barbara and Patricia HENNESSEY (1975) "Small Claims, Complex Disputes: A Review of the Small Claims Literature," 9 *Law & Society Review* 219.

ZIMMERMAN, Don H. (1970) "The Practicalities of Rule Use," in J. Douglas (ed.), *Understanding Everyday Life: Toward the Reconstruction of Sociological Knowledge.* Chicago: Aldine.

ZIMMERMAN, Don H. and Melvin POLLNER (1970) "The Everyday World as a Phenomenon," in J. Douglas (ed.), *Understanding Everyday Life: Toward a Reconstruction of Sociological Knowledge.* Chicago: Aldine.

ZURCHER, Louis, George KIRKPATRICK, Robert G. CUSHING and Charles K. BOWMAN (1973) "The Anti-Pornography Campaign: A Symbolic Crusade," in C.M. ViVona (ed.), *The Meanings of Deviance.* New York: MSS Information Corp.